Civic Media

Civic Media

Technology | Design | Practice

edited by Eric Gordon and Paul Mihailidis

The MIT Press
Cambridge, Massachusetts
London, England

This book was set in Stone Sans and Stone Serif by Toppan Best-set Premedia Limited. Printed and bound in the United States of America.

Library of Congress Cataloging-in-Publication Data

Names: Gordon, Eric, 1973- editor. | Mihailidis, Paul, 1978- editor.
Title: Civic media : technology, design, practice / Eric Gordon and Paul Mihailidis, eds.
Description: Cambridge, MA : MIT Press, [2015] | Includes bibliographical references and index.
Identifiers: LCCN 2015039701 | ISBN 9780262034272 (hardcover : alk. paper)
Subjects: LCSH: Mass media–Political aspects. | Digital media--Political aspects. | Political participation. | Political participation--Technological innovations. | Internet in public administration.
Classification: LCC P95.8 .C4858 2015 | DDC 302.23–dc23 LC record available at http://lccn.loc.gov/2015039701

10 9 8 7 6 5 4 3 2 1

Dedicated to all those who have inspired us by inventing, adopting, or adapting media to make positive change in the world.

Contents

Acknowledgments

Civic Media: Technology, Design, Practice is the largest, most collaborative intellectual project we have ever attempted. To get to publication, it has taken inspiration, collaboration, consultation, and criticism. It has taken scores of authors to trust in the idea and contribute their work, an editor to believe in the project, extensive comments from anonymous reviewers, and students and research assistants toiling away because they truly care about the work.

We are grateful to the dozens of contributing authors, who, when approached in 2013 about an ambitious project that would attempt to map the growing space of research and practice of civic media, enthusiastically agreed to contribute. Their collective effort and enthusiastic engagement in the project has been inspiring to us and has served as a constant source of motivation throughout the long editorial process. We are so grateful to all the contributors and their persistent passion and professionalism during our seemingly endless barrage of comments and requests.

We want to acknowledge all those who have read drafts, discussed ideas, and generally tolerated our obsession over the last several years. Our colleagues and fellows at the Engagement Lab at Emerson College, including Catherine D'Ignazio, Miranda Banks, Russell Newman, Vincent Reynauld, and Sarah Zaidan, provided valuable feedback on an early draft of the introduction. Engagement Lab staff Stephen Walter and Christina Wilson provided feedback and support throughout. Jay Vachon provided technical support, Aidan O'Donahue created the beautiful artwork on the website, and Jedd Cohen led the design of the learning guide that accompanies the case studies. But everything would have been at a standstill, if not for project manager Becky Michelson, and research assistants Roma Dash and Marissa Koors, who worked on the details, day in and day out, with such professionalism and passion for the end product.

In addition to the print book, this project has a significant online component called *The Civic Media Project*. Launching in early 2015 with nearly 100 case studies, this compendium to the book is meant to flesh out the context of civic media by providing a space for the rigorous documentation and discussion of examples. To host this project, we partnered with the team at the University of Southern California who built the online publishing platform Scalar. Pushing on the boundaries of publishing, Scalar helped us imagine the multimedia form that the "book" would ultimately take. None of this would have been possible without the support from that magnificent team, including Tara McPherson, Steve Anderson, Lex Taylor, and Craig Dietrich, who provided technical, content, and moral support throughout production. And of course, we are greatly indebted to all the case study authors who provided compelling portraits of civic media in action from around the world.

Finally, we want to acknowledge our friends and family who have been hearing about this project for some time, and who traveled along that sometimes-rocky path from interest to acceptance as the years dragged on. For Eric, his wife Justeen Hyde has been an inspiration and critic, and has provided moral, emotional, and intellectual guidance throughout. And his kids, Elliot and Adeline, are the two biggest reasons he does this work: the promise of ethically being in the world in spite of and because of the media they produce and consume, is what drives him every day. And for Paul, his wife Amy, working in public education, has been a source of inspiration and reflection, and his daughters, Emma and Mae, whose budding engagement with media for civic life make this work all the more meaningful.

Introduction

What does civic engagement look like in a digital age? What does it mean to participate in civic life when the lines between online and offline, political and social, organization and network are increasingly blurred? And what happens when civic life is professionalized, when institutions and communities seek to understand and capitalize on motivations for people to engage in public matters offices of civic engagement are cropping up in universities, governments, and corporations, to communicate that the institution is connected and relevant to social life. Many university offices of service learning, focused on "giving back," have transformed to offices of civic engagement, focused on involving outside communities in the mission of teaching and research. Municipal governments have made a similar transition from neighborhood services to hubs of civic engagement and community action. Cities throughout the world have opened "civic innovation" offices. The White House now houses an office of social innovation and civic participation to support bottom-up, community-driven civic engagement initiatives. Civic engagement is increasingly part of the discourse of civil society programs in international development organizations (Edwards 2014). So, too, has the private technology sector embraced the language of civics. Microsoft founded a dedicated office of "civic technology," and companies like Facebook, Google, and Twitter have put resources into civic innovation, blurring the lines between customers and citizens. While these offices and initiatives were once primarily considered community benefits (often a form of charitable afterthought), in recent years they have migrated to the center of institutions, suggesting that civic life is part of the infrastructure of consumerism and governance. At a time when information is so easily accessible to so many, when connections are so easily formed, and when the porousness between work life and personal life is so significant, the space of civics has become integrated into the norms of work, social, and personal life. Civic engagement, in this regard, expands beyond its traditional manifestations of voting, paying taxes, volunteerism, and town meeting attendance, and comes to represent the texture of everyday life—the interface among individuals, their communities, and public institutions.

While one can argue that civic life is simply a promotional trend—concepts of connectivity, sharing, community, and democracy, so well rehearsed in Silicon Valley conversations about market valuation, have seeped into other institutional forms and emerged within a watered-down discourse of civic engagement—one can just as easily make the case that this discourse represents a structural shift toward participatory and accessible institutions, and heightened citizen expectations that they embrace such shifts. The reality is likely a bit of both: the structural transformation of institutions to accommodate greater participation and feedback, and the corresponding commodification and promotion of that transformation. In any case, the result is a dramatic increase in the channels available to people to participate in what we now call civic life. So whether the language of civic engagement is mobilized to sell a product or change policy, there is need to understand it in the new situated space of digital culture. In its newly centralized position, civics has moved from a space of duty and virtue, facilitated by traditional mechanisms of participation, to a space of personal interest, care, and self-actualization, facilitated by a multitude of media platforms (Dalton, 2008). Corporate and government players are acknowledging, celebrating, and exploiting these new platforms as the expansive interface between private life and public institutions (Gordon and Walter, chapter 15); underrepresented populations are imagining how they can obtain a voice (Mihailidis and Gerodimos, chapter 24); and global networks of activists are connecting and assembling to force change (Bennett and Segerberg, chapter 3; Milan, chapter 4). In this formulation, there is little distinction between civic life and the media that facilitate it. We call this *civic media*—the technologies, designs, and practices that produce and reproduce the sense of being in the world with others toward common good. While the concept of "common good" is deeply subjective, we use the term to invoke the good of the commons, or actions taken that benefit a public outside of the actor's intimate sphere. To this end, the *civic* in civic media is not merely about outcomes, but about process and potential. It is about the mechanics of acting in the world with the tools and conditions available. Civic media, then, are any mediated practice that enables a community to imagine themselves as being connected, not through achieving, but through striving for common good.

Why Civic Media?

The term civic media has been used in education and media literacy discussions for decades. It has referred to everything from advocacy journalism to e-government, and has defined both a genre of media and an approach to media making. Media scholar (and contributor to this book) Henry Jenkins defined civic media in 2007 as "any use of any medium which fosters or enhances civic engagement." This intentionally broad definition was meant to expand the term from traditional conceptions of civics such as political news, town halls, and voting booths to online advocacy, fan culture, and public performance. Jenkins argued that civic engagement is more than just actions taken; it is inclusive of and formed by the rituals associated with those actions. Likewise, the media that facilitate civic engagement are not just objects or texts; they represent "communities of practice," which Lave and Wenger define as "an intrinsic condition for the existence of knowledge" and one "that implies participation in an activity system about which participants share understanding concerning what they are doing and what that means in their lives and for their communities" (1991, 122). A community of practice is a group of people invested in the maintenance of their own connectedness. The concept has been used to describe all variations of online (Rheingold 1993) or offline groupings (Brody 2012), and it typically refers to the social ties built on common practices or shared goals (i.e., matters of preference, not circumstance).

One could argue that all communities require some form of practice—even close neighbors do the work of imagining the whole of which they are a part (Anderson 1983). Whether this happens through verbal communication, online social networking, or mass media representation, communities are mediated by some tool, process, or mechanism. So what is unique about civic media practice? Why is it important to understand these practices as related to each other and distinct from other practices in the world? How does the term *civic media* differ from other monikers such as political communication, civic technology, community media, educational media, and citizen journalism? We contend that the value of the umbrella term is its ability to disentangle media practice from its outcomes. Its power lies in the potential to identify civic communities that form around the production or use of media technologies, without making claims about the technologies themselves or their formal and aesthetic composition. We are not interested in defining a genre of media and technology; instead, we are interested in identifying common practices, dispositions, and motivations that organize communities toward achieving civic outcomes around a common good.

One of the early uses of the term was in 2007 with the founding of the Center for Future Civic Media at MIT. This center, launched with support from the Knight Foundation, and situated within the Media Lab, was motivated by the general ethos of "inventing the future" of civics through technology. This was a unique perspective, because at the time, many scholars and pundits were reflecting on the negative impact of the media on civic engagement. This context was heavily influenced by Robert Putnam's influential book *Bowling Alone,* where he demonstrated a drastic decline in voter turnout and public meeting attendance in the United States (Putnam 1995). Notably, he made specific reference to television, arguing that the medium perpetuated civic decline through the facilitation of public gathering without physical co-presence; television enabled a bypassing of civic infrastructure including town halls, front porches, and bowling leagues. This argument was consistent with media scholars such as Joshua Meyrowitz who, a decade earlier, wrote of television's role in decentralizing place in social and civic life (Meyrowitz 1985). The general premise was that television became a kind of civic prosthesis, displacing the need for the physical co-presence most recognizable as civic engagement. In many ways, social media added to this anxiety—while its connective capacity was evident, the ease with which people could connect across space and time further challenged appearances of civic life. People no longer needed to gather in the town square if they could coordinate on Facebook. They no longer needed to march on Main Street if they could retweet something and advocate online. This tension between civic and media became common sense, one that was given a shot of reinforcement by Malcolm Gladwell's 2010 *New Yorker* article, where he criticized the role of social media in political activism and claimed that, because of the placelessness of digital social networks, "we seem to have forgotten what activism is." And Gladwell was not alone. Media critic Evgeny Morozov characterized the Internet as a space for "cyber utopianism."[1] And communication scholar Jose Van Dijck (2013) referred to social networks not as open spaces for active participation, but as increasingly co-opted and commoditized connective platforms for data gathering.

The sociologist Barry Wellman (2002) provides an important counterpoint to this criticism. As a scholar of social networks prior to the rise of social media, Wellman asked how new technology was changing the way that people associated with each other. He introduced the concept of the networked individual, which suggests that people are less likely to limit their group associations because of physical proximity; online they can seamlessly and flexibly move between groups. His work built off of Granovetter's (1973) seminal study that argued for the strength of linking members of different small groups around relevant issues. The concept of the networked individual influenced a large amount of scholarship in areas such as mobile media (Gordon and de Souza e Silva 2011; Ling 2009), activism (Zhang, Johnson, Seltzer, and Bichard 2010), social media (Marwick and boyd 2011), social capital (see Ellison et al. 2010; Steinfeld et al. 2008), and civic engagement (Gil de Zuñiga, Jung, and Valenzuela 2012), all areas that sought to explore the roles of proximity and formal institutions in the formation of social networks. The placelessness lamented by Meyrowitz, Putnam, Gladwell, and others was a quality of everyday life in Wellman's formulation. Media was not in conflict with civic life, but was constitutive of its structure.

It is evident that the term civic media emerged within a polarized context in which can be seen the traces of two contradictory assumptions: (1) all media are civic (media define the structures of social interaction) and (2) all media are the antithesis of civic (media detract from the communities and the public institutions that comprise democracy). Early attempts at defining a field of practice captured the inevitability of a civic framework of media while simultaneously positioning technology as a possible future intervention to solve civic ills. The 1999 protests at the World Trade Organization gathering in Seattle, where protesters established a media center and facilitated the exchange of thousands of hours of video, created a common reference point for the debate about the potential civic impact of networked media. Of course, it did not create common meaning. The story of what became known as the "Battle in Seattle" was framed as both the triumph of community organizing that just happened to involve media, and the triumph of portable, connectable media that just happened to involve community organizing. A decade later, civic uprisings in Moldova, Iran, Tunisia, and Egypt were commonly referred to as "Social Media Revolutions," invoking a similar uneasiness about the role of technology. While the mainstream media was quick to jump on the technological angle, critics were quick to criticize the technological determinism of such approaches. So, in 2007, when the Center for Future Civic Media (now the Center for Civic Media) was established, it was deliberately positioned within this discourse, capitalizing on the enthusiasm of a technological shift as well as providing a critical lens from which to make and observe these phenomena. At that moment in time, the term civic media carved out a possibility space, a way of imagining a future of technology that was pro-social and for public benefit.

But why does the designation of *civic* media matter in 2016? Certainly, the novelty of the civic application of media and the political tensions in which that novelty existed is the justification for early work in this space. But we would not claim that that novelty persists today. In fact, we believe that the term civic media now has very different connotations but remains important. Today, there is widespread recognition that online spaces hold considerable potential for civic life (Banaji and Buckingham 2013), and in fact they are central to institutional and political transformations (Smith 2009). The possibility space of civic media has become normalized in certain sectors, as the discourse surrounding civic or government technology demonstrates, and reduced to a set of assumptions about the composition of tools. That national and local government offices are routinely developing civic technology departments, coupled with their emphasis on democracy and community, demonstrates a mainstreaming of the civic potential of digital technologies. *No longer struggling for attention, civic media is now struggling for differentiation.* The danger, then, is in the term ossifying to mean very specific things, in its reduction to the instrumental functionality of tools or the assumption of access and participation. In some very important ways, the work of civic media now is to combat its success, to identify a space of criticality as well as instrumentality, which moves beyond the normalizing value of the term.

For as much as civic media are celebrated for their scale and inclusion, they are prone to reifying some of the social and political ills that digital culture has cast on contemporary democracies. The reality is that digital media still primarily serve and address communities of privilege, even as marginalized communities are actively inventing and appropriating new tools (see Levine, chapter 1; McDowell and Chinchilla, chapter 30). So there is increased urgency in establishing a space for the study and practice of civic media that can accommodate some organizing questions: How do mediated communities form and maintain themselves? How do people interact with tools or systems, high-tech or low-tech, meant to facilitate community connection or common good? What are the impacts of these mediated practices on sense of community and citizenship? What are the connective practices and critical discourses that drive the adoption of civic tools? And what are the pedagogies and support structures that cultivate knowledge of and criticality towards the media? These questions strategically counteract the functionalist paradigm of applied civic technologies emerging across domains, wherein technological solutions dominate discourse. The authors in this book provide an example-rich, conceptual framework from which to question the assumptions of technological determinism and solutionism (Morozov 2013) and they represent a range of scholarly discourses that explore the critical thinking and making which happens at the intersection of civic and media.

The Structure of the Book

The book is organized into six thematic sections—The Big Picture, Systems + Design, Play + Resistance, Learning + Engagement, Community + Action, and Research + Funding—with three cross-cutting analytical modalities: technology, design, and practice. The modalities do not have their own sections, as they are implied within the analysis of each of the essays and case studies. Technology is in reference to tools or mechanics. The authors question the nature of tools or mechanisms that facilitate civic life. Design is the intentionality of an intervention or civic action. The authors explore the role of intention and accident, the role of conscious design, and responsive appropriation. And practice refers to the routine actions people take with media to enact identities or effect social change. Each of the authors represented in this volume uses one or all of these analytical modalities.

What follows is a collection of nineteen essays and twenty-three case studies from leaders in their respective academic and professional disciplines.[2] We strongly believe that for civic media to be relevant, it needs to be theoretically informed *and* applied. That belief has guided our design of this book. In order to capture the productive collision between academic theory and the nuance of application, we have juxtaposed two very different forms—the long academic essay with the short case study. While academics usually write long essays and practitioners short case studies, we sought crossover in this as well. Some of the essays are written by practitioners and some of the case studies are written by academics. And some of the contributing authors would reject this binary all together. The case studies offer a look into how civic media are being designed, implemented, and practiced in the world. Not all of the examples are successes. Some show failure, intractable challenges, and the shortcomings of civic technologies implemented without care. The case studies represent real world accounts of civic media in practice, from social justice campaigns to the amplification of minority voices, and expand the purview of the book to issues and geographies well beyond what the essays can cover by themselves. The result, we hope, is an honest articulation of the challenges and opportunities associated with the practice and theory of civic media, including deep questioning of what it is, why it matters, and how it is practiced in the world.

Section I: The Big Picture

The first section of the book provides a conceptual framework by putting a few different approaches into dialogue. It begins with the essay written by philosopher and civic engagement scholar Peter Levine in which he questions commonly held assumptions about the structures of technology and democracy. He identifies four "perennial challenges of the digital age": the disaggregation of choice, the increased ambiguity of state sovereignty, the legibility of society to the state, and the state's decreasing reliance on people. He urges a sobriety about the new media environment. "It may empower some ordinary people," Levine says, but "it also disempowers many and offers unprecedented influence to the small groups who control governments and companies." Rooted in a deep understanding of political philosophy, Levine contextualizes civic media in long running debates about democracy, the state, and the public sphere. Ethan Zuckerman, a media activist cum academic, who now directs the Center for Civic Media at MIT, takes a much more enthusiastic position about technology, grounded in practical sense, to articulate a way of thinking about a diversity of participation practices enabled by connective technologies. He identifies three characteristics through which to examine the effectiveness of digital participation: "their 'thickness,' or the demands they put on the participant; their use of different levers of chance to seek specific impacts; and their reliance on voice as a path towards change." Zuckerman's essay provides a robust analytical framework through which to understand motivation and incentives of digital civic participation. Communication scholars W. Lance Bennett and Alexandra Segerberg contribute an updated version of what has become a seminal text in the field about the logic of connective action. They argue that connective technologies have created a context for activism and collective action wherein large-scale social change is often motivated by individuals sharing and connecting. And finally, Stefania Milan offers a critical narrative on the emancipatory potential of civic media, looking at social movements and their "liberated technologies," and providing a compelling historical perspective through which to understand how contemporary media activism has taken shape. Milan argues that emancipatory communication activism must work beyond and outside of the structures that support dominant, mainstream media and communication practices.

There are also three case studies included in this section, including a piece by Chris Peterson that analyzes counter speech in a right-wing community on the website Digg; a piece by Brady Robards and Bob Buttigieg that looks at the effort to achieve marriage equality through the deliberate changing of Facebook profile pictures; and Erhardt

Graeff's detailed look at a self-organizing group of young people that mobilized to resist their own financial debts and the perceived abuses of capitalism. These four foundational essays and three case studies question the role of civic media in theories of democracy, engagement, and activism, and provide a context through which to view the book in its entirety.

Section II: Systems + Design

A system is a set of principles or procedures according to which something is done. And design is the intentional production of an artifact or process. In this section, each of the authors questions how design interventions into civic processes can change the function and nature of civic systems. They explore how the culture of technology design has gained influence on policy making within government (Noveck, chapter 8), how visualizations of massive amounts of data transform the everyday work of governments and NGOs (Williams, chapter 9), and how persuasion and digital connectivity are transforming political campaigning (Karpf, chapter 10). Much of what is addressed in this section falls into the category of civic technology or "civic tech." Civic tech includes such design interventions as mobile websites for government services, social media tools to connect local neighborhoods, data visualization tools to map urban infrastructure, and transportation apps to track buses and trains (Open Plans 2012)— and while it typically refers to work within government, it is increasingly representative of private sector entrepreneurs, activists and artists.

The space of civic tech has grown significantly over the past several years (Sifry, 2014).[3] There are powerful examples of governments adopting new tools for streamlining process and increasing civic engagement (Blake and Epstein, chapter 12; Lackoff, chapter 13, CITRIS, chapter 14). The effort has been anchored by organizations like Code for America (Shrock, chapter 11) (and the international "Code for [your country] movement") and citywide independent initiatives like Civic Hall in New York City or the Smart Chicago Collaborative. The enthusiasm around civic tech has motivated scores of municipal governments to form "innovation offices" charged with inventing and integrating technologies that enable and streamline the work of government (*New Tech City Report* 2012), including notable organizations like New Urban Mechanics in Boston or the *Laboratorio para la Ciudad* in Mexico City. These offices are focused on inventing new tools or creatively adapting existing tools (i.e., Facebook or Twitter), and generally bridging the organizational cultures of government bureaucracy with tech-sector entrepreneurialism (Jacob, 2015; Poje, 2011). The technology evangelist Tim O'Reilly's concept of "government as platform" has guided much of this work, and advocates for government to be a more nimble staging area for experimentation and innovation by serving as a platform for services (internal or third-party) and not simply a provider of services (O'Reilly, 2010).

The transformation of public sector systems through the deliberate design of civic media tools is rich with opportunities and challenges. Just as the need to reimagine systems of democracy and governance is amplified through new technological practices, so are the real threats to basic democratic principles such as privacy, inclusion, and sovereignty. While the authors in this section are largely enthusiastic about the possibilities of new technologies and practices for civic life, these essays and case studies present a complex tension between the desire to be responsive to changing social and cultural trends and the need to cautiously preserve or ensure foundations of democracy. And as the space of civic tech continues to expand, there is need to conceptualize how these technological innovations generate interest, get deployed, get used in practice both intra- and extra- organizationally, and how they are sustained over time within or alongside the social, civic and political realities of systems of governance.[2]

The Systems + Design section provides a unique perspective on the relationship between the design of tools and the systems they are meant to impact. Beth Noveck, a legal scholar and former White House Deputy Chief Technology Officer, provides an institutional perspective on how civic media tools and approaches can "transform and reboot democratic institutions as well as reinvigorate civil society." She explicitly addresses the tensions between new technologies and government bureaucracies and the ways in which design interventions can serve to negotiate those tensions. The next essay, by planning scholar and technologist Sarah Williams, looks at how large data sets get communicated to decision-makers and the public and how the aesthetics of data can impact the decisions people make. She describes four categories in which data are impacting civic processes: (1) the use of previously unavailable datasets, (2) the ability to better communicate complexity, (3) the opportunity for people to explore data and make their own stories, and (4) the ease in which institutions can solicit and represent public input. The third essay in this section, written by political communication scholar David Karpf, examines the use of new technologies in American political campaigns. Karpf argues that political technologies are distinct from other modes of civic technology, because of the element of competition baked into their function. "Unlike government service delivery or civic volunteering," Karpf says, "electoral and advocacy campaigns have strong incentives to construct competing technology platforms and capitalize on technological advances." Karpf makes clear that political technologies are always embedded within value systems; his essay reinforces the connection between individual acts of design and the political, social and cultural systems in which they exist.

In addition to these essays, there are four case studies featured in this section. Andrew Schrock details the history and development of Code for America and discusses the organization's relevance to the field. Dmitry Epstein and Cheryl Blake write about "RegulationRoom," which is a platform designed at Cornell University to bring "missing stakeholders" into regulatory policymaking. Derek Lackaff discusses the exceptional buy-in of participatory policy-making in Reykjavik, Iceland, specifically through the use of a mobile app called Better Reykjavik. And the CITRIS Connected Communities Initiative at UC Berkeley presents an effort from the State of California to solicit and use input in rating government service delivery. Taken together, these essays and case studies provide an overview of civic tech in the context of large systems, public influence, and bureaucratic decision-making.

Section III: Play + Resistance

Civic life is often associated with hard work, risk, boredom, and sacrifice. The consequences of participating (or not participating) are real and have impact on livelihoods, structures of governance, and/or quality of life. Or this is the narrative that has traditionally defined the discourse of civics. But as people find other avenues to engage in civic processes, whether through social media campaigns or occupying urban space, the serious work of civic engagement is complicated by playful activities and creative approaches to problem solving. The increasing role of humor in political discourse (Graeff 2015), the production of activist fan videos (Jenkins et al., chapter 17), or the seemingly simple act of changing one's Facebook profile picture (Robards and Buttigieg, chapter 6), point to a legitimization of play as a context for civic participation and a mode of resistance to normalized power structures.

Play provides opportunity for experimentation, reflection, and failure without traditional consequence. It is a state wherein players can try new identities or practices outside of the rules and restrictions of everyday life—what anthropologist Johan Huizinga famously called the "magic circle" (1950). Huizinga was interested in the ritual aspects of play; building off a Durkheimian notion of the lifeworld, he focused on how play has become a structural necessity in social life, worked into institutions like community governance and religion.

The psychologist Jean Piaget argues that, for children, play is an essential means of problem solving, where most matters of physical, emotional, and social context are explored and mastered (1985). Ranging from imaginative play to daydreaming, video games, and sport—play enables spaces where children confront the problems of the world in a fashion that is set aside, on their own terms, and strictly voluntary. But play is not simply for coping with past and present concerns. As Bruno Bettleheim argues, "play is the child's most useful tool for preparing himself for the future and its tasks" (1987). Play provides a foundation of knowledge and experience that is carried over into non-play activities throughout one's life. In many ways, play is the most serious of human endeavors. Even when it comes to matters of politics and civics, where the inclination is to associate those domains with serious work, there is room to play. And in fact, according to the authors represented in this section, there is *need* to play. Civic communities of practice, through media, are increasingly exploring play as a modality of interaction, from civic games (Gordon and Baldwin-Philippi 2014; Ruiz, Stokes, and Watson 2003) to fan cultures (Jenkins and Shresthova 2012) and social media memes (Shifman 2011).

The sociologist Pierre Bourdieu famously uses the framework of games to describe the *habitus,* or the subjectivity of the individual as she interacts with social structures (1992). Play and the player are implied in his use of games. Every habitus, or subjectivity, is situated in a field (or board); a player is on the field or the board, and has a "feel for the game," he says. Bourdieu refers to this as the *near miraculous encounter* between incorporated history and objectified history. In other words, in "playing the game," there is always a collision between the player (as conceived by the designer) and the player (as enacted through play). In this encounter Bourdieu suggests that players have a sense of the judiciousness of their actions wherein things "make sense"—where history meets situation and is negotiated without articulation. However, he warns that sense is easily disrupted: "One only has to suspend the commitment to the game that is implied in the feel for the game in order to reduce the world, and the actions performed in it, to absurdity, and to bring up questions about the meaning of the world and existence which people never ask when they are caught up in the game" (1992, 66–67).

After describing the games metaphor using examples such as the Olympics, Bourdieu says the following: "By contrast, the social fields, which are the products of a long, slow process of autonomization, and are therefore, so to speak, games 'in themselves' and not 'for themselves,' one does not embark on the game by a conscious act, one is born into the game, with the game" (1992, 67). If social life comprises games in themselves, then games for themselves are self-contained systems wherein people have to consciously step. By this logic, civic media can be considered games "for themselves," and require a shift in player sensibility from one field to another. Civic media can push on Bourdieu's notion of the *"miraculous encounter between habitus and field,"* where media are not disembodied systems, but designed encounters that hinge on the variability of players and designers. In this sense, play allows for a resistance to the normative rules of the game. It provides a critical opportunity to step outside the bounds of everyday reality.

The three essays included in this section address how play, as a mode of resistance, expands the discourse of what is possible in civic media design and practice. Media scholar Eric Gordon and civic designer Stephen Walter contribute an essay entitled "Meaningful Inefficiencies," which warns against the conflation of technological efficiencies with discourses of community and democracy. Gordon and Walter question the characterization of the citizen as the technologically compatible user, where systems are conceived as containing prescribed citizen actions instead of enabling citizens to explore and discover. They make the argument that the player, instead of the user, might in fact be a better metaphor to guide the creation of civic systems, and one way of facilitating this is through the intentional design of *meaningful inefficiencies* into civic technologies. The next essay is a contribution from artist and technologist Beth Coleman. Her piece entitled "Let's Get Lost" examines the way that new-media artists are generating civic spaces through a cartographic imagination or sense of geographic play. She looks closely at several art interventions that seek to alter how people perceive and occupy urban spaces and she makes the argument that creative exploration is generative of civic action taking. In the section's last essay, entitled "Superpowers to the People! How Young Activists Are Tapping the Civic Imagination," media scholars Henry Jenkins, Sangita Shresthova, Liana Gamber-Thompson, and Neta Kligler-Vilenchik look at the power of what they call the civic imagination, or the collective ability to imagine common futures. Specifically, they show how young activists are shaping their imagination of the real world through the appropriation of fan cultures, such as superhero texts. They focus primarily on the Dreamers, an immigrant rights community founded and run by the children of illegal immigrants in the United States, and how superhero stories, such as Superman's immigration to Earth, come to define the stories they are able to tell about themselves.

Five case studies round out this section. Roy Bendor writes about "Mashnotes," which is a playful input mechanism and public art display in Vancouver, Canada. Jessica McLean and Sophia Maalsen document the use of the #destroythejoint hashtag in Australia in reaction to conservative politicians claiming that women in politics were "destroying the joint" by their efforts to support women's equality. Laurie Phillips Honda contributes a piece about the "It Gets Better Campaign" (IGBC), which "is an ongoing campaign to combat suicide among lesbian, gay, bisexual, transgender, and queer (LGBTQ) youth comprised of videos created by LGBTQ individuals and allies of all ages." Catherine D'Ignazio describes a browser plug-in she designed to generate serendipity in news consumption, pushing readers to play with and explore parts of the world they would not otherwise consider. And finally, Nicole Stremlau contributes a piece on mobile money in the Somali territories. The reason we include this in the play and resistance section is to highlight this bold case of creative problem solving as an act of playful resistance. What binds these essays and cases together is an attention to the constraints of traditional civic systems and an exploration of the possibility space opened up through play and imagination. In essence, this section seeks to acknowledge the *miraculous encounter* between players and systems and the consequent re-imagination of civic life.

Section IV: Learning + Engagement

The centrality of digital media, or more specifically, connective technologies, in the lives of young people today, has surfaced important questions about the competencies—or literacies—needed to effectively navigate digital spaces in everyday life. As youth generate a growing dependence on social networks to facilitate communication and sense of belonging (Deuze 2006; Christakis 2011; Turkle 2012), they also develop a sense of agency that exists outside of the traditional structures of civic life (boyd 2014). The essays in this section examine how young people develop and disseminate civic competencies (Hobbs, chapter 23), both within educational institutions and outside of them (Soep, chapter 25), and the role of formal and informal pedagogies in support of engagement in civic life (Mihailidis and Gerodimos, chapter 24).

The connection between civic engagement and education is nothing new. John Dewey said that "as a society becomes more enlightened, it realizes that it is responsible not to transmit and conserve the whole of its existing achievements, but only such as make for a better future society. The school is its chief agency for the accomplishment of this end" (2011, 24). Dewey's successors, notably Freire (2000), Postman (1996), Ong (2002), and McLuhan (1994), all offered their distinct narratives that support his claim that "the devotion of democracy to education is a familiar fact." Freire, in particular, encompasses the civic aim of education in his understanding of "education as the practice of freedom" where learning is embedded in the social, political and cultural realities of civic life that reflect "people in their relations with the world" (2000, 81).

The political theorist Benjamin Barber suggests, "because democracy depends on citizenship, the emphasis then was to think about how to constitute a competent and virtuous citizen body. That led directly … to the connection between citizenship and education" (2002, 22). Citizenship and education are tied to media literacies because civic life is composed of the skills and dispositions that young people use to engage with media for personal and public means. As the spaces for formal education have trouble keeping pace with technological advancements (Rheingold, 2012), how students learn to participate in civic life becomes a question of increasing importance, and that is less dependent on formal schooling alone. Education scholar Renee Hobbs summarized the aims of media and digital literacy in a report for the Aspen Foundation, in which she highlights the need for young people to "recognize personal, corporate and political agendas" and be "empowered to speak out on behalf of the missing voices and omitted perspectives in our communities" (2010, 17). These abilities have been supported by scholarship that has moved discussions about learning and engagement in civic life from a set of constructs embedded in the analysis of media texts to an analysis of media's impact on identity and agency in civic life. Notably, Mimi Ito's notion of connected learning repositions education as more than the ability "to access serious online information and culture." She argues that "youth could benefit from educators being more open to forms of experimentation and social exploration that are generally not characteristic of educational institutions" (2012, 2). Ito's work in this space has been complemented by movements in participatory politics (Middaugh and Kahne 2013), new literacies (Lankshear and Knobel 2011); and digital citizenship (Hobbs

2010), that have at their core a more robust and dynamic approach to learning about media, moving beyond normative approaches to the critical analysis of texts.

Each of the essays in this section explores the connection between engaging in civic life and the structures and institutions of learning that support it. They also address the moral responsibilities that bubble to the surface as the media transform traditional interfaces between private and public, formal and informal, social and political. As Ethan Zuckerman writes in his book *ReWire:* "If we want to maximize the benefits and minimize the harms of connection, we have to take responsibility for shaping the tools we use to encounter the world" (2013, 40). To begin this section, media education scholar Renee Hobbs contributes an essay called "Capitalists, Consumers, and Communicators: How Schools Approach Civic Education," wherein she explores three specific literacies—financial, news, and digital. She argues that these literacies are central to civic education in public schools today. She questions the ability of the educational system to respond and adapt to students' media practices, and whether or not teachers possess the skills to activate a more functional, dynamic and forward looking approach to civic education guided by learners' engagement with news, finance, and technology. Media scholars Paul Mihailidis and Roman Gerodimos, in their essay entitled "Connecting Pedagogies of Civic Media," argue for a need to better connect scholarship and practice in education about media to the expanding domain of civic engagement. Their argument focuses on the constraints that formal spaces of learning place on activist and engaged forms of pedagogy. They propose a focus on civic voice through which youth agency connects with pedagogy to generate the possibility space of civic media. To round out this section, youth media activist Elizabeth Soep contributes an essay called "Youth Agency in Public Spheres: Emerging Tactics, Literacies, and Risks," which asks three questions that have emerged from her work at Youth Radio in San Francisco. What specific tactics are young people experimenting with to exercise agency and intervene in public affairs? How can these activities grow in quality? What work is required to ensure that opportunities to engage in participatory politics are equitably distributed among youth including those marginalized from digital and other forms of privilege? She's interested in how young people "engage with and remake public spheres, often deploying digital and social media tools in intriguing ways." She offers five specific tactics that can be used to better facilitate youth driven activities in support of community engagement, action, and participation.

Finally, this section is rounded out with three case studies. Katie Day Good documents the Flat Stanley Project, a networked initiative where kids all over the world cut out and photograph a paper doll in places where they live or travel. Daniela Gerson, Nien-Tsu Nancy Chen, Sandra Ball-Rokeach, and Michael Parks document a story of police in a small Southern Californian city, with a significant Chinese immigrant population, using the Chinese social network Weibo to facilitate deep local and diasporic community connections. It provides a rich example of meaningful learning and engagement outside of formal institutions. And Jennifer Gabrys, Nerea Calvillo, Tom Keene, Helen Pritchard, and Nick Shapiro contribute a case study on citizen environmental sensing, wherein the act of contributing and reading environmental data is characterized as civic. The three essays and three case studies featured in this section examine the complex intersection between formal education, community life, and civic action-taking through media.

Section V: Community + Action

Examples of mass assembly, connection, and protest facilitated by social networks are abundant. The Arab Spring, Occupy Wall Street, Hong Kong's Umbrella revolution, and protests in Greece, Turkey, and Ukraine, are but a few of the civic movements supported by people's ability to tap into networks through YouTube, Facebook, Twitter, and Instagram, among others, both for the coordination of physical gatherings and for garnering global attention and support for a cause. Manuel Castells, in *Networks of Outrage and Hope* (2012), details the rise of "networked social movements" which he argues are a new, distributed form of action for the people and by the people. This narrative has been supported by research that shows civic applications of social networks and connective technologies are increasingly central facilitators for the public to engage in activism and disruption (Chadwick 2009; Garrett 2006; Mercea 2013; Siegel 2009). Evidence of civic action has been more prominent when explored in the context of reaction to oppression and injustice. Cases of social networks facilitating civic protest in Chile (Valenzuela 2012), Turkey (Tufekci and Wilson 2012), and the United States (Thorson 2013), have provided a strong set of models for the ecosystem of civic action driven by what Stuart Allan (2012) believes is a "need to better understand how personal experience gives shape to the ways young people relate to their communities beyond 'citizenship' narrowly defined" (36).

What constitutes civic *action* and its relationship to community or publics is the topic of this section. danah boyd's notion of a "networked public" (boyd 2014) representing "the imagined community that emerges as a result of the intersection of people, technology, and practice" (19) provides a useful frame for understanding motivations for participating in a digital culture (Burgess 2006), in everyday civic life (Silverstone 2007; Bennett and Segerberg, 2012), and it is particularly relevant to a contemporary understanding of citizenship. Sociologist and civic scholar Michael Schudson (1998) has traced the notion of citizenship through a historical look at civic life in the United States, starting with the ideas of *good* and *informed citizenship*—bound to both an obedience to democratic power structures and an adherence to the need to make informed decisions about the duties that contemporary civic life entails. Schudson concludes that traditional concepts of "good citizenship" marked by the duties traditionally reserved for civic engagement—voting, paying taxes, volunteering, military duty, jury duty, and the like—are no longer sufficient for meaningful civic contributions in a democratic society. Instead, Schudson suggests a "monitorial" form of citizenship, where citizens monitor "the informational environment in a way so that he or she may be alerted on a very wide variety of issues for a very wide variety of ends and may be mobilized around those issues in a large variety of ways." This concept has been supported by Jenkins (2006), Papacharissi (2009), and Zuckerman (chapter 2), who note that while the monitorial citizen perhaps does not serve democracy better or worse than another form of citizen, the concept forces a discussion about what community, participation, and action mean for civic life.

Bennett (2008) extends this debate by differentiating the dutiful citizen, who understands civic action as a set of prescribed duties to one's community, from the actualizing citizen, who views civic action through a personal lens that focuses on notions of agency, protest, justice, rights, and inclusion (also see Bennett and Segerberg, chapter 3). In *The Good Citizen,* Dalton (2008) cites a host of social shifts that have re-framed what it means to be a civic actor. Dalton's engaged citizen sees their primary form of contribution to make the world a better place, to advocate for rights, diversity, and social justice. This concept "emphasizes a more assertive role for the citizen and a broader definition of the elements of citizenship to include social concerns and the welfare of others" (2008, 5). Dalton, like Bennett, invokes duty-based citizenship as a counter example in order to create a clear distinction from more traditional approaches to civic engagement.

The authors in this section take three distinct approaches to the topic of community and action. Media scholar Molly Sauter looks at the phenomenon of distributed denial of service attacks (DDoS) to provide a framework for where the personal and community meet. She interrogates how digital activists, through computer-generated actions meant to overwhelm and shut down servers, have contested the distinction between private and public spaces online by pushing on the boundaries of free speech, vandalism, and civic participation. Scholar activists Ceasar McDowell and Melissa Chinchilla, in "Partnering with Communities and Institutions," approach community and action through the lens of inclusion. They write, "to promote democracy in a diverse society, civic technology must design for civic inclusion instead of civic engagement." McDowell and Chinchilla understand civic inclusion as a designed process where "all individuals learn to engage with established organizational structures, and that institutions become adept in serving an increasingly heterogeneous membership." To make this argument, they provide an action research perspective through their own community engagement work that identifies five challenges they see as central to civic inclusion in digital culture. Lastly, information science scholar Colin Rhinesmith explores the structure of community-based media as civic engagement. His essay, "Community Media Infrastructure as Civic Engagement," urges readers to "look beyond Facebook, YouTube, and other participatory media platforms in order to focus on the underlying civic communications infrastructure that makes free speech possible in many communities around the world." He presents the public, educational, and government (PEG) access television model developed in the United States as a paradigmatic framework of sustainable community media infrastructure. But Rhinesmith notes the challenges that this infrastructure poses in the context of a shift to open, digital culture. He argues that there is an explicit need "to rethink localism and self-determination in discussions of Internet policy in order to engage more people in deciding the future of free speech in the digital age."

There are five case studies in this section, which include two examples of hashtag activism, Emiliano Treré's piece on the #YoSoy132 movement in Mexico, and Sarah Whitcomb Lozier's detailed analysis of #MyNYPD in New York. Tad Hirsch introduces what he calls "surreptitious communication design" in a project called Pivot, which provides rescue information in menstrual pads for victims of sex trafficking. Stuart Davis details the "rise of citizen journalism in Brazil" through his case study of the MídiaNINJA project. And Sebastian Kubitschko looks closely at a hacker collective in Europe called the Chaos Computer Club, and its efforts to "hack politics."

Section: VI: Research + Funding

The central challenge with any new interdisciplinary set of practices is establishing commonly held questions and methods. What are problems that existing approaches and disciplines cannot address and what research methods are appropriate? This is most often done through a combination of academic journals, foundation partners, and university leadership, and is very rarely a smooth or even necessary process. Civic media finds itself in an interesting position, as a handful of foundations, notably MacArthur, Knight, Omidyar, Sunlight, Rockefeller, and Ford, came to the table early on, eager to motivate or solidify emerging practices around technology and civic engagement. The Knight Foundation provided funding for the MIT Center for Future Civic Media in 2007 as well as the Emerson Engagement Lab in 2010 (which is directed by the editors of this volume), and through its *Technology for Engagement* program, gave the initial funding to Code for America and other landmark non-university organizations such as Open Plans. Likewise, the MacArthur Foundation, through its Digital Media and Learning (DML) program, made a substantial investment in building a field of practice and research around digital literacies and young people. The DML conference remains one of the most interesting annual meetings for exploring these issues. Topics of civic media are often addressed, but they have not been the primary concern of the community. Seeing an opportunity, several years ago the MacArthur foundation began investing specifically in the intersections of digital learning and civic practices. They funded the Youth and Participatory Politics (YPP) research network in 2011 (which includes several of this book's authors, including Henry Jenkins, Joe Kahne, and

Elisabeth Soep) and the Governance network in 2014 (which includes Beth Noveck, and which was supported by Valerie Chang on the foundation side, both of whom are contributors to this volume). Each of these networks explores some aspect of civic media (youth and government respectively), and has productively contributed to scholarship and practice in these areas. But while foundation dollars can be instrumental in field building (Petrovich 2013), they can also generate confusion as to the role of research in facilitating social change and, indeed, the role of social change in shaping research. When funders want immediate results, or specific uses of data, researchers and their institutions tend to accommodate, potentially compromising the quality of research and its potential impact.

Application and scholarship are often uneasy bedfellows. And civic media is almost necessarily crammed between them in what turns out to be a rather rickety bed, as academic institutions struggle to situate themselves within a context of foundation funding, private sector enthusiasm, and public sector transformations (O'Toole, Aaron, Chin, Horowitz, and Tyson 2003). The role of the university has been unclear in these shifts for both university researchers and practitioners as they each struggle with the substantive disconnect between knowing and doing, each operating with a different language, different incentives, and different timelines. For academics, the notion of *doing* civic media is caught between the creation of tools, the activation of communities, and the production of knowledge (Foth and Brynskov, chapter 38). This is not to suggest that the entirety of civic media research is applied. In fact, this book represents a range of scholars from academic disciplines where application is not a central concern. However, it is safe to assume that for the authors represented in this volume, while application may not guide their research, they are concerned with the use of academic knowledge. As contributors to a volume on civic media, they are all investigating some aspect of media practice—how are people using media to achieve civic outcomes? And how are media defining the terms of use?

We do not want to suggest that these tensions are unique to civic media; in fact, there is tension in any applied field, or any field that has direct consequence for application, between rigor and usefulness of research (Atkinson and Blanpied 2008). In a university context, usefulness can have negative connotations for tenure committees, as it is assumed to degrade the integrity of knowledge production.[4] But for many applied fields such as health and policy, areas of economics, applied anthropology, political science, and certain areas of communications and media studies, the connection between knowledge and practice is central. And in each case, the relationship between universities and practitioners needs to be negotiated. Policymakers, entrepreneurs, service providers, and activists want research, but they need it today; they are unwilling or unable to wait a year for a journal article to be published. And university researchers are under pressure to publish and are given little or no credit for the application of their ideas. What's happened in many fields is an adoption of applied methodologies or approaches, such as, Participatory Action Research (Bilandzic and Venable 2011; Hearn, Tacchi, Foth, and Lennie 2009), Human Centered Design (Simonsen & Robertson 2012) or Community-based Participatory Research (Hacker 2013; O'Toole et al. 2003), that aim to bring research subjects into a partnership with the researcher as a means of situating knowledge in the world and in practice. There is a substantial body of academic work from methodologists that has attempted to bridge the gap between the researcher and the researched, which has undoubtedly been important for the development of a civic media field. But as academic researchers struggle with shifting university leadership, more pressure to secure external funding in the humanities and social sciences, and increasing porousness in town/gown relations, the tension between rigor and usefulness remains front and center.

It is for this reason that we end the book with a section on research and funding. While this section is necessarily incomplete for the reasons we discuss above (we could write an entire book about this), we felt it was important to pull back the camera and get a wide angle on the practice of doing the kind of work that this book represents. As an academic work published by a prestigious academic press, we are very aware of this book's position in the lexicon of civic media objects. We understand it as making a contribution to research, but we also understand it as a useful object. Quite honestly, this is the tension that motivated us to put this volume together in the first place, as each of us found ourselves struggling with the use value of doing scholarship about civic media while making the very tools about which we were writing and teaching. In some very real ways, we founded the Engagement Lab (a research organization) at Emerson College (a school with a heavy emphasis on media production) precisely so we could sit in that uneasy position between making things, impacting communities, and producing knowledge.[5]

The three essays and four case studies in this section provide a meta-perspective to the other pieces in the book. The section begins with an essay from education scholars Joseph Kahne and Benjamin Bowyer, who look at the challenges and opportunities of doing survey research in ways that can deductively address the shifting domain of form and practice. While the essay focuses specifically on survey research, Kahne and Bowyer address the need for qualitative and interpretative research alongside surveys as a means of mapping out the complexity of emerging civic practices. In the following essay, Human Computer Interaction scholars Marcus Foth and Martin Brynskov focus on Participatory Action Research for new media, and introduce methods of meaningfully involving communities and users in both knowledge production and design. The last essay is from philanthropists Valerie Chang and Beth Gutelius from the MacArthur Foundation. It makes a unique contribution in a volume otherwise focused on the research and practice of civic media by highlighting the organizational politics of funding the research and practice. The essay provides an overview of philanthropy's role in shaping the field over the last decade, and then provides an in-depth analysis of the specific decisions made by the MacArthur Foundation.

Three case studies round out this section. Glenda Amayo Caldwell, Lindy Osborne, Inger Mewburn, and Ben Kraal discuss what they call "Guerrilla Research Tactics," exploring alternative ways to work with communities in collecting data. Carl DiSalvo and ken anderson look at Hackathons as research, and explore the what, when, and how of collecting knowledge within collective efforts. And finally, Rodrigo Davies looks at how creative crowdfunding mobilized a movement in support of *catadores* or "waste pickers" in São Paulo, Brazil.

Each of the essays and case studies in this section represents an aspect of the increasingly complex terrain of applied scholarship. When the production of knowledge is intended to have direct impact in the world and when impact is intended to produce knowledge, the traditional structures of research, including its methods and funding, are challenged. This section is the ideal conclusion of a volume that seeks to contribute new knowledge and, at the same time, question how knowledge is contributed.

To the Book

As we write this introduction, there are countless examples of people around the world harnessing the affordances of digital media to enable democratic participation, coordinate disaster relief, advocate for policy change, empower marginalized communities, or simply to strengthen local advocacy groups (Foth, Forlano, Satchell, and Gibbs, 2011; Goldstein and Dyson 2013; Gordon, Baldwin-Philippi, and Balestra 2013; Meier, 2015; Mihailidis 2014; Nabatchi and Leighninger 2015; Zuckerman 2013). And there are just as many examples of corporations, universities, and governments using the language of participation to rethink their relationship to customers, students, and constituents. By bringing together scholars from multiple academic disciplines and practitioners from an array of organizations, *Civic Media* seeks to establish an interdisciplinary conversation, spanning departmental and institutional boundaries, that at once motivates more scholarly work about tools and practices and provides a critical language to its application.

Civic media are all the technologies, designs, and practices that connect people to government, institutions, and more generally, the practice and promise of contemporary democracy. This book is at once a record of the past and a road map to the future of civics. It is just one small piece of a very large puzzle, and while it alone cannot solve the big challenges outlined in its pages, we embrace its potential as a civic media object, one that will hopefully enable a community of scholars and practitioners to imagine themselves as being connected, not through achieving, but through striving for common good.

Notes

1. Morozov's perspective generated considerable debate, nicely represented here: http://www
.cjr.org/cover_story/evgeny_vs_the_internet.php.

2. In addition to the twenty-three case studies collected here, a hundred more exist online at
http://civicmediaproject.org. The Civic Media Project is a living collection of civic media case
studies with an actively curated conversation and curriculum that guides its use in the classroom.

3. More than $695 million was invested in civic tech start-ups from 2011 to the end of 2013,
according to a February 2014 update to the Knight Foundation report, "The Emergence of Civic
Tech: Investments in a Growing Field."

4. For example, the Consortium of Practicing and Applied Anthropology Programs (COPAA) has
existed since 2003 and has sought to respond to tenure and promotion concerns by establishing
professional standards or research and application.

5. The Engagement Game Lab (http://elab.emerson.edu) was founded by Eric Gordon at Emerson College in 2010, with a unique focus on games and civic engagement. It has since expanded
its purview to include other modalities of civic media with the addition of new affiliated faculty,
including Paul Mihailidis (this book's co-editor). It officially changed its name to the Engagement
Lab in 2013.

References

Allan, Stuart. 2012. "Civic Voices: Social Media and Political Protest." In *News Literacy: Global
Perspectives for the Newsroom and the Classroom*, ed. P. Mihailidis. New York: Peter Lang.

Anderson, B. 1983. *Imagined Communities: Reflections on the Origin and Spread of Nationalism.*
London: Verso.

Atkinson, R. C., and W. A. Blanpied. 2008. "Research Universities: Core of the US Science And
Technology System." *Technology in Society* 30 (1): 30–48. doi:10.1016/j.techsoc.2007.10.004

Barber, Benjamin. 2002. The Educated Student—Global Citizen or Global Consumer? *Liberal Education* (*Spring*).

Bennett, W. Lance. 2008. "Changing Citizenship in the Digital Age." In *Civic Life Online: Learning
How Digital Media Can Engage Youth*, ed. W. L. Bennett. Cambridge, MA: MIT Press.

Bettleheim, B. 1987. "The Importance of Play." *Atlantic Monthly,* March. Retrieved from http://
www.theatlantic.com/magazine/archive/1987/03/the-importance-of-play/305129.

Bilandzic, M., and J. Venable. 2011. "Towards Participatory Action Design Research." *Journal of
Community Informatics* 7 (3). Retrieved from files/1931/Journal of Community Informatics 2011
Bilandzic.pdf.

Bourdieu, P. 1992. *The Logic of Practice*. Palo Alto: Stanford University Press.

boyd, danah. 2014. *It's Complicated: The Social Lives of Networked Teens*. New Haven, CT: Yale University Press.

Brody, S. 2012. "How the Sausage Is Made: The Inside Story on Community Organizing." *Analyses of Social Issues and Public Policy (ASAP)* 12 (1): 412–416. doi:.10.1111/j.1530-2415.2011.01260.x

Burgess, Helen G. 2006. "Everyday Creativity as Civic Engagement: A Cultural Citizenship View of New Media." In *Communications Policy & Research Forum*. Sydney.

Castells, Manuel. 2012. *Networks of Outrage and Hope: Social Movements in the Internet Age*. Cambridge: Polity Press.

Chadwick, Andrew. 2009. "The Internet and Politics in Flux." *Journal of Information Technology & Politics* 6:195–196.

Costanza-Chock, S. 2014. *Out of the Shadows, Into the Streets!* Cambridge, MA: MIT Press.

Christakis, J. 2011. *Connected: How Your Friends' Friends' Friends Affect Everything You Feel, Think, and Do*. New York: Penguin.

Dalton, R. J. 2008. *The Good Citizen: How a Younger Generation Is Reshaping American Politics*. Revised Edition. Washington, DC: CQ Press.

de Zuñiga, G., H. Jung, and S. Valenzuela 2012. "Social Media Use for News and Individuals' Social Capital, Civic Engagement and Political Participation." *Journal of Computer-Mediated Communication* 17 (3): 319–336. Retrieved from http://onlinelibrary.wiley.com/doi/10.1111/j.1083-6101.2012.01574.x/full.

Deuze, M. 2006. Collaboration, Participation and the Media. *New Media & Society* 8 (4): 691–698. doi:.10.1177/1461444806065665

Dewey, John. 2011. *Democracy and Education*. New York: Simon and Brown.

Edwards, M. 2014. *Civil Society*. 3rd ed. London: Polity.

Ellison, N. B., C. Steinfield, and C. Lampe. 2010. Connection Strategies: Social Capital Implications of Facebook-Enabled Communication Practices. *New Media & Society* 13 (6): 873–892.

Foth, M., L. Forlano, C. Satchell, and M. Gibbs, eds. 2011. *From Social Butterfly to Engaged Citizen: Urban Informatics, Social Media, Ubiquitous Computing, and Mobile Technology to Support Citizen Engagement*. Cambridge, MA: MIT Press.

Freire, Paulo. 2000. *Pedagogy of the Opressed*. New York: Bloomsburg Academic.

Garrett, R. K. 2006. "Protest in an Information Society : A Review of Literature on Social Movements and New ICTs." *Information, Communication & Society* 9 (2): 202–224. doi:.10.1080/13691180600630773.New

Gladwell, M. 2010. "Small Change: Why the Revolution Will Not Be Tweeted." *The New Yorker*, October 4.

Goldstein, B., and L. Dyson. 2013. *Beyond Transparency: Open Data and the Future of Civic Innovation*. Ed. B. Goldstein and L. Dyson. San Francisco: Code for America Press.

Gordon, E., and A. de Souza e Silva. 2011. *Net Locality: Why Location Matters in a Networked World*. Boston, MA: Blackwell.

Gordon, E., and J. Baldwin-Philippi. 2014. "Playful Civic Learning: Enabling Lateral Trust and Reflection in Game-based Public Participation." *International Journal of Communication*, February 26. Retrieved from http://ijoc.org/index.php/ijoc/article/view/2195.

Gordon, E., J. Baldwin-Philippi, and M. Balestra. 2013. "Why We Engage: How Theories of Human Behavior Contribute to Our Understanding of Civic Engagement in a Digital Era." *SSRN Electronic Journal* (21). doi:.10.2139/ssrn.2343762

Graeff, E. 2015. "Binders Full of Election Memes: Participatory Culture Invades the 2012 US Election." In *The Civic Media Project*, ed. E. Gordon and P. Mihailidis. Cambridge, MA: MIT Press.

Granovetter, M. S. 1973. The Strength of Weak Ties. *American Journal of Sociology* 78 (6): 1360–1380.

Hacker, K. 2013. *Community-Based Participatory Research*. New York: Sage Publications.

Hearn, G., J. Tacchi, M. Foth, and J. Lennie. 2009. *Action Research and New Media*. New York: Hampton Press.

Hobbs, Renee. 2010. *Digital Media Literacy: A Plan of Action*. Aspen, CO: Aspen Institute.

Huizinga, J. 1950. *Homo Ludens: A Study of the Play-Element in Culture*. Boston, MA: Beacon Press.

Ito, Mizuko, Kris Gutiérrez, Sonia Livingstone, Bill Penuel, Jean Rhodes, Katie Salen, Juliet Schor, Julian Sefton-Green, and S. Craig Watkins. 2012. *Connected Learning. An Agenda for Research and Design*. Digital Media and Learning Research Hub. http://dmlhub.net/publications/connected-learning-agenda-for-research-and-design.

Jacob, N. 2015. Living Cities. *Guide for Embedding Breakthrough Innovation in Local Government*. Retrieved from https://www.livingcities.org/resources/286-city-accelerator-guide-for-embedding-innovation-in-local-government.

Jenkins, H. 2006. *Convergence Culture: Where Old and New Media Collide*. New York: New York University Press.

Jenkins, Henry. 2007. "What Is Civic Media?" Confessions of an Aca-Fan. http://henryjenkins.org/2007/10/what_is_civic_media_1.html.

Jenkins, H., and S. Shresthova. 2012. "Up, Up, and Away! The Power and Potential of Fan Activism." *Transformative Works and Cultures*, 10. Retrieved from http://journal.transformativeworks.org/index.php/twc/article/view/435/305.

Lankshear, Colin, and Michele Knobel. 2011. *New Literacies: Everyday Practices and Social Learning*. New York: Open University Press.

Lave, J., and E. Wenger. 1991. *Situated Learning: Legitimate Peripheral Participation*. New York: Cambridge University Press; Retrieved from http://books.google.com/books?id=CAVIOrW3vYAC andpgis=1.

Ling, R. 2009. *Mobile Communication*. New York: Polity.

Marwick, A. E., and boyd, d. 2011. "I Tweet Honestly, I Tweet Passionately: Twitter Users, Context Collapse, and the Imagined Audience." *New Media & Society* 13 (1): 114–133.

McLuhan, Marshall. 1994. *Understanding Media: The Extensions of Man*. Cambridge, MA: MIT Press.

Meier, P. 2015. *Digital Humanitarians: How Big Data Is Changing the Face of Humanitarian Response*. New York: CRC Press.

Mercea, D. 2013. "Probing the Implications of Facebook Use for the Organizational Form of Social Movement Organizations." *Information, Communication & Society* 16 (8): 1306–1327.

Meyrowitz, J. 1985. *No Sense of Place: The Impact of Electronic Media on Social Behavior*. New York: Oxford University Press.

Middaugh, Ellen, and Joseph Kahne. 2013. "New Media as a Tool for Civic Learning." *Comunicar* 20 (40): 99–107. http://www.revistacomunicar.com/pdf/comunicar40-en.pdf#page=99.

Mihailidis, P. 2014. *Media Literacy and the Emerging Citizen: Youth, Engagement and Participation in Digital Culture*. New York: Peter Lang.

Morozov, E. 2013. *To Save Everything, Click Here: The Folly of Technological Solutionism*. New York: PublicAffairs.

Nabatchi, T., and M. Leighninger. 2015. *Public Participation for 21st Century Democracy*. New York: Jossey-Bass.

New Tech City Report. (2012). Center for an Urban Future. Retrieved from http://nycfuture.org/research/publications/new-tech-city.

O'Reilly, T. 2010. Government as platform. In *Open government: Collaboration, transparency, and participation in practice*, ed. D. Lathrop and L. Ruma, 12–39. Sebastopol, CA: O'Reilly.

O'Toole, T., K. F. Aaron, M. Chin, C. Horowitz, and F. Tyson. 2003. "Community-based Participatory Research: Opportunities, Challenges, and the Need for a Common Language." *Journal of General Internal Medicine* 18 (7): 592–594.

Ong, Walter. 2002. *Orality and Literacy*. 2nd ed. New York: Routledge.

Open Plans. 2012. *Field Scan of Civic Technology*. New York.

Papacharissi, Zizi. 2009. "The Citizen Is the Message: Alternative Modes of Civic Engagement." In *Journalism and Citizenship: New Agendas in Communication*, ed. Zizi Papacharissi, 29–43. New York: Routledge.

Petrovich, J. 2013. *Building and Supporting Sustainable Fields: Views from Philanthropy*. New York: Robert Wood Johnson Foundation.

Piaget, J. 1985. *Equilibration of Cognitive Structures: The Central Problem of Intellectual Development*. Chicago: University of Chicago Press.

Poje, J. (2011). Gov 2.0: Interaction, Innovation and Collaboration. (Cover story). *Public Lawyer, 19*(1), 2–11.

Postman, Neil. 1996. *The End of Education: Redefining the Value of School*. New York: Vintage Books.

Putnam, R. 1995. "Bowling Alone." *Journal of Democracy* 6 (1). Retrieved from http://xroads.virginia.edu/~HYPER/DETOC/assoc/bowling.html.

Rheingold, H. 1993. *The Virtual Community: Homesteading on the Electronic Frontier*. Boston, MA: Addison-Wesley.

Rheingold, H. 2012. *Net Smart: How to Thrive Online*. Cambridge, MA: MIT Press.

Ruiz, S., B. Stokes, and J. Watson. 2003. "The Civic Tripod for Mobile and Games." *International Journal of Learning and Media*, January 1. Retrieved from http://civictripod.com.

Schudson, Michael. 1998. *The Good Citizen: A History of American Civic Life*. New York: Free Press.

Shifman, L. 2011. "An Anatomy of a YouTube Meme." *New Media and Society,* October 3. Retrieved from http://nms.sagepub.com/content/early/2011/09/27/1461444811412160.abstract.

Siegel, D. A. 2009. "Social Networks and Collective Action." *American Journal of Political Science* 53 (1): 122–138.

Sifry, M. 2014. *The Big Disconnect: Why the Internet Hasn't Transformed Government (Yet)*. New York: OR Books.

Silverstone, R. 2007. *Media and Morality*. Cambridge: Polity.

Simonsen, J., and T. Robertson, eds. 2012. *Routledge International Handbook of Participatory Design*. New York: Routledge.

Smith, A. 2009. *The Internet's Role in Campaign 2008*. Pew Research Center.

Steinfield, C., N. B. Ellison, and C. Lampe. 2008. Social Capital, Self-Esteem, and Use of Online Social Network Sites: A Longitudinal Analysis. *Journal of Applied Developmental Psychology* 29:434–445.

Thorson, C. 2013. "YouTube, Twitter and the Occupy Movement." *Information, Communication & Society* 16 (3): 421–451.

Tufekci, Zeynep, and Christopher Wilson. 2012. "Social Media and the Decision to Participate in Political Protest: Observations From Tahrir Square." *Journal of Communication* 62 (2): 363–379.

Turkle, Sherry. 2012. *Alone Together: Why We Expect More from Technology and Less from Each Other*. New York: Basic Books.

Valenzuela, A. 2012. "The Social Media Basis of Youth Protest Behavior: The Case of Chile." *Journal of Communication* 62 (2): 299–314.

Van Dijck, J. 2013. *The Culture of Connectivity: A Critical History of Social Media*. Oxford: Oxford University Press.

Wellman, B. 2002. "Little Boxes, Glocalization and Networked Individualism." In M. Tanabe, P. van den Besselaar, and T. Ishida (eds.), *Digital Cities II: Computational and Sociological Approaches: Second Kyoto Workshop on Digital Cities, Kyoto, Japan, October 18–20, 2001*. London: Springer.

Zhang, W., T. J. Johnson, T. Seltzer, and S. L. Bichard. 2010. "The Revolution Will Be Networked : The Influence of Social Networking Sites on Political Attitudes and Behavior." *Social Science Computer Review* 28 (1): 75–92. Retrieved from http://blaz.lasi.cc/TheRevolutionWillBeNetworked.pdf.

Zuckerman, E. 2013. *Rewire: Digital Cosmopolitanism in the Age of Connection*. New York: W. W. Norton & Co. Inc.

I   The Big Picture

1 Democracy in the Digital Age

Peter Levine

To write a chapter about democracy in the digital age invites ridicule. The digital media change so rapidly that bold predictions set on paper in one year can look quaint by the next. Democracy is also changing rapidly, and not only because of media and technology; witness the rise of neo-authoritarian regimes in many countries (Ignatieff 2014) and increasing economic inequality in societies such as the United States (Piketty 2014).

The question of anonymity illustrates how quickly our sense of the situation can change. Since ancient times, participants in public debates had been known by name and face, but that has not always been the case since message boards and blogs arose. Anonymity promises freedom and equality but also irresponsibility and incivility. These were prominent concerns in the literature on civil society and the Internet at the turn of our century (e.g., Naughton 2001). But then Facebook built a network of 1.5 billion active users, capitalizing on an apparently irrepressible impulse to share one's real name and appearance with "friends" whom you actually know. Instead of opting for pseudonyms, Facebook users were sharing unprecedented amounts of actual personal information with their social circles—and beyond. The handwringing shifted from concerns about anonymity to the supposed death of privacy.

Another example of rapid change is the quickly evolving nature of American political campaigns. Barack Obama's success in 2008 seemed to suggest that political campaigns would now be able to raise their funds from millions of small donors and push their power out to the edges of their networks by allowing ordinary volunteers to choose their own messages and strategies. Obama's victory promised an end to the era of campaigns dominated by big funders and mass media. But by 2012, the same candidate presided over a reelection campaign that raised $715 million (not counting so-called independent expenditures), almost two thirds of which came from large individual donors,[1] and he spent that money on a combination of mass media and finely tuned, data-driven, targeted outreach *from* the campaign *to* individual citizens. Now the Internet was being used not to push power out to the edges of the network, nor to promote discussion, but to harvest consumer data for campaign HQ, a place of "whiz-bang technologies and startup geniuses," where "every possible organizational and statistical tool that a campaign wonk could dream up is being marshaled by the campaign ten-fold" (Cherlin 2012). To be sure, a year later, scholars were already raising doubts about the real impact of this marketing wizardry on the 2012 election (Sides and Vavreck 2013). But that just underlines how rapidly the conversational pendulum swings.

I would therefore like to step back and suggest some underlying principles that may help us assess the relationship between digital media and democracy even as both continue to change rapidly.

What Is Democratic Politics?

A government, Max Weber argued, is an organization that has a monopoly on the legitimate use of violence within its jurisdiction (Weber 1918, 83). Because the government owns the police and the military (or their functional equivalents), its decisions are final and can take the form of binding laws.

To be sure, the state is never unified; it always consists of separate offices, branches, and officers who also have private interests and private lives. Further, governments are never capable of ruling except with the willing collaboration of some other sectors of society. These observations blur the line between government and the rest of a community (V. Ostrom 2007), yet the Weberian concept of government remains a valid starting point.

A democracy is a system in which the government is accountable to the people, who each have roughly equal say. Democracy therefore characteristically involves popular votes to choose officials, laws, or policies. However, it has often been noted that voting alone will not suffice, even for the bare purpose of making the state answerable to the people. The people must have a free and informed discussion of public issues before they vote. That requires, at a minimum, freedom of speech. Some would argue that democracy has much broader requirements, extending to the economic and social equality necessary to make everyone's voice roughly equal (Dewey 1927, 143). And since not only the state but also workplaces and families are locations of power, a case can be made that those institutions should also become more democratic (e.g., Pateman 1970).

The public sphere is that metaphorical space in which individuals share ideas and information in order to form public opinion, without which the state cannot be made accountable to the people (Habermas 1974). In the public sphere, we discuss in order to decide who we are, what we want, what problems we face, and what we should do. The public sphere always depends on some kind of infrastructure, whether the literal marketplace of an ancient city, the coffee houses of seventeenth-century Istanbul or eighteenth-century Paris, or the Internet today. One unresolved issue is whether we should strive for a single public sphere or welcome the emergence of multiple spheres and numerous "publics" (Cohen 1999, 73–75).

Finally, civil society is that set of organizations and less-formal networks and groups that bring people out of their private domains and involve them both in directly solving common problems (with or without the government) and in forming public opinion that can influence the state.

We are thus considering a system—"politics" broadly defined—that involves civil society, the public sphere, democracy, and government. It relates to other systems, such as markets/exchange and nature/ecosystems. The design of a worthy political system involves tradeoffs among genuine goods, such as individual liberty versus group decision-making and social equality versus prosperity. I stand with those who think that the state should be more accountable to citizens, citizens should be more equal to each other, and the public sphere should be freer and more robust than it is today, notwithstanding the necessary tradeoffs. Those objectives also imply that we need a stronger civil society to underpin the public sphere and a more effective state for the people to control democratically.

The Perennial Challenges of Democratic Politics

In designing, reforming, or assessing a political system with those goals in mind, we must consider several perennial challenges.

First, it is not in an individual's narrow self-interest to participate in civil society, the public sphere, democracy, or government. The paradox of voting (Downs 1957) illustrates this problem. If one assumes that citizens vote to maximize their own good, then it is irrational for them to vote at all. Their odds of affecting the outcome are low (less than one in 100 million in the US), and voting costs time. The costs are even higher if one is considering becoming informed about public issues, engaging in public conversations, encouraging others to participate, seeking public office, joining a social movement, or defending the country.

If we relax the assumption of selfishness and allow that some individuals may act in the public interest, it is still not evident that they ought to vote or otherwise participate in politics. A saint might decide that she should not vote because the impact is small and the time would be better spent on direct service to the poor and oppressed. In other words, voting not only costs the individual but also creates moral opportunity costs in the form of time that could have been used for altruistic purposes.

As a matter of fact, many people do vote: more than half of the US population in presidential elections. In all likelihood, voters do not carefully weigh the benefits versus the costs of voting and decide that the net favors voting. Rather, they may feel a sense of solidarity and "we-ness," an obligation to participate in a national ritual, a feeling that they are playing a part in the community's story, or a sheer burst of satisfaction from casting the vote. But the fact that many individuals vote despite a collective action problem doesn't show that the problem was a myth to start with. It is difficult to persuade the public to hold the government accountable (by voting or by many other forms of participation) when each individual's actions have very limited impact. It is only thanks to the persistent efforts of schools, political parties and campaigns, the media, parents, and other organizations and networks that we see much engagement at all—and we do not see enough of it.

Second, we would like people to participate in more than their narrow self-interest. They should demonstrate some concern for other people and for general principles of fairness and justice. After all, politics confers power, and if we use our power selfishly or destructively, the results can be costly, unjust, or even cruel. Thus a good society must address the problem of *faction* in the sense that James Madison meant when he defined a faction as "a number of citizens, whether amounting to a majority or a minority of the whole, who are united and actuated by some common impulse of passion, or of interest, *adversed to* the rights of other citizens, or to the permanent and aggregate interests of the community" (Madison 1787, emphasis added). Madison proposed various solutions, including checks and balances within the government, limitations on the powers of the state as a whole, and a large enough republic that no narrow economic interest would be able to dominate it. Madison wrote in opposition to traditional solutions that emphasized changing people's characters to make them substantially more public-spirited. Although the best solutions may vary, the problem of faction is perennial.

A third challenge is inequality. Democracy means equal voice, but there are many sources of inequality, including differences in social standing and prestige as well as in expertise, skill, and commitment. I would especially emphasize what Charles Lindblom called "the privileged position of business" (Lindblom 1977). People and firms that can make substantial investments have more influence in a democracy than individuals who must simply sell their labor, let alone the indigent. Investors need not act or speak in order to have influence; governments and communities want them to invest and will defer to their interests. That problem would vanish under conditions of perfect economic equality, but markets are popular with democratic peoples because they generate prosperity. Since markets also yield inequality, inequality is a perennial problem (Elkin 2006).

Finally, we would like to retain in the political domain some of the ethical values that we prize in everyday human interactions. In small-scale forms of politics, such as community organizing, deliberative democracy, or the management of common resources such as ponds and forests, the participants can explain what they believe and value to one another and can tangibly affect the outcomes with their own words and work. Participants can genuinely listen, offer their labor, and form relationships of reciprocity, loyalty, and trust (Levine 2013). Their political action is thus continuous with their everyday lives and relationships, potentially manifesting the same virtues and satisfactions (but also the same exclusions and animosities). I would not want the government to address all our social problems, even if it could, because small-scale voluntary groups are domains of ethical interaction and tangible human agency.

Yet we cannot stop at the small scale, because the national and global economy and environment are crucial. If we only do what is right, we leave most of the world unchanged. If we seek to change the world at large scale, we must get others to do what we favor as well. That requires leverage. As the Archimedean metaphor suggests, to use leverage is to manipulate—to treat something as a means. In the social world, that something will have to be human: a person or a group. For the most part, our leverage in the social world comes from creating, using, and changing institutions. But institutions are relatively impersonal. They do not promote or even permit relationships of mutual understanding and trust.

In short, leverage is necessary if you care for the world at any significant scale. But leverage is also risky and ethically problematic because it cannot be fully reciprocal and relational.

The Perennial Challenges in the Digital Age

I could have written all of the above—outlining the four problems of collective action, faction, inequality, and leverage—a century ago. The Internet and other digital media have not changed the list of fundamental issues. Instead, the new media affect these issues in varied and unpredictable ways. Still, I think we can risk some generalizations about how the digital media are influencing politics.

1. When choice is massively disaggregated

First, the new media offer individuals unprecedented array of choices. Making a choice by clicking, searching, or contacting someone is perhaps the most basic action we take when using a computer or mobile technology. It might seem that choice is always at the heart of human action—but not so. In the United States and many other countries before 1900, citizenship was less about choice than about expressing and exercising responsibility to ascribed groups, such as nations, communities, religions, races, or classes. For example, as Michael Schudson notes, voting was not the private act of an individual who selected representatives. It was generally an expression of loyalty: groups or whole communities would all publicly vote for the same candidates to demonstrate their shared commitment. Parties were coalitions of demographic groups, so that Southern Whites voted Democratic and New England Yankees voted Republican as matters of identity more than of preference. Newspapers were often named *The Republican* or *The Democrat*, and even if they had other names, they were openly recognized as vehicles for partisan mobilization. Meanwhile, schools and colleges taught loyalty and duty to their relatively homogeneous student bodies; many college presidents were clergymen who personally taught a required "morals" course (Schudson 1998).

The Progressive reformers of ca. 1900–1924 challenged all of these norms and practices because they valued the independent choice of informed individuals. They fought to make ballots secret and to disaggregate political choices so that citizens could vote separately on each referendum and office. They promoted the independent and non-partisan press, at least as an ideal. In 1933, University of Chicago President Robert Hutchins announced, "'education for citizenship' has no place in the university" (Talcott 2005). He really meant that there was no place in his university for explicit appeals to loyalty and duty. Students should rather obtain information that would enable them to make free and wise choices. For that purpose, they ought to be able to choose their classes, which would be taught by professors whose intellectual freedom protected them to make their own decisions.

One can certainly sympathize with the motives of the Progressive reforms, but they coincided with a sharp drop in political participation, which some have attributed to the shift from duty to choice (Schudson 1998, 190). If political participation requires collecting information to make many disaggregated choices, and if you can choose whether to participate at all, fewer people will participate.

We see the same pattern continue in the last quarter of the twentieth century, when rates of attending community meetings and working on community projects declined badly. I have argued that a contributing factor was again a shift to choice (Levine 2013, 91–96). At the beginning of that period, many people took jobs that happened to be unionized, subscribed to the local daily newspaper to get classified advertisements and comics, went to church because their parents had attended or to save their own souls, and belonged to a political party because it represented their demographic identity group. In short, they did not originally choose to be "civically engaged," but the union, the newspaper, the church, and the party all offered concrete benefits and then sought to interest people in public life, making appeals to duty and group interest. By the end of the century, you could still choose to engage in the affairs of your democracy and community if you wanted to, but now that was up to you. Fewer people did. Furthermore, civil society was now funded by philanthropists rather than members, meaning that it depended on the discretionary choices of donors (Skocpol 2004).

The Internet is thus a continuation of longer-term shifts from duty to choice and from loyalty to information. Whereas a metropolitan daily newspaper put the front-page headlines on your doorstep, a Web search can yield almost anything you want. The choice used to be to subscribe to the newspaper or not; now it is whether to read a given paragraph in a particular article in a specific publication. For an individual who wishes to participate in public life, having countless options of news sources, organizations, and networks is empowering. But many people do not want to participate politically, and for them, having choice means that they do not engage at all. Further, we can choose to consume only ideas with which we agree, thereby avoiding the stress of cognitive dissonance. Choices to filter information and ideas create cyber-balkanization, which is a hypercharged version of Madisonian factionalism (Sunstein 2001; Zuckerman 2013).

Traditionally, we combat individuals' unwillingness to participate by creating and sustaining organizations that enlist them, and we check factionalism by constructing representative organizations and institutions, including metropolitan daily newspapers, legislatures, and broadly-based social movements. Such organizations pose a classic problem of collective action, because they depend on individual contributions to the public good. We have been able to solve that problem under favorable conditions (E. Ostrom 1990), but unconstrained choice makes the challenge harder.

As Lance Bennett and Alexandra Segerberg note, a framework of collective action "stresses the organizational dilemma of getting individuals to join in actions where personal participation costs may outweigh marginal gains, particularly when people can ride on the efforts of others for free." Bennett and Segerberg suggest that we expand our framework in the digital age to encompass *connective* action, which can flourish under conditions of rampant choice. In connective action, "contributing to the public good becomes an act of personal expression and recognition or self-validation achieved by sharing ideas in trusted relationships. … In place of the initial collective action problem of getting the individual to contribute, the starting point of connective action assumes contribution: the self-motivated (though not necessarily self-centered) sharing of already internalized or personalized ideas, plans, images, actions, and resources with networks of others" (Bennett and Segerberg 2013, 27, 36).

Politically oriented networks can quickly become large and powerful, especially in the new media environment. Bennett and Segerberg cite, for example, *los Indignados*, a movement composed of 15 million protesters in 60 Spanish cities that arose in 2011. These protesters kept "political parties, unions, and other powerful political organizations out: indeed, they were targeted as part of the political problem. … The most visible organization consisted of the richly layered digital and interpersonal communication networks centering around the media hub of *Democracia real YA!*" (Bennett and Segerberg 2012). Bennett and Segerberg argue that connective action capitalizes on "personalization." Individuals need not change their identities to participate in connective politics but can rather choose an array of issues, slogans, and network partners that express their existing personas. Personalization is another way to describe the disaggregation of choice that has been a trend of the last century.

In a related argument, Clay Shirky notes that organizations were traditionally required to reduce transaction costs. That was Ronald Coase's explanation for why firms existed, instead of markets in which individuals would exchange labor and goods (Coase 1937). But digital media have cut transaction costs so much that it is now possible to produce goods and achieve other ends without firms or other organizations, simply through networked voluntary action (Shirky 2008; cf. Benkler 2006).

I agree that networks have become more important, and organizations less so, because digital media have cut transaction costs. The question is whether networks can achieve the *political* purposes of organizations. Political action typically provokes counter-action; politics is contentious. It is one thing to build a network of voluntary contributors to a community news portal or Wikipedia, relatively uncontroversial public goods. It is quite another to "crowdsource" resistance to an organized foe.

Thus, for instance, an ideologically diverse network of committed protesters brought down the corrupt government in Egypt in 2011, but that network was displaced by the highly disciplined Muslim Brotherhood, which, in turn, was overthrown and persecuted by the even better-organized Egyptian army (Ruthven 2014). Narrow, factional organizations defeated broad-based and public-spirited networks. That is just one example—other cases will turn out differently—but I think it will be a durable question whether networks can sustain themselves, create and distribute resources, and protect rights, especially in the face of disciplined opposition. If not, the decline of organizations in the face of individualized choice will harm democracy.

In considering any political institution, organization, movement, or network, we might hope for four virtues (among others). (1) The entity should be large, so that it can have influence and serve many members. (2) It should be unified, so that it can move effectively toward a goal. (3) It should be "deep," causing significant changes in its own members and giving them satisfaction and meaning. And (4) it should encompass a diversity of views, so that it can avoid narrow perspectives and factionalism.

Perhaps some political systems and social movements have achieved all of these virtues at once. At its peak around 1960, the American Civil Rights Movement drew millions, offered many of them profound experiences, encompassed a wide range of philosophies (from the Nation of Islam to the Southern Christian Leadership Conference), and yet managed to attain what Charles Tilly deemed "WUNC"—worthiness, unity, numbers, and commitment—valuable assets for any social movement (Tilly 2004).

But the movement's unity was short-lived; the coalition dissolved. On the whole, groups must *choose* among these four goods. Given limited resources, they cannot be both large and deep. For instance, Scott Reed, who leads the faith-based community-organizing network known as PICO, recently described to me the deep and transformative work that PICO does with its grassroots leaders. But "scale is what we are trying to figure out," he said. "How do you get to scale, because we are nowhere near where we want?" Meanwhile, Anna Galland, who leads the online network, MoveOn, told me that her organization has "tremendous scale and little depth." MoveOn's goal, she said, is to "move from a list of 8 million to horizontal connectivity."

Groups like MoveOn choose unity over viewpoint diversity. Galland explained that her organization has developed a "threshold of torque." When one third of the members dissent on an issue, it triggers a formal process. "We are member-led," she said, and one-third disagreement is too much. Other groups prefer diversity over unity. Martha McCoy, executive director of Everyday Democracy, described to me the painstaking efforts her organization takes to bring together people who sharply disagree. But Everyday Democracy is far smaller than MoveOn.

If you think of these as two dimensions—ideological unity versus diversity, and scale versus depth—it produces an array of four kinds of organizations. I can name examples of three of the four types. There are deep and unified groups, deep and diverse groups, and large and unified groups. But I do not believe we have any large and ideologically diverse groups like the Civil Rights Movement at its apogee or like a political party that has a robust internal public sphere. The digital media seem to support evanescent networks that enlist many diverse people, but these networks fade. It remains an open question whether we can sustain scale *and* diversity or scale *and* depth online.

2. When sovereignty is ambiguous

The dominant theory of democracy used to be the sovereignty theory. A "people" would consist of a bounded group, all of whose members would have equal rights to discuss and decide the issues that came before them. Such groups might be nation-states bounded by international borders, but they might also be organizations or associations; they were sovereign to the extent that they could make decisions about categories of issues. They would thus exercise what the French Revolutionary theorist Benjamin Constant called the "liberty of the ancients," meaning the right "to deliberate, in a public space, about war and peace, to ratify treaties of alliance with foreigners, to vote laws, pronounce decisions, examine the accounts, actions, and management of officials, to compel them to appear before the whole people, to accuse them, to condemn or acquit them" (Constant 1819).

Two problems arise for all such sovereign groups: (1) they may not have a legitimate moral basis to exclude outsiders from their decisions, and (2) they may not have actual control over the situations that they confront. For example, the United States may not have a legitimate moral justification to exclude Germans from influencing our government's surveillance policy, which also affects Germany; and the US government *cannot* control capital markets or pollution flows that cross its borders.

These problems have become more severe and more evident in a highly interconnected world. A traditional justification for the sovereignty theory presumed that nation-states could safeguard the interests of their own members without impinging often on others. But, as Archon Fung writes, "If there once was a time when the laws of a nation-state could adequately protect the fundamental interests of its citizens, many argue that such time is past" (Fung 2009). One factor is the increasingly privileged position of business at a time when digital networks (abetted by favorable state policies) are making capital and information globally mobile even as people remain relatively stationary. Fung and others argue that we should shift from a sovereignty theory to a "theory of affected interests," or at least add the latter to our understanding of democracy.

According to a theory of affected interests, a democracy is not a group of people who constitute a fixed polity that has a right to decide on everything that comes before it. In fact, if Americans can decide every topic under our government's control, we will violate non-Americans' rights to be consulted on matters that affect them as much or more than they affect us. Rather, each person has a potentially unique set of interests and a right to be consulted on all the decisions that affect those interests. For example, I have interests in clean and safe streets in my neighborhood and also in the amount of carbon produced by Chinese industry. Fung proposes as the basic democratic principle that "An individual should be able to influence an organization if and only if that organization makes decisions that regularly or deeply affect that individual's important interests." On that basis, I may have a right to influence Cambridge, MA, and the People's Republic of China, as well as Microsoft, the National Security Agency (NSA), and the American Political Science Association. The world becomes more democratic to the extent that each person has influence over the various overlapping organizations that affect him or her.

Empirically, this seems to be one direction politics is taking in our digitally enabled, global world. Social movements now draw people from a range of political jurisdictions who share a common interest. Movements target the appropriate organizations, which may be governments, corporations, or NGOs. They work like networks rather than institutions: people who share interests connect up to protest, boycott, or otherwise confront organizations.

Fung cites the example of the Coalition of Immokalee Workers, farm laborers in the Florida tomato industry who were subject to terrible pay, stolen wages, and even documented cases of slavery. The sovereignty theory of democracy would not work for them because they were mostly not US citizens; they would be badly outvoted even if they were citizens; and they worked in a global market.[2] Instead, the workers identified consumers from many nations who felt a moral stake in not supporting oppression. (The consumers had an interest, but not a purely selfish one.) The workers organized a boycott that forced the major buyers to negotiate. The result was a binding code of conduct that the workers can help enforce (Ríos 2011).

In essence, the workers identified a common interest with global consumers, targeted a set of international companies, and created a new micro-democracy just for their issue, in which they have considerable clout. One could define a more democratic world as one in which there are more such movements that represent more interests more effectively. Digital media would make that version of democracy more attainable than it ever was in the past. The democratic nation state would be decreasingly relevant.

However, we should consider what would be lost if the sovereignty theory gave way entirely to a theory of affected interests. Constant spoke for a long line of civic republican theorists who envisioned citizens as groups of people who do *not* assess their individual interests in an ad hoc way and decide what affects them. Rather, they take responsibility for forming opinions about all matters that involve the group, giving at least some attention to abstract principles of justice as well as interests. Because they are responsible for considering a wide range of issues, they can weigh conflicting claims. For example, they should not only care about the farmworkers but also industry, the environment, and consumers. They should make laws that govern not only the tomato industry but the whole economy. And they should be subject to the laws that they influence, consistent with Aristotle's definition of a citizen as one who both rules and obeys (*Politics* III:5).

So far, the democratic nation state has provided the main venue for this kind of citizenship. It has the two limitations named above: it may not have legitimate reasons to exclude outsiders, and it may not be capable of addressing all of its own problems. Therefore, the state should not be the only venue for democracy. Yet the democratic state is an achievement that we should not casually discard. Nations are big enough that they encompass some diversity of culture and class, and the successful ones have been able to organize one reasonably representative national discussion about justice. That requires an inclusive public sphere, a powerful and accountable legislature, and a sense of "shared fate" that draws people's attention to the public good (Ben-Porath 2012). I see works as diverse as the "Gettysburg Address" and *Bleak House* as contributions to building that sense of common fate at the national level. Perhaps we should now *also* understand ourselves as global citizens (Zuckerman 2013), but we are not literally people who both rule and obey at that scale. Meanwhile, we are at some risk of losing the national solidarity that underlies hard-won sovereign democratic institutions.

3. When society is legible to the state

In order for a state to govern, it must be able to see what it rules and make sense of the data. It would be an analytical mistake to *assume* perfect information; governments need rules and tools to make their societies legible; and people must cooperate (to a degree) if the state is to see them accurately.

According to many ancient stories, one of a ruler's first tasks is to count his people and objects. For instance, the biblical Book of Numbers relates the journey of the newly formed people of Israel to take possession of the land that they believe is theirs. In the very first verse, the Lord tells Moses: "Take ye the sum of all the congregation of the children of Israel, after their families, by the house of their fathers, with the number of their names, every male by their polls" (Numbers 1:2). Likewise, near the beginning of Luke, we are told, "And it came to pass in those days, that there went out a decree from Caesar Augustus that all the world should be taxed." The emperor needed information, and the people complied: "All went to be taxed, every one into his own city" (Luke 2:1–3). And not long after William the Conqueror seized England, he "sent his men over all England, into every shire, and caused them to ascertain how many hundred hides of land it contained, and what lands the king possessed therein, what cattle there were in the several counties, and how much revenue he ought to receive yearly from each" (Giles 1914, A1085).

Since these are stories about monarchs, we might have mixed feelings about their ability to count and read their societies. In a democracy, the state is supposed to do the people's will, and it cannot do that unless it can see the society clearly. For example, unless it knows how much money each individual earns, it cannot implement an income tax and use the revenues for popular purposes. In turn, the people must be able to see what the democratic state does in order to hold it accountable. Some degree of transparency and legibility (in both directions) is necessary for a democracy to function.

However, even a democratic state should not be able to see everywhere all the time. Jeremy Bentham was a proponent of democracy (defined as majority-rule) who pushed the ideal of transparency to a horrifying conclusion. His famous model of the ideal prison was the "Panopticon," which he sketched thus:

The building circular—the cells occupying the circumference. ... One station in the inspection part affording the most perfect view of two stories of cells, and a considerable view of another. ... By blinds and other contrivances, the keeper concealed from the observation of the prisoners, unless where he thinks fit to show himself: hence, on their part, the sentiment of an invisible omnipresence.—The whole circuit reviewable with little, or, if necessary, without any, change of place. (Bentham 1843, n. 25, order changed)

For most readers, however, the Panopticon is a nightmare. What is wrong with it? First, it makes power pervasive and reduces human agency to a minimum. Michel Foucault observed:

The major effect of the Panopticon: to induce in the inmate a state of conscious and permanent visibility that assures the automatic functioning of power. So to arrange things that the surveillance is permanent in its effects, even if it is discontinuous in its action; that the perfection of power should tend to render its actual exercise unnecessary; that this architectural apparatus should be a machine for creating and sustaining a power relation independent of the person who exercises it; in short, that the inmates should be caught up in a power situation of which they are themselves the bearers. (Foucault 1977)

In a society that is completely legible to the state, we cannot have private spaces in which to develop beliefs and interests so that we can participate in the public realm as distinct individuals. The result is a far poorer public sphere. Hannah Arendt was a great defender of public life, but she wrote that the "four walls, within which people's private life is lived, constitute a shield against the public aspect of the world. They enclose a secure place, without which no living thing can thrive" (Arendt 1954, 186). The Panopticon's cells have three walls, so that the prisoners cannot communicate with each other; the fourth is deliberately missing to allow the keeper to see in.

In the digital age, the problem of legibility has become much more severe. We now use computers, mobile phones, and other electronic devices in almost all aspects of our lives, for work, exchange, health, recreation, and intimacy. Each call placed, character typed, and site visited leaves a digital trace. Those traces can be collected and analyzed by firms and governments—or first by firms and then by the governments that seize or penetrate their data. Because most content on the Internet is free but supported by advertising, and because the actual financial returns from advertising are poor, Web companies face relentless pressure to collect information on customers to make advertising more effective. People accept that data will be collected because that is how the Internet is funded. And then governments harvest the data (Zuckerman 2014).

We do not know whether our behavior is being analyzed at any time, but it could be. That is the principle of the Panopticon. I think Foucault was too quick to see power as determinative and was not optimistic enough about people's capacity to resist surveillance through our creativity and our sheer recalcitrance. But the threat is real.

One aspect of the threat is pervasiveness. Hannah Arendt's four walls cannot shield you against surveillance if inside your house you are typing emails that Google analyzes and the NSA reads (Sanger and Perloth 2014). As long as you are using a digital device, there is no secure refuge from surveillance. The chilling effect may take many forms. As one example, journalists now say that government sources are more reluctant to come forward than they used to be because they believe their communications are being monitored. "Many journalists reported a strong preference for meeting sources in person in large part for reasons of security. 'I don't think there's anything ironclad you can do except [meet] face to face,' remarked Jonathan Landay. 'Maybe we need to get back to going to sources' houses,' added Peter Finn. Indeed, several journalists expressed a marked reluctance to contact certain sources by email or phone" (Human Rights Watch and American Civil Liberties Union 2014, 35).

A second aspect of the problem is precision. Today, analysts no longer rely on samples of information taken from random surveys, observations, or audits, which they would analyze using statistical techniques that depend on probability. Now they can get *all* the data. For example, social scientists working in academia, business, or the government can collect and analyze all the votes in cast in an election, all the job openings advertised in newspapers, or all the social media postings that include a given phrase. They can also merge these data, so that we can know, for instance, detailed consumer and employment information about each voter. The result is a wealth of information about small groups and their behavior that yields remarkably accurate predictions. Those predictions would have been unthinkable when we relied on samples and on statistics based on probability (King 2014).

Pervasiveness and precision relate to a third aspect of the threat: manipulability. Behavioral economics, prospect theory, and the latest marketing science combine to tell us that: (1) people's behavior is predictable, but it does not depend on rational calculations of benefits versus costs; (2) we can get people to do what we want by understanding their history of behavior so far and then subtly shifting messages or the way we frame choices; and (3) this is all *good* because we can attain desirable social outcomes without paying people or threatening people to do the right thing. Governments needn't ban or tax harmful products; they can "nudge" citizens into avoiding them (Thaler and Sunstein 2008). According to Katrin Bennhold (Bennhold 2013),

In 2010, [the British Prime Minister] Mr. Cameron set up the Behavioral Insights Team—or nudge unit, as it's often called. Three years later, the team has doubled in size and is about to announce a joint venture with an external partner to expand the program. The unit has been nudging people to pay taxes on time, insulate their attics, sign up for organ donation, stop smoking during pregnancy, and give to charity—and has saved taxpayers tens of millions of pounds in the process, said David Halpern, its director. Every civil servant in Britain is now being trained in behavioral science.

From Bentham's perspective, it is excellent news that a democratically elected government can make people act better without threats or bribery, just by observing them more accurately and tweaking choices or messages to nudge them in the right direction. Democracy benefits because the people can decide what counts as "better" and can monitor the state, and the government will be more efficient and effective thanks to its use of data. But from Foucault's perspective, the new data-driven behavioral economics is the epitome of a Panopticon. Precisely because the power is soft, imperceptible, cheap, and ubiquitous, we don't resist it.

4. When the state no longer needs the people

The previous section suggested that elites and publics are locked in a power struggle. That is not necessarily the case. The elites in charge of Weberian states needed their people to pay taxes, lend money, and serve in militaries. Sometimes, the public actively, authentically, and enthusiastically responded. When that happened, nations were highly successful. For example, the Dutch Republic bankrupted the greatest empire in the world (Spain), despite the Spanish king's silver mines, because Dutch citizens willingly lent their government money to fight for Dutch independence. The Dutch did not invent accountable, representative government as a strategy for defeating Spain. The basis of Dutch republicanism lay in old traditions of municipal self-government, plus Calvinist theology. We could view those causes as akin to random mutations in Darwinian evolution. They produced a system that happened to be more fit than a monarchy in the competition among states. The Dutch beat the Spanish, and then, by late the 1700s, the French revolutionary democracy could field an army of 1.3 million against the largest monarchical army of the same time (Prussia's) at 80,000 men (Crenson and Ginsberg 2002, 38). The social contract involved enthusiastic support from the citizens and accountability by the government, cemented by votes.

By the 1900s, the remaining viable options were tyrannies, which mobilized through fear, and democracies, which received active support. Both worked in the period 1900–1950, but democracies prevailed because fear proved unsustainable. Wars typically saw the expansion of the franchise because elites needed popular support. Thus African Americans won a (paper) right to vote after serving in the Civil War, and women obtained suffrage in the United States and Britain around World War I. In both instances, the elites in charge of the state needed these populations' support and were willing to promise them some power. The relationship was not zero-sum but win/win.

Today, however, democracies no longer need many soldiers. Even while fighting two simultaneous wars in Asia during the 2000s, the United States had only about 0.5 percent of its population in active military service. Technology and skilled specialists, not great numbers of conscripts, win wars. Governments also no longer need individual lenders to finance their national debts; bonds are floated on global markets. And they do not need willing compliance with taxation, because taxes are drawn automatically, and a state can be financed with income taxes from a wealthy minority. States that do not need people have no incentives to consult people.

We are confronted with a situation in which sovereign states are less able to rule within their jurisdictions than they were in the past—and are seen as less legitimate when they try to rule—and yet they are also less dependent on the people within their jurisdictions and more capable of conducting surveillance on their own citizens and potentially anyone else in the world. Democratic states have less authority over their own publics but more capacity to intervene against individuals, using information and sometimes-deadly power; and citizens have less control over their own governments but more opportunities to act globally through voluntary networks. These are rough waters.

Conclusion

This chapter has been intentionally rather dark. I have not cited inspiring examples in which people deliberately use digital media to improve the world. Such examples figure prominently in subsequent chapters and in the case studies that accompany this volume. I believe they offer grounds for optimism—or at least hope.

But we should be sober about the new media environment. It may empower some ordinary people; it also disempowers many and offers unprecedented influence to the small groups who control governments and companies. We should celebrate the victories of digitally enabled networks. For instance, the "DREAMers" are young people who started by advocating for the Development, Relief and Education for Alien Minors (DREAM) Act and have been able to influence public opinion about immigration in the United States and gain recognition as legitimate participants in public life even though they lack citizenship (Nicholls 2013). Yet at the same time, the US Congress was failing to reform immigration policy, and the executive branch was effectively deporting nearly 400,000 aliens per year (Lopez and Gonzalez-Barrera 2013), taking advantage of expensive and sophisticated digital technologies to identify and remove them. I think that if we tallied the score so far, the undemocratic users of the new media would be far ahead of the democrats. Of course, not all uses of the digital media are zero-sum. Wikipedia, as just one example, shows that people can cooperate to make a free resource of enormous value without coercion or financial reward. But some political struggles do have winners and losers, and although it is far too soon to conclude that the ordinary people of the world will be the net losers overall, they do face serious challenges that we must address head on.

Notes

1. Author's calculation from Center for Responsive Politics data, https://www.opensecrets.org/pres12.

2. Fung used this example in a Tufts University seminar, July 2014.

References

Arendt, Hannah. 1954. "The Crisis in Education." In *Between Past and Future: Eight Exercises in Political Thought*. New York: Penguin.

Benkler, Yochai. 2006. *The Wealth of Networks: How Social Production Transforms Markets and Freedom*. New Haven, CT: Yale University Press.

Bennett W. L., and Alexandra Segerberg. 2012. "The Logic of Connective Action: Digital Media and the Personalization of Contentious Politics." *Information Communication and Society* 15 (5): 739–768.

Bennett, W. L., and Alexandra Segerberg. 2013. *The Logic of Connective Action: Digital Media and the Personalization of Contentious Politics*. New York: Cambridge University Press.

Bennhold, Katrin. 2013. "Britain's Ministry of Nudges." *New York Times*, December 7. http://www.nytimes.com/2013/12/08/business/international/britains-ministry-of-nudges.html.

Ben-Porath, S. R. 2012. "Citizenship as Shared Fate: Educating for Membership in a Diverse Democracy." *Educational Theory* 62 (4): 381–395.

Bentham, Jeremy. 1843. "Appendix: Selections from Bentham's Narrative Regarding the Panopticon Penitentiary Project, and from the Correspondence on the Subject." In *The Works of Jeremy Bentham*, vol. 11: *96ff*. Edinburgh: William Tait. Public Domain.

Cherlin, Reid. 2012. "Yes They Can (They Think)." *GQ*, October 31. http://www.gq.com/news-politics/blogs/death-race/2012/10/president-obama-appears-under-the.html.

Coase, Ronald. 1937. "The Nature of the Firm." *Economica* 4 (16): 386–405.

Cohen, Jean L. 1999. "American Civil Society Talk." In *Civil Society, Democracy, and Civic Renewal*, ed. Robert K. Fullinwider, 55–85. Lanham, MD: Rowman & Littlefield.

Constant, Benjamin. 1819. *De la liberté des anciens comparée à celle des modernes*. Translated by the author. http://www.panarchy.org/constant/liberte.1819.html.

Crenson, M., and Benjamin Ginsberg. 2002. *Downsizing Democracy: How America Sidelined Its Citizens and Privatized the Public*. Baltimore: The Johns Hopkins University Press.

Dewey, John. 1927. *The Public and Its Problems*. New York: Henry Holt.

Downs, A. 1957. *An Economic Theory of Democracy*. New York: Harper & Row.

Elkin, Stephen L. 2006. *Reconstructing the Commercial Republic: Constitutional Design after Madison*. Chicago: University of Chicago Press.

Foucault, Michel. 1977. "Discipline and Punish, Panopticism." In *Discipline & Punish: The Birth of the Prison*, ed. Alan Sheridan, 195–228. New York: Vintage Books.

Fung, Archon. 2009. "The Principle of Affected Interests: An Interpretation and Defense." In *Representation: Elections and Beyond*, ed. Jack H. Nagel and Rogers M. Smith, 236–268. Philadelphia: University of Pennsylvenia Press.

Giles, J. A., ed. 1914. *The Anglo-Saxon Chronicle*. London: Bell & Sons.

Habermas, Jürgen. 1974. "The Public Sphere: An Encyclopedia Article." *New German Critique, NGC* 3:49–55.

Human Rights Watch and American Civil Liberties Union. 2014. *With Liberty to Monitor All: How Large-Scale US Surveillance is Harming Journalism, Law, and American Democracy*. http://www.hrw.org/reports/2014/07/28/liberty-monitor-all-0.

Ignatieff, Michael. 2014. "Are the Authoritarians Winning?" *New York Review of Books*, July. http://www.nybooks.com/articles/archives/2014/jul/10/are-authoritarians-winning/.

King, Gary. 2014. "Restructuring the Social Sciences: Reflections from Harvard's Institute for Quantitative Social Science." *PS*, January. http://gking.harvard.edu/files/gking/files/king14.pdf.

Levine, Peter. 2013. *We Are the Ones We Have Been Waiting For: The Promise of Civic Renewal in America*. New York: Oxford University Press.

Lindblom, Charles. 1977. *Politics and Markets: The World's Political-Economic Systems*. New York: Basic Books.

Lopez, Mark Hugo, and Ana Gonzalez-Barrera. 2013. "High Rate of Deportations Continue under Obama Despite Latino Disapproval." Pew Research Center. http://www.pewresearch.org/fact -tank/2013/09/19/high-rate-of-deportations-continue-under-obama-despite-latino-disapproval/.

Madison, James. 1787. "The Same Subject Continued: The Union as a Safeguard Against Domestic Faction and Insurrection." (Now generally known as "Federalist 10.") *The New York Packet*, Nov. 23. http://thomas.loc.gov/home/histdox/fedpapers.html.

Naughton, John. 2001. "Contested Space: The Internet and Global Civil Society." In *Global Civil Society*, ed. Helmut Anheier, Marlies Glasius, and Mary Kaldor, 147–168. Oxford: Oxford University Press.

Nicholls, Walter. 2013. *The DREAMers: How the Undocumented Youth Movement Transformed the Immigrant Rights Debate*. (Google eBook). Redwood City, CA: Stanford University Press.

Ostrom, Elinor. 1990. *Governing the Commons: The Evolution of Institutions for Collective Action*. Cambridge: Cambridge University Press.

Ostrom, Vincent. 2007. *The Intellectual Crisis in Public Administration*. 3rd ed. Tuscaloosa: University of Alabama Press.

Pateman, Carole. 1970. *Participation and Democratic Theory*. Cambridge: Cambridge University Press.

Piketty, Thomas. 2014. *Capital in the Twenty-First Century*. Trans. A. Goldhammer. Cambridge, MA: Harvard University Press.

Ríos, Kristofer. 2011. "After Long Fight, Farmworkers in Florida Win an Increase in Pay." *New York Times*, January 18. http://www.nytimes.com/2011/01/19/us/19farm.html.

Ruthven, Malise. 2014. "What Happened to the Arab Spring?" *New York Review of Books,* July 20: 72–75.

Sanger, D. E., and N. Perloth. 2014. "Internet Giants Erect Barriers to Spy Agencies." *New York Times*, June 14. http://www.nytimes.com/2014/06/07/technology/internet-giants-erect-barriers -to-spy-agencies.html?_r=0.

Schudson, Michael. 1998. *The Good Citizen: A History of American Civic Life*. New York: The Free Press.

Shirky, Clay. 2008. *Here Comes Everybody*. New York: Penguin.

Sides, John, and Lynn Vavreck. 2013. *The Gamble: Choice and Chance in the 2012 Presidential Election*. Princeton, NJ: Princeton University Press.

Skocpol, Theda. 2004. *Diminished Democracy: From Membership to Management in American Civic Life*. Norman: University of Oklahoma Press.

Sunstein, Cass. 2001. *Republic.com*. Princeton, NJ: Princeton University Press.

Talcott, William. 2005. "Modern Universities, Absent Citizenship? Historical Perspectives." CIRCLE Working Paper 39. www.civicyouth.org.

Thaler, Richard H., and C. R. Sunstein. 2008. *Nudge: Improving Decisions about Health, Wealth, and Happiness*. New Haven, CT: Yale University Press.

Tilly, C. 2004. *Social Movements 1768–2004*. Boulder, CO: Paradigm.

Weber, Max. 1918. "Politics as a Vocation." In *Max Weber: Essays in Sociology*. Translated, edited, and with an introduction by H. H. Gerth and C. Wright Mills, 77–128. Oxford: Oxford University Press.

Zuckerman, Ethan. 2013. *Rewire: Digital Cosmopolitans in the Age of Connection*. New York: Norton.

Zuckerman, Ethan. 2014. "The Internet's Original Sin." *Atlantic* (August): 14.

2 Effective Civics

Ethan Zuckerman

Introduction: Ferguson and the Range of Reactions

On August 9, 2014, police officer Darren Wilson fatally shot Michael Brown, an unarmed African American teenager, in Ferguson, Missouri. After Brown's body had lain in the hot sun for four hours, citizens of Ferguson took to the streets to protest. The protests, initially peaceful, took a violent turn on August 10, with businesses looted and burned. Ferguson police in riot gear attempted to quell the protests using tear gas and rubber bullets. Journalists covering the story were arrested and shot at by police. Faced with extensive criticism, on August 14 Missouri governor Jay Nixon turned over the policing of Ferguson to Captain Ron Johnson of the highway patrol, an African American and a long-time resident of the city, who used community-policing tactics to calm crowds. The following day, Ferguson police chief Tom Jackson released the name of the officer who shot Brown, but he preceded the announcement by accusing Brown of robbing a convenience store. Anger over the announcement sparked another wave of violence, which continued through August 18.

The protests in Ferguson brought media and public attention to a wide range of contemporary social issues: the ways in which young African American males are widely viewed (and portrayed in media) as threatening; racial disparities in arrest and treatment by police; poverty in inner-ring suburbs of American cities; decreasing social mobility in the wake of a "jobless recovery"; the adoption of military-style equipment and tactics by US law enforcement. Much as the killing of Trayvon Martin, another unarmed African American teenager, in February 2012 had opened a national dialog about racism and private gun ownership in America, the death of Michael Brown opened a set of parallel conversations about race, policing, and the future of American cities.

The reactions to Michael Brown's death in Ferguson offer not just a window on pressing issues Americans face regarding racism, violence, and the culture of policing, but a picture of how citizens engage in civics in the wake of a high-profile event.

Reactions to Brown's death in Ferguson unfolded locally and globally, in the media as well as in the streets.

The most visible form of engagement came through participation in rallies and vigils, and, unfortunately, in violence and looting. Protesters were not just making their presence felt in the streets. They were also documenting the events as they transpired. On August 9, the day of Brown's killing, no cable news channels or national newspapers had covered the shooting and its aftermath. For those who wanted to follow events in Ferguson in real time, tweets from St. Louis rapper Tef Poe and others at the scene were required reading. Even as professional reporters for national newspapers came to Ferguson to report, Twitter and other digital media were where stories unfolded moment by moment. When *Washington Post* reporter Wesley Lowery was arrested in a Ferguson McDonalds, he yelled to his colleague Ryan Reilly, "Ryan, tweet that they're arresting me, tweet that they're arresting me," knowing that those following the story closely would mobilize for his release (Fung 2014).

Twitter was not just a channel to follow reports from Ferguson. It quickly became a space to organize responses to events on the ground and to media coverage of Ferguson. When television stations and websites began accompanying stories of Michael Brown's death with a photo of the teenager, wearing baggy clothing and scowling at the camera, some Twitter users began asking whether this was an appropriate photo to portray a murder victim. Some users unearthed another recent photo of Brown, looking shy and unthreatening, and asked whether the photo chosen by news outlets to portray Brown had been chosen to look as menacing as possible. Others began tweeting pairs of photos from their Facebook timelines. One photo portrayed the subject as an upstanding citizen, graduating from high school or appearing in military dress uniform. The other showed the same person drinking with friends, menacing the camera, or striking a thuggish pose. Captions asked: "#iftheygunnedmedown which picture would they use?"(Stampler 2014; Rhoades and Carrasquillo 2014)

The protests in the streets documented online and the online protests calling attention to events in the streets represent some of the ways in which "civic media"—the use

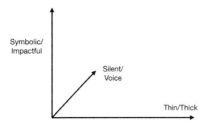

Figure 2.1
Three axes that characterize different forms of civic engagement.

of participatory media technologies for civic participation, political engagement, or social change—has become a routine part of protest movements, opening participation in protests far beyond those physically present. The diversity of participation in response to Michael Brown's shooting offers a picture of the many ways in which civic engagement takes place in the early twenty-first century. We are seeing not just a range of actors and venues—those proximate and distant, online and in the physical world—but multiple forms of civic participation.

Understanding these forms of civic participation requires moving beyond conventional ideas of what constitutes legitimate civic participation and exploring questions about which forms of participation are effective. To examine effectiveness, I propose understanding participation in relation to three characteristics: the "thickness," or the demands put on the participant; the use of different levers of change to seek specific impacts; and the reliance on voice as a path toward change.

The model outlined here is illustrated with examples primarily from the context of US civic engagement, but it is likely that many of the ideas outlined here apply outside the US context. The specifics of the US situation, where a decline in public trust combined with pervasive digital technologies is opening new paths to civic engagement, has parallels in many advanced and emerging democracies. These circumstances are not universal, and the models suggested are likely less applicable in societies where online speech is sharply constrained, or where baseline trust in institutions is so low that activists reject the utility of influencing existing institutions.

Changing Times, Changing Civics

The protests that demanded the identification and arrest of the officer who shot Michael Brown, and later the withdrawal of militarized police from Ferguson, used time-honored tactics of nonviolent resistance popularized in the civil rights movement of the 1950s and '60s. Their theories of change sought justice within the existing legal system, seeking an independent investigation of the shooting of Brown and demanding that Darren Wilson, the officer who shot Brown, be indicted by a grand jury. The protesters' skillful use of nonviolent confrontation with heavily armed police, and documentation of the asymmetry of these forces in broadcast media, also hearkens back to civil rights protests and reinforces the possibility of judicial action by shaping public opinion (Sledge and Kassie 2014).

Social media campaigns like #iftheygunnedmedown unfold using a different theory of change. Those tweeting contrasting self-portraits and asking which the media would pick to memorialize them aren't seeking Darren Wilson's arrest or demanding an investigation. Instead of using media to demand enforcement of the law, they are using media to influence media. The question asked by #iftheygunnedmedown is all too easy to answer, argue the protesters: media has a systemic bias against African Americans and will choose the image that transfers blame onto a person of color, even if he is the victim of a crime. The goal of the campaign is to change media behavior and, in turn, to challenge a social norm in which young black men tend to be viewed as dangerous. Criticizing those who tweet #iftheygunnedmedown photos as "slacktivists" who are not engaged with the real-world issues unfolding in Ferguson (Story 2014) misses the point—these activists are using media to challenge media and norms, not to seek an arrest or an investigation. Instead, it is helpful to see these campaigns as part of a broad set of "civic media" interventions—ways of using participatory media to seek social change.

Within ten days of Brown's death, activists were leading voter registration efforts in Ferguson. Reverend Al Sharpton, in a sermon at Greater Grace Church in Ferguson, pointed out that voter turnout in the city was a scant 12 percent and urged those in the pews to vote (Lapidos 2014). Reverend Jesse Jackson announced a door-to-door voter registration drive in conjunction with local clergy, telling listeners at an interview at the Ferguson McDonalds, "Five thousand new voters will transform the city from top to bottom" (Brown 2014). The strategy behind voter registration as a response to Michael Brown's shooting is clear: Jackson, Sharpton, and others believed that increased black voter participation would change Ferguson from a city in which a black majority (67 percent) is policed and governed by a white minority (29 percent) into one where the majority population is better represented in positions of power (Smith 2014). Critics of Sharpton, Jackson, and voter registration included conservatives who saw voter registration as "politicizing" the tragedy of Michael Brown's death—Missouri RNC executive director Matt Wills told reporters, "If that's not fanning the political flames, I don't know what is. I think it's not only disgusting but completely inappropriate" (Spiering 2014). Those promoting voter registration argue that Brown's death was an outcome of political inequities and that increased engagement in representative democracy is precisely how Brown's death should be honored.

These different theories of change and the multilayered civics that they drive are anticipated by Michael Schudson's 1998 book, *The Good Citizen.* Schudson's book is a history of civic participation in America that argues that our collective understanding of what it means to be a good citizen has changed over time. In Schudson's telling, we've moved from a vision of citizenship centered on representation by the most socially prominent individuals, to representation through the machinery of patronage-fueled political parties, to a more recognizable model he calls "the informed citizen" (Schudson 1998, 69). The informed citizen model is a product of the Progressive era and puts a heavy set of expectations on the citizen to help reform the excesses of machine-era party politics. The informed citizen relies on investigative journalism to understand the issues of the day and is prepared to vote directly on legislation in referenda or to pick specific politicians she favors by voting split tickets on secret ballots.

Schudson worries that our understanding of civic participation has stalled with the informed citizen paradigm, which underlies much of the debate around "a crisis in civics"(Dillon 2011). The expectations of citizens in the Progressive vision were too high—Walter Lippmann suggests that reformers imagined an impossibly "omnicompetent citizen"(Lippmann 1922)—and voting rates dropped sharply as elections felt less like daylong political celebrations and more like civics exams. In overfocusing on citizenship as conceived of by Progressives, Schudson worries that we may fail to consider subsequent redefinitions of good citizenship. The civil rights movement shifted battles from the election booth into the streets and into the courts for the simple reason that African Americans could not achieve representation within the voting booth due to violations of their voting rights.

Key to Schudson's argument is the idea that the shape of civic participation continues to change, and that multiple paradigms of citizenship coexist, with some declining in prominence as others grow. In examining the responses to Ferguson, I see at least four of these paradigms at work: machine politics of the late 1800s, "informed citizenship" of the Progressive era, court-based citizenship strategies from the civil rights era, and a new model of monitorial citizenship. Voter registration drives focused on bringing African American citizens informed about racial imbalances of power in Ferguson to the voting booth map neatly to Progressive visions of informed citizenship. The reactions from some on the right who saw this as a tactic of pure political mobilization invoke memories of the age of machine politics. Mobilization in the streets in response to lack of confidence in elected officials and demands for relief through the judicial process invoke the rights-based citizenship of the civil rights struggle and help explain the prominent role played by civil rights organizations of that era.

While *The Good Citizen* was published in 1998, Schudson offers a possible framework for understanding contemporary phenomena like the hashtag activism in reaction to Michael Brown's death: monitorial citizenship. Schudson's monitorial citizen is not omnicompetent, but continually scans the media for issues she is concerned about and where she might be able to have an influence (301–311). Building on Schudson's notion, John Keane has posited monitorial citizenship as a new era of civic engagement where citizens focus on exerting power through oversight of powerful institutions, in government and in the private sector (Keane 2009).

Activism around the #iftheygunnedmedown hashtag is well explained by the model of monitorial citizenship. "Black Twitter" has been credited with popularizing Ferguson-related hashtags (Marfo 2014). The community is a loose, informal network of Twitter users who monitor news and social media for racist statements and actions and respond by confronting or ridiculing those who've erred (McDonald 2014). Outrage from Black Twitter helped prevent George Zimmerman juror "B37" from selling her memoir about acquitting Trayvon Martin's killer (Sugerman 2013), and the spread of links within the community helped draw media attention to events in Ferguson and encouraged participation in campaigns like #iftheygunnedmedown. By monitoring media to confront instances of systemic bias, and by challenging racist norms with alternative images, the Twitter users behind #iftheygunnedmedown demonstrated a civics that scans the horizon to find issues of interest, monitors powerful institutions, and intervenes by shaping norms through the creation and dissemination of media.

Schudson invokes monitorial democracy as a way both to explain apparent deficits in contemporary civics and to legitimate this new form of participation. Legitimation is a key first step toward a more nuanced dialog about the shortcomings of our contemporary civics. Acknowledging that civics not only includes those attending school board meetings and running for office but also encompasses those making media and monitoring powerful institutions broadens the base of those engaged in civics and widens the toolkit accessible to civic actors. But such a broadening opens a new set of questions about civic efficacy. Hashtag activism may be a manifestation of monitorial citizenship and an emergent form of civic participation, but critics are justified in asking whether such engagement is effective in bringing about the changes its proponents imagine.

On the surface, #iftheygunnedmedown was highly effective in confronting a mainstream media narrative and in gaining coverage. In the days after the hashtag came to prominence, CNN, *Time,* the *New York Times*, and dozens of other news outlets referenced the campaign directly in stories about Ferguson and online activism. (Media Cloud, http://mediacloud.org, finds more than a hundred mentions of the tag on US mainstream media and political blogs in the week after the campaign launched.) But the longer-term effects of the campaign won't be clear for months and years to come, and even if media outlets are more careful in photo selection in stories about African American victims, it will be difficult to determine whether this campaign was the decisive cause of the change.

The #iftheygunnedmedown campaign can be thought of as a single incident within the larger narrative of the #BlackLivesMatter movement, a protest movement that began as a hashtag and has become a major force in organizing protests and demonstrations. Started by activists and organizers Alicia Garza, Patrisse Cullors, and Opal Tometi after the acquittal of George Zimmerman for the death of Trayvon Martin (Garza 2014), the campaign seeks to connect individual instances of police violence into a larger narrative of state violence against black people. Patrisse Cullors sees the movement as drawing connections between the death of Oscar Grant at the hands of the Oakland Police in 2009 and the deaths of Trayvon Martin, Eric Garner, and dozens of others, with the individual deaths leading toward 2015 as a year of protest (Garza 2014). As of February 2015, 23 chapters of Black Lives Matter in the United States, Canada, and Ghana were organizing protests and marches demanding the release of US government information about police violence against black people, as well as a shift in investment from law enforcement to community development. Tens of thousands of people have been involved with Black Lives Matter protests, with varying motivations, but monitoring abuse of power by federal and local governments is a major focus of the ongoing movement.

Civic Efficacy

Given a range of possible methods of civic participation, questions of efficacy come to the fore. If I care about racial justice, should I work to elect candidates from a particular political party, run for local office, participate in a march, write an op-ed or a blog post? Given my skills, capabilities, and time, am I likely to be effective in bringing about the changes I wish to see through a given civic act?

In 1957, Anthony Downs attempted to answer this question from the perspective of a voter deciding whether or not she should participate in an election. In *An Economic Theory of Democracy* (Downs 1957), Downs models the calculations a rational voter makes in terms of the benefit she would see from electing her preferred candidate, the probability that her vote will determine the course of the election, and the cost of participation. Since cost is relatively high and close elections are relatively rare, Downs's calculus suggests that voter turnout should be much lower than it actually is. Challenged by this finding, Downs suggests that voters may turn out simply to support the democratic exercise, as a way of voting for the process of representative democracy through their presence.

Building on Downs's work a year later, William Riker and Peter Ordeshook formalized Downs's model into an equation: $R = PB - C + D$ (Riker and Ordeshook 1968, 25–42). A rational voter will participate in an election when the probability (P) of her participation in delivering the benefit (B) she desires outweighs the cost (C) of participation. While Riker and Ordeshook use calculus to demonstrate that there are moments when PB is very high in contested elections, their main contribution may be in adding a new variable to the equation: duty (D). D represents the sense of civic duty one feels from participating in an election, which includes the "satisfaction from compliance with the ethic of voting," "satisfaction from affirming allegiance to the political system," "satisfaction from affirming a partisan preference," the possible enjoyment of the experience of going to the polls, and the satisfaction that comes from affirming one's efficacy.

Community organizer, technologist, and political theorist Anthea Watson Strong invoked Riker and Ordeshook in a 2014 speech about increasing civic participation. In her work on open government projects for Google, Watson Strong encourages her teammates to consider the equation: $C < PB + D$ (Watson Strong 2014a).

People will participate in a particular civic action, she argues, if the cost to do so is lower than the sum of their sense of duty plus the combination of probability of having an effect and the magnitude of the benefit in question. Watson Strong defines D more

C < BP + D

B = Benefit
P = Probability of having benefit
C = Cost
D = Duty

Figure 2.2
Watson Strong's rewriting of Riker and Ordeshook's equation to understand civic efficacy.

broadly than Riker and Ordeshook, as not just a duty to civic process, but a loyalty toward friends who are taking action or the desire to be part of a broader movement.

Watson Strong's reworking of decades-old equations of civic efficacy retains some of the assumptions and challenges associated with these formulations. Given mounting evidence that humans are far from rational economic actors, a theory that posits rational calculations about thousands of possible civic actions may not model reality as well as theories that look at the power of peer influence and mass movements—an idea we'll return to later in this chapter. As Downs (1957) discusses at length in his book, voters lack perfect information about which candidate will give the largest benefits; in considering Watson Strong's formulation, it is worth considering all variables—cost, probability, benefit, and duty—in terms of an individual's perception.

Shortly before reading Watson Strong's formulation, I attended a town meeting in my hometown, joining a few hundred voters to vote on the town's annual budget. I live in Massachusetts, where many towns hold open town meetings, in which any taxpayer can vote on individual line items in the town's budget as well as any other legislative matters under consideration by the town. (Towns with a population under 6,000 are required to have open town meetings. Many larger towns hold open town meetings as well, while still-larger towns elect representatives to the town meeting, and cities are governed by a mayor and a city council.) Town meetings have been celebrated as an especially "pure" form of participatory democracy, including by Henry Thoreau, who declared, "When, in some obscure country town, the farmers come together to a special town-meeting, to express their opinion on some subject which is vexing the land, that, I think, is the true Congress, and the most respectable one that is ever assembled in the United States" (Thoreau 1854). However, many towns are finding they cannot assemble sufficient participants to hold town meetings and are moving to less participatory, more streamlined, forms of governance.

Neighbors warned me over a brewing fight about our town's participation in a regional school district, where we pay high tax rates to send our children to a high-quality high school nearby. Remaining in this district had high B for me, as I plan to send my son to public high school, and friends persuaded me that the vote would be very close, which meant I had high P, a strong chance that my vote would be decisive. This was strong enough to motivate me, despite my apparently low D (I'd not previously attended a town meeting) and a non-zero C (I had to hire a babysitter to watch my child). Once the votes were counted, over 300 had voted to remain in the district and less than a dozen had voted against—had I had perfect knowledge of P, I might well have stayed at home (Zuckerman 2014). But citizens are neither omniscient nor omnicompetent and efficacy must be calculated in terms of perception, not reality.

Reducing Cost, Increasing Duty, Increasing Efficacy

With these amendments to the formulation, Watson Strong's formula offers three ways to increase participation in civics: lower the costs of participation, increase the sense of duty, or increase the sense of efficacy that results from participation. Much of Watson Strong's work at Google focuses on reducing the cost of participation, ensuring that Google searches provide citizens with the information they need to find a polling place or a town meeting. A great deal of the excitement about the digital revolution of the past twenty years has focused on lowering transaction and coordination costs, so it is unsurprising that many new civics efforts focus on reducing cost.

Projects like SeeClickFix and FixMyStreet make it easier for citizens to report flaws in local infrastructure, with the hopes of increasing citizen engagement with and faith in local government. Indirectly, these projects educate their users in how local government works, so they understand who is responsible for different aspects of a community's infrastructure, and who they would need to influence or oust to achieve change on a given issue. Tim O'Reilly's call for government as a platform (O'Reilly 2010), where open government data is delivered via applications and tools developed in the private sector, operates on the same logic: if government operated as efficiently and elegantly as our best commercial applications, citizens would engage with government services more often and more easily. Code for America, which brings programmers into city governments to build new tools and services, offers a path toward making O'Reilly's prescription a reality.

The danger of cost-based approaches to increasing civic participation is that they can increase participation in broken systems. Rock the Vote and other projects focused on voter registration do an admirable job of reducing the cost of participation through voting. But as partisanship and procedural maneuvering have reduced the ability of Congress to pass legislation to historic lows (Bump 2014), increased participation in legislative elections may increase civic participation without increasing civic effectiveness. (It is also possible that a large-scale transformation of the electorate is one thing that could transform the functioning of Congress.) In the case of an underfunded and overburdened city government, reducing transaction costs and making government services more accessible could have the unintended consequence of revealing the limitations and shortcomings in government services, decreasing trust and confidence in government in the long run.

Other approaches to increased civic participation focus on increasing a sense of duty—to the democratic process, to geographic communities, as well as to communities of interest, religion, or ethnicity. The humble "I Voted" sticker handed out at polling places is a classic technique to increase D, advertising the act of voting to encourage others to do their civic duty. Meetup, founded by Scott Heiferman in response to concerns in the decline of community capital (Sundwall, n.d.), as expressed in Robert Putnam's influential *Bowling Alone* (Putnam 2000), increases a sense of duty through helping people organize and identify with affinity groups. Meetup groups have been credited with helping both Obama presidential campaigns (Baumgartner and Morris 2010) and with helping to create the Tea Party (Williamson, Skocpol, and Coggin 2011, 25–43). Organizations and strategies that try to increase patriotism, or more local senses of city identity and civic pride, or to urge members of a religious congregation toward political participation are all leveraging duty to increase the likelihood of civic action.

A danger of duty-based strategies is that they are often deployed to encourage participation in forms of civics that may be ineffective but have strong historical grounding. You are more likely to encounter an appeal to your sense of civic duty to encourage you to vote than to encourage you to participate in a demonstration or a sit-in. Schudson warns of "political piety"(Schudson 1998, 137), the danger of accepting a set of political practices and origin myths as the time-honored and right way of conducting our civic lives. Duty, applied incautiously, could limit our ability to explore and embrace new forms of civics.

The remaining factors in Watson Strong's formulation demand the closest exploration. As the range of civic responses to Ferguson suggests, citizens now have a wide and varied toolkit of ways to engage, far beyond the possibilities modeled by Downs or Riker and Ordeshook. Determining whether a method of engagement is effective requires considering how a participant calculates the benefit of her actions, and the probability that her actions will have benefit. This requires more careful analysis than is often applied to civic participation, where counting attendance at a rally or turnout in an election often serves as a shortcut to evaluating success or failure. Understanding whether a civic act has a probability of succeeding and what benefits it might engender involves closely considering actions in terms of theories of change, theories of how change will come about, who is influenced by a civic action, how citizens evaluate if they were effective influencers, and whether theory initial theories of change were correct.

Evaluating Efficacy through Theories of Change

The voter registration campaigns promoted by Reverends Jackson and Sharpton are part of a set of interventions focused around representative democracy as a primary theory of change: when a large population is empowered to vote in a fair electoral system, they can elect representatives who will advocate for their interests in local, state, and federal venues. The advantages of this theory of change include its familiarity and strong cultural currency—most efforts to promote engagement in civics or increase a sense of civic duty encourage participation in acts focused on representative democracy. Success is relatively easy to measure in these interventions, as elections are easily quantified and reported, and the binary nature of most of our elections makes it reasonably easy to determine which candidate is more likely to support your goals as a citizen. Most importantly, many of the resources of a democratic society are controlled by elected representatives and those they appoint, suggesting that the benefits of electing representatives who share a citizen's values and concerns is very high in comparison to other forms of engagement.

Unfortunately, as Downs and others have explained, high B is accompanied by low P—it is unlikely that your individual vote will sway the outcome of a political campaign. Low P suggests that those seeking change through representative democracy are well served to build movements, as a large group of voters is much more likely to sway an election than an individual. The need to assemble large groups to exercise power suggests another limit to democratic representation as a theory of change: it is far more powerful for asserting the will of majorities than of minorities. Most functioning democracies balance majority rule with strong protections for the rights of minorities to ensure against the downside of majoritarianism, but this imbalance suggests that democratic representation isn't the ideal strategy for groups who hold views or opinions well outside of the mainstream of discourse.

Democratic representation as a pathway to individual civic engagement has two other key downsides that are more apparent now than at the formation of the American republic. First, politics has become highly professionalized, in terms of both standing for office and managing political campaigns. An increasing percentage of congresspeople list their profession, pre-election, as "public service," while decreasing numbers report prior careers in business, education, or the military (Ornstein et al. 2013). Candidates for state- and national-level office are usually supported by a team of political professionals who apply a refined set of skills to different campaigns each year. As a result, it's easy for citizens to feel like political campaigns are something the pros do, rather than something an ordinary citizen can participate in. Second, the United States is experiencing a widespread loss of faith in governing institutions, especially at the federal level. Pew Research Center finds that Americans' trust in government has experienced steady declines from 73% during the Eisenhower administration to a level of 24% under the Obama administrations (People Press 2014). With congressional approval levels plumbing historic depths and a deep partisan split in evaluating presidential performance, it's not hard to see why some American citizens would feel frustrated at their ability—or lack thereof—to make change through engagement in representative democracy.

The street protests in Ferguson evoked memories of the civil rights protests that took place throughout the American South, protests that led to both legislative and judicial changes that enshrined rights of access to courts, classrooms, public spaces, the workplace, and the polling booth. Seeking change by demanding that courts enforce or extend these rights has become a primary tactic for social change advocates from all corners of the political spectrum; activists on the left seek court rulings that seek ongoing enforcement of the 1965 Voting Rights Act while some on the right are seeking a constitutional amendment restricting abortion. It's easy to understand why, as winning a battle in a state or federal court brings the government's entire enforcement apparatus to bear on an issue, even if the issue does not enjoy widespread popular support. As a result, judicial theories of change are especially important and useful for those seeking to protect human rights and the rights of minorities. Furthermore, it's fairly easy to measure the success of activism in this space. Advocates for the right to spend private money to support political campaigns saw the Supreme Court's decision in Citizens United v. Federal Election Commission as a stunning success, and campaign reform advocates nearly universally saw it as a catastrophe.

If one of the flaws of representative democracy as a theory of change for civic participation is that politics is highly professionalized, the problem is more acute with judicial theories of change. While a huge number of advocacy organizations seek cases they can litigate to set precedent, participation in this space is limited largely to a subset of lawyers with experience and skills around a specific set of political issues. The process of public interest litigation is opaque compared with the process of political campaigning, complicated by restrictions on reporting from courtrooms and the difficulties reporters have in making legal processes understandable to their readers. Compared to elections where people put signs on their lawn or canvass their neighbors, litigation is relatively nonparticipatory. In the wake of Bush v. Gore and other Supreme Court decisions with partisan political implications, only 36 percent of Americans believe that the Court decides cases based purely on the facts rather than considering political views (Fuller 2014). Americans don't yet have as much disdain for the Supreme Court as they do for other branches of government, but approval ratings for the courts are just above 50% and trending downward. So while B is high for judicial theories of change, P is even lower, for most citizens, than in theories of change centered on representative democracy.

Theories of Change and the Affordances of Digital Media

In considering the other theories of change that activists and citizens are bringing to bear in the wake of Ferguson and around other contemporary issues, it's useful to put some limits on the scope of activism to consider. Social change through coordinated prayer has become a popular tactic for Christian activists from different positions on the political spectrum. (While B is likely high, calculating P is beyond the theological scope of this chapter.) In considering civic media specifically, it's helpful to consider theories of change where the affordances of digital technology are making these strategies more common and more visible.

Lawrence Lessig offers a helpful framework for considering forms of civics that are advanced through the rise of pervasive computing, though his goal was not to provide a framework for understanding participation, but for understanding how governments and companies can control the adoption of technology. In *Code and Other Laws of Cyberspace* (Lessig 2000), which Lessig wrote after serving as special master in United States v. Microsoft, a case that centered on Microsoft's power to control technical innovation, Lessig offers the idea that there are multiple ways to regulate new technologies. Regulation occurs through law, making certain behaviors (such as sharing child pornography or transmitting money to terrorist organizations) illegal. But regulation also happens through markets, making some behaviors cheap and others expensive, to encourage certain behaviors. Norms are another form of regulation, where society collectively decides that some behaviors are unacceptable (e.g., watching as people type in passwords) and others laudable (retweeting a friend's witty comment). Finally, regulation takes places through code, making it difficult to do some things (sharing copyprotected movies) and easy to do others (posting content and allowing the hosting service to "monetize" it.) All these methods can be profoundly effective in regulating speech and behavior, leading to the quip, "code is law."

I propose inverting Lessig's framework and considering his regulatory strategies as theories of change useful for civic engagement. The representative democracy and judicial theories of change map neatly to law in Lessig's framework, as core functions in a representative democracy are creation, enforcement, and review of law. The three remaining theories of change—code, markets, and norms—offer help in evaluating the effectiveness of emerging forms of civic behavior.

Code

Seeking change through code has been a galvanizing idea for computer programmers since Richard Stallman first promoted free software as a force for economic and social change in the 1980s, but as Biella Coleman notes in *Coding Freedom* (2012, 40), *Code* has become a bible for activist geeks. The appeal of change through code—and more broadly, through technological and architectural affordances—is largely the same as the appeal of innovation to investors and financial markets. Software companies promise sustained returns for a modest upfront effort—adoption of a technology in the marketplace does the lion's share of the work. It required enormous effort to make Facebook accessible to the first million users and significantly less effort for each additional million, which has allowed early investors in the company to realize massive returns on their investment. The creator(s) of Bitcoin likely had similar aspirations in creating a currency free of the influence of governments and central banks: the upfront effort to create a novel set of transaction tracking mechanisms would be counterbalanced by the promise that the currency would spread and be adopted with little or no additional ongoing effort.

Change through code is potentially deep, long lasting, and often destabilizing. The rise of zero-cost Internet telephony and videoconferencing through Skype and other services has not only halted the growth of long-distance telephone companies (Malik 2012), but has changed the structure of corporations and organizations, massively lowering barriers to international cooperation and weakening the paradigm of the office-bound worker. Activists who bet on pervasive encryption as a way of frustrating government surveillance of communications anticipate a range of pro-civic behaviors that come from establishing both public and private spaces online.

Finally, code opens the field of social change to new actors. Satoshi Nakamoto (or whoever actually created Bitcoin) had strong feelings about fiat currency and central banking, and might have channeled his opinions into letters to the editor or his congressperson. By creating Bitcoin, he has opened a debate about the future of banking, money, and governments that would have been very difficult to accomplish through lobbying or legislation. For technically savvy people who find politics inaccessible and opaque, the idea of change through code is liberating in the extreme, as B is high but unpredictable, and P is higher than change through other means.

Unfortunately, change through code is only open to a small subset of people who can create truly novel systems. This number is smaller than one might expect. Truly transformative systems like Bitcoin or Skype are rare, and are often the product of years of work by very talented programmers. It is possible that change through code is at least as professionalized as change through the courts or elections, although a different group of experts works within this framework. It is also likely that change through code is overhyped and that coders imagine more interventions in the space than will succeed as standalone systems. Finally, new technologies tend to be usable by many different actors in different contexts. The strong encryption systems that protect individuals from NSA spying are also powerful tools to conceal criminal activities. It is difficult, if not impossible, to prevent the use of technologies to advance antisocial ends without crippling those technologies and banning important novel uses for them.

Code-centric theories of change share certain drawbacks with other approaches to increasing individual civic engagement. Software systems often focus on reducing transaction costs, which suggests that these theories of change, like approaches that focus on reducing the cost of civic action, run the risk of making broken systems more efficient. And because some of the impacts of novel technologies are unintended consequences, it is difficult to design strategies to evaluate the impact of code-based civic engagement.

Markets

Seeking social change through markets is a strategy for social change that clearly precedes the rise of the commercial Internet: the boycott of public buses in Montgomery, Alabama, in 1955–1956 is seen as one of the turning points of the civil rights movement in the US. However, the rise of widely accessible digital technologies has made it easier to coordinate actions like boycotts or buycotts (Shirky 2008), making such campaigns more common. Crowdfunding platforms like Kickstarter and Indiegogo are lowering barriers to entry in starting new businesses and bringing products to the market. The success of Internet-based businesses has led to a wave of enthusiasm for entrepreneurship as a career, and to the emergence of new training programs focused specifically on social entrepreneurship.

Market-based theories of change are bringing new actors into the space of organized social change, new activists who believe in the power of markets and are skeptical of legal and regulatory approaches to change around environmental issues, for instance. Business-based approaches to change have the advantages of scalability and sustainability since, to succeed as businesses, they need to reach large audiences and support their own costs. It's possible that market-based theories of change may serve as an end run around dysfunctional legal regimes; consider Uber as a market-based strategy to reforming dysfunctional taxi medallion legislation as well as a disruptive for-profit startup.

That said, market-based strategies may be most powerful when accompanied by law-based strategies. The Toyota Prius is an effective market-based tool for reducing carbon emissions in part due to Corporate Average Fuel Economy standards that have encouraged Toyota to bring efficient cars to market. Market-based approaches, like the renting of residential rooftop space to install solar panels, would be unlikely to gain traction without legislation that offers tax credits and rebates to participating homeowners.

There likely are sharp limits to how effective market-based theories of change can be without deeper structural changes to existing economic systems. Proponents of a "stakeholder" theory of capitalism suggest that many corporations will be limited in their ability to bring about positive social impacts due to concerns of maximizing "shareholder value" without considering the broader social and environmental impacts on a broader set of stakeholders (Donaldson and Preston 1995, 65–91). Accounting for social and environmental benefits within traditional market systems may require accountants to consider a "triple bottom line" that considers social, environmental, and fiscal returns on investment (Elkington 1999), which may be difficult or impossible to calculate (Norman and MacDonald 2004, 243–262).

Market-based theories of change raise difficult questions about the relationship between markets and governments. If markets become increasingly successful at helping communities raise money and purchase public goods through mechanisms like civic crowdfunding, it is possible that there will be further decay in trust in govern-ment, as citizens see governments as incapable of providing community projects with-out private aid (Zuckerman 2012). Governments are generally held to closer monitorial scrutiny than private sector actors, and the rise of market-based approaches to social change raises the possibility that new pseudopublic services may benefit only those who can afford them, while traditional public services benefit a broad swath of society and are monitored to ensure fairness of distribution. (It is likely that this objection to change through markets is particularly specific to the US, the UK, and other "advanced democracies" where neo-liberal reforms of the 1980s have favored provisions of ser-vices through commercial over governmental systems.)

Norms

The ability to seek social change by challenging and changing norms may be the most powerful theory of change implied by Lessig's framework. Michael Brown's death is a key demonstration: it is illegal for law enforcement officers to shoot unarmed people who do not present a clear and present danger, yet a 2007 investigation by *Color Lines* and the *Chicago Reporter* finds that African Americans are overrepresented in sets of police shooting victims throughout the United States, suggesting that implicit bias may play a role in whom the police shoot (Lowenstein 2007). Passing new laws that require the police to wear body cameras that activate once guns are unholstered may help reduce police shootings, but changing a pattern of police violence against African Americans requires strategies that challenge cultural perceptions of African American men as dangerous and potentially violent in the hopes of preventing future tragedies.

Shaping social norms is a time-honored technique in the public health community, where social marketing of health initiatives is a common means of achieving wide-spread behavioral change. The Harvard Alcohol Project pioneered the use of promo-tional messaging in entertainment content, working with television sitcom *Cheers* to mention designated drivers as a plot point in an attempt to normalize the intervention (Winsten 1994, 11–14), while social marketing campaigns in sub-Saharan Africa show evidence of changing norms and behaviors around condom use (Eloundou-Enyegue, Meekers, and Emmanuèle Calvès 2005, 257–268). Advocates for gays and lesbians see the possibility of expanded support for equal rights through pop culture exposure to homosexual characters (Schiappa, Gregg, and Hewes 2006, 15–37) even as the move-ment debates whether bringing gay culture into the mainstream ends up enforcing heterosexism (Battles and Hilton-Morrow 2002, 87–105).

If one major selling point for norms-based theories of change is the possibility of widespread social transformation (high B), another benefit it its accessibility to a gen-eration of "digital natives," a term that is both an unhelpful simplification as well as an acknowledgment that norms around media production have changed radically in the past two decades. Campaigns like #iftheygunnedmedown are not unusual within social media. In a sense, they are an outgrowth of quotidian uses of social media to express opinions and group affiliation, made visible by organizing personal actions around a shared search term. Barriers to entry for this sort of engagement are extremely low, leading to the viral spread of interventions like the Human Rights Campaign's effort to spread their logo to call attention to issues of marriage equality (HRC, n.d.). For a generation of social media users, shaping norms through participating in hashtags and spreading images may be a natural modus operandus.

But while norms-based theories of change can have high benefits and low barriers to participation, it is extremely difficult to evaluate the success of norms-based campaigns at the time a campaign is launched. Changing social norms is a slow process; acceptance of black-white marriage in the United States has grown, year on year, from 4 percent in 1958 to 87 percent in 2013 (Newport 2013), and acceptance of equal marriage rights for same-sex couples has changed dramatically in the past two decades and is likely to continue to increase. Measuring norms change is difficult and generally requires large-scale public polling carried out over many years, an expensive proposition. Determining whether a specific intervention was effective is even more difficult, as it requires careful examination of agenda setting (did my action get people talking about this issue) and framing (when discussing the issue, are people taking my side and promoting my understanding of the issue) as well as values change. It's one thing to measure how many millions of Facebook users changed their profile photo to the logo of an equality campaign; it is another to determine whether those profile changes led to a change in public acceptance of equal marriage rights.

There's another serious shortcoming to norms-based theories of change, which results directly from the strategy's low barrier to entry. Widespread adoption of this theory of change is likely to complicate existing problems of attention scarcity. As campaigns similar to HRC's Marriage Equality campaign or Kony2012 (which sought to publicize the crimes of Lord's Resistance Army warload Joseph Kony in the hopes of leading to his arrest) become models for future activism, I expect more individuals and groups to launch similar efforts. The capacity to produce these campaigns is distributed over the billions of social media users, but our individual attention for these campaigns is finite. Social media users face a future—and perhaps a present—in which we all may be overwhelmed by demands to pay attention to pressing social issues by friends, family, politicians, brands, and activist organizations.

One likely outcome of this overabundance is a further corrosion of deliberative democracy. It is already difficult for elected representatives to agree on which pressing issues should be the subject of national debate. The eroding reach of broadcast media means that newspapers and television newscasts are less powerful in setting the agenda for national debate. As the capacity to control the news and opinions each of us encounters wanes, it is likely to be harder to have a "national conversation" about critical issues. Partisan divides over which problems governments should tackle may be superseded by even more complex, multifaceted debates over which issues merit public discussion and government intervention.

Participation as a Dimension of Civic Engagement

Understanding civic engagement through the lenses of cost, duty, and the probabilities and benefits of various theories of change may be helpful in analyzing the range of reactions to the events in Ferguson, but this language is incomplete in understanding how different individuals choose different forms of civic participation. Some choices are constrained by questions of capability and skillset: not everyone who wants to reform banking is capable of programming a novel cryptocurrency. Other choices are constrained by the cost of a given engagement: a working single mother is less likely to participate in town meetings than a retiree without children. But understanding civic participation also requires close consideration of what capacities a civic act asks of us.

Some of the debate surrounding online activism dismisses online participation in social movements as a statement of fashion, a desire to be aligned with one's peers, rather than a serious attempt to make change in the world (Morozov 2011). As I've argued above, it is possible that changing your Facebook icon to support equal marriage, or authoring an #iftheygunnedmedown tweet, could have impact through the long, slow process of shaping norms. But it's also worth considering these acts in terms of the demands they make on participants. In his critique of slacktivism, Malcolm Gladwell rightly celebrates Freedom Riders and other civil rights activists as being willing to take on significant risks to forward their cause, but he unfairly dismisses online supporters of the Save Darfur movement as being unwilling to make the same commitment (Gladwell 2010).

Gladwell is correct that the 1.3 million members of Save Darfur on Facebook were not, on average, as committed to their cause as Freedom Riders who knew that they faced arrest or murder for their participation. This disparity can be explained with the "ladder of engagement," a tool frequently used by social organizers, descended from the Ladder of Citizen Participation that Sherry Arnstein proposed in 1969 to warn of the long path from governments consulting citizens on proposed social changes to authentic citizen control of those decisions (Arnstein 1969, 216–224). As adopted by organizers, the ladder of engagement has become a less challenging, more manageable way of understanding different levels of participation in a movement. For every ten Facebook supporters of Save Darfur, movement leaders hoped that one would write online about the organization and its issues. For every ten who wrote online, perhaps one would donate. For every ten who donated, perhaps one would be willing to host a meeting in their house. For every ten meeting hosts, one might become a leader of a regional chapter. Cultivating an activist movement becomes the process of leading people up the ladder of engagement from affiliates to opinion leaders, to donors, to movement organizers. In theory, as participants climb the ladder, they take on responsibility for the strategy of the organization; in practice, Arnstein's warnings about cooption and manipulation apply as much to engagement with NGOs as they do to engagement with governments in neighborhood planning.

Considered in terms of the ladder of engagement, those 1.3 million Save Darfur supporters represented an opportunity to move hundreds or thousands into positions of leadership, while hundreds of thousands failed to become fully engaged. There is another way to consider those supporters that doesn't presuppose massive failure: the idea of thick and thin participation.

Thin forms of civic engagement are ones that require minimal effort from a participant. They gain their strength through scale. A few dozen Facebook users changing their profile pictures is unlikely to have any effect on shaping norms, but millions of Facebook users doing so may alert many other Facebook users to the fact that they have lots of friends who support equal marriage (Matias 2013). Because thin forms of engagement depend on widespread participation, organizers of thin forms of engagement work to keep costs of participation very low. Typically, thin forms of engagement promise participants that if they show up and take part, they will be able to have a cumulative impact.

In thin forms of engagement, someone else has done the thinking; your job is to show up and carry out your role. Thick engagement begins by considering what needs to be done. It demands your head as well as your feet. Occupy encampments, where participants worked to determine how camps would run, what issues they would focus on, and how to feed and shelter participants, offer an example of why thick engagement is simultaneously compelling and challenging. Many civic participants want their thinking and creativity to be part of what they give to a cause, not just signatures or donations. At the same time, most of the people who supported Occupy weren't able to give the time necessary for truly thick engagement, and some have argued that Occupy would have had more political impact had it demanded less thick engagement from its supporters.

There is a tendency to privilege thick engagement over thin, as Gladwell does. But thin engagement is critically important, as most people cannot engage in thick ways on all the issues they care about. The public benefits when people are capable of participating in meaningful ways at a cost of time and effort that they can afford. Making engagement too thick breaks forms of engagement that demand participation at scale. When it requires thick engagement to cast a vote, the situation is best understood as "voter suppression." Understanding that thin engagement is not necessarily a step on the path to thick engagement, but a legitimate form of participation that may be particularly useful at the scale of Web-based movements is a key step toward being able to evaluate the efficacy of participating in campaigns like #iftheygunnedmedown.

Distinguishing between thin and thick engagement does not exempt all participation from the "slacktivism" critique. It is certainly possible for engagement to be too thin to be effective, most likely when engagement is thin and not well attached to a theory of change. #iftheygunnedmedown may have, in fact, convinced participants that they were doing something relevant while they were wasting their time tweeting. But understanding this civic engagement that unfolds through media requires consideration of another factor: the importance of voice.

Voice

In considering #iftheygunnedmedown and other forms of civic participation that center on generating and disseminating media, I have focused primarily on the ways in which this media could be an instrument for change. If enough people share pictures that challenge the portrayal of people of color in the news media, news outlets may change their behavior, which may help slowly erode a norm in which African American men are viewed by law enforcement as more dangerous than other groups, and therefore more likely to be violently confronted. This analysis may be plausible, but it misses other key ways in which expressions of voice can indirectly, but powerfully, lead to change.

After I tweeted about Watson Strong's C < PB + D framework, I found myself in a Twitter debate with her and with Zeynep Tufekçi, a Turkish-American academic who studies protests movements (Watson Strong 2014b). Tufekçi worried that Watson Strong overestimated the importance of rational choice in making civic decisions: "Most people, historically, participate in most stuff, because their friends are or [it] feels like the right moment." In other words, individuals don't make a rational calculation before joining the protests in Gezi Park or Tahrir Square; instead, they look closely at what their friends are doing and often follow their lead. Tufekçi's objection recalls the insight of another great Turkish scholar, Timur Kuran, who explained that "preference falsification," where people lie about what they really believe in order to maintain social cohesion, can collapse in sudden, revolutionary changes if peers start expressing their true opinions. Given their lead, the rest of us are free to take to the streets and express our opposition (Kuran 1997).

Watson Strong explained that her use of "duty" was broad enough to include considerations of what our friends cared about and were doing, and that her model allowed for actions where the main motivator was one of duty to one's friends. I think the idea of duty may be best understood as aggregate peer influence, and that thinking of duty this way helps us understand the particular power of civic media. Deleting D and adding a new variable, I propose rewriting Watson Strong's equation as follows:

I will act if

C < BP + ΣI

*the cost is lower than the sum of
my perceived efficacy (BP) and what my
influencers signal they are doing*

Figure 2.3
My proposed rewriting of Watson Strong's equation.

I will take a specific civic action if the cost is lower than the sum of my perceived efficacy (the probability P that my action will lead to probable benefit B and my interpretation of the aggregate of what my peers and influencers signal they are doing.

Voice is how people signal their affiliations, their priorities, and the issues they care sufficiently about that they share them with friends in the hope of influencing their actions. Voice may be honest or deceptive. I may retweet voices from Ferguson because I want to be perceived as being enlightened on racial issues while harboring racist thoughts; I've still sent a signal to those who listen to me that they interpret as part of their ΣI (sum of peer influences).

Voice can be powerful enough to invalidate calculations of effectiveness. Kony2012, a social media campaign designed to rally support for the capture and arrest of a little-known Central African warlord, was carefully designed and launched by activist group Invisible Children so that social media users would hear about the campaign from different members of their social network at the same time (Lotan 2012). If you were a teenage social media user, particularly if you knew evangelical Christians, it was easy to feel like everyone you knew was posting about stopping Joseph Kony. Given such a powerful signal from ΣI, participants were spared the calculation of PB (a calculation that would be quite difficult to make), as the collective signal from one's friends was high enough to overcome the low cost of posting a status update. When criticisms of the Kony2012 campaign came to light, ΣI quickly shifted, and voicing your support for the campaign may have signaled to your friends that you were a bandwagon-joiner and an uncritical thinker, instead of a caring person trying to make a change in the world.

The ability of voice in aggregate to trigger civic engagement in ways that look more like social fads than carefully considered campaigns helps fuel the skepticism around civic media as a path toward social change. However, voice is often the precursor to other forms of instrumental engagement. Each of us turn to our friends, our family, and our colleagues when we look for the most effective ways to engage with an issue we care about, and increasingly, we make this journey from interest to engagement online and in public. And while there are certainly important civic actions planned in secret, expressions of voice through social media have become a critical tool in organizing social movements, as Rheingold (2002), Shirky (2008), and others have explored.

Voice begets voice. The DREAM activists—undocumented youth brought to the United States by their parents, youth who are now seeking the right to become citizens—often begin their "biographies of engagement" with a video "coming out," identifying themselves as "undocumented and unafraid"(Costanza-Chock 2011, 29–35). As with the gay and lesbian rights movement, which the DREAM movement consciously parallels, identifying as a visible member of a marginalized group is a first step toward deeper involvement. As with coming out in the gay and lesbian community, the visibility of DREAM activists is designed to help others identify themselves and make it safer to raise their own voices. The shift toward visibility on social media, to using voice to build a movement, is a radical shift in strategy within US immigration activism, where the undocumented have long been represented by activists who are US citizens, who do not face the threat of deportation and who feel more free to speak (Beltrán, 2015). As DREAM activists show themselves willing to speak, others are raising their voices as well.

Finally, voice may be the only form of civic engagement that is possible for those who feel truly disempowered. Economist Albert Hirschman introduces voice as an alternative to exit to explain a thorny problem in economics: why do customers remain loyal to a firm when the quality of their goods drops? (Hirschman 1970) Classical economics predicts that customers are rational actors and will turn to the market to seek an alternative when their needs are not met. Hirschman explores voice as a way of explaining the cases where a customer—or a citizen—would protest, and try to help a firm—or a country—improve, instead of exiting. Voice, Hirschman explains, is the province of political science rather than economics, because it presumes that exiting a state is difficult, if not impossible. Individuals may disengage from political discussion, but they are still affected by the decisions the government makes, which gives them a strong incentive to voice dissent and seek change.

Philosopher Tommie Shelby uses Hirschman's formulation of voice to help explain "impure dissent." Shelby asks readers to take seriously the angry, violent, and sometimes misogynistic voices of hiphop, not just the "pure" voices of nonviolent civil rights activists. Principled, "pure" dissent is possible when one believes that change within existing systems is possible. When one believes the system to be so flawed that one has no ability to make change, expressing opposition—even in ways that offend and marginalize others—may feel like the only effective way to engage (Shelby, 2015).

The challenge of impure dissent exposes the most important implication of taking voice seriously. It turns listening into a core civic duty—listening broadly, diversely to a range of perspectives and opinions. To make change in ways that reach beyond an immediate circle of friends, participants need to escape the echo chambers (Sunstein 2001) that are becoming all too common with digital media and to ensure they are also listening to those they disagree with, if only to understand those who oppose the sought-after changes.

While impure dissent proposes voice as a path toward change for participants with no trust in existing institutions, the strategy of "coming out" demands a certain baseline of trust, a belief that it is possible to raise one's voice without suffering grave harm. A society that imprisons people on the basis of their sexuality is one where coming out is an extremely dangerous expression of voice, just as a society that routinely deports nonviolent undocumented immigrants is one where the DREAMers' tactics would be significantly more dangerous. Voice as a path toward change requires not just brave speakers and engaged listeners, but a baseline of social trust that makes such dialogs possible.

An Equation and a Matrix

To understand civic media and the changing shape of civics, I propose modeling individual civic actions in terms of their cost, their possible benefits, and the odds that actions will lead to those benefits. A full model would consider the role that the opinion of friends and peers plays in driving individuals toward action, and consider the ways that producing and disseminating media influence peers.

I suggest evaluating individual acts of civic participation in terms of a matrix defined by three axes. Asking if an act has a well-defined theory of change is asking whether it is instrumental or symbolic, whether the action is designed to influence people through passing laws, influencing norms, leveraging markets, or coding new possibilities, or whether an act's importance is through the raising of voice. Evaluating an action considers whether an action is thin, demanding little more than an actor's presence, or thick, asking for creativity as well as participation. Finally, I suggest we ask if an act is silent or uses voice, whether it seeks to influence the perceptions of the audience or whether it avoids notice.

It is easy to turn these axes into value judgments, favoring thick acts over thin, impactful over symbolic, public acts of voice over the silent. This matrix is a far more useful tool when it allows for successful and failed forms of civic engagement across the spectrum of each axis and in every corner of the matrix. A campaign that is thin, symbolic, and silent is probably doomed to failure, while some of the most powerful norms-based engagement—diplomacy and other "insider" theories of change—often take place in silence.

As civic media grows and matures as a field, experiments with digital technologies will likely push toward all corners of this matrix. At the heart of this examination of the changing nature of civics is a simple question: is this an effective way to participate as a citizen? I hope these early steps toward a language of civic efficacy make this an easier question to answer.

References

Arnstein, Sherry R. 1969. "A Ladder of Citizen Participation." *Journal of the American Institute of Planners* 35 (4): 216–224.

Battles, Kathleen, and Wendy Hilton-Morrow. 2002. "Gay Characters in Conventional Spaces: Will and Grace and the Situation Comedy Genre." *Critical Studies in Media Communication* 19 (1): 87–105.

Baumgartner, Jody C., and Jonathan S. Morris. 2010. "Who Wants to Be My Friend? Obama, Youth, and Social Networks in the 2008 Campaign." In *Communicator-in-Chief: How Barack Obama Used New Media Technology to Win the White House*, ed. John Allen Hendricks and Robert E. Denton, Jr. Lanham, MD: Lexington Books.

Beltrán, Cristina. 2015. "'Undocumented, Unafraid, and Unapologetic': DREAM Activists, Immigrant Politics, and the Queering of Democracy." In *From Voice to Influence: Understanding Citizenship in a Digital Age*, ed. Danielle Allen and Jennifer Light. Chicago: University of Chicago Press.

Brown, Lisa. 2014. "Jesse Jackson Talks Voter Registration at Ferguson's McDonalds." *St. Louis Post-Dispatch*, August 18. http://www.stltoday.com/news/local/jesse-jackson-talks-voter -registration-at-ferguson-mcdonald-s/article_d789a49e-4957-5ba2-ae16-e03af805f00f.html.

Bump, Philip. 2014. "The 113th Congress Is Historically Good at Not Passing Bills." *Washington Post*, July 9. http://www.washingtonpost.com/blogs/the-fix/wp/2014/07/09/the-113th -congress-is-historically-good-at-not-passing-bills.

Coleman, Gabriella. 2012. *Coding Freedom: The Ethics and Aesthetics of Hacking*. Princeton, NJ: Princeton University Press.

Costanza-Chock, Sasha. 2011. "Digital Popular Communication: Lessons on Information and Communication Technologies for Social Change from the Immigrant Rights Movement." *National Civic Review* 100 (3): 29–35.

Dillon, Sam. 2011. "Failing Grades on Civics Exam Called a 'Crisis.'" *New York Times*, May 4. http://www.nytimes.com/2011/05/05/education/05civics.html?_r=0.

Donaldson, Thomas, and Lee E. Preston. 1995. "The Stakeholder Theory of the Corporation: Concepts, Evidence, and Implications." *Academy of Management Review* 20 (1): 65–91.

Downs, Anthony. 1957. *An Economic Theory of Democracy*. New York: Harper.

Elkington, John. 1999. *Cannibals with Forks: Triple Bottom Line of 21st Century Business*. Oxford: Capstone.

Eloundou-Enyegue, Parfait M., Dominique Meekers, and Anne Emmanuèle Calvès. 2005. "From Awareness to Adoption: The Effect of AIDS Education and Condom Social Marketing on Condom Use in Tanzania (1993–1996)." *Journal of Biosocial Science* 37 (3): 257–268.

Fuller, Jamie. 2014. "Have American Politics Killed the Impartial Supreme Court?" *Washington Post*, May 8. http://www.washingtonpost.com/blogs/the-fix/wp/2014/05/08/have -american-politics-killed-the-impartial-supreme-court.

Fung, Brian. 2014."How Social Media Freed Reporters Wesley Lowery and Ryan Reilly from Ferguson Police." *Washington Post*, August 14. http://www.washingtonpost.com/blogs/ the-switch/wp/2014/08/14/how-social-media-freed-reporters-wesley-lowery-and-ryan-reilly -from-ferguson-police.

Garza, Alicia. 2014. "A Herstory of the #BlackLivesMatter Movement." *The Feminist Wire*, October 7. http://www.thefeministwire.com/2014/10/blacklivesmatter-2.

Gladwell, Malcolm. 2010. "Small Change: Why the Revolution Will Not Be Tweeted." *New Yorker*, October 4. http://www.newyorker.com/magazine/2010/10/04/small-change-3.

Hirschman, Albert O. 1970. *Exit, Voice, and Loyalty: Responses to Decline in Firms, Organizations, and States*. Cambridge, MA: Harvard University Press.

Human Rights Campaign. n.d. "HRC Goes Viral." http://www.hrc.org/viral.

Keane, John. 2009. *The Life and Death of Democracy*. New York: Simon & Schuster.

Kuran, Timur. 1997. *Private Truths, Public Lies: The Social Consequences of Preference Falsification*. Cambridge, MA: Harvard University Press.

Lapidos, Juliet. 2014. "Voter Registration in Ferguson Called 'Disgusting.'" *New York Times*, August 19. http://takingnote.blogs.nytimes.com/2014/08/19/voter-registration-in-ferguson-called -disgusting.

Lessig, Lawrence. 2000. *Code and Other Laws of Cyberspace*. New York: Basic Books.

Lippmann, Walter. 1922. *Public Opinion*. New York: Harcourt, Brace and Company.

Lotan, Gilad. 2012. "[Data Viz] KONY2012: See How Invisible Networks Helped a Campaign Capture the World's Attention." *Gilad Lotan*, March 14. http://giladlotan.com/2012/ 03/data-viz-kony2012-see-how-invisible-networks-helped-a-campaign-capture-the-worlds -attention.

Lowenstein, Jeff K. 2007. "Killed by the Cops." *Color Lines*, November 4. http://www .colorlines.com/archives/2007/11/killed_by_the_cops.html.

Malik, Om. 2012. "Skype Is Killing Long Distance, One Minute at a Time." *Gigaom*, January 10. https://gigaom.com/2012/01/10/skype-is-killing-long-distance-one-minute-at-a-time.

Marfo, Amma. 2014. "Why #BlackTwitter Was Essential to Media Outrage over Ferguson." *Talking Points Memo*, August 16. http://talkingpointsmemo.com/cafe/why-blacktwitter-was-essential-to -media-outrage-over-ferguson.

Matias, Nathan. 2013. "Green vs. Pink: Change Your Picture, Change the World." MIT Centre for Civic Media, March 28. https://civic.mit.edu/blog/natematias/green-vs-pink-change-your-picture -change-the-world.

McDonald, Soraya Nadia. 2014. "Black Twitter: A Virtual Community Ready to Hashtag Out a Response to Cultural Issues." *Washington Post*, January 20. http://www.washingtonpost.com/ lifestyle/style/black-twitter-a-virtual-community-ready-to-hashtag-out-a-response-to-cultural -issues/2014/01/20/41ddacf6-7ec5-11e3-9556-4a4bf7bcbd84_story.html.

Morozov, Evgeny. 2011. *The Net Delusion: The Dark Side of Internet Freedom.* New York: PublicAffairs.

Newport, Frank. 2013. "In U.S., 87% Approve of Black-White Marriage vs. 4% in 1958." *Gallup*, July 25. http://www.gallup.com/poll/163697/approve-marriage-blacks-whites.aspx.

Norman, Wayne, and Chris MacDonald. 2004. "Getting to the Bottom of 'Triple Bottom Line.'" *Business Ethics Quarterly* 14 (2): 243–262.

O'Reilly, Tim. 2010. "Government as a Platform." In *Open Government: Collaboration, Transparency, and Participation in Practice*, ed. Daniel Lathrop and Laurel Ruma. Sebastopol, CA: O'Reilly Media. http://chimera.labs.oreilly.com/books/1234000000774/ch02.html.

Ornstein, Norman J., Thomas E. Mann, Michael J. Malbin, Andrew Rugg, and Raffaela Wakeman. 2013. "Vital Statistics on Congress," July. http://www.brookings.edu/research/reports/2013/07/vital-statistics-congress-mann-ornstein.

People Press. 2014. "Public Trust in Government: 1958–2014," November 13. http://www.people-press.org/2013/10/18/trust-in-government-interactive.

Putnam, Robert D. 2000. *Bowling Alone: The Collapse and Revival of American Community.* New York: Simon & Schuster.

Rheingold, Howard. 2002. *Smart Mobs: The Next Social Revolution.* New York: Basic Books.

Rhoades, Logan, and Adrian Carrasquillo. 2014. "How the Powerful #IfTheyGunnedMeDown Movement Changed the Conversation about Michael Brown's Death." *Buzzfeed*, August 13. http://www.buzzfeed.com/mrloganrhoades/how-the-powerful-iftheygunnedmedown-movement-changed-the-con.

Riker, William H., and Peter C. Ordeshook. 1968. "A Theory of the Calculus of Voting." *American Political Science Review* 62 (1): 25–42.

Schiappa, Edward, Peter B. Gregg, and Dean E. Hewes. 2006. "Can One TV Show Make a Difference? Will & Grace and the Parasocial Contact Hypothesis." *Journal of Homosexuality* 51 (4): 15–37.

Schudson, Michael. 1998. *The Good Citizen.* New York: The Free Press.

Shelby, Tommie. 2015. "Impure Dissent: Hip Hop and the Political Ethics of Marginalized Black Urban Youth." In *From Voice to Influence: Understanding Citizenship in a Digital Age*, ed. Danielle Allen and Jennifer Light. Chicago: University of Chicago Press

Shirky, Clay. 2008. *Here Comes Everybody: The Power of Organizing Without Organizations.* New York: Penguin Press.

Sledge, Matt, and Emily Kassie. 2014. "Ferguson Protestors Have Some Demands (VIDEO)." *Huffington Post*, August 22. http://www.huffingtonpost.com/2014/08/22/ferguson-protest-demands_n_5701847.html.

Smith, Jeff. 2014. "In Ferguson, Black Town, White Power." *New York Times*, August 17. http://www.nytimes.com/2014/08/18/opinion/in-ferguson-black-town-white-power.html.

Spiering, Charlie. 2014. "Missouri GOP: Michael Brown Voting Registration Booths 'Disgusting.'" *Breitbart*, August 18. http://www.breitbart.com/Big-Government/2014/08/18/Missouri-GOP-Michael-Brown-Voting-Registration-Booths-Disgusting.

Stampler, Laura. 2014. "Twitter Users Ask What Photo Media Would Use." *Time,* August 11. http://time.com/3100975/iftheygunnedmedown-ferguson-missouri-michael-brown.

Story, Mark. 2014. "The Damage Done to the Ferguson Debate by Slacktivism." *LinkedIn*, August 29.https://www.linkedin.com/pulse/article/20140829102300-10273678-the-damage-done-to-the-ferguson-debate-by-slactivism.

Sugerman, Mike. 2013."'Black Twitter' Credited with Torpedoing Zimmerman Juror Book Deal." *CBS, Bay Area*, July 18. http://sanfrancisco.cbslocal.com/2013/07/18/black-twitter-credited-with-torpedoing-zimmerman-juror-book-deal.

Sundwall, Jed. n.d. "Making People Powerful: Interview with Scott Heiferman from Meetup." *NetSquared*. http://www.netsquared.org/blog/jedsundwall/making-people-powerful-interview-scott-heiferman-meetup#.VCW5r-dbenY.

Sunstein, Cass. 2001. *Republic.com*. Princeton, NJ: Princeton University Press.

Thoreau, Henry David. 1854. "Slavery in Massachusetts." Lecture delivered July 4. http://www.transcendentalists.com/slavery_in_ma.htm.

Watson Strong, Anthea. 2014 a. "The Three Levers of Civic Engagement." *Anthea Watson Strong*, June 9. http://www.antheawatsonstrong.com/writing/2014/6/8/the-three-levers-of-civic-engagement.

Watson Strong, Anthea. 2014 b. Twitter post, June 9, 2014. https://twitter.com/antheaws/status/476085729827639298.

Williamson, Vanessa, Theda Skocpol, and John Coggin. 2011. "The Tea Party and the Remaking of Republican Conservatism." *Perspectives on Politics* 9 (1): 25–43.

Winsten, Jay. 1994. "Promoting designated drivers: the Harvard Alcohol Project." *American Journal of Preventive Medicine* 10 (3): 11–14.

Zuckerman, Ethan. 2012. "How Do We Make Civic Crowdfunding Awesome?" *Ethan Zuckerman*,August10.http://www.ethanzuckerman.com/blog/2012/08/10/how-do-we-make-civic-crowdfunding-awesome.

Zuckerman, Ethan. 2014. "Town Meeting and a Lesson in Civic Efficacy." *Ethan Zuckerman*, June 11. http://www.ethanzuckerman.com/blog/2014/06/11/town-meeting-and-a-lesson-on-civic-efficacy.

3   The Logic of Connective Action: Digital Media and the Personalization of Contentious Politics

W. Lance Bennett and Alexandra Segerberg

From the Arab Spring and *los indignados* in Spain, to Occupy Wall Street (and beyond), large-scale, sustained protests are using digital media in ways that go beyond sending and receiving messages. Perhaps the quality that most distinguishes these protests is that they are populated largely by young citizens armed with all manner of digital media devices and the apps that make them go. For example, the Hong Kong protests of 2014 began with high school students and soon attracted crowds of other young people protesting the restrictions on Hong Kong electoral democracy imposed by Beijing. In Australia rising discontent with an unpopular government produced a series of marches in dozens of cities that became established as March Australia. Examining photos from the crowds reveals a broad age spectrum, with young people waving homemade signs and posting them on social media sites and the March organizing site. The Do It Yourself quality of these protests stands in sharp contrast to the more standardized event formats organized by conventional social movement organizations. Indeed the banners, slogans, and leaders of formal organizations are conspicuously absent or downplayed in many of these movements.

Each such protest becomes a model for others, as they are easy to find online via personal devices. People around the world can follow them, participate from afar, and organize their own versions. There is by now a large literature on how young people have gone digital and become skeptical of conventional politics, parties and politicians. The emerging protest and "lifestyle politics" trends suggest that young citizens are reinventing politics through creative uses of media to organize public spheres, generate frames for action and organize a variety of activities both on and offline (Bennett and Segerberg 2013). It is important to note that the so-called millennials who came of age in the digital era are now aging themselves. Thus, trends that once applied to those under twenty-five soon applied to those under thirty, and now capture much of the population under forty in an impressive variety of national settings from the OECD democracies to China and Russia (ibid., 2013). The implications for democratic politics are not settled, but it is increasingly clear that we need to expand our frameworks for thinking about how movements and protests work in this changing civic media environment.

If we step back and survey the broader spectrum of citizen activism today, we see that there are varieties of organizational forms, ranging from technology enabled crowds that are largely self-organized, to more conventional movements organized by formal bureaucratic organizations with resources, leaders and established agendas. In the middle of this spectrum are hybrid forms that involve conventional organizations deploying rather less conventional and highly individualized social media networks to engage citizens who may not wish to join formal organizations or subscribe to their agendas. This chapter examines the organizational dynamics that emerge when communication becomes a prominent part of these different organizational structures. It argues that understanding such variations in large-scale action networks requires distinguishing between at least two logics that may be in play: the familiar logic of collective action associated with high levels of organizational resources and the formation of collective identities, and the less familiar logic of connective action based on personalized content sharing across media networks. In the former, introducing digital media does not change the core dynamics of the action. In the case of the latter, it does. Building on these distinctions, the chapter presents three ideal types of large-scale action networks that are becoming prominent in the contentious politics of the contemporary era.

Understanding Digitally Networked Action

With the world economy in crisis, the heads of the 20 leading economies held a series of meetings beginning in the fall of 2008 to coordinate financial rescue policies. Wherever the G20 leaders met, whether in Washington, London, St Andrews, Pittsburgh, Toronto, or Seoul, they were greeted by protests. During the London summit in April 2009, anti-capitalist, environmental direct activist, and non-governmental organization (NGO)–sponsored actions were coordinated across different days. The largest of these demonstrations was sponsored by a number of prominent NGOs including Oxfam, Friends of the Earth, Save the Children, and World Vision. This loose coalition launched a Put People First (PPF) campaign promoting public mobilization against social and environmental harms of "business-as-usual" solutions to the financial crisis. The website for the campaign carried the simple statement:

Even before the banking collapse, the world suffered poverty, inequality, and the threat of climate chaos. The world has followed a financial model that has created an economy fuelled by ever-increasing debt, both financial and environmental. Our future depends on creating an economy based on fair distribution of wealth, decent jobs for all, and a low carbon future. (Put People First, 2009)

The centerpiece of this PPF campaign was a march of some 35,000 people through the streets of London a few days ahead of the G20 meeting, to give voice and show commitment to the campaign's simple theme.

The London PPF protest drew together a large and diverse protest with the emphasis on personal expression, but it still displayed what Tilly (2004, 2006) termed "WUNC": worthiness, embodied by the endorsements by some 160 prominent civil society organizations and recognition of their demands by various prominent officials; unity, reflected in the orderliness of the event; numbers of participants, that made PPF the largest of a series of London G20 protests and the largest demonstration during the string of G20 meetings in different world locations; and commitment, reflected in the presence of delegations from some 20 nations who joined local citizens in spending much of the day listening to speakers in Hyde Park or attending religious services sponsored by faith-based development organizations.[1] The large volume of generally positive press coverage reflected all of these characteristics, and responses from heads of state to the demonstrators accentuated the worthiness of the event (Bennett and Segerberg 2011).[2]

The protests continued as the G20 in 2010 issued a policy statement making it clear that debt reduction and austerity would be the centerpieces of a political program that could send shocks through economies from the United States and the UK, to Greece, Italy, and Spain, while pushing more decisive action on climate change onto the back burner. Public anger swept cities from Madison to Madrid, as citizens protested that their governments, no matter what their political stripe, offered no alternatives to the economic dictates of a so-called neoliberal economic regime that seemed to operate from corporate and financial power centers beyond popular accountability and, some argued, even beyond the control of states.

Some of these protests seemed to operate with surprisingly light involvement from conventional organizations. For example, in Spain *"los indignados"* (the indignant ones) mobilized in 2011 under the name of 15M for the date (May 15) of the mass mobilization that involved protests in some 60 cities. One of the most remarkable aspects of this sustained protest organization was its success at keeping political parties, unions, and other powerful political organizations out: indeed, they were targeted as part of the political problem. There were, of course, civil society organizations supporting 15M, but they generally stayed in the background to honor the personalized identity of the movement: the faces and voices of millions of ordinary people displaced by financial and political crises. The most visible organization consisted of the richly layered digital and interpersonal communication networks centering around the media hub of ¡Democracia real YA![3] This network included links to more than 80 local Spanish city nodes, and a number of international solidarity networks. On the one hand, ¡Democracia real YA! seemed to be a website, and on the other, it was a densely populated and effective organization. It makes sense to think of the core organization of the *indignados* as both of these and more, revealing the hybrid nature of digitally mediated organization (Chadwick 2013).

Given its seemingly informal organization, the 15M mobilization surprised many observers by sustaining and even building strength over time, using a mix of online media and offline activities that included face-to-face organizing, encampments in city centers, and marches across the country. Throughout, the participants communicated a collective identity of being leaderless, signaling that labor unions, parties, and more radical movement groups should stay at the margins. A survey of 15M protesters by a team of Spanish researchers showed that the relationships between individuals and organizations differed in at least three ways from participants in an array of other more conventional movement protests, including a general strike, a regional protest, and a pro-life demonstration: (1) where strong majorities of participants in other protests recognized the involvement of key organizations with brick-and-mortar addresses, only 38 percent of *indignados* did so; (2) only 13 percent of the organizations cited by 15M participants offered any membership or affiliation possibilities, in contrast to large majorities who listed membership organizations as being important in the other demonstrations; and (3) the mean age range of organizations (such as parties and unions) listed in the comparison protests ranged from 10 to more than 40 years, while the organizations cited in association with 15M were, on average, less than three years old (Anduiza et al. 2014). Despite, or perhaps because of, these interesting organizational differences, the ongoing series of 15M protests attracted participation from somewhere between 6 and 8 million people, a remarkable number in a nation of 40 million (RTVE 2011).

Similar to PPF, the *indignados* achieved impressive levels of communication with outside publics both directly via images and messages spread virally across social networks, and indirectly when anonymous Twitter streams and YouTube videos were taken up as mainstream press sources. Their actions became daily news fare in Spain and abroad, with the protesters receiving generally positive coverage of their personal messages in local and national news, again defying familiar observations about the difficulty of gaining positive news coverage for collective actions that spill outside the bounds of institutions and take to the streets (Gitlin 1980).[4] In addition to communicating concerns about jobs and the economy, the clear message was that people felt the democratic system had broken to the point that all parties and leaders were under the influence of banks and international financial powers. Despite avoiding association with familiar civil society organizations, lacking leaders, and displaying little conventional organization, *los indignados*, similar to PPF, achieved high levels of WUNC.

Two broad organizational patterns characterize these increasingly common digitally enabled action networks. Some cases, such as PPF, are coordinated behind the scenes by networks of established issue advocacy organizations that step back from branding the actions in terms of particular organizations, memberships, or conventional collective action frames. Instead, they cast a broader public engagement net using interactive digital media and easy-to-personalize action themes, often deploying batteries of social technologies to help citizens spread the word over their personal networks. The second pattern, typified by the *indignados* and the Occupy protests in the United States, entails technology platforms and applications taking the role of established political organizations. In this network mode, political demands and grievances are often shared in very personalized accounts that travel over social networking platforms, e-mail lists, and online coordinating platforms. For example, the easily personalized action frame, "We are the 99 percent," that emerged from the US Occupy protests in 2011 quickly traveled the world via personal stories and images shared on social networks such as Tumblr, Twitter, and Facebook.

Compared to many conventional social movement protests, with identifiable membership organizations leading the way under common banners and collective identity frames, these more personalized, digitally mediated collective action formations have frequently been larger; have scaled up more quickly; and have been flexible in tracking moving political targets and bridging different issues. Whether we look at PPF, Arab Spring, the *indignados*, or Occupy, we note surprising success in communicating simple political messages directly to outside publics using common digital technologies such as Facebook or Twitter. Those media feeds are often picked up as news sources by conventional journalism organizations.[5] In addition, these digitally mediated action networks often seem to be accorded higher levels of WUNC than their more conventional social movement counterparts. This observation is based on comparisons of more conventional anti-capitalist collective actions organized by movement groups, in contrast with both the organizationally enabled PPF protests and the crowd-enabled 15M mobilizations in Spain and the Occupy Wall Street protests, which quickly spread to thousands of other places. The differences between both types of digitally mediated action and more conventional organization-centered and brokered collective actions led us to see interesting differences in underlying organizational logics and in the role of communication as an organizing principle.

The rise of digitally networked action (DNA) has been met with some understandable skepticism about what really is so very new about it, mixed with concerns about what it means for the political capacities of organized dissent. We are interested in understanding how these more personalized varieties of collective action work: how they are organized, what sustains them, and when they are politically effective. We submit that convincingly addressing such questions requires recognizing the differing logics of action that underpin distinct kinds of collective action networks. This chapter thus develops a conceptual framework of such logics, on the basis of which further questions about DNA may then be tackled.

We propose that more fully understanding contemporary large-scale networks of contentious action involves distinguishing between at least two logics of action that may be in play: the familiar logic of collective action, and the less familiar logic of connective action. Doing so in turn allows us to discern three ideal action types, of which one is characterized by the familiar logic of collective action, and two other types involve more personalized action formations that differ in terms of whether formal organizations are more or less central in enabling a connective communication logic. A first step in understanding DNA, the DNA at the core of connective action, lies in defining personalized communication and its role along with digital media in the organization of what we call connective action.

Personal Action Frames and Social Media Networks

Structural fragmentation and individualization in many contemporary societies constitute an important backdrop to the present discussion. Various breakdowns in group memberships and institutional loyalties have trended in the more economically developed industrial democracies, resulting from pressures of economic globalization spanning a period from roughly the 1970s through to the end of the last century (Bennett 1998; Putnam 2000). These sweeping changes have produced a shift in social and political orientations among younger generations in the nations that we now term the post-industrial democracies (Inglehart 1997). These individualized orientations result in engagement with politics as an expression of personal hopes, lifestyles, and grievances. When enabled by various kinds of communication technologies, the resulting DNAs in post-industrial democracies bear some remarkable similarities to action formations in decidedly undemocratic regimes such as those swept by the Arab Spring. In both contexts, large numbers of similarly disaffected individuals seized upon opportunities to organize collectively through access to various technologies (Howard and Hussain 2011). Those connectivities fed in and out of the often intense face-to-face interactions going on in squares, encampments, mosques, and general assembly meetings.

In personalized action formations, the nominal issues may resemble older movement or party concerns in terms of topics (environment, rights, women's equality, and trade fairness) but the ideas and mechanisms for organizing action become more personalized than in cases where action is organized on the basis of social group identity, membership, or ideology. These multifaceted processes of individualization are articulated differently in different societies, but include the propensity to develop flexible political identifications based on personal lifestyles (Giddens 1991; Inglehart 1997; Bennett 1998; Bauman 2000; Beck and Beck-Gernsheim 2002), with implications in collective action (McDonald 2002; Micheletti 2003; della Porta 2005) and organizational participation (Putnam 2000; Bimber et al. 2012). People may still join actions in large numbers, but the identity reference is more derived through inclusive and diverse large-scale personal expression rather than through common group or ideological identification.

This shift from group-based to individualized societies is accompanied by the emergence of flexible social "weak tie" networks (Granovetter 1973) that enable identity expression and the navigation of complex and changing social and political landscapes. Networks have always been part of society, to help people navigate life within groups or between groups, but the late modern society involves networks that become more central organizational forms that transcend groups and constitute core organizations in their own right (Castells 2000). These networks are established and scaled through various sorts of digital technologies that are by no means value-neutral in enabling quite different kinds of communities to form and diverse actions to be organized, from auctions on eBay to protests in different cultural and social settings. Thus, the two elements of "personalized communication" that we identify as particularly important in large-scale connective action formations are:

1. Political content in the form of easily personalized ideas such as PPF in the London 2009 protests, or "We are the 99 percent" in the later Occupy protests. These frames require little in the way of persuasion, reason, or reframing to bridge differences in how others may feel about a common problem. These personal action frames are inclusive of different personal reasons for contesting a situation that needs to be changed.
2. Various personal communication technologies that enable sharing these themes. Whether through texts, tweets, social network sharing, or posting YouTube mashups, the communication process itself often involves further personalization through the spreading of digital connections among friends or trusted others. Some more sophisticated custom coordinating platforms can resemble organizations that exist more online than off.

As we followed various world protests, we noticed a dazzling array of personal action frames that spread through social media. Both the acts of sharing these personal calls to action and the social technologies through which they spread help to explain both how events are communicated to external audiences and how the action itself is organized. Indeed, in the limiting case, the communication network becomes the organizational form of the political action (Earl and Kimport 2011). We explore the range of differently organized forms of contention using personalized communication up to the point at which they enter the part of the range conventionally understood as social movements. This is the boundary zone within which what we refer to as connective action gives way to collective action.

The case of PPF occupies an interesting part of this range of contentious action because there were many conventional organizations involved in the mobilization, from churches to social justice NGOs. Yet, visitors to the sophisticated, stand-alone, PPF coordinating platform (which served as an interesting kind of organization in itself) were not asked to pledge allegiance to specific political demands on the organizational agendas of the protest sponsors. Instead, visitors to the organizing site were met with an impressive array of social technologies, enabling them to communicate in their own terms with each other and with various political targets. The centerpiece of the PPF site was a prominent text box under an image of a megaphone that invited the visitor to "Send Your Own Message to the G20." Many of the messages to the G20 echoed the easy-to-personalize action frame of PPF, and they also revealed a broad range of personal thoughts about the crisis and possible solutions.

PPF as a personal action frame was easy to shape and share with friends near and far. It became a powerful example of what students of viral communication refer to as a meme: a symbolic packet that travels easily across large and diverse populations because it is easy to imitate, adapt personally, and share broadly with others. Memes are network-building and bridging units of social information transmission similar to genes in the biological sphere (Dawkins 1989). They travel through personal appropriation, and then by imitation and personalized expression via social sharing in ways that help others to appropriate, imitate, and share in turn (Shifman 2013). The simple PPF protest meme traveled interpersonally, echoing through newspapers, blogs, Facebook friend networks, Twitter streams, Flickr pages, and other sites on the Internet, leaving traces for years after the events.[6] Indeed, part of the meme traveled to Toronto more than a year later where the leading civil society groups gave the name "People First" to their demonstrations. And many people in the large crowds in Seoul in the last G20 meeting of the series could be seen holding up red and white "PPF" signs in both English and Korean (Weller 2010).

Something similar happened in the case of the *indignados*, where protesters raised banners and chanted "Shhh ... the Greeks are sleeping," with reference to the crushing debt crisis and severe austerity measures facing that country. This idea swiftly traveled to Greece where Facebook networks agreed to set alarm clocks at the same time to wake up and demonstrate. Banners in Athens proclaimed: "We've awakened! What time is it? Time for them to leave!" and "Shhh ... the Italians are sleeping" and "Shhh ... the French are sleeping." These efforts to send personalized protest themes across national and cultural boundaries met with varying success, making for an important cautionary point: we want to stress that not all personal action frames travel equally well or equally far. The fact that these messages traveled more easily in Spain and Greece than in France or Italy is an interesting example pointing to the need to study failures as well as successes. Just being easy to personalize (for example, I am personally indignant about x, y, and z, and so I join with *los indignados*) does not ensure successful diffusion. Both political opportunities and conditions for social adoption may differ from situation to situation. For example, the limits in the Italian case may reflect an already established popular anti-government network centered on comedian–activist Beppe Grillo. The French case may involve the ironic efforts of established groups on the left to lead incipient solidarity protests with the *indignados*, and becoming too heavy-handed in suggesting messages and action programs.

Personal action frames do not spread automatically. People must show each other how they can appropriate, shape, and share themes. In this interactive process of personalization and sharing, communication networks may become scaled up and stabilized through the digital technologies people use to share ideas and relationships with others. These technologies and their use patterns often remain in place as organizational mechanisms. In the PPF and the *indignados* protests, the communication processes themselves represented important forms of organization.

In contrast to personal action frames, other calls to action more clearly require joining with established groups or ideologies. These more conventionally understood collective action frames are more likely to stop at the edges of communities, and may require resources beyond communication technologies to bridge the gaps or align different collective frames (Snow and Benford 1988; Benford and Snow 2000). For example, another set of protests in London at the start of the financial crisis was organized by a coalition of more radical groups under the name G20 Meltdown. Instead of mobilizing the expression of large-scale personal concerns, they demanded ending the so-called neoliberal economic policies of the G20, and some even called for the end to capitalism itself. Such demands typically come packaged with more demanding calls to join in particular repertoires of collective action. Whether those repertoires are violent or non-violent, they typically require adoption of shared ideas and behaviors. These anarcho-socialist demonstrations drew on familiar anti-capitalist slogans and calls to "storm the banks" or "eat the rich" while staging dramatic marches behind the four horsemen of the economic apocalypse riding from the gates of old London to the Bank of England. These more radical London events drew smaller turnouts (some 5,000 for the Bank of England march and 2,000 for a climate encampment), higher levels of violence, and generally negative press coverage (Bennett and Segerberg 2011). While scoring high on commitment in terms of the personal costs of civil disobedience, and displaying unity around anti-capitalist collective action frames, these demonstrations lacked the attributions of public worthiness (for example, recognition from public officials, or getting their messages into the news) and the numbers that gave PPF its higher levels of WUNC.

Collective action frames that place greater demands on individuals to share common identifications or political claims can also be regarded as memes, in the sense that slogans such as "eat the rich" have rich histories of social transmission. This particular iconic phrase may possibly date to Rousseau's quip: "When the people shall have nothing more to eat, they will eat the rich." The crazy course of that meme's passage down through the ages includes its appearance on T-shirts in the 1960s and in rock songs of that title by Aerosmith and Motorhead, just to scratch the surface of its history of travel through time and space, reflecting the sequence of appropriation, personal expression, and sharing. One distinction between personal action and collective action memes seems to be that the latter require somewhat more elaborate packaging and ritualized action to reintroduce them into new contexts. For example, the organizers of the "storm the banks" events staged an elaborate theatrical ritual with carnivalesque opportunities for creative expression as costumed demonstrators marched behind the four horsemen of the financial apocalypse.[7] At the same time, the G20 Meltdown discourse was rather closed, requiring adopters to make common cause with others. The Meltdown coalition had an online presence, but they did not offer easy means for participants to express themselves in their own voices (Bennett and Segerberg 2011). This suggests that more demanding and exclusive collective action frames can also travel as memes, but more often they hit barriers at the intersections of social networks defined by established political organizations, ideologies, interests, class, gender, race, or ethnicity. These barriers often require resources beyond social technologies to overcome.

While the idea of memes may help to focus differences in transmission mechanisms involved in more personal versus collective framing of action, we will use the terms "personal action frames" and "collective action frames" as our general concepts. This conceptual pairing locates our work alongside analytical categories used by social movement scholars (Snow and Benford 1988; Benford and Snow 2000). As should be obvious, the differences we are sketching between personal and collective action frames are not about being online versus offline. All contentious action networks are in important ways embodied and enacted by people on the ground (Juris 2008; Routledge and Cumbers 2009). Moreover, most formal political organizations have discovered that the growing sophistication and ubiquity of social media can reduce the resource costs of public outreach and coordination, but these uses of media do not change the action dynamics by altering the fundamental principles of organizing collectivities. By contrast, digital media networking can change the organizational game, given the right interplay of technology, personal action frames, and, when organizations get in the game, their willingness to relax collective identification requirements in favor of personalized social networking among followers.

The logic of collective action that typifies the modern social order of hierarchical institutions and membership groups stresses the organizational dilemma of getting individuals to overcome resistance to joining actions where personal participation costs may outweigh marginal gains, particularly when people can ride on the efforts of others for free, and reap the benefits if those others win the day. In short, conventional collective action typically requires people to make more difficult choices and adopt more self-changing social identities than DNA based on personal action frames organized around social technologies. The spread of collective identifications typically requires more education, pressure, or socialization, which in turn makes higher demands on formal organization and resources such as money to pay rent for organization offices, to generate publicity, and to hire professional staff organizers (McAdam et al. 1996).[8] Digital media may help to reduce some costs in these processes, but they do not fundamentally change the action dynamics.

As noted above, the emerging alternative model that we call the logic of connective action applies increasingly to life in late modern societies in which formal organizations are losing their grip on individuals, and group ties are being replaced by large-scale, fluid social networks (Castells 2000).[9] The organizational processes of social media play an important role in how these networks operate, and their logic does not require strong organizational control or the symbolic construction of a united "we." The logic of connective action, we suggest, entails a dynamic of its own and thus deserves analysis on its own analytical terms.

Two Logics: Collective and Connective Action

Social movements and contentious politics extend over many different kinds of phenomena and action (Melucci 1996; McAdam et al. 2001; Tarrow 2011). The talk about new forms of collective action may reflect ecologies of action that are increasingly complex (Chesters and Welsh 2006). Multiple organizational forms operating within such ecologies may be hard to categorize, not least because they may morph over time or context, displaying hybridity of various kinds (Chadwick 2013). In addition, protest and organizational work is occurring both online and off, using technologies of different capabilities, sometimes making the online/offline distinction relevant, but more often not (Earl and Kimport 2011; Bimber et al. 2012).

Some observers mark a turning point in patterns of contemporary contentious politics, which mix different styles of organization and communication, along with the intersection of different issues with the iconic union of "teamsters and turtles" in the "Battle of Seattle" WTO protests in 1999, during which burly union members marched alongside environmental activists wearing turtle costumes in battling a rising neoliberal trade regime that was seen as a threat to democratic control of both national economies and the world environment. Studies of such events show that there are still plenty of old-fashioned meetings, and issue brokering and coalition building, going on (Polletta 2002). At the same time, however, there is increasing coordination of action by organizations and individuals using digital media to create networks, structure activities, and communicate their views directly to the world. This means that there is also an important degree of technology-enabled networking (Livingston and Asmolov 2010) that makes highly personalized, socially mediated communication processes fundamental structuring elements in the organization of many forms of connective action.

How do we sort out which organizational processes contribute which qualities to collective and connective action networks? How do we identify the borders between fundamentally different types of action formations: that is, what are the differences between collective and connective action, and where are the hybrid overlaps? We propose a starting point for sorting out some of the complexity and overlap in the forms of action by distinguishing between two logics of action. The two logics are associated with distinct dynamics, and thus draw attention to different dimensions for analysis. It is important to separate them analytically as one is less familiar than the other, and this in turn constitutes an important stumbling block for the study of much contemporary political action that we term connective action.[10]

The more familiar action logic is the logic of collective action, which emphasizes the problems of getting individuals to contribute to the collective endeavor that typically involves seeking some sort of public good (for example, democratic reforms) that may be better attained through forging a common cause. The classical formulation of this problem was articulated by Olson (1965), but the implications of his general logic have reached far beyond the original formulation. Olson's intriguing observation was that people in fact cannot be expected to act together just because they share a common problem or goal. He held that in large groups in which individual contributions are less noticeable, rational individuals will free-ride on the efforts of others: it is more cost-efficient not to contribute if you can enjoy the good without contributing. Moreover, if not enough people join in creating the good, your efforts are wasted anyway. Either way, it is individually rational not to contribute, even if all agree that all would be better off if everyone did. This thinking fixes attention on the problematic dynamics attending the rational action of atomistic individuals, and at the same time makes resource-rich organizations a central concern. Both the solutions Olson discerned—coercion and selective incentives—implied organizations with substantial capacity to monitor, administer, and distribute such measures.

In this view, formal organizations with resources are essential to harnessing and coordinating individuals in common action. The early application of this logic to contentious collective action was most straightforwardly exemplified in resource mobilization theory (RMT), in which social movement scholars explicitly adopted Olson's framing of the collective action problem and its organization-centered solution. Part of a broader wave rejecting the idea of social movements as irrational behavior erupting out of social dysfunction, early RMT scholars accepted the problem of rational free-riders as a fundamental challenge and regarded organizations and their ability to mobilize resources as critical elements of social movement success. Classic formulations came from McCarthy and Zald (1973, 1977) who theorized the rise of external support and resources available to social movement organizations (SMOs), and focused attention on the professionalization of movement organizations and leaders in enabling more resource-intensive mobilization efforts.

The contemporary social movement field has moved well beyond the rational choice orientation of such earlier work. Indeed, important traditions developed independently of, or by rejecting, all or parts of the resource mobilization perspective and by proposing that we pay more attention to the role of identity, culture, emotion, social networks, political process, and opportunity structures (Melucci 1996; McAdam et al. 2001; della Porta and Diani 2006). We do not suggest that these later approaches cling to rational choice principles. We do, however, suggest that echoes of the modernist logic of collective action can still be found to play a background role even in work that is in other ways far removed from the rational choice orientation of Olson's original argument. This comes out in assumptions about the importance of particular forms of organizational coordination and identity in the attention given to organizations, resources, leaders, coalitions, brokering differences, cultural or epistemic communities, the importance of formulating collective action frames, and bridging of differences among those frames. Connective action networks may vary in terms of stability, scale, and coherence, but they are organized by different principles. Connective action networks are typically far more individualized and technologically organized sets of processes, that result in action without the requirement of collective identity framing or the levels of organizational resources required to respond effectively to opportunities.

One of the most widely adopted approaches that moved social movement research away from the rational choice roots toward a more expansive collective action logic is the analysis of collective action frames, which centers on the processes of negotiating common interpretations of collective identity linked to the contentious issues at hand (Snow et al. 1986; Snow and Benford 1988; Hunt et al. 1994; Benford and Snow 2000). Such framing work may help to mobilize individuals and ultimately lower resource costs by retaining their emotional commitment to action. At the same time, the formulation of ideologically demanding, socially exclusive, or high-conflict collective frames also invites fractures, leading to an analytical focus on how organizations manage or fail to bridge these differences. Resolving these frame conflicts may require the mobilization of resources to bridge differences between groups that have different goals and ways of understanding their issues. Thus, while the evolution of different strands of social movement theory has moved away from economic collective action models, many still tend to emphasize the importance of organizations that have strong ties to members and followers, and the resulting ways in which collective identities are forged and fractured among coalitions of those organizations and their networks.

Sustainable and effective collective action from the perspective of the broader logic of collective action typically requires varying levels of organizational resource mobilization deployed in organizing, leadership, developing common action frames, and brokerage to bridge organizational differences. The opening or closing of political opportunities affects this resource calculus (Tarrow 2011), but overall, large-scale action networks that reflect this collective action logic tend to be characterized in terms of numbers of distinct groups networking to bring members and affiliated participants into the action and to keep them there. On the individual level, collective action logic emphasizes the role of social network relationships and connections as informal preconditions for more centralized mobilization (for example, in forming and spreading action frames, and forging common identifications and relations of solidarity and trust). At the organizational level, the strategic work of brokering and bridging coalitions between organizations with different standpoints and constituencies becomes the central activity for analysis (see also Diani 2015). Since the dynamics of action in networks characterized by this logic tends not to change significantly with digital media, it primarily invites analysis of how such tools help actors do what they were already doing (see also Bimber et al. 2009; Earl and Kimport 2011).

Movements and action networks characterized by these variations on the logic of collective action are clearly visible in contemporary society. They have been joined by many other mobilizations that may superficially seem like movements, but on closer inspection lack many of the traditional defining characteristics. Efforts to push these kinds of organization into recognizable social movement categories diminish our capacity to understand one of the most interesting developments of our times: how fragmented, individualized populations, that are hard to reach and even harder to induce to share personally transforming collective identities, somehow find ways to mobilize protest networks from Wall Street to Madrid to Cairo. Indeed, when people are individualized in their social orientations, and thus structurally or psychologically unavailable to modernist forms of political movement organization, resource mobilization becomes increasingly costly and has diminishing returns. Organizing such populations to overcome free-riding and helping them to shape identities in common is not necessarily the most successful or effective logic for organizing collective action. When people who seek more personalized paths to concerted action are familiar with practices of social networking in everyday life, and when they have access to technologies from mobile phones to computers, they are already familiar with a different logic of organization: the logic of connective action.

The logic of connective action foregrounds a different set of dynamics from the ones just outlined. At the core of this logic is the recognition of digital media as organizing agents. Several collective action scholars have explored how digital communication technology alters the parameters of Olson's original theory of collective action. Lupia and Sin (2003) show how Olson's core assumption about weak individual commitment in large groups (free-riding) may play out differently under conditions of radically reduced communication costs. Bimber et al. (2005) in turn argue that public goods themselves may take on new theoretical definition as erstwhile free-riders find it easier to become participants in political networks that diminish the boundaries between public and private; boundaries that are blurred in part by the simultaneous public–private boundary crossing of ubiquitous social media.

Important for our purposes here is the underlying economic logic of digitally mediated social networks, as explained most fully by Benkler (2006). He proposes that participation becomes self-motivating as personally expressive content is shared with, and recognized by, others who in turn repeat these networked sharing activities. When these interpersonal networks are enabled by technology platforms of various designs that coordinate and scale the networks, the resulting actions can resemble collective action, yet without the same role played by formal organizations or transforming social identifications. In place of content that is distributed and relationships that are brokered by hierarchical organizations, social networking involves co-production and co-distribution, revealing a different economic and psychological logic: co-production and sharing based on personalized expression. This does not mean that all online communication works this way. Looking at most online newspapers, blogs, or political campaign sites makes it clear that the logic of the organization-centered brick-and-mortar world is often reproduced online, with little change in organizational logic beyond possible efficiency gains (Bimber and Davis 2003; Foot and Schneider 2006). Yet, many socially mediated networks do operate with an alternative logic that also helps to explain why people labor collectively for free to create such things as Wikipedia, WikiLeaks, and the free and open source software that powers many protest networks (Calderaro 2011).

In this connective logic, taking public action or contributing to a common good becomes an act of personal expression and recognition or self-validation achieved by sharing ideas and actions in trusted relationships. Sometimes the people in these exchanges may be on the other side of the world, but they do not require a club, a party, or a shared ideological frame to make the connection. In place of the initial collective action problem of getting the individual to contribute, the starting point of connective action is the self-motivated (though not necessarily self-centered) sharing of already internalized or personalized ideas, plans, images, and resources with networks of others. This 'sharing' may take place in networking sites such as Facebook, or via more public media such as Twitter and YouTube through, for example, comments and re-tweets.[11] Action networks characterized by this logic may scale up rapidly through the combination of easily spreadable personal action frames and digital technology enabling such communication. This invites analytical attention to the network as an organizational structure in itself.

Technology-enabled networks of personalized communication involve more than just exchanging information or messages. The flexible, recombinant nature of DNA makes these web spheres and their offline extensions more than just communication systems. Such networks are flexible organizations in themselves, often enabling coordinated adjustments and rapid action aimed at often shifting political targets, even crossing geographic and temporal boundaries in the process. As Diani (2015) argues, networks are not just precursors or building blocks of collective action: they are in themselves organizational structures that can transcend the elemental units of organizations and individuals.[12] As noted earlier, communication technologies do not change the action dynamics in large-scale networks characterized by the logic of collective action. In the networks characterized by connective action, they do.

The organizational structure of people and social technology emerges more clearly if we draw on the actor-network theory of Latour (2005) in recognizing digital networking mechanisms (for example, various social media and devices that run them) as potential network agents alongside human actors (that is, individuals and organizations). Such digital mechanisms may include organizational connectors (for example, web links), event coordination (for example, protest calendars), information sharing (for example, YouTube and Facebook), and multifunction networking platforms in which other networks become embedded (for example, links in Twitter and Facebook posts), along with various capacities of the devices that run them. These technologies not only create online meeting places and coordinate offline activities, but they also help to calibrate relationships by establishing levels of transparency, privacy, security, and interpersonal trust. It is also important that these digital traces may remain behind on the web to provide memory records or action repertoires that might be passed on via different mechanisms associated with more conventional collective action such as rituals or formal documentation.

The simple point here is that collective and connective logics are distinct logics of action (in terms of both identity and choice processes), and thus both deserve analysis on their own terms. Just as traditional collective action efforts can fail to result in sustained or effective movements, there is nothing preordained about the results of digitally mediated networking processes. More often than not, they fail badly. The transmission of personal expression across networks may or may not become scaled up, stable, or capable of various kinds of targeted action depending on the kinds of social technology designed and appropriated by participants, and the kinds of opportunities that may motivate anger or compassion across large numbers of individuals. Thus, the Occupy Wall Street protests that spread in a month from New York to more than 80 countries and 900 cities around the world might not have succeeded without the inspiring models of the Arab Spring or the *indignados* in Spain, or the worsening economic conditions that provoked anger among increasing numbers of displaced individuals. Yet, when the Occupy networks spread under the easy-to-personalize action frame of "We are the 99 percent," there were few identifiable established political organizations at the center of them. There was even a conscious effort to avoid designating leaders and official spokespeople. The most obvious organizational forms were the layers of social technologies and websites that carried news reported by participants and displayed tools for personalized networking. One of the sites was "15.10.11 united for #global change."[13] Instead of the usual "Who are we" section of the website, #globalchange asked: "Who are you?"

Collective and connective action may co-occur in various formations within the same ecology of action. It is nonetheless possible to discern three clear ideal types of large-scale action networks. While one is primarily characterized by collective action logic, the other two are connective action networks distinguished by the role of formal organizations in facilitating personalized engagement. As noted above, conventional organizations play a less central role than social technologies in relatively crowd-enabled networks such as the *indignados* of Spain, the Arab Spring uprisings, or the

Occupy protests that spread from Wall Street around the world. In contrast to these more technology-enabled networks, we have also observed hybrid networks (such as PPF) where conventional organizations operate in the background of protest and issue advocacy networks to enable personalized engagement. This hybrid form of organizationally enabled connective action sits along a continuum somewhere between the two ideal types of conventional organizationally brokered collective action and relatively more crowd-enabled connective action. The following section presents the details of this three-part typology. It also suggests that co-existence, layering, and movement across the types becomes an important part of the story.

A Typology of Collective and Connective Action Networks

We draw upon these distinct logics of action (and the hybrid form that reveals a tension between them) to develop a three-part typology of large-scale action networks that feature prominently in contemporary contentious politics. One type represents the brokered organizational networks characterized by the logic of collective action, while the others represent two significant variations on networks primarily characterized by the logic of connective action. All three models may explain differences between and dynamics within large-scale action networks in event-centered contention, such as protests and sequences of protests as in the examples we have already discussed. They may also apply to more stable issue advocacy networks that engage people in everyday life practices supporting causes outside of protest events, such as campaigns. The typology is intended as a broad generalization to help understand different dynamics. None of the types are exhaustive social movement models. Thus, this is not an attempt to capture, much less resolve, the many differences among those who study social movements. We simply want to highlight the rise of two forms of digitally networked connective action that differ from some common assumptions about collective action in social movements and, in particular, that rely on mediated networks for substantial aspects of their organization.

Figure 3.1 presents an overview of the two connective action network types and contrasts their organizational properties with more familiar collective action network organizational characteristics. The ideal collective action type at the right side in the figure describes large-scale action networks that depend on brokering organizations to carry the burden of facilitating cooperation and bridging differences when possible. As the anti-capitalist direct action groups in the G20 London summit protests exemplified, such organizations will tend to promote more exclusive collective action frames that require frame bridging if they are to grow. They may use digital media and social technologies more as means of mobilizing and managing participation and coordinating goals, rather than inviting personalized interpretations of problems and

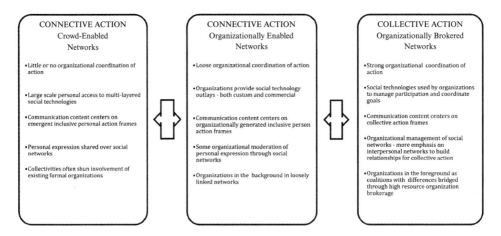

Figure 3.1
Elements of collective and connective action networks.

self-organization of action. In addition to a number of classic social movement accounts (for example, McAdam 1986), several of the NGO networks discussed by Keck and Sikkink (1998) also accord with this category (Bennett 2005).

At the other extreme, on the left side in the figure we place connective action networks that self-organize largely without central or lead organizational actors, using technologies as important organizational agents. We call this type crowd-enabled connective action. While some formal organizations may be present, they tend to remain at the periphery or may exist as much in online as in offline forms. In place of collective action frames, personal action frames become the transmission units across trusted social networks. The loose coordination of the *indignados* exemplifies this ideal type, with conventional organizations deliberately kept at the periphery as easily adapted personal action frames travel online and offline with the aid of technology platforms such as the ¡Democracia real Ya! organization.[14]

In-between the organizationally brokered collective action networks and the crowd-enabled connective action network is the hybrid pattern introduced above. This middle type involves formal organizational actors stepping back from projecting strong agendas, political brands, and collective identities in favor of using resources to deploy social technologies enabling loose public networks to form around personalized action themes. The middle type may also encompass more informal organizational actors that develop some capacities of conventional organizations in terms of resource mobilization and coalition building without imposing strong brands and collective identities.[15] For example, many of the general assemblies in the Occupy protests became resource centers, with regular attendance, division of labor, allocation of money and food, and coordination of actions. At the same time, the larger communication networks that swirled around these protest nodes greatly expanded the impact of the network. The surrounding technology networks invited loose-tied participation that was often in tension with the face-to-face ethos of the assemblies, where more committed protesters spent long hours with dwindling numbers of peers debating on how to expand participation without diluting the levels of commitment and action that they deemed key to their value scheme. Thus, even as Occupy displayed some organizational development, it was defined by its self-organizing roots.

Networks in this hybrid model engage individuals in causes that might not be of such interest if stronger demands for membership or subscribing to collective demands accompanied the organizational offerings. Organizations facilitating these action networks typically deploy an array of custom-built (for example, "send your message") and outsourced (for example, Twitter) communication technologies. This pattern fit the PPF demonstrations discussed earlier, where some 160 civil society organizations—including major NGOs such as Oxfam, Tearfund, Catholic Relief, and World Wildlife Fund—stepped back from their organizational brands to form a loose social network inviting publics to engage with each other and take action. They did this even as they negotiated with other organizations over such things as separate days for the protests (Bennett and Segerberg 2011).

The formations in the middle type reflect the pressures that Bimber et al. (2005) observed in interest organizations that are suffering declining memberships and have had to develop looser, more entrepreneurial relations with followers. Beyond the ways in which particular organizations use social technologies to develop loose ties with followers, many organizations also develop loose ties with other organizations to form vast online networks sharing and bridging various causes. Although the scale and complexity of these networks differ from the focus of Granovetter's (1973) observations about the strength of weak ties in social networks, we associate this idea with the elements of connective action: the loose organizational linkages, technology deployments, and personal action frames. In observing the hybrid pattern of issue advocacy organizations facilitating personalized protest networks, we traced a number of economic justice and environmental networks, charting protests, campaigns, and issue networks in the UK, Germany, and Sweden (Bennett and Segerberg 2013).[16] In each case, we found (with theoretically interesting variations) campaigns, protest events, and everyday issue advocacy networks that displayed similar organizational signatures: (1) familiar NGOs and other civil society organizations joining loosely together to provide something of a networking backbone; (2) for digital media networks engaging publics with contested political issues; yet with (3) remarkably few efforts to brand the issues around specific organizations, own the messages, or control the understandings of individual participants. The organizations had their political agendas on offer, to be sure, but as members of issue networks, put the public face on the individual citizen and provided social technologies to enable personal engagement through easy-to-share images and personal action frames.

The organizations that refrain from strongly branding their causes or policy agendas in this hybrid model do not necessarily give up their missions or agendas as name-brand public advocacy organizations. Instead, some organizations interested in mobilizing large and potentially "WUNC-y" publics in an age of social networking are learning to shift among different organizational repertoires, morphing from being hierarchical, mission-driven NGOs in some settings to being facilitators in loosely linked public engagement networks in others. As noted by Chadwick (2007, 2013), organizational hybridity makes it difficult to apply fixed categories to many organizations as they variously shift from being issue advocacy NGOs to policy think tanks, to SMOs running campaigns or protests, to multi-issue organizations, to being networking hubs for connective action. In other words, depending on when, where, and how one observes an organization, it may appear differently as an NGO, SMO, INGO, TNGO, NGDO (non-governmental organization, social movement organization, international non-governmental organization, transnational non-governmental organization, non-governmental development organization), an interest advocacy group, a political networking hub, and so on. Indeed, one of the advantages of seeing the different logics at play in our typology is to move away from fixed categorization schemes, and observe actually occurring combinations of different types of action within complex protest ecologies, and shifts in dominant types in response to events and opportunities over time.

The real world is of course far messier than this three-type model. In some cases, we see action formations corresponding to our three models side by side in the same action space. The G20 London protest offered a rare case in which organizationally enabled and more conventional collective action were neatly separated over different days. More often, the different forms layer and overlap, perhaps with violence disrupting otherwise peaceful mobilizations as occurred in the Occupy Rome protests on October 15, 2011, and in a number of Occupy clashes with police in the United States. In still other action cycles, we see a movement from one model to another over time. In some relatively distributed networks, we observe a pattern of informal organizational resource-seeking, in which informal organizational resources and communication spaces are linked and shared (for example, re-tweeted), enabling emergent political concerns and goals to be nurtured without being co-opted by existing organizations and their already fixed political agendas. This pattern occurred in the crowd-enabled Twitter network that emerged in 2009 around the 15th UN Climate Change Conference in Copenhagen. As the long tail of that network handed its participants off to the Twitter stream devoted to the next summit in Cancun, we saw an increase in links to organizations of various kinds, along with growing links to and among climate bloggers (Segerberg and Bennett 2011). Such variations on different organizational forms offer intriguing opportunities for further analyses aimed at explaining whether mobilizations achieve various goals and attain different levels of WUNC.

In these varying ways, personalized connective action networks cross paths (sometimes with individual organizations morphing in the process) with more conventional collective action networks centered on SMOs, interest organizations, and brand-conscious NGOs. As a result, while we argue that these networks are an organizational form in themselves, they are often hard to grasp and harder to analyze because they do not behave like formal organizations. Most formal organizations are centered (for example, located in physical space), hierarchical, bounded by mission and territory, and defined by relatively known and countable memberships (or in the case of political parties, known and reachable demographics). By contrast, many of today's issue and cause networks are relatively decentered (constituted by multiple organizations and many direct and cyber activists), distributed, or flattened organizationally as a result of these multiple centers, relatively unbounded, in the sense of crossing both geographical and issue borders, and dynamic in terms of the changing populations who may opt in and out of play as different engagement opportunities are presented (Bennett 2003, 2005). Understanding how connective action engages or fails to engage diverse populations constitutes part of the analytical challenge ahead.

Compared to the vast number of theoretically grounded studies on social movement organizing, there is less theoretical work that helps to explain the range of collective action formations, running from relatively crowd-enabled to organizationally enabled connective action networks. While there are many descriptive and suggestive accounts of this kind of action, many of them insightful (for example, Castells 2000; Rheingold 2002), we are concerned that the organizational logic and underlying dynamic of such action is not well established. It is important to gain clearer understandings of how such networks function and what organizing principles explain their growing prominence in contentious politics.

Conclusion

DNA is emerging during a historic shift in late modern democracies in which, most notably, younger citizens are moving away from parties, broad reform movements, and ideologies. Individuals are relating differently to organized politics, and many organizations are finding that they must engage people differently: they are developing relationships to publics as affiliates rather than members, and offering them personal options in ways to engage and express themselves. This includes greater choice over contributing content, and introduces micro-organizational resources in terms of personal networks, content creation, and technology development skills. Collective action based on exclusive collective identifications and strongly tied networks continues to play a role in this political landscape, but this has become joined by, interspersed with, and in some cases supplanted by personalized collective action formations in which digital media become integral organizational parts. Some of the resulting DNA networks turn out to be surprisingly nimble, demonstrating intriguing flexibility across various conditions, issues, and scales.

It has been tempting for some critics to dismiss participation in such networks as noise, particularly in reaction to sweeping proclamations by enthusiasts of the democratic and participatory power of digital media. Whether from digital enthusiasts or critics, hyperbole is unhelpful. Understanding the democratic potential and effectiveness of instances of connective and collective action requires careful analysis. At the same time, there is often considerably more going on in DNA than clicktivism or facile organizational outsourcing of social networking to various commercial sites.[17] The key point of our argument is that fully explaining and understanding such action and contention requires more than just adjusting the classic social movement collective action schemes. Connective action has a logic of its own, and thus attendant dynamics of its own. It deserves analysis on its own terms.

The linchpin of connective action is the formative element of "sharing": the personalization that leads actions and content to be distributed widely across social networks. Communication technologies enable the growth and stabilization of network structures across these networks. Together, the technological agents that enable the constitutive role of sharing in these contexts displace the centrality of the free-rider calculus and with it, by extension, the dynamic that flows from it; most obviously, the logical centrality of the resource-rich organization. In its stead, connective action brings the action dynamics of recombinant networks into focus, a situation in which networks and communication become something more than mere preconditions and information. What we observe in these networks are applications of communication technologies that contribute an organizational principle that is different from notions of collective action based on core assumptions about the role of resources, networks, and collective identity. We call this different structuring principle the logic of connective action.

Developing ways to analyze connective action formations will give us more solid grounds for returning to the persistent questions of whether such action can be politically effective and sustained (Tilly 2004; Gladwell 2010; Morozov 2011). Even as the contours of political action may be shifting, it is imperative to develop means of thinking meaningfully about the capacities of sustainability and effectiveness in relation to connective action and to gain a systematic understanding of how such action plays out in different contexts and conditions.

Part of the challenge ahead is therefore to understand when DNA becomes chaotic and unproductive, and when it attains higher levels of focus and sustained engagement over time. Moving in this direction, our studies suggest that differing political capacities in networks depend, among other things, on whether: (1) in the case of organizationally enabled DNA, the network has a stable core of organizations sharing communication linkages and deploying high volumes of personal engagement mechanisms; or (2) in the case of crowd-enabled DNA, the digital networks are redundant and dense with pathways for individual networks to converge, enabling broad transmission of personally appealing action frames to occur.

Attention to connective action will neither explain all contentious politics nor replace the model of classic collective action that remains useful for analyzing social movements. But it does shed light on an important mode of action making its mark in contentious politics today. In recent years, we have seen more conventional political organizations stepping back from trying to own and brand their issues, and centrally manage the activities of their memberships. Instead, many are learning how to engage diverse publics who participate through their own social networks in organizing civic actions. This model may include a prominent NGO partnering with a rock band to use the band's fan networks to spread the word about world food shortages. In other contexts, loose coalitions of civic actors may step behind a commonly constructed online organization and run a campaign that personalizes engagement in the issue of debt relief for poor nations, or tax policies to limit financial speculation that destabilizes economies. Some of these hybrid forms of political organization appear to offer stable and effective bases of civic engagement in an era of democratic transition. This suggests that understanding how connective action works can help to illuminate how civic engagement evolves in changing political systems as well as in shifting political times.

Acknowledgment

The original version of this chapter was published as: W. Lance Bennett and Alexandra Segerberg (2012), "The Logic of Connective Action: Digital Media and the Personalization of Contentious Politics." *Information, Communication & Society*, 15(5), 739–768. The authors are grateful for permission from Taylor & Francis (http://www.tandfonline.com) to reprint the article as this chapter. This version has been updated to reflect changes that appear in *The Logic of Connective Action* (Bennett and Segerberg, 2013).

Notes

1. Simultaneous protests were held in other European cities with tens of thousands of demonstrators gathering in the streets of Berlin, Frankfurt, Vienna, Paris, and Rome.

2. US Vice President Joe Biden asked for patience from understandably upset citizens while leaders worked on solutions, and the British Prime Minister at the time, Gordon Brown, said: "the action we want to take (at the G20) is designed to answer the questions that the protesters have today" (Vinocur and Barkin 2009).

3. http://www.democraciarealya.es.

4. Beyond the high volume of Spanish press coverage, the story of the *indignados* attracted world attention. BBC *World News* devoted no fewer than eight stories to this movement over the course of two months, including a feature on the march of one group across the country to Madrid, with many interviews and encounters in the words of the protesters themselves.

5. For example, our analyses of the US Occupy protests show that increased media attention to economic inequality in the USA was associated with the coverage of the Occupy protests (Bennett and Segerberg 2013). While political elites were often reluctant to credit the occupiers with their newfound concern about inequality, they nonetheless seemed to find the public opinion and media climate conducive to addressing the long-neglected issue.

6. A Google search of "put people first g20" more than two years after the London events produced nearly 1.5 million hits, with most of them relevant to the events and issues of those protests well into 75 search pages deep.

7. We would note, however, that carnivalesque or theatrical expressions may entail strategically depersonalized forms of expression in which individuals take on other personae that often have historically or dramatically scripted qualities. We thank Stefania Milan for this comment.

8. We are not arguing here that all contemporary analyses of collective action rely on resource mobilization explanations (although some do). Our point is that whether resource assumptions are in the foreground or the background, many collective action analyses typically rely on a set of defining assumptions centered on the importance of some degree of formal organization and some degree of strong collective identity that establishes common bonds among participants. These elements become more marginal in thinking about the organization of connective action.

9. While we focus primarily on cases in late modern, post-industrial democracies, we also attempt to develop theoretical propositions that may apply to other settings such as the Arab Spring, where authoritarian rule may also result in individualized populations that fall outside of sanctioned civil society organization yet may also have direct or indirect access to communication technologies such as mobile phones.

10. Routledge and Cumbers (2009) make a similar point in discussing horizontal and vertical models as useful heuristics for organizational logics in global justice networks (see also Robinson and Tormey 2005; Juris 2008).

11. We are indebted to Bob Boynton for pointing out that this sharing occurs both in trusted friends networks such as Facebook and in more public exchange opportunities among strangers of the sort that occur on YouTube, Twitter, or blogs. Understanding the dynamics and interrelationships among these different media networks and their intersections is an important direction for research.

12. We have developed methods for mapping networks and inventorying the types of digital media that enable actions and information to flow through them. Showing how networks are constituted in part by technology enables us to move across levels of action that are often difficult to theorize. Network technologies enable thinking about individuals, organizations, and

networks in one broad framework. This approach thus revises the starting points of classic collective action models, which typically examine the relationships between individuals and organizations and between organizations. We expand this to include technologies that enable the formation of fluid action networks in which agency becomes shared or distributed across individual actors and organizations as networks reconfigure in response to changing issues and events (Bennett and Segerberg 2013; Bennett et al. 2014).

13. http://www.15october.net (accessed 19 October 2011). The website is no longer active, but versions from 2011 are available on the Internet Archive (https://archive.org).

14. We wish to emphasize that there is much face-to-face organizing work going on in many of these networks, and that the daily agendas and decisions are importantly shaped offline. However, the connectivity and flow of action coordination occurs, importantly, online.

15. We thank an anonymous referee for highlighting this subtype.

16. Our empirical investigations focused primarily on two types of networks that display local, national, and transnational reach: networks to promote economic justice via more equitable North–South trade norms (fair trade) and networks for environmental and human protection from the effects of global warming (climate change). These networks display impressive levels of collective action and citizen engagement and they are likely to remain active into the foreseeable future. They often intersect by sharing campaigns in local, national, and transnational arenas. As such, these issue networks represent good cases for assessing the uses of digital technologies and different action frames (from personalized to collective) to engage and mobilize citizens, and to examine various related capacities and effects of those engagement efforts.

17. Technology is not neutral. The question of the degree to which various collectivities have both appropriated and become dependent on the limitations of commercial technology platforms such as Flickr, Facebook, Twitter, or YouTube is a matter of considerable importance. For now, suffice it to note that at least some of the technologies and their networking capabilities are designed by activists for creating political networks and organizing action (Calderaro 2011).

References

Anduiza, Eva, Camilo Cristancho, and José M. Sabucedo. 2014. "Mobilization Through Online Social Networks: The Political Protest of the *Indignados* in Spain." *Information Communication and Society* 17 (6): 750–764.

Bauman, Z. 2000. *Liquid Modernity*. Cambridge: Polity.

Beck, U., and E. Beck-Gernsheim. 2002. *Individualization: Institutionalized Individualism and its Social and Political Consequences*. London: SAGE.

Benford, R. D., and D. A. Snow. 2000. "Framing Processes and Social Movements: An Overview and an Assessment." *Annual Review of Sociology* 26:611–639.

Benkler, Y. 2006. *The Wealth of Networks: How Social Production Transforms Markets and Freedom*. New Haven: Yale University Press.

Bennett, W. L. 1998. "The Uncivic Culture: Communication, Identity, and the Rise of Lifestyle Politics." Ithiel de Sola Pool Lecture, American Political Science Association, published in *P.S.: Political Science and Politics* 31: 41–61.

Bennett, W. L., 2003. "Communicating Global Activism: Strengths and Vulnerabilities of Networked Politics." *Information, Communication & Society,* 6(2): 143–168.

Bennett, W. L., 2005. "Social Movements beyond Borders: Organization, Communication, and Political Capacity in Two Eras of Transnational Activism." In *Transnational Protest and Global Activism*, ed. D. della Porta and S. Tarrow, 203–222. Boulder, CO: Rowman & Littlefield.

Bennett, W. L., S. Lang, and A. Segerberg. 2014. "European Issue Publics Online: The Cases of Climate Change and Fair Trade." In *European Public Spheres: Politics Is Back*, ed. Thomas Risse, 108–137. Cambridge: Cambridge University Press.

Bennett, W. L., and A. Segerberg. 2011. "Digital Media and the Personalization of Collective Action: Social Technology and the Organization of Protests against the Global Economic Crisis." *Information, Communication & Society* 14: 770–799.

Bennett, W. L., and A. Segerberg. 2013. *The Logic of Connective Action: Digital Media and the Personalization of Contentious Politics*. New York: Cambridge University Press.

Bimber, B., and R. Davis. 2003. *Campaigning Online: The Internet in US Elections*. New York: Oxford University Press.

Bimber, B., A. Flanagin, and C. Stohl. 2005. "Reconceptualizing Collective Action in the Contemporary Media Environment." *Communication Theory* 15:389–413.

Bimber, B., A. Flanagin, and C. Stohl. 2009. "Technological Change and the Shifting Nature of Political Organization." In *Routledge Handbook of Internet Politics*, ed. A. Chadwick and P. Howard, 72–85. London: Routledge.

Bimber, B., A. Flanagin, and C. Stohl. 2012. *Collective Action in Organizations: Interaction and Engagement in an Era of Technological Change*. New York: Cambridge University Press.

Calderaro, A. 2011. "New Political Struggles in the Network Society: The Case of Free and Open Source Software (FOSS) Movement." Paper presented at ECPR General Conference, Reykjavik, August 25–27.

Castells, M. 2000. *The Network Society*. 2nd ed. Oxford: Blackwell.

Chadwick, A. 2007. "Digital Network Repertoires and Organizational Hybridity." *Political Communication* 24 (3): 283–301.

Chadwick, A. 2013. *The Hybrid Media System: Politics and Power*. New York: Oxford University Press.

Chesters, G., and I. Welsh. 2006. *Complexity and Social Movements: Multitudes at the End of Chaos*. London: Routledge.

Daily Show. 2009. "Tea Partiers Advise G20 Protesters." *Daily Show*, October 1. http://www.thedailyshow.com/watch/thu-october-1-2009/tea-partiers-advise-g20-protesters.

Dawkins, R. 1989. *The Selfish Gene*. Oxford: Oxford University Press.

della Porta, D. 2005. "Multiple Belongings, Flexible Identities and the Construction of 'Another Politics': Between the European Social Forum and the Local Social Fora." In *Transnational Protest and Global Activism*, ed. D. della Porta and S. Tarrow, 175–202. Boulder, CO: Rowman and Littlefield.

della Porta, D., and M. Diani. 2006. *Social Movements: An Introduction*. 2nd ed. Malden, MA: Blackwell.

Diani, Mario. 2015. *The Cement of Civil Society: Studying Networks in Localities*. Cambridge: Cambridge University Press.

Earl, J., and K. Kimport. 2011. *Digitally Enabled Social Change: Online and Offline Activism in the Age of the Internet*. Cambridge, MA: MIT Press.

Foot, K., and S. Schneider. 2006. *Web Campaigning*. Cambridge, MA: MIT Press.

Giddens, A. 1991. *Modernity and Self-Identity: Self and Society in the Late Modern Age*. Stanford, CA: Stanford University Press.

Gitlin, T. 1980. *The Whole World Is Watching: Mass Media in the Making and Unmaking of the New Left*. Berkeley, CA: University of California Press.

Gladwell, M. 2010. "Small Change: Why the Revolution Will Not Be Tweeted." *New Yorker*, October 4.

Granovetter, M. 1973. "The Strength of Weak Ties." *American Journal of Sociology* 78:1360–1380.

Howard, P., and M. Hussain. 2011. "The Role of Digital Media." *Journal of Democracy* 22 (3): 35–48.

Hunt, S., R. D. Benford, and D. A. Snow. 1994. "Identity Fields: Framing Processes and the Social Construction of Movement Identities." In *New Social Movements: From Ideology to Identity*, ed. E. Laraña, H. Johnston, and J. R. Gusfield, 185–208. Philadelphia, PA: Temple University Press.

Inglehart, R. 1997. *Modernization and Post-Modernization: Cultural, Economic, and Political Change in 43 Societies*. Princeton, NJ: Princeton University Press.

Juris, J. 2008. *Networking Futures: The Movements against Corporate Globalization*. Durham, NC: Duke University Press.

Keck, M., and K. Sikkink. 1998. *Activists beyond Borders: Advocacy Networks in International Politics*. Ithaca, NY: Cornell University Press.

Latour, B. 2005. *Reassembling the Social: An Introduction to Actor-Network-Theory*. Oxford: Oxford University Press.

Livingston, S., and G. Asmolov. 2010. "Networks and the Future of Foreign Affairs Reporting." *Journalism Studies* 11 (5): 745–760.

Lupia, A., and G. Sin. 2003. "Which Public Goods Are Endangered? How Evolving Communication Technologies Affect 'The Logic of Collective Action.'" *Public Choice* 117:315–331.

McAdam, D. 1986. "Recruitment to High-Risk Activism: The Case of Freedom Summer." *American Journal of Sociology* 92:64–90.

McAdam, D., J. D. McCarthy, and M. N. Zald. 1996. "Opportunities, Mobilizing Structures, and Framing Processes: Toward a Synthetic, Comparative Perspective on Social Movements." In *Comparative Perspectives on Social Movements: Political Opportunities, Mobilizing Structures, and Cultural Framings*, ed. D. McAdam, J. D. McCarthy, and M. N. Zald, 1–20. New York: Cambridge University Press.

McAdam, D., S. Tarrow, and C. Tilly. 2001. *Dynamics of Contention*. New York: Cambridge University Press.

McCarthy, J. D., and M. N. Zald. 1973. *The Trend of Social Movements in America: Professionalization and Resource Mobilization*. Morristown, NJ: General Learning Press.

McCarthy, J. D., and M. N. Zald. 1977. "Resource Mobilization and Social Movements: A Partial Theory." *American Journal of Sociology* 82 (6): 1212–1241.

McDonald, K. 2002. "From Solidarity to Fluidarity: Social Movements beyond 'Collective Identity'—The Case of Globalization Conflicts." *Social Movement Studies* 1 (2): 109–128.

Melucci, A. 1996. *Challenging Codes: Collective Action in the Information Age*. Cambridge: Cambridge University Press.

Micheletti, M. 2003. *Political Virtue and Shopping*. New York: Palgrave.

Morozov, E. 2011. *The Net Delusion: How Not to Liberate the World*. London: Allen Lane.

Olson, M. 1965. *The Logic of Collective Action: Public Goods and the Theory of Groups*. Cambridge, MA: Harvard University Press.

Polletta, F. 2002. *Freedom Is an Endless Meeting: Democracy in American Social Movements*. Chicago, IL: University of Chicago Press.

Putnam, R. 2000. *Bowling Alone: The Collapse and Revival of American Community*. New York: Simon & Schuster.

Put People First. 2009. Accessed July 6, 2011. http://www.putpeoplefirst.org.uk/.

Rheingold, H. 2002. *Smart Mobs: The Next Social Revolution*. Cambridge, MA: Perseus Pub.

Robinson, A., and S. Tormey. 2005. "Horizontals, Verticals and the Conflicting Logics of Transformative Politics." In *Confronting Globalization*, ed. C. el-Ojeili and P. Hayden, 208–226. London: Palgrave.

Routledge, P., and A. Cumbers. 2009. *Global Justice Networks: Geographies of Transnational Solidarity*. Manchester: Manchester University Press.

RTVE. 2011. "Más de seis millones de españoles han participado en el movimiento 15M." August 6. Accessed September 18, 2011. http://www.rtve.es/noticias/20110806/mas-seis-millones-espanoles-han-participado-movimiento-15m/452598.shtml.

Segerberg, A., and W. L. Bennett. 2011. "Social Media and the Organization of Collective Action: Using Twitter to Explore the Ecologies of Two Climate Change Protests." *Communication Review* 14 (3): 197–215.

Shifman, L. 2013. *Memes in Digital Culture*. Cambridge, MA: MIT Press.

Snow, D. A., and R. D. Benford. 1988. "Ideology, Frame Resonance, and Participant Mobilization." *International Social Movement Research* 1:197–217.

Snow, D. A., B. Rochford, Jr., S. K. Worden, and R. D. Benford. 1986. "Frame Alignment Processes, Micromobilization, and Movement Participation." *American Sociological Review* 51:464–481.

Tarrow, S. 2011. *Power in Movement: Social Movements in Contentious Politics*. 3rd ed. New York: Cambridge University Press.

Tilly, C. 2004. *Social Movements, 1768–2004*. Boulder, CO: Paradigm.

Tilly, C. 2006. "WUNC." In *Crowds*, ed. J. T. Schnapp and M. Tiews, 289–306. Stanford, CA: Stanford University Press.

Vinocur, N., and N. Barkin. 2009. "G20 Marches Begin Week of Protests in Europe." *Reuters,* March 28. Accessed July 9, 2011. http://www.reuters.com/article/2009/03/28/us-g20-britain-march-idUSTRE52R0TP20090328.

Weller, B. 2010. "G20 Protests in Seoul." *Demotix*, November 11. Accessed July 9, 2011. http://www.demotix.com/photo/504262/g20-protests-seoul.

4 Liberated Technology: Inside Emancipatory Communication Activism

Stefania Milan

"Your radio dial was made for revolution!" read the mission statement of a pirate signal, appropriately named Radio Mutiny, broadcasting on 91.3 FM, in the 1990s in Philadephia, Pennsylvania. The "rabidly non-hierarchical, decisively anti-authoritarian, avidly pro-feminist, staunchly anti-racist, and flamboyantly anti-homophobic" volunteer group operated a micro-powered transmitter "for people who are denied a voice in the mainstream media" (Milan 2013, 78). Some of its founders went on to organize "radio barnraisings" across the United States, in which communities gathered to build together their low-power radio transmitter and station (Dunbar-Hester 2014).

In November 1999 protesters managed to block the summit of the World Trade Organization. For the first time in history, they were able to report directly from the streets using open source software that allowed them to bypass the editorial filters of mainstream media. Three years after its foundation, the open publishing platform of the Independent Media Center, or Indymedia, already counted 89 nodes in six continents (Kidd 2010). Around that time, the pirate TV stations of the Telestreet movement mushroomed in various metropolitan areas in Italy. They used self-made micro-transmitters to exploit the "shadow zones" of the public broadcaster's signal (Pelizza 2006).

Radio Mutiny, Indymedia, Telestreet, and their many siblings across the world challenged on their own terrain the power of media corporations and state-owned broadcasters. Over the years, they have allowed broader sectors of the citizenry to reclaim their voice and access unfiltered media production. Fast forward to today, and many of these projects have disappeared, succumbing in the face of commercial "free" services and social networking platforms. Many others, however, have evolved to meet the changing needs of citizens and activists alike, and thrive in the fringes of our mediascape.

These experiments in media and social justice offer alternatives to existing commercial infrastructure, often operating across media platforms and involving non-professional producers. They emerge within, and are strictly linked to, the global struggle for social justice, contributing to the efforts of progressive movements to shape the world according to principles of equality, participation, and horizontality. In other words, they constitute what DeeDee Halleck of the Deep Dish Satellite Network, the first US grassroots community television network, calls "infrastructures of resistance" (Halleck 2002, 191) to neoliberal media.

I like to think of these "liberated technologies" as the outcome of emancipatory communication practices. "Practice" evokes the hands-on approach of grassroots groups in promoting reform-from-below of the communications system. "Emancipatory" denotes their promise to share and redistribute technical knowledge, in order to extend also to non-experts the possibility to control communicative actions bypassing commercial and state-owned platforms. Emancipation is strictly linked to the notion of empowerment, seen as "freedom to" communicate in one's own terms. In this sense, emancipatory communication projects should be seen as a space for people to enact their democratic agency and "spin transformative processes that alter people's sense of self, their subjective positioning, and therefore their access to power" (Rodriguez 2001, 18). By enacting their citizenship, activists "contest social codes, legitimized identities, and institutionalized social relations [...] to the point where these transformations and changes are possible" (2001, 20).

Emancipatory communication activism seeks to create alternatives to existing media and communication infrastructure. It includes a variety of self-organized media outlets, often small-scale and run by volunteers, but active in broader transnational networks. Examples range from independent information platforms on the Web such as Indymedia and the Global Voices network to alternative press, radio, and video production (Downing 1984; Downing 2011), from community radio and television stations (Rennie 2006; Rodriguez 2011) to self-organized wireless networks (Powell 2008), open source software development projects (Coleman 2013), and nonprofit Internet service providers (Milan 2013). Artistic forms of direct action, such as billboard liberation and culture jamming, also belong to the realm of emancipatory communication activism, to the extent that they expose the contradictions of the system by encouraging public participation and critical thinking, and opposing the frantic media consumption promoted by commercial media. By engaging in these practices, activists aim to bypass the politics of enclosure and control enacted by states and corporations. Rather than engaging in advocacy work and policy reform, their primary strategy is structural reform at the grassroots level through the creation of autonomous spaces of communication. By emancipating other social actors from commercial communication services, they aim to empower them to articulate, voice, and convey their own messages without filters.

Emancipatory communication practices represent a challenge to dominant powers in the communications and media realm. Up for grabs is the power of participation, which refers to the possibility of making informed contributions to democratic decision making and public life, but also to access public communication more generally: in other words, the power of deciding who should speak, what messages should be transmitted, and on what conditions. Both are linked to the democratic agency of individuals and groups, as they articulate their identities and roles through interpersonal and public communication.

At the macro level, challenging the power structure means resisting the concentration of media and communication platforms held by a handful of global corporations such as Google, News Corp, and Facebook. It means resisting the securitization of interpersonal communications operated by security agencies, the police, and the industry, as they exploit the power of massive data collection to monitor citizens (Deibert 2013). It implies pressuring national regulators to warrant some space of autonomy on the Internet, license nonprofit media, or protect the right to anonymity and freedom of expression online (Hintz 2012). At the micro level, emancipatory communication practices challenge power structures in the media realm by creating alternative spaces of communication where freedom of expression, participation, and self-organization are practiced independently of social norms and legislations (Milan and Hintz 2013). It involves defending the right of disadvantaged communities and minorities to make their voices heard. It implies protecting local content and independent producers and voices, and fighting "the escalating cultural and mediatic censorship of imagination, and the attempts to sell us pre-digested dreams" (Milan 2013, 3). It includes finding new ways of sharing content and knowledge, rejecting the ever-tightening intellectual property regimes.

Technology is the backbone of the struggle of emancipatory communication activism. Far from being an end in itself, however, technology is a means to a political end, whose scope goes well beyond a national mediascape or the Internet. In other words, it is "politics by other means" (Flacks 2005, 6), and as such, emancipatory communication activism should be seen as a subdivision of the growing number of social mobilizations addressing democracy and participation in public life more broadly. But this special intertwining of the social and the technical affects also our way of understanding the same emancipatory practices. Analytically, they are artifacts that are simultaneously technical and semiotic and are meant for communication between people; their use "implies combined technical and communicative actions" (Goldkuhl 2013, 90). Thus, creating and engaging with these practices is of sociotechnical nature, and the two sides cannot be addressed in isolation. Here, emancipatory communication practices are acknowledged to be first and foremost ways of social organizing and of articulating the relation between tactics and values, tools and identities.

This chapter looks at civic media in their guise of emancipatory communication practices. The two intersect in that they both are mediated practices of participation in civic life. However, the latter are collectively created and oriented to collective use; they are explicitly concerned with progressive social change, and emerge rigorously from the non-governmental and nonprofit realm. In addition, emancipatory communication practices are sites of contestation, and encompass a crucial element of protest and/

or reform of the existent. Today they extensively take advantage of the possibilities of experimenting, designing, and networking offered by digital technology. However, as we shall see, their practices, principles, and approaches are deeply grounded in earlier, analog experiences of autonomous communication. As such, they can be seen as both a protest-laden approach to civic media, and a subgroup within this umbrella notion. Here I present an empirical overview of emancipatory communication activism in view of offering a specific theoretical lens through which we can look at social justice–oriented civic media. In particular, this chapter takes a micro-sociological approach to explore their emergence and flourishing with the global struggle for social justice. Instead of focusing on the content they broadcast or host in their wires, it investigates the sociotechnical processes behind their creation: why and how these practices emerge, who is behind them, how activists interact with institutions and norms, and what these projects mean for contemporary societies.

The chapter is organized as follows. First, it offers a historical perspective on the emergence and evolution of forms of emancipatory communication activism over time, from miners' radio stations in Latin America to present-day "liberation technology" projects. Second, it illuminates the micro-sociological processes that sustain emancipatory communication activism and the complex relations with their communities of reference. Third, it explores their organizational forms, and the relation between groupings and technology. It then articulates the connection between the micro and local dimensions of emancipatory communication activism and the transnational perspective of mobilization and exchange around issues of media democracy, citizenship, and participation. Finally, it connects the global mobilization around alternative communication to contemporary challenges like surveillance, corporatization, and the role of the industry in the post-Snowden era.

The Long Walk of Emancipatory Communication Activism

The history of civic media is strictly connected to that of social movements and citizen-led social change initiatives. Although waves of creation of "movement media" (Downing 2011) include, for instance, the nineteenth-century labor press in the UK and the US and the 1940s miners' radio stations in rural Colombia (see for example Downing 1984; Gumucio-Dagron 2001), contemporary emancipatory communication practices have their roots in the 1970s. Over the last half-century, and with a significant acceleration toward the end of the 1990s, initiatives to democratize public communication have mushroomed in both Western democracies and postcolonial societies. In order to make sense of such a dense recent history, we can identify four decades of contention in the period of time running from 1975 to present. Each phase is characterized by a combination of political opportunities, that is to say formal or informal dimensions of the political struggle that encourage people to take action (Tarrow 1998); a distinct socio-cultural *esprit du temp*; and the emergence of new technology and the emancipatory discourses it inspired. While this is little more than an arbitrary classification, it has the power to shed light on the unique combination of these three elements (institutional processes, socio-cultural climate, and technology) as they contribute to shape activism in the field.

1975–1985: The "institutional" period and the emergence of the free radio movement. In a 1970s Cold War context, the first institutional wave of debates on media democratization and development emerged within the United Nations Educational, Scientific and Cultural Organization (UNESCO). Promoted by the Non-Aligned Movement, the debate on the New World Information and Communication Order (NWICO) and the subsequent publication of the controversial MacBride report (1980) on the status of the world's communications exposed the imbalances in global information flows and raised attention on the opportunities for development brought about by recent evolutions in media technology, including satellites. Advocates started speaking of a proactive "right to communicate," moving beyond the passive right to information enshrined in the 1948 Universal Declaration of Human Rights (D'Arcy 1969). On the technology front, in the industrialized West, television was slowly moving from natural monopoly to a privatized endeavor, and the first modern computers entered the small circles of research institutions. Meanwhile, the so-called new social movements emerged in Europe and the US: they addressed immaterial interests and values such as peace, the environment, and gender equality (Melucci 1989). In this period civic media flourished in Western democracies and Latin America, mainly in the form of self-printed pamphlets and local nonprofit radio stations. The movement probably started in Italy with the so-called *radio libere* (free radio stations) following the liberalization of the Italian airwaves in 1976. Italian and later French stations inspired pirates all over the world (Downing 2001). In 1983, the GNU Project called for software writers to contribute to the compilation of an operating system free from constraints on the use of its source code (Free Software Foundation 1987). It was the start of the free software movement, which spread across the globe in the second half of the 1980s. In 1984, a group of grassroots non-governmental organizations from four continents active in the sustainable development and women's movements signed the Velletri Agreement (from a city outside Rome, Italy), committing to use telephone lines to network their computers (Murphy 2005). As a result, a series of experiments in computer-mediated communication emerged, including Interdoc, PeaceNet (US), GreenNet (UK), and the European Counter Network, connected to the most radical fringes of European social movements (see Interdoc 1984).

1985–1995: An autonomous civil society agenda. Following the NWICO failure, the idea of the democratic reform of the global communications system disappeared from the institutional agendas, surviving within civil society and journalists' associations that continued gathering in the MacBride Roundtables, an advocacy group that met annually from 1989 to 1999 (Nordenstreng and Traber 1992). On the technology front, states set the basis for the concentration of media ownership; personal computers started entering households, and in 1985 Microsoft introduced its Windows operating system. From civic renewal movements in Eastern Europe to the Zapatista indigenous struggle in Mexico in 1994, civil society started organizing autonomously and across borders. In the US, a democratic media activism movement made its voice increasingly heard at Congress (McChesney and Nichols 2002), while faith-based associations and advocacy groups began to address issues of media concentration, pluralism, and copyright. The first grassroots Internet Service Providers were founded, among which was London-based GreenNet, serving the environmental community (Hintz and Milan 2009). The People's Communication Charter (1993) advocated for people's empowerment through media access (Hamelink 1983). The first open source Linux operating system was released in 1991. In 1988, inspired by "the Internet vision of global communications unfettered by commercial barriers" (Murphy 2000), PeaceNet and Green-Net teamed up to create the first NGO-owned transatlantic digital communication network. Community radio stations began to organize in national and international coalitions, such as the UK Community Radio Association and the World Association of Community Broadcasters, often to lobby for their legalization. A new discourse on tactical media emerged: at the crossroads between arts and activism, situationist tactical media fostered "a critical usage of media practices that draw on all forms of old and new, both lucid and sophisticated media, for achieving a variety of specific noncommercial goals and pushing all kinds of potentially subversive political issues" (Critical Art Ensemble 2001, 5).

1995–2005: The self-organized Internet. By the mid-1990s, the Internet entered the everyday lives of ordinary people, accelerating communications across the globe and fostering connections among dispersed activists. Laptops, camcorders, and digital cameras became available at lower prices. This was the decade of alter-globalization protests (della Porta and Tarrow 2005). Exchanging information and organizing via the Internet, activists began to target supranational institutions and attack global summits, and a "global civil society" emerged (Kaldor 2003). Civil society created also autonomous spaces like social forums (Juris 2008), which developed around the utopia of "another possible world." Many emancipatory media saw the light in this period, allowing readers and listeners to become writers and producers (Atton 2002; Atton 2004). The praxis-oriented emancipatory approach to media activism became visible in a myriad of autonomous projects such as Indymedia. It inherited the values and tactics of pirate stations, community media, and pamphlets produced over the years by an array of social movements worldwide. The figure of the media activist embodying critical practices of autonomous communication, able to report on movement issues and from demonstrations, became a distinct identity within social movements. Electronic civil disobedience, email bombing, and net strikes attacking corporate and governmental websites became widespread forms of digital resistance (Milan 2015). Meanwhile, institutions rediscovered the importance of communication for the development of people and nations. In 2003–2005, the World Summit on the Information Society was the first United Nations summit to address communication issues and the role of new technologies in development. Its multistakeholder approach allowed for broad civil society participation, which mobilized in big numbers within and beyond the official process.

2005–2015: The era of transparency and social media activism. The global quest for democracy and the financial crisis that broke loose in 2008 encouraged people to eventually take back to the street again. From the North African Arab Spring (2011) to the Spanish Indignad@s (literally, the enraged), to the global wave of protests that started in New York City and became known as Occupy, people protested austerity measures and reclaimed their democratic agency. These mobilizations were linked to the emergence of social media activism, where "connective action" has replaced more traditional forms of collective action (Bennett and Segerberg 2013). The availability of "free" social media resulted in the progressive disaffection for self-organized small media, in favor of individualized point-to-point communication mediated by the omnipresent smartphone. While the role of the media activist became diffused, social media are increasingly used as broadcast media to reach the masses where people hang out, notwithstanding the capitalist nature of those venues—a move in radical contraposition with the alternative-media project of the earlier decades. However, emancipatory media continue thriving, such as privacy-minded social networking services Crabgrass and Diaspora. Mobile apps and online platforms are often equaled to "liberation technology" able to "expand political, social, and economic freedom" (Diamond 2010, 70)— again, a far cry from the *liberated* technology approach of emancipatory communication practices. Social media activism, although increasingly popular and able to speak to a broader audience, exposes the contradictions inherent in the technology people so much rely upon. Meanwhile, technology is increasingly used to support transparency and the monitoring of power holders: think of WikiLeaks, a whistleblowing platform publishing classified information from anonymous sources (Brevini, Hintz, and McCurdy 2013). In 2013 whistleblower Edward Snowden revealed the presence of massive surveillance programs enacted by the US National Security Agency and its siblings with the connivance of corporate players. Civil society slowly started to mobilize for digital rights with the help of online hacktivist communities like Anonymous (Coleman 2014), and so did some governments: for example, Brazil organized the NetMundial event to discuss the future of Internet governance, which set a high bar for the communications governance to come (Milan 2014).

In the next section, I look to emancipatory communication activism and explore individual motivations for engagement, ideological references of activists, and collective identity mechanisms deployed in practice.

Roots of Emancipatory Communication Activism

Why do emancipatory communication practices emerge? Where do they come from? How is a group identity created around technology?

The rise of emancipatory media has been linked to the perception of some form of injustice, and more precisely to the presence of a democratic deficit affecting the field of public communication. This democratic deficit spans the failure to foster a public sphere, the homogenization of discourses in society, inequality in access to means and content, the corporate enclosure of knowledge, and policy making conducted behind closed doors (Carroll and Hackett 2006, 2–10). Emancipatory communication activists frame injustice broadly as a matter of social, economic, and cultural inequality pertaining to different sectors of society. Nonetheless, the focus is on media-related injustice, which is believed to play a crucial role in perpetuating other forms of structural injustice. Thus, fighting the injustice embedded in the mediascape means addressing other inequalities in society. Activists tend to distinguish between a content- and a structure-related injustice, where the former indicates the homogenization of discourses, and the latter concerns both the architecture of technologies and institutional and commercial arrangements and relations. Emancipatory media activists, however, tend to emphasize structural injustice, believed to underpin all other inequalities—and this is why they engage at the level of media infrastructure, rather than solely content.

Among the most often cited motivations for engagement are political and social change, freedom of expression and self-determination, the possibility to take part in a collective experience; the fascination for experimenting and learning, curiosity, and even individualism for the more techie tasks. Often activists are driven by a sort of craftsman urge, that is to say a passion for making and creating, and by the idea of self-determination as control over technologies. Also, activists highly value their function as service providers and view their self-organized infrastructure as open channels that allow other people to voice their messages without filters or monitoring.

Emancipatory communication activism is a field of social action filled with emotions, despite it being so technology-driven. Emotions offer the "possibility of referring to a love-object ('Us' against 'Them')" which "continuously reduces ambivalence and fuels action with positive energies" (Melucci 1996, 83). Emotions are first and foremost individual, but they are also a relational experience that binds people together. Emotions linked to the perception of injustice, such as anger and moral outrage, are negative emotions and speak to the normative dimension of engagement. Positive emotions connected to the sense of togetherness that derives from collective action (e.g., happiness, empathy, gratification, a sense of worth) address the expressive dimension of activism. Fun and leisure as ends in themselves, too, perform an expressive function.

It is important to note that emancipatory communication activism is not usually the first and/or only field of activism people are engaged in. Activists are often also squatters, community advocates, or engage in environmental or direct action activism. These other subcultures influence the sphere of emancipatory communication activism with their practices and values. Human rights activism, people-centered approaches to development, the experiences of free radio in the 1970s and 1980s, but also do-it-yourself culture, the punk and squatter subcultures, cyber-libertarianism, the hacker and free software culture, anarchism, and the Zapatista struggle all contribute to shape the worldview of emancipatory communication practitioners.

Finally, how does a subjective sociotechnical experience such as that of infrastructure activism become collective? Collective action scholarship posits the presence of a shared identity through which individuals recognize themselves in some sort of "we-ness" (real or imagined) that stands for collective agency (Snow 2001). Identity work is situated at the crossroads of the private sphere of individuals and the collective dimension of action. It is not merely an individual process concerning the psychology of the self, but also a social process (Polletta and Jasper 2001). In this respect, emancipatory communication activism is experiential in nature, in that it is the private and subjective experience of the individual that takes central stage. But collective action in the field has some peculiarities, if compared to other mobilizations: the centrality of expertise, which is owned first at the individual level although it becomes meaningful in relation to the group of peers; the frequency of actions performed individually, such as coding, hacking, broadcasting, editing; and the role of cultural and ideological references that emphasize the individual component and subcultural elements such as lifestyle (see for example the do-it-yourself or the hacker approach). Under such conditions, the collective dimension is experienced through the individual involvement, and not vice versa as we would expect. Collective identity results from encounters between self-contained individuals, rather than from the collapsing of the individual into the group. In sum, the experiential dimension of the individual can be understood in the guise of "stories of 'I' encountering others" (McDonald 2004, 589), and as such is rooted in the "public experience of the self" (McDonald 2002, 125).

It is worth noting that the specificities of the medium (television, radio, Internet, print, etc.) are likely to have an impact on the way a collective identity is experienced—and on the degree of internalization versus externalization a group might adopt. For example, Internet and tech projects tend to emphasize individualism even further, while radio stations lean toward privileging more inclusive approaches. In addition, the peculiar relation with the community of reference typical of emancipatory communication projects more generally contributes to offset the individualistic tensions, as it fosters an externalized and inclusive collective identity that extends to incorporate user communities.

Organizing for Communicative Justice

What do emancipatory communication activism groupings look like? Organizational forms usually follow from the way the shared identity of a group is developed and experienced by social actors. In other words, organizations are a source of identity reproduction, and, at the same time, identity works as an organizing principle (c.f. Polletta 2002). But within emancipatory communication activism, organizational forms tend to reflect also the dynamics proper of the technology around which practitioners mobilize: in other words, whether you work in print, broadcasting, or the Internet affects the way you organize as a group.

We find a plurality of organizational models within emancipatory communication practices, with a predominance of grassroots, informal organizations. While there are a few semi-professional groups, generally groups are characterized by the "creative transposition of familiar but apolitical models of organizations to politics" (Clemens and Minkoff 2004, 158): in other words, they resemble groups of friends or the neighborhood or the local community. As such, they are regulated by trust and loyalty, and their boundaries are only relatively permeable, although nominally access barriers are low.

As is typical with experiential forms of activism, emancipatory communication groupings signal a preference for "the event and the experience" (McDonald 2006, 84) over "the power to represent" (37). As a result of this focus on experience, the informal collectives of emancipatory communication activists resemble affinity groups. Affinity groups are temporary action-oriented clusters that "reflect the convergence of the people who act through them," as opposed to being the organized expression of a group (McDonald 2002, 115). Involvement "is experienced as personal, as opposed to acting out one's role as a member of a group or association" (116).

Tech and Internet-inspired groupings share a number of characteristics. First, the group can be viewed as a "community of practice" (Husband 2005) that aims to reproduce a collective identity through joint action, experimenting, and learning. Second, the group functions through a division of labor model where individual skills are valued. Third, the group is based on the principles of equality among its members, horizontality, and decentralization in decision making. Fourth, the group is invisible, precisely because what is visible are its actions. The group works as a functional unit, and action is the only justification for its existence.

How does decision making unfold in emancipatory communication groups? In principle, groups implement horizontality, decentralization, and equality, and reject mechanisms of representation and delegation. Typically, they implement a participatory decision-making method rooted on consensus. However, the small size of the groups and the significant amount of individual energies invested in running infrastructure occasionally result in distortions of the decision-making process known in the literature as the "tyranny of structurelessness" (Freeman 1972). There is a pragmatic motivation for this, which points to the centrality of action within these groups. However, because activists share a set of tacit values as a precondition for collective action, whoever decides can reasonably assume that the other members will support the decision, in a sort of inferred consensus mechanism. An activist described this approach as a "dictatorship of action," whereby "those who decide to organize something, are in charge of their own project and get support of the others of the group" (Milan 2013, 93–94).

Mobilizing "beyond" Institutions and Norms

Tactics adopted by activists are "alternative means of acting together on shared interests" in order to "make a statement of some kind" (Tilly 1983, 463–464). They provide a "moral voice," giving activists "an opportunity to articulate, elaborate, alter, or affirm one's moral sensibilities, principles, and allegiances" (Jasper 1997, 15). Disruptive protest, advocacy campaigning, norm change, resistance, and direct action constitute the action repertoire of emancipatory communication activists, that is to say "sites of contestation in which bodies, symbols, identities, practices, and discourses are used to pursue or prevent changes in institutionalized power relations" (Taylor and van Dyke 2004, 268).

When addressing collective actors engaged in political processes, scholars typically distinguish between "insiders" and "outsiders" (Tarrow 2005). While insiders adopt cooperative approaches trying to exert influence from within, outsiders prefer to apply pressure from the outside by engaging in direct action. Typically they have no access to institutions, or reject the rules of the game, refusing to get involved.

Emancipatory communication activists, however, hardly fall within this dichotomy. Rather, they operate "beyond" institutions and norms. They tend to refuse to stay within the rules of the game of the known social system. For them, action is not merely a matter of rejecting institutions, nor one of interacting with them within a stable social system that is taken for granted. Instead, it is a matter of discarding that social system itself. In short, they reject both insider and outsider tactics because both of them stay within the boundaries of the system as it is, rather than subverting it. As an activist explained, "Trying to have a voice from below within the spheres of 'mainstream politics' […] just legitimates those power structures" (Milan 2013, 126). Mobilizing beyond institutions and social norms is a process of "redefinition or explosion of power" as we know it (Jordan 2002, 33).

Alongside refusing direct interaction with institutions, these groups have a message for society: they want a different social order. But rather than building influence or creating special-interest organizations, they attempt to create parallel *prefigurative realities*. These attempt to achieve here and now the principles (of horizontality, equality, participation, etc.) advocated by activists. In doing so, they aim to generate a new world, and to redefine social structures from scratch. In the words of the activists, "the political goal is to create counter-power, not to oppose it but … like in the Indymedia slogan: 'don't hate the media, become the media'" (Milan 2013, 127).

The creation of prefigurative realities has emancipatory, signaling, expressive, and even a support function for activists. In this sense, Porter's observations on anarchist "liberated areas" can apply to the "liberated spaces" of emancipatory communication practices. Porter wrote that "any liberated areas, however limited, are a challenge to the capitalist order. The challenge lies in their visceral resistance to and struggle against the system, and in their offering time and space for potentially less sublimated behaviors. […] Such zones sustain the energies of militants" (Porter 1979, 223–224). Emancipation, as taking control over one's communications, is achieved through participation, and is attained whenever individuals and groups directly experience the alternative.

According to Downing (1984), the creation of radical media signals the need to think of liberation as an everyday process that disrupts immediate realities. Activists attempt to "create little islands of prefigurative politics with no empirical attention to how these might ever be expanded into the rest of society" (Downing 2001, 72). These "little islands" closely resemble the prefigurative actions of social actors that position themselves beyond institutions and social norms. Not surprisingly, the notion of prefigurative realities is strictly linked to anarchism, and feminist anarchism in particular. Quoting the feminist thinker Sheila Rowbotham, Downing stressed how the vision of a more just society cannot be detached from the process of its making. Politics "must provide staging posts along the way, moments of transformation, however small" (Downing 2001, 72).

Emancipatory communication initiatives might occasionally break the law, as they operate on the basis of alternative sets of values. They position themselves as independent from other social structures and institutional processes in general. As an activist explains: "My main focus is bypass the mainstream by creating living alternatives to it. Our job, as activists, is to create self-managed infrastructures that work *regardless of* 'their' regulation, laws, or any other form of governance" (Milan 2013, 130). The "regardless of" evokes autonomy, independence, and self-determination, but it also indicates a disregard for societal norms and rules. Frequently, emancipatory communication activists see institutions and norms as potential interference that can endanger the prefigurative autonomous zones (Hintz and Milan 2009).

However, emancipatory communication activists do react when laws, regulations, or police repression threaten their activities and values, acting as moral shocks fostering collective action. Their tactical repertoire in such cases includes avoiding control, the creation of technical bypasses to evade legislation, the hacking of norms and conventions, re-appropriation, and all those "obscure technically savvy ways of circumventing limitations" (Milan 2013, 132). It is the "engineering philosophy to 'make things work'" that encounters an "insistence on adopting a technocratic approach to solving societal problems and to bypassing ('hacking') legislative approaches" (Berry 2008, 102).

New Geographies between Local and Transnational

Emancipatory communication projects are often small in scale and operate locally, but they typically share values and practices with like-minded groups and individuals across borders. These values are rooted on the very same properties of the medium they mobilize around: for example, openness and making for tech projects, and grassroots participation and communitarian ethos for radio and television stations. They identify a sort of transnational imaginary that fosters mutual recognition, which works as a transnational framing mechanism "through which physically, socially, and culturally dispersed social actors develop a degree of common understanding" (Olesen 2005, 22) that originates informal transnational networks. Infused with a strong global consciousness, or "the ability to think about the world and humankind as a single entity" (17) typical of progressive activists, these networks are embedded in broader social movement arrangements working for social justice.

These networks are mobilized at need, in occasion of knowledge-exchange events or in the presence of threats. Events like the World Summit on the Information Society—which attracted the attention of many radical techies that mobilized at its margins and rigorously outside the summit compound, or threats like server seizure or repression, function as catalyzing moments that coalesce these transnational networks. Groups exploit these moments to interact, get to know each other, and create the basis for mutual recognition, joint agendas, and shared discourses. They are instrumental in creating and reproducing linkages across borders, and in promoting a common belief system. They represent the physical and symbolic space within which practitioners, who are usually grounded in bounded communities, experience the transnational dimension of their activism.

Peer networks are crucial for skills sharing and self-defense purposes. Networks can be national, regional, and international, and they often overlap; they can be online and offline, and can connect both individuals and/or groups. They strengthen the position of otherwise fragile projects, functioning as an alert and self-defense mechanism to be mobilized in the case of repression. More often than not, these networks are informal; sometimes they take the shape of membership associations, and occasionally they operate underground.

It is worth noting that individuals play a crucial role in network creation and maintenance. Usually experts, they act as norm entrepreneurs and connection nodes able to bind together the local and the transnational dimension. They can be seen as "rooted cosmopolitans" (Tarrow 2005, 42), because they are able to connect their groups with transnational networks.

According to their function, we can distinguish between three types of networks: instrumental, exchange-based, and self-defense networks. Instrumental networks are those asymmetrical linkages that are established between emancipatory media as service providers and their users. These networks are rooted in a set of shared values, on the basis of which the service (e-mail accounts, web space, broadcasting, etc.) is required and offered. Networks of peers are created on an affinity basis, while we have exchange-based networks when individuals with similar expertise are connected to enable knowledge sharing and capacity building. These networks also tend to be online, and are visible offline only at convergence spaces. Finally, self-defense networks are often created on a need basis, and act as safety nets. To be sure, networking is a "condition for sustainability" (Milan 2013, 144) for emancipatory communication projects.

In Conclusion: Emancipatory Communication and Civic Media after Snowden

The Snowden revelations have made clear that, as Braman put it, "governments deliberately, explicitly, and consistently control information creation, processing, flows, and use to exercise power" (Braman 2009, 1). States and security agencies rely on "corporate collaboration" (MacKinnon 2012, 56) to monitor their citizens and implement regulations (c.f. Deibert 2013). In times of aggressive corporatization, increasing enclosure of communication spaces, and blanket surveillance, emancipatory communication practices appear to be particularly well suited to offer concrete alternatives to activists and citizens alike. With their focus on the reconfiguration of power through prefigurative action, practitioners take action against a mainstream system that they consider to be governed by distorted values and illegitimate actors. They seek to expand unregulated spaces, and often bypass threats through technical fixes. In other words, they seek to defend the civil and digital rights of citizens as they meet communication rights (see Brevini, Hintz, and McCurdy 2013; Padovani and Calabrese 2014) and the exercise of democratic participation in the mediascape.

While emancipatory communication practices and civic media more generally are not new, today's scale, autonomy, and self-sufficiency of the phenomenon is unprecedented. It is a function of the availability and diffusion of digital technology, which opens up spaces for experimentation and engagement. Far from operating exclusively on the fringes of society, emancipatory communication projects and activists have started to intervene in public debates, as WikiLeaks and Anonymous have shown. Their importance in this historical moment is dual: on the one hand, they offer options for participation in civic life, and secure, commercial-free spaces where people can communicate on their own terms, and on the other, their prefigurative realities are the harbinger of a more just and more secure mediascape to come. They show that an alternative, safer space for communication and democratic participation is not only possible, but probably also desirable.

References

Atton, Chris. 2002. *Alternative Media*. London: Sage.

Atton, Chris. 2004. *An Alternative Internet: Radical Media, Politics and Creativity*. Edinburgh: Edinburgh University Press.

Bennett, Lance W., and Alexandra Segerberg. 2013. *The Logic of Connective Action: Digital Media and the Personalization of Contentious Politics*. Cambridge: Cambridge University Press.

Berry, D. M. 2008. *Copy, Rip, Burn: The Politics of Copyleft and Open Source*. London: Pluto Press.

Braman, Sandra. 2009. *Change of State: Information, Policy, and Power*. Cambridge, MA: MIT Press.

Brevini, Benedetta, Arne Hintz, and Patrick McCurdy. 2013. *Beyond WikiLeaks: Implications for the Future of Communications, Journalism and Society*. Basingstoke, UK: Palgrave Macmillan.

Carroll, William K., and Robert A. Hackett. 2006. "Democratic Media Activism through the Lens of Social Movement Theory." *Media, Culture & Society* 28 (1): 83–104.

Clemens, E. S., and D. C. Minkoff. 2004. "Beyond the Iron Law: Rethinking the Place of Organizations in Social Movements Research." In *The Blackwell Companion to Social Movements*, ed. D. A. Snow, S. A. Soule, and H. Kriesi, 155–170. Oxford: Blackwell.

Coleman, Gabriella. 2013. *Coding Freedom: The Ethics and Aesthetics of Hacking*. Princeton: Princeton University Press.

Coleman, Gabriella. 2014. *Hacker, Hoaxer, Whistleblower, Spy: The Many Faces of Anonymous*. New York: Verso.

Critical Art Ensemble. 2001. *Digital Resistance: Explorations in Tactical Media*. New York: Autonomedia.

D'Arcy, J. 1969. "Direct Broadcast Satellites and the Right of Man to Communicate." *EBU Review* 118:14–18.

Deibert, Ronald J. 2013. *Black Code: Inside the Battle for Cyberspace*. Toronto: McClelland & Stewart.

della Porta, Donatella, and Sidney Tarrow, eds. 2005. *Transnational Protest and Global Activism*. Lanham, MA: Rowman & Littlefield.

Diamond, L. 2010. "Liberation Technology." *Journal of Democracy* 3:69–83.

Downing, John D. H. 1984. *Radical Media: The Political Experience of Alternative Communication*. Boston: South End Press.

Downing, John D. H. 2001. *Radical Media: Rebellious Communication and Social Movements*. Thousand Oaks, CA: Sage.

Downing, John D. H. 2011. *Encyclopedia of Social Movement Media*. Thousand Oaks, CA: Sage.

Dunbar-Hester, Christina. 2014. *Low Power to the People! Pirates, Protest, and Politics in FM Radio Activism*. Cambridge, MA: MIT Press.

Flacks, R. 2005. "The Questions of Relevance in Social Movement Studies." In *Rhyming Hope and History: Activists, Academics, and Social Movement Scholarship*, ed. D. Croteau, W. Hoynes, and C. Ryan, 3–19. Minneapolis: University of Minnesota Press.

Freeman, Jo. 1972. "The Tyranny of Structurelessness." *Berkeley Journal of Sociology* 17:151–165.

Free Software Foundation. 1987. "The GNU Manifesto." http://www.gnu.org/gnu/manifesto.html.

Goldkuhl, Göran. 2013. "The IT Artefact: An Ensemble of the Social and the Technical? A Rejoinder." *Systems, Signs & Actions* 7:90–99.

Gumucio-Dagron, A. 2001. *Making Waves: Stories of Participatory Communication for Social Change: A Report to the Rockefeller Foundation*. New York: Rockefeller Foundation.

Halleck, D. 2002. *Hand-Held Visions: The Impossible Possibilities of Community Media*. New York: Fordham University Press.

Hamelink, C. 1983. *Cultural Autonomy in Global Communications*. London: Longman.

Hintz, Arne. 2012. "Challenging the Digital Gatekeepers: International Policy Initiatives for Free Expression." *Journal of Information Policy* 2:128–150.

Hintz, Arne, and Stefania Milan. 2009. "At the Margins of Internet Governance: Grassroots Tech Groups and Communication Policy." *International Journal of Media & Cultural Politics* 5 (1/2): 23–38.

Husband, C. 2005. "Minority Ethnic Media As Communities of Practice: Professionalism and Identity Politics in Interaction." *Journal of Ethnic and Migration Studies* 31 (3): 461–479.

Interdoc. 1984. *The Velletri Agreement*. Neijmegen: Antenna.

Jasper, James. 1997. *The Art of Moral Protest: Culture, Biography, and Creativity in Social Movements*. Chicago: Chicago University Press.

Jordan, Tim. 2002. *Activism! Direct Action, Hacktivism and the Future of Society*. London: Reaktion Books.

Juris, Jeffrey S. 2008. *Networking Futures: The Movements Against Corporate Globalization*. Durham, NC: Duke University Press.

Kaldor, M. 2003. *Global Civil Society: An Answer to War*. Cambridge: Polity Press.

Kidd, Dorothy. 2010. "Indymedia (The Independent Media Center)." In *Encyclopedia of Social Movement Media*, ed. John D. H. Downing, 267–270. Los Angeles: Sage.

MacBride, S. 1980. *Many Voices, One World: Report of the International Commission for the Study of Communication Problems*. Paris: UNESCO.

MacKinnon, Rebecca. 2012. *Consent of the Networked: The Worldwide Struggle for Internet Freedom*. New York: Basic Books.

McChesney, R. W., and J. Nichols. 2002. "The Making of a Movement." *Nation,* January 7.

McDonald, Kevin. 2002. "From Solidarity to Fluidarity: Social Movements Beyond 'Collective Identity'—the Case of Globalization Conflicts." *Social Movement Studies* 1:109–128.

McDonald, Kevin. 2004. "One as Another: From Social Movement to Experience Movement." *Current Sociology* 52 (4): 575–593.

McDonald, Kevin. 2006. *Global Movements: Action and Culture.* Malden, MA: Blackwell.

Melucci, Alberto. 1989. *Nomads of the Present: Social Movements and Individual Needs in Contemporary Society.* London: Hutchinson Radius.

Melucci, Alberto. 1996. *Challenging Codes: Collective Action in the Information Age.* Cambridge: Cambridge University Press.

Milan, Stefania. 2013. *Social Movements and Their Technologies: Wiring Social Change.* London: Palgrave Macmillan.

Milan, Stefania. 2014. "NETmundial: Is There a New Guard of Civil Society Coming to the Internet Governance Fore?" *CGCS Media Wire,* April 24. http://www.global.asc.upenn.edu/netmundial-is-there-a-new-guard-of-civil-society-coming-to-the-internet-governance-fore/.

Milan, Stefania. 2015. "Hacktivism as a Radical Media Practice." In *Routledge Companion to Alternative and Community Media,* ed. Chris Atton, 550–560. New York: Routledge.

Milan, Stefania, and Arne Hintz. 2013. "Networked Collective Action and the Institutionalized Policy Debate: Bringing Cyberactivism to the Policy Arena?" *Policy & Internet* 5 (1): 7–26.

Murphy, Brian M. 2000. "The Founding of APC: Coincidences and Logical Steps in Global Civil Society Networking." Association for Progressive Communications Annual Report 2000. Association for Progressive Communications. http://www.apc.org/about/history/coincidences-and-logical-steps-in-networking.

Murphy, Brian M. 2005. "Interdoc: The First International Non-Governmental Computer Network." *First Monday* 10 (5). http://firstmonday.org/ojs/index.php/fm/article/view/1239/1159.

Nordenstreng, K., and M. Traber. 1992. *Few Voices, Many Worlds: Towards a Media Reform Movement.* London: World Association of Christian Communications.

Olesen, T. 2005. *International Zapatismo: The Construction of Solidarity in the Age of Globalization.* London: Zed Books.

Padovani, C., and A. Calabrese. 2014. Communication Rights and Social Justice: Historical Accounts of Transnational Mobilizations. London: Palgrave Macmillan.

Pelizza, Annalisa. 2006. "Comunicare L'immediatezza. Una televisione di strada a Rotterdam." *Inchiesta: Rivista di Studi Politici* 152.

Polletta, Francesca. 2002. *Freedom Is an Endless Meeting: Democracy in American Social Movements.* Chicago: University of Chicago Press.

Polletta, Francesca, and James M. Jasper. 2001. "Collective Identity and Social Movements." *American Review of Sociology* 27:283–305.

Porter, D. 1979. "Revolutionary Realization: The Motivational Energy." In *Reinventing Anarchy*, ed. H. J. Ehrlich, 214–228. London: Routledge and Kegal Paul.

Powell, A. 2008. "Co-Productions of Technology, Culture and Policy in the North American Community Wireless Networking Movement." *Information, Communication and Society* 11 (8): 1068–1088.

Rennie, E. 2006. *Community Media: A Global Introduction*. Lanham, MA: Rowman & Littlefield.

Rodriguez, C. 2001. *Fissures in the Mediascape: An International Study of Citizens' Media*. Cresskill, NJ: Hampton Press.

Rodriguez, C. 2011. *Citizens' Media Against Armed Conflict: Disrupting Violence in Colombia*. Minneapolis: University of Minnesota Press.

Snow, David A. 2001. "Collective Identity and Expressive Forms." In *International Encyclopedia of the Social and Behavioral Sciences*, ed. Neil J. Smelser and Paul B. Baltes, 2212–2219. London: Elsevier.

Tarrow, S. 1998. *Power in Movement: Social Movements and Contentious Politics*. Cambridge: Cambridge University Press.

Tarrow, Sidney. 2005. *The New Transnational Activism*. New York: Cambridge University Press.

Taylor, Verta, and Nancy van Dyke. 2004. "'Get Up, Stand Up': Tactical Repertoires of Social Movements." In *The Blackwell Companion to Social Movements*, ed. David A. Snow, Sarah A. Soule, and Hanspeter Kriesi, 262–293. Malden, MA: Blackwell.

Tilly, Charles. 1983. "Speaking Your Mind Without Election, Surveys, and Social Movements." *Public Opinion Quarterly* 47 (4): 461–478.

5 Case Study: "Bury until They Change Their Ways"—The Digg Patriots and/as User-Generated Censorship

Chris Peterson

Introduction to the Digg Patriots and User-Generated Censorship

In May 2009, an *ad hoc* coalition of politically conservative members of the social news site Digg collectively founded a Yahoo! Group community and mailing list, calling it the Digg Patriots. The Patriots were united by a shared self-identification with movement conservatism, a belief that liberal users of Digg were profoundly wrongheaded, and a desire to terraform the political landscape of Digg to be more consonant with their conservatism.

SUBJ: Re: DiggPatriots-Whining again

I'll continue to bury their submissions until they change their ways and become conservatives. =^)

—VRayZ, June 6, 2010[1]

As a graduate student at MIT, I studied the Digg Patriots as a case of what I call *user-generated censorship:* a mode of political activism through which actors manipulate the affordances of social media to suppress speech.[2] I argue that the same tools and systems designed to facilitate speech can be and have been repurposed to suppress it, through "flagging" campaigns on Facebook,[3] downvote bots on reddit,[4] NegativeSEO on Google Search,[5] and other similar approaches. Because their mailing lists were leaked in August 2010,[6] the Digg Patriots present an unusually well-documented case of user-generated censorship. I reviewed nearly 13,000 emails exchanged among the Patriots over the course of 11 months as they coordinated their campaign to make Digg more conservative.

"Any Chair in a Bar Fight": Strategy and Tactics of the Digg Patriots

Digg was one of the most popular websites in the world during the Patriots' campaign to make it more conservative.[7] A "social news" site, Digg allowed users to submit links

Figure 5.1
The homepage of the Digg Patriots Yahoo! Group in August 2010.

to external content such as news stories or videos. Other users would then vote to "digg" or "bury" the links, which, along with other factors including recency and comment activity, would algorithmically cause those links to rise or fall in an ordinal ranking and becoming more or less visible to Digg's ~30 million monthly visitors. The Digg Patriots developed a set of crude-but-effective and even-a-bit-ingenious techniques, which let them leverage these algorithmic inputs to alter the political composition of Digg.

Coordinated Digging and Burying

The Patriots' primary method was to coordinate votes through the Yahoo! Group. When a Patriot identified a newly submitted link as liberal he or she would quickly forward the link to the entire group with a synopsis and an urgent call for burying. The Patriots also coordinated "up" votes for conservative links, particularly posts made by fellow Patriots. Although almost 7,000 targeted links are included in the corpus, this drastically *underrepresents* the total activity of the Patriots: from April 2009 to August 2010 a single Patriot dugg an astounding 76,000 links and submitted over 1,600 articles, 20 percent of which made the front page with assistance from her allies.[8]

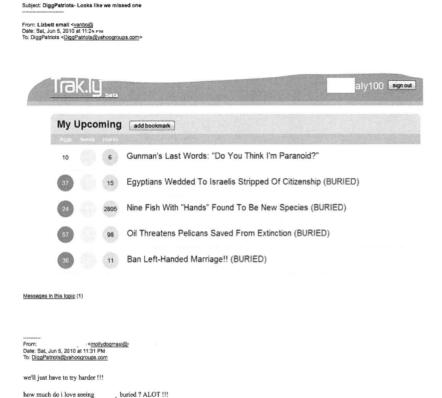

Subject: DiggPatriots- Looks like we missed one

From: Lizbett email <vanbo@
Date: Sat, Jun 5, 2010 at 11:24 PM
To: DiggPatriots <DiggPatriots@yahoogroups.com>

From: <mollydogmaxi@
Date: Sat, Jun 5, 2010 at 11:31 PM
To: DiggPatriots@yahoogroups.com

we'll just have to try harder !!!

how much do i love seeing   _ buried ? ALOT !!!

Figure 5.2
A screenshot circulated among the Patriots celebrating they had successfully buried four of the
five most recent articles submitted by a liberal user they tracked.

Strategic Comment Activity

SUBJ: Re—BurY Mutual?

Please, Please, stop the discussions. You are playing right into their hands. If you just can't help
yourself, then Maybe you should find another outlet for your frustration. I spend far too much
time on Digg to see it wasted by immature sniping. I hope no one is offended, but remember why
we are here. We want to Depress the progressive stories, while encouraging conservative ones.

—rgcmsg G, March 29, 2010[9]

Digg allowed users to comment on links and incorporated comment activity as an
index of interest such that, all things being equal, links with more comments would
rise, and links with fewer would fall. The Patriots harnessed this dynamic to their

advantage, discouraging members from commenting on liberal posts ("Venting here, so I don't violate DP discipline and comment on a submission we're trying to bury")[10] and purposefully trolling the comments of conservative posts to bait liberals into responding ("We probably should concentrate on … creating conversational comments to pull in more people to comment when they come by to digg on our stories").[11] By doing so, the Patriots inverted the conception of the comment section, flipping its function from a *sphere* of deliberative discourse to an *instrument* of its suppression.

Cultivating Alliances to Extend Influence

SUBJ: RE: FP for J!

Okay folks, want to hit FP often? Follow J's lead. He's got 90+ friends all who digg early (this is key). If you can cultivate 90–100 friends like this your subs will hit on a regular basis, but cultivating this many GOOD friends requires you to do the same for them. Gotta digg 'em early and never miss.

—phil d., June 17, 2010[12]

The Patriots expanded their ranks by recruiting small armies of "mutuals," unaffiliated users at the other end of a symmetrical relationship, which allowed two Digg users to see what the other had submitted. A Patriot would identify highly active Diggers to request mutual status. The Patriot would then groom the mutuals, monitoring how rapidly and regularly they (the mutuals) would upvote Patriot submissions, retaining those who reliably did so quickly and dropping those who did not. The Patriots, who were in other respects ultrapartisans, adopted a highly pragmatic approach when it came to grooming their mutuals ("I don't befriend based on someone's politics. I look at their stats").[13] The most highly prized mutuals were also (and because of) the most dehumanized: those which could be treated as black boxes, mechanical reproducers of input -> output, almost an extension of the Digg algorithm itself.

"A Rude Wake-Up Call": Reading the Digg Patriots

SUBJ: Re: Digg Patriots

In short, the Digg Patriots was a response to a wave of leftism that had grown smug and arrogant in its presence on Digg. We were a rude wake-up call that there were those who felt otherwise within Digg.

—R.J. Carter, February 12, 2013[14]

On August 5, 2010, a muckraking blogger and progressive activist writing under the name of OleOleOlson revealed the existence of the Patriots in a blog post for *Alternet*.[15]

Since Olson's exposé, the Patriots have been considered mostly unsympathetically by the few popular press articles which have referenced them. When you read the emails, especially those excerpts Olson chose to highlight, it's easy to see why: many are rife with the worst sexist, racist, and homophobic slurs characteristic of the rotten base of contemporary movement conservatism. Yet the character of their cause is, from the perspective of digital civics, more complex:

SUBJ: Re: Bury Now Novahater's sub

Again the question arises about the validity of us organizing through email …

I feel we are far outnumbered. So does that make what we do right?

To fight for what is right and just, I would say yes. Hopefully more people will see our beliefs as the right way. We're called the right for a reason.

—R.J.C., October 29, 2009[16]

The Patriots understood that the authorized logic of Digg, which both designed for and demanded "independent," uncoordinated voters, was a crudely majoritarian model, and thus not "neutral" in its effect but in fact reproductive of the majority's politics. Since (they believed) liberals outnumbered conservatives on Digg, without coordination the conservative viewpoint would lose, and so they needed to support each other to give their perspective a fighting chance. Both Olson and I have characterized the Patriots as censors, but from a different perspective they could be read as a determined minority mobilizing a fully sympathetic Get Out the Vote effort to "wake up" other users and have their voices heard.

The story of the Digg Patriots, like any text, can be and in fact is read differently by different readers: how you feel about their mission and methods says rather less about the Patriots themselves than about how you believe digital civics should properly be practiced. The hotly contested case of the Patriots, along with many analogues across civic media, reminds us that we have still not yet settled on a stable consensus on how these new sociotechnical systems ought to work, and ought to *be* worked, as critical levers of power in our emerging networked political apparatus.

Notes

1. Document 20100606-DiggPatriots-Whining-again-1877.html, on file with the author.

2. Chris Peterson, "User-Generated Censorship: Manipulating the Maps of Social Media" (master's thesis, Massachusetts Institute of Technology, 2007), esp. at 9–10, http://dspace.mit.edu/handle/1721.1/81132.

3. Jillian York, "Policing Content in the Quasi-Public Sphere," *OpenNet Initiative*, September 2010. https://opennet.net/sites/opennet.net/files/PolicingContent.pdf; Jillian York, "AllFacebook

.com Editor Uses Bully Pulpit in Attempt to Remove Facebook Page," March 21, 2011, http://jilliancyork.com/2011/03/21/allfacebook-com-editor-uses-bully-pulpit-to-remove-facebook-page.

4. Chris Peterson, "The Fault, Dear Reddit, Is Not in Our Bots, But in Ourselves: The Case of LibertyBot," *MIT Center for Civic Media,* March 22, 2013, http://civic.mit.edu/blog/petey/the-fault-is-not-in-our-bots-dear-reddit-but-in-ourselves-the-case-of-libertybot.

5. Chris Peterson, "Google NegativeSEO: Case Study in User-Generated Censorship," *MIT Center for Civic Media*, March 20, 2013, http://civic.mit.edu/blog/petey/google-negativeseo-case-study-in-user-generated-censorship.

6. For information about the origins, controversies, and considerations of the corpus, please see Peterson, *supra* at 3, Appendix A.1.

7. Sara Lacy and Jessi Hempel, "Valley Boys," *BusinessWeek*, August 13, 2006, http://www.businessweek.com/stories/2006-08-13/valley-boys.

8. For Lizbett's statistics, see http://socialblade.com/digg/top1000users.html under name "bettverboten." Statistics for her original account, "lizbett," can be seen at http://socialblade.com/digg/topgraveyard.html. Both links accessed on May 24, 2013.

9. Document 20100329-DiggPatriots-BurY-Mutual-12404.html, on file with the author.

10. Document 20100326-DiggPatriots-Bury-12308.html, on file with the author.

11. Document 20100212-DiggPatriots-Re-Novahators-Sub-More-BURY-13994.html, on file with the author.

12. Document 20100617-DiggPatriots-FP-for-J-1836.html, on file with the author.

13. 20091219-DiggPatriots-Re-Bury-9896.html.

14. R. J. Carter, in email to the author, February 12, 2013.

15. OleOleOlson, "Massive Censorship of Digg Uncovered," *Alternet*, August 5, 2010, http://blogs.alternet.org/oleoleolson/2010/08/05/massive-censorship-of-digg-uncovered.

16. Document 20091029-DiggPatriots-Bury-Now-Novahaters-sub-14422.html, on file with the author.

6 Case Study: Marriage Equality, Facebook Profile Pictures, and Civic Participation

Brady Robards and Bob Buttigieg

On March 25, 2013, the Human Rights Campaign (HRC)—a lesbian, gay, bisexual, and transgender (LGBT) lobby—urged people to change their Facebook profile pictures to a pink-on-red equals sign to show support for marriage equality (see figure 6.1). The campaign corresponded with a U.S. Supreme Court meeting to debate the issue. Shortly after, on March 30, Eytan Bashky (2013) from the Facebook data science team reported that "roughly 2.7 million (120%) more [users], updated their profile photo on Tuesday, March 26, compared to the previous Tuesday," which was roughly attributed to the HRC push. The campaign to change Facebook profile pictures spread to become a global phenomenon. Variations on the HRC profile picture emerged, some in support of the campaign, others opposing it, and others critiquing the impact changing one's profile picture can have. In this case study, we explore the campaign through the lens of the "actualizing citizen" (Miegel and Olsson 2007) and discourses around "slacktivism" (Christensen 2011).

Variations on a Meme

After posting their call to action, a range of variations to the HRC's image emerged, notably including several brands that sought to "hitch their wagon" to the campaign, such as Maybelline, Absolut Vodka, and Bud Light (see figure 6.2). These brands were able to associate themselves with the goodwill of the campaign, and also "plug into" its viral spread.

Critiques

Other variations were created, some seemingly critical of the effectiveness of the campaign itself (see figure 6.3). In the first example from this figure, a critique against assimilating into the heteronormative institution of marriage is mounted, inviting viewers (especially queer viewers) to re-think the value of marriage as an institution itself. In other words, "to extend the conformist embrace of marriage to same-sex

Figure 6.1
Screen capture from the public HRC Facebook page, taken July 1, 2014.

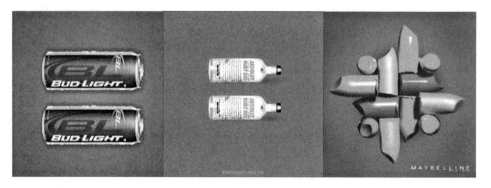

Figure 6.2
Branding: Variations on a meme.

couples is to lack imagination" (Jagose 2013). In the second example from this figure, the "spectre of the slacktivist" is invoked, representing a pessimistic reading of the HRC's movement as an effective form of civic participation and ridiculing the people who have "done [their] part" by simply changing their profile pictures.

Defining Civic Participation

How, then, can the effectiveness of forms of civic participation that play out online—as per the HRC case study—be measured? What actually constitutes civic participation? The Australian Bureau of Statistics (ABS) uses the following definition:

In measuring civic participation, we consider collective and individual activities that reflect interest and engagement with governance and democracy: for example, membership of civic organisations such as political parties and trade unions; serving on committees or clubs, voluntary organisations, and associations; contacting members of parliament; participating in demonstrations and rallies; and attending community consultations.

This definition silences informal modes of civic participation such as conversations that occur in everyday settings, in schools, pubs, and over dinner tables. As per this case study, informal acts of civic participation are also mediated online, but rather than vanishing into the ether or human memory, as with physical conversations (that are not recorded), conversations mediated online leave "digital traces" (Bowker 2007), and this is a reality with which we are still coming to terms. The profile picture is one such digital trace. Recently, scholars have argued for a broader definition of civic participation. Christensen (2011) argues that even though we cannot effectively measure the impact of online political activities on traditional forms of civic participation (as per the ABS definition above, for instance), the activities of whom he describes as "internet activists" can serve to "invigorate" and "reinforce" a broader sense of civic participation. Similarly, Vie (2014) argues that "digital activism made possible through social media memes can build awareness of crucial issues, which can then lead to action."

In studying how young people engage in democracy online, Miegel and Olsson (2007, 231) consider a shift in conceptualisations of citizenship from what they describe (via Bennett 2008) as the "dutiful citizen" toward the actualizing citizen. Whereas voting and joining a political party are at the core of civic participation for the dutiful citizen (as per the ABS definition), the actualizing citizen participates in civic life differently, favoring loose networks of community action and "personally defined acts of participation" (Miegel and Olsson 2007, 231) over voting, rigid party-based politics, and other traditional, institutionally sanctioned forms of action.

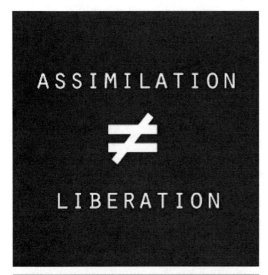

Figure 6.3
Critiques: (a) "Assimilation does not equal liberation"; and (b) "Welp, I've done my part!"

Conclusion

What constitutes civic participation is clearly changing, and the social web is part of this. As Harris, Wyn, and Younes (2010, 27) argue, the social web can allow people a place to "have a say," giving them a voice in an arena (civic life) that is otherwise dominated by people with power. Thus, perhaps changing a Facebook profile picture to support marriage equality can constitute a valid, generative, and even "invigorating" (Christensen 2011) form of civic engagement. Even though these performances of civic participation are mediated online, they should not be rendered less valuable, as somehow "not real." Indeed, visibility (and the awareness that comes with being seen) does not just lead to action, but it is also a form of action in itself. While it is difficult to quantify the full outcome of this social media campaign for the HRC, even commandeered (figure 6.3a) or critical (figure 6.3b) reinterpretations of the pink-on-red equals sign contain important semiotic links back to the HRC, to the movement in support of marriage equality, and to the historic contexts in which the movement arose, elevating the campaign's visibility. The figure of 2.7 million more U.S. users changing their profile pictures on March 26, 2013, compared with the previous Tuesday (Bashky 2013) is presumably only the tip of the iceberg here, as the meme continued to circulate in the days (and weeks) following, across the globe. Indeed, among our own networks in Australia, the original image is still set as the profile picture for some users. Viewers are engaged to consider these images by the prominence and importance of profile images on Facebook, potentially sparking discussion and reflection both on- and offline. Individual-centered, personally motivated forms of civic participation mediated online can represent an important part of a reconceptualisation of civic life. By adjusting the lens through which civic participation is measured, a rich terrain of engagement will be made visible.

References

Australian Bureau of Statistics. 2010. "1370.0—Measures of Australia's Progress," *Democracy, Governance, and Citizenship*. http://www.abs.gov.au/ausstats/abs@.nsf/Lookup/by%20Subject/1370 .0~2010~Chapter~Democracy%20governance%20and%20citizenship%20and%20progress%20 %284.6.1%29.

Bashky, Eytan. 2013. "Showing Support for Marriage Equality on Facebook." *Facebook.* https:// www.facebook.com/notes/facebook-data-science/showing-support-for-marriage-equality-on -facebook/10151430548593859.

Bennett, W. Lance. 2008. "Changing Citizenship in the Digital Age." In *Civic Life Online: Learning How Digital Media Can Engage Youth*, ed. W. Lance Bennett, 1–24. Cambridge, MA: MIT Press.

Bowker, Geoffrey C. 2007. "The Past and the Internet." In *Structures of Participation in Digital Culture*, ed. Joe Karaganis, 20–36. New York: Columbia University Press.

Christensen, Henrik S. 2011. "Political Activities on the Internet: *Slacktivism* or Political Participation by Other Means?" *First Monday* 16 (2). doi: Accessed June 3, 2012.10.5210/fm.v16i2.3336.

Harris, Anita, Johanna Wyn, and Salem Younes. 2010. "Beyond Apathetic or Activist Youth: 'Ordinary' Young People and Contemporary Forms of Participation." *Young* 18 (1): 9–32.

Jagose, Annamarie. 2013. "The trouble with gay marriage." *The Conversation.* http://theconversation.com/the-trouble-with-gay-marriage-19196.

Miegel, Fredrik, and Tobias Olsson. 2007. "Invited but Ignored. How www.ungtval.se Aimed to Foster but Failed to Promote Youth Engagement." In *Young People, ICTs and Democracy*, ed. Tobias Olsson and Peter Dahlgren, 231–246. Gothenburg: Nordicom.

Vie, Stephanie. 2014. "In Defense of 'Slacktivism': The Human Rights Campaign Facebook Logo as Digital Activism." *First Monday* 19 (4). doi: Accessed June 28, 2014.10.2139/ssrn.2179035.

7 Case Study: Strike Debt and the Rolling Jubilee—Building a Debt Resistance Movement

Erhardt Graeff

From *The Debt Resisters' Operations Manual*:

There are countless ways to "strike" debt: demanding a people's bailout and an end to corporate welfare; collectively refusing to pay illegitimate loans; targeting and shutting down collections agencies, payday lenders, or for-profit colleges; regulating loan speculators out of business; reinstating limits on usurious interest rates; defending foreclosed homes; fighting tuition hikes and school budget cuts; resisting austerity policies; fighting militarism, which accounts for half of our nation's discretionary spending; organizing debtors' associations and unions; and more. On the constructive side, building an alternative economy run for mutual benefits is a long-term goal. (Strike Debt 2014, 213)

Growing out of Occupy Wall Street, Strike Debt has been working since May 2012 to build a social movement through various forms of media and market-based activism under the banner of "debt resistance." They cite the history of Biblical jubilees that canceled debt to normalize society (Graeber 2011), the debtor movement like El Barzon in Mexico (Caffentzis 2013), and "mortgage strikes" by Empowering and Strengthening Ohio's Peoples (Strike Debt 2014, 93), to make an intellectual and moral argument for debt resistance against the contemporary *system* of debt, which in their analysis causes dehumanizing shame and suffering. They describe debt as a weapon and a web that catches you—as soon as you pay off one loan you are indebted for another reason (Graeff and Bhargava 2014).

Prehistory of Strike Debt

In the midst of Occupy Wall Street (OWS) on October 23, 2011, at ContactCon, artist and activist Thomas Gokey, inspired by his own struggles with student debt, his participation in "war tax resistance," and conversations with others at Zuccotti Park, proposed building a reverse KickStarter or "Kick-Stopper," a platform for organizing a large scale debt strike that could collect pledges from participants and coordinate the payment of debt into escrow rather than to big banks (2011a; n.d.). It went on to win

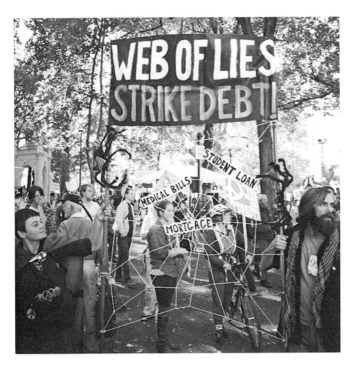

Figure 7.1
Strike Debt banner at S17 (photograph by Chase Wilson in Portland, Oregon, September 17, 2012).

acclaim as one of the most actionable ideas at the conference (Jaffe 2011). While Kick-Stopper was in development via a mailing list,[1] Gokey had started working on a related idea for buying and forgiving debt with Adbusters's Micah White (Gokey 2011b; White 2014). White had imagined the idea back in 2009,[2] and later received input from David Graeber, who wrote about the history of debt forgiveness "jubilees" in his book *Debt: The First 5,000 Years* (White 2014).

Back at Zuccotti Park, the Occupy Student Debt Campaign (OSDC) formed from assemblies involving sociologist and activist Andrew Ross (Larson and Smith 2014). Growing out of Occupy Wall Street's Education & Empowerment Working Group, OSDC developed a debt refusal pledge campaign, which they launched November 21, 2011. The campaign called for one million signatories, who would pledge to default on their debt en masse once the million person threshold was met. OSDC distributed the pledge and related information and collected stories of indebtedness through their website.[3] Their focus on debt refusal as an explicit alternative strategy to legislative action differentiated OSDC from prior initiatives like Student Loan Justice[4] (n.d.), and gained enough notoriety to merit the inclusion of their "debt strike" as a new tactic in

Andrew Boyd's *Beautiful Trouble* (Jaffe and Skomarovsky 2012). However, the OSDC pledge was ultimately unsuccessful.

In response to OWS's disaggregation after actions on May Day 2012, Occupy Theory, the working group of OWS publication *Tidal,* held a series of assemblies in Washington Square Park. One of the early assemblies co-organized with OSDC and Free University was on Education and Debt in solidarity with student strikes in Montreal; it attracted many OWS-affiliated organizers and participants looking at mortgages, education, or other debt-related and social justice issues (Hiscott 2013; Strike Debt 2014; Larson and Smith 2014). The resonance of the assembly and subsequent conversations indicated to the organizers in attendance that there was common interest in broadening their analyses to look at the whole debt *system* (Larson and Smith 2014). This was the genesis of Strike Debt.

Building the Movement

Strike Debt's Facebook page[5] was created on June 6, 2012, and its website's domain names[6] were registered on June 11–12. Their first events were "debt assemblies" in parks, starting on June 11, 2012, in Washington Square Park (McKee 2012). The debt assemblies gave a safe space for debtors to come and share their stories of indebtedness and build community and solidarity. They also continued their analysis of the debt system, and started to draft the Debt Resisters' Operations Manual[7] (DROM) to offer advice on how to escape all types of debt and urge individuals to join in collective action, in a debt resistance movement (Ross 2013).

During Strike Debt's first few weeks, a friend recommended to organizer Aaron Smith that he contact Gokey (Larson and Smith 2014). Smith and a former OSDC organizer who had previously spoke to Gokey invited him to travel from Syracuse and pitch his idea for buying debt on the secondary market, like debt collectors do, and then canceling it (Ibid.). Despite reservations by other Strike Debt organizers who thought the idea was too capitalistic, they pushed ahead with meeting Gokey, hoping the tactic could at least raise awareness (Ibid.).

By mid-July, the idea of the Rolling Jubilee, then known as the "debt fairy" campaign, was added to Strike Debt's game plan (McKee 2012). From the beginning, they argued it was not an end-game strategy, as Strike Debt organizer Yates McKee noted in a July 13 essay,

While not a structural solution—and not applicable to student loans—scaled up it could become what David Graeber imagines as a "moving jubilee" capable of both garnering media attention around debtors' struggles and taking business away from the intermediary companies that profit from hounding and penalizing those unable to pay. (Ibid.)

Gokey had already successfully tested the debt-buying idea using $500 of his own money. To effectively scale the action, Strike Debt reached out to lawyers and accountants for help with the details, and set a goal of raising $50,000 with the hope of buying $1,000,000 worth of debt at the going rate of ~5 cents on the dollar (Larson and Smith 2014).

Strike Debt continued to organize debt assemblies over the summer (Ross 2013), building toward OWS's anniversary on September 17, 2012 (S17), where they would officially launch the DROM. Strike Debt was deeply involved with the planning of and media activism around S17, where one of the "quadrants" was dedicated to the theme of "debt"; they hoped to unite Occupy Movement participants around the issue (Taylor 2012; Graeber 2012; Konczal 2012a).

The Rolling Jubilee and Its Limits

Following S17 and the launch of DROM, Strike Debt focused on planning a launch for the Rolling Jubilee to coincide with the November 15, 2012, anniversary of OWS's eviction from Zuccotti Park. The Rolling Jubilee Facebook page[8] had already been registered August 14, and its website's domain names[9] were registered September 26–27. On October 22, they shared a screenshot of the teaser page on their website via Facebook.

Returning to the successful tactic of story sharing employed by OSDC and the debt assemblies, on October 29, Strike Debt started curating stories arguing for debt resistance on Tumblr[10]. Using a mailing list of organizers from the Occupy Movement's network of encampments, a larger social media bomb via Twitter and blogs was planned for the launch of the Rolling Jubilee—a strategy inspired in part by the Kony2012 campaign's successful construction and activation of on-the-ground networks to make their video go "viral" (Larson and Smith 2014).

The launch was designed as a "telethon" entitled "The People's Bailout," featuring musicians and comedians taking the stage and a livestream simulcast—all ticket proceeds went to the Rolling Jubilee fund and online donations were tallied with updates punctuating the acts. The social media bomb was planned for a week ahead of time. Organizers created a promotional video[11] and poster for the event, and drafted a press release for their network for promotional use. Unexpected social media success came on November 8 as co-organizer and co-host of the telethon David Rees posted the announcement to his well-followed Tumblr blog the night before the bomb;[12] it piqued the interest of actor and writer Wil Wheaton who re-blogged it,[13] putting the press release in front of his large audience of followers. Within 48 hours, the online donations surpassed the $50,000 goal (Larson and Smith 2014).

By the end of its first push, the Rolling Jubilee took in $435,000 (Tepper 2012), well surpassing its goal. However, critics dismissed the Rolling Jubilee as a "gimmick," arguing it was at a scale too small to have impact and was a distraction from more useful

Figure 7.2
Rolling Jubilee teaser page screenshot shared on Facebook, October 22, 2012.

tactics like educating people about strategic bankruptcy (Henwood 2012; Smith 2012). They also questioned its ability to build a movement through debt forgiveness (Konczal 2012b). Strike Debt organizers reiterated that it was never meant to be a large-scale solution (Ross and Ackerman 2012; Ross and Taylor 2012), as McKee had noted early on. Instead, Ross and Taylor's piece in *The Nation* emphasized that the Rolling Jubilee was "an act of solidarity and an opportunity for public education," and introduced the broad set of debt resistance strategies and the long-term vision of a system of positive credit through mutual aid (2012).

These response articles and interviews also publicized the creation of Strike Debt chapters in cities and on campuses across the country, inspired by the DROM (Ross and Taylor 2012; Tepper 2012). This is Strike Debt's real end-game strategy: build a networked social movement around debt resistance by correcting the information asymmetry between the lenders and the indebted while promoting a wide variety of actions.

The Rolling Jubilee stopped collecting donations on December 31, 2013. The donations totaled $701,317. And as of the writing of this case study, they had purchased and

Figure 7.3
The People's Bailout, Rolling Jubilee "telethon" poster.

"abolished" \$14,734,569.87, with one more jubilee announcement on the way. The first four debt purchases, detailed on the "Transparency" page of the Rolling Jubilee website,[14] went to medical debt, the accrual of which can be argued to be rarely the fault of the debtor, which helps reinforce Strike Debt's moral argument against the debt *system*.

Next Steps

With the Rolling Jubilee ending, the Strike Debt organizers I spoke to in May 2014 say they will miss the massive media attention delivered by the debt buys, but they are eager to focus on creating a more sustainable structure for Strike Debt and building the on-the-ground network of debt resisters (Larson and Smith 2014). They want to grow the number of chapters, especially on college campuses, and get the DROM, which had been expanded into a full book, into more hands. They continue to analyze the debt system and write reports to support their intellectual and moral argument (Graeff and Bhargava 2014). Additionally, they are exploring new forms of action and public education, currently working with an NYU law student to develop "debt clinics" (Ibid.).

Market-Based Activism, Media Activism, or Both?

In his book *Code and Other Laws of Cyberspace*, Lawrence Lessig contends that there are four ways contemporary society is regulated: law, norms, markets, and architecture (2006). Ethan Zuckerman argues that these also represent opportunities for citizens to effect change in complex systems by treating each of them as levers (2013). Strike Debt as a debt resistance movement and an offshoot of Occupy Wall Street has a particular focus on the market-based lever, generally used to punish corporations by affecting the cost of doing business. The goal of debt resistance as practiced by Strike Debt is to undermine and destroy the system of lenders that prey on debtors, ideally drying up their market through non-participation. The Rolling Jubilee is a tactic that tried to subvert the system by using its own market structure to cancel debt. But as the organizers confess, this is symbolic; its utility is its ability to draw attention to the issue, like a creative spectacle in the service of media activism.

Analyzing Strike Debt's tactics using Albert Hirschman's framework of exit, voice, and loyalty, debt resistance looks like an exit from the relationship with big banks and the debt system (1970). This is the long-term goal of an alternative economy for mutual benefit. But this is not easy to achieve because of the laws, norms, markets, and architectures that govern the system and everyone who touches it. Thus, it becomes an exercise in voice, confronting the system designed to bind people to it, as in the "web" metaphor Strike Debt uses. This requires media activism to affect norms and perhaps laws—fortunately, one of the great successes of the Occupy Movement has been to move anti-capitalism and class inequality into the "sphere of legitimate controversy" from the "sphere of deviance," to use Daniel Hallin's terms for how the media covers different issues (1986).

If Strike Debt can succeed where OSDC failed, as Gokey aspired to do with Kick-Stopper, building a large enough network of debt resisters willing to form a debtor's union and refuse to pay up, then perhaps we will see a full exit from the debt system and a "salvaging" of popular democracy to quote Ross (2013). At the very least, Strike Debt's tactics for both media activism and market-based activism add to a creative repertoire for manipulating Lessig's and Zuckerman's levers, being pioneered by contemporary networked social movements.

Notes

1. https://groups.google.com/forum/#!forum/debt-strike-kick-stopper.

2. https://www.adbusters.org/blogs/blackspot_blog/debtors_union_and_bank_strike.html.

3. http://www.occupystudentdebtcampaign.org.

4. http://studentloanjustice.org.

5. https://www.facebook.com/pages/Strike-Debt/244850825627699.

6. http://strikedebt.org.

7. http://strikedebt.org/drom.

8. https://www.facebook.com/RollingJubilee.

9. http://rollingjubilee.org.

10. http://whystrikedebt.tumblr.com.

11. https://www.youtube.com/watch?v=1Qs9w1XlJKE.

12. http://howtosharpenpencils.tumblr.com/post/35285338188/the-peoples-bailout.

13. http://wilwheaton.tumblr.com/post/35309150177/the-peoples-bailout.

14. http://rollingjubilee.org/transparency.

References

Caffentzis, George. 2013. "Reflections on the History of Debt Resistance: The Case of El Barzon." *South Atlantic Quarterly* 112 (4): 824–830. doi:.10.1215/00382876-2345315

Gokey, Thomas. n.d. "A Debt Strike Vision." https://docs.google.com/document/d/1o6J0ITG JReByTHjX9B1UyLOTcyRMHcih-8psAw7G_0g/edit.

Gokey, Thomas. 2011 a. "Kick-Stopper," October 23. *ContactBBS*. *Internet Archive*. https://web .archive.org/web/20111220011757/http://forum.contactcon.com/discussion/33/kick-stopper.

Gokey, Thomas. 2011 b. "Volunteer Programmer Needed for a Debt Forgiveness Project," November 1. https://groups.google.com/d/topic/debt-strike-kick-stopper/8H8pA91_sDo/discussion.

Gokey, Thomas. 2012. "Debt Strike Update," August 20. https://groups.google.com/d/topic/debt-strike-kick-stopper/_d2dssJHlF8/discussion.

Graeber, David. 2011. *Debt: The First 5,000 Years*. New York: Melville House.

Graeber, David. 2012. "Can Debt Spark a Revolution?" *Nation*, September. http://www.thenation.com/article/169759/can-debt-spark-revolution.

Graeff, Erhardt, and Rahul Bhargava. 2014. "Strike Debt and the Moral Argument for Debt Resistance." *MIT Center for Civic Media Blog*. http://civic.mit.edu/blog/erhardt/strike-debt-and-the -moral-argument-for-debt-resistance.

Hallin, Daniel C. 1986. *The Uncensored War: The Media and Vietnam*. New York: Oxford University Press.

Henwood, Doug. 2012. "The Problem with (Strike) Debt." *Jacobin*, November 14. https://www.jacobinmag.com/2012/11/the-problem-with-strike-debt/.

Hirschman, Albert O. 1970. *Exit, Voice, and Loyalty: Responses to Decline in Firms, Organizations, and States*. Cambridge, MA: Harvard University Press.

Hiscott, Rebecca. 2013. "Defined by Debt: How the Strike Debt Movement Redefined Occupy." *Truthout*, May 30. http://truth-out.org/news/item/16671-defined-by-debt-how-the -strike-debt-movement-redefined-occupy.

Jaffe, Sarah. 2011. "Debtor's Revolution: Are Debt Strikes Another Possible Tactic in the Fight Against the Big Banks?" *AlterNet*, November 3. http://www.alternet.org/story/152963/ debtor%27s_revolution%3A_are_debt_strikes_another_possible_tactic_in_the_fight_against_the_ big_banks/?page=entire.

Jaffe, Sarah, and Matthew Skomarovsky. 2012. "Debt Strike." In *Beautiful Trouble: A Toolbox for Revolution*, ed. Andrew Boyd, 24–26. New York: OR Books. http://beautifultrouble.org/tactic/ debt-strike/.

Konczal, Mike. 2012 a. "On the Occupy/Strike Debt 'Debt Resistors' Manual." *Next New Deal*. http://www.nextnewdeal.net/rortybomb/occupystrike-debt-debt-resistors-manual.

Konczal, Mike. 2012 b. "Keep Calm and Get Excited About the Rolling Jubilee." *Next New Deal*. http://www.nextnewdeal.net/rortybomb/keep-calm-and-get-excited-about-rolling-jubilee.

Larson, Ann, and Aaron Smith. 2014. *Interview with Strike Debt Organizers*. Interview by Erhardt Graeff.

Lessig, Lawrence. 2006. *Code Version 2.0*. New York: Basic Books.

McKee, Yates. 2012. "With September 17 Anniversary on the Horizon, Debt Emerges as Connective Thread for OWS." *Waging Nonviolence*, July 13. http://wagingnonviolence.org/feature/with-september-17-anniversary-on-the-horizon-debt-emerges-as-connective-thread-for-ows/.

Ross, Andrew. 2013. "Democracy and Debt." *Is This What Democracy Looks Like ?* http://what-democracy-looks-like.com/democracy-and-debt/.

Ross, Andrew, and Seth Ackerman. 2012. "Strike Debt and Rolling Jubilee: The Debate." *Dissent,* November. http://www.dissentmagazine.org/online_articles/strike-debt-the-debate.

Ross, Andrew, and Astra Taylor. 2012. "Rolling Jubilee Is a Spark—Not the Solution." *Nation,* November. http://www.thenation.com/article/171478/rolling-jubilee-spark-not-solution.

Smith, Yves. 2012. "Occupy Wall Street's Debt Jubilee: A Gimmick with Tax Risk." *Naked Capitalism.* http://www.nakedcapitalism.com/2012/11/occupy-wall-streets-debt-jubilee-a-gimmick-with-tax-risk.html.

Strike Debt. 2014. *The Debt Resisters' Operations Manual.* Oakland, CA: PM Press.

Taylor, Astra. 2012. "Occupy 2.0: Strike Debt." *Nation,* September 5: http://www.thenation.com/article/169760/occupy-20-strike-debt.

Tepper, Fabien. 2012. "The 'People's Bailout' Was Just the Beginning: What's Next for Strike Debt?" *YES!,* December 13. http://www.yesmagazine.org/new-economy/peoples-bailout-just-the-beginning-whats-next-strike-debt-rolling-jubilee.

White, Micah. 2014. "On the Origins of the Rolling Jubilee (Solving a Movement Mystery with History)." *Boutique Activist Consultancy*, May 3. http://www.activistboutique.com/leaderless-revolution/origin-rolling-jubilee.

Zuckerman, Ethan. 2013. "The 'Good Citizen' and Effective Citizen." *… My Heart's in Accra.* http://www.ethanzuckerman.com/blog/2013/08/19/the-good-citizen-and-the-effective-citizen/.

II Systems + Design

8 Re-Imagining Government through Civic Media: Three Pathways to Institutional Innovation

Beth Simone Noveck

The Fire Department of San Ramon, California, created the PulsePoint app to enable the public to save lives in medical emergencies. Each year, 424,000 people in the United States suffer sudden cardiac arrest and 1,000 die each day. Effective CPR administered immediately after a cardiac arrest can potentially double or triple the victim's chance of survival, but less than half of victims receive that immediate help because they have to rely upon the arrival of a small number of official first responders, such as paramedics or police, to administer aid. PulsePoint takes this function typically performed exclusively by government officials and decentralizes it by enabling citizens to serve as first responders.

By tapping into a feed of the 911 calls, PulsePoint is able to notify registered and trained CPR users—off-duty doctors, nurses, police, and trained amateurs, for example—near the victim to come to the aid of stricken neighbors. PulsePoint sends them a text message in capital letters: "CPR NEEDED!" A trained bystander can do three things to improve a victim's chances for survival: call 911, start chest compressions, and/or use a defibrillator. If a bystander who knows how to do these things arrives in the first few minutes, the odds of death go down 50 percent. According to the American Heart Association, bystander CPR gets performed only one-quarter of the time. PulsePoint aims to change this. Now the program is in use in 1,100 communities in the United States. The app has been used in 11,000 cases to activate citizen responders in response to more than 4,000 cardiac emergencies.[1]

PulsePoint is paradigmatic of the new models and approaches for using citizen engagement and collaboration to improve how government makes policies and delivers public services. Throughout the world, governments are struggling to address increasingly complex problems with dwindling resources. From sustainability to security, these challenges demand not simply different decisions but changes in how institutions make decisions. The same digital tools that enable greater engagement by citizens in civic life are also facilitating systematic collaboration and engagement between citizens and government agencies and authorities in the formal practices of governing. We call such institutional innovations "open government."

Open government blurs the boundaries between the public and civic sectors. Greater engagement between citizens and the state enhances legitimacy but, as we shall explore, also has the potential to lead to more-effective problem solving and more-efficient functioning of institutions, which, in turn, bolsters legitimacy.

In this chapter, we explore some of the existing modalities by which civic media are being applied to transform institutions and portend some of the future ways that civic media have the potential to reboot democratic institutions as well as reinvigorate citizenship and civil society.[2] Solving complex challenges requires many people with diverse skills and talents working together. By providing the "conversational infrastructure" to enable leaders and citizens to work together with the public to tackle society's biggest problems, these tools for engagement are accelerating access, not merely to information, which would only drown decision-makers, but to the collective knowledge and creativity needed to curate and filter innovative and out-of-the-box solutions to hard problems.

We explore three ideal types of open government—that is, three paradigms by which institutions are introducing citizen engagement into governing practices: open data governance, smarter governance, and distributed governance. Illustrating each with examples of current practice, the aim is to offer a picture of the unfolding transformation of democratic institutions and the evolution of more active and collaborative forms of citizenship that go beyond voting to enable robust participation in government, not only in civic life. Even the most ardent democrats (with a small d) often waver in their faith that citizens possess the knowledge and the competence needed for participation in governing. In "Federalist 57," Madison suggested that peoples' virtues lie primarily in their capacity to choose "rulers who possess the most wisdom" but not in the capacity to make their own decisions among the common good.[3] Technology is changing the way people and institutions can collaborate and driving the adoption of open government innovations that are proving Madison wrong.

Open Data Governance

On January 21, 2009, as his first executive action, President Obama signed the Memorandum on Transparency and Open Government, committing his administration to "establish a system of transparency, public participation, and collaboration" for government. The Memorandum set in motion a national and, subsequently, an international effort to encourage public institutions to innovate to improve people's lives. The vision underlying the Open Government Memorandum was a commitment to move away from governing behind closed doors through a limited set of public policy professionals and their adjutants. The explicit goal (as head of the White House Open Government Initiative, I was responsible for the implementation of the Memorandum) was a radical reinvention of government: fundamentally redesigning, not merely reforming, how institutions make decisions by opening them up to systematic conversation and collaboration with the public.

As John Dewey wrote a century ago: "There is no sanctity in universal suffrage, frequent elections, majority rule, congressional and cabinet government. These things are devices evolved in the direction in which the current was moving, each wave of which involved at the time of its impulsion a minimum of departure from antecedent custom and law. The devices served a purpose; but the purpose was rather that of meeting existing needs, which had become too intense to be ignored, than that of forwarding the democratic idea. In spite of all defects, they served their own purpose well."[4] The aim of open government policy was not, in fact, to increase transparency to the end of making government more accountable—the age-old goal of good government—but, instead, to introduce greater citizen engagement on an ongoing basis to give our governing institutions access to innovative thinking from more diverse sources in order to overcome complex challenges from climate change to poverty.

The first prong of the Memorandum and hence the first tool in the toolkit of institutional transformation was open data, one of the primary drivers of citizen engagement in governing today. The Memorandum stated that: "Government should be transparent. Transparency promotes accountability and provides information for citizens about what their Government is doing. Information maintained by the Federal Government is a national asset. My Administration will take appropriate action, consistent with law and policy, to disclose information rapidly in forms that the public can readily find and use. Executive departments and agencies should harness new technologies to put information about their operations and decisions online and readily available to the public. Executive departments and agencies should also solicit public feedback to identify information of greatest use to the public."[5] Since then, more than a million datasets have been opened for free public use and re-use by governments around the world at every level.[6] These include data sets about the workings of government, such as budgets and data about government spending on contracts and grants. But open data is much broader than data about the workings of government[7]—such as politicians' tax returns,[8] who-met-with-whom,[9] and even spending data.[10] Rather, it includes any data that can be publicly released that government collects about the economy, the environment, and the marketplace.

For example, the Canadian Open Government Directive calls for releasing government "information and data of business value to support transparency, accountability, citizen engagement, and socio-economic benefits through reuse, subject to applicable restrictions associated with privacy, confidentiality, and security."[11] The United States Open Government Directive, the policy which directed federal agencies in how to implement the Open Government Memorandum, defines the data to be opened as "high value data," which is any information "to increase agency accountability and responsiveness; improve public knowledge of the agency and its operations; further the core mission of the agency; create economic opportunity; or respond to need and demand as identified through public consultation."[12]

The last decade or so has seen a data explosion around the world. In late 2012, it was estimated that there existed some 2.8 zettabytes (2.8 trillion GB) of data; this was expected to grow to 40ZB by 2020.[13] Until recently, much of this data was closed to public access—hidden behind firewalls and passwords, protected by copyright or other legal barriers. In addition, some of the data was kept from the public due to legitimate concerns over privacy or national security. Recent years have witnessed something of a sea change in the way data is treated, particularly by governments and (to a lesser extent) private companies. Across the world, there has been a gradual—and sometimes not so gradual—transition underway from what McKinsey calls a culture of "protect" to one of "share, with protections."[14]

Forty-five countries and hundreds of cities and states now have open data portals where government data can be searched and downloaded.[15] It is this move toward greater data transparency that marks what some observers have called an open data revolution. Where Big Data is the information science trend of being able to collect, transmit, visualize, and mash up ever-larger quantities of information, Open Data refers to the policy of making data available such that it can be readily accessed, used, and re-distributed free of charge, often via a one-stop data sharing platform.[16] The technology of Big Data fits hand in glove with the policy of Open Data.

Data is a transformative tool for changing how we govern, first, because it enables more evidence-based decision making, including new forms of pattern detection (sometimes called predictive analytics) to spot problems and target solutions even without knowing what to look for. Following flooding in Rio de Janeiro in 2010, for example, where torrential rains left thousands homeless and more than 70 dead, the city created one-stop access to geo-spatial information on issues such as the position of public transport, tidal levels, and real-time traffic data to enable more-agile decision making and coordination between departments such as police and health, especially when crises occur.[17]

But open data is important for a second reason, namely it fosters citizen engagement. Open data can provide the raw material to convene informed conversations inside and outside institutions about what's broken and about the empirical foundation for developing solutions together.[18] The ability of third parties to participate is what makes open data truly transformative. When Rio opened that same crisis data, it was then able to host several hackathons to encourage citizens to create applications that solve additional social problems such as The BUUS, which gives the location of the nearest bus and its current status—full or empty.

The underlying rationale behind opening data is that the organization that collects and maintains information is not always in the exclusive position to use it well. For example, US regulators have compiled hospital infection rates for a long time.

Previously accessible only to government professionals, bureaucrats had limited resources to make adequate use of the information. When the Department of Health and Human Services (HHS) made the data publicly available by publishing the data online in a computable format, Microsoft and Google were then able to mash up that information with mapping data. Now these companies' search engines allow anyone— from the investigative journalist to the parent of the sick child—to decide which hospital to choose (or whether it is safer to stay home). Similarly, the National Health Service (NHS) in the United Kingdom has long collected prescription records. But it was only when a startup called Mastodon-C analyzed that information that the public was able to see wild variations in the pattern of prescribing name-brand versus generic cholesterol-lowering drugs called statins—variations that are potentially costing the NHS £200 million a year.[19]

When data are open—namely legally and technically accessible and capable of being machine processed—those with technical know-how can create sophisticated and useful tools, visualizations, models, and analysis, as well as spot mistakes or mix and mash across datasets to yield insights. Open data create obvious new ways for geeky citizens to play a role in governance. All over the world, from Zurich to San Francisco to Hong Kong, local transportation authorities are making schedules available for free and then inviting tech savvy citizens—civic coders—to create smartphone apps that tell commuters when their bus or train is coming[20] or how to plan their daily commute.[21] There's obvious value to the public as well as to institutions from having better data to inform planning, policymaking, and the expenditure of resources. But what's exciting when the White House holds a hackathon[22] or the Department of Health and Human Services convenes an annual datapalooza[23] is that these are intelligible models for civic engagement with government institutions.

Hackathons aren't the only model for participatory governance but they are one way for some within civil society to get involved directly in governing. By pushing data out, open government has created a way to bring citizens in, showcasing new mechanisms for distributed and collaborative ways of working. Philadelphia has 41 active improvement projects that the city is undertaking with citizens, using meet-ups to get people together on a regular basis to open up data and collaborate around using that information to help citizens, for example, detect the safest way to travel from your house to your child's school based on crime and traffic and safety data.

Moving toward open innovation as a default way of working in government is not easy. It takes a religious fervor (hence the sense of movement that exists around the #opendata hashtag) for those who want to open up data. It requires doing the hard and costly work of persuading data owners to shift from paper to digital and machine-readable formats and then to release that data despite political and technical challenges. It requires thoughtful decision making about how and how often to release data and how to ensure its reliability, accuracy, and quality. But, above all, realizing the value in open data requires ensuring participation to get subject matter experts, stakeholders, data geeks, activists, designers, computer scientists, data junkies, and entrepreneurs to work together.

Creating a participatory innovation ecosystem is about a lot more than just publishing data sets. It requires doing the hosting, convening, persuading, and demonstrating. The institutional players have to be prepared to collaborate with the innovators; those outside government have to know how to collaborate; civil society activists have to ensure that innovators know the problems that need solving. Such curation is about devising strategies for using data to develop innovative solutions to protect consumers and serve the public interest. If we merely throw data over the transom, few entities outside of government will have the wherewithal to do anything with the raw information. Rather, open data becomes a tool for better governance when it is combined with active curation practices to invite outside engagement by diverse participants.

The Economist has called open data "a new goldmine."[24] The consulting firm McKinsey has predicted the possible global value of open data to be over $3 trillion annually.[25] Likewise, a study commissioned by the Omidyar Network concluded that open data could increase the output of G20 countries by some $13 trillion over five years (equivalent to a growth rate of 1.1 percent, more than half the G20's collective growth target).[26] Yet for all the enthusiasm about open data's potential, we in fact know very little about how open data works—what kinds of data are most in demand, what supply of data is most effective, and under what conditions it has maximum impact. Across the world, the nascent field of open data is still characterized by a form of market failure in which there is a mismatch between the *supply* (or availability) of data and its actual *demand* (and subsequent use). This mismatch potentially limits the impact of open data, and inhibits its ability to effect social, economic, political, cultural, and environmental change. More generally, the field is characterized by a broad (yet untested) assumption akin to the "build it and they'll come" logic of much technology thinking: a faith that if data is simply "opened," it will achieve impact because people will engage with it. Much more research and evidence are necessary to test this assumption and understand when open data works as a mechanism for translating civic engagement into improved institutional practice.

Smarter Governance

Pushing data out encourages participation by giving people the raw material to spot and solve problems. Open data is also a mechanism for getting information and intelligence back into institutions to inform how they govern. In Uganda, more than a quarter of the caloric intake in the national diet comes from bananas. Over the last decade, Banana Bacterial Wilt (BBW) has been wiping out crops, costing hundreds of millions in economic losses and threatening public health.[27] But thanks to the United

Nations' mobile SMS-based reporting tool Ureport, the Ugandan government has been able to engage 300,000 citizens in reporting and sharing data back about the state of BBW, giving the government insight into on-the-ground conditions and enabling officials to communicate back to citizens together with recommendations for how to treat crops and combat the disease.

Like open data, smarter governance is another tool in the toolkit for change that also depends upon connecting up civic engagement to institutions. Rather than big data, however, smarter governance depends upon new kinds of communication and collaboration tools such as social media and expert networks to enable institutions to get input from distributed lay and expert citizens to inform decision making. As the Open Government Memorandum stated: "Knowledge is widely dispersed in society, and public officials benefit from having access to that dispersed knowledge. Executive departments and agencies should offer Americans increased opportunities to participate in policymaking and to provide their Government with the benefits of their collective expertise and information."

Electronic petitions are one example of using new technology for getting better information into government. Whereas previously, a citizen had no way to put an issue on the policy agenda, petitions websites are opening up a new channel of communication. In 2012, the White House established an online petitions website, *We the People*.[28] Like its British counterpart, *e-Petitions*, the American website allows members of the public to solicit signatures in support of a petition for government action. Petitions have been launched on such diverse topics as enacting Federal gun control reforms, legalizing marijuana, supporting mandatory labeling of genetically engineered foods, and building a "Death Star," like that in the movie *Star Wars*. Initially, only 5,000 signatures were needed to prompt a response from the executive branch, but the popularity of the system—it is the only way to communicate with the White House directly other than by mail—led to the requirement being raised to 100,000 signatures.

We the People is a mass-based engagement tool, designed to reach large audiences and connect them to the White House. As a means of engagement, the petitions website can sometimes enable individuals and interest groups to raise awareness of an issue among media or political elites, as was the case with cell phone unlocking in 2013. A petition on the website demanded that the White House call upon the Librarian of Congress to rescind a copyright decision that made it possible for phone companies to prevent consumers from unlocking their mobile phones for use on a competitor's network without the carrier's permission, even after their contract had expired or, at least, to champion legislation to legalize cell phone unlocking. The petition, which garnered 114,000 signatures, drew significant attention to the far-reaching impact of a previously obscure and technical copyright policy.

Such petitions enhance direct participation in the political process, opening a channel of communication for getting a topic onto the public agenda other than through lobbying or appeal to congressional officials.[29] But at most it may force a press release by the White House; it has no real impact on policymaking. As of the last time the White House made the data from the website available (in May 2013), there had been 200,000 petitions with 13 million signatures, yet only 162 have received a response—and none can be directly connected to a decision made, dollar spent, or action taken.[30] A year and a half later, there were still only 165 responses. It is probably no wonder that use on the site dropped off precipitously. Few petitions reached the required signature threshold, and close to half of the petitions made requests for actions outside the scope of presidential powers.[31]

The limitations of the petitions websites in the United States (and the United Kingdom) stem less from the technology than from the lack of a process to make use of the information supplied by citizens. Petitions websites are glorified suggestion boxes that demand little more of citizens than offering a naked idea without evidence or support to guide policymakers wishing to implement the suggestion. By contrast, an online social media game by the Engagement Lab called Community PlanIt: Youth@Work Bhutan gave Bhutanese youth the ability to deliberate on issues involving youth unemployment. Players were posed questions in the form of challenges and earned points over three week-long "missions." What makes this different is that the country's Ministry of Labor committed to using the proposed ideas in its policymaking.[32] Ideation platforms (also known as brainstorming websites) are also now in widespread use in the public sector. On these sites, citizens respond to *specific* requests from officials, where input is intended to inform a decision-making process. Ideation tools generally enable the public to propose an idea, offer short supporting arguments, and then enable the public to view the suggestions and vote them up or down, allowing ideas to be rated and prioritized.

Prize-backed challenges—the policies to encourage their use and the platforms to make those challenges findable—go beyond petition and ideation sites. Although there has been little research to date of the impact of challenges to help us understand in which contexts they work better than traditional contracting mechanisms, challenges seem to be starting to channel more systematic engagement toward problem solving.[33] Use by government of prize-backed challenges to spur innovation is not a new idea. Prizes have long been used to recognize past achievement. What is particularly salient about how prizes are being used in government is that they are a mechanism to induce participation to the end of solving future, unsolved problems rather than merely rewarding past performance.

Back in 1714, the British Government introduced the Longitude Prize to induce the identification of a precise way to measure a ship's position and thereby to accelerate trade. But today new technology has made it possible to engage more people in challenges. In September 2009, as part of his Strategy for American Innovation, President Obama called upon "all agencies to increase their use of prizes to address some of our

Nation's most pressing challenges" in his Strategy for American Innovation.[34] The launch of Challenge.gov the following year created a one-stop shop where agencies could post public-sector prize competitions and entrepreneurs and citizens could find them. As of March 2015, there were almost 400 competitions run by 40 agencies.

Twenty-three of those competitions had a prize purse of over $1 million. These "Grand Challenges" are a variation on prize-backed challenges, which offer large purses to make specific, quantifiable progress against a measurable and important target. For example, the Progressive Insurance Automotive X Prize, sponsored in part by Department of Energy together with private sector partners, induced the development of new production-capable super fuel-efficient vehicles using a $10 million prize. The European Commission's €2 million Horizon Prize was awarded in 2014 to a German biopharmaceutical company for "progress towards a novel technology to bring life-saving vaccines to people across the planet in safe and affordable ways."[35]

There are myriad rationales for using prizes as a way to solve problems better and faster than the government can do alone. By opening the challenge of how to stop a rogue vehicle at a military checkpoint, for example, the Air Force Research Laboratory was able to identify a solution to a problem that had "vexed military security forces and civilian police for years" in only 60 days. In addition to inducing a faster way to work, prizes can help to diversify the pool of respondents and proposed solutions and give government access to a far wider range of expertise. NASA, for example, received 400 responses to its Asteroid Grant Challenge, which sought to identify and address threats to humanity from asteroids. Prizes are also a way to encourage collaboration among those who might, in a procurement context, otherwise be competitors.

Whereas government agencies and public sector organizations typically work confidentially and behind closed doors, referring primarily to their own rolodexes to solicit advice and expertise to inform how they work, challenges and challenge platforms represent a move away from closed-door bureaucracy. Prize-backed challenges create an incentive to attract people, whether students or start-ups or large companies, to participate in public life. Just as the hackathon complements open data policy by encouraging engagement with and the use of open government data, prize policy (which makes the use of such challenges legal) complemented by a platform to post challenges, offers another mechanism for citizen engagement in government. This result is engagement that is not only designed to improve the legitimacy of decision making but to improve the efficacy of problem solving by opening up decision-making processes to a more diverse pool of solvers outside the boundaries of the public sector.

Citizen engagement—getting information in—does not have to come simply in the form of suggesting ideas through brainstorming or challenges. It can also include asking citizens to supply data, such as in the case of the Ugandan Banana Bacterial Wilt problem, or to undertake a task like digging out a fire hydrant after a snowstorm using the Adopt-a-Hydrant tool. It is often in these task-based scenarios that these open call approaches work and really work well. Galaxy Zoo is a platform to help scientists tackle the problem of going through a large quantity of data, namely pictures of galaxies, and trying to sort and categorize them to the end of identifying how old each galaxy is. Using crowdsourcing, it took 24 hours to get 70,000 pictures classified. There were more than 50 million classifications done in the first year of the project most notably by volunteers in New Zealand and in Leicester, England, where people seem to have a penchant for galaxy classification in their leisure time.

Coincidentally, people from New Zealand were also active participants in the crowdsourcing project of transcribing death records from the State of Missouri (so they can be digitized). The public translated the corpus of historical death records from the state in a matter of a few days. When the challenge is specific, hard, interesting, and in the public interest, people will participate regardless of whether the state or another institution is the host. Motivations for engagement include the intrinsic joy of solving a problem for the common good and demonstrating mastery in a subject of interest but also the extrinsic incentives of a cash prize or the credential that comes from such participation, which can translate into professional advancement and further monetary gain.

Open call approaches, however, have their limitations in that they depend upon the "right" people knowing about the opportunity to participate. As such, these open call approaches are often too ad hoc and too unsystematic to become the basis for sustained institutional practice. If we "build it," we don't know that "they will come" in every instance. For every successful crowdsourcing program that invites citizens to participate, they are ten more that yield few submissions and none of the appropriate quality. These open calls are inspiring when they work but they do not guarantee that a large enough or diverse enough mix of people will come together on a regular basis.

Open call approaches to engagement are, in the future, likely to be supplemented by the use of new tools to connect citizens to opportunities to participate more systematically. Tools like expert networks and digital badges—what I call the technologies of expertise—are making it possible to match the supply of citizen knowledge to the demand for it in government.[36] With recent advances in information retrieval technology and the large-scale availability of digital traces of knowledge-related activities, platforms such as LinkedIn that can fully automate the process of expressing, locating, and matching expertise within and across organizations have become a reality. Such practices are already in widespread use in business. Banks turn to a company like Gerson Lehrman when trying to find an expert to advise them prior to an investment, and start-ups like Ideoba out of Wales are trying to automate that process by making it possible to identify expertise from searches on the open web.

We are still evolving the tools and approaches for making what people know systematically searchable, but we are on the cusp of an expertise revolution, not just an information revolution that could expand participatory democracy beyond the paltry act of occasional voting or the serendipity of crowdsourcing to take account of people's talents, skills, abilities, and interests.

Distributed Governance

The Memorandum on Transparency and Open Government intentionally went beyond championing open data or participation to include a commitment to *collaboration* as well. Collaboration is not the same as participation, which is about getting information back *into* government. Rather, collaboration emphasizes new ways of tackling challenges outside of government. The President said: "Collaboration actively engages Americans in the work of their Government. Executive departments and agencies should use innovative tools, methods, and systems to cooperate among themselves, across all levels of Government, and with nonprofit organizations, businesses, and individuals in the private sector. Executive departments and agencies should solicit public feedback to assess and improve their level of collaboration and to identify new opportunities for cooperation."

Collaboration—new forms of public-private partnership whereby government distributes responsibility for tackling problems to those outside its walls whether collaboration across government agencies, or involving both the private sector and the research community—can build a bigger knowledge base and generate more innovative solutions than would be possible working in isolation. PulsePoint, the example with which this chapter opened, and initiatives like it involving distributed disaster relief and recovery, is paradigmatic of this new wave of distributed and shared governance.

The most widespread and well-known example of the collaboration paradigm of open government is, of course, participatory budgeting. Fifteen hundred local legislatures from New York City to Seville, Spain, to Porto Alegre, Brazil, are now experimenting with handing control over millions of dollars of budgetary spending to citizens, not professional politicians and officials. But participatory budgeting remains extremely localized and limited only to a small range of a simple capital spending projects, such as fixing a school or building a soccer pitch. However, by handing the purse strings and thereby a small amount of the power of government over to citizens to decide how money gets spent in their communities, PB—as it is known—has the potential to make decisions more legitimate but also to decrease fraud and abuse and bring communities together around a shared purpose and process. PBs, like PulsePoint, are not freestanding civic projects but depend squarely on collaboration with public sector institutions to succeed. PulsePoint could not work without a feed of official 911 data and coordination with state first responders. Similarly, participatory budgeting is part of larger bureaucratic process.

Like open data and prize-backed challenges—seemingly unthinkable innovations but a few years ago—new forms of collaboration *could* represent another new tool in the "innovation toolkit" that could make government work better. In addition to participatory budgeting, data collaboratives are perhaps the most exciting new addition to the toolkit of governance innovation. Data collaboratives involve private sector companies sharing data *back* and combining it with government open data for public good. In Europe, for example, phone companies in Norway and Italy have made anonymized datasets available, making it possible for researchers to track calling and commuting patterns and gain better insight into myriad social problems from unemployment to mental health. In the United States, LinkedIn is providing free data about demand for IT jobs in different markets, which, when combined with Department of Labor data, has the potential to help communities target efforts around training and hiring. Thanks to the open availability of Twitter data, to take another example, it is becoming possible to predict elections, analyze the unfolding of revolutions, and assess the performance of government agencies.

No one needs convincing that private data represents a tremendous business asset. But collaboration between public and private and academic sectors to combine their rich, growing, and dispersed bodies of data can—with the right governance frameworks, standards, and incentives in place—do double duty as an invaluable social asset. "Data collaboratives"—an innovative way of working together and combining abilities to leverage data, wherever it's stored and whoever collects it, for the public good—has the potential to provide an unprecedented picture of on-the-ground conditions that could enable better governing.

As participatory practices like data collaboratives, participatory budgeting, and decentralized disaster relief and recovery become more systematic and reliable, these new forms of collaboration point the way toward a future in which policies get made, services get delivered, and problems get solved in more-distributed fashion through collaboration between the public and professional public servants, rather than by either sector working in isolation. As with other new open government tools, most of which have only been in use for five years or less, there is too little experience yet to have more than an anecdotal and descriptive understanding of what kinds of problems lend themselves to solving better as a result of these more collaborative approaches and contexts.

We also do not yet have a good picture of whether and how institutional entanglement creates or depresses incentives to participate over the use of similar techniques in the civic space divorced from state action. Whether pushing data out through open data, getting information back in through ideation or prize-backed challenges, or distributing governance by means of participatory budgeting, we are still just getting a handle on what is underway and what might soon be tried without a thorough grasp yet of what will become possible if we systematically introduce the tools of civic media and practices of civic engagement into the working fabric of governing institutions.

Open Government: Re-Imagining the State, Re-Inventing Citizenship

Of course, the ideal of greater openness and collaboration—government of the people, by the people, *with* the people—resonates in all democracies. Yet poll after poll reveals deep distrust of institutions that seem largely to have left "the people" out of the governing equation.[37] For the most part, governing is the still the domain of professionals working largely behind closed doors. For those who do not take full-time jobs in the administration of government, stand for office, or work in a quasi-governmental, federally funded R&D center, or who do not get hand-picked for one of a few advisory committees that meet in Washington, D.C., or in state capitals a few times a year, there are few obvious channels to participate in governing. Public consultation is routinely practiced in connection with agency rulemaking, of course, but typically only after the fact, as a way to fine-tune an already formulated plan or to sell the public on it to ease subsequent implementation. Voting is still the *non plus ultra* of democracy. Seymour Martin Lipset, in his canonical *Political Man*, defines democracy as "a system of elections."[38] Voting asks citizens to express their opinions and only then in the form of a yea or nay choice between candidates or ratification of a ballot measure. But voting does very little to tap the full gamut of citizens' abilities and expertise nor does it enable citizens to devote their time and attention to those public interest topics of greatest interest to them.

The opportunity to contribute to the common good has been largely the province of the civic and voluntaristic domain separate from government. With the advent of new technologies—so-called civic technologies and civic media—there has been an explosion of these occasions to participate in community life. Civic engagement affords the public a wider palette of options for participation that speak to their interests, talents, and ability while advancing the common good. The limitation of civic engagement, however, is that it has typically been disconnected from institutions and hence from the power that government can wield to convene, coordinate, and amplify good works.

Government bureaucracies that are supposed to solve critical problems on their own are a troublesome outgrowth of the professionalization of public life in the industrial age. They are especially ill suited to confronting today's complex challenges as evidenced by mounting levels of distrust of all branches of government and in all nations.

Institutional innovation—changing how we make policy not which policies we make—is imperative. Online tools for collaboration and engagement, previously the basis for civic engagement, are increasingly serving as the basis for open government as well, enabling those outside government to take part in every stage of decision making from problem spotting to problem solving, from drafting to implementtion, whether in the executive or the legislative branch.

When government adopts the practices of civic engagement, citizenship, in turn, ceases to become something associated exclusively with the act of voting and legitimated by membership in a geographical community. Rather, it becomes a richly textured, robust, and meaningful form of collaboration between citizen, state, and society tethered to day-to-day practices of governing, not merely the once-a-year act of politicking. What makes this kind of engagement truly democratic—and citizenship in this vision more active, robust, and meaningful—is that it multiplies the number and frequency of ways to engage productively in a manner consistent with each person's talents, abilities, and interests. When we embrace the truism that the smartest people are those who don't work in government but who may work for somebody else; when we recognize the joy that comes from collaboration—that many hands make light work—then we begin to embrace the future of 21st-century government.

Notes

Many thanks to Stefaan Verhulst for his helpful insights and improvements to an earlier draft. This chapter has benefited greatly from his work on data collaboratives, in particular.

1. *PulsePoint,* http://www.physio-control.com/PulsePoint.

2. John Boik, Lorenzo Fioramonti, and Gary Milante, "Rebooting Democracy," *Foreign Policy,* March 16, 2015, http://foreignpolicy.com/2015/03/16/rebooting-democracy-participatory-reform-capitalism.

3. James Madison, "Federalist 57," 1778, in *The Federalist Papers* (Toronto: Bantam Books, 1982). "The aim of every political constitution is, or ought to be, first to obtain for rulers men who possess most wisdom to discern, and most virtue to pursue, the common good of the society; and in the next place, to take the most effectual precautions for keeping them virtuous whilst they continue to hold their public trust."

4. John Dewey, *The Public and Its Problems: An Essay in Political Inquiry,* (New York: H. Holt and Sons, 1927; Pennsylvania State Press, 2012), 20.

5. Barack Obama, "Memorandum on Transparency and Open Government," January 21, 2009, https://www.whitehouse.gov/sites/default/files/omb/assets/memoranda_fy2009/m09-12.pdf.

6. Tetherless World Constellation, International Open Government Dataset Search, logd.tw.rpi.edu/page/international_dataset_catalog_search.

7. Tom Lee, "Defending the Big Tent: Open Data, Inclusivity and Activism," Sunlight Foundation, May 2, 2012, http://sunlightfoundation.com/blog/2012/05/02/defending-the-big-tent-open-data-inclusivity-and-activism.

8. Ethics.Data.gov, http://www.ethics.gov.

9. The White House Visitor Access Records, http://www.whitehouse.gov/briefing-room/disclosures/visitor-records.

10. USAspending.gov, http://www.usaspending.gov.

11. Treasury Board of Canada, "Directive on Open Government," October 9, 2014, http://www.tbs-sct.gc.ca/pol/doc-eng.aspx?id=28108.

12. Peter Orzag, "Memorandum on Open Government Directive," December 8, 2009, http://www.whitehouse.gov/omb/assets/memoranda_2010/m10-06.pdf.

13. John Burn-Murdoch, "Study: less than 1% of the world's data is analysed, over 80% is unprotected," *The Guardian,* December 19, 2012, http://www.theguardian.com/news/datablog/2012/dec/19/big-data-study-digital-universe-global-volume.

14. James Manyika, Michael Chui, Diana Farrell, Steve Van Kuiken, Peter Groves, and Elizabeth Almasi Doshi, "Open Data: Unlocking Innovation and Performance with Liquid Information," McKinsey, October 2013, http://www.mckinsey.com/insights/business_technology/open_data_unlocking_innovation_and_performance_with_liquid_information.

15. Data.gov, Open Government, http://www.data.gov/open-gov.

16. Beth Simone Noveck and Daniel L. Goroff, *Information for Impact: Liberating Nonprofit Sector Data* (Washington, DC: The Aspen Institute, 2013). http://www.aspeninstitute.org/sites/default/files/content/docs/psi/psi_Information-for-Impact.pdf.

17. The Open Data Institute, "Supporting sustainable development with open data," http://theodi.org/supporting-sustainable-development-with-open-data.

18. Beth Noveck, "Open Data—The Democratic Imperative," *Crooked Timber,* July 5, 2012, http://crookedtimber.org/2012/07/05/open-data-the-democratic-imperative.

19. "Beggar thy neighbour: How Scrutiny of Freely Available Data Might Save the NHS Money," *The Economist,* December 8, 2012, http://www.economist.com/news/britain/21567980-how-scrutiny-freely-available-data-might-save-nhs-money-beggar-thy-neighbour.

20. Bruce Sterling, "Urban Data Challenge: Zurich, San Francisco, Geneva," *Wired,* February 6, 2013, http://www.wired.com/2013/02/urban-data-challenge-zurich-san-francisco-geneva.

21. Data.gov.hk, "Traffic Speed Map," http://www.gov.hk/en/theme/psi/datasets/speedmap.htm.

22. Leigh Heyman, "Announcing the White House's Second Annual Civic Hackathon," The White House Blog, May 1, 2014, https://www.whitehouse.gov/blog/2014/05/01/announcing-white-houses-second-annual-civic-hackathon.

23. Health Datapalooza, http://healthdatapalooza.org.

24. "A New Goldmine: Making Official Data Public Could Spur Lots of Innovation," *The Economist,* May 18, 2013, http://www.economist.com/news/business/21578084-making-official-data-public-could-spur-lots-innovation-new-goldmine.

25. James Manyika, Michael Chui, Diana Farrell, Steve Van Kuiken, Peter Groves, and Elizabeth Almasi Doshi. "Open Data: Unlocking Innovation and Performance with Liquid Innovation," McKinsey, October 2013, http://www.mckinsey.com/insights/business_technology/open_data_unlocking_innovation_and_performance_with_liquid_information.

26. Nicholas Gruen, John Houghton, and Richard Tooth, "Open for Business: How Open Data Can Help Achieve the G20 Growth Target," Omidyar Network, June 2014, https://www.omidyar.com/sites/default/files/file_archive/insights/ON%20Report_061114_FNL.pdf.

27. Anna Scott, "Open Data: How Mobile Phones Saved Bananas from Bacterial Wilt in Uganda," *The Guardian,* February 11, 2015, http://www.theguardian.com/global-development-professionals-network/2015/feb/11/open-data-how-mobile-phones-saved-bananas-from-bacterial-wilt-in-uganda.

28. "We the People, Your Voice in Government," Petitions, The White House. Available at: https://petitions.whitehouse.gov.

29. John W. Kingdon, *Agendas, Alternatives, and Public Policies*, Longman Classics edition (London: Longman Publishing Group, 2002), 3.

30. Leigh Heyman, "There's Now an API for We the People," The White House Blog, May 1, 2013, http://www.whitehouse.gov/blog/2013/05/01/theres-now-api-we-people.

31. Dave Karpf, "How the White House's E-People Petition Site Became a Virtual Ghost Town," *TechPresident,* June 20, 2014, http://techpresident.com/news/25144/how-white-houses-we-people-e-petition-site-became-virtual-ghost-town.

32. Youth@Work Bhutan, https://communityplanit.org/youthbhutan.

33. Stefaan Verhulst, "Governing through Prizes and Challenges," GovLab Blog, January 29, 2015, http://thegovlab.org/governing-through-prizes-and-challenges.

34. Tom Kalil and Cristin Dorgelo, "Identifying Steps Forward in Use of Prizes to Spur Innovation," Office of Science and Technology Policy, April 10, 2012, http://www.whitehouse.gov/blog/2012/04/10/identifying-steps-forward-use-prizes-spur-innovation.

35. European Commission, Research & Innovation Horizon Prizes, http://ec.europa.eu/research/horizonprize/index.cfm?pg=home.

36. See Beth Simone Noveck, *Smart Citizens, Smarter State: The Technologies of Expertise and the Future of Governing* (Cambridge, MA: Harvard University Press, 2015).

37. Gallup Poll, "Confidence in Institutions," June 2013.

38. Seymour Martin Lipset, *Political Man: The Social Bases of Politics* (Baltimore: The Johns Hopkins University Press, 1981), 45.

9 Data Visualizations Break Down Knowledge Barriers in Public Engagement

Sarah Williams

Data visualizations are rapidly being disseminated to large publics through online forums and are breaking down the power relationships typically associated with the use of data for public engagement. In her seminal work "A Ladder of Citizenship Participation," Arnstein (1969) states that proper public engagement strategies should reduce the knowledge barriers created between the "powerful" and the "powerless." Embedded in this statement is the message that public participation processes should educate and create literacy around civic topics in order for the public to make informed decisions about civic issues (Glass 1979). Data visualizations are effective tools for creating this literacy as they help the public to literally see underlying systems that generate planning policies (Williams 2015).

Traditionally data visualizations have been used to support decisions made by those in power (Forester 1988). New forms of data visualizations are changing this traditional power relationship, as they now allow the public to acquire information for their own uses and generate a debate about what they have visualized, creating a literacy around civic topics. At the same time, data visualizations can reach larger publics than the traditional method of in-person public forums, with new visualization technologies that allow easy distribution through online communities and the social web. This media distribution allows the visualizations to achieve collective learning around planning processes, as these sites often facilitate public debate through interactive commenting.

The increased interest in the use of "big data" for planning decisions and the ease in which data visualizations can be generated has caused an exponential increase their use to describe and argue for policy decisions. However, it should be noted that data visualizations still hold the potential to exclude populations who cannot understand or access the visualizations (Elwood 2002). This makes teaching the public how to read and understand data by increasing data literacy essential for using data visualization to increase involvement in civics.

Recent experiments in data visualization leverage new tools and software to translate big data into interactive public engagement tools that can describe policy and be used as evidence for decision making. These new visualizations can be categorized as those that: (1) employ previously unavailable datasets to expose policy issues; (2) teach civic issues through guided interactive learning facilitated by data visualizations; (3) allow the public to explore data and generate their own stories; and (4) visualize solicited public input or crowdsourcing, exposing individual perspectives collectively. Inherent in all these data visualization categories is the ability to generate literacy about planning processes and to narrow the knowledge gap necessary for making informed decisions about civic processes by providing greater access to the information (Harvery and Chrisman 1998). These categories will be used as a guide for arguing how current data visualizations have changed the public dialog in civic engagement.

Engaging the public with data visualization is not new. In fact, some might say the use of data visualizations for public engagement is as old as the map itself. What is new is the public's ability to consume, access, and work with data that was previously inaccessible, which has created new experiments in the use of data visualization for public policy debates. This is largely due to the explosion of big data now collected by governments and organizations (Lane et al. 2014; Lindquist 2011), the open data movement that provides greater access to data (Bourgault 2013; Goldstein and Dyson 2013), new tools for developing static and interactive data visualizations that invite public participation, and the current media culture that supports the consumption of information through visual snapshots (Bekkers and Moody 2011).

Data visualizations are essential for communicating in a society that has become increasingly dependent on using data to make decisions. Data analytics are used for everything from managing police strategies to suggesting books on Amazon (boyd and Crawford 2012). Data visualizations transform the complexity of this data into something that is easy to understand thereby facilitating a conversation and a public debate (Segel and Heer 2010; Bekkers and Moody 2011). Visualizations have therefore become essential tools for public engagement as they are necessary to communicate data-driven policies by making them more transparent and accessible to broader publics (Bekkers and Moody 2011).[1] Borrowing techniques from advertising, data visualizations help inform, and sometimes sway, the public (Harley 1992). Their ability to reach broad groups of people through social media and news venues allows them to have a larger impact, making them effective tools for policy making. Data visualizations are not only useful for communicating policy plans—they can start a public debate and generate the interactive knowledge sharing important for public engagement.

Public Engagement, Civic Engagement, and Civic Culture

It is important to have a working definition of public engagement in order to frame how data visualization and public engagement are associated. The term public engagement has varied—and often conflicting—definitions, and public "participation" might be an easier way to understand the term. One of the clearest definitions comes from *Public Participation Handbook: Making Better Decisions Through Citizen Involvement* by

James L. Creighton in which he states "Public participation is the process by which public concerns, needs, and values are incorporated into governmental and corporate decision making. It is two-way communication and interaction, with the overall goal of better decisions that are supported by the public" (Creighton 2005, 7). Public engagement is different from public participation as this two-way participation is not always incorporated in public engagement strategies. Those often involve more-passive interaction, although this is not recommended. Important to this definition is the idea that public participation is about making decisions and communicating those decisions. Data visualizations are important to facilitating that type of dialog.

In this chapter, the term public engagement is often used interchangeably with civic engagement because data visualizations not only impact our involvement with public decisions, they also affect engagement in civics. Adler and Goggin in their review of civic engagement define it as "the ways in which citizens participate in the life of a community in order to improve conditions for others or to help shape the community's future" (Adler and Goggin 2005, 236). Here "civic" relates to one's role as a citizen, and "engagement" is synonymous with interaction.

Some see civic engagement as working within a framework of creating a civic culture. Civic culture is the merging of different types of relationships within our roles as citizens, both passive activities and action (Almond and Verba 1989). Data visualization contributes to this integration through its ability to communicate complex geographic research in a way that is understandable and relatable to a diverse set of residents. This increases our sense of obligation and competence when it comes to being politically active. The act of learning about our local environment and community may be passive in nature, but as Almond and Verba state in their widely cited piece on the topic, "there would be no civic culture without them" (Almond and Verba 1989). Therefore, one form of civic engagement is learning through the transfer of knowledge provided by data visualizations.

Data Visualizations Are Essential in a Data-Centric Society

Using data for effective governance has gained popularity because of the exponential increase in the amount of data we now collect and store. According to the International Data Corporation (IDC), "In 2011 alone, 1.8 zettabytes (or 1.8 trillion gigabytes) of data will be created, the equivalent to every U.S. citizen writing 3 tweets per minute for 26,976 years" (Merian 2011). This data is collected through devices embedded in common items such as clothing, cell phones, vehicles, roads, and buildings, and through our everyday interactions with the digital environment, which records interactions at a scale previously unachievable (Mayer-Schönberger and Cukier 2013). One of the fundamental problems associated with this massive collection of data, also referred to as big data, is that it is difficult to analyze and convey the results for use in decision making. Data visualizations have become an essential tool for communicating the quantitative insights of big data because they translate raw data into easily understood information using imagery. This transformation allows data to be used for civic engagement and policy change by clearly exposing hidden patterns to audiences inside and outside the policy arena (Williams 2015).

Recent interest in using data to drive government policies is evidenced in Stephen Goldsmith and Susan Crawford's recent book *The Responsive City: Engaging Communities Through Data-Smart Governance*, which illustrates how governments are harnessing the power of big data to increase efficiency in the delivery of city services. In the foreword, Michael Bloomberg, the former mayor of New York, explains why he thinks data is essential when he states "If you can't measure it, you can't manage it." He goes on to say that, "Harnessing and understanding data helped us to decide how to allocate resources more efficiently and effectively, which allowed us to improve the delivery of services from protecting children to fighting crime" (Goldsmith and Crawford 2014, v). For Bloomberg, data analytics are essential for proper governance and data visualizations explain the policy choices made.

The increased availability of data supported through governmental open data policies has broadened public access to data and allowed citizens to use it to develop their own stories. These policies, often framed as the "open data movement," are designed to increase transparency in government as well as spur innovations in the use of data for civic applications (Robinson et al. 2009; Goldstein and Dyson 2013). Technology experts have been successful at using open data in developing applications for increasing access to transportation, providing evacuation tools for Hurricane Sandy, mapping crime, and creating web interfaces for city complaint hotlines or 311-call centers, among numerous other examples (Kalin 2014; Goldstein and Dyson 2013). Software applications and data visualizations developed with open data have been largely inclusive because they usually provide tools that bring data to the broader public. However, open data has been criticized as generating barriers to civic engagement as it is restricted to those who know how to work with data to generate value (Gurstein 2011; Kitchin 2014). Even with this limitation, open data allows groups beyond the government to develop, disseminate, and acquire data visualizations to understand policy positions from their perspective.

Data visualizations are effective at communicating because they hold the legitimacy of data and convince the consumer of their truth. Maps are a good example—data read on maps is rarely questioned because it is often equated with the presentation of fact (Monnmonier 1991; Wood 1992). Data still holds biases generated through the collection purpose and survey methods used (boyd and Crawford 2012). For example, cell phone data analysis can only provide insight about those populations that own a cell phone. Biases are also inherent in data visualizations as they synthesize and edit data to help explain its complexity. This simplification can obfuscate other patterns that the data might expose. Therefore, it is important to be critical of the data visualization we use for public engagement as the messages are still highly controlled.

Current media culture suits the use of data visualizations for telling stories and generating a debate. This is because the consumption of news and information has shifted toward using small discrete visual packages posted on social media sites and blogs (Castells 2013; Bekkers and Moody 2011). Data visualizations fit this medium well because they create visual snapshots of complex ideas. Acquiring visuals through the "social web," consumers add both their critiques and analysis by posting comments and sharing the images online. A quick web search for "data visualization" produces results on everything from scientific data to mentions of Barack Obama on Twitter. Many websites, such as Information Aesthesis, Flowing Data, Junk Art, Vizwonk, and Policyviz, plot the development of these visualizations. Even the U.S. Census Bureau has created a data visualization website which helps to connect them to the public and promotes the use of their data (United States Census Bureau 2014). The explosion of data visualization in these mediums shows that the public is clearly interested in how big data can be used to gain new insights. Social media helps the public share those insights through interactive commenting, which can help form a debate.

Visualizations Strategies for Public Engagement Have Been Controversial

Visualizations are useful for public engagement as they are easy to consume and provide a common language among stakeholders (King et al. 1989; Al-Kodmany 1999). The use of data visualization to affect public policy has been controversial. Traditionally only a select few, largely those in power, had access to data about civic issues, including basic information on socioeconomic, and the ability to create data visualizations from that data (Forester 1988). Modern public engagement strategies in the United States are attributed to the engagement process necessary for the Federal Urban Renewal program started in 1954 (Krueckeberg 1983; Hall 2000; Gordon, Schirra, and Hollander 2011). These early strategies largely employed visualizations, drawings, models, plans, interactive games, and maps at community meetings to garner public support for federal development programs. The results were often criticized for being one-sided, allowing little interaction with the community, and having predetermined agendas that encouraged particular development strategies (Forester 1988; Jacobs 2002; Whyte 1980). This is because the developers and city officials were largely in charge of the data presented.

Reactions to what was seen as top-down strategies for public engagement encouraged the development of equity-driven public participation strategies as early as the 1960s. These experiments largely called for processes that helped to narrow the gap between those who had control of information and decisions and those who did not. Shelly Arnstein (1969) notably advocated for greater knowledge sharing between what she called the "power-holders" and the "powerless" in public participation. Inherent in Arnstein's approach was the need to engage broader publics, including communities typically marginalized by public participation processes, because they do not have resources and data to advocate for their needs (Forester 1988). Interactive education and community dialog became important tools to fill that gap. Glass (1979) believed that information exchange that involved education, building support, supplemental decision-making, and representational input could change power relationships within public engagement strategies. Critical planning theorist John Forester believed that through interactive dialog power could be transferred, as dialog allows groups to present their perspectives and ideas and thereby educate each other on critical issues (Forester 1999).

Literacy and Civic Engagement

Inherent in engagement strategies developed since the late 1960s is the idea that the public needs a certain level of literacy in urban planning processes to interpret information presented to them and make informed decisions. Gordon, Schirra, and Hollander (2011) interpret urban planning as a semiotic domain in which participants must understand a set of "oral or written language, images, equations, symbols, sounds, gestures, graphs, or artifacts" (Gee 2007, 19), yet participants in the urban-planning decision making might not possess these literacies. Several strategies have been developed to help the public acquire these skills. Perhaps the most common are design charrettes, where participants work interactively with architects and planners to develop new planning strategies.

One limitation of design charrettes and other public forums is the public's ability to attend meetings in person. Digital media allow for a new form of civic engagement where participants can become more literate about planning processes through online visualizations and conversations on the social web. The benefits of these tools have been cited as generating cooperative production (Benkler 2006; Lessig 2008), the ability to crowdsource ideas (Howe 2008; Surowiecki 2005), and transforming the role of the audience to knowledge producer through their collective commenting on information presentations (Shirky 2010).

Media theorist Paul Mihailidis (2014) argues that being able to use new digital technologies for active civic engagement is dependent on users being media literate, which he defines as the ability to think critically about media that is consumed and to be able to communicate and interpret ideas using the media as evidence. What is important about media literacy for civic engagement is that it allows the public to acquire, interpret, and generate positions for active social change by developing media-based argument that can then be further disseminated through digital technology (Mihailidis 2014).

The current trend to present planning issues through data visualization means that citizens not only need to be media literate, they need to be data literate so they can be critical of the data they consume and use it to make informed arguments. The definition of data literacy has a relationship to media literacy as it also requires citizens to think critically about the information they are presented with, to have the ability to develop interpretations of that data, and to use data visualization to make arguments (Williams et al. 2014).

Data Visualization Tools Can Transform Power Relationships

Data visualizations have become an important tool in engaging communities in civic topics as they provide a way to clearly communicate and educate various publics on issues using data (King et al. 1989; Al-Kodmany 1999). However, the use of data has been controversial as it was traditionally seen as a tool of the powerful as only few people had the ability to access data and the tools to analyze it. (Harvery and Chrisman 1998). The debate was perhaps most pronounced in the use of Geographic Information Systems (GIS), where many believed it was hard to use maps developed by GIS to address social agendas because they were operated from a position of power (Pickles 1995; Harris and Weiner 1998; Elwood 2002).

GIS can both marginalize and empower different populations depending on how it is used (Pickles 1999; Koti and Weiner 2006). Given these competing results, and the possible social implication of this new tool, a series of workshops were held during GIS's early development to address its effects on society. The first, "Ground Truth: The Social Implications of Geographic Information Systems," often referred to as the Friday Harbor meeting, was held in 1993. This was followed in 1996 by "GIS and Society: The Social Implication of How People, Space, and Environment Are Represented in GIS," organized by the National Center for Geographic Information and Analysis (NCGIA) (Harris and Weiner 1996). The National Research Council then organized "The Future of Spatial Data and Society" (National Research Council 1997). While these workshop discussions documented how spatial data can contribute to marginalization, participants also recognized that there was a possibility to empower populations by developing ways that communities could generate and maintain their own Geographic Information Systems (Harris and Weiner 1998).

These discussions led to the development of Public Participation Geographic Information Systems (PPGIS), which attempts to address the power dynamics involved in spatial analysis and mapping by providing a methodology with which the public can more easily engage and learn about the data used to make decisions with GIS (Gordon, Schirra, and Hollander 2011). PPGIS was originally defined as "a variety of approaches to make GIS and other spatial decision-making tools available and accessible to all those with a stake in official decisions" (Schroeder 1996). Since the late 1990s, PPGIS projects have sought to change the public's relationship with data by creating data literacy and allowing citizens to work interactively with information and generate their own opinions (Sieber 2006). This data literacy allows for a more-engaged citizenry as they can now think critically and make arguments with the data they are presented with.

PPGIS projects are based on the premise that when community groups actively engage in data analysis and collection efforts, they have more power in the political decision-making process (Elwood and Leitner 2003; Bailey and Grossardt 2010). Since its development, PPGIS has been used by governments and Non-Governmental Organizations (NGOs) to share data with wider audiences and thereby influence national-level policies (Alcorn 2000; Rambaldi 2005). Community-based organizations have also used GIS within their own organizations to develop maps that represent their own perspectives and voice to influence neighborhood-level planning initiatives (Sawicki and Craig 1996; Ghose 2007; Kellogg 1999; Elwood 2002). PPGIS projects empower citizens by creating a process through which the public can work with GIS systems and the data they hold and use that information for decision making.

While PPGIS projects have been successful in providing increased access to information to the powerless, many still need a data operator to help community members understand the data presented (Brown and Kytta 2014). The data operator can choose what the community will see and understand and, therefore, maintains some level of control over the data. Even with this level of control, the relationship between the data operator and the public is often one that involves education and interactive knowledge sharing, which is an important component to successful public engagement strategies.

Gordon, Schirra, and Hollander (2011) include PPGIS projects in a conceptual public engagement model called "immersive planning," in which public participation strategies focus on the depth and breadth of user experience to generate new literacies around the ideas presented. The model is framed within three categories of immersion: challenge-based, sensory, and imaginative. Visualization tools can help to create this immersive experience by allowing participants to imagine different scenarios and creating ways for them to interactively generate and visualize planning options. CommunityViz, a GIS-based software, helps users understand planning proposals by allowing them to change zoning, land-use regulations, and amenities, and to visualize the potential results of those decisions (figure 9.1) (Walker and Daniels 2011). Others have sought to use 3D space to visualize planning outcomes, including using virtual reality programs such as Second Life and computer games to help generate a sensory understanding of planning options and to assist with the development of alternative ideas (Gordon and Koo 2008). These visualizations educate participants about the data presented and provide them the ability to add their own input to the plans; and, perhaps most importantly, they generate debate around the proposals and encourage new

Figure 9.1
Image of community members using CommunityViz to develop Build-out Scenarios for a green community in Utrecht, Netherlands. (ESRI 2008)

opinions about urban planning initiatives. The conversations generated by these tools are more important than the scenarios they create as they provide a way for communities to actively communicate their interests through interactive knowledge sharing.

New Visualization Tools Can Create New Innovation

From advances in the printing press in the 1800s, which propagated the use of line and pie charts developed by William Playfield in 1786 and 1801, to John Snow's cholera map, to the proliferation of word clouds, the popularity of data visualizations has grown alongside the advances in technology that make it easier to create them (Friendly and Denis 2008). Current data visualizations are easy to consume because the web has made them more accessible. At the same time, and perhaps more importantly, there has been an explosion of visualization tools (Bekkers and Moody 2011) such as Many Eyes, Tableau, Visual.ly, Lyra, and Google Charts. The development of open source programming languages has also made it easier to visualize data, including the recent creation of languages such as D3, Processing, and Open Frameworks. The ability to develop maps is also becoming more accessible. Here too new software packages are leading the way. Google Earth, Cartodb, Mapbox, and Tilemill, to name of few, have made it easier to stylize and add data to maps to generate quick data visualizations.

There is software designed specifically to generate information visualizations for government. Policy Map, an online data and mapping tool, was designed for government agencies to access everything from health to census data and to generate compelling maps for policy reports. These tools help to remove some of the technical barriers created by data visualization software, such as GIS, by providing a way to more easily develop visuals using publicly accessible data. (Moody 2010). While these tools are easier to use, they still present some challenges as users need training and the funds to purchase subscriptions. Even with these caveats, the tools help loosen professionals' control over data, allowing anyone to create their own impressions of civic decisions through readily accessible visual tools.

A Picture Is Worth a Thousand Words: Data Visualization Can Affect Policy

One interesting development of data visualizations is the ability to acquire new forms of data or use openly available governmental data sets to expose policy issues that were previously difficult to discern. Visualizations developed from these data sets can help generate a debate and can change policies. A notable example of this is Million Dollar Blocks, a project developed by the Justice Mapping Center and the Spatial Information Design Lab at Columbia University, in which data visualizations developed for this project were used as evidence for the Criminal Justice Reinvestment Act of 2009 and 2010. The project takes government criminal intake records and transforms them to expose how funding is allocated to prisons rather than communities (Kurgan et al. 2006; Kurgan 2013). Million Dollar Blocks transformed governmental data into a picture of fiscal spending and illustrated the cost of incarceration from the perspective of the communities that many prisoners come from, helping to generate debate about the inequity of resource allocation in those communities.

Governmental prisoner intake data from New York City; Wichita, Kansas; New Haven, Connecticut; New Orleans, Louisiana; and Phoenix, Arizona, were used to plot the locations of where prisoners lived before they went to prison. This data was cross-tabulated with the cost of incarcerating these people and then summed by the blocks where they had lived. The results exposed that in some communities over a million dollars is spent to incarcerate residents of single blocks. The visualization illustrated that these "million dollar blocks" were concentrated in communities that often have limited resources allocated to social programs, including job training or prison reentry services that could alleviate some of the systemic issues behind the high incarceration rates (Kurgan 2013).

Presented in the original visualization as red blocks against a dark background, the images were at once alarming and captivating because they scale prison policy down to the size of a city block—something that everyone can understand (figure 9.2). Visualizing the data on the scale of the block was an important tool for contextualizing the vast sums of money spent on incarceration. Instead of asking the reader to understand a billion-dollar figure for an entire state, the data was transformed to the scale of a city block, connecting it to a particular place. Reading the dollar amounts in millions instead of billions allowed the public to connect with the scale of the spending as it is easier to conceive of a million-dollar figure. The data visualizations allowed the public to see the spatial patterns associated with prison spending and develop their own interpretations based on their knowledge of those places. Maps showing race and poverty were presented alongside prison spending maps providing demographic context. Areas with high concentrations of prison spending usually had high rates of poverty.

The use of the map was also an important tool for creating a sense of legitimacy in the data presented. This is because people often believe evidence presented on maps is proven fact rather than interpreted results created from the perspective of the map-maker (Wood 1992). In his book *How to Lie with Maps*, Mark Monmonier explains how map readers rarely question data on maps because they are often see them as representation of what exists on the ground such as is seen in a road map (Monmonier 1991).

The Million Dollar Blocks' message was at once both simple and complicated. Through the collection process itself, the data revealed that our response to poverty is often incarceration. In many ways, this result is unintentional as it is driven by diverse policy-based spending decisions. The maps have been exhibited widely, starting at the Architectural League of New York in 2006, and in the "Design and the Elastic Mind" exhibition at the Museum of Modern Art (MoMA) in New York City in 2008. The maps have also been included in the permanent collection of the MoMA and have been on display multiple times where audiences can continue to experience the message they present—we spend millions of dollars to incarcerate people in the United States, and the cycling of people in and out of prison has become a big business. The Million Dollar Blocks visualizations not only supported a public debate in the media, they also provided accessible evidence to support congressional funding for the Criminal Justice Reinvestment Act of 2009, which allocated funding to prisoner reentry programs.

Data Visualization Can Facilitate Interactive Knowledge Sharing on Civic Topics

Interactive education on civic issues is important to public engagement processes as it allows the public to understand an issue, start a dialog, and narrow the information gap

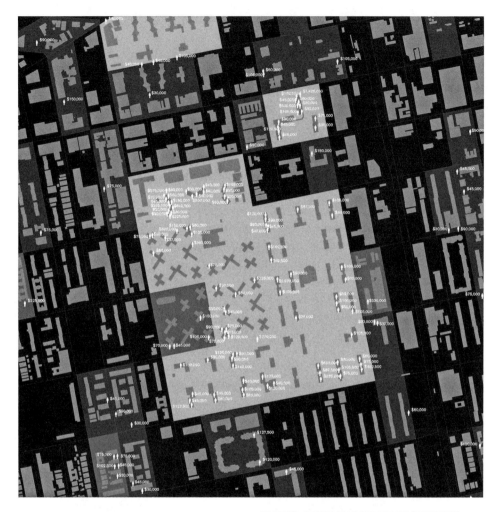

BROWNSVILLE, BROOKLYN

IT COST 17 MILLION DOLLARS TO IMPRISON 109 PEOPLE FROM THESE 17 BLOCKS IN 2003. WE CALL THESE MILLION DOLLAR BLOCKS. ON A FINANCIAL SCALE PRISONS ARE BECOMING THE PREDOMINANT GOVERNING INSTITUTION IN THE NEIGHBORHOOD.

Figure 9.2
The above image of the Million Dollar Blocks project was used to help argue for prisoner re-entry funding in Congress. Image provided by the Spatial Information Design Lab.

between the public and those who develop policy. Data visualizations are increasingly being used to develop this type of knowledge sharing. An organization that uses data visualization in this way is the Center for Urban Pedagogy (CUP). According to their website (http://welcometocup.org/About), this nonprofit organization "uses design and art to improve civic engagement. CUP projects demystify urban policy and planning issues that impact our communities, so that more individuals can better participate in shaping them." CUP's projects break policies down into "simple, accessible, visual explanations." What captivates people about CUP's projects is that they often ask the public to both gather and interpret information they acquire on policy issues and to develop visual representations through conversation with the CUP team. This forces the public to educate themselves on the topic, creating a literacy on the topic.

One of CUP's projects that best illustrates how interactive visualization can educate the public about policy and generate a conversation about its use is the Affordable Housing Toolkit, which teaches affordable housing policies in New York City. Affordable housing is complex; as CUP's website explains, it "doesn't always mean what people think it does. It is actually a technical definition, which can determine what gets built and who gets to live there." This is because affordable housing is defined by the proportion of income a family can feasibly spend on rent, which is defined by the Area Median Income (AMI). Understanding how New York City derives the AMI is not easy as it changes depending on family size. However, it is important to identify AMI as it is used to determine whether a family qualifies for New York City's various housing programs. The toolkit and its associated website use neighborhood-level visualizations to explore U.S. Census data on median household income, average family size, and housing costs (figure 9.3). Interaction with the tool teaches how income and family size affect eligibility for the program. For example, in 2013, a family of three needed to earn $46,440 or less (60% of the AMI) to qualify for the Low-Income Affordable Marketplace Program (LAMP) program (New York City Housing Development Corporation 2014). Users can also see neighborhoods where there are more residents in need of affordable housing programs. The tool allows anyone to explore the affordable housing programs he or she may be able to participate in, from subsidized housing to Section 8 (City Atlas New York 2014).

The toolkit, which in its physical form looks like a felt game board, initiates conversations when used (figure 9.4). Participants are asked to reorganize felt markers on a graph to show the distribution of income and determine the affordable housing options available in different neighborhoods. CUP staff often provides support, and the process begins a discussion about how income relates to available housing options. Participants come to understand their options and the trade-offs associated with various housing policies. They also learn how they can qualify for specific housing programs. The toolkit simplifies the complexity of affordable housing policies through discussion about

Figure 9.3
Affordable Housing Toolkit online tool. Image provided by the Center of Urban Pedagogy.

Figure 9.4
Affordable Housing Toolkit felt "game board." Image provided by the Center of Urban Pedagogy.

options and the ability to visualize those options. The process educates participants in the planning processes, which allows them to make more-informed decisions.

Teaching socially relevant topics through data visualization can also increase data literacy by translating raw numbers into information easily understood by laypeople. Data literacy is the ability to work with, analyze, and make arguments with data (Williams et al. 2014). It has become an essential skill in a society that increasingly depends on data to make decisions (Philip, Schuler-Brown, and Way 2013). One model for using data visualization to teach data literacy is City Digits: Local Lotto, a high school curriculum and its accompanying web application that supports students in building data literacy by allowing them to collect, explore, and form opinions about a civic topic—the lottery (Williams et al., 2014). Inherent in teaching data literacy is the ability to generate arguments about quantitative and qualitative data. In Local Lotto, these arguments tackle whether the lottery is "good" or "bad" for communities. The data visualization web tool facilitates the development of arguments by drawing a clearer picture of the how different communities are affected by lottery sales. The dialog developed while students construct their arguments helps to teach students the policy issues behind the lottery and create a dialog that is important for community engagement.

The Local Lotto mapping tool was piloted in Bushwick School for Social Justice in New York City in 2013 and allows students to explore maps of the New York Lottery's sales and winnings data. The lottery data was obtained through the New York State Gaming Commission, who openly shared five years of winning and sales data. Varying circle sizes illustrate the amount each lottery retailer sells and pays out in winnings by address (figure 9.5). The visualization clearly shows that the odds of winning are the same at every location. Students zoom in to navigate the data plotted on a digital street map and explore the neighborhood around their school. The data is also aggregated by neighborhood boundaries to illustrate that different communities spend different proportions of their income on lottery tickets. Students can also explore the sociodemographic characteristics of communities, which allows them to draw conclusions about who plays the lottery.

After the students explore the maps in the classroom, they head out into the neighborhood with mobile tablets and conduct interviews with lottery players and retailers using a recorder built into the application. The interview results go directly onto the map and web application. After the students work through the curriculum, they are asked to synthesize the data collected, both in the field and during map exploration, and use it to develop an argument about whether they think the lottery is good or bad (figure 9.6). The resulting stories are added to the web tool, allowing anyone to see the students' interpretations of the data. The process of developing these stories by exploring visuals allows the students to bring together multiple viewpoints on how the lottery affects their community and helps them form their own opinions on a civic topic (Williams et al. 2014). The process teaches the students data literacy because they have

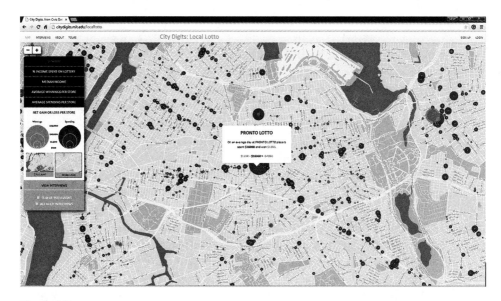

Figure 9.5
Net gain or loss map, zoomed into the street level. The darker circles represent the amount of money spent on lottery tickets at individual retail stores. The lighter circles represent the amount of money won from lottery tickets at the same stores. Images provided courtesy of Sarah Williams, Civic Data Design Lab.

to interpret and understand the data they worked with to make a cohesive argument using the information they collected.

CUP's Affordable Housing Toolkit and City Digits: Local Lotto both teach civic topics and provide a way for the public to form their own questions, develop their own opinions, and ultimately generate a conversation. The data visualizations facilitate education on a civic topic, as participants must communicate with the visualization to show how a policy affects them. This helps to break down the knowledge barriers associated with civic engagement and helps to create a more informed public. This type of information sharing is an important component to successful civic engagement strategies. Perhaps more importantly, the interactive and graphic nature of the visuals make the education experience fun and increases interest in the topics (Williams et al. 2014).

Media-Generated Data Visualizations Allow the Public to Discover Their Own Stories

Newspapers and other forms of media have long been used as outlets for public debate. Recent web-based interactive technology such as D3 programming language has increased the media's ability to develop interactive "data stories" that allow users to

Figure 9.6
A group of students works together on constructing their arguments.

explore data, ask their own questions, and generate new conversations. These visualizations do not provide one story line; rather they allow readers to find their own. The resulting stories help create a debate on civic topics.

The *New York Times* has generated many of these kinds of visualizations. After the release of the 2010 U.S. census data, they created a series called "Mapping America" that looked at race, income, family status, and housing issues. In 2012, the *Times* created a map called the "Geography of Benefits," which shows concentrations of Medicaid, food stamps, and social security payments along with other state and federal benefits. In 2013, they created a series called "Mapping Poverty." All three of these projects have been successful in providing information to the public, and the visualizations have created a way for readers to use data for their own public debate.

A quick web search shows the number of people who have taken snapshots of the data visualizations developed by the *Times* to tell their own stories. For example, a blog in Denver uses a screen grab (figure 9.7) of a map on race to highlight the segregation between Latinos and whites, concluding that the city is more divided than they had

DENVER RACIAL BOUNDARIES: *NEW YORK TIMES* CENSUS MAPS SHOW MASSIVE URBAN SEGREGATION

A A   **BY JOEL WARNER**   MONDAY, DECEMBER 20, 2010 | 5 YEARS AGO

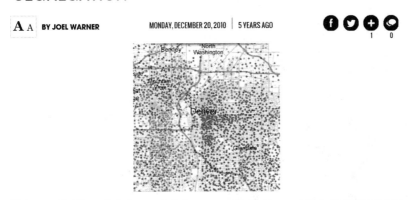

It's no secret that Denver is far from perfectly homogenous. But just how racially divided is the city? As illustrated by new, interactive, nationwide population maps developed by the *New York Times*, Denver's Hispanic and white populations are starkly segregated, with I-25 serving as the proverbial "wrong side of the tracks" boundary line.

Figure 9.7
Screen grab of a Denver blog that used the *New York Times* maps to create discussion of race in Denver.

thought (Warner 2010). Another blog uses the maps to highlight poverty in the South and to show that income disparity between the North and the South is more significant than originally thought (Badger 2013). *Radar,* a blog from O'Reilly Media, which is a leader in emerging technologies, cites the tools as being faithful to the original data and states that its "ease of use" opens up a new range of ways to see the data. The blog author believes the visualization "makes complex information simpler to understand" (Pierre 2011). The repurposing of these maps is widespread both online and in teaching environments, creating a public resource that gives anyone access to the power data holds in order to communicate stories.

One notable case in which a *New York Times* interactive map was acquired for public debate was a graphic titled "How Minorities Have Fared in States with Affirmative Action Bans," which was used in a Supreme Court decision (Fessenden and Keller 2014). The graphic, developed in April 2014, allowed readers to explore the percentage of Hispanic and black students accepted to state universities in Washington, Florida, Texas, California, and Michigan before and after affirmative action bans were established. Overall, the charts and accompanying graphics showed decreases in minority enrollment after affirmative action bans were set in place.[2] At the time the graphic was published, the Supreme Court was set to hear the case of Schuette v. Coalition to Defend Affirmative Action, which would decide whether to uphold the affirmative action ban in Michigan. The visualizations were generated by the *Times* so readers could better understand the questions put before the Supreme Court.

These data visualizations became part of a historical public debate when Sonya Sotomayor used the graphic as part of her official dissent to the ruling to uphold the ban. In her document, a screenshot (figure 9.8) of the *New York Times* visualization was used to support her position that the removal of affirmative action does, in fact, affect minority enrollment in college. She noted, "the proportion of black students among those obtaining bachelor's degrees was 4.4 percent, the lowest since 1991." Using the graphs as evidence, she goes on to say "At UCLA, for example, the proportion of Hispanic freshman among those enrolled declined from 23 percent in 1995 to 17 percent in 2011, even though the proportion of Hispanic college-aged persons in California increased from 41 percent to 49 percent during that same period" (Schuette v. Coalition to Defend Affirmative Action 2014, 51). Sotomayor has always been a supporter of affirmative action so the graphic most likely did not inform her decision, but she hoped it would sway others by illustrating the relationship between policies and minority enrollment.

The *New York Times* received some criticism that the graphics were biased toward lifting affirmative action bans, which helped to further the public debate generated by

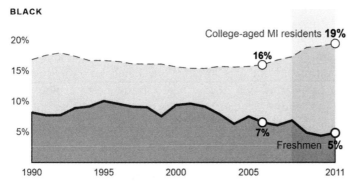

Figure 9.8
Screenshot from Sotomayor's dissent.

the images. One article in the *Independent Voter Network* claimed, "All of these numbers have left off something very important; the students that leave those states to attend a university in another state and the students from other states that go to those particular universities. Should they be used to help show if a university is measuring up in minority enrollment to the state's total minority population?" (Spurgeon 2014). Others found the arguments misleading because they believed the data should have compared college-ready minority students rather than college-age students (Weiser 2013). More articles point out that the *Times* did not include Asians or other minorities in their definition, and, therefore, the story is misleading (Howley 2014). The debate generated over the "fairness" of the graphic allowed those that supported the Supreme Court's decision to use the same data visualizations to argue their position.

The inclusion of the *New York Times* affirmative action data visualization in a public media forum allowed it to be acquired and used as evidence for divergent stories. The graphics generated a debate, which is important for public engagement. However, it should be noted that this debate was largely developed by those who could understand the visualizations and the data behind them. While public engagement processes encourage a conversation between the powerful and powerless, the conversation generated by these graphics was more a debate among those who knew how to operationalize the data visualization. This is why data literacy is important if we are going to use data visualization for public engagement.

Crowdsourced Data Visualizations Create Public Debates

There is a trend to develop data visualizations that collect and solicit public input. These crowdsourcing sites are different from many of the other visualizations mentioned in this chapter because they focus on communicating collective opinions rather than presenting predetermined stories. These visualizations largely use maps to organize user-generated data illustrating place-specific community issues. Assembling the data in this way allows the public to see the locations where there are overlapping interests, thereby encouraging a debate on the problems visualized. The data itself is often left in its raw form, and the users are asked to find their own meaning from the narratives left on the site. Ultimately, the sites become visual databases of the community's collective thoughts, complaints, and ideas—there for anyone to explore. The sites also often become a form of advertising for the topics they address. There are benefits and disadvantages to using these types of collective visualizations to make decisions. They help to engage people who might not have traditionally gone to a public meeting or review by creating a captivating way to engage the community. However, at the same time, they can exclude people who might not typically participate in an interactive online format, making it hard to use the data to develop decisions.

Some of the first applications developed to crowdsource civic data were complaint sites focused on community issues, usually known as 311 hotlines. These hotlines started in Baltimore in 1996 and are now popular in most large cities in the United States. 311 hotlines allow the public to receive information about city services such as trash collection times. They also provide the ability to report incidents or register complaints about everything from potholes to excessive noise. In the summer of 2014, a National 311 Executive Council was formed to develop "best practices, standards, and policies" for 311 to help coordinate a growing interest in using the data (Shueh 2014). Many cities have generated online tools to collect and visualize data from 311 programs.

One of the first online 311 tools developed is SeeClickFix, a web and mobile application that allows citizens to report and review community issues online. Originally developed for New Haven, Connecticut, the service thrived because citizens realized they could use the space to advocate community ideas and, more importantly, to meet others who had similar interests and concerns. Users in the Downtown-Wooster Square area all realized they were concerned about the lack of a full-service grocery store and sufficient street lighting in the neighborhood. They came together and created the Downtown-Wooster Square Management Team after reading each other's messages on the SeeClickFix site (figure 9.9) (Williams 2014). They now advocate issues in their neighborhood both virtually and digitally. SeeClickFix provided a way for people who might not have traditionally attended community meetings to come together and

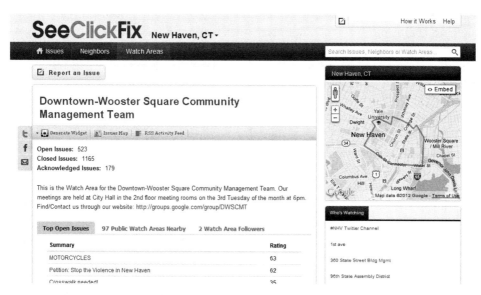

Figure 9.9
Screenshot from SeeClickFix. Images courtesy of SeeClickFix.

work on an idea in the virtual world. Publicizing and visualizing the data about the community, rather than entrusting it to the vault of 311 phone complaints, has allowed the community to organize itself rather than wait for the city to respond. Here the digital technology allowed for the collective cooperation needed for civic change.

SeeClickFix is both a data collection and visualization tool. The visualization aspect of the tool creates meaningful results for public engagement as it allows users to see common interest and goals using a map as the exploration framework. The visualization openly shares user generated data making civic issues more transparent. City officials, as well as the public, have a greater ability to learn from other members of the community and form common goals, which is an important component of public engagement process.

The popularity of the SeeClickFix has led many cities to develop sites that allow citizens to engage with information in similar ways. One group that often works in this medium is OpenPlans, a nonprofit that "develops tools that help planners communicate better" (OpenPlans 2014). Similar to SeeClickFix, OpenPlans's Shareabouts tool allows users to geolocate their opinions and share them via an online map. The OpenPlans team has worked with several cities to build Shareabouts-based sites, creating visualizations of community input on everything from the location of bike share docking stations to participatory budgeting projects.[3]

The New York City Department of Transportation's Vision Zero Action Plan used Shareabouts to facilitate the presentation and collection of community input on street safety. The online mapping tool combines city data sets on traffic accidents and allows users to comment on the conditions of street intersections (figure 9.10). Public data was collected through an online and in-person community engagement process that generated over 10,000 comments. The tool facilitated increased public engagement as it allowed people who might not come to a community meeting to participate online. Users of the site can post and comment on street safety issues (figure 9.11). The online visualization of the data allows users as well as city officials to see streets with particularly high traffic problems, empowering them with information to help suggest solutions to those problems.

Crowdsourced data visualization tools allow communities to input and visualize community issues; however, the data, which is often presented in its raw form as points on a map, could benefit from further synthesis to use it to generate meaningful action. For example, a New York City Department of Transportation crowdsourcing site that asks "Where do you want bike share?" lacks visual order (figure 9.12), making it is hard to see locations where the most users might be requesting the program.[4] The same is true for New York City's Vision Zero project (figure 9.11). SeeClickFix users were able to visualize common concerns and come together to take action on those issues; not all crowdsourcing sites operate in this way. This means the data is often controlled by the organization that developed the site. Some crowdsourcing sites allow the public to download and work with the data generated. However, this type of interaction needs

Figure 9.10
New York City's Department of Transportation Vision Zero web map, which allows users to provide community input about safe streets.

technical expertise. Visualizations developed on crowdsourcing sites still need refinement in order for communities to truly engage with the some of the questions they seek to answer. They are still useful for obtaining and sharing feedback from populations that might not engage in the typical community forum. They help to engage the public in community issues and start a debate. However, it is important to remember that the public is limited to those who know about the site and can use the technology. While crowdsourced visualizations try to break down the barriers in public engagement, the visualizations themselves are not always effective in achieving that goal.

Discussion

Public engagement strategies have always used data visualizations as a way to communicate ideas because they are easy to consume (King et al. 1989; Al-Kodmany 1999), yet these strategies have often been criticized for upholding the position of those who

Figure 9.11
Users of New York City's Vision Zero program can post and add to other users' comments. The image above shows a speeding program on Canal Street in New York City and user remarks that better traffic light timing might help the problem.

control the data (Jacobs 2002; Whyte 1980; Harvery and Chrisman 1998; Elwood 2002). The volumes of data we now collect and the openness in which governments are sharing that data have caused and increased interest in using data visualization for public engagement as they help to communicate the complexity of data. These visualizations are being rapidly disseminated to large publics through social media and news outlets. Online data visualization tools developed by nonprofits to educate the public about civic topics using data have increased knowledge sharing important for successful community engagement. The accessibility of these tools has helped to break down the typical power relationships associated with the use of data for public engagement, as the visualizations allow the public to acquire the data visualizations for their own uses and to generate a debate about what they have visualized.

An emphasis on the need to change the power dynamics associated with public engagement processes was led by Arnstein (1969), who advocated greater information exchange between the "powerful" and the "powerless" in her article "A Ladder of Citizenship Participation." One way this has been accomplished is through involved

Figure 9.12
Screenshot of New York City's bike share suggest-a-location portal. Although this visualization helps anyone see where potential users are interested in the program, the visualization overall is hard to read and would benefit from further synthesis to show where the most users are requesting a location.

education and building support for decision-making and representation strategies (Glass 1979). Data visualization helps facilitate learning about civic topics essential to the generation of civic engagement (Almond and Verba 1989; Gordon, Schirra, and Hollander 2011). Openly shared data presented through news venues and social media sites allows for this kind of interactive learning by exposing policy issues. The availability of these visualizations allows the public to acquire and use them for their own purposes. This is true of the examples seen in the *New York Times*. Justice Sotomayor was able to use the visualizations to present her own argument, as did the people who opposed her position.

Data visualizations help facilitate knowledge sharing through education and outreach programs that help the public understand the complexity of civic topics while also teaching data literacy. The Center for Urban Pedagogy's Affordable Housing

Toolkit teaches the public how data is used in New York City's Affordable Housing Program. The conversation generated through interaction with the toolkit creates a greater understanding of both policy and the data it is based on. Interactive data visualization tools are also being used more in traditional education learning environments such as the City Digits: Local Lotto project, which allows participants to form an opinion on whether the lottery is "good" or "bad" for their community. Both projects help the public increase their data literacy skills by asking them to interpret the data that is presented and derive new meaning. Using data visualization to teach about policy is also important in a world that increasingly depends on data to make decisions (Philip, Schuler-Brown, and Way 2013). Teaching the public to be more data literate by actively asking questions about the information they are presented helps them learn about civic topics and can allow them to be more critical of data.

New tools have also allowed the public to generate a collective representation of their opinions and interests as seen in some of the crowdsourcing projects presented. These sites allow the public to give data back to the government to collectively inform policy. In these projects, citizens who might not typically attend public meetings are able to participate in the debate. These tools change the structural limitations often associated with civic engagement by giving the public an increased ability to provide their input.

The power dynamics within data still exist. While governments have opened up data, the ability to interact with visualizations is still available only to those who have access to them. Furthermore, the control of the data lies in the ability to interpret it. While there are new tools such as Cartodb, Many Eyes, Tableau, and Visual.ly that facilitate access to visualization creation, these tools can only be used by those who have the necessary skills. The examples shown here often work to address the needs of those with less power, yet visualizations are still controlled by those that create them. A person skilled in working with data, or a data operator, is necessary to translate the data for the public, and it can be difficult for data interpreters to be entirely neutral (Brown and Kytta 2014). Data visualizations are powerful tools for swaying public opinion (Harley 1992), which makes it essential to know the purposes and perspectives of the person creating them. This is why data literacy is necessary—to ensure that the public can analyze the data visualizations they consume. Even with these potential biases, it is clear that the explosion of data visualizations driven by increased access to data and tools to generate them has had the ability to generate public debates about policy initiatives essential for successful public engagement.

Acknowledgments

I want to thank Eric Gordon, Paul Mihailidis, and the MIT Press for including my thoughts on data visualization in their manuscript. The works could not have been completed without the helpful assistance of my research assistants Karuna Mehta and Elizabeth Early.

Notes

1. The term data visualization has varied definitions depending on the application of its use. Some define it as a graphic exercise, while others define it as a way to facilitate discussion or explain complexity (Lindquist 2011 and Friendly and Denis 2008).

2. Florida was the only state where their affirmative action ban did not seem to affect the minority enrollment in state schools.

3. Participatory budgeting allows users to vote on the allocation of capital development projects in their neighborhood under $1 million. The community generates ideas for these projects and votes on which idea they like the best. The online maps built in Shareabouts help to generate public debate on the topics to be included.

4. In many ways the data collected on these sites is presented in a neutral way as it has not been synthesized to tell a story. Yet the data itself still holds the biases of the users who come to the site and add their input.

References

Adler, Richard, and Judy Goggin. 2005. "What Do We Mean by 'Civic Engagement'?" *Journal of Transformative Education* 3 (3): 236–252.

Alcorn, Janis B. 2000. "Borders, Rules, and Governance: Mapping to Catalyze Changes in Policy and Management." International Institute for Environment and Development, *Gatekeeper Series*, no. 91. http://pubs.iied.org/pdfs/X180IIED.pdf.

Al-Kodmany, Kheir. 1999. "Using Visualization Techniques for Enhancing Public Participation in Planning and Design: Process, Implementation, and Evaluation." *Landscape and Urban Planning* 45 (1): 37–45.

Al-Kodmany, Kheir. 2002. "Visualization Tools and Methods in Community Planning: From Freehand Sketches to Virtual Reality." *Journal of Planning Literature* 17 (2): 189–211.

Almond, Gabriel A., and Sidney Verba. 1989. The Civic Culture: Political Attitudes and Democracy in Five Nations. Atlanta, GA: Sage.

Arnstein, Shelly. 1969. "A Ladder of CItizenship Participation." *Journal of the American Institute of Planners* 35 (4): 216–224.

Badger, Emily. 2013. "5 Maps That Show How Divided America Really Is." *CityLab*, June 7. Accessed January 2, 2015. http://www.citylab.com/work/2013/06/5-maps-show-2-different-americas/5824.

Bailey, Keiron, and Ted Grossardt. 2010. "Toward Structured Public Involvement: Justice, Geography and Collaborative Geospatial/Geovisual Decision Support Systems." *Annals of the Association of American Geographers* 100 (1): 57–86.

Bekkers, Victor, and Rebecca Moody. 2011. "Visual Events and Electronic Government: What Do Pictures Mean in Digital Government for Citizen Relations?" *Government Information Quarterly* 28 (4): 457–465.

Benkler, Yochai. 2006. *The Wealth of Networks: How Social Production Transforms Markets and Freedom.* New Haven, CT: Yale University Press.

Bourgault, Jeanne. 2013. "How the Global Open Data Movement Is Transforming Journalism." *Wired,* May 31. www.wired.com/2013/05/how-the-global-open-data-movement-is-transforming-journalism.

boyd, danah, and Kate Crawford. 2012. "Critical Questions for Big Data: Provocations for a Cultural, Technological, and Scholarly Phenomenon." *Information Communication and Society* 15 (5): 662–679.

Brail, Richard K., and Richard E. Klosterman. 2001. *Planning Support Systems: Integrating Geographic Information Systems, Models, and Visualization Tools.* Redlands, CA: ESRI Press.

Brown, Greg, and Marketta Kyttä. 2014. "Key Issues and Research Priorities for Public Participation GIS (PPGIS): A Synthesis Based on Empirical Research." *Applied Geography* 46:122–136.

Castells, Manuel. 2013. *Communication Power.* Oxford: Oxford University Press.

Center for Urban Pedagogy. 2015. http://welcometocup.org/About.

City Atlas New York. 2014. "Talking Affordable Housing with CUP." http://newyork.thecityatlas.org/lifestyle/talking-transitions-talks-affordable-housing.

Creighton, James L. 2005. *The Public Participation Handbook: Making Better Decisions Through Citizen Involvement.* Hoboken, NJ: John Wiley & Sons.

Elwood, Sarah. 2002. "GIS and Collaborative Urban Governance: Understanding Their Implications for Community Action and Power." *Urban Geography* 22 (8): 737–759.

Elwood, Sarah, and H. Leitner. 2003. "GIS and Spatial Knowledge Production for Neighborhood Revitalization: Negotiating State Priorities and Neighborhood Visions." *Journal of Urban Affairs* 25 (2):139–157.

ESRI. 2008. CommunityViz Case Studies Web App. http://placeways.maps.arcgis.com/apps/MapTour/index.html?appid=8471e8a44a6646148df7e467dd1e91db&webmap=fd881fc619a54af7b29c97bae02af413.

Fessenden, Ford, and Josh Keller. 2013. "How Minorities Have Fared in States with Affirmative Action Banks." *New York Times,* June 24. Last modified June 30, 2015. http://www.nytimes.com/interactive/2013/06/24/us/affirmative-action-bans.html.

FlowingData. 2014. http://flowingdata.com.

Forester, John. 1988. *Planning in the Face of Power*. Berkeley: University of Califonia Press.

Forester, John. 1999. *The Deliberative Practitioner: Encouraging Participatory Planning Processes*. Cambridge, MA: MIT Press.

Friendly, Michael, and Daniel Denis. 2008. *"Milestones in the History of Thematic Cartography, Statistical Graphics, and Data Visualization." Seeing Science*. Today American Association for the Advancement of Science. http://www. datavis. ca/milestones.

Gebeloff, Robert, Haeyoun Park, Matthew Bloch, and Matthew Ericson. 2013. "Where Poor and Uninsured Americans Live." *New York Times*, October 2. http://www.nytimes.com/interactive/2013/10/02/us/uninsured-americans-map.html?_r=0.

Gee, James Paul. 2007. *What Video Games Have to Teach Us About Learning and Literacy*. New York: Palgrave.

Ghose, R. 2007. "Politics of Scale and Networks of Association in Public Participation in GIS." *Environment and Planning A* 39:1961–1980.

Glass, James J. 1979. "Citizen Participation in Planning: The Relationship Between Objectives and Techniques." *Journal of the American Planning Association* 45 (2): 180–189.

Goldstein, Brett, and Lauren Dyson. 2013. *Beyond Transparency: Open Data and the Future of Civic Innovation*. San Francisco, CA: Code for America Press.

Goldsmith, Stephen, and Susan Crawford. 2014. The Responsive City: Engaging Communities Through Data-Smart Governance. Hoboken, NJ: John Wiley & Sons.

Gordon, Eric, and Gene Koo. 2008. "Placeworlds: Using Virtual Worlds to Foster Civic Engagement." *Space and Culture* 11 (3): 204–221.

Gordon, Eric, Steven Schirra, and Justin Hollander. 2011. "Immersive Planning: A Conceptual Model for Designing Public Participation with New Technologies." *Environment and Planning* B 38 (3).

Gurstein, Michael B. 2011. "Open Data: Empowering the Empowered or Effective Data Use for Everyone?" *First Monday* 16 (2).

Hall, Peter. 2000. *Cities of Tomorrow: An Intellectual History of Urban Planning and Design in the Twentieth Century*. Malden, MA: Blackwell.

Harley, John. 1992. *The Politics of Pictures: The Creation of the Public in the Age of Popular Media*. London: Routledge.

Harris, T., and D. Weiner. 1996. "GIS and Society: The Social Implications of How People, Space, and Environment Are Represented in GIS." Scientific Report for the Initiative 19 Specialist Meeting, March 2–5, 1996, Koinonia Retreat Center, South Haven, Minnesota. National Center for Geographic Information and Analysis.

Harris, T., and D. Weiner. 1998. "Empowerment, Marginalization, and 'Community-Integrated' GIS." *Cartography and Geographic Information Systems* 25 (2): 67–76.

Harvery, F., and N. Chrisman. 1998. "Boundary Objects and the Social Construction of GIS Technology." *Environment and Planning A* 30 (9): 1683–1694.

Howe, J. 2008. *Crowdsourcing: Why the Power of the Crowd Is Driving the Future of Business*. New York: Three Rivers Press.

Howley, Patrick. 2014. "New York Times Excludes Asian-Americans from Affirmative Action Study." *Daily Caller*, April 23. http://dailycaller.com/2014/04/23/new-york-times-excludes-asian -americans-from-affirmative-action-study.

Income Eligibility. 2014. http://www.nychdc.com/Contact_Us.

Information Aesthetics. 2014. http://infosthetics.com.

Information Is Beautiful. 2014. http://www.informationisbeautiful.net.

Jacobs, Jane. 2002. *The Death and Life of Great American Cities*. New York: Random House.

Kalin, Ian. 2014. "Open Data Policy Improves Democracy." *SAIS Review of International Affairs* 34 (1): 59–70.

Kellogg, Wendy. 1999. "From the Field: Observations on Using GIS to Develop a Neighborhood Environmental Information System for Community-Based Organizations." *Journal of the Urban and Regional Information Systems Association / URISA* 11:15–32.

King, Stanley, Merinda Conley, Bill Latimer, and Drew Ferrari. 1989. *Co-Design: A Process of Design Participation*. New York: Van Nostrand Reinhold.

Kitchin, Robert. 2014. *The Data Revolution : Big Data, Open Data, Data Infastructures & Their Consequences*. London: SAGE.

Koti, F., and D. Weiner. 2006. "(Re) Defining Peri-Urban Residential Space Using Participatory GIS in Kenya." *The Electronic Journal on Information Systems in Developing Countries* 25: 1–12.

Krueckeberg, D. A. 1983. *Introduction to Planning History in the United States*. New Brunswick, NJ: The Center for Urban Policy and Research.

Kurgan, Laura. 2013. *Close Up at a Distance: Mapping, Technology, and Politics*. Cambridge, MA: MIT Press.

Kurgan, Laura, Erica Cadora, Sarah Williams, and David Reinfurt. 2006. *Architecture and Justice*. New York: Columbia University Graduate School of Architecture, Planning, and Preservation (GSAPP).

Lane, Julia, Victoria Stodden, Stefan Bender, and Helen Nissenbaum. 2014. *Privacy, Big Data, and the Public Good: Frameworks for Engagement*. Cambridge: Cambridge University Press.

Lessig, Lawrence. 2008. *Civic Engagement on the Move: How Mobile Media Can Serve the Public*. Washington, DC: Aspen Institute.

Mearian, Lucas. 2011. "World's Data Will Grow by 50X in Next Decade, IDC Study Predicts." Computerworld, June 28, http://www.computerworld.com/article/2509588/data-center/world-s-data-will-grow-by-50x-in-next-decade--idc-study-predicts.html.

Lindquist, Evert. 2011. *Surveying the World of Visualization.* Australian National University, HC Coombs Policy Forum.

Mayer-Schönberger, Viktor, and Kenneth Cukier. 2013. *Big Data: A Revolution That Will Transform How We Live, Work, and Think.* Boston: Houghton Mifflin Harcourt.

Mihailidis, Paul. 2014. *Media Literacy and the Emerging Citizen: Youth, Engagement and Participation in Digital Culture.* Peter Lang Publishing Inc.

Monmonier, Mark. 1991. *How to Lie with Maps.* Chicago: University of Chicago Press.

Moody, Rebecca F.I. 2010. *"Mapping Power: Geographical Information Systems, Agenda-Setting and Policy Design." PhD. diss.,* Erasmus University.

National Research Council, Mapping Science Committee. 1997. "The Future of Spatial Data and Society: Summary of a Workshop." Washington, DC: National Academy Press.

New York City Housing Development Corporation. 2014. Income Eligibility. http://www.nychdc.com/pages/Income-Eligibility.html.

OpenPlans. 2014. http://openplans.org.

Philip, Thomas M., Sarah Schuler-Brown, and Winmar Way. 2013. "A Framework for Learning About Big Data with Mobile Technologies for Democratic Participation: Possibilities, Limitations, and Unanticipated Obstacles." *Technology, Knowledge and Learning* 18 (3): 103–120.

Pickles, John. 1999. "Arguments, Debates, and Dialogues: The GIS–Social Theory Debate and the Concern for Alternatives." In *Geographic Information Systems: Principles and Technical Issues*, 47–59. New York: John Wiley and Sons.

Pickles, John, ed. 1995. *Ground Truth: The Social Implications of Geographic Information Systems.* New York: Guilford Press.

Pierre, Sébastien. 2011. "Visualization Deconstructed: New York Times 'Mapping America.'" *Radar: Insights, Analysis, and Research About Emerging Technologies,* January 7. Accessed January 2, 2015. http://radar.oreilly.com/2011/01/visualization-mapping-america.html.

Rambaldi, G. 2005. "Who Owns the Map Legend?" *URISA Journal* 17 (1): 5–13.

Robinson, David, Harlan Yu, William P. Zellar, and Edward W. Felton. 2009. "Government Data and the Invisible Hand." *Yale Journal of Law and Technology* 11:159–175.

Rojas, Francisca M. 2012. *"Transit Transparency: Effective Disclosure through Open Data." Report of Transparency Policy Project*, Ash Center for Democratic Governance and Innovation, Taubman Center for State and Local Government, Harvard Kennedy School.

Sawicki, D., and W. Craig. 1996. "The Democratization of Data: Bridging the Gap for Community Groups." *Journal of the American Planning Association* 62 (4):512–523.

Schroeder, Paul. 1996. "Report on Public Participation GIS Workshop." In Harris, T., and D. Weiner, "GIS and Society: The Social Implications of How People, Space, and Environment Are Represented in GIS." Scientific Report for the Initiative 19 Specialist Meeting, March 2–5, 1996, Koinonia Retreat Center, South Haven, Minnesota. National Center for Geographic Information and Analysis.

Schuette v. Coalition to Defend Affirmative Action, Integration and Immigration Rights and Fight for Equality by Any Means Necessary (BAMN) et al. 572 U.S. (2014).

SeeClickFix. http://seeclickfix.com/watch_area/1044-downtown-wooster-square-community-management-team.

Segel, Edward, and Jeffrey Heer. 2010. "Narrative Visualization: Telling Stories with Data." *IEEE Transactions on Visualization and Computer Graphics* 16 (6): 1139–1148.

Shirky, Clay. 2010. *Cognitive Surplus: How Technology Makes Consumers into Collaborators*. New York: Penguin.

Shueh, Jason. 2014. "6 Cities and a County Share 311 Data, Best Practices." *Government Technology,* October 30. Accessed Januaury 2, 2015. http://www.govtech.com/local/6-Cities-and-County-Share-311-Data-Best-Practices.html.

Sieber, Renee. 2006. "Public Participation Geographic Information Systems: A Literature Review and Framework." *Annals of the Association of American Geographers* 96 (3): 491–507.

Spurgeon, James. 2014. "Do Affirmative Action Bans Hurt Minority Students?" *IVN*, April 29. http://ivn.us/2014/04/29/affirmative-action-bans-hurt-minority-students-states-show-mixed-results.

Surowiecki, James. 2005. *The Wisdom of Crowds*. New York: Anchor Books.

United States Census Bureau. 2014. Data Visualization Gallery. https://www.census.gov/dataviz.

Walker, Doug, and Thomas L. Daniels. 2011. *The Planners Guide to CommunityViz: The Essential Tool for a New Generation of Planning*. Orton Family Foundation Books, American Planning Association.

Warner, Joel. 2010. "Denver Racial Boundaries: *New York Times* Census Maps Show Massive Urban Segregation. *Denver Westword,* December 20. http://blogs.westword.com/latestword/2010/12/denver_racial_boundaries_new_y.php.

Weiser, Jay. 2013. "Correcting the New York Times on College 'Enrollment Gaps'." *AEI*, June 25. http://www.aei.org/publication/correcting-the-new-york-times-on-college-enrollment-gaps.

Whyte, William H. 1980. *The Social Life of Small Urban Spaces*. New York: Project for Public Places.

Williams, Sarah. 2015. "More Than Data: Working with Big Data for Civics." *I/S: A Journal of Law and Policy for the Information Society* .

Williams, Sarah. 2014. "The Responsive City: The City of the Future Re-Imagined from the Bottom Up." In *Emergent Urbanism: Urban Planning & Design in Times of Structural and Systemic Change*, ed. Tigran Haas and Krister Olsson. Farnam, UK: Ashgate Publishing, Ltd.

Williams, Sarah, Erica Deahl, Laurie Rubel, and Vivian Lim. 2014. "City Digits: Local Lotto: Developing Youth Data Literacy by Investigating the Lottery." *Journal of Digital and Media Literacy*, December 15.

Wood, Denis. 1992. *The Power of Maps*. New York: Guilford Press.

10   The Partisan Technology Gap

David Karpf

Introduction

Political technology behaves differently than most other areas of civic technology. Civic technology holds the general promise that digital tools can help solve collective action problems and improve society as a whole. Political technology holds out a different, specific promise: digital tools can yield a set of incremental efficiencies and advantages, helping you to *beat your opponent*. At least within the arenas of electoral and issue-based mobilization, political technology is partisan technology. The result is a set of competitive practices that give rise to a partisan technology gap. This chapter will discuss the roots and evidence of the partisan technology gap in America. It discusses two cases from 2012 that illuminate what happens when a company seeks to bridge the partisan technology gap. It concludes by discussing what partisan technology implies about the promise, potential, and limitations of this emerging sector.

The promise of most civic technology is that it can be used equally by all. From social networks to crowdfunding, new technologies promise to lower the barriers to civic participation, rebuild social institutions, and improve social trust. Civic technologies like Meetup.com are helping to reknit the fabric of civil society, replacing some of the lost "middle spaces" where citizens used to congregate and engage with one another (Evans and Boyte 1992). Civic technologies like Peer-to-Patent (Noveck 2010) make government processes faster, cheaper, and more efficient. Civic crowdfunding tools lower the barrier-to-entry for citizen financial collaboration, giving more power to small donors (Davies 2014). The growing field of civic technology is rife with examples of how a mix of networked technologies and smart user-oriented designs can provide novel solutions to old institutional failings.

In game theoretic terms, civic technology is primarily a *positive-sum game*: the more people who use a piece of civic technology, the more everyone benefits. Positive-sum games tend to encourage collaboration. It may be difficult to coordinate a large populace to partake in the game to begin with, but the more we all play, the better we all do.

Take SeeClickFix.com as an example (Berkowitz 2014). SeeClickFix was originally launched in New Haven, CT, as an app that lets people report problems in their neighborhood. It now has a foothold in 170 U.S. cities. The app applies the logic of crowdsourcing to government service delivery, improving the lines of communication between everyday citizens and government officials. SeeClickFix lets people report potholes and busted streetlamps without navigating any government bureaucracy. In his book, *The Big Disconnect* (2014), Micah Sifry describes some of the benefits that have come out of SeeClickFix: "The result [of SeeClickFix] is a kind of 'thick' civic engagement between ordinary residents, elected representatives, and city officials that merges the online and offline worlds and, in the best of cases, is helping cities like New Haven do something more important than just save money or respond more quickly to residents' complaints: it is growing social capital" (Sifry 2014, 180). The more people use SeeClickFix, the more social value the app generates. Your use of the app benefits me, and my use benefits you.

Much of politics, however, is a *zero-sum game*. Elections, for instance, feature a clear winner and a clear loser. This introduces a competitive, partisan dynamic into the political technology space—particularly within the confines of America's two party–dominated system. Democrats and Republicans don't just benefit from having improved digital campaign technologies, they also look for incremental advantages where one party has better technology than the other. If I am working on a campaign that has a great, new database, that benefits me. If my opponent is stuck relying upon a dial-up modem and an old copy of Windows 95, that benefits me as well. Technology alone does not determine the outcome of elections, but effective campaign technologies can produce more efficient targeting, persuasion, and mobilization efforts, yielding a marginal, incremental advantage that can help swing close elections to one party or the other (Issenberg 2012).

Neither political party has an inherent advantage at technological innovation. In the brief history of the Internet, Republicans and Democrats have each experienced periods of dominance (Kreiss 2012; Karpf 2012a; Stromer-Galley 2014). The history of campaign technology in the U.S. is like a pendulum, swinging back and forth from one party's advantage to the other's advantage. Though Democrats and Republicans make use of the same Internet, and use it for largely the same purposes, they are driven to develop incremental comparative advantages, and to wield these technological advantages for as long as they can. Firms that do business with both sides are a rarity, and are stridently attacked as turncoats and traitors for "giving away partisan secrets." This helps explain why (as detailed below), when NationBuilder.com signed a technology contract with the Republican State Leadership Committee in 2012, outraged progressives threatened a mass boycott. "Progressives should think carefully about who they're helping when they use NationBuilder," said Jason Rosenbaum of the Progressive

Change Campaign Committee. "Every dollar you spend directly aids your opponents" (Stirland 2012). And this was not an empty threat: Rosenbaum would go on to help build The Action Network, an award-winning competitor to NationBuilder that explicitly promises to do business only with progressives and Democrats. And the same pattern appears in contentious politics *outside* the electoral arena, as we will see in the case of Change.org (detailed below). Politics is a harsh, zero-sum competition, and political technology adopts that same competitive culture.

This chapter details the implications of these partisan competitive dynamics in political technology. Unlike government service delivery or civic volunteering, electoral and advocacy campaigns have strong incentives to construct competing technology platforms and capitalize on technological advances. Cross-partisan services are rare, and bipartisan civic technologies often fall prey to the "Field of Dreams Fallacy" (Karpf 2012b), in which appeals to the moderate, centrist American public fail for lack of interest and participation. Meanwhile, politically adjacent civic technologies face an altered competitive landscape, with unexpected challenges and rewards.

The Partisan Technology Pendulum

In light of recent political history, one might assume that democrats are simply "better" at using digital communications technologies in politics. The 2004 Howard Dean presidential campaign harnessed the Internet to raise millions of dollars and engage hundreds of thousands of volunteers (Hindman 2005). Though Dean failed to translate online momentum into election day votes, the members of his campaign team went on to launch firms like Blue State Digital and EchoDitto that were responsible for many of the Obama campaign's vaunted digital innovations (Kreiss 2012). The Democratic Party's digital advantage has become a commonplace observation ever since.

The 2008 and 2012 Obama campaigns have been heralded as technological marvels. Daniel Kreiss notes in *Taking Our Country Back* (2012) how the Presidential campaign infused online metrics, testing, and data into all facets of its decision-making process. This integration, which Kreiss refers to as "computational management," produced clear results—$57 million in increased online donations, according to Michael Slaby, the Chief Technology Officer of the 2008 Obama campaign (Kreiss 2012, 145). From voter targeting and persuasion to offline field coordination and mobilization, the Obama campaign demonstrated a pervasive advantage over Republican opponents John McCain and Mitt Romney (Judd and Sifry 2012; Madrigal 2012). It is particularly noteworthy that Romney's 2012 campaign did not mimic the 2008 Obama campaign's successful data practices (Stromer-Galley 2014). The Obama campaign maintained a well-publicized technological advantage across multiple electoral cycles, despite a motivated and well-resourced opposition.

This partisan advantage is not limited to Presidential campaigns. As I document in *The MoveOn Effect* (Karpf 2012a), conservative partisan activists have repeatedly tried and repeatedly failed to build their own equivalents to progressive online institutions like ActBlue.com, MoveOn.org, and DailyKos.com. ActBlue is an online fundraising portal that has raised over $500 million for Democratic candidates and PACs from 10.3 million donors since it was founded in 2004. The hallmarks of the site are its ease of use and the ability for users to launch their own fundraising pages. When an advocacy organization wants to bundle small-dollar donations to a candidate, it can do so through a simple ActBlue page. When a state or local candidate wants cheap fundraising utilities, they can turn to the same toolset used by Senators and major PACs. Republicans have attempted in every election cycle since 2004 to launch their own ActBlue competitor. Sites like RightRoots in 2008 and SlateCard in 2010 specifically promoted themselves as conservative mirrors of ActBlue, but failed to achieve anywhere close to the same results (Karpf 2012a, 133). MoveOn.org has built a member list of over 8 million progressive supporters, making it one of the largest progressive advocacy organizations in the country. Though Tea Party conservatives have had some modicum of success building large supporter lists, their ongoing attempts to "build a conservative MoveOn" have resulted in a string of public failures (Karpf 2012a, 130–132). And while the progressive community blog DailyKos.com has built a multimillion-person following since its founding in 2003, conservative analogues like RedState.com have repeatedly failed to gather the same momentum. From electoral campaigns to electoral infrastructure to advocacy organizations and political blogs, conservatives have publicly proclaimed the Democratic advantage, then tried and failed to close the gap.

But it would be a mistake to conclude from past Presidential electoral cycles that Democrats hold an immutable advantage online. From 1996 to 2004, it was widely assumed that the new medium in fact had a *conservative* lean to it. Well before Howard Dean and ActBlue, the 2000 John McCain primary campaign was once viewed as *the* trailblazer in online fundraising. The 2004 Bush campaign relied on superior databases to engage in sophisticated microtargeting that yielded dividends for its 36-hour Get-Out-The-Vote field program (Nielsen 2012). Well before left-leaning news blogs like the Huffington Post and Talking Points Memo rose to prominence, the conservative Drudge Report broke news of the Monica Lewinsky scandal, nearly resulting in the abrupt end of Bill Clinton's Presidency. In 2004, *Time* magazine dubbed the conservative political blog PowerLine as "blog of the year" over progressive rivals like DailyKos. And throughout the late 1990s, conservative activists mobilized online through the discussion forum "Free Republic," engaging in mass online actions that predated the rise of MoveOn.org. The Democratic tilt of current partisan technology is still a relatively recent occurrence.

This pendulum-swing pattern can best be understood as a process driven by "Out-party Innovation Incentives" (Karpf 2012a). At three levels—candidate, interest group, and party network—the party that is out of power tends to have strong incentives to pursue innovative strategies and invest in new technologies.

Outparty innovation is primarily the result of a repeated, zero-sum game: at the candidate level, it is the candidate who *expects* to lose, under prevailing conditions, that will look to new strategies and technologies in a bid to change those prevailing conditions. We can see evidence through Presidential primaries, where the best-known tech innovators have been McCain (2000), Dean (2004), Obama (2008), and Ron Paul (2008). Each of these candidates was viewed as an outsider or "dark horse" candidate, and gained (at least) brief notoriety through their investment in new campaign technologies (Trippi 2004; Alexander 2011; Kreiss 2012; Vaccari 2010; and Stromer-Galley 2014).

At the interest group level, it is a well-established finding that the membership rolls of mass membership-based interest groups swell during periods of opposition. This pattern is often demonstrated with the Sierra Club, whose member rolls rapidly expanded in the early 1980s during the Reagan administration, dramatically declined during the Clinton era, and rose again early in the George W. Bush administration. Likewise, the rise and fall of grassroots conservatism is tied to the Presidency—both Jimmy Carter and Bill Clinton faced waves of conservative political mobilization (McGirr 2001; Rozell and Wilcox 1995), just as Barack Obama's election spurred the immediate rise of the conservative Tea Party movement (Skocpol and Williamson 2012; Parker and Barreto 2013). So outparty status is useful to new organizations seeking to raise funds and assemble a mass following. It is easier to say "no" than "go" in American politics, and the politics of opposition provide strong opportunities for new political organizations, armed with new information and communication technologies, to establish a base of support. As one Republican technology consultant told me in 2008, "While the Right has been in power, defending the status quo, the Left has been storming the castle. Storming the castle is *much* more fun" (Karpf 2012a).

At the party network level, outparty status also matters a great deal. It is important to keep in mind that political candidates do not run for election alone. They rely upon political "assemblages" (Nielsen 2012), which include a host of consultants, volunteers, part-time and full-time staff. Political consultants in elections are a lot like coaches in professional sports—they determine a strategy and participate in resource allocation decisions, but it is devilishly hard to assess the effectiveness of any particular strategic choice. Did the candidate win because she used the right message? Did she lose because she had the wrong television ads, or because she didn't have *enough* television ads? Like the coaches in professional sports, political consultants develop their reputations based upon retrospective victories. James Carville helped Bill Clinton win the Presidency in 1992, so he is hailed as a genius. Karl Rove created George W. Bush's base-mobilization strategy of 2000. Bush narrowly won, so Rove was elevated to the status of a modern-day Nostradamus. Had Clinton or Bush lost, Carville and Rove would have had a much tougher time finding their next jobs.

Also like professional sports coaches, political consultants aren't immediately blamed for individual losses. It is only after several losing election seasons that a party network starts rewarding new consultants. This happened in the Democratic Party network after the disappointing 2004 election—the fourth consecutive election in which Democrats had failed in their goals (1998, 2000, 2002, 2004). Amy Sullivan wrote a call to arms in 2005 titled "Fire the Consultants," which specifically asked, "Why do Democrats promote campaign advisors who lose races? ... Every sports fan knows that if a team boasts a losing record several seasons in a row, the coach has to be replaced with someone who can win. Yet when it comes to political consultants, Democrats seem incapable of taking this basic managerial step" (Sullivan 2005). Howard Dean was soon installed as the new chair of the Democratic National Committee, and alumni of the Dean campaign would go on to build several successful technology consultancies (Kreiss 2012). By comparison, Republicans reacted to their 2012 loss—which had been preceded by a 2010 "wave" of electoral victories—by promising more resources to their losing technology "coaches" of the past several years.

Within party networks, consulting contracts are another form of zero-sum game. New technologists try to attract contracts where they can provide improved services to a campaign. But every contract awarded to a new consultant is a contract lost by an old consultant. And at the party network level, it is only after repeated "losing seasons" that we are likely to see new tech firms attract substantial new business.

This outparty innovation pattern drives the pendulum swing of partisan technological advantages in politics. There is evidence that this same pattern can be found both cross-nationally and historically. Cross-nationally, it is noteworthy that, during the period of progressive blogosphere dominance in the United States, conservative bloggers developed a stronger following in the Labour Party–governed United Kingdom. Historically, it is noteworthy that Rush Limbaugh and other conservative talk radio hosts experienced a surge in listenership during the early Clinton era. The institutional development of the conservative talk radio empire was juxtaposed against the Clinton bogeyman. And progressive attempts to duplicate that talk radio empire a decade later repeatedly foundered, in much the same way that conservative attempts to mimic ActBlue, MoveOn, and DailyKos have failed to gain traction.

There is nothing *inherently* partisan about political technology, though. Democrats and Republicans use the same email, the same Twitter, the same Facebook. They have the same needs from a database or constituent relationship management (CRM) software program. Why don't more technology firms provide services to both ideological coalitions? Why doesn't profit-maximizing behavior lead naturally to cross-partisan consulting organizations? It turns out that there are a small number of technology providers who *have* sought to bridge the Republican-Democrat/Conservative-Progressive gap. The following section describes what happens when they do.

NationBuilder and The Action Network

NationBuilder offers virtually every tool you might need to run an electoral or issue-based political campaign, at a lower price than most of its competitors. It was founded in late 2009 by Jim Gilliam, a brilliant coder with deep ties to both Silicon Valley and progressive politics. Today it is used by over 4,000 organizations and campaigns, both in the United States and across the world (McKelvey and Piebak 2014). But it has also attracted public boycott threats, losing customers in the process. And it has attracted new, sophisticated competitors based *solely* on its policy of selling technology initially developed in Democratic campaigns to any client, regardless of political affiliation.

Gilliam cut his teeth as a software developer in the 1990s, working at Lycos, eCompanies, and Business.com. Even by Silicon Valley standards, he was known as a phenomenal coder. In a 2013 profile of Gilliam for *The American Prospect*, journalist Andy Kroll interviewed many of Gilliam's former colleagues. Lycos's former vice president of engineering told Kroll described Gilliam as a brilliant coder. "Stuff that takes weeks or months to do, he'd do it in an all-night session. ... There are people who are 10 times or 100 times more productive than others. Jim falls into that category" (Kroll 2013). In the aftermath of September 11th, Gilliam became more political. He began blogging and creating software for groups like MoveOn.org. He cofounded Brave New Films with progressive filmmaker Robert Greenwald. He created individual tools, like the Twitter petition site Act.ly and the crowdsourcing experiment Whitehouse2.org, practically on a whim.

Gilliam created NationBuilder as a competitor to the expensive CRMs being offered to nonprofits and political campaigns. The company has experienced rapid growth and is generally well regarded by political operatives. NationBuilder offers a full suite of tools: customer/constituent relationship management, social sharing, mass email, fundraising, analytics, blogging, and event planning. For smaller organizations, these tools are offered for as low as $19 per month.[1] Larger organizations incur sliding-scale pricing, up to $999 per month for organizations with 100,000 people on their email list. The company also offers customized "enterprise edition" services for massive organizations and campaigns. These price points were developed with an eye toward disrupting the existing marketplace. Competing companies charge several thousand dollars per month for their services. Gilliam loudly proclaimed from the start that he could offer a platform that was both higher quality and much cheaper than the existing offerings.

But Gilliam, with his roots in progressive/Democratic politics, didn't design NationBuilder just for progressives and Democrats. In the summer of 2012, Gilliam signed "probably the largest deal ever struck in political technology" (Fitzpatrick 2012). The Republican State Leadership Committee (RSLC) signed an exclusive deal for

NationBuilder's customized (and more expensive) enterprise-level services for the 7500 Republican races that the RSLC coordinates. Joe Green, NationBuilder's president at the time, told a reporter at *Mashable.com*, "Everyone else has built partisan technology while we're building nonpartisan technology. I think people are tired of technology wielded as a partisan weapon. Our fundamental belief is that everyone should have access. This is the technology of democracy, everyone should have equal access" (Fitzpatrick 2012). In a separate interview, Green claimed "Our ultimate goal is simply to level the playing field and let the people decide based on the strength of the arguments, not based on who has the biggest TV ad budgets. We're proving that political software can and will be nonpartisan" (Friess 2012). The RSLC contract signaled that NationBuilder would aggressively attempt to bridge the partisan technology gap. But the question still remained, is "leveling the playing field" a *good thing* in zero-sum electoral competitions? Many progressives and Democrats felt that it was not.

The blowback was both immediate and spectacular. Raven Brooks, the executive director of Netroots Nation (an annual convention of left-leaning political organizers, campaigners, bloggers, and technologists), called for a boycott of NationBuilder. He told reporter Sarah Lai Stirland, "At this point, I don't think it's in the interest of progressive causes and candidates to keep supporting a platform that's basically taking a side. … This isn't Google Docs, where anyone can sign up for free. This is a specific set of tools that draws on a body of knowledge that's been built up on the progressive side primarily over a number of years." He also told Stirland, "This is like Blue State Digital saying: 'Here Mitt Romney, you can have Obama's technology.' It's an advantage for Democratic campaigns—we've had a technology advantage that we've built up over the years, and to just hand that off to the Republican party—it could be the difference-maker in some elections" (Stirland 2012).

Matt Browner-Hamlin, who helps run the progressive advocacy incubator Citizen Engagement Lab, called for a boycott as well. Writing at the popular progressive site AmericaBlog.com, Browner-Hamlin announced, "My recommendation is to deny business to technologists who are working with conservatives […]. If you are a client of NationBuilder, fire them. If you are considering hiring them, don't. Make your decision public and make sure that even if NationBuilder isn't going to change, other technologists will know that progressives won't work with the people whose code is being used to attack the human and civil rights of women, gays, immigrants, people of color, and workers" (Browner-Hamlin 2012). NationBuilder did indeed begin to lose contracts, and immediately went on the defensive.

Competitor companies like NGP VAN and Blue State Digital were quick to capitalize on this controversy. Gilliam accused NGP VAN of "bullying" NationBuilder clients and suggesting that NationBuilder data might be leaked to Republican opponents. NGP VAN denied the accusation (and no specific support for it has surfaced). But critics like NGP VAN did aggressively point out a broader problem. As Andrew Kroll explains it, "… When Democratic candidates use Democratic-only tools and the party voter file, they improve that data with information gleaned during canvasses and phone calls. By continually updating their in-house data, Democrats better know whom to target with ads and whom to turn out on Election Day. The more Democrats use NationBuilder […] the less they improve the party's data, which only helps the GOP" (Kroll 2013).

Companies like Blue State Digital and NationBuilder function under a "software as a service" model (Kreiss 2012). Blue State Digital, for instance, develops websites and other digital organizing tools for Democratic candidates. Over the course of an election cycle, it makes improvements to those digital tools. And since Blue State Digital owns the underlying codebase, those improvements function as learning and experimentation opportunities for the broader Democratic ecosystem. Local candidates cannot deploy the digital sophistication of the Obama campaign, but they benefit from the Obama campaign's sophistication by deploying products that were tested and developed in that high-stakes, high-attention, high-priced setting. NationBuilder operates under the same model. So, while NationBuilder does not sell or leak user data about Democrats to Republicans, or vice versa, it does use the *results* of Democratic campaigns to improve its product, which is then marketed to Democratic opponents.

Gilliam responded to the criticisms from his former friends and colleagues with a mix of anger and hostility. He took to Twitter, writing "some progressive operatives are freaking out cause we at @nationbuilder are leveling the playing field of democracy" (Gilliam 2012a) and "to all the elites who think they get to decide who can organize … suck it. Your days are numbered. Power to the people" (Gilliam 2012b).

Notice the shift in tone here: In Gilliam's framing, progressive nonprofit leaders have turned into "elites," while the Republican State Leadership Committee has become "the people." Gilliam is making the normative democratic claim that everyone (who runs for elective office) should have equally cheap, high-quality communication tools. Implicit in this claim is, arguably, a larger political critique of a two-party electoral system that leaves the great mass of minority viewpoints un- or under-represented in elected office. The digital revolution has disrupted many traditional gatekeeping institutions in the media, culture, and business sectors. Why should it be constrained to the two existing dominant parties? Yet Gilliam's detractors maintain that campaign communications are a form of partisan competition. America's electoral systems are embedded in its Constitution; its first-past-the-post electoral rules ensures two-party dominance. And with the Republican Party actively pursuing state-level legislation that restricts voting rights, leveling the technological "playing field" may only further exacerbate deep inequalities in America.

The public calls for a boycott were one *predictable outcome* of NationBuilder's bipartisan business strategy. The boycott itself had limited direct impact. It sparked long debates on listservs like Progressive Exchange, where software developers and political organizers debated whether technology should be partisan or not. It led NationBuilder to lose a few contracts, and hurt its public branding when competing for others. But the company has held firm to its bipartisan commitment. Its product is effective and affordable, and the business has continued to grow. So one potential lesson from this case might be that political technology does not *have* to be partisan technology, so long as the product is good enough to absorb the inevitable criticism.

There was a second response to NationBuilder, however. Where Brooks, Browner-Hamlin, and others called for a Democratic boycott of NationBuilder, technologist Jason Rosenbaum took a different approach. Rosenbaum was outraged by the RSLC contract, initially calling what NationBuilder was doing "evil." In an interview with Sarah Lai Stirland, Rosenbaum said "As it stands now, progressives should think carefully about who they're helping when they use NationBuilder—every dollar you spend directly aids your opponents. The [RSLC] are the folks who helped pass [Wisconsin Governor] Scott Walker's [anti-union] agenda, who want to give transvaginal ultrasounds to women, who want to disenfranchise the minorities, who want to keep the rich rich and the poor poor. Helping them win elections is pretty evil. ... Fortunately, there are competitive toolsets at competitive prices available to campaigns, especially on the new media side. Progressives don't have to work with a company like Nation-Builder" (Stirland 2012).

At the time of the RSLC controversy, Rosenbaum was employed as the online campaign director for the Progressive Change Campaign Committee (PCCC), a progressive advocacy group that works to elect and support "bold progressives" in government. After the 2012 election, Rosenbaum left PCCC and helped found The Action Network, a nonprofit NationBuilder competitor that offered similar tools at even lower prices, restricted solely to leftwing partisans. ActionNetwork.org launched one year later, in September 2013 (Karpf 2013).

The Action Network offers practically all of the same features as NationBuilder. But where Gilliam's NationBuilder offers a starter package for $19 per month, Rosenbaum's Action Network offers all of the basic services for free. Larger organizations, including national campaigns and advocacy organizations, receive customized features and support for a fee. But Action Network actively boasts about its selectivity, touting on its landing page that "We're a nonprofit and only work with progressives."[2]

At the time of this writing, The Action Network has received ample praise and national awards. It was named "Most Valuable Technology" at the New Organizing Institute's 2013 RootsCamp, and won two awards in the Google-sponsored "New Tools Shootout" at Netroots Nation 2014. National political campaigns and nonprofits have moved to The Action Network as well. For these organizations, it appears as though the Partisan Technology Gap is a feature, not a bug.

So it appears from this case that Joe Green and Jim Gilliam were wrong in their assessment that "... people are tired of technology wielded as a partisan weapon."

Political technology yields partisan benefits, and the market for political technology vendors is made up of partisans. Faced with a nonpartisan political technology, some partisans chose to boycott, and others chose to launch new competing services based on the promise of partisan exclusivity.

Change.org and the Dangers of Neutrality

Change.org is the world's largest online petition platform. With over 70 million users in 196 countries, the site has been described as "the go-to site for Web uprisings" (Kristof 2012). Anyone is free to launch a petition at Change.org, and the site employs hundreds of organizers who aid petition creators in refining their language, connecting with reporters, and reaching out to powerful decision makers. Unlike NationBuilder, Change.org's petition platform is not used for deciding American elections. It is political technology, but it is focused on issue politics, rather than electoral politics. Issue politics are less of a zero-sum competition than electoral politics—it is at least conceivable that competing issue advocates can come together and find common ground, even if the recent history of American politics has mostly featured scorched-earth competition. Change.org occupies a niche that is more civic and less partisan than Nation-Builder. Nonetheless, Change.org is political technology. When Change.org tried to embrace political neutrality and openness by offering its services to citizens of all ideological stripes, it encountered the very same challenges we saw in the NationBuilder example.

According to its founder, Ben Rattray, Change.org is built to help everyday citizens address big problems through small solutions:

The thing about big problems is they exist for a reason. There are powerful forces resisting change. If you try to hit them head on, directly, meeting force with force, you very rarely win. So I have no doubt the Internet has huge potential to empower people to address these big problems, but not primarily in the way most people think. I think primarily it's the internet's ability to organize around small solutions. Tens of thousands. (Rattray 2011)

Rattray's organization is not a traditional nonprofit or NGO (non-governmental organization). It is a for-profit company, registered as a "b-corp" (or "benefit corporation"), which seeks both to maximize profits and to maximize social good. While anyone can create and sign petitions at Change.org for free, the company's primary business model is lead generation through "sponsored petitions" from nonprofits, campaigns, and companies. After a visitor has signed a few user-generated petitions, they are presented with sponsored petitions, which are functionally the same as advertisements from a business or nonprofit. If the visitor signs that sponsored petition, their email address is acquired by the sponsoring organization, and Change. org is paid a fee per email address. Online fundraising is a growth industry, and since

2011 Change.org has grown into a rich source of potential supporters for social change organizations.

Change.org is rooted in progressive politics. There were initially several limitations on what sort of sponsored petitions Change.org would accept. In its early years, the company's client policy stated "We accept sponsored campaigns from organizations fighting for the public good and the common values we hold dear—fairness, equality, and justice. We do not accept sponsored campaigns from organizations that consistently violate these values, support discriminatory policies, or seek private corporate benefit that undermines the common good" (Karpf 2012c). Change.org hired many organizers from traditional progressive nonprofits, and those organizers comfortably found the for-profit company to be well aligned with their ideological leanings.

As the company grew, though, the client policy came under pressure for being overwhelmingly vague. What counts as "fighting for the public good?" What counts as "seek[ing] corporate benefit?" As a practical matter, just how *open* does Change.org want to be? It is easy enough to prohibit explicit hate groups from doing business with the organization, but what about Republicans, libertarians, abortion opponents, second amendment advocates, or other organizations whose vision of "the public good" stands starkly at odds with left wing/progressive interests? Online petitions, writ large, are not partisan technology. But petitions that build mass support for these charged issue spaces are deeply political and firmly partisan. As Change.org grew, the zero-sum elements of political technology created pressure on the company's business model.

In the summer of 2012, these questions were pushed to the forefront by an active online petition campaign targeting Change.org itself. At issue was a sponsored petition from the education reform organization Stand For Children. The petition was titled "Tell Chicago Board of Education and Teachers' Union: Get Back to the Table," and it was created in response to a strike-authorization vote. From Stand For Children's perspective, a teachers' strike in Chicago would undermine the public good. Stand For Children has a long history of fighting with teachers unions. From the American Federation of Teachers's perspective, Stand For Children was calling for union-busting activity—the polar opposite of "fairness, equality, and justice." Stand For Children and American Federation of Teachers are engaged in a pitched political battle with one another, just as fierce as the electoral fights between local Democrats and Republicans.

Over the course of several months, Change.org engaged in a leadership-wide discussion of the client policy. In the end, the company decided to expand the policy, replacing the ideologically progressive language of "fighting for the common good" with language that instead embraced an ideology of openness. The current advertising guidelines, adopted in October 2012, read, "As an open platform with tens of millions of diverse users, Change.org hosts sponsored petitions representing a wide range of viewpoints. We do not endorse nor are we affiliated with any sponsored petition or associated organizations." The new policy language carves out only one exemption, stating, "Change.org does not accept ads from hate groups, or persons/entities directly associated with them" (Change.org 2014).

The internal debate over these advertising guidelines was heated. Several staff members resigned in the wake of the new advertising policy, and one went so far as to leak an internal memo about the discussion to Jeff Bryant, an associate fellow at Campaign for America's Future (the leaker was quickly discovered and promptly fired). In an interview with Ryan Grim, Washington Bureau Chief at the *Huffington Post*, Bryant expressed disappointment, noting, "Change.org built its reputation on arming Davids to take on the Goliaths of the world. Now it seems that the company thinks David and Goliath should be on the same team" (Grim 2012). Several left-leaning nonprofits responded by ending their contracts with Change.org. If Change.org was open to accepting sponsored advertisements from coal industry "astroturf" groups, then many climate advocacy organizations would find some other venue for lead generation.

As with NationBuilder, partisan technologists also stepped into this breach. MoveOn. org had already created its own Change.org competitor system, called SignOn.org. SignOn is an open petition platform where individuals or organizations can launch their own petition-based campaigns. MoveOn emails these petitions to small subsets of its membership. Those campaigns that prove popular are then ratcheted up, with the potential of reaching MoveOn's entire 8 million–person member list. Two months after Change.org announced its new neutral advertising policy, MoveOn announced a major upgrade to SignOn.org. The platform was rebranded as MoveOn Petitions, and became the centerpiece of MoveOn's "million leader strategy" for citizen campaigning. Like Change.org's sponsored petitions, MoveOn Petitions allows partner organizations to create their own petitions on the site, and supports a two-step lead generation process that gives progressive peers access to the new email addresses. But unlike the sponsored petitions at Change.org, MoveOn doesn't charge its allies for this service. Likewise, large progressive organizations like Credo Action, Avaaz.org, and Democracy For America all launched open petition platforms after Change.org's policy change, creating additional market competition for the Change.org model. By moving to the center, Change.org left itself vulnerable to explicitly partisan competitors.

Change.org had planned to make their advertising policy revisions quietly, but the leaked memo led to a public uproar and resulted in an organized crisis communication response. Rattray wrote a piece for the *Huffington Post* where he described the decision as "embracing openness." "If we weren't open to everyone, and if we limited access based on a set of political viewpoints, we would undercut the power of our petition creators and users. We would be perceived as an advocacy group ourselves, and the media and decision makers would often typecast petition creators as players in our supposed issue agenda, rather than the independent agents of change they are. The result would be to strip our petition creators of the power of telling their own story on their own terms, making them less likely to gather broad support and less likely to win" (Rattray 2012). In Rattray's view, Change.org is a platform for civic engagement. In his critics' view, Change.org is political technology, and must chose to side either with the "Davids" or with the "Goliaths." Philosophically, there are strong arguments that can be made for either of these positions. But, empirically, the main lesson is that technologies like Change.org and NationBuilder invite these types of intense debate. If Change.org stayed away from traditional politics, then it would be shielded from these partisan market pressures. But the more a site like Change.org or NationBuilder links its business model to politics (electoral or issue-based), the stronger the calls for partisan alignment will be.

Can Political Technology Be Politically Neutral?

Change.org and NationBuilder both behaved as though their products were contributing to a positive-sum game—as though, in other words, they were producing civic technologies. This perspective is perhaps best summarized by Ben Joffe-Walt, Change.org's Communications Director. In the face of the threatened boycott of Change.org, Joffe-Walt described the new client policy as "Google-like," stating, "If Google will allow it, we would allow it" (Grim 2012).

The Google analogy is particularly worth considering: Republicans and Democrats both use GoogleDocs and Gmail. Likewise, Facebook and Twitter provide the same resources to liberals and conservatives alike (see Vaidhyanathan 2011 for a thorough critique of Google and its peers). Apple offers the same student discounts to Oberlin College and Liberty University. Why should partisans expect anything different from a CRM or online petition site?

There is a legitimate argument that they should not. Digital tools are just tools. Companies, even those with a social mission, should be allowed to pursue business wherever they can. Democracies work best when everyone has the capacity to make their voice heard. Openness and neutrality are themselves powerful and compelling values.

But the counterargument is that political competition, both in elections and in issue advocacy, is primarily a zero-sum affair. Social movements have a long tradition of trying to confront the concentrated power of monied interests with the diffuse power of citizen engagement. And when for-profit companies provide their services "neutrally" (for a price) to all competitors in an issue arena, the comparative advantage of social movement organizations is eroded. It is too easy for an "astroturf" front group to purchase an online membership base and use these numbers to muddy the effectiveness of grassroots citizens groups (Walker 2014). Critics of Change.org hold that the partisan ideological stance of these sites is an important precondition for building movements for large-scale social change. The partisan technology pendulum will eventually swing back to favor conservatives and Republicans. The question is how quickly it will swing, and what sort of social change is accomplished in the meantime.

Change.org and NationBuilder are trying to prove that political technology does not have to be partisan technology. Change.org is attempting to be the petition platform/ lead generation site for Democrats and Republicans, for unions and union-busters, for second amendment enthusiasts and for gun violence prevention advocates. Nation-Builder is trying to level the electoral playing field, putting the same tools for campaign communications, mobilization, and fundraising in both parties' hands. Both companies have experienced some growth while carving out that nonpartisan niche. But both companies have also faced fierce partisan criticisms, brand damage, and organized boycotts. And both companies, in moving to the center, invited new rivals built upon the promise of partisan exclusivity. When explicitly political technology providers seek to bridge the partisan divide, they invite organized outrage. Seasoned political campaigners, who are the most reliable clients of these companies, are well schooled in applying pressure and causing reputational harm to companies. Bridging the partisan technology gap comes at a cost.

This pattern renders political technology different from other forms of civic technology. Crowdsourcing information and crowdfunding art projects do not emerge in such polarized spaces. Even digital government service delivery promises civic responsiveness, rather than partisan control. Political competition determines a different type of power than other areas of social life, and this results in a visible, repeatable pattern: political technology yields valuable partisan advantages in zero-sum political competition. These partisan advantages exhibit a pendulum-like swing over time, sometimes benefiting Republicans/conservatives and sometimes benefitting Democrats/ progressives. Those technology providers that pursue an open or neutral strategy by serving both ideological party coalitions can expect intense pressure campaigns and competition from new technology providers that (correctly) view neutrality as a market risk.

Notes

1. NationBuilder, http://nationbuilder.com/pricing.

2. The Action Network, https://actionnetwork.org.

References

Alexander, Jeffrey. 2011. *Performance and Power*. New York: Polity Press.

Berkowitz, Ben. 2014. "Love Thy Neighbor … Hood." Keynote address, Personal Democracy Forum, New York, NY, June 2014. https://www.youtube.com/watch?v=uE6s0P9OGGY.

Browner-Hamlin, Matt. 2012. "Another Liberal Tech Company Doing Work for Conservatives." *Americablog.com*, June 28. http://americablog.com/2012/06/another-liberal-tech-company-doing -work-for-conservatives.html.

Change.org, 2014. "Advertising Guidelines." http://www.change.org/about/advertising -guidelines.

Davies, Rodrigo. 2014. "Civic Crowdfunding: Participatory Communities, Entrepreneurs and the Political Economy of Place." *SSRN,* May 9. http://papers.ssrn.com/sol3/papers.cfm?abstract_id =2434615.

Evans, Sara, and Harry Boyte. 1992. *Free Spaces: The Sources of Democratic Change in America.* Chicago: University of Chicago Press.

Fitzpatrick, Alex. 2012. "NationBuilder Makes 'Largest Deal Ever Struck in Political Technology.'" *Mashable.com*, July 11. http://mashable.com/2012/07/11/nationbuilder-republicans.

Freiss, Steven. 2012. "NationBuilder Upgrades the Campaign Game." *Politico.com*, June 27. http:// www.politico.com/news/stories/0612/77899.html#.T-uJP2eHsoM.twitter.

Gilliam, Jim. 2012 a. "Some progressive operatives are freaking out cause we at @nationbuilder are leveling the playing field of democracy." Tweet, December 16, 2012. https://twitter.com/ jgilliam/status/280373817845624832.

Gilliam, Jim. 2012 b. "To all the elites who think they get to decide who can organize … suck it. Your days are numbered. Power to the people." Tweet, July 12, 2012. https://twitter.com/jgilliam/ status/223588071139057664.

Grim, Ryan. 2012. "Change.org Changing: Site to Drop Progressive Litmus Test for Campaigns, Say Internal Documents (UPDATE)." *HuffingtonPost.com*, October 10. http://www.huffingtonpost .com/2012/10/22/changeorg-corporate-gop-campaigns-internal-documents_n_1987985.html.

Hindman, Matthew. 2005. "The Real Lessons of Howard Dean: Reflections on the First Digital Campaign." *Perspectives on Politics* 3 (1): 121–128.

Issenberg, Sasha. 2012. *The Victory Lab: The Secret Science of Winning Campaigns.* New York: Broad-way Books.

Judd, Nick, and Micah Sifry. 2012. "Obama Campaign's Legacy: Listen, Experiment, and Analyze Everything." *TechPresident.com*, November 21. http://techpresident.com/news/23173/ obama-campaigns-legacy-listen-experiment-and-analyze-everything.

Karpf, David. 2012 a. *The MoveOn Effect: The Unexpected Transformation of American Political Advo-cacy.* New York: Oxford University Press.

Karpf, David. 2012 b. "[OP-ED] Americans Elect: They Built It, and Nobody Came." *TechPresi-dent.com*, May 4. http://techpresident.com/news/22148/op-ed-americans-elect-they-built-it-and -nobody-came.

Karpf, David. 2012 c. "Change.org and the Dilemmas of Success." *TechPresident.com*, June 19. http://techpresident.com/news/22396/op-ed-changeorg-and-dilemmas-success.

Karpf, David. 2013. "4 Things to Watch for with ActionNetwork.org, The New Online Organizing Platform." *TechPresident.com*, September 13. http://techpresident.com/news/24345/4-things -watch-actionnetworkorg-new-online-organizing-platform.

Kreiss, Daniel. 2012. *Taking Our Country Back: The Crafting of Networked Politics from Howard Dean to Barack Obama*. New York: Oxford University Press.

Kristof, Nicholas. 2012. "After Recess: Change the World." Op-Ed, *New York Times*, February 5. http://www.nytimes.com/2012/02/05/opinion/sunday/kristof-after-recess-change-the-world. html?_r=1&.

Kroll, Andy. 2013. "The Evangelist." *American Prospect,* October 9. http://prospect.org/article/ evangelist.

Madrigal, Alexis. 2012. "When the Nerds Go Marching In." *TheAtlantic.com*, November 15. http:// www.theatlantic.com/technology/archive/2012/11/when-the-nerds-go-marching-in/265325/.

McGirr, Lisa. 2001. *Surburban Warriors*. Princeton, NJ: Princeton University Press.

McKelvey, Fenwick, and Jill Piebak. "Porting the Good Campaign: American Campaign Management Software in Canada." Paper presentation, Qualitative Political Communication Preconference, International Communication Association Annual Meeting, Seattle, WA, May 2014.

Nielsen, Rasmus Kleis. 2012. *Ground Wars*. Princeton, NJ: Princeton University Press.

Noveck, Beth. 2010. *Wiki Government: How Technology Can Make Government Better, Democracy Stronger, and Citizens More Powerful*. Washington, DC: Brookings Institution Press.

Parker, Christopher, and Matt Barreto. 2013. *Change They Can't Believe In : The Tea Party and Reactionary Politics in America*. Princeton, NJ: Princeton University Press.

Rattray, Ben. 2011. "How Hyperlocal Online Organizing Is Disrupting Traditional Advocacy." Keynote speech, Personal Democracy Forum, New York, NY, June 2011. https://www.youtube .com/watch?v=WV2XK46LkQE.

Rattray, Ben. 2012. "The Case for Change." *HuffingtonPost.com*, October 25. http://www .huffingtonpost.com/ben-rattray/the-case-for-change_b_2018554.html.

Rozell, Mark, and Clyde Wilcox, eds. 1995. *God at the Grassroots: The Christian Right in the 1994 Elections*. Lanham, MD: Rowman & Littlefield.

Sifry, Micah. 2014. *The Big Disconnect: Why The Internet Hasn't Transformed Politics (Yet)*. New York: O/R Books.

Skocpol, Theda, and Vanessa Williamson. 2012. *The Tea Party and the Remaking of Republican Conservatism*. New York: Oxford University Press.

Stirland, Sarah Lai. "NationBuilder Signs Software Deal with RSLC, Some Progressives Call for a 'Boycott.'" *TechPresident.com*, July 12, 2012. http://techpresident.com/news/22556/nationbuilders -mammoth-deal-state-level-republican-committee-sparks-calls-boycott.

Stromer-Galley, Jennifer. 2014. *Presidential Campaigning in the Internet Age*. New York: Oxford University Press.

Sullivan, Amy. 2005. "Fire the Consultants!" *Washington Monthly*, January/February. http:// www.washingtonmonthly.com/features/2005/0501.sullivan.html.

Trippi, Joe. 2004. *The Revolution Will Not Be Televised: Democracy, the Internet, and the Overthrow of Everything*. New York: Harper Collins.

Vaccari, Cristian. 2010. "'Technology is a Commodity': The Internet in the 2008 United States Presidential Election." *Journal of Information Technology & Politics* 7 (4): 318–339.

Vaidhyanathan, Siva. 2011. *The Googlization of Everything: (And Why We Should Worry)*. Berkeley: University of California Press.

Walker, Edward. 2014. *Grassroots for Hire: Public Affairs Consultants in American Democracy*. New York: Cambridge University Press.

11   Case Study: Code for America—Scaling Civic Engagement through Open Data and Software Design

Andrew Richard Schrock

Introduction

Code for America (CfA) is devoted to improving government effectiveness, fostering transparency, and increasing communication around civic issues in local communities. The non-profit organization operates a range of programs, such a peer network and yearly summit. Historically, the organization became known for fellowships, brigades, and an accelerator. This case study considers how these programs fostered organizational partnerships and created channels for participation in designing digital infrastructure through software production and open data. In the context of CFA, civic engagement is thick and impactful online and in-person collaboration on topics of public concern outside of deliberative modes or electoral politics. Code for America's rapid scaling up and record of working with municipal governments provide examples of how technology design can be integrated with mechanisms for collective action and improving government responsiveness.

Connecting Code with Civic Engagement

Code for America (CfA) was founded as a non-profit organization in 2009 by Jennifer Pahlka, drawing on ideas such as Tim O'Reilly's "gov 2.0" and "government as a platform." CfA has grown to be an essential bridge between community needs and local government. The primary activities of Code for America involve technology design and implementation leading to increased transparency, process change, and increased communication among residents around issues of public interest. Altering the infrastructure for governance marks CfA as different from other progressive organizations focused on, for example, electoral politics or youth mobilization. Participation entails personalized involvement where individuals create or alter digital infrastructures to support community needs. In practice this resembles an algorithmic citizenry: monitorial citizens (Schudson 2004) surveil communities and bring about social change through direct action. Their voices can be heard in new modalities of data manipulation, design, and software production.

Code for America's efforts tend to be applied interventions oriented to mitigate suffering around specific societal issues, echoing Popper's notion of "piecemeal engineering" (Popper 1957). Online and offline communication mutually reinforce each other. Tools such as meet-ups, discussion forums and code repositories exist as part of a larger mobilization effort. Precursors to CfA include Ethan Zuckerman's Geek Corps and previous hackthons overtly oriented towards civic goals such as Random Hacks of Kindness. Participation ranges from peripheral to more long-term service through a range of technical and nontechnical roles. From least to most involved, CfA's primary programs have been brigades, fellowships, and a yearly accelerator/incubator, which ran from 2012–2014.

Brigades

Brigades are community-based groups that count activists, organizers and residents in their ranks. Compared with fellowships, which are arranged by CfA, brigades arise more organically. They become officially recognized by Code for America when they have met certain milestones, such as having a brigade leader and demonstrating sustainability. Brigades act rather autonomously, often running what Carl DiSalvo terms "issue-oriented hackathons" (DiSalvo 2014)—day-long processes where teams design solutions to address issues of public concern. Brigades are designed to have low barriers to participation and encourage both technical and non-technical roles in group activities. Employing open data and creating apps that act as tools often comes with opportunities for civic learning and community sharing. For example, assembling a list of open data government resources raises community awareness among participants about connection points between residents and their government.

Fellowships

The fellowship program connects technologists from a diverse array of backgrounds with city governments. Early to mid-career fellows devote a year to completing a major project. Typically they immerse themselves in the community, analyze their needs, prototype ideas, and meet with government stakeholders. They may bring about secondary effects such as changing public opinion and promoting communication between government agencies. Support for fellows comes from a mixture of funding from Code for America, the local government, and industry partnerships. In 2014 there were 10 cities and 30 fellows across the United States working on projects to improve health care, transportation and communication among residents. Fellows particularly advocate for improved transparency and improved effectiveness of local government services through open government data (Maruyama, Douglas, and

Robertson 2013). After finishing the year fellows pursue a range of non-profit and for-profit career paths.

Accelerator and Incubator (2013–2014)

Code for America's accelerator and incubator programs offered routes for "civic tech" companies to receive small grants and operational support. Civic tech is an elastic category that encompasses a range of projects, many with a local dimension. For example, Seeclickfix allows citizens to report neighborhood issues in need of repair, while Civic Insight provides information on under-utilized properties. CfA is not alone in speculating that civic tech might be a growth industry where non-profit and for-profit companies operate in an informational ecosystem with government open data to produce software that acts in the public good.

Conclusion

Code for America is devoted to supporting and implementing institutional and resident collaboration across several programs. Brigades pursue a diverse set of goals and are often responsible for setting up hackathons and guiding local projects. Fellowships facilitate more empathic design of government services and training of leaders. The accelerator program supported "civic tech" with small grants. In the future, Code for America is likely to pursue further ways for participants to learn and translate civic values of local communities across institutional, technical and humanistic registers.

References

DiSalvo, Carl. 2014. "Exploring Civic Imaginaries in Issue-Oriented Hackathons." Annual Conference of the Society for the Social Studies of Science, San Diego, CA, October 9–12, 2013.

Maruyama, Misa, Sara Douglas, and Scott Robertson. 2013. "Design Teams as Change Agents: Diplomatic Design in the Open Data Movement." 46th Hawaii International Conference on System Sciences, Honolulu, HI.

Popper, Karl. 1957. *The Poverty of Historicism*. London: Routledge.

Schudson, Michael. 2004. "Click Here Democracy: A History and Critique of an Information-Based Model of Citizenship." In *Democracy and New Media*, ed. Henry Jenkins and David Thorburn, 49–59. Cambridge, MA: MIT Press.

12   Case Study: RegulationRoom

Dmitry Epstein and Cheryl Blake

Rulemaking, the process used to make new health, safety, and economic regulations, is among the most open and participatory mechanisms in US federal policymaking.[1] Its formal legal structure establishes robust requirements for transparency and public participation. Government agency rulemakers are required to notify the public of what is being proposed, explain the underlying legal and policy rationales, and provide supporting data. Participation is formally guaranteed by a period during which anyone may comment on a proposed rule. Further, all comments must be reviewed and considered by the agency.

However, in practice, meaningful public comment has been highly selective, dominated by industry groups, professional associations, and other well-resourced entities.[2] Both the Bush and Obama Administrations have tried to remediate this and broaden public participation in rulemaking through Regulations.gov, a government-wide rulemaking portal where people can find rulemaking documents and submit comments. Still, observers generally agree that, while the overall number of comments has increased—principally from mass, form-comment campaigns led by advocacy organizations[3]—*effective* participation by individuals, small businesses, non-governmental organizations, and other missing stakeholders remains elusive.[4]

CeRI (the Cornell e-Rulemaking Initiative), a cross-disciplinary group of researchers in law, communication, conflict resolution, and computing and information science, created RegulationRoom with the goal of engaging missing stakeholders in the policymaking process.[5] As an action-research platform for online civic engagement, RegulationRoom can reach stakeholders nationwide in ways that would not be possible offline. In collaboration with the Department of Transportation and the Consumer Financial Protection Bureau, six live rulemakings have been hosted on the platform.

The use of web-based tools has long been promoted as a means to lower the cost of public engagement in policymaking and other forms of political action.[6] RegulationRoom is unique, however, in its conception as a socio-technical system. Some civically oriented platforms, such as Ideascale and Change.org, rely primarily on technological tools rather than human support to structure participants' engagement with

Figure 12.1
Developing law and policy requires significant research, as well as consultation with experts and the public.

policymakers. In contrast, RegulationRoom calls for a more hands-on approach to engagement engineering where technological tools and facilitative engagement practices are closely intertwined.

Drawing on the design-based research paradigm, the RegulationRoom team pursues iterative analysis, design, development, and implementation based on experimentation and observation in the field.[7] To these ends, we employ a range of mixed methods including web-analytics, surveys, and online ethnographies. Our research so far suggests that supporting broader, better public participation involves a combination of strategically designed technology and human effort over five stages: (1) choosing an appropriate rule, (2) identifying, alerting, and engaging missing stakeholders, (3) information design, (4) facilitative moderation, and (5) closing the loop.[8]

Choosing a Rule

Getting public input that is more thoughtful and nuanced than mere expressions of outcome preferences takes time and effort. Not all rulemakings justify this resource investment. Some proposals require specialized technical expertise or impact only a narrow range of stakeholders who are already engaged in the traditional process. Investing in broader public participation is most likely to yield value where there exist (1) one or more substantial groups of missing stakeholders (2) who are likely to have relevant "situated knowledge" (i.e., information about likely impacts, causation, etc., based on first-hand experience with the problems the rule addresses and the circumstances of its implementation).[9]

Table 12.1
RegulationRoom site statistics for rulemaking discussions to date

	Ban on texting by commercial truckers	Airline passenger rights	Commercial trucker electronic driving time recorders	Check-in kiosk and air travel website accessibility	Consumer protections for home mortgages	Consumer debt collection practices
Days open for comment	34	110	106	112	61	115
"Visits"	3,729	24,441	8,855	12,631	12,665	12,629
"Visitors"	1,999	24,441	5,328	7,949	8,908	8,480
Registered users	54	1,189	121	68	144	377
Comments	18 users submitted 32 comments	348 users submitted 931 comments	68 users submitted 235 comments	31 users submitted 103 comments	67 users submitted 236 comments	224 users submitted 956 comments
Users reporting this as first rulemaking experience	98%	94%	73%	64%	79%	83%

Figure 12.2
Visitors to the RegulationRoom website are encouraged to ask questions, engage with the agency documents, and consider how to balance various aspects of the proposal.

Identifying, Alerting, and Engaging New Voices

RegulationRoom works with agency partners to identify missing stakeholder groups and determine where and how these groups get information. Targeted conventional and social media outreach, based on this research, tries to motivate participation by (1) explaining how the proposed rule would affect these stakeholders and (2) emphasizing their legal right to participate and the government's legal responsibility to review every comment before making a final decision.[10] The ability to recruit participants using social media has provided the research team with opportunities to experiment with the framing of calls to action, with the goal of determining effective frames to motivate engagement in policy deliberation.

Information Design

Effective participation is informed participation.[11] RegulationRoom's platform design encourages participants to engage with the government's proposal through a side-by-side format, which features text explaining the proposal on the left and the comment stream on the right. Unlike a traditional blog format, this model highlights the centrality of the proposal text. As such, participants are better able to learn about and critique the agency proposal with specificity. Additionally, participants must attach their comments to particular sections of text (targeted commenting); this helps participants identify sections of interest to them and provide detailed comments about their experiences or concerns related to the issue in that section. Targeted commenting also helps agencies use public input in their decision-making process, because comments are automatically organized by substantive issues. Finally, threaded commenting encourages interactive discussion.

A major information design challenge is that the original rulemaking documents often total hundreds of pages of dense, jargon-filled text. Several techniques are used to render this text into site content that participants can read, understand, and discuss effectively:

• Information triage: identifying the most relevant information needed for effective commenting, and packaging it in thematic topic posts of manageable length
• Signposting: cues that help participants rapidly proceed to the issues that interest them most (e.g., an index of topic posts; subtopics with short descriptive titles)
• Translation: creating shorter, simpler text using plain-language writing principles
• Layering: using hyperlinks, glossaries, and other hypertext functionality to embed information in ways that allow each participant, at his/her own choice, to get deeper or broader information (e.g., reading the original rulemaking document)—or to find more help than triage and translation have already provided (e.g., definitions; background explanations)[12]

Each of the strategies described above applies existing technological and design tools to a new problem: how to make complex policymaking processes accessible to stakeholders who possess relevant knowledge and concerns, but lack the resources to engage in the traditional process without additional support.

Facilitative Moderation

To actually influence the rulemaking outcome, commenters must substantiate claims with facts and reasons, acknowledge competing arguments, discuss alternatives, etc. RegulationRoom provides educational materials about effective commenting in text and video formats,[13] but also relies on human moderators to mentor participants new to the process. Trained in conflict resolution and group facilitation techniques, moderators help participants who lack, or misunderstand, important information about the proposal by replying with clarification or providing links to additional information. To help participants articulate their knowledge, concerns, and arguments as fully as possible, moderators will pose neutral, but probing, questions for more details and the implications of a participant's comment. Additionally, moderators may encourage knowledgeable participants to engage more deeply with the government's analytical documents; point out other issues, and other comments, that relate to the participant's interests or concerns; and, where necessary, emphasize norms of candid but civil discussion.

Closing the Loop

At the close of the comment period, the RegulationRoom team creates a detailed summary of the comments; this is vetted by the community of commenters and submitted

Figure 12.3
Screenshot of a RegulationRoom topic post showing information layering and moderation.

to the government as formal public input in the rulemaking process. When a rule is finalized, participants receive an email notice and can visit the site to find a description and text of the final rule, as well as pointers to where RegulationRoom commenters were mentioned.

The RegulationRoom experience is rooted in and enabled through the use of social media. It demonstrates that broader, meaningful public engagement in complex policymaking is possible, but it requires more than mainly technical solutions. Instead, designing for such participation requires thoughtfulness, commitment, and resources on the part of engagement engineers. Unlike less effortful forms of public participation like voting thumbs up or thumbs down on crowdsourced ideas, which rely on aggregation of preferences or sentiment expression, genuine substantive engagement with complex policy proposals builds on socio-technical design that lowers barriers to entry and bolsters effective participation. Though brainstorming and preference aggregation tools have roles to play in civic participation, engagement engineers must ensure that participants have adequate technical and human support to effectively engage in a process—whether it is petitioning, participatory budgeting, or commenting on proposed regulations. Ultimately, they should be guided by the principle that a democratic government should not actively facilitate civic participation it does not truly value.

Notes

1. *What Is Rulemaking?* Video recording, 3:42, edited by Margaret Storms (Cornell eRulemaking Initiative, 2013). http://regulationroom.org/learn/what-rulemaking or https://www.youtube.com/watch?v=lLQJpAJEQhI.

2. Cornelius M. Kerwin, *Rulemaking: How Government Agencies Write Law and Make Policy*, 3rd ed. (Washington, DC: CQ Press, 2003).

3. Stuart W. Shulman, "The Case against Mass E-mails: Perverse Incentives and Low Quality Public Participation in U.S. Federal Rulemaking," *Policy & Internet*, 1, no. 1 (2009): 23–53.

4. Steven. J. Balla and Benjamin. M. Daniels, "Information Technology and Public Commenting on Agency Regulations," *Regulation & Governance*, no. 1 (2007): 46–67; and Cary Coglianese, "Citizen Participation in Rulemaking Past, Present, and Future," *Duke Law Journal* 55, no. 5 (2006): 943–968.

5. *What Is RegulationRoom?* Video recording, 3:42, edited by Margaret Storms (Cornell eRulemaking Initiative, 2013), http://regulationroom.org/learn/what-regulationroom or https://www.youtube.com/watch?v=mKVI-aGHrLk.

6. Clay Shirky, *Here Comes Everybody: The Power of Organizing Without Organizations* (New York: Penguin, 2008).

7. Feng Wang and Michael J. Hannafin, "Design-Based Research and Technology-Enhanced Learning Environments," *Educational Technology Research and Development*, 53, no. 4 (January 01, 2005): 5–24.

8. Cynthia R. Farina, Paul Miller, Mary J. Newhart, Claire Cardie, Dan Cosley, and Rebecca Vernon, "Rulemaking in 140 Characters or Less," *Pace Law Review* 31, no. 1 (2011): 382–463.

9. Cynthia R. Farina, Dmitry Epstein, Josiah Heidt, and Mary J. Newhart, "Knowledge in the People: Rethinking 'Value' in Public Rulemaking Participation," *Wake Forest Law Review* 47, no. 5 (2012): 1185–1241; Dmitry Epstein, Josiah Heidt, and Cynthia R. Farina, "The Value of Words: Narrative as Evidence in Policymaking," *Evidence and Policy* 10, 2 (2014): 243–258; Cynthia R. Farina and Mary J. Newhart, *Rulemaking 2.0: Understanding and Getting Better Public Participation* (Washington, DC: IBM Center for the Business of Government, 2013).

10. Cynthia R. Farina, Dmitry Epstein, Josiah Heidt, and Mary J. Newhart, "Designing an Online Civic Engagement Platform: Balancing 'More' vs. 'Better' Participation in Complex Public Policy-making," *International Journal of E-Politics* 5, no. 1 (2014): 16–40.

11. *What Is Effective Commenting?* Video recording, 2:12, edited by Margaret Storms (Cornell eRulemaking Initiative, 2013), http://regulationroom.org/learn/what-effective-commenting or https://www.youtube.com/watch?v=kppUJY9S-V4; *Why Should You Participate?* Video recording, 1:36, edited by Margaret Storms (Cornell eRulemaking Initiative, 2013), http://regulationroom.org/learn/why-participate or https://www.youtube.com/watch?v=Uu55nVXimpk.

12. Cynthia R. Farina, Mary J. Newhart, and Josiah Heidt, "Rulemaking vs. Democracy: Judging and Nudging Participation That Counts," *Michigan Journal of Environmental and Administrative Law* 2, no 1 (2012): 123–217.

13. Cynthia R. Farina, Dmitry Epstein, Josiah Heidt, and Mary J. Newhart, "Designing an Online Civic Engagement Platform.

13   Case Study: Better Reykjavik—Open Municipal Policymaking

Derek Lackaff

Following an economic crisis which swept away much of their wealth, international regard, and trust in established political institutions, Icelanders were in a unique position to experiment with radical new approaches to governance and citizenship. As one of the world's most highly developed nations (95 percent of Icelanders are "regular users" of the Internet, the highest percentage in Europe),[1] several Icelandic grassroots initiatives attempted to leverage digital platforms to improve governmental access, transparency, and accountability.

Better Reykjavik (Betri Reykjavík, https://betrireykjavik.is) is one such socio-technical initiative designed to promote citizen participation and collaborative problem solving in city governance. Better Reykjavik is a website that allows citizens to submit policy proposals to the municipal government. These ideas are publically accessible, and may be debated by other participants and revised. The public is also encouraged to make a simple vote on each proposal—support or oppose. Over time, a body of proposals emerges, each idea refined by debate, with the aggregate list ordered by the number of votes it has received. Better Reykjavik is an "e-petition" or "open innovation" website that enables citizens to submit, debate, and prioritize policy proposals and ideas.

Launched in 2009 by grassroots activists as a platform for a frustrated citizenry to express their views about how to move forward, the project was subsequently endorsed by a new political party , the Best Party, that went on to win the Reykjavik municipal government election. The platform was later formally adopted as an official channel for citizen petitions of the government. In its four years of operation, over 70,000 people have used the platform to propose and discuss over 1,800 policy proposals and ideas, of which nearly 450 have received formal consideration from the municipal government and over 350 have been implemented or are in the process of implementation. The nonprofit Citizens Foundation[2] maintains the codebase as an open source project[3] and has assisted in the launching of similar projects in locations ranging from the United Kingdom[4] to the Balkans[5] to rural North Carolina.[6]

Better Reykjavik has several qualities that distinguish it from similar projects: it (1) is developed and maintained by a grassroots nonprofit organization, and not by a

Figure 13.1
One of the thousands of policy proposals submitted on the Better Reykavik site for deliberation and endorsement by the public.

government, (2) rapidly achieved significant buy-in from citizens, policymakers, and public administrators, and (3) has been normalized as an ongoing channel for citizen-government interaction. The citizen engagement and policy development process it facilitates more closely resembles crowdsourcing and aggregation platforms like Reddit than established e-petition sites such as the Obama administration's We The People site[7] or the German Bundestag's e-petitions site.[8]

Building a Better Reykjavik: From e-Governance to e-Democracy

Iceland is among the world's "most connected" nations, and has a strong tradition of official initiatives at both the national and municipal levels to provide services to citizens via the Internet, a project often termed "e-government." A 2005 study identified Reykjavik as one of the top 20 municipalities worldwide in digital governance, including high rankings for the privacy and security, content, and service delivery provided via its website.[9] At the end of 2013, 96 percent of Icelandic households had a broadband Internet subscription, and 81 percent of citizens used e-government services.[10] An e-government benchmark report in May 2014 characterized Iceland as a "steady performer" with "good performance, consistently, across all priorities" in e-government implementation.[11]

The development of new models for more open institutions and infrastructures has emerged as an important goal of both official and grassroots efforts, indicating a potential shift from service provision to civic participation and engagement. Following the 2008 economic crisis, Iceland's political context was characterized by a massive decline in trust for incumbent politicians and institutions. A unique characteristic of many post-crisis Icelandic political initiatives is that individuals and groups without direct policymaking authority developed them: not politicians and government officials, but grassroots activists, hackers, and entrepreneurs. The "interfaces" between these projects and Icelandic policymaking institutions developed following popular interest and success.

Much Icelandic attention has focused on allowing citizens easier and more-effective ways to make their opinions, and more importantly, their ideas, apparent to politicians. A 2009 "National Assembly" was organized by tech entrepreneurs and activists, and brought together 1,500 Icelanders for a multimodal "envisioning" summit focused on the future of the country—the results of which were subsequently endorsed by the national parliament. A second, similar, assembly in 2010 with 950 participants launched the nation's (in)famous "crowdsourced" constitution-crafting project.[12]

Better Reykjavik did not emerge fully formed, but is one of the longest lasting and most impactful of the projects that emerged from this particular milieu for innovative civic technology. It evolved from a previous initiative called the Shadow City (*Skuggaborg*), which was opened created by grassroots activists shortly before the Reykjavík municipal elections in May 2010. Each of the eight political parties vying for seats on the council was provided with a "branded" section of the site to use to connect with potential voters, who were encouraged to submit their political priorities for debate and voting. While most of the parties utilized the site little or not at all, supporters of "anarcho-surrealist" comedian Jón Gnarr's[13] Best Party were encouraged to help set the agenda by using the site, and approximately 1,400 citizens joined in this process.

On May 29, 2010, the Best Party defeated the incumbent Independence Party in the city council election, and subsequently entered into coalition talks with the Social Democrats. The dense social networks within the small society contributed to high awareness of the Shadow City among new city councilors. Best Party officials, having been impressed with the system and its possibilities, asked the Shadow City developers to create a website devoted to soliciting the opinions of the citizens of Reykjavík on their pact for their coalition city council. A new section of the Shadow City website called Better Reykjavík was opened, and the coalition partners encouraged citizens to use the site to share their priorities for the new government. Soon over 5,000 users were participating on the site—an impressive figure in a municipality where 56,897 votes were cast in total. Within months, several of the highest-rated ideas from the Better

Reykjavík site had been placed at the top of the policy agenda listed on the Best Party website, and many were soon implemented.[14]

Following completion of the coalition talks, citizens continued to use the Better Reykjavik site to petition the new government. In October 2011, the City of Reykjavik entered into a formal partnership with the Citizens Foundation. One component of this partnership was a commitment by the city council to address the top five priorities posted to the site each month, as well as the top priorities in each of the 13 topical categories on this site (e.g., "environment," "transportation," "education").[15] Over the next several years, tens of thousands of participants engaged with the site. Reykjavik city committees formally evaluated and processed hundreds of these citizen-submitted ideas, issued an official response to each, and implemented those deemed feasible.

The popularity of the project with residents and city administrators alike led to further initiatives for innovative governance. In 2012, Reykjavik started using the Better Reykjavik site to support its participatory budgeting initiative Better Neighborhoods (*Betri Hverfi*).[16] Through 2014, the city allocated ISK 900 million (nearly USD 8 million) to the best ideas submitted for neighborhood beautification and improvement. Residents with digitally verified residential addresses cast their votes on the site to select projects to implement in their neighborhoods.

In the May 2014 municipal election, Gnarr declined to stand for office, and his Best Party was dissolved. A new government was formed in June 2014, with the Social Democrats entering a coalition with the colorfully named Bright Future, Left-Green, and Pirate parties. In their joint platform statement, the parties reiterated their commitment to using and developing the Better Reykjavik platform during the next four years.[17]

Why has the Better Reykjavik initiative been successful while similar initiatives elsewhere have faltered?

First, the initiative was implemented quickly, and is subject to a fast iterative process where successful projects attract attention and meaningful resources. This model is greatly supported by the fact that most key software technologies are open source, which supports a grassroots development and participation model with very low upfront costs. Those projects that prove especially useful, such as Better Reykjavik, have successfully attracted more formal forms of financial and political support.

Second, the scale of the project was clear, and goals were clearly defined. Better Reykjavik offers an effective user experience of online engagement that is not simply symbolic, but leads directly to policy outcomes. Disruptive users have not been a major problem because participants understand and accept both the overall agenda and the technical process. This success might be contrasted, for example, against the debacle of the U.S. Republican National Committee's technically similar open innovation site *America Speaking Out*, which was overrun by pranksters and ideologues within days of its launch in 2010.[18]

Third, a direct connection with social media networks like Facebook and Twitter reduces barriers to participation while situating policy discussions within the users' real social networks. Users may quickly and easily engage their online network via "likes" and "shares" with the ideas that are important to them.

Although many of the nation's political and cultural divisions have been laid bare by the crisis and its aftermath, Icelanders and their governments increasingly share a commitment to high-tech engagement and transparency. Better Reykjavik provides a useful demonstration of how new interfaces between fast-moving digital participation systems and slow-moving governmental institutions can be successfully negotiated.

Notes

1. "Computer and Internet Usage in Iceland the Highest in Europe," *Statistics Iceland*, January 27, 2014, http://www.statice.is/Pages/444?NewsID=10790.

2. Citizens Foundation, http://citizens.is.

3. Your Priorities, https://github.com/rbjarnason/your-priorities.

4. National Health Service (NHS) Citizen, https://nhs-citizen.yrpri.org.

5. Balkan e-Democracy Startup project, https://balkan-startup.yrpri.org.

6. Better Alamance: Ideas, http://betteralamance.org.

7. We The People, https://petitions.whitehouse.gov.

8. Deutscher Bundestag: Petitionen, https://epetitionen.bundestag.de.

9. Tony Carrizales, Marc Holzer, and Aroon Manoharan, "Worldwide E-Governance: A Longitudinal Assessment of Municipal Websites and the Digital Divide," *E-Government Research: Policy and Management,* IGI Global, 2008, 98–119. doi:10.4018/978-1-59904-913-7.ch004.

10. "Digital Agenda Scoreboard," *Digital Agenda for Europe*, ec.europa.eu//digital-agenda/en/digital-agenda-scoreboard.

11. European Commission, *Delivering on the European Advantage? "How European Governments Can and Should Benefit from Innovative Public Services": eGovernment Benchmark Final Insight Report*, Digital Agenda for Europe, 2014. http://bookshop.europa.eu/en/delivering-on-the-european-advantage-how-european-governments-can-and-should-benefit-from-innovative-public-services-egovernment-benchmark-pbKK0114450.

12. Hélène Landemore, "Inclusive Constitution-Making: The Icelandic Experiment," *Journal of Political Philosophy*, February 25, 2014. doi:10.1111/jopp.12032.

13. Jón Gnarr, *Gnarr: How I Became the Mayor of a Large City in Iceland and Changed the World* (Brooklyn, NY: Melville House, 2014).

14. "Fyrir Gangandi Og Hjólandi Fólk," *Visir.is*, July 12, 2010, http://www.visir.is/fyrir-gangandi-og-hjolandi-folk/article/2010583635150; "Nætursund Í Laugardalslaug," *Mbl.is*, July 20, 2010, http://www.mbl.is/frettir/innlent/2010/07/20/naetursund_i_laugardalslaug.

15. Anna Anderson, "E-Democracy Takes Off in Reykjavík," *Reykjavík Grapevine*, January 30, 2012, http://www.grapevine.is/Features/ReadArticle/e-democracy-takes-off-in-reykjavik.

16. Seehttps://ylstrondin-i-nautholsvik.betrireykjavik.is/pages/6.

17. "Samstarfssáttmáli: Við Myndun Meirihluta Borgarstjórnar Reykjavíkur 2014–2018," June 11, 2014, http://www.dv.is/media/attachments/samstarf.pdf.

18. Charles Babington, "New Republican Agenda, or Lack of One, Divides Party," *Huffington Post*, June 20, 2010, http://www.huffingtonpost.com/2010/06/21/new-republican-agenda-or_n_618964 .html.

References

Anderson, Anna. 2012. "E-Democracy Takes Off in Reykjavík." *Reykjavík Grapevine*, January 30. http://www.grapevine.is/Features/ReadArticle/e-democracy-takes-off-in-reykjavik.

Babington, Charles. 2010. "New Republican Agenda, or Lack of One, Divides Party." *Huffington Post*, June 20. http://www.huffingtonpost.com/2010/06/21/new-republican-agenda-or_n_618964 .html.

"Computer and Internet Usage in Iceland the Highest in Europe." 2014. *Statistics Iceland*, January 27. http://www.statice.is/Pages/444?NewsID=10790.

European Commission. 2014. *Delivering on the European Advantage? "How European Governments Can and Should Benefit from Innovative Public Services": eGovernment Benchmark Final Insight Report. Digital Agenda for Europe.* http://bookshop.europa.eu/en/delivering-on-the-european -advantage-how-european-governments-can-and-should-benefit-from-innovative-public-services-egovernment-benchmark-pbKK0114450.

"Digital Agenda Scoreboard." *Digital Agenda for Europe.* http://ec.europa.eu//digital-agenda/en/ digital-agenda-scoreboard.

"Fyrir Gangandi Og Hjólandi Fólk." 2010. *Visir.is*, July 12. http://www.visir.is/fyrir-gangandi-og-hjolandi-folk/article/2010583635150.

Gnarr, Jón. 2014. *Gnarr: How I Became the Mayor of a Large City in Iceland and Changed the World.* Brooklyn, NY: Melville House.

Landemore, Hélène. 2014. Inclusive Constitution-Making: The Icelandic Experiment. *Journal of Political Philosophy, February 25.* doi:.10.1111/jopp.12032

"Nætursund Í Laugardalslaug." 2010. *Mbl.is*, July 20. http://www.mbl.is/frettir/innlent/ 2010/07/20/naetursund_i_laugardalslaug.

"Samstarfssáttmáli: Við Myndun Meirihluta Borgarstjórnar Reykjavíkur 2014-2018," June 11, 2014. http://www.dv.is/media/attachments/samstarf.pdf.

14 Case Study: The California Report Card Version 1.0

CITRIS Connected Communities Initiative at UC Berkeley[1]

Introduction

Mobile technology offers new opportunities for the public to express views and insights, consider the views of others, and directly engage with political leaders (e.g., Hemphill and Roback 2014; Himmelroos and Christensen 2014; Graham et al. 2013; Landemore 2013).

However, the volume and diversity of ideas can be difficult to manage or may not result in actionable suggestions. A specific and timely response from government leaders is important to close the loop to sustain engagement (NDI 2014; Newsom 2013).

The California Report Card (CRC) v1.0 is an experimental platform that streamlines public input by openly encouraging suggestions from a broad range of participants, and by combining peer-to-peer review with statistical models to identify and highlight the most insightful ideas.

The CITRIS (Center for Information Technology Research in the Interest of Society) Connected Communities Initiative developed the CRC in collaboration with the office of California Lt. Governor Gavin Newsom to explore how technology can improve communication among voters and public officials. The CRC aims to increase public engagement with government and to tap California's collective intelligence. In CRC v1.0, participants graded the State of California on six timely issues and suggested topics that deserve increased priority at the state level.

Between January and June 2014, more than 9,000 California residents from all 58 counties assigned over 23,000 grades to the state and suggested over 300 issues for increased priority. Among other topics, the CRC revealed strong interest in statewide disaster preparedness, prompting a specific response from Lt. Governor Newsom on March 20, 2014, when he announced that this issue would become a top priority for him and his staff. The CRC v1.0 and associated data can be accessed at Californiareportcard.org.

Figure 14.1
Graphic summary of the California Report Card v1.0. Illustration courtesy of Grace Jang.

The California Report Card v1.0

The CRC integrates elements of two projects: the Opinion Space project developed at UC Berkeley between 2009 and 2013 (Faridani et al. 2010) and the Citizen Report Card concept developed by the World Bank in 1993 to assess government performance in developing economies (World Bank 2014). To increase accessibility, the CRC was built using HTML5 to enable access across mobile and desktop devices.

The CRC v1.0 is available to anyone online. It asked participants to grade the state on six timely issues:

1. Implementation of the Affordable Care Act ("Obamacare")
2. Quality of K–12 public education
3. Affordability of state colleges and universities
4. Access to state services for undocumented immigrants
5. Laws and regulations regarding recreational marijuana
6. Marriage rights for same-sex partners

In contrast to traditional polls and surveys, the CRC provides instant feedback by revealing the median grade from all participants each time a grade is entered (see figure 14.2a). The system measures changes in grades to evaluate the effect of social influence bias (Krishnan et al. 2014).

Participants were then invited to evaluate and suggest issues to be considered on the next CRC (figure 14.2b–c). In the "CAFE" ideation space, participants can suggest an issue for priority at the state level. This phase is illustrated as a café table, where participants can discuss issues over a cup of coffee. Suggestions are displayed as mugs (see figure 14.2b) and are positioned using Principal Component Analysis (using grades assigned on the initial six issues)—mugs in closer proximity represent participants who graded the six issues similarly. Participants evaluate others' suggestions by assigning

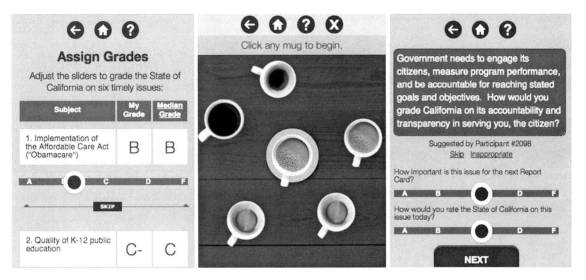

Figure 14.2

The California Report Card v1.0 User Interface. (a) Grading the State of California; (b) the CAFE (Collaborative Assessment and Feedback Engine); (c) grading an issue suggested by a participant.

grades on two axes: "How important is this issue for the next report card?" and "How would you grade the State of California on this issue today?" (figure 14.2c). An earlier study showed that participants explore more divergent ideas using such a graphical display instead of list-based approaches (Faridani et al. 2010).

Responses from the 9,000 participants confirm approval of California's rollout of the Affordable Care Act, but convey mixed sentiment on California's education system. To evaluate the representativeness of these results, a reference-randomized survey was conducted with 611 participants. A comparison of the mean grades on the CRC and the reference survey showed remarkable similarity: over the six issues, the average difference between the mean CRC grades and the mean reference survey grades was 3%. In the ideation space, suggestions from a broad cross section of Californians revealed new insights on statewide concerns, including widespread interest in greater statewide disaster preparedness. All research was conducted with approval from the Institutional Review Board at UC Berkeley.

Two participant comments: (1) "This is the first system that lets us directly express our feelings to government leaders. I also really enjoy reading and grading the suggestions from other participants"; and (2) "This platform allows us to have our voices heard. The ability to review and grade what others suggest is important. It enables us and elected officials to hear directly how Californians feel."

Conclusion

The CRC v1.0 demonstrates how mobile technology can improve public communication and bring the government closer to the people it represents. The CRC v1.0 facilitated identification of statewide concern for disaster preparedness and prompted a direct response from the office of Lt. Governor Gavin Newsom to identify methods to improve statewide disaster preparedness.

While elections, opinion polls, and surveys produce valuable information, they tend to be infrequent, costly, and are often conducted at the convenience of government or special interests. We believe that new technology has the potential to increase public engagement by tapping the collective intelligence of California residents every day, not just on Election Day.

Data are available at Californiareportcard.org/data.

Note

1. Authors of the article are Brandie Nonnecke, Tanja Aitamurto, Daniel Catterson, Camille Crittenden, Chris Garland, Allen Ching-Chang Huang, Sanjay Krishnan, Matti Nelimarkka, Gavin Newsom, Jay Patel, John Scott, and Ken Goldberg.

References

Faridani, Siamak, Ephrat Bitton, Kimiko Ryokai, and Ken Goldberg. 2010. "Opinion Space: A Scalable Tool for Browsing Online Comments." In *Proceedings of the ACM International Conference on Computer Human Interaction (CHI).* New York: ACM Press.

Graham, Todd, Marcel Broersma, Karin Hazelhoff, and Guido van 't Haar. 2013. "Between Broadcasting Political Messages and Interacting with Voters: The Use of Twitter during the 2010 UK General Election Campaign." *Information Communication & Society* 16 (5): 692–716.

Hemphill, Libby, and Andrew J. Roback. 2014. "Tweet Acts: How Constituents Lobby Congress via Twitter." In *Proceedings of the 17th ACM Conference on Computer Supported Cooperative Work & Social Computing—CSCW '14,* 1200–1210. New York: ACM Press.

Himmelroos, Staffan, and Henrik Serup Christensen. 2014. "Deliberation and Opinion Change: Evidence from a Deliberative Mini-Public in Finland," *Scandinavian Political Studies* 37 (1) (March 11): 41–60.

Krishnan, Sanjay, Jay Patel, Michael Franklin, and Ken Goldberg. 2014. "Social Influence Bias in Recommender Systems: A Methodology for Learning, Analyzing, and Mitigating Bias in Ratings." Working paper. Retrieved June 27, 2014, from http://goldberg.berkeley.edu/pubs/sanjay-recsys-v10.pdf.

Landemore, Helene. 2013. *Democratic Reason: Politics, Collective Intelligence, and the Rule of the Many*. Princeton, NJ: Princeton University Press.

National Democratic Institute (NDI). 2014. *Citizen Participation and Technology: An NDI Study*. Retrieved from http://bit.ly/1hePZuM.

Newsom, Gavin, with Lisa Dickey. *Citizenville: How to Take the Town Square Digital and Reinvent Government*. 2013. New York: Penguin Press.

World Bank. 2014. *Citizen Report Card and Community Score Card*. Retrieved from http://bit.ly/1hwn0kt.

III Play + Resistance

15   Meaningful Inefficiencies: Resisting the Logic of Technological Efficiency in the Design of Civic Systems

Eric Gordon and Stephen Walter

We are making government more user-friendly. …
—San Francisco Mayor Ed Lee in "A Start-Up Called Government," the first annual report of the Mayor's Office of Civic Innovation (2013)

In the early 2000s, the City of Baltimore became the first big American city to organize all its major services under a single digital system and to utilize the collection and reporting of big data to increase efficiency in all aspects of government (O'Connell 2001). This program, called CitiStat, winner of the 2004 Innovations in American Government Award, originally made use of existing, yet closed, data streams collected by 16 agencies across the city. However, CitiStat would make two paradigm-shifting enhancements to the system. The first was the opening of a new, citizen-sourced data stream, a 311 citizen-reporting hotline—similar to 911 but for non-emergency calls— that linked directly to city service management; the second was opening up the data to the public and using it as a "civic communication tool." This helped usher in a new age of e-reporting that soon spread to related data programs in New York, Chicago, and elsewhere. Now, as both data producers and data consumers, citizens ostensibly became partners to the government in making the basic functioning of the city more efficient (Ackerman 2004). This model of co-governance was met with much praise by tech-industry leaders. The IBM Center for The Business of Government sponsored a report praising the City of Baltimore for becoming "increasingly customer-friendly" as a result of its data-driven programs and "the higher level of agency performance in delivering critical goods and services to citizens in the metropolitan area" (Henderson 2003, 6).

In the decade that followed, social networks such as Facebook and Twitter, publishing platforms from Patch to Tumblr, and mobile web-connected smart devices all worked to set new standards for how people communicate with each other. In April 2015, partly facilitated by these connective technologies, multiple videos captured by onlookers went viral showing an unarmed black man named Freddie Gray as he was dragged screaming into a police van by Baltimore police officers. Freddie Gray would later die due to the injuries he sustained during his arrest.

Inspired by the videos captured by smartphones and amplified on social media, these same technologies were then utilized to coordinate widespread protests against police brutality across Baltimore, which would ostensibly "shut the city down." Certain city services were canceled, and a curfew was imposed. These events, and the often disquieting and extraordinary images, stories, and commentaries produced and shared from them, pushed the national conversation and media coverage about police brutality, mass incarceration, and urban inequality, to the center of attention. In a marked shift from other recent episodes of police brutality in the United States (e.g., in Ferguson, MO, and New York City), the state's attorney for the City of Baltimore, Marilyn Mosby, conducted a news conference where she both publicly ruled the death a homicide, charging the six officers involved, and, in unity with the protestors, openly acknowledged the "structural and systemic" racial issues present in policing, and the need for them to be broadly changed.[1] Though the decision was a result of many disparate current and historical factors, connective technologies played a part in the telling and reflection of the story. Without the capturing of video, without the amplification on social media, and without the tech-coordinated protests, this may have become another buried case of police brutality. Instead, it became a highly visual moment of reflection on the inequality inherent in Baltimore's systems of governance.

CitiStat in the early 2000s and the protests in 2015 represent two starkly different cases of technologies used to "efficiently" enhance or intervene in civic systems. With CitiStat, the notion of efficiency is born out of the technical and industrial sectors, defined by cost-effectiveness, speed, and market distribution. These efficiencies were intentionally designed into the system by a central design team. With the protests, efficiency is tied to what John Dewey (2011) has called "civic efficiency," or the ability to get things done with others, even if disruptive, messy, and unpredictable. In this case, existing technology was appropriated in an unexpected context, and civic efficiency emerged through its unique use by disparate actors. These two cases bring up important questions as to what efficiency means, for whom systems are efficient, and how efficiencies are designed into a civic technology. When the application of technology to civic life is celebrated purely for its expediency, transactionality, and instrumentality, then other uses and users are potentially sidelined. Civic technology is running on two parallel tracks—technological efficiency and civic efficiency—where an emerging technology sector is forming around streamlining government operations, and worldwide social movements are forming around unexpected uses of existing technology. While the latter track often produces dramatic images and stories that draw media attention and public conversation, the former track is becoming increasingly profitable and, we argue, dangerously overtaking the narrative of civic technology *design* and shifting the intentional mobilization of efficiency by designers, implementers, and funders to focus more on helping users of a technological system than citizens of a democracy.

The philosopher Hannah Arendt, writing in the 1950s in response to postwar industrialism in Europe and the United States, provides important insight into the logic of human systems, specifically the way tools and functions conceive of and mobilize their human users. Arendt (1998) argues that all human activity falls within three categories: *labor, work,* and *action.* Labor is fundamental activity that maintains human life, activity that caters to biological needs of production and consumption (the actual human effort that is mobilized toward work); work is activity that contributes to the world that humans occupy (everything from building tools to thinking ideas); finally, action is the birth of a new political current in the world, a social means for change with no neatly predictable or prescribed ends.

The problem with many contemporary systems built purely with a focus on labor or work is that they too often view humans as interchangeable units, and imposed civic *behavior* replaces civic action. Arendt criticizes the rationalizing systems under which modern humans live for their tendency to elicit "from each of its members a certain kind of behavior, imposing innumerable and various rules, all of which tend to 'normalize' its members, to make them behave, to exclude spontaneous action or outstanding achievement" (1998, 41). Technology critic Evgeny Morozov echoes this in 2013 in the context of digital technology: "recasting all complex social situations either as neatly defined problems with definite, computable solutions or as transparent and self-evident processes that can be easily optimized—if only the right algorithm is in place!—" is likely not even to achieve its predicted purpose, for the "solutions" are often more tied to techno-utopian values than the realities of a messy, real world democracy (Morozov 2013, 5).

It is perhaps an irony then that modern web technologies might be the most effective medium ever to exist to facilitate action as Arendt defines it. Open, interconnected, mobile, complex, chaotic: the Web not only provides potential for action through its ability to connect disparate people and to propagate ideas at an energy never before realized, but it is also perfectly fitted to integrate into the contours of a democratic system—one complex pluralistic system intertwined with another. The job of civic systems can be to promote and curate this action while at the same time establishing stable "islands of predictability" through institutions, laws, and promises (1998, 244). When we invoke "civic systems," we mean any designed series of social interactions aimed at facilitating collective governance or action, be it a constituted system of national government aimed at sustaining integral institutions, a grassroots collective aimed at radically altering how voices are counted in a deliberative process, or an online forum dedicated to establishing and maintaining the rules and etiquette of a website. It is imperative that the designers of civic systems leverage web-based technology not for imposing behaviors, but for facilitating action.

In this chapter, we analyze the narrative of technological efficiency in the civic space. Contributing to what Elizabeth Losh calls the *Virtualpolitik,* the narrative of technological efficiency has become part of everyday governance, impacting decisions made by the "managers of the nation state" (2009, 12). We seek to recognize where the narrative is challenged through alternative actions and designs. We introduce what we call *meaningful inefficiencies* as an emerging design paradigm for civic technology, which accommodates the possibility of messiness, disruption, and the playing with rules and boundaries. Borrowing from game design and game studies, meaningful inefficiencies is a way of thinking about civic systems that are open to the affordances of play (what Roger Caillois refers to as an "occasion of pure waste" (2001, 5)), where users have the option to *play* within and with rules, not simply to *play out* prescribed tasks (Sutton-Smith 1997; Sicart 2014). While we argue for the value of play in the design and implementation of civic systems, we do not want to suggest that there is something inevitable in the playful (or ludic) paradigm (Raessens 2006; Walz 2010; Zimmerman 2015). Instead we seek to understand play not as a paradigmatic shift, but as a characteristic of systems that has been overlooked in the current discourse surrounding technology and governance. Ultimately, in this chapter we present a call to action to understand civic technologies not simply in terms of what they do, but what people do with them. Designing for meaningful inefficiencies is a way of expanding technological civic systems to accommodate more than just the "good user" of systems, but also the marginalized, the emergent, and the playful.

User-Friendliness

While civic technology, or civic tech, in its current form is a new phenomenon, the insertion of technological efficiency into civic life is hardly new. Consider the design of cities. Twentieth-century urbanism has ushered in an understanding of cities as complex and rational systems (Mumford 2010) wherein the networks of buildings and roads could be conceptualized as a structure or language with which humans could interact (Alexander et al. 1977). But the end logic of the modernist city, the master-planned Brasilia or Robert Moses's rationalized sanitation of New York City, is what by today's standards would be called a dumb city, as they were systems designed and fixed in place with the premise of full automation without responsiveness to their human occupants. These mid-century modernist utopias were human systems designed for the abstracted and generic human user (Gordon 2010). More recently, discourses of the smart city, or the smarter city, have dominated contemporary city planning efforts around a simple premise—data generated through users of systems can inform the design and iteration of such systems (Townsend 2013; IBM 2012). In a big data environment, where mobile devices and sensors can capture movements, purchases and, social interactions, and where data from property, crime, and taxes are available and usable in aggregate, the promise of data-driven design is motivating change in urban systems and their governance (Ratti and Townsend 2011; Caragliu, Del Bo, and Nijkamp 2009).

The individual is no longer the primary subject of governance; instead, governments have sought to become responsive to the aggregate data traces they leave behind (Whitson 2015; de Souza e Silva and Gordon 2013). Data sourced in aggregate, and the users that enable efficient data access, are the subjects directly addressed by government and organizations all within the celebrated framework of the "user-friendly city." This rhetoric was apparent in Baltimore's early CitiStat program, but questions about which customer was being served, and to whom the government was being friendly, arose with dramatic poignancy during the 2015 protests. The only people that get counted in aggregate, it would seem, are those who are good users of the systems provided.

Inequality and access have been insufficiently addressed in the context of "smart" governance and city building, largely because it has been so heavily influenced by private sector–sponsored infrastructure projects, including IBM's Smarter Cities initiative, or contemporary master-planned city environments such as New Songdo City in South Korea. While the modernist representations of urbanism are apparent in these projects—skyscrapers, plazas, and highways—a central part of the infrastructure is the data scraped from citizens as they occupy these representations. Residents are conceived as users of systems, and most importantly, creators and users of data. Governing this

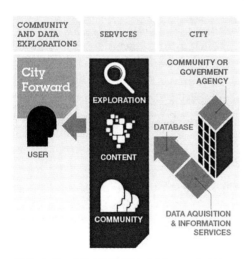

City Forward is a platform that enables users to uncover insights about cities and engage in the ecosystem of people working to move cities forward.

Figure 15.1
A screenshot of an early logic model for City Forward, an IBM web-based platform from 2010 for analyzing and visualizing data from cities. The program has since evolved into the Smarter Cities Challenge, where IBM experts help cities "[reimagine] their relationships with citizens, leveraging them as both sources of data—the pulse of the city—and as partners in seeding change."

smarter city, therefore, requires access, production, and analysis of data, and the conceptualization of the citizen as a producer of data within the confines of systems.

The city as system, much like any designed technical system, is designed for the user who uses the system well, or one who enters into the system in good faith to accomplish prescribed tasks. Users of technological systems often accommodate those systems *in order* to use them well (Lanier 2010) and the underlying code of systems become a kind of hidden legal framework that shapes social actions (Lessig 2006). For example, users learn how to navigate automated telephone lines in order to speak to a human, or learn how to use Facebook to reach their friends. Technological systems are always guiding and "reskilling" their users as much as they are facilitating pre-mediated social actions (Latour 1988). Thus, technology that focuses only on designing more efficiency into civic life runs the risk of altering, without deliberation or oversight, the very constitution of what a citizen is and what they can or cannot do.

So when city government is framed as a user-friendly technological system, the characteristics of the "good user" become the legible stand-in for the citizen. The concept of the "good user" is based on normative structures of citizenship that situate the user solely within abstracted procedures, such as attending a meeting or voting or registering a complaint about a pothole. The users, conceived within the systems they use well, are necessarily articulated outside of any other modes of social integration such as place or cultural lineage that might otherwise compose political and civic identities (Habermas 2001), and determine patterns of inclusion or exclusion (Fraser 1990). Mechanisms of crafting citizenship such as formal or informal education (Callan 1997; Guttman 1999) and civic voice and activism (Habermas 2001; Manin 1997; W. Lance Bennett 2008) are potentially sidelined in the minds of system architects to accommodate those already producing the appropriate data or those data-producing practices that can best accommodate new technological systems. The "good user" is the rational, self-interested customer who demands efficient services toward prescribed ends. Similar to the concept of "political consumerism," or the buying or boycotting of products for political purposes (Stolle, Hooghe, and Micheletti 2005), the production or use of aggregate data is a form of consumerism that has direct impact on one's sense of engagement (or lack of same) in civic life (de Zuniga, Copeland, and Bimber 2013).

Hackability

One of the first major instances of a city actively publicizing its ability to leverage private sector innovations occurred with CompStat in New York City. Originally developed for the NYPD in 1994, CompStat aimed to modernize the department through a "continuous improvement of performance" by employing "a variety of corporate strategies" to make its organizational structure more efficient (O'Connell 2001). At the core of CompStat is the requirement of routine data-based meetings

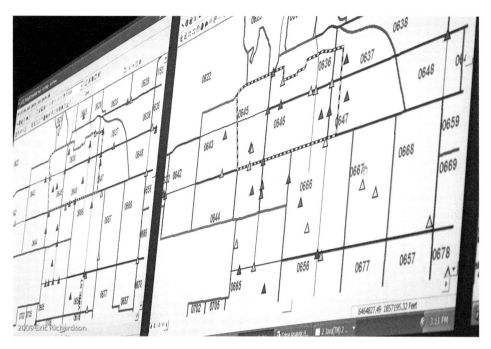

Figure 15.2
A CompStat data interface.

where field commanders were mandated to both report and react to data generated from their precincts. This data resulted from a requirement that all precincts record a number of crime statistics on a neighborhood basis. The reaction to the data would trigger a street-by-street response, with the goal of rewarding commanders not on the number of arrests their staff made, but on a drop in specific crime statistics.

Winner of the 1996 Innovations in American Government Award from the Harvard Kennedy School of Government, CompStat represents one of the first major city systems to fully embrace an emerging focus of the private sector: the collection and leveraging of big data. Soon, this data-driven approach to service management was adopted by other New York City departments—"ParkStat" for the Department of Parks and Recreation, "TrafficStat" for the traffic division, "JobStat" for the Human Resources Administration, and "HealthStat" for health insurance enrollment—and by other cities throughout the U.S. It was Baltimore that fused all this together in Citistat.

E-government, Government 2.0, open government: these are all terms used to describe the "digital revolution" in government function and operation, in no small way influenced by Citistat (Poje 2011; Misuraca 2009; Ressler 2009). Chun et al. (2010) identify several stages of e-government, ranging from the basic digitization of government records, to simple web-based transactions with available data, to more complex transactions such as paying taxes and fines. These early stages of e-government were focused solely on the efficiency of transactions at the municipal level, as we saw with the first 311 services. The current stage, they argue, is focused on interaction. It is about the quality of citizen interaction with government and the opportunities for collaborative decision making through social media and open data. These three stages make clear the logical slippage between digitization of records and citizen engagement. For e-government practitioners, these very different activities are placed under the umbrella of government efficiency and speak directly to the rhetorical promise of networked, web-based technologies for everyday governance.

This declarative position is in part fueled by the Obama administration's 2009 open government initiative (Noveck, chapter 8), which established three principles for governing in the digital age: transparency, participation, and collaboration. According to the document, governments should make more data available to the public; they should make it easy to access basic services and information; and they should foster possibilities for inter-departmental and inter-agency collaboration. The initiative was directed to the federal government, but it has served as a justification for municipal government to devote resources to "opening up." As these principles of open government translate to the local level, they have maintained their focus on internal efficiency and appropriation of private sector rhetoric, but have also been refined to focus on direct service provision and citizen participation.

"Opening up" and empowering citizens has dominated the discourse of civic technology. But just as the civic tech community has celebrated these possibilities, they have also situated that openness within a language of control, specifically, in the discourse of technology, through the metaphor of *hacking*. According to Shannon Spanhake, San Francisco's deputy innovation officer, "Cities are like living machines, and policy making in government is like writing the code that governs how a city operates. This city is the most complex machine I have ever had the opportunity to hack and it is what inspired my shift from the private sector to the public sector. #helloworld" (Innovate SF 2013). Big data production and consumption has enabled the opening up of channels of communication, but at the same time, it has enabled designers of civic systems to control and *hack* the system. As a result of this conceptual framing, the citizen as user of a hackable system, is disciplined through procedures of what philosopher Michel Foucault describes as governmentality (1991), whereby under the promise of collaboration, governments redouble their hold on power by dispersing it to the governed. In the actual operation of governments, this does not represent "a diminishment or a reduction of state sovereignty and planning capacities but a displacement from formal to informal techniques of government and the appearance of new actors on the scene of government (e.g., NGOs), that indicate fundamental transformations in statehood and a new relation between state and civil society actors" (Lemke 2002,

11). In this sense, government power can be maintained far more efficiently and pervasively not through external force, but by tacitly managing the possible forms of self-government and fields of action available to citizens (Klauser, Paasche, and Söderström, 2014). Hackability, according to the discourse of the smarter city, is often employed as a means of exerting control, as opposed to challenging it. It invokes an internal to government strategy that becomes a way of managing social difference, including race, class, and gender, by streamlining the good user into normative, technical activities.

Civic Labor and Civic Work

The designers and proponents of civic technology too often articulate participation and openness within the framework of efficiency and control. This approach to governance is premised on defining a very specific user, one that is compelled to operate as an individual, presumably for personal benefit, but in the service of a system. Hannah Arendt's conceptions of labor and work provide useful frameworks for understanding this design paradigm.

When civic technologies are designed for labor, users are conceived as components of an efficient system, laborers in achieving prescribed ends (i.e., 311 systems). Systems designed to cultivate civic labor tend to be transactional, focusing on the curation of good habits and slipping into the background of everyday routine. Citizen mobile reporting apps and APIs such as Boston 311, NYC 311, or Chicago Works outsource the identification of problems directly to laborers. According to Arendt, to labor is "meant to be enslaved by necessity, and this enslavement was inherent in the conditions of human life" (1998, 83–84). Labor is the basic contribution to the maintenance of survival. No longer needing to attend extensively to biological survival, modern labor in post-industrial nations can be equated to the continual repetitive processes with which the status quo of any system is maintained. Not only does outsourcing labor to citizens increase efficiency and decrease costs for government if done correctly, but it also defines citizenship in transactional terms and as something done purely "in service" to the basic continuation of the status quo and its existing power structures.

Systems designed with civic work in mind tend to consider the outcomes of labor and the use of those outcomes in the world. For example, public planning processes are typically framed as a collective effort toward designing a particular policy document through input and analysis. Contrary to simply using citizens as laborers for increasing efficiency of civic life, civic designers deploy interventions that help to *fabricate solutions* and *make* citizens better users of existing civic systems. Whether traditional public information campaigns, education programs, and mandatory requirements for participation, or web-enabled education and discussion apps, civic work aims to construct an artifice of efficient citizenship required by all in order to optimize the way civic systems are used. As opposed to using citizens to generate big data, here data is used to optimize citizens through systems of education or activity. For example, the attempt at crowd-sourcing a new constitution in Iceland after the protests in 2008/9 is a good example of civic tech directed toward a specific work product. While the effort was ultimately rejected by parliament in 2012, the process of using networked technology to steer collective labor toward specific ends is clearly represented in this example. However, being that the new constitution, whose ratification was supported by 67 percent of voters, was rejected because of a few disenchanted MPs, the value of such efforts should be questioned. Despite the "opening up" through consolidating work efforts, the system remained *hackable* by its architects, essentially under the control of those already in power. Iceland, perhaps because of its highly connected (95 percent broadband use) and highly homogenous population, has continued to explore and support similar civic tech efforts such as Better Reykjavik (Lackaff, chapter 13), which is a mobile input system that has sourced over 1700 policy recommendations (with over 400 of them formally considered by government) since its start in 2010. The example of Iceland demonstrates both the extraordinary affordances of streamlining civic work and the risk of it simply reifying existing power structures through governmentality.

Increasingly, practitioners in and out of government are looking to behavioral science for insights and for approaches to encouraging civic labor and work. In the UK, for example, the Behavioral Insights Team (sometimes called the "Nudge Unit") was established in 2010 through the Prime Minister's Office to apply behavioral science to policy enforcement and service delivery. In the United States, the Obama adminis-tration established a similar office in 2014 called the Social and Behavioral Science Team (SBST). The notion of "nudging" people as an approach to social policy was popu-larized by economist Richard Thaler and former Administrator of the White House Office of Information and Regulatory Affairs, Cass Sunstein. Nudging seeks to alter "people's behavior in a predictable way without forbidding any options or significantly changing their economic incentives" so that "consistent and unwavering people, in the private or public sector, can move groups and practices in their preferred direction" (Thaler and Sunstein 2009, 58). With this subtle coercion of citizens into governing their behaviors more efficiently through the internalization of mechanisms of control (as in governmentality), the citizen again takes on the qualities of a good user: predict-ably acting within a pre-defined system and pushed to act primarily in their own self-interest.

Many of these efforts have produced clear outcomes: for example, the benchmark program for the new SBST, in partnership with the US Department of Education, sought to increase rates of federal loan repayment among those who have fallen behind. The team experimented with email communication to understand what form of address and frequency of email had most impact on loan repayment. The results of the pilot demonstrated that sending emails to borrowers in delinquency for 90–180 days resulted in a statistically significant increase in repayment applications, with 6,000 additional completed applications in the first month. These sorts of results hold significant promise for making government more efficient insofar as they seek to understand and iterate on the measurable behaviors of citizens. But they also reinscribe the notion of a citizen as a user of a system, as a consumer of services, engaging in the activities of labor and work. In so doing, they bracket out the nuance, the unmeasurable, the actions through which citizens construct meaning and form identities. By making civic systems more user-friendly, they ultimately make users more friendly to civic systems.

Civic Action and Meaningful Inefficiencies

Democracy does not always appear to be efficient. As the events in Baltimore demonstrate, anger and feelings of exclusion can lead to disruption of otherwise streamlined systems. But those same feelings, bolstered by social media and connective technologies, create what John Dewey (2011) calls civic efficiency, or the working with others to achieve public ends. "If democracy has a moral and ideal meaning," Dewey states, "it is that a social return be demanded from all and that the opportunity for development of distinctive capacities be afforded all ... the adoption of the narrower meaning of efficiency deprives it of its essential justification" (2011, 117). Dewey here is distinguishing technological efficiency from the kind of "civic efficiency" that makes social experiences valuable and educative. Both technological efficiency and civic efficiency are present in any democratic context, even as civic technologies push to produce and reproduce the former. The activities associated with Dewey's version of civic efficiency are born of Arendt's third category: *action*.

Democracy needs to allow for unpredictable, chaotic, novel *civic action* to occur, in which even "the smallest act in the most limited circumstance" and even "one deed, and sometimes one word, suffices to change every constellation" (Arendt 1998, 190). Action, as Arendt defines it, is the birth of a new political current, as small as a word or as large as a declaration, that reverberates through a human collective and interacts with everything and everyone, often imperceptibly. Allowing the freedom and providing a medium through which these waves can flow enables the chaotic emergence of new ideas, new experiences, and new actions that a single individual, group, or data model could never achieve. The consequences are "boundless, because action, though it may proceed from nowhere, so to speak, acts into a medium where every reaction becomes a chain reaction and where every process is the cause of new processes" and that "no matter what its specific content, always establishes relationships and therefore has an inherent tendency to force open all limitations and cut across all boundaries" (1998, 190). An action can be set into motion by a single person, but it reverberates and grows in the social world where it takes on a character that transcends its initial design or intention through pluralistic, collective force. A system that allows for action in

Arendt's sense allows for collective contributions to a process or a cause to become more than the sum of its parts. From people in the Roxbury neighborhood of Boston commandeering the 311 system to focus the city's attention on blighted properties, to a simple hashtag, #blacklivesmatter, created by a few activists after the acquittal of George Zimmerman in the wrongful death trial of African American teenager Trayvon Martin in Sanford, Florida—each action is a meaningful inefficiency with clear outcomes. One forced a city government to act on long ignored blighted properties and the other mobilized a global campaign to highlight racial injustices. While vastly different in scale, each is disrupting norms and challenging efficiencies in systems of governance.

To counteract technological efficiency as the dominant design value of civic systems, we suggest a concerted effort to design meaningful inefficiencies into human systems. Meaningful inefficiencies represent the design of systems for civic action, not behaviors. They can be civic tools, systems, or events, etc., that temporarily halt normal civic processes and create a delineated time or place in which play, disorder, messiness, and the ability to experiment and fail safely are utilized in productive—though not necessarily practical—ways. The results of this play can be increased civic learning, reflection, empathy, and increased awareness of civic systems and their effects—which citizens can then leverage in creating new action in the normal processes of civic life.

A meaningful inefficiency, like Dewey's civic efficiency, ultimately aims to increase "neither more nor less than capacity to share in a give and take of experience. It covers all that makes one's own experience more worthwhile to others, and all that enables one to participate more richly in the worthwhile experiences of others" (Dewey 2011, 116). In the near dominance of technological efficiency in the design of civic systems today, meaningful inefficiency is necessarily an oppositional term, bringing to light the collapsing of the "range and accuracy [of a citizen's] perception of meanings" into machine-readable, hackable, and simplistic *features* (2011, 119).

We are not suggesting the design or cultivation of inefficiencies out of context. The fundamental requisite for a civic inefficiency to be "meaningful" is that it is productively *in tension* with a new or existing efficiency. It would not necessarily be meaningful to create more inefficiencies where inefficiencies run rampant, such as in a situation where basic civic and social services do not exist. An inefficiency becomes meaningful once it either provides a respite from efficiency, where citizens can share in a give and take of experience and increase their range and perception of meanings with each other, or when it provides a new view of the efficiency, where citizens are able to more fully understand how they are being shaped by the system—or how they might in turn be able to shape it. By doing so, this prompt allows for systems to make the uncertainties of variables fertile; the unexpectedness of outcomes revelatory; the opportunities for waste and the failure of resources and efforts constructive; the stakeholder complexities of interests and goals nourishing; and the deliberate misuses of the system

Figure 15.3
Media artist Catherine D'Ignazio's 2011 project *The Border Crossed Us* at the UMass Amherst campus. In the middle of a busy route on campus, she installed a to-scale replica of a US border fence that divides the Tohono O'odham Nation—the second-largest Native American reservation in the country—into two parts. People are literally stopped in their tracks and prompted to text a number and join a conversation about what happens when we divide a territory that the community imagines as contiguous and how the international border in Arizona touches lives on a college campus in New England.

constructive. Common to all meaningful inefficiencies, as we shall see below, is an element of play, or playfulness.

Play

Play is, in a sense, the mechanism of action in meaningful inefficiencies. Play can be defined as an activity in which the means are more valuable than the ends—that is, it is *autotelic*, it is done first and foremost for its own sake. Anthropologist Johan Huizinga writes that "in play there is something 'at play' which transcends the immediate needs of life and imparts meaning to the action. All play means something" (1950, 1). Thus, regardless of outcome—which certainly can be important—play itself is its own point. Players voluntarily enter into a system ostensibly in pursuit of some goal, but participation is not wholly dependent on the outcome of achieving that goal. For example, in a good game, players elect to play and the reward for playing is play itself. If one were to start a game of chess and beat their opponent in less than two minutes, the game would likely be unsatisfying for both the loser and the winner, because while the goal of winning provides direction, the goal of simply playing is not achieved. The uneven game of chess disallows the experience of play. The good user of chess is the one who beats her opponent in less than two minutes. The good player, however, is one that generates meaning from actions taken within the inefficiencies in the system—the circuitous paths one often takes to achieve victory in the face of unnecessary obstacles (Suits 2005).

While play is "an action accomplishing itself outside and above the necessities and seriousness of everyday life," at the same time it can, and often is, employed as a "helping-out of the action" of everyday life, beyond traditional play contexts (Huizinga 1950, 26, 15). Miguel Sicart suggests *playfulness* as the term for using play in a "context that is not created or intended for play" (2014, 27). Fundamental to this act is the "appropriation of what should not be play." It is this act of appropriation, of bringing to bear on a serious situation in life, play—a mode of experience so fundamental to how we make meaning in the world as we grow, but so stamped out of adult life—that "we bring freedom to a context." Play is "personal, and playfulness is used to imbue the functional world with personal experience," while at the same time "revealing the seams of behaviors, technologies, or situations that we take for granted" (2014, 29).

When playfulness is recognized and accommodated within civic systems, the result is a meaningful inefficiency, where the good user is propelled toward action, not just work and labor. In this sense, the notion of a user of a meaningfully inefficient civic system is not sufficient; when a system enables playfulness, either by design or accident, the user acts as a player with freedom to explore meaning well beyond the confines of the system in which they are operating. As such, the recognition of meaningful inefficiencies suggests the recognition of a playful citizen, not simply a good user.

The playful citizen, as a subject of civic systems, is able to more fully participate in that give and take of experience that Dewey declares so fundamental to democratic and personal growth. Acknowledging the playful citizen means recognizing that people actively play with and within systems, which necessitates being adaptable and responsive to unpredictable appropriations. This means that one should not, as Internet scholar Yochai Benkler puts it, utilize "a straightforward, uncomplicated theory of human nature that reduces our actions as simple, predictable responses to punishments and incentives and helps us explain away confusing and even disturbing behaviorism," but that designers of civic technologies and citizens alike can learn from each other in a constant play of inventive meanings (Benkler 2011, 18).

"Vibrancy and efficiency may not be diametrically opposed," says Ethan Zuckerman, "but the forces are clearly in tension" (2013, 220). This tension can be productive; and, while challenging for designers, it is only through designing for the play of these and the other forces that facilitate and are moved by citizen action that it is possible to

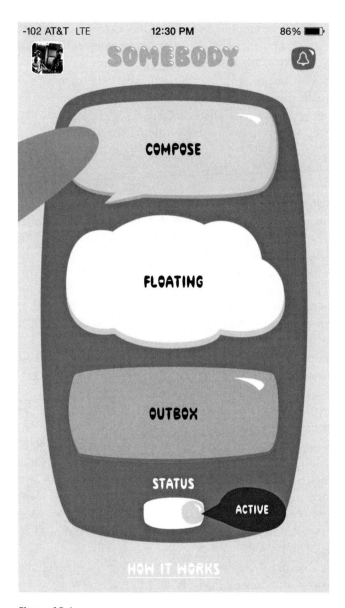

Figure 15.4
Somebody, an app designed by artist and author Miranda July, allows people to ask strangers who are nearby to contacts in one's phone to physically deliver a message or perform an action. Here, smartphone technology, including location services, SMS, and an app, are used to facilitate an (ironically) inefficient face-to-face connection between two strangers. Might there be an application for this sort of functionality in the civic realm?

think about and build systems that "let our humanity find a fuller expression; systems that tap into a far greater promise and potential of human endeavor than we have generally allowed in the past" (Benkler 2011, 26). Instead of using new technological innovations to structure behavior so as to impose transactionality, efficiency, and predictability operating on that technology's own terms, it is possible to commission the chaos and emergent play of appropriations when new technology enters civic life, and to use citizen action to steer systems in new, unconventional directions.

Meaningful Inefficiencies: An (Im)practical Example

The concept of disruptive design is nothing new. In the art world, examples abound in the twentieth century, from the Dadaists to the Situtationists. And more specifically in the realm of design, Carl DiSalvo's (2012) concept of adversarial design or Dunne and Raby's (2013) concept of speculative design each point to an interventionist practice in relation to dominant systems. What is unique about the concept of meaningful inefficiencies is its distinct focus on play and civic action taking, not only as an interventionist and deliberate act of design, but also as a characteristic that is inherent within existent systems. Our own experience in designing civic technologies is illustrative of the relevance of meaningful inefficiencies.

Motivated by a lack of community feedback systems in urban planning, in 2010 we were funded by the Knight Foundation to build a public dialogue game. The project, called Community PlanIt, was an online social network meant to bring the public planning meeting online, increase the diversity of those who participated, and to scaffold the process with learning in order to enhance deliberation (Gordon and Baldwin-Philippi 2014). We were interested in making people more informed about the planning issues at hand, more capable of understanding the nuances and rules of a public planning process, and more congenial and empathetic toward other deliberators and decision makers. Following this, our goal, ultimately, was to create a new public planning process and to concurrently cultivate a good user of it. In other words, if we were to successfully introduce a new platform for public engagement, we would need to engage the public in using the platform well.

But, as happens in the early days of a design project, our focus lingered upon all the bad users we seemed to be getting, and how we might be able to make them go away. Because of this, many of our early design iterations were about stamping out opportunities where bad users could unexpectedly appropriate our system and do something we hadn't planned on. After some pilot tests in the Boston area, we set out to design a system that was more efficient, had more features, and eliminated uncertainty—not so much in the content people could put in to the system, but rather the *way* in which people could use the system. The value of the system, we suspected, was the layering of the social values of the Internet (efficiency, archivability, searchability) onto the practical outcomes of most planning processes (conflict avoidance, ephemerality, and confusion).

However, as we deployed the game in two initial implementations (in Boston as part of a school policy planning process and in Detroit as part of an urban planning process), it was clear that the efficiencies so painstakingly built into the system were perhaps the least interesting (and least impactful) qualities of the game experience. While the efficiencies of online participation were an appealing selling point to funders and partners (each game attracted over 1,000 players), in fact, the inefficiencies of gameplay created the greatest amount of interest. Ranging from humorously spamming the system with good-natured community event posts (which then created another tangent where participants deliberated about the unsaid rules of civil Internet etiquette), to stepping away from the planning issues and talking about the game system itself, the role of youth in civic planning, what it meant to digitally engage with stakeholders or to imbue serious issues with a sense of fun, etc.—these actions were intentional means of appropriating the system to bring some other meaning to it. The best conversations and the most interesting insights did not occur from prompts by the designers, but rather the prompts or provocations created when users disrupted the normal use of the system and did something slightly different with it.

This sort of thing had occurred with virtually all the games or game-like systems we had created for civic engagement up to this point (Gordon and Manosevitch 2010; Gordon and Schirra 2012). But never was it clearer than in this experiment that perhaps our use of games was actually inadvertently doing something else that we weren't taking into account; perhaps it wasn't the games themselves that offered the biggest value to these civic engagement processes, but rather something that emerged because of the very use of a game in this particular sociotechnical context. When tasked with organizing and finding a pattern to the most impactful moments for participants during the process, we realized it wasn't when the system was working fully, or during the moments when it was working but doing nothing more than facilitating simple transactional interactions such as liking comments or answering yes or no to a prompt; it also wasn't when a part of the system was simply broken, or was functionally pointless or redundant. The most impact, defined as opportunities to increase trust and efficacy, occurred in moments that were meaningfully inefficient—where either an existing inefficiency itself prompted the user to appropriate it to create some new meaning or action within the system, or when users were able to bring in some inefficiency of their own, and use that to temporarily disrupt the system and cause others to reflect upon what it is that is happening under their noses—how they have been *designed* and how they might be able to build off, or resist, such a design. If this observation was correct, and in fact community engagement matters most when the systems through which people engage are intentionally inefficient (in the technological sense), then our challenge became how to design for these meaningful inefficiencies. Indeed, in the years since Community PlanIt was first deployed, there has been a marked increase in the desire to see technologically efficient systems in processes of public engagement and civic life more generally. The use of games or game mechanics to achieve these ends was gaining popularity among marketing consultants and policy makers alike (McGonigal 2011; Zichermann and Cunningham 2011), even as it developed its very vocal critics in academia (Bogost 2015). But what made our project unique, and perhaps not as scalable as other solutions, was the inherent inefficiency in the system that compelled the user to explore alternative meanings. It was the experience of play, buried within our own gamified design and replete with messiness and ambiguity, that positioned us, inadvertently, in a discursive battle emerging within the conflation of technological efficiency and civic life.

Thus, when we set out to design a game to make planning more efficient, we found ourselves pushing up against the very affordances of games. Games are built to be inefficient as the player seeks to overcome unnecessary obstacles to reach her goal and to engage in the process of play for itself (Suits 2005). Civic tech, on the other hand, is steeped in the discourse of efficiency, with a laser focus on the instrumentality of activity. We became very aware of the tensions inherent in the system we designed—wanting to cultivate civic action through play, and at the same time appeal to funders and partners (foundations, municipal governments, and development organizations) to appease their sense of value through efficiency.

Applied games are often characterized as gamified systems (Deterding et al. 2011). In 2011, the term gamification saw a significant surge in popularity, most commonly applied to the use of game mechanics for specific behavior modifications, ranging from business to healthcare. The early location-based social network, Foursquare, used points and badges to motivate digital check-ins, and major corporations began using similar social incentives to increase productivity in the workforce. Gamified systems are widely considered to do three things: 1) they give users motivation to do something; 2) they give users the ability to complete the action; and 3) they give users a trigger or cue to complete the action (Laja 2012). Gamified systems, by this definition, are no different than the ideal systems conceived through the lens of civic tech. This is what makes our early design work with Community PlanIt so contradictory: it was a gamified system that promised some level of increased efficiency, but was framed around the possibilities of play.

We began teasing out these distinctions very slowly. Our initial studies of Community PlanIt were focused on its capacity to increase efficiency in what we understood to be a dangerously inefficient system of urban planning (Gupta, Bouvier, and Gordon 2012). We sought to measure participation rates, reciprocity on the part of government stakeholders, and trust among users. It was not until later implementations and years of being steeped in discourses of gamification, that all the fissures and intentional

Figure 15.5
Players of the online Community PlanIt game met at a game finale event at the Detroit Public Library. The meeting was a messy mix of technology, face-to-face interaction, and online and offline tools.

ellipses that Community PlanIt brought to planning narratives demonstrated their value. The messy data of deliberation, the playful competition, and the creative storytelling were not simply artifacts of a system, but were central to its design.

The tensions that emerged in the implementation of Community PlanIt have been central to our evolved understanding of what it takes to recognize civic action and design for it. Characteristics of play and playfulness were emergent within this system. While clearly also designed for labor and work, valued for the data produced by users, the system's incorporated elements of play, of encouraging exploration and discovery, were meaningful inefficiencies that came to define it. Or at least came to define our sense of what made it valuable. With the promise of the good user so persistent in civic tech discourse—a user self-disciplined through data production and consumption—the playful citizen became a necessary design prompt for us as a means of cultivating better, more humane systems that are scalable, meaningful, and allow for novel action to emerge.

Conclusion

The example of Community PlanIt represents our "aha moment" in designing technologies that are meaningfully inefficient. We do not present it as a case study with particular observable outcomes, but as a study in process, wherein our expectations were subverted by the logics we had inadvertently designed into the system. Civic life is composed of actions, even if they are masked by the efficient presentation of labor and work. And civic technologies, properly conceived, should acknowledge and nurture the actions that are expressive and potentially transformative. We began this chapter by talking about the contrast present in the civic technology landscape of 21st-century Baltimore. On one hand, CitiStat represents a triumph of technological efficiency, where good users are effectively defined and governed through promises of "user-friendliness" and "hackability." And on the other hand, the 2015 protests prompted by the unlawful death of Freddie Gray represent a triumph of civic efficiency led by those historically excluded from the category of "good user." The latter definition of efficiency is often realized in opposition to existent systems of governance, and for that reason, it is, in practice, a meaningful inefficiency. Civic technologies have the capacity to cultivate meaningful inefficiencies within a system that enables playful citizens to electively explore, experiment, resist, and reimagine the systems that govern their collective actions.

We advocate for policy makers and civic technologists alike to incorporate meaningful inefficiencies into the design of civic systems in order to allow for emergent qualities and experiences beyond those prescribed to the good user. Civic systems should accommodate play through embracing: (1) uncertainties (of variables); (2) unexpectedness (of outcomes); (3) opportunities for waste and failure (of resources and efforts); (4) stakeholder complexity (of interests and goals); and (5) deliberate non-use or misuse (of the system). These qualities of play function as a kind of safety valve for the dominance of technological efficiency in civic design and encourage an evolution of democratic practices not absolutely contained by the rational means of their distribution.

We do not mean to suggest that technological efficiency lacks importance or that programs like CitiStat cannot contribute productively to civic life. The efficient delivery of basic services such as access to housing, policing, and healthcare, is essential. This sort of efficiency is a fundamental and important part of civic life and human activity, and certainly something not to be snuffed out. The danger is when technological efficiency goes unchecked, and the rigid systems are designed only for "good users"—where the slightest unexpected use of the system by a user operating outside of the accepted norms is not accommodated or acknowledged. Ultimately, we suggest that designers, implementers, and funders of civic technologies take into account the existent qualities of labor, work, and action to more accurately pinpoint the function(s) of human activity they are meant to address. The future of civic technology needs to be critical of its ascending values of technological efficiency and not allow a technomentality to obscure relevant intervention points, contexts, and communities in need that may not play well with the rules of good use that have been articulated by the technology of the time. The basic question in civic tech today—how can we make civic life more efficient with technology—must be changed to, how can we use technology to make civic life more meaningful.

Notes

1. "WATCH: Baltimore Prosecutor Charges Six Police Officers, Calls Freddie Gray's Death a 'Homicide'," *Democracy Now!*, May 1, 2015, http://www.democracynow.org/blog/2015/5/1/ watch_baltimore_prosecutor_charges_six_police.

References

Ackerman, John. 2004. "Co-Governance for Accountability: Beyond 'Exit' and 'Voice'." *World Development* 32 (3): 447–463.

Alexander, Christopher, Sara Ishikawa, Murray Silverstein, Max Jacobson, Ingrid Fiksdahl-King, and Shlomo Angel. 1977. *A Pattern Language: Towns, Buildings, Construction.* Oxford: Oxford University Press.

Arendt, Hannah. 1998. *The Human Condition.* 2nd ed. Chicago: University Of Chicago Press.

Benkler, Yochai. 2011. *The Penguin and the Leviathan: How Cooperation Triumphs over Self-Interest.* New York: Crown Business.

Bennett, W. Lance. 2008. "Changing Citizenship in the Digital Age." In *Civic Life Online: Learning How Digital Media Can Engage Youth*, ed. W. L. Bennett. Cambridge, MA: MIT Press.

Bogost, Ian. 2015. "Why Gamification Is Bullshit." In *The Gameful World: Approaches, Issues, Applications*, ed. Steffen Walz and Sebastian Deterding, 65–79. Cambridge, MA: MIT Press.

Callan, E. 1997. *Creating Citizens.* Oxford: Oxford University Press.

Caillois, Roger. 2001. *Man, Play and Games.* Chicago: University of Illinois Press.

Caragliu, Andrea, Chiara Del Bo, and Peter Nijkamp. 2009. "Smart Cities in Europe." Series Research Memoranda 0048, VU University Amsterdam, Faculty of Economics, Business Administration and Econometrics. http://www.inta-aivn.org/images/cc/Urbanism/background%20 documents/01_03_Nijkamp.pdf.

Chun, Soon Ae, Stuart Shulman, Rodrigo Sandoval, and Eduard Hovy. 2010. "Government 2.0 : Making Connections between Citizens, Data and Government." *Information Polity* 15 (1,2): 1–9.

De Souza e Silva, Adriana, and Eric Gordon. 2013. "The Waning Distinction Between Private and Public: Net Locality and the Restructuring of Space." In *International Encyclopedia of Media Studies*, ed. Kelly Gates. Vol. 6. Malden, MA: Wiley-Blackwell Publishing.

De Zúñiga, H. G., L. Copeland, and B. Bimber. 2013. "Political Consumerism: Civic Engagement and the Social Media Connection." *New Media & Society*, June 7. doi:.10.1177/1461444813487960

Deterding, Sebastian, Dan Dixon, Rilla Khaled, and Lennart Nacke. 2011. "From Game Design Elements to Gamefulness: Defining 'Gamification.'" In *Mind Trek '11: Proceedings of the 15th International Academic MindTrek Conference: Envisioning Future Media Environments*, 9–15. New York: ACM Press.

Dewey, John. 2011. *Democracy and Education*. New York: Simon and Brown.

DiSalvo, Carl. 2012. *Adversarial Design*. Cambridge, MA: MIT Press.

Dunne, Anthony, and Fiona Raby. 2013. *Speculative Everything*. Cambridge, MA: MIT Press.

Foucault, Michel. 1991. "Governmentality." In *The Foucault Effect: Studies in Governmentality*, ed. Graham Burchell, Colin Gordon, and Peter Miller, 87–104. Chicago, IL: University of Chicago Press.

Fraser, N. 1990. "Rethinking the Public Sphere : A Contribution to the Critique of Actually Existing." *Social Text* 26 (25): 56–80.

Gordon, Eric. 2010. *The Urban Spectator: American Concept-Cities from Kodak to Google*. Hanover, NH: Dartmouth University Press.

Gordon, Eric, and Jessica Baldwin-Philippi. 2014. "Playful Civic Learning: Enabling Lateral Trust and Reflection in Game-Based Public Participation." *International Journal of Communication* 8. http://ijoc.org/index.php/ijoc/article/view/2195.

Gordon, Eric, and E. Manosevitch. 2010. "Augmented Deliberation: Merging Physical and Virtual Interaction to Engage Communities in Urban Planning." *New Media & Society* 13 (1): 75–95. doi:.10.1177/1461444810365315

Gordon, Eric, and Steven Schirra. 2012. "Playing with Empathy: Digital Role Playing Games in Public Meetings." In *Communities and Technologies 2011*, Proceedings of the 5th International Conference on Communities and Technologies, 179–185. http://dl.acm.org/citation.cfm?doid=2103354.2103378.

Gupta, Jyoti, Jassica Bouvier, and Eric Gordon. 2012. *Exploring New Modalities of Public Engagement: An Evaluation of Digital Gaming Platforms on Civic Capacity and Collective Action in the Boston Public School District*. Public Agenda. http://elab.emerson.edu/wp-content/uploads/2011/03/Engagement_Game_Lab_CPI-Eval_6.11.12.pdf.

Guttman, A. 1999. *Democratic Education*. Princeton, NJ: Princeton University Press.

Habermas, Jurgen. 2001. *The Postnational Constellation: Political Essays*. Ed. M. Pensky. Cambridge, MA: MIT Press.

Henderson, Lenneal. 2003. "The Baltimore CitiStat Program: Performance and Accountability." New York: IBM Center for The Business of Government. http://www.businessofgovernment.org/report/baltimore-citistat-program-performance-and-accountability.

Huizinga, Johan. 1950. *Homo Ludens: A Study of the Play-Element in Culture*. Boston, MA: Beacon Press.

IBM. 2012. *Smarter, More Competitive Cities: Forward-Thinking Cities Are Investing in Insight*. New York: IBM Corporation.

Innovate SF. 2013. "The San Francisco Mayor's Office of Civic Innovation: A Start-up Called Government—Our First Year in Retrospect." San Francisco.

Klauser, Francisco, Till Paasche, and Ola Söderström. 2014. "Michel Foucault and the Smart City: Power Dynamics Inherent in Contemporary Governing through Code." *Environment and Planning D: Society and Space* 32 (5):869–885.

Laja, Peep. 2012. *"How To Use Gamification For Better Business Results"*. Kissmetrics blog. https://blog.kissmetrics.com/gamification-for-better-results/

Lanier, Jaron. 2010. *You Are Not a Gadget: A Manifesto*. New York: Thorndike Press.

Latour, Bruno. 1988. "Mixing Humans and Non-Humans Together: The Sociology of a Door Closer." *Social Problems* 35 (3): 298–310.

Lemke, Thomas. 2002. Foucault, Governmentality, and Critique. *Rethinking Marxism* 14 (3): 49–64.

Lessig, Laurence. 2006. *Code: Version 2.0*. New York: Basic Books.

Losh, Elizabeth. 2009. *Virtualpolitik: An Electronic History of Government Media-Making in a Time of War, Scandal, Disaster, Miscommunication, and Mistakes*. Cambridge, MA: MIT Press.

Manin, Bernard. 1997. *Principles of Representative Government*. Cambridge: Cambridge University Press.

McGonigal, Jane. 2011. *Reality Is Broken: Why Games Make Us Better and How They Can Change the World*. New York: Penguin Press.

Misuraca, Gianluca C. 2009. "E-Government 2015: Exploring M-Government Scenarios, between ICT-Driven Experiments and Citizen-Centric Implications." *Technology Analysis and Strategic Management* 21 (3): 407–424.

Morozov, Evgeny. 2013. *To Save Everything, Click Here: The Folly of Technological Solutionism*. New York: PublicAffairs.

Mumford, Lewis. 2010. *Technics and Civilization*. Chicago: University of Chicago Press.

O'Connell, Paul E. 2001. "Using Performance Data for Accountability : The New York City Police Department's CompStat Model of Police Management Department of Criminal Justice." New York: IBM Center for The Business of Government.

Poje, Joshua. 2011. "Gov 2.0: Interaction, Innovation and Collaboration." *Public Law* 19 (1): 2–11.

Raessens, J. 2006. "Playful Identities, or the Ludification of Culture." *Games and Culture* 1:52–57.

Ratti, Carlo, and Anthony Townsend. 2011. "Harnessing Residents' Electronic Devices Will Yield Truly Smart Cities." *Scientific American,* September. http://www.scientificamerican.com/article .cfm?id=the-social-nexus.

Ressler, Steve. 2009. "The Rise of Gov 2.0—From GovLoop to the White House." *Public Management* 38 (3): 10–13.

Sicart, Miguel. 2014. *Play Matters.* Cambridge, MA: MIT Press.

Stolle, Dietland, Marc Hooghe, and Michele Micheletti. 2005. "Politics in the Supermarket: Political Consumerism as a Form of Political Participation." *International Political Science Review* 26 (3): 245–269.

Suits, Bernard. 2005. *The Grasshopper: Games, Life and Utopia.* Peterborough, ON: Broadview Press.

Sutton-Smith, Brian. 1997. *The Ambiguity of Play.* Cambridge, MA: Harvard University Press.

Thaler, Richard, and Cass Sunstein. 2009. *Nudge: Improving Decisions About Health, Wealth, and Happiness.* New York: Penguin Books.

Townsend, Anthony. 2013. *Smart Cities: Big Data, Civic Hackers, and the Quest for a New Utopia.* New York: W. W. Norton & Company.

Walz, Steffen. 2010. *Toward a Ludic Architecture: The Space of Play and Games.* Pittsburgh: ETC Press.

Whitson, Jennifer. 2015. "Foucault's Fitbit: Governance and Gamification." In *The Gameful World: Approaches, Issues, Applications,* ed. Steffen Walz and Sebastian Deterding. Cambridge, MA: MIT Press.

Zichermann, Gabe, and Chris Cunningham. 2011. *Gamification by Design: Implementing Game Mechanics in Web and Mobile Apps.* Seabastopol, CA: O'Reilly.

Zimmerman, Eric. 2015. "Manifesto for a Ludic Century." In *The Gameful World: Approaches, Issues, Applications,* ed. Steffen Walz and Sebastian Deterding, 19–22. Cambridge, MA: MIT Press.

Zuckerman, Ethan. 2013. *Rewire: Digital Cosmopolitanism in the Age of Connection.* New York: W. W. Norton & Co. Inc.

16   Let's Get Lost: Poetic City Meets Data City

Beth Coleman

Each inhabitant can enjoy every day the pleasure of a new itinerary to reach the same places. The most fixed and calm lives in Esmeralda are spent without any repetition. ... A map of Esmeralda should include, marked in different coloured inks, all these routes, solid and liquid, evident and hidden.

—Italo Calvino, *Invisible Cities*

One of the basic situationist practices is the dérive, a technique of rapid passage through varied ambiences. Dérives involve playful-constructive behavior and awareness of psychogeographical effects, and are thus quite different from the classic notions of journey or stroll.

—Guy Debord, "Theory of the Dérive"

Generative Mappings of New Civic Publics

In *Invisible Cities*, the famous literary text on the intractable difficulty and irresistible lure of knowing all of a territory, Italo Calvino asks, What is the task of knowing cities? What is the endeavor of vast knowledge? He writes of an ancient age of empire, when Kublai Khan ruled in 1260 from Siberia to what would be Afghanistan (one fifth of the inhabited land area of the world) (Calvino 1972). The text traces a long history of networks that well precede the digital ones of the contemporary epoch. These are the markings of Kublai's empire or the ferreting of trade routes by European contenders like Marco Polo, who acts as the emperor's avatar, a proxy, in the field. The phenomenon is not a new one: the digital age of networks is not the first age to extend an individual's (or a nation's) power beyond the reach of site and touch.

Today, like the great emperors of legend, one finds oneself facing *boundless territories* of information and potential connection. This moment of Big Data exceeds the boundaries of what any one person can know or control. We are in a state of "too big to know," as media theorist David Weinberger has argued, characterizing the network age as an epistemological shift in how we know a place, not simply a matter of having more things to know (Weinberger 2014). Yet, as a society, at least in terms of mapping technologies, we have what appears to be the inverse problem of too much information:

using massively adopted platforms such as Google maps and Google Earth with which we simulate a total rendering of a territory, we have gained a new dilemma—perhaps a unique one. In a time where wayfinding is built into one's handheld device, what does it meant to get lost? And more to the point, what would be the virtue of getting lost?

In this essay, I argue for a vital relationship between how we understand Big Data and how we might move forward with valuable experience that may not appear as what is currently configured as a "data set." I outline a program that takes into account the poetic, the whimsical, and the activist assumptions of mobile and locational media design. These are experimental interfaces that point to critical knowledge and a legacy of mapping territories, as Calvino writes, "solid and liquid, evident and hidden." I look at the intersection of the Poetic City and the Data City, marking the generative mappings of new civic publics (Mitchell 1995; Sassen1992; Thrift 2006; Varnelis 2008; Virilio 1986). In asking, What does it mean to know a city?, I am also asking, What does it mean to design for greater civic engagement? How might one leverage the inventions of information communication technologies (ICTs) and art toward an idea of civic media and new networked publics?

To discuss these questions, I look at projects that primarily use the city as a living laboratory, including the Dérive mobile app; City as Platform's (my own research group) social media mapping *Ceci n'est pas une Tweet* (This is not a Tweet); *Shadowing*, an Internet of Things (IoT) installation; and *Level of Confidence*, an artwork that uses surveillance technology. I chose these four examples—an app "to get lost with," a psychogeographic "small data" map of a city, an IoT sensor-based street interaction, and a networked countersurveillance project—to point to the diversity of experimental civic media work that engages affective and immersive aspects of interaction and spatial design. They all experiment with IxD (interaction design) forms, transforming data through different modes of interaction. Uniformly, from the Situationist International dérive of the 1950s to contemporary mobile apps, the media design invokes a disruptive use of technology and the city. These are, in fact, not apps for wayfinding, but apps for getting lost.

I focus primarily on artistic assumption of locative design, as the design innovation is clearly articulated away from a mimetic representation of place in terms of the design interface. What I mean by that is the aesthetics and the politics of these projects happen on the street—not on the screen. And one sees this resonance in the broader adoption of these design methods by political activist movements of the early part of the twenty-first century, such as Occupy Wall Street and the Egyptian occupation of Tahrir Square during the "Arab spring."[1] The reference of these projects remains necessarily local as opposed to the ubiquity of Big Data, that is, the designs are specific in application and not generic in interpretation. The implications of these projects on the other hand, work on a large scale, playing with the fabric of ICTs and public space. Or, to put it another way, they manifest techniques of civic imagining that engender new publics modeled on critical principles of civic design. In short, what I stage is a defense of the urban poetic, calling on the power of ICT and art to transform the built environment and the kinds of interactions prescribed therein.

I frame generative design as an imperative of twenty-first-century civic media. In the language of computationally modeled objects, generative design describes the algorithmic production of unique variation in forms such as sound, 3D models, etc. Working against this definition, I see an affective relation *between* the algorithmic and the human agent; this is a return to local variation as contextually experienced and embodied in relation to the material world *with the supplement of networked media technologies*. In this sense, generative design designates a *productive* relationship between user and ICT application—not a generative one exclusively within the computational context—that moves beyond the norms of interaction design (IxD) procedures such as keyword search or location mapping. Generative design commands an X-reality function where the impact of virtual information on located experience creates new values (as opposed to simply annotating existing ones). The condition of this phenomenon is the technological infrastructure of pervasive networked media embedded in the landscape and the cultural conditions established around such mobile, real-time, augmented, and addressable engagements (Coleman 2011; de Souza e Silva 2006; Meyrowitz 1985; Ohta and Tamura 1999). This is an effect that transposes data back into experience—the indexical maneuvered toward the generative.

This is a computational and cultural mash-up born of networked publics that have been practiced primarily online for two decades. These publics have begun porting their interactions over to geolocated events in the terrestrial world. These technologies are the technologies of a post-Web era, populated by the "everyware" of ubiquitous computing and Internet of Things that affect not just the techno-utopic city but the quotidian experience of nearly every city (de Certeau 1984; Greenfield 2006, 2013). The relation between user and machine described by IxD increasingly becomes an urban interaction design (UxD), wherein the user is resituated as "player"—one who interacts with the environment. The important change in interaction design—the shift from IxD to UxD—is signaled not in the exchange between player and device but between player and context. By broadening the field of interaction, these designs address a valuable reordering of the informational device; instead of the computational view as the primary information framing, one finds a system view impacted by diverse conditions and agents.

I list here four progressive steps that move from design of mobile media applications to a critical framing of Big Data and the importance of small data to expand the conceptual framework and applied experience of civic media. I develop these points of argument in case studies of recent applications.

1. **Generative design**: the shift in interaction design (IxD), where actionable information is not held exclusively on the screen (between device and user). Rather, the player *in her interaction with the street* generates the information. The generative is informed by the concept of *poiesis*.

2. **Poetic City**: a shift in mobile design that offers a type of immersive experience outside of the normative design practice of Cartesian mapping. It is an affective and immersive turn of mobile locative design, using its affordances and interaction toward aesthetic ends that expand beyond an indexical capacity.

3. **Distributed storytelling as a data set**: first, with an affective turn in mobile locative design, there is no content without context. Information is both networked and situationally inscribed. Second, this is also a civic turn in mobile media where the player's action *in public space* constitutes a civic view of the city. The type of data generated is necessarily small data, locative and contextually bound.

4. **The interrelation of Big Data and small data:** as a mode of participatory democracy or a form of generating new publics, civic media shifts the framework of the "informational" and the "contextual" value of data toward an interrelation of established Big Data practices and emergent small data protocols.

In the era of Big Data, as we develop technological and cultural standards for engaging ubiquitous networked technologies, I identify the necessary emergence of small data in mobile, locational media design. Historically speaking, the first decade of the millennium demonstrated global mobile and locational ICT penetration at an unprecedented rate. These devices transmit ever-increasing amounts of information (Castells et al. 2007; GSMA). As a result, this population of mobile and locational ICTs presents a body of Big Data that is also without equal. In other words, as we have more information-transmitting devices, we transmit more information. Of course, the question is, What do we make of this information? How should the data be read? The preliminary answer has been a positivistic application with which data scientists (and others) make increasingly hegemonic claims on the truth of human behavior and society as "impartially" demonstrated in the data.

In light of the dominant ontology of Big Data, the affective turn in a civic mobile media reminds us—the "we" in this case being researchers and citizens alike—to remember the importance of small data. To this effect, I argue that twenty-first-century civic media must hail a generative design principle that invites not only the informational but also a mode of *poiesis*. The ancient Greek term *poiesis* means "to make" or "to create" and is the root of the more modern concept of "poetry." In philosophical discourse, from Plato to Heidegger, there is a fundamentally generative condition to the word that posits a relation between creator and world: an always already-situated context. In this sense, the assignment of *civic* media is to engage a situated context of media use that resists certain a priori considerations of data. This is not so much a re-humanization of networked media technologies, at least not in a purely nostalgic way. Rather, it is a reframing of complex systems in which "agents" or "actors" are most certainly not exclusively human (Latour 2005). Nonetheless, the artworks and media design I look at do critically engage the play of affect and experience (phenomena still largely attributed to human subjects) in an understanding of the possibilities and responsibilities of civic media for a networked age.

Theory of the Digital Dérive: Distributed Storytelling as a Data Set

In spring of 2013, the news media story on mobile took a turn toward a narrative of chance encounter outside of the conscripted behaviors of alternate reality games (ARGs), which had been the primary form of mobile and transmedia engagement used by Hollywood, game companies, and artists before that moment. It was a declaration that exploded existing contours of mobile social media use; the status update marking location and orientation was abandoned for a kind of dislocation, a drift. "Apps that lead you off the beaten path," wrote CNN. "Doing a Dérive," the urban poetics journal *Common* announced. Popucity, the trend-spotting blog wrote, "Want To Claim Your City? There's An App For That." And the BBC Travel blog reported "Four Apps encourage Smarter Detours," outlining apps that actually take one off route entirely.[2] In aggregate, they were mobile applications for losing one's way.

As I speak to people—daily users of smartphone technology—about this mode of mobile app, often they scoff, "Why not just turn off your phone if you want to get lost?" But this is not exactly a question of having a real-time map of a place or not having one. Rather, it is a question of what can be known of a territory and what kind of map holds that knowledge. The 2013 crop of apps signaled a shift from the indexical to the generative in the use of mobile media. This reorientation of IxD paradigms sets the groundwork for a mode of distributed storytelling toward a generative design aesthetic and the imagination of a poetic city. From the perspective of longitudinal impact on civic media, I am suggesting that historically this is an important moment to attend to.

If a narrative is an account of connected events (or an accounting of possible connections), then a distributed narrative is marked by its existence *across* place and form. The difference might be described as one between a love note contained on a piece of paper and one written across the walls of a city. With the former, there is a coherence of message and format. With the latter, an inherent fragmentation of traditional narrative form is raised by the event of content in distributed context. In regard to the emergence of a mobile media culture, the practices I describe speak to narrative construction as a form of geolocated storytelling. It is a shift away from mobile ICTs for "purely" informational exchanges to a form of subjective relation that falls outside of the established patterns of mobile locative media use.

Distributed storytelling as a data set outside of the normative framing of traditional urban Big Data can be characterized by two traits. First, it is transmedia by nature, playing like an ARG across platforms and diverse formats of broadcast. Second, no-content-without-context becomes the very condition of the dataset. That is to say, no Tweet is broadcast without a temporal and geolocational orientation, whether or not the meta-data reflects those conditions. If there is missing information, such as location, or time, or provenance of a posted image or video, then the absence of framing information must be part of that set: in correcting for what is *unknown*, one recalibrates the notion of the "complete dataset" for the available or apparent data set. This allows for a con-ditionality of assumptions and conclusions when analyzing datasets big or small.

As global media technologies continue to expand in the form of Smart City and Smart Things (i.e., IoT) distribution, I am suggesting that distributed storytelling is part of an affective turn in media design that invites (and values) the inclusion of small datasets—the local, the temporary, and the resolutely subjective. With the explicitly artistic and avant-garde applications of this design turn, the important part to recog-nize is the reappropriation of form (mobile locative apps) toward new ends: not real-time wayfinding but an experiential way-losing, a drift across the city, as it were.

Effectively, what I am describing is a *détournement*—to appropriate a form and pro-duce an inversion of its effect—of the general principles of mobile design as established at the end of the twentieth century. (This is a concept developed and enacted by the Situationist International, the avant-garde Parisian art collective who also promulgated the concept of the dérive.) The *détournement* of mobile app design takes the affordances and interaction procedures that have become standards of locative media and turn them inside out. Instead of using mobile devices and locational data to create an index of place, meaning, and value mapped onto a latitude/longitude axis, they facilitate interaction with location without a predetermined outcome. In other words, there is always "information" at play. In this sense, the mobile app user is also always a player, one who *affects* the outcome. The difference in IxD is that the information is *generated by the play* and not a priori by the app. Thus inherent to the design, one encounters the possibility of feedback loops and recursive logic beyond the confines of algorithmically generated "recommendations." That opens the field of mobile design to worlds of possibilities.

In the common recommendation system, only known quantities can be recom-mended; for example, a book title must be in the database for the book to be recom-mended. Anything outside of the dataset cannot be mapped as a recommendation. One is familiar with this mode of Big Data and corresponding modes of algorithmic generation with online databases such as Amazon or Soundcloud, respectively shop-ping and music streaming platforms. One encounters the same mode of analysis with locational mapping and recommendation systems: territories for which there is no data do not exist on the map. And the primary reason they do not appear is that they are statistically invisible. Such phenomena are, at best, anomalous and, at worst, unchartable ephemera of the most transient nature.

The possible intervention into the meaning of civic data that a generative civic design offers—as networked, digital artifacts—is precisely the located, temporal, and ethnographic view of a city (or neighborhood) from the view of its constituents. How that new information is interpreted in relation to the tradition of Big urban data is a key challenge for knowing a city (Hemment and Townsend 2014; Picon 2008; Townsend 2013). Big Data, despite its seeming infinity of points, describes a logic of the cul-de-sac unless it allows for information that is not—perhaps cannot—be mapped on the traditional grid. Unless it allows for the messy, the local, the specific of the situated action—the experience of content in context.

With the distributed narrative, other issues come to the foreground, such as urban exploration as the experience of a detour, self-reflection in civic space, and affective mappings. These are transmedia endeavors, as most things are now, that cut across visual, platform, and rhetorical dimensions, building on many collective years of Internet-based practices of user-generated content, participatory culture, and manifestations of copresence (Farman 2012; Gordon and de Souza e Silva 2011; Ito, Okabe, and Matsuda 2005). The strong difference here is that it is located. The discursive space of narrative becomes literally the city which one moves through, hailing a long-standing and disruptive tradition of urban drift. I make the claim this is a way to know a city. It is a necessarily partial one, tied to place and contextual meaning, but also a powerful one.

This may not be the dataset upon which one designs the underground metro system for a 50-year projection of city growth. But it is a "dataset" that should be ignored at the peril of city planners if, indeed, the plan includes a multiplicity of city dwellers, as all cities do. This small dataset of the anomalous and local also offers an opportunity for citizen action that articulates futures of participatory democracy. In understanding these new civic publics as sites of engagement, one encounters a way of knowing a city and how its citizens shape it. This is an affective and civic turn in locational design in the sense that the player acts in public space, constituting a civic view of the city.

Big Data, Small Data Ontologies

The dominant form one finds of mobile media mapping of a territory—the Google map one might use to find a best route or the recommendations maps of good coffee shops—demonstrates an indexical knowledge of space and place (Gitelman 2013; Reades et al. 2007, Calabrese et al. 2012; Vermesan and Friess 2013). Such an index illustrates the established interaction design practices of ubiquitous computing (pervasive sensor and autonomous computational objects) and Big Data (large-scale data, e.g., transportation data, population statistics, etc.). In this ontology, the user is framed as someone who enters a query and, essentially, passively waits for the computational outcome. There is no play as such and no player; it is the agency of the algorithm that is paramount.

The rapid-fire spread of ICTs, such as mobile phones, speaks to the emergence of urban Big Data, where massive data sets are generated by an environment increasingly defined by ubiquitous computing technologies, such as intelligently connected infrastructure, sensor networks, radio-frequency identification (RFID), satellite, and WiFi (Bijker et al. 1987; Dourish and Bell 2011; Ling 2010; Ling and Donner 2009; Katz and Aakhus 2002). Associated with the phenomenon of Big Data is the emergence of a Big Data analytical hegemony, where more information (of a certain type) is equated with more knowledge (of all types)—in fact, it is often seen as an index of total knowledge. The nineteenth-century panoptical view or city panorama has been transformed into the invisible structures of city data. One finds with the Big Data Smart Cities information architecture of multinational groups such as IBM or Cisco an ethos of total dataset that is equated with total efficiency and total knowledge (IBM 2012).

To make sense—to be statistically valuable for mayor's offices and city planners—civic data is often read along a bell curve to describe normal distributions of resources, leaving aside outlier instances. The focus is on the normative *as a representative* of the greater good, where the exceptional is usually a problem to be fixed, such as a bottleneck in public transportation. And certainly this framing of the data has great value for

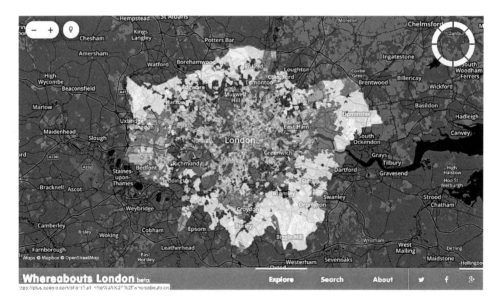

Figure 16.1
Whereabouts city data map of London.

many things pertaining to urban infrastructure and delivery of services. A project such as Whereabouts London interactive map works to correlate people and location using city Big Data (primarily census) as the basis of the interactive map (Catapult 2015). When one moves the cursor over the map, color codes appear linking location and demographic information such as, "Whereabouts [area] 7 residents are, on average, the most well off of all the Whereabouts with the highest proportion of company directors this West London group" (Catapult 2015). The text goes on to describe this group as 8 percent of the city population, with the highest portion of degree-level qualifications, and that this group is most likely to work more than 49 hours a week.

The open civic database on which the map is based is one of the most radical aspects of the project.[3] It does make far more easily accessible information that rests in the public domain. Nonetheless, what I focus on is the affordances of the map and the limitations of Big Data in relation to knowing a city. In effect, in this example, the map has located the upwardly mobile professional sector of the city, as might be done with other kinds of groups or phenomena. Citing historical precedent, the creators of Whereabouts refer to the data maps of John Snow (cholera) and Charles Booth (UK poverty) to frame the value of visualization toward civic good. And the design value of visualized information in Whereabouts certainly helps the viewer understand the city data more easily. But, in terms of urban data and ways of knowing a city, in a direct sense I do not know anything *new* about London outside of the normative values of census data.

In other words, the kind of statistics about a city that urban planners have regularly relied on since the invention of the national census are made more easily available to the user as searchable, digital assets that have been interpreted as a data graphic. That civic dataset does not include information that has not been filtered through the traditional government channels, which means that only an overview of the neighborhoods of London is available as opposed to the small data of a local view. In fact, the importance of small data to the civic is not to simply replicate what is known in the bell curve of urban Big Data. Rather, it can work as a countermeasure to such a median, as urban theorist Jane Jacobs advocated in the 1960s (Jacobs 1992).

In the context of networked cities, increasingly—across disciplinary boundaries— the framework of "knowing a city" is knowing the Big Data of a city: how massively scaled information marks the relations to the built and lived environment. I am also suggesting that to know a city is also to know its poetics, its routes of situated action (Suchman 2006) that are both designed and serendipitous. I argue for a poetic imperative in the face of a growing hegemony of urban Big Data. Indeed, the projects I cite all manifest a type of "urban hack"—a repurposing of networked media technologies or public space—that I see as resistance to a quantified self in a quantified city as the dominant mode of understanding the daily life of a city. There are very strong reasons, such as participatory democracy, to work against a hegemony of Big Data: for all its possible benefits, the narrow version of Big Data is also characterized by state surveillance, objectification of the subject, and invisible citizens. In defense of a capacious view of new data publics, I posit a data poetics that informs a reorientation of ICTs and locative design toward an ontology of the partial view. Fundamentally, it is an argument for the necessity of small data in relation to Big Data. How that relationship is managed is something of an art of new publics, new media, and new methodologies.

Of course, there is a value of Big Data for big infrastructure that continues to be critical to urban planning and management. It does not, though, give its analysts any new information outside of the established framework of urban demographics. It does not, for example, broadcast how subjects know their city outside of crime statistics and the cost of housing. This other knowledge of cities, I am arguing, is no longer exclusively the demimonde of artists, avant-gardists, novelists, activists, and the itinerant; it is increasingly the signal broadcast from millions of cell phones and serendipitous interactions on a daily basis. In other words, one knows more about what the street sounds and feels like at the level of affective narrative because people are constantly describing it.

In speaking of a "new data publics," I do not mean to present a false binary (Bail 2014; Lin 2015).[4] There is no clean apposition of Big and small data, pervasive media used by the state and the same technologies used by civic hackers. If information has been "free" during the first decades of large-scale Internet adoption, one can reflect, in the new millennium, on the public price of "free" services where dollars are a mere microcurrency in relation to the value of data. The pervasive presence of networked media platforms, addressable objects, and mobile applications speak to critical questions regarding civic participation, civic data, and policy. How might this informational framing facilitate media technology design that forwards civic ends? Thus, the first mandate of the new data public is to step outside of the normative view, to get lost.

The Naked City: Passional Terrain

I describe above an affective turn in mobile and locative media design that moves toward creating narrative around place, as opposed to the exclusively social (e.g., Foursquare check-ins) or informational (Yelp, Google Maps, etc.). The timing of this shift—the second decade of pervasive mobile technology—and the sector from which it hails—the artistic, the activist, and generally critically minded—are traits that describe the societal role of the historical avant garde even as they mark a new prospect, or at least newly computational prospect, in IxD. The traditional positivistic framing of scale and reproducibility of results, respectively in free market and scientific ontologies, have little bearing in this case. As with historical, avant-garde civic disruptions, such as the Situationist International dérive I discuss below, the question of societal impact cannot be gauged simply by scale (how many people use it or do it) or in a timeframe of immediacy. The hallmark of artistic innovation continues to rest with an ethos of singularity: a work or an artist or a collective is important because it triggers a kind of cultural response, a broader conversation in society, even if the object or event actually involve few.

Even as the terms of artistic innovation continue to shift, as does the medium of art, this hallmark of cultural influencer seems to abide. For example, Magritte's iconic painting *La trahison des images* (*The Treachery of Images*, 1928), describing the semiotic slippage between word-image-meaning, gained renown for the painter's aesthetically deft depiction of a referential conundrum. When someone says, "this is not a pipe," the reference is to this work of art and the puzzle it poses. On the level of artistic genius, the painter's style was original and winning. At a second level of cultural impact, Magritte's concept (and image) has been broadly disseminated over time and continues to be referenced and remixed for close to a hundred years. *Ceci n'est pas une Tweet*, the civic mapping project I discuss below certainly builds on the fame of the original work. In this vein, how one might measure the importance of generative mobile design may not be in terms of its early adoption by many but, rather, its strategic use by a few. The analogy between the Magritte painting and an app to get lost with is the *singular intervention* as critical to an understanding of self and world.

I describe the phenomenon of generative civic computational design as one that combines the affordances of new technology (locative computing) with a renewed imagination of public space. Effectively, the relationship between *affective* and *generative* might be described as two species in the genus of *poiesis*. If affect is the experience of feeling (Hogg, Abrams, and Martin 2010; Roelvink and Zolkos 2014), then we might call generative the creation of an emotional context or ... a design impetus. As Dourish and Bell write, "Emotion is ... interactional as opposed to representational. This conclusion does not simply *raise* implications for design; it *is* an implication for design" (2011, 77–78). In this sense, generative design is a discursive practice; it is a practice of distributed storytelling and placemaking that falls outside of a Cartesian coordinate system. Wayfinding becomes an act of *poiesis*. For these reasons, the midcentury avant-garde notion of the dérive has returned in the form of mobile locative design.

Fundamentally, a dérive describes the act of willfully getting lost. That is its key generative procedure: a *knowing step toward unknowing*, toward disorientation. It is an avant-garde sensibility (and critique of capitalism) that often coincides with a political one of reclaiming public space and occupying the streets. This blueprint for much contemporary civic interaction design hails from French artist Guy Debord's theorization of the dérive or urban "drift" made renowned by the Situationist International (Debord 1958; Sadler 1999). In its essence the dérive is an argument for the power of art to transform the environment into an affective landscape. It is an *action* in defense of the urban poetic. Debord writes in this ur-text of the psychogeographic understanding of terrain (how a neighborhood sees itself and also how it is seen by its neighbors) that all techniques are aimed toward the rapid and total disorientation of the urban subject in motion.

The dérivist is a player in a total, immersive scenario in which all things, places, and objects may be aspects of a mysterious rendezvous simply because they have drifted across one's path … or one's path has drifted across them. For example, in the gambit of the "possible rendezvous" the player is sent to a train station to meet an unspecified person who, possibly, may not even be there. With that readjustment of the psycho-geographic apprehension of waiting for someone (but not knowing who), the player is pricked into excitement with the approach or glance of every passerby. This is a scenario that reflects a local counterinsurgency of players rediscovering and reclaiming the neighborhoods of Paris half a century into the industrialization of urban space and the continued expansion of global markets (key subjects Debord revisits [1994]). On the level of the anecdotal, the singular experience of the drifting subject reinscribes the transformative importance of the local view *as well as* reflects the state of the alienated subject buffeted by the immensity of a post-war military industrial complex.

Both of these aspects, a salutary local resistance and the recognition of a system beyond any "one" to control (or know), are at work in the midcentury instantiation of the dérive, even as they are previsioned, as such, in earlier assessments of industrialization and later post-modern, post-technological reflections on the power of urban drift. In the 1840 short story "The Man of the Crowd," Edgar Allan Poe conjured the every-man of the industrial crowd as a fiend of listless motion caught up in a fever dream of modernity. Similarly, in an end-of-the-millennium work of fiction, Neil Stephenson places his protagonist of *The Diamond Age* (1992) in the middle of a drama of smart objects and trickster agents that has no start or stop, just a jangle of motion and revelation that plays out the ethos of dérive to perfection. In a related mode but different medium, the 2002 "discovery" browser StumbleUpon held its 15 minutes of Internet fame by bringing users a psychogeographic web: the experience was not based on what one searched but, rather, what one came upon. And the delight of that experience gained the browser its renown (StumbleUpon 2002). All of these works—from the turn-of-the-century literary to networked media interaction—describe worlds of immersion in spaces framed by the structures of new technological regimes, be it the factory or the Internet. They also describe a continually emergent role of the subject finding his way often by losing his way in these new worlds.

It is important to note though that in the seductive call to get lost—one that spans periods and genre—what has been distinctly absent from the legacy of the dérive is Debord's scientific drive: his call for a new method of information acquisition that respects data and its purported other, affect. In direct terms, Debord frames the dérive, this circumlocution of the city, as a mode of data acquisition. "The spatial field of a dérive may be precisely delimited or vague, depending on whether the goal is to study a terrain or to emotionally disorient oneself," he writes, directing the reader to the *logically inclusive* disjunction of "study of" or "emotional disorientation" (Debord 1958). Both operands or either may come into play. Debord goes on to outline a set of rules for locative disorientation that is exhaustive and confounding. A dérive can be short *or* long; it can include one *or* several participants, and so on.

One suspects that Debord's sense of paradox and play are at work in his instructions. Nonetheless, this "or/both" function proceeds with a strong logistical method to its madness. In other words, the theory of the dérive offers an ontology that includes both the objective data, as one might study a landscape in a sociological sense (as he cites), and the subjective data of the player's affective relation to the landscape. The mercurial rules do not make the dérive into nonsense or the Surrealist chance operation (an operation Debord thoroughly mocks in the text). Rather, it aids in the production of psychogeographic "data." On the subject of data, Debord writes, "But the dérive includes both this letting-go and its necessary contradiction: the domination of psychogeographical variations by the knowledge and calculation of their possibilities. In this latter regard, ecological science … provides psychogeography with abundant data" (Debord 1958). What the quotation calls attention to is the *evidentiary* aspect of the dérive along with its playfulness.

In the cultural and design history of the dérive, I wish to revive the important interaction of objective and subjective data that Debord's method of psychogeography frames as a critical to the operation. I would extend the logic of Debord's argument to say that the two knowledge systems—the objective and the subjective—are not merely inclusive but actually constitutive—they produce each other. Ideally, they function as a type of Big and small data set in concert. At the core of this theoretical model is the idea that cultural production frames the production of space, in this case an urban, civic space. In fact, such a notion of space being a constitutive phenomenon, not an a priori, has a long history in spatial theory, particularly with the Marxist sociologist Henri Lefebvre (who, in the 1960s, called for the citizen's "right to the city" [Lefebvre 1991]). Psychogeography adds back into the conceptual frame of objective knowledge the salutary effect of "messy" data. In his prescription of the dérive, Debord weaves across objective and subjective modes of knowing. And, I would suggest, it is this same lattice of engagement across heterogeneous information that is critical to the history and future of civic media design.

The theory of the dérive has been put in motion across various trajectories. The one I am most interested in is its history in experimental mappings with mobile technologies. The first of these I would cite as Debord's own indelible situationist mapping, "The Naked City," a scrawled collage that renders in two dimensions Debord's drunken meander across Paris of an evening. "The Naked City" is, at the very least, a non-Cartesian map of place. But it is also a mapping of an event (a walk home) and an experience (perception of Paris) as, one might argue, in the end all maps in effect are. Debord describes such a mapping process as representing an "objective passional

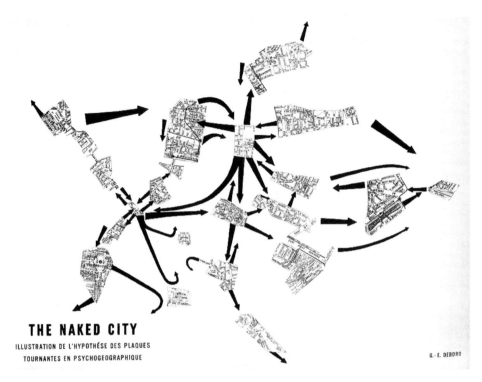

Figure 16.2
"The Naked City."

terrain" (Debord 1958). He utilizes a representational technique, the two-dimensional map, and transforms it into a pliant form, a *generative mapping*, that must be rendered by its viewer to fathom the data stored there. It is an interactive map before the fact of mobile computational media.

Case Studies: Content in Context

1.   Dérive app

Debord describes a "passional terrain" that opens the possibility of an extraordinary engagement with the urban. So when architect Eduardo Cachucho created a Dérive app for mobile phones in 2012, he designed a procedure (a set of rules and commands) that detour the iconic and expected interaction of contemporary mapping applications toward the passional terrain. The Dérive app is made up of "decks," groups of cards with text and image that prompt an action. For example, the Urban deck of 64 cards can be played in any city. There are also decks customized for particular cities, such as Abu Dhabi, Johannesburg, New York, and Paris, among others.

One downloads a deck to a mobile device—which means, effectively, a player does not need a network connection to play through the dérive. This aspect of IxD makes the app old-fashioned in not leveraging real-time and locative data; it also makes it cheap and easy to use by many. Most importantly though, the work of creation is not embedded in the interaction between the mobile device and the player; rather, it is between the player and the street. The significance of this is enumerated in the play. The primary point is to get one's head up and to look around a place. When one plays through a deck, the experience is of an app that revels in the quotidian, transforming the daily into a pretext for action and objects of passion. For example, one might pull up a card that reads, "Pick a flower," with an image of flowers drawn with a fat black magic marker on a photograph of gray garbage strewn on an anonymous city street. How one judges a task accomplished is entirely up to the player, as there is no referee, no guidelines for scoring, and only the slightest framing of start and stop. It is a direct transmission of the psychogeographic gestalt. The city-specific decks hold content

Figure 16.3
"Let your mind lead you."

Figure 16.4
"Pick a flower."

resonant of that environment (e.g., Paris deck: "Look out for space invaders," referring to the famous tile graffiti by the eponymous street artist). The cards can also invoke a poetic or contemplative state: "Let your mind lead you," reads one card accompanied by an image of Debord's dérive map of the "Naked City."

The Dérive app gives direction in a manner distinctly different from the tradition of real-time mapping. The act of wayfinding quickly and abruptly steps off a Cartesian grid. Finding a flower orients toward an act, and often an interpretive one at that: a flower may be scarce in certain locales, which invites the subject to move neither left nor right nor forward. Rather, the player is the agent of the action. Wayfinding, in the palm of one's hand, becomes pathmaking. Despite sharing an apparatus and, to an extent, an interface with other mobile apps, these are different orders of self-orientation to the geographic and built environments.

The phenomenon of using apps to "get lost" reflects an important turn in civic media design, urban hacking, and the reappropriation of public space away from an indexical, purely informational, and cognitivist use of mobile computing, and toward the affective and often normatively disruptive acts of distributed storytelling. Other mobile locative design in this camp includes Mark Shepard's Serendipitor, part of the artists/theorists Sentient City Survival Kit (Shepard 2010). Random GPS, by artist Stéphane Degoutin, hacks the GPS system of cars, randomizing the route one takes (2013). Broken City Lab's Drift app prompts the user to "unfamiliarize" with a known environment (2013). Two things are clear in this suite of apps for getting lost. First, there is a sneaking sense of the "actual," of an experience as it exists outside of the confinement of the informational. Second, the counterintuitive nature of such design tickles one's fancy even if it is by no means the stuff daily life is made of. In fact, that's the whole point. One is invited to venture outside the habitual, to generate new experiences if not understandings.

2. Small Data Mapping: Ceci n'est pas une Tweet

The second example I discuss of generative design and affective (psychogeographic) mapping is a project developed with my research group, City as Platform (PI Coleman, collaborating artist Howard Goldkrand, and graduate researchers Adam Bradley and Anne Hammoud). *Ceci n'est pas une Tweet*, a situated installation that connected networked social media to a geographic context, was developed in consortium with an ICT&Art Connect workshop supported by the European Union Parliament, Brussels, Belgium, in November 2013 (Coleman 2013). In this project, we use networked social media (Tweets, Tumblrs, and so on) to create a geotagged map of Brussels. The procedure was to capture the location of each media utterance and to map it in relation to where geographically it had been posted. Following that process, we then went into the streets of Brussels and wrote the networked message by hand in the location that best approximated the coordinates from which the message had been posted. In other words, we put in public places, such as walls, a post from the neighborhood in which it originated.

The goal of the piece was to experiment with evocative, poetic uses of social media data. Explicitly, we were asked to create scenarios of new publics and participatory democracy using networked media tools. In the four-day period from workshop to presentation at Parliament and museum installation, we explored affordances of real-time geolocative social data to describe how a city represents itself, developing a short-form project that addressed concepts of the poetic city in relation to the data city. The framework for data engagement was a translation of Big (social media broadcast) to small (located utterances). Unlike work in "sentiment mapping," instead of making a broad claim about neighborhood or region, we used the data in a pointillist and

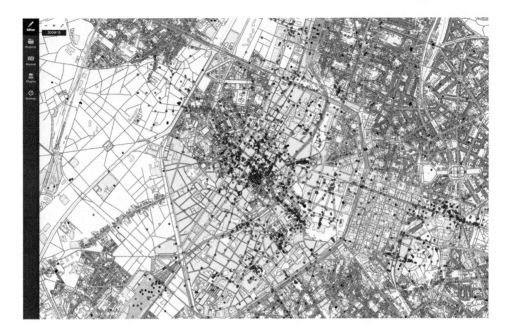

Figure 16.5
Social media map of Brussels.

Situationist manner: we took information that floated in the twittersphere ("unlocated" social media utterances) and framed them in relation to place and time.

The concept of distributed storytelling was critical to how we approached the
engagement of art and technology for the project; we viewed the social media utterances as stories (short self-portraits) that were about the identity of the poster but also
about the identity created *in situ*—in relation to being someone *somewhere*. In our view,
the piece reflected a mode of Situationist mapmaking. *Ceci n'est pas une Tweet* put social
media into dialogue with location and a new public by connecting the informational
and the geolocated.

The project evokes the Magritte painting (*This Is Not a Pipe*) for two reasons. Brussels,
the city we were psychogeographically mapping, was the birthplace of the painter. But
more importantly, the provocation we offered was that these messages were actually no
longer "tweets" or "check-ins" or "likes" or other shorthand of social media vernacular.
They were signs of a public in conversation locally as well as across a network. The
simple act of relocating what people had said on the Internet to the streets was an
opportunity to move outside of both the habit of social media and neighborhood, if
only for a moment. If the dérive dislocates the player to disrupt habit, this tracking of
small data into a poetics of place—a relocating of the unlocated—also produced a sense
of disorientation by collapsing contexts between the informational and the lived. We

Figure 16.6
#brusselair "You could have said that as well: hey I think you are boring so get out of my life."

marked the chalked messages with the hashtag #brusselair in order to graphically tag the relocated utterance and would then retweet it (resend it) to the person who had originally posted it, with an attached image.[5] In this way, we closed the virtual-geolocated loop by making the terrestrial data available in the online network.

In relation to a civic data mapping project like Whereabouts, discussed earlier, *Ceci n'est pas une Tweet* endeavors to make visible what one might call, with all respect to Calvino and Latour, the invisible city—the city inscribed on its walls and other physical spaces that mark the diverse routes of its players (citizens, visitors, auditors, artists, scientists, and so on). It is a project that works to reframe Big Data of a particular unredacted flavor, networked social media, and frame it in a location view as a mode of small data that tells a local story.

3.   Shadow City and Civic Publics

Bringing a mode of generative IxD to the street, Canadian and British interaction designers/urbanists/artists Jonathan Chomko and Matthew Rosier installed the IoT work, *Shadowing*, in Bristol, UK, in the fall of 2014 (Chomko and Rosier 2014). Winner of the Playable City design competition, *Shadowing* used sensors attached to city lampposts to catch the motion of a passerby and then project that person's shadow a few

Figure 16.7
The Street Plays Along, *Shadowing* IoT installation.

seconds later in the place of the pedestrian's journey across the networked space *but with a new pattern of movement*. Similar to how other IoT projects behave, *Shadowing* captures the urban data of peoples' location and movement (Kuniavsky 2010; Anzelmo, et al. 2011). But unlike many IoT projects, *Shadowing* takes the data capture and translates it into poetic form. In effect, *Shadowing* takes its unsuspecting user by surprise, animating the shadow as a kind of short-form puppet show.

As a form of play, this animation raises specters of Peter Pan's shadow getting away from him and launching the famous fairytale adventure in Neverland. And that is the point of the piece: to play on the city street with one's shadow. As multiple players join the scenario, a kind of shadow dance ensues with the duration of each animated shadow lasting around half a minute. The artists describe the project as something a person living in a city might "wander into," where the interface and the experience are immediately clear. Additionally, *Shadowing* raises questions about how a city street, embedded with smart sensor technology, can create a site of gaming and delight or surveillance and fear. It is essentially the same technology embedded in the light post, only designed toward different ends.

Along similar lines of public interaction, using surveillance software, Mexican artist Rafael Lozano-Hemmer created a poetic imagination around countersurveillance and issues of social justice. An international figure, Lozano-Hemmer has created a well-known series of interactive urban public artworks, under the title *Relational Architecture*, since the late 1990s,[6] which hail as an antecedent for projects such as *Shadowing*. With that said, I address a different project of Lozano-Hemmer's to look at a compelling and critical manifestation of a new public, or a networked civic body, in his 2015 work *Level of Confidence*.

Level of Confidence uses biometric surveillance algorithms (Eigen, Fisher, and LBPH) to make facial characteristic matches between individuals in the group of 43 students kidnapped from the Ayotzinapa normalista school in Iguala, Guerrero, Mexico, on September 26, 2014, and the viewer of the piece (Lozano-Hemmer 2015). As the artist notes, these are matches that will never be actually made, as the students are assumed dead. The best the surveillance software can do is produce a "level of confidence" of a match. Police and other surveillance bodies, such as military, use this mode of machine visioning increasingly to identify individuals. In Lozano-Hemmer's reversal, it is now a public searching for victims (or the terrible impossibility of that search) instead of the police surveilling for suspicious individuals.

The entire artwork is open source and free to download. Since the spring of 2015, the project has been exhibited internationally, including in Mexico, at museums, galleries, and universities. Thus, in a literal sense, Lozano-Hemmer has created a new public for the particular issue of the missing Mexican students, the global issue of people missing in relation to state violence, and exposure to new technologies of surveillance that are defining how civic publics might exist.

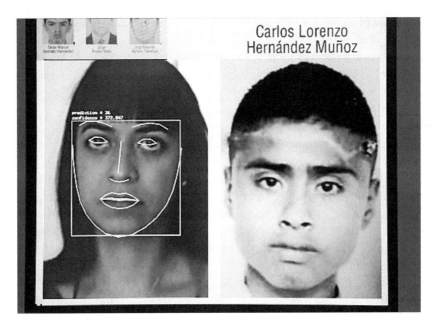

Figure 16.8
Level of Confidence, image-matching software.

Both *Level of Confidence* and *Shadowing* play with the boundaries of self (with image-matching algorithms or IoT shadows) in a manner that also begs the issue of civic borders: What is the limit of play in the street? Can it only exist as part of a festival or is it otherwise conscripted as suspicious activity? Who are the publics participating in immersive poetic designs? The projects reconfigure urban Big Data (in the form of surveillance footage) and repurpose it toward a small data poetic experience. It is disorienting and magical to have one's shadow dance on its own. Even as it is powerfully moving to have one's face searched for the traces of lost people.

Across the projects I outline, the shift in IxD focus is clear: as opposed to finding the information on the device screen, one finds the information, or rather makes it, in the street. Design applications such as these are also an invitation to *use* the street, to take up the civic and public domain as one of tactical engagement. This is both a profound and direct *détournement* of mobile mapping protocols, where Cachucho and the others take the technological affordances and interface design expectations and turn them around. As Debord's map of the "naked city" illuminates, it is always a passional terrain one moves through when one moves through a city.

The consequence of this psychogeographic reflection is a hasty reembodiment of the player. It's not that one ever really left the body behind with earlier mobile media experiences. But, with the affective turn, the interpolation of the subject as citizen comes to bear with weight. The sociopolitically located body that one inhabits on the street comes slamming into the psychogeographic "user experience" with an unrelenting reality drive. For example, a dérive for a student of architecture versus a homeless person may play out very differently in terms of leeway to "drift" in public.

With the same token (the embodied space token), the question also arises of what streets? A dérive for a woman in Tehran may have a powerfully different affective register than the same deck played out in New York. This affective and embodied turn of generative design speaks to a constitutionally civic view, as the pyschogeographic reflects the player in the landscape she plays in. In this sense, there is no content without context; and it is this aspect of the affective and immersive—the interaction between outside and in, the objective and the subjective phenomenon—that describes a generative aesthetic in action.

Open City: Conclusion

In an iconic image from the early 2000s the Graffiti Research Lab, using their mobile L.A.S.E.R. Tag system and the input from passersby, wrote in script the height of a building the words "Open City" (Roth and Powderly 2005).[7] This was a guerilla artwork, appropriating public space and interactions therein. Additionally, the group has historically taken an activist civic media approach to technical and aesthetic production: code and hardware are open source and the works crowdsourced. Graffiti Research Lab works in a mode of civic media that speaks to an age of ubiquitous computing and expansive networks (Castells 2000; Weiser 1999). Their work contributes to a legacy of urban interventions that strategically offer poetic and political reimaginings of the civic (Bachelard 1964; Forlano 2009, 2011; Foth 2008). With generative design across periods, as I have argued, one finds a strategic reordering of content in context such as with the work of Graffiti Research Lab that goes beyond a Cartesian mapping of place.

In looking at contemporary instantiations of the civic, one can easily excavate a long history of splintering between the model city of planners, a virtual form "from which all possible cities can be deduced" and the Situationist city made only of "exceptions, exclusions, incongruities, contradictions" (Calvino 1972). Of course, living in a city one finds an interrelation (if not a synthesis) of the poetic and the practical ideal in the actual. One of the critical issues is how such a balance might be struck in the emergence of cities increasingly full of autonomous or "smart" technologies that report on its citizens. As the theoretical works, literatures, and art projects I have discussed demonstrate, to support new civic publics is to invite diverse forms of participation and dissent, poetics and technologies. It is to locate generative mappings of a territory.

Notes

1. I refer to the use of social media by Egyptian activists as an organizational tool but also as an emotive tool to signify local presence across a network.

2. For another example see: "4 Apps That Get You Lost, So You Can Have Actual Experiences," Ben Schiller, *Coexist*, August 19, 2014, http://www.fastcoexist.com/3034121/4-apps-that-get-you-lost-so-you-can-have-actual-experiences.

3. The Whereabouts map is based on the public Datastore initiative established by the city of London, http://data.london.gov.uk.

4. In reference to my discussion of Big Data versus small data, in the first decades of the 2000s there has been a heated debate around issues of collection, interpretation, and framework of data. Data scientists and data sociologists may conclude that the relationship is more of a continuum than oppositional. In any case, that is a closer approximation of my position.

5. The French #brusselair means "native to Brussels," even though natives of the city might post in multiple languages, including Flemish, Arabic, and Kituba (Congo). We developed the hashtag in collaboration with Director Yves Bernard and his colleagues at the iMal media center, over the course of the workshop.

6. These projects span crowd-controlled lasers in Abu Dhabi (*Pulse Corniche*, 2015) to the peer-sourced 3D light sculptures over Mexico City (*Vectorial Elevation*, 1999).

7. L.A.S.E.R. Tag from Graffiti Research Lab, https://www.youtube.com/watch?v=cY6vfJAxtH8.

References

Anzelmo, E., 2011. "Discussion Paper on the Internet of Things." Institute for Internet and Society, Berlin.

Arnall, T. 2011. *Immaterials: Light Painting WiFi*. Laboratori, Arts Santa Mònica, Barcelona.http://www.ub.edu/opensystems/en/site/project/14.

Arnall, T. 2013. "Making Visible: Mediating the Material of Emerging Technology." http://www.elasticspace.com/downloads/Making_Visible_Timo_Arnall_2014.pdf.

Bachelard, G. 1964. *The Poetics of Space*. Trans. Maria Jolas. Boston: Beacon Press.

Bail, C. 2014. "The Cultural Environment: Measuring Culture with Big Data." *Theory and Society* 43 (3–4):465–482.

Bijker, W. E., T. P. Hughes, and T. Pinch. 1987. *The Social Construction of Technological Systems*. Cambridge, MA: MIT Press.

Broken City Lab. 2013. Drift app. http://www.brokencitylab.org.

Calabrese, F., M. Diao, G. Lorenzo, J. Ferreira, and C. Ratti. 2012. "Understanding Individual Mobility Patterns from Urban Sensing Data: A Mobile Phone Trace Example." SENSEable City Lab, MIT, Cambridge, MA. http://senseable.mit.edu/papers/pdf/2012_Calabrese_Mobile_TRC.pdf.

Calvino, I. 1972. *Invisible Cities. Trans. William Weaver*. New York: Harcourt Brace Jovanovich.

Cachucho, E. 2012. Dérive app. http://deriveapp.com/s/v2.

Catapult. 2015. Whereabouts London Map. http://whereaboutslondon.org/#/map.

Castells, M. 2000. *The Rise of the Network Society*. Oxford: Blackwell.

Castells, M., M. Fernández-Ardèvol, J. Linchuan Qiu, and A. Sey. 2007. Mobile Communication and Society: A Global Perspective. Cambridge, MA: MIT Press.

Chomko, J., and M. Rosier. 2014. *Shadowing* installation, Bristol, UK. https://www.youtube.com/watch?v=qYlJ-m40Ewk.

Coleman, B. 2011. *Hello Avatar*. Cambridge, MA: MIT Press.

Coleman, B. 2013. *"Ceci n'est pas une Tweet* (This Is Not a Tweet): Modeling Participatory Culture." Proceedings Information and Communications Technologies and Art presentation, European Union Parliament, Brussels, Belgium, November. http://www.slideshare.net/cityasplatform/ceci-nest-pas-une-tweet.

de Certeau, M. 1984. *The Practice of Everyday Life*. Berkeley: University of California Press.

Debord, G. 1956 [1958]. "Theory of the Dérive." Trans. Ken Knabb. *Les Lèvres Nues* #9, Paris; *Internationale Situationniste* #2, Paris. http://www.bopsecrets.org/SI/2.derive.htm#1.

Debord, G. 1994. *The Society of the Spectacle*. New York: Zone Books.

Degoutin, S. 2013. Random GPS. http://nogovoyages.com/random_gps.html.

de Souza e Silva, A. 2006. "From Cyber to Hybrid: Mobile Technologies as Interfaces of Hybrid Spaces." Space and Culture 9 (3): 261–278.

Donner, J., and C. Tellez. 2008. "Mobile banking and economic development: Linking adoption, impact, and use." *Asian Journal of Communication* 18 (4): 318–332.

Dourish, P., and G. Bell. 2011. *Divining a Digital Future: Mess and Mythology in Ubiquitous Computing*. Cambridge, MA: MIT Press.

Farman, J. 2012. *Mobile Interface Theory: Embodied Space and Locative Media*. New York: Routledge.

Forlano, L. 2009. "WiFi Geographies: When Code Meets Place." *Information Society* 25 (5):1–9.

Foth, M. 2008. *Handbook of Research on Urban Informatics: The Practice and Promise of the Real-Time City*. Hershey, PA: IGI Global.

Foth, M., L. Forlano, M. Gibbs, and C. Satchell. 2011. *From Social Butterfly to Engaged Citizen*. Cambridge, MA: MIT Press.

Free Art and Technology Collective (F.A.T.). 2010. http://fffff.at.

Gitelman, L. 2013. *"Raw Data" Is an Oxymoron*. Cambridge, MA: MIT Press.

Google. 2012. Field Trip app. https://www.fieldtripper.com.

Gordon, E., and A. de Souza e Silva. 2011. *Net Locality: Why Location Matters in a Networked World*. Hoboken, NJ: Wiley-Blackwell.

Greenfield, A. 2006. *Everyware: The Dawning Age of Ubiquitous Computing*. San Francisco: New Riders Publishing.

Greenfield, A. 2013. *Against the Smart City*. N.p.: Do Projects.

GSMA Intelligence, https://gsmaintelligence.com.

Hemment, D., and A. Townsend, eds. 2014. *Smart Citizens*. Manchester: FutureEverything Publications. http://futureeverything.org/wp-content/uploads/2014/03/smartcitizens1.pdf.

Hogg, M. A., D. Abrams, and G. N. Martin. 2010. "Affect." In *Psychology*, ed. G. N. Martin, N. R. Carlson, and W. Buskist, 646–677. Harlow: Pearson Education.

IBM. 2012. Smarter Cities. http://www.ibm.com/smarterplanet/us/en/smarter_cities/overview.

Ito, M., D. Okabe, and M. Matsuda. 2005. *Personal, Portable, Pedestrian: Mobile Phones in Japanese Life*. Cambridge, MA: MIT Press.

Jacobs, J. 1992. *The Death and Life of Great American Cities*. New York: Vintage.

Katz, J., and M. Aakhus. 2002. *Perpetual Contact: Mobile Communication, Private Talk, Public Performance*. Cambridge, UK: Cambridge University Press.

Kuniavsky, M. 2010. *Smart Things: Ubiquitous Computing User Experience Design*. Amsterdam: Morgan Kaufmann Publisher.

Latour, B. 2005. *Reassembling the Social: An Introduction to Actor-Network-Theory*. Oxford: Oxford University Press.

Latour, B., and E. Hermant. 1998. Paris: Invisible City. http://www.bruno-latour.fr/virtual/EN/index.html.

Lefebvre, H. 1991. *The Production of Space*. Trans. Donald Nicholson-Smith. Oxford: Blackwell.

Lin, J. 2015. "On Building Better Mousetraps and Understanding the Human Condition: Reflections on Big Data in the Social Sciences." *Annals of the American Academy of Political and Social Science* 659 (1): 33–47.

Ling, R., and J. Donner. 2009. *Mobile Phones and Mobile Communication*. Cambridge, MA: Polity.

Ling, R. 2010. *New Tech, New Ties: How Mobile Communication Is Reshaping Social Cohesion*. Cambridge, MA: MIT Press.

Lozano-Hemmer, R. 2015. *Level of Confidence* installation, various sites. http://www.lozano-hemmer.com/level_of_confidence.php.

Meyrowitz, J. 1985. *No Sense of Place: The Impact of Electronic Media on Social Behavior*. New York: Oxford University Press.

Mitchell, W. J. 1995. *City of Bits: Space, Place, and the Infobahn*. Cambridge, MA: MIT Press.

Ohta, Y., and H. Tamura. 1999. *Mixed Reality: Merging Real and Virtual Worlds*. New York: Springer.

Picon, Antoine. 2008. "Toward a City of Events: Digital Media and Urbanity." *New Geographies* 0:31–43.

Reades, J., F. Calabrese, A. Svetsuk, and C. Ratti. 2007. "Cellular Census: Explorations in Urban Data Collection." *IEEE Pervasive Computing* 6 (33): 10–17.

Roelvink, G., and M. Zolkos. 2014. "Affective Ontologies: Post-Humanist Perspectives on the Self, Feeling and Intersubjectivity." *Emotion, Space and Society* 14 (February): 47–49.

Roth, E., and J. Powderly. 2005. Graffiti Research Lab. http://www.graffitiresearchlab.com.

Sadler, S. 1999. *The Situationist City*. Cambridge, MA: MIT Press.

Sassen, S. 1992. *The Global City: New York, London, Tokyo*. Princeton, NJ: Princeton University Press.

Shepard, M. 2010. Serendipitor. http://serendipitor.net/site/?page_id=2.

StumbleUpon. 2002. https://www.stumbleupon.com.

Suchman, L. 2006. *Human-Machine Reconfigurations: Plans and Situated Actions*. Cambridge: Cambridge University Press.

Thrift, N. 2006. "Space." *Theory, Culture & Society* 23 (2–3): 139–155.

Townsend, A. 2013. *Smart Cities: Big Data, Civic Hackers, and the Quest for a New Utopia*. New York: Norton.

Vermesan, O., and P. Friess. 2013. *Internet of Things: Converging Technologies for Smart Environments and Integrated Ecosystems*. Aalborg, Denmark: River.

Varnelis, K. 2008. *Networked Publics*. Cambridge, MA: MIT Press.

Virilio, P. 1977 [1986]. *Speed and Politics: An Essay on Dromology*. New York: Semiotextet.

Weinberger, D. 2014. *Too Big to Know: Rethinking Knowledge Now That the Facts Aren't the Facts, Experts Are Everywhere, and the Smartest Person in the Room Is the Room*. New York: Basic Books.

Weiser, M. 1999. "The Computer for the 21st Century." *Mobile Computing and Communications Review* 3 (3): 3–11.

Whereabouts: London. 2015. http://whereaboutslondon.org/#/map.

17 Superpowers to the People! How Young Activists Are Tapping the Civic Imagination

Henry Jenkins, Sangita Shresthova, Liana Gamber-Thompson, and Neta Kligler-Vilenchik

Scratch an activist and you're apt to find a fan. It's no mystery why: fandom provides a space to explore fabricated worlds that operate according to different norms, laws, and structures than those we experience in our "real" lives. Fandom also necessitates relationships with others: fellow fans with whom to share interests, develop networks and institutions, and create a common culture. This ability to imagine alternatives and build community, not coincidentally, is a basic prerequisite for political activism.

—Steven Duncombe (2012a)

Like many other fellow members of the American Sikh community, Vishaljit Singh experienced post-9/11 xenophobia and racism first hand. As a bearded and dastar- (or turban-) wearing Sikh, he became an easily recognizable and completely misidentified face for those who were terrified, ignorant, and seeking scapegoats. Thinking back on that period, Singh recalls being called "Osama" and "towelhead," and being told to "go home" in no uncertain terms. Though things have definitely changed since then, Singh and other members of the Sikh community still endure persistent verbal (and other) abuse, which now tends to ebb and flow in response to news coverage on terrorism. Determined to take action to counter the misinformation and ignorance that fueled such outbursts, Singh turned to popular culture to counter existing stereotypes about Sikhs. In addition to launching sikhtoons.com (a site that uses cartoons to as commentary on being Sikh in America), Singh also mashed up the turban-wearing Sikh with Captain America, to create a character to drive home his message that: "A Sikh is just as American as an iconic superhero" (Singh in interview with Hills 2014). Initially a cartoon character, the Sikh Captain America came to life when Singh started dressing as his character when making public appearances to drive home the point that an American Sikh man can also be a superhero.

Singh's story is a provocative example of what this essay will call the civic imagination at work. We are interested in understanding the ways that young activists, especially in North America, are conducting politics through images and narratives drawn from popular culture; encouraging other youth to "imagine better," to envision alternatives to current conditions and develop new pathways into political and civic engagement. Singh's story also gives us a way to start to answer a core question: What is an essay about superheroes doing in a book about civic media? Often, discussions about civic media focus on creating an independent communication infrastructure, a way of routing around concentrated media, so that citizens can share information, minority voices can be heard, and we can access alternative perspectives. Often, as Stephen Duncombe (2007) has noted, the focus is on how we "get the facts out" yet, in practice, politics may also consist in the ways we deploy participatory culture, narrative, fantasy, the imagination, toward civic and political ends.

Superheroes are, for sure, the stuff of Hollywood blockbusters and prime time television series, of adolescent power fantasies where might makes right and everyone looks better in tights and capes. Five of the ten highest grossing films since 2010 have featured superheroes. Superhero series, from *Arrow* to Marvel's *Agents of S.H.I.E.L.D.*, are becoming more common on American television. Superheroes are also increasingly tools that grassroots networks are appropriating and repurposing for their own political ends. Superhero stories offer a shared vocabulary for talking about personal and cultural identity, differing conceptions of justice and the social good, the nature of power and responsibility. Many different groups, but especially those engaging with youth, have tapped into the superhero mythology as a means of empowering their members to think differently about their place in society.

Over the past few decades, we've seen dramatic increases in grassroots access to the means of cultural production and circulation and improvements to the infrastructure required for collective action (Jenkins, Ford, and Green 2013). Henry Jenkins first introduced the concept of "participatory culture" in his book, *Textual Poachers*, in 1992, and has elaborated it across a range of subsequent publications (Jenkins 2006; Jenkins et al. 2007; Jenkins, Ford, and Green 2013; Jenkins et al. 2013), each describing the changes in how creative industries, politics, and education have operated in response to the public's expanded communicative capacities. He ended *Convergence Culture* (2006) with the suggestion that we would soon be deploying for politics skills, practices, and resources that had emerged from our play. Almost a decade later, we can see that this participatory turn in culture has been mirrored by shifts in the ways citizens exert power within the political process. Young men and women who learned how to use their cameras recording skateboarding videos or taking cute cat pictures, are now turning their skills toward political speech and grassroots mobilization. These "creative activists" often speak through images borrowed from commercial entertainment but remixed to communicate their own messages; they are often deploying social media tools and platforms, sometimes in ways that challenge corporate interests, and they are forging communities through acts of media circulation.

In a white paper for the MacArthur research network on Youth and Participatory Politics (YPP), Cathy J. Cohen and Joseph Kahne (2012) define participatory politics as "interactive, peer-based acts through which individuals and groups seek to exert both voice and influence on issues of public concern" (vi). Citing data from a survey of more than 4000 respondents aged 15–25, Cohen and Kahne found that those who engaged in participatory politics (roughly 40–45 percent across all racial categories) were almost twice as likely to vote as those who did not. Their report identified various forms of participatory politics, including sharing of information through social media, engaging in digital forums or blogs and podcasts, creating online videos or Photoshopped memes to comment on a current issue, using microblogging tools to rally a community toward collective action, or deploying databases to investigate an ongoing concern. Cohen and Kahne (2012, 3) explain, "The participatory skills, norms, and networks that develop when social media is used to socialize with friends or to engage with those who share one's interests can and are being transferred to the political realm. ... What makes participatory culture unique is not the existence of these individual acts, but that the shift in the relative prevalence of circulation, collaboration, creation, and connection is changing the cultural context in which people operate."

Building on (and contributing to) this concept of participatory politics, our team, based at the Annenberg School for Communication and Journalism at the University of Southern California, has been tracking a range of different organizations and networks that have been effective at getting young people involved in civic and political activities through their deft use of networked political practices and participatory culture frameworks. As part of a research initiative funded by the MacArthur Foundation, we've interviewed more than 200 young activists drawn from Invisible Children, the Harry Potter Alliance, Nerdfighters, Students for Liberty, networks of American Muslim youth, and young people supporting the DREAM act, often referred to as DREAMers. Any quote here not otherwise specified emerged from those interviews, but for this project, we've supplemented that research through media audits and field observation as we've collectively identified rich examples for comparison. Many of these groups emphasize personal and collective storytelling, often through grassroots media production and circulation, as well as the deployment of content worlds, often drawn from popular culture.

In this chapter, we will examine a range of different ways that the iconography and narrative conventions of the superhero genre have been deployed by the various activist networks we've researched, using these appropriations and repurposing to illustrate some core findings about the nature of participatory politics—particularly the importance of the civic imagination. We can imagine other pop culture figures that can and have done some of this same political work—the zombie (as in *The Walking Dead*), the vampire (as in *Twilight* and *True Blood*), the wizard (as in Harry Potter), come to mind. These icons are culturally pervasive and thus handy for political deployment; each figure extends beyond a single text and thus carries a mix of intertextual and generic associations; each represents either the potential for empowerment or risk and catastrophe; and thus they constitute useful resources for discussing the state of our society. But none runs across as many different movements as the superhero does.

Throughout this discussion, the core of our examples come for the United States, which has been the focus of our current research. We've certainly seen rich examples of the deployment of the civic imagination elsewhere around the world—such as the use of the Three Finger Salute from *The Hunger Games* by Thai student rebels, or the adoption of the identity of the zombie for protest against student loan cutbacks in Chile, or the use of the Na'vi from James Cameron's *Avatar* for indigenous rights movements around the globe. However, more work would need to be done before we can fully understand the similarities and differences in how these practices operate across various national contexts, so our focus here remains on the United States.

DREAMing about the Man of Steel

We first began to ponder the political uses of superheroes when we encountered multiple appropriations within the DREAMer movement. The DREAMers are undocumented youth who were raised in the United States and who are seeking greater educational and citizenship rights. Many of them have been, as they describe it, "hiding in the shadows" with their legal status unknown to many of the most important people in their lives. Tactics like the production and circulation of "coming out" videos have played an important role in allowing them to share their stories with others. So far, they have been held hostage by the failure of the U.S. Congress to pass comprehensive immigration reform. For the most part, forced to survive on low incomes as a consequence of the constraints on their employment, DREAMers often have only limited access to forms of digital production and circulation many other groups take for granted. Yet, they have been among the most adept digital strategists we've encountered.

And, one more thing, many of them are fans of superhero comics. To explain his undocumented experiences, Erick Huerta, an immigrant rights advocate and blogger, referenced Superman who was "from another planet … and grew up in the United States, just like me." Superman was created by two Jewish high school students, both immigrants from Eastern Europe, in the 1930s; he has become a key vehicle by which another generation of immigrants seeks to understand their place in American society. If ever there was an illegal alien, it is Kal-El from the planet Krypton whose parents sent him away from his native world in search of a better life, who slipped across the border (via spaceship) in the middle of the night, got adopted by an Anglo family, has had to hide his true identity, but has been deeply dedicated to promoting and defending American values. Amid a controversy over Superman's decision in an alternative universe DC Comics story to renounce his American citizenship, Huerta and other undocumented youth argued that there was no evidence that Superman was anything other than undocumented, no signs he had the right papers, no evidence that he had ever applied for citizenship.

In "What Makes Superman So Darned American?," Gary Engle (1987) explores how Superman's saga taps into the classic American immigrant narrative:

> Like the peoples of the nation whose values he defends, Superman is an alien, but not just any alien. He's the consummate and totally uncompromised alien, an immigrant whose visible difference from the norm is underscored by his decision to wear a costume of bold primary colors so tight as to be his very skin. … Superman's powers—strength, mobility, x-ray vision and the like—are the comic-book equivalents of ethnic characteristics, and they protect and preserve the vitality of the foster community in which he lives in the same way that immigrant ethnicity has sustained American culture linguistically, artistically, economically, politically, and spiritually. The myth of Superman asserts with total confidence and a childlike innocence the value of the immigrant in American culture.

The DREAMers are reclaiming meanings that have been embedded within the superhero narrative since its origins as a means of connecting their current struggles to a larger history of immigration politics and of making common cause with other Americans whose immigrant backgrounds are no longer so visible or so pressing.

Huerta was not alone in connecting the DREAMers' struggles with the Superman saga. Hari Kondabolu (Jenkins and Shresthova 2012), a South Asian comedian, recorded a video asking why no one ever tried to deport Superman for "stealing jobs." Photographer Dulce Pinzon (2010) depicted a range of superheroes performing the jobs often done by undocumented workers: Spider-man washes windows, Mr. Fantastic waits tables, The Thing joins a construction crew. Pinzon explains, "The principal objective of this series is to pay homage to these brave and determined men and women that somehow manage, without the help of any supernatural power, to withstand extreme conditions of labor in order to help their families and communities survive and prosper."

Thomas Andrea (1987) has shown how, in his earliest incarnations, the 1930s Superman was described as "protector of the oppressed," a language that would have sounded "too radical" even a few years later. Superman challenged the powerful, smashing down doors in the governor's office to insist that a wrongfully convicted man be rescued from death row, calling attention to the corrupt motives that contributed to a mining disaster, or stopping domestic abuse. Over time, Superman was stripped of this overtly political role, subordinated to governmental authorities: "Superman no longer operates outside the law but is made an honorary policeman. … His struggle against evil becomes confined to the defense of private property and the extermination of criminals. It is no longer a struggle against social injustice, an attempt to aid the helpless and oppressed" (131).

Insofar as the superhero genre emerged as other creators sought to reverse engineer what was popular about Superman, other superheroes have followed a similar path.

Ironically, this shift from a political to a civic vision has not prevented the superhero character from becoming a political symbol for a range of different movements. One could argue that the broad, yet ultimately empty, gestures linking superheroes to the nation-state have left the figure more open to diverse ideological uses. Forrest Phillips (2013), for example, has written about how Captain America has been deployed as a symbol by opposing political groups (including the Tea Party and Occupy): "Captain America's owners have crafted an icon of Americanness whose bipartisan popularity rivals or surpasses that of our nation's founders. ... Each poacher considers the elements of Cap's character that conform to his or her own perspective to be essential, while casting aside those that conflict."

The superhero has become such an effective resource because his political significance has been underspecified; even as many people have grown up with an intense emotional investment to these characters who have been a part of our individual lives since childhood and our collective memory since the late 1930s. Matt Yockey (2012) makes a similar claim about the roles Wonder Woman has played in debates about gender politics over the past fifty years: "While the visual and narrative excesses of the genre speak directly to the affective capacity of childhood play, the superhero also speaks specifically to the transcendent agency of imagining a new social self."

For the DREAMers, the issue of what makes one American and what constitutes a meaningful contribution to society are key concerns, so the superhero represents a very useful resource through which to conduct these essential conversations.

A Figment of Our (Civic) Imagination

As our team has sought to understand the nature of participatory politics, we've increasingly been drawn toward the concept of the "civic imagination," which we define as the capacity to imagine alternatives to current social, political, or economic conditions. One cannot change the world unless one can imagine what a better world might look like, and too often, our focus on contemporary problems makes it impossible to see beyond immediate constraints. One also can't change the world until one can imagine oneself as an active political agent. For many of the young people we spoke with, the message they received on a daily basis was that what they had to say didn't matter; the social change organizations we studied work hard to help participants learn to trust their own voice. Here, we are drawing on Nick Couldry (2010), who describes political voice as the process of "giving an account of oneself," in ways which can help others to engage with your concerns and learn from your experiences. Such accounts may be autobiographical (as they often are among the DREAMer youth we have studied) but they may also involve sharing fantasies (as is more the case in the DREAMers' use of the superhero genre). For youth, this focus on potential civic roles is important since, as writers like Shakuntala Banaji and David Buckingham (2013) have suggested, young

people are often excluded from playing an "actual" or "meaningful" role in the processes associated with institutionalized politics, their agendas are marginalized, and, as
in current voter suppression efforts that make it harder for American youth to register
to vote through their schools, they are disenfranchised. All of this is certainly true for
young DREAMers who are fighting for their right to stay in this country and to participate in the "American Dream."

Yet, we've found that young people are learning to identify and frame political issues
in language that speaks to them and their peers. Many of the youth we've interviewed
told us that they felt discomfort embracing contemporary political rhetoric they found
exclusive (insofar as you have to know much about the political system in order to
understand what is being discussed) and repulsive (insofar as it is bound up with partisan struggles for power rather than an effort to find a consensus). In turning toward
icons and narratives borrowed from popular media to express their civic identities and
political concerns, they were seeking a way to bridge across divisions and differences
that are making it hard for the political establishment to move forward to solve persistent problems.

This movement from private toward public imagination often depends on images
already familiar to participants from other contexts, images drawn not from political
rhetoric but popular fantasy. The image bank through which we forge the civic imagination shifts from generation to generation: for the civil rights movement in the 1950s,
it might have been formed around the rhetoric of the black church with its talk of
"crossing the River Jordan" and entering the "promised land," while for the American
founding fathers, it might have been formed around motifs from classical history and
mythology. But, the emerging generation of young activists maintains a strong, close
relationship to American popular culture, and that shared vocabulary helps them to
broker relations across different political groups.

Immigration IS "the American Way"

Robert Putnam (2000) has made a distinction between bonding social capital (which
creates a shared framework of meanings among the members of a group or community) and bridging social capital (which allows the group to find common ground with
others). In this case, the superhero narrative performs both functions, allowing the
young DREAMers to share common experiences through reference to a shared symbol
system, while also allowing them to speak in meaningful ways to others who may
never have thought about their experiences in such terms before.

One example of the bridging function the superhero performs can be found in
"Superman is an Immigrant," an awareness and public education campaign around the
release of *Man of Steel*, a 2013 revamp of the basic Superman origin story. The campaign
was conducted in cooperation between Define American, a project founded by

immigrant rights activist—and undocumented American—Jose Antonio Vargas, and Imagine Better, a fan activist network, an offshoot of the Harry Potter Alliance (HPA). The HPA was started by community organizer and Harry Potter fan Andrew Slack as a means of rallying young people in support of a range of human rights related issues. Today, the group has more than 100,000 members in chapters across the US and has conducted campaigns against genocide, and for disaster relief, marriage equality, labor rights, and fair trade, among many other issues (Jenkins 2012; Kligler-Vilenchik 2013). With Imagine Better, the HPA sought to broaden its base through outreach to fans of many other media franchises. Within Imagine Better, the key figure behind the "Superman is an Immigrant" campaign was Julian Gomez, a vlogger for the Harry Potter Alliance who "came out" as undocumented in an HPA video blog a year earlier. In a *Huffington Post* piece (Gomez 2013), 20-year-old Julian describes his personal connection to Superman: "In the summer blockbuster *Man of Steel*, Superman struggles with his identity as an immigrant, terrified that if he tells the American people that he's from another place, they will reject him. I felt that same fear when I was old enough to understand what it meant to be undocumented. Last year, I finally found the courage to publicly speak about my undocumented status in a video blog that has now been watched over 16,000 times."

Gomez's story captured the interests of HPA members, many of whom may not have known of anyone who was undocumented before. Meghan, an HPA member, shared:

> Immigration was one of those things that I never really thought too much about before. I never really truly took a stance on it, because I just didn't know anything about it. I've never known anybody who was a legal or an illegal immigrant, one way or another, or that came to this country, at least to my knowledge I didn't know. To have somebody who had come to this country, they're an undocumented citizen, and being able to tell their story gave me a lot of perspective very quickly about that subject.

Imagine Better and Define American encouraged people to share their stories of heritage and identity, inspired by the connection to Superman, and to spark a conversation around immigration reform.

On wearetheamericanway.tumblr.com, young people uploaded pictures of themselves holding descriptions of their family heritage, signing with "I am the American way" and the Superman's signature S, branded with the colors of the American flag. One young woman's hand-written and hand-decorated sign reads: "I am a 1st generation Salvadorian-American. My mom came to the States at 15 and then got pregnant when she was 16 years old. She didn't finish high school, but she helped me to. I'm two years away from a Bachelors. I am the American Way." Sitting in a dimly lit room, a young man's modest sign reads: "Born & raised in Honduras. America is my home. I am the American Way." Here, again, this approach is consistent with the film's own messages—at one point, Superman is asked to prove his commitment to American values, and he defines his citizenship not based on a birthright but on his experiences of growing up in Kansas, the same kind of claims which the DREAMers have made for their rights to become citizens. Beyond the personal immigration stories, the Tumblr website links to "5 facts about immigration" (e.g., "By today's rules, your great-grandmother may have been denied at Ellis Island") as well as a call to "Tell Obama: Stop Deportations!" In the page's comment section, immigration reform advocates engaged with opponents to the DREAMer movement, who claimed, "there are laws that govern entry and citizen status in this country. EVERYONE must follow the rules." These sometimes heated conversations, interestingly, never referenced the Superman metaphor.

Mechanisms of Translation and Connection

As we seek to understand the nature of participatory politics, a key challenge is to identify the mechanisms that help young people move from being socially and culturally active to being politically and civically engaged. Current scholarship from the United States, Canada, and Great Britain (Gibson 2003; Bennett 2008; Wattenberg 2008; Buckingham 2000; Levine 2007) suggests that young people in those contexts are most apt to become politically involved if they come from families with a history of citizen participation and political activism, if they encounter civics teachers who encourage them to reflect on and respond to current events, if they attend schools where they are allowed a voice in core decisions, and if they participate in extracurricular activities and volunteerism that gives back to their community. Most forms of activism reach the same core group of participants, who already are politically engaged, and redirects them toward new issues. But both the Harry Potter Alliance and the Nerdfighters (a group discussed in more depth later) often target young people who are engaged culturally as fans and help them to extend their engagement into politics, often deploying existing skills and capacities in new ways. Kahne, Lee, and Feezell (2011, 2) discovered that involvement in online interest-based networks (fandom, for example) also shapes political identities: "Online, nonpolitical, interest-driven activities serve as a gateway to participation in important aspects of civic and, at times, political life, including volunteering, engagement in community problem-solving, protest activities, and political voice."

The Imagine Better Network connects different popular texts to contemporary social issues. As a movement, it is based on the notion that, as HPA founder Andrew Slack described in an email to the HPA mailing list, "Fantasy is not an escape from our world, but an invitation to go deeper into it." The Imagine Better Network emerged from the Harry Potter Alliance that. since 2005, has been mobilizing fans of the young adult franchise to engage in civic action, using metaphors from the wizarding world. While the Harry Potter Alliance has been mostly focused on fans, Imagine Better seeks to engage wider audiences by tapping the attention paid to popular media texts, at a time when they're most resonating culturally. Andrew Slack (2010) calls this process cultural acupuncture:

Finding where the psychological energy is in the culture, and moving that energy towards creating a healthier world. … We activists may not have the same money as Nike and McDonald's but we have a message that actually means something. … What we do not have is the luxury of keeping the issues we cover seemingly boring, technocratic, and inaccessible. With cultural acupuncture, we will usher in an era of activism that is fun, imaginative, and sexy, yet truly effective.

The HPA realized that the news media was more likely to cover the launch of the next Harry Potter film than the genocide in Darfur. Imagine Better works through the model of cultural acupuncture, pinning political and social causes to content worlds that have fan followings, are familiar to wide audiences, and attract media interest. Imagine Better uses popular culture narratives—including superhero stories—as a form of cultural currency, bringing the group's messages to many who would not hear them otherwise.

Imagine Better's metaphoric use of Superman is an example of what we call "mechanisms of translation" (Kligler-Vilenchik 2013). Mechanisms of translation describe the ways that such groups deploy cultural investments and social connections to support participatory politics outcomes. Mechanisms of translation straddle and connect the worlds of participatory culture and participatory politics, where group members are highly invested participants in the cultural realm, even as they also seek political change. This use of superhero references also represents an example of what Mizuko Ito and Elisabeth Soep et al. (2015) have described as "consequential connections," a concept which has emerged from the MacArthur Foundation's Connected Learning Initiative. Connected Learning research (Ito et al. 2015) seeks to identify and map "the constructed features of the cultural and social environment that support connections, brokering, and translations across spheres of activity," primarily in terms of the ways young people's interests and activities within their homes or their peer culture relates to what gets valued by schools and other powerful institutions in their lives.

A white paper on Connected Learning (Ito et al. 2013, 42) describes some underlying assumptions: "Connected learning is socially embedded, interest-driven, and oriented toward expanding educational, economic, or political opportunity. It is realized when a young person is able to pursue a personal interest or passion with the support of friends and caring adults, and is in turn able to link this learning and interest to academic achievement, career success, or civic engagement." Noting that many young people have been turned off politics as it has traditionally been defined, Connected Learning researchers (Ito et al. 2015) suggest a more expansive understanding of the civic, which "include[s] involvement in state apparatuses (what is traditionally deemed "politics"), as well as activities tied to community problem-solving and social justice that do not necessarily lead to or even involve direct governmental action."

Here, the goal is to move from materials that young people explore in their imaginations to their active engagement with real world problems, and as this occurs, they often also find themselves applying skills they acquired through their recreational lives—producing videos, writing stories, using social media, constructing memes— toward political and civic ends. Writing about the Race-Bending movement, which has sought to direct attention to the racial politics around Hollywood casting decisions, Lori Kido Lopez (2011) explains, "Some of the organization's strongest and most effective tactics rely on the skills developed as members of the fan community: honing their arguments through community discussions, producing and editing multimedia creations, educating themselves about every facet of their issue, and relying on their trusted networks to provide a database of information" (432).

This fusion of the fan and the activist reflects the models of social change that animate many of the young people we interviewed. Many feel frustrated with the current state of the American government and are thus turned off by the mechanisms of institutional politics—whether through a distaste for the impasse and bickering of a government too invested in partisanship, for the corruption which has occurred as campaign finance reform provisions have been overturned and the role of major funders in the political process has become more explicit, or for the voter suppression efforts being conducted by many states. Instead, these young people are following the news closely, are anything but apathetic, but are turning to cultural and educational mechanisms rather than institutional politics as the primary means by which to change the political climate and reshape public opinion.

Often, these youths' media production practices involve a complex blending of culture jamming ("high jacking the signs" to express opposition to dominant value) and fan mastery (showcasing their expertise over the fictional universe.) For example, the Hawkeye Initiative encourages feminist critique within comics fandom, as female artists challenge the stereotypical, sexist, and simply awkward positions in which female superheroes get depicted within mainstream comics. A conversation on Tumblr suggesting that male characters never get depicted in such a fashion led to a grassroots project to reproduce classic superhero images, swapping out female superheroes for second-tier Marvel protagonist, Hawkeye. As one female participant explained, "If your female character can be replaced by Hawkeye in the same pose without looking silly or stupid, then it's acceptable and probably non-sexist" (Know Your Meme 2014). At a time when young people are struggling to articulate their relationship with feminism, when female comics fans are struggling against sexual harassment as they venture into comics conventions and retailers, and when the major studios still are not featuring female superheroes on the big (or small) screen, the Hawkeye Project gives these young feminists a chance to conduct a conversation about gender politics and command the attention of other comics fans.

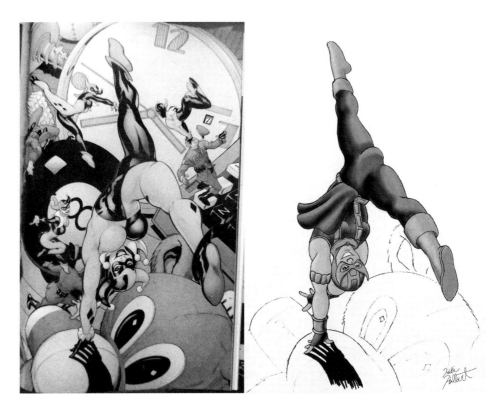

Figure 17.1
Artwork created by Kathryn Halbert for the Hawkeye Initiative.

The First Knight of Ramadan: Holding Out for a (Muslim) Hero

Those groups who feel most marginalized in American society often turn to popular culture as a means of negotiating their differences and forging some sense of belonging. We can observe this process through some examples of the ways superhero narratives entered the lives of American Muslim youths. In the first example, we see young people struggling to reconcile the particular practices of their religion with their desire to share experiences with others of their generation. For example, when the first night of the holy month of Ramadan (a month defined by abstention and fasting) coincided with the opening night for *The Dark Knight Rises* (2012), many young American Muslims turned to their social media networks to debate whether or not it would be acceptable to see the film as observant Muslims. The discussion even surfaced during an American Muslim forum organized by the Muslim Public Affairs Council in Washington D.C. that July: an exasperated senior Muslim leader exclaimed that he just refused to discuss this topic on Twitter any more. Aman Ali, one of the founders of the 30Mosques storytelling project, took a more playful approach when he posted "First Knight of Ramadan—A Muslim Nerd's Dilemma" on YouTube. The short begins with Ali moving through an urban landscape dressed in a Batman costume: "Like a lot of nerds, I often imagined myself as Batman, a reluctant hero," Ali shares through a voice over. The audience learns that he has seen all the films and is very excited about this latest one. But, he explains, "Unlike a lot of other nerds, I am a Muslim … and Ramadan, the holiest month for Muslims also starts on July 20th. This is a Muslim nerd's nightmare." Aman seeks advice on what to do, consulting his social media networks and querying religious leaders. In the end, Ali's decision is made for him when he discovers that opening night tickets are sold out. "I will get another chance to watch the movie," he concludes as he begins his Ramadan fast, "but for now it's time for me to be the hero."

Not surprisingly, many American Muslim youth also responded actively to the news that Marvel was introducing a new superhero character, Kamala Khan—the new Ms. Marvel—an American Muslim of Pakistani descent. Sana Amanat, the series editor, was interviewed on Marvel's site: "As much as Islam is a part of Kamala's identity, this book isn't preaching about religion or the Islamic faith in particular. It's about what happens when you struggle with the labels imposed on you, and how that forms your sense of self. It's a struggle we've all faced in one form or another, and isn't just particular to Kamala because she's Muslim. Her religion is just one aspect of the many ways she defines herself."

Sabaa Tahir, a young adult author of Pakistani origin, discussed Kamala Khan's politicized identity in a *Washington Post* editorial: "As a Pakistani American female, I can relate to Kamala. … At age 10, or even 15, it would have meant the world to me to see a Pakistani girl portrayed positively, let alone as a comic book superhero." Marvel's choice to introduce this character has already inspired other American Muslim youth to imagine how they might fit within the Marvel universe. In the summer of 2014, for example, Nour Saleh, a British Muslim teen, sparked widespread interest among comics fans when she responded to a Draw Yourself challenge on Tumblr, depicting herself in the garb of various superheroes, male and female.

As she explained, "I am a Muslim girl (who wears a hijab) and I prefer to wear long/loose things that go below the butt" so that's how she drew herself, reimagining both classic Marvel and DC superheroes as they might appear if they had a similar cultural identity and fashion sense (Pahle 2014). The images' publication on a range of fan-oriented blogs sparked further discussions about whether a Muslim can occupy the role of a superhero in contemporary American culture. We have found that American Muslim identities are always already political, even when—especially when—they seek to do things that are normal for other American youth: in this context, acts of self-expression (such as drawing pictures of superheroes) or everyday life (such as the choice

Figure 17.2
Artwork created by Nour Saleh in response to the Draw Yourself challenge.

of whether or not you should go to a movie opening) are also political, in that they have implications for how American Muslims get perceived by others and how they fit into American culture.

Kamala Khan's image has been used to shine light on the politicized nature of these so-called "personal" acts, but it has also been in employed toward other forms of activism. For instance, when the American branch of the Freedom Defense Initiative, an anti-Muslim organization, placed posters on buses around San Francisco, Ms. Marvel inspired young activists to take action to "stop the hate" (Whitbrook 2015). Anonymous activists printed up images of Kamala Khan and plastered them on top of the offending advertisements, "calling all bigotry busters" to speak out against such hate speech wherever they encountered it, a message endorsed by the comic's writer, G. Willow Wilson.

"Waiting for Superman" Is a Bad Idea!

Marvel's efforts to incorporate American Muslim experiences into its superhero universe was a logical outgrowth of the efforts of the U.S. comic books industry to move beyond its jingoistic past in the wake of 9/11. As Henry Jenkins (2006, 79) wrote in an overview of how the comics industry depicted the tragedy, "Comic book artists rejected fisticuffs or vigilante justice in favor of depicting the superheroes as nurturers and healers. They are more likely to be standing tall against domestic racial violence than punching out terrorists." Making Ms. Marvel an American Muslim girl paralleled other recent decisions to grant an African American youth the mantle of Spider-Man or for Thor to adopt a female persona. Jenkins (2006) summed up his argument this way:

Popular culture is the space of dreams, fantasies, and emotions. In that space, it matters enormously whether Captain America stands for fascism or democracy, whether Wonder Woman represents the strong arm of American cultural imperialism or whether she respects and understands third world critiques of her mission, whether Superman is more important than the average men and women who are accidental casualties of his power struggles or whether everyday people have the power to solve their problems without turning to superheroes for help. (98)

And for this reason, superheroes often get pulled into debates about what actions are appropriate for responding to contemporary social problems. We saw two rich examples of such debates in the course of our research.

The first involved the Nerdfighters. Nerdfighters participate in an informal online community revolving around the YouTube channel of the "VlogBrothers," John and Hank Green. Nerdfighters are united by a broad but shared identity as "nerds," as well as by a loosely defined civic mission to "decrease world suck." When Nerdfighters talk about "decreasing world suck," they may mean a broad range of things—helping a friend in need, creating a funny video to make others happy, or activities more traditionally conceived as civic engagement, such as donating to nonprofits and charities. Nerdfighters have shown impressive abilities to mobilize quickly with high impact, for example when in 2013 they raised over $870,000 in two days, which were then divided between charities for which Nerdfighters voted.

Uniting all these actions is a belief in a model of change in which every person counts, and small acts add up to make big change. Such an approach may be at odds with the superhero model, in which an extraordinary character saves the world, while ordinary people are powerless bystanders. This possible contradiction inspired a 2011 discussion entitled "I don't like superheroes," on a popular Nerdfighter forum, nerdfighters.ning.com. Nerdfighter Kat posted: "I don't hate them, it's just I don't like the idea of how one person wields the power to change things and fight crime, while the ordinary citizens are always sort of helpless and expect the superhero to save them; in real life, it's the ordinary people who change things, and they don't get special powers or are 'chosen,' and very often, they can't do it alone and have to band together."

Some Nerdfighters agreed with Kat. Other forum participants used the question of superheroes' popularity to make a wider statement about how humans respond to what often seems a chaotic and unjust world: "Superheroes are present for the same reason religions are, to restore order where we may see chaos. To enact morals where there may be none, to punish and reward." Others used superheroes as role models for "ordinary people," to make the argument that every person can make a difference—if they try hard enough. Another Nerdfighter, with the username Calibran explained: "Each and every one of those people has all the power they need to become a superhero in their own right." Superheroes thus offered the Nerdfighters a lens through which to discuss ideas about individual agency, civic responsibility, and models of change and thus to think more deeply about what motivates their own civic activities.

Similar analysis about which superheroes most embody a libertarian belief system can be found across the web, penned by range of libertarian authors, from casual bloggers to professional journalists. Witness writer and editor Franklin Harris's 2009 blog post from the Young Americans for Liberty website, "We Don't Need Another Hero." Harris focuses mostly on the libertarian appeal of Alan Moore and Dave Gibbons' 1986 graphic novel, *Watchmen*, adapted for film in 2009, but also identifies libertarian elements in the 2008 *Dark Knight* and *Iron Man* films: "While *Iron Man* and *The Dark Knight* both deal with issues of power and corruption, they ultimately side with their vigilante protagonists." The superheroes in *Watchmen*, on the other hand, have a more ambiguous relationship to social good, and they are often as vulnerable to established power structures as their human counterparts or, worse, wield their powers for evil and corruption. Following a similar logic to Thomas Andrea's critique of Superman as a law enforcer rather than as a champion of justice, Harris argues that *Watchmen* is so appealing to libertarians (and anti-statists in particular) because it is an allegory for the misuse of power:

What are superheroes anyway, except unauthorized, unaccountable law-enforcement agents? Superheroes don't obtain search warrants. They don't read suspects their Miranda rights. If they screw up, they don't face disciplinary action. And it's almost impossible for a wronged party to sue them for misconduct. Just try serving a court summons to the Hulk. In short, all of the real-world problems associated with police misconduct are potentially worse when it comes to superheroes. They exist outside the rule of law.

Other libertarian writers have a less dystopian take on superheroes. Stacy Litz, a Drexel University student writing for *Examiner.com* in 2010, makes a case for the libertarianism of Iron Man, Tony Stark, who uses his private means to battle the military-industrial complex: "So, what did *Iron Man 2* prove to viewers? Government intervention results in a lot of unnecessary explosions. When striving to 'protect the country,' those in power will go through 'any means necessary' to achieve a sense of security, even by faking deaths, working with the enemy and stealing Iron Man suits. … Private security is a reliable asset while public law enforcement is less than trustworthy."

Fred Roeder, blogging for Students for Liberty, agrees with Litz's assessment, including Stark in his June 2014 listicle/photo essay of "16 Libertarian Sci-Fi Heros." Roeder also includes the likes of V from *V for Vendetta*, Dr. Jean Grey from *X-Men*, Steve Rogers from *Captain America*, and even Unikitty from *The Lego Movie*.

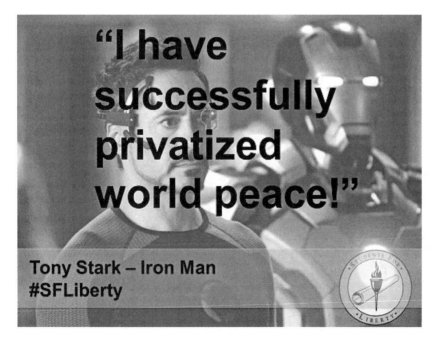

Figure 17.3
Artwork created by Fred Roeder of Students for Liberty.

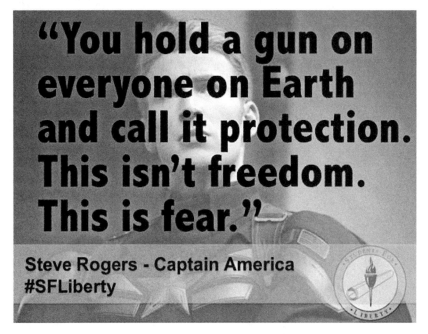

Figure 17.4
Artwork created by Fred Roeder of Students for Liberty.

Figure 17.5
Artwork created by Fred Roeder of Students for Liberty.

Both the Nerdfighters and the libertarians saw the superhero mythos as raising some core questions informing their civic and political lives. For the Nerdfighters, the key issue was whether change might come through the actions of everyday people working together toward common ends or whether it necessarily rested in the hands of elite institutions or exceptional individuals. For the libertarians, the question was how we should deal with the risks of concentrated power (especially when aligned with state interests).

Because participants already knew who these superheroes were, they were able to use them to encourage analysis and, through this process, to identify points of agreement or conflict in their underlying models of political life. Such debates may or may not spark action; they can also distract from more-grounded discussions of tactics for mobilization. Our focus on the civic differs from traditional understandings of ideology because of our focus on the bottom-up, participatory shaping of these narratives as part of larger cultural struggles over meaning and representation. We might read the superhero narrative as embodying particular ideologies about American exceptionalism and manifest destiny, meanings that can often be located in the official texts surrounding these characters. Superhero characters were deployed as part of propaganda campaigns during World War II, for example. Across the varied examples in this essay, we've also seen that these same figures can be and are deployed by a broader range of groups toward their own political ends—many of which challenge, contest, or even reverse that particular frame, allowing the superhero saga to speak for Sikhs, undocumented immigrants, or American Muslims who might otherwise be excluded from dominant ideological understandings of what constitutes an American hero. Any act of appropriation involves some reproduction of prevailing ideology but these examples also involve a remixing or rethinking of these core myths to express alternative perspectives. Our next section considers more fully what it means to "act" as superheroes in the political realm, looking at examples of performances within the Occupy Wall Street and Invisible Children movements.

Occupying Gotham

In an age when new media platforms have lowered the transaction costs for collective action and made it easier to share grassroots media with dispersed networks, young activists are often taking the civic imagination to the next level—performing these imagined identities through what Stephen Duncombe has described as "ethical spectacle." Duncombe (2012b) defines this concept in *Beautiful Trouble*, an online resource for contemporary activists:

An ethical spectacle is a symbolic action that seeks to shift the political culture toward more progressive values. An ethical spectacle should strive to be:

Participatory: Seeking to empower participants and spectators alike, with organizers acting as facilitators.

Open: Responsive and adaptive to shifting contexts and the ideas of participants.

Transparent: Engaging the imagination of spectators without seeking to trick or deceive.

Realistic: Using fantasy to illuminate and dramatize real-world power dynamics and social relations that otherwise tend to remain hidden in plain sight.

Utopian: Celebrating the impossible—and therefore helping to make the impossible possible.

Beautiful Trouble offers its own examples of the ways that the superhero has been mobilized for grassroots politics. On November 17, 2011, a coalition of labor organizers seeking to challenge austerity measures and to demand more jobs projected a Bat Signal on the side of Brooklyn's Verizon Building. As one of the event organizers (Read 2012) explained:

The "bat signal" itself required no translation. It's a part of our cultural commons, part of the "spectacular vernacular" of global pop culture, a symbol we all understand to be a call for aid and an outlaw call to arms—after all, isn't that precisely what the Occupy movement is? Of course Batman is actually a quasi-sociopathic millionaire vigilante. A one-percenter, you might say. But by filling that symbol—by occupying it—with our own content—"99%"—we appropriated it for the rest of us. And in this reconfiguration, we were no longer waiting for some superhero, be it a masked vigilante or the first black president, to swoop in and save the day. Rather, we were the response to our own call for aid.

In his analysis of the Occupy movement, Manuel Castells (2012) talks about how its discursive and organizational practices created spaces for imagining alternatives, for expressing the movement's shared concerns about wealth inequalities, and for innovating new mechanisms for collaboration and deliberation. The Bat Signal, and especially the group's acknowledgment of its contradictory meanings, is a great illustration of these practices at work.

A Movement Has Got to Move

If the 99% Bat Signal demonstrates the participatory dimensions of Duncombe's "ethical spectacle" model, Invisible Children has showcased spectacular performance through its events as a means of inspiring its members to do more within their own communities. Based in San Diego, Invisible Children is a non-profit that strives to end the violence and atrocities perpetrated by Joseph Kony's Lord's Resistance Army in central Africa. IC has often invited the Legion of Extraordinary Dancers (LXD) to perform at their gatherings. Initially founded as a Hulu web series, LXD, a fictional epic tale spanning hundreds of years, centers on dancers who discover their superhero-like extraordinary dance abilities. LXD's relationship with the superhero genre is hinted at in their original advertising pitch, cited on IMDb.com: "Join seemingly ordinary people who discover they have extraordinary powers in a groundbreaking mythology about hope, greed, love, and the force that moves us all." The initial 10 episodes of the series introduced members of the LXD through origin stories that reveal their dance powers, which include incredible flexibility, extreme robot dance moves, head spins, and ballet-style grand battements. This set-up leads to an epic conflict between good and evil that gets staged through (dance) battles in later episodes as LXD members use their dance abilities as supernatural weapons. Since LXD's creation in 2011, the dancers featured in the series have continued to create and perform under the LXD banner—including regular appearances at IC events, where dance often functions in cathartic finales. Those who learned about IC through the media frenzy that surrounded Kony2012 might be surprised to learn that IC actually sees its roots in face-to-face interactions with its mostly young supporters. Jason Russell, one of IC's founders, explains that to him a social "movement actually moves your body, physically from one location to another." Russell believes that in order to move people's minds and hearts, you also need to move their bodies. At all events that we witnessed, including MoveDC in 2012 and the Fourth Estate leadership conferences of 2011 and 2013, IC supporters responded enthusiastically to LXD performances, which invariably crescendoed to an almost ecstatic participatory moment when everyone in the audience joined in the dance.

The IC/LXD partnership can be partially explained by the close friendship, dating back to their undergraduate days, between Jason Russell and Jon Chu, founder of LXD, but also by strong underlying commitments connecting the groups. When Sangita Shresthova interviewed Chu, he explained: "I think when you know an IC person, you know an LXD person. ... It's the type of person who will so work extremely hard to move that you can break your neck. ... Then they get it, they will just do it over and over again."

Galen, a lead LXD dancer and choreographer, also sees a connection between IC's humanistic goals and LXD's commitment to recognizing diverse dance superpowers: "That's the bottom line ... we're all human. ... If we went over to Africa there'd be some interaction there trying to feel out the different cultures ... but then in the end, everyone comes together. We're all one, we're all unified. We're all doing the same choreography and it's powerful."

Just as Occupy supporters saw the Bat Signal as a call to arms, IC supporters seek inspiration from the collective energies, discipline and dedication, and commitment to diversity they observed from LXD's performances. In both cases, performing the superhero mythology becomes a way of bringing those powers into the real world and allowing them to work for the collective good. Whether participatory or spectatorial, these spectacles do political work, empowering these movements to go out and change the world. We understand this deployment of the superhero mythology as enabling the kind of "affective attunement" Zizi Papacharissi (2014) has argued is central to contemporary political movements, constituting what she describes as "stories of connection and expression" that help people to "feel their way" into identification with their causes. She rejects classically maintained oppositions between affect and reason, suggesting that the two can work hand in hand in order to enable political movements to attract members. No one rationally believes that dancing superheroes can combat evil warlords, but Duncombe would argue that this is part of the point: by depicting impossible or improbable solutions, participants free their imaginations from constraints, and thus, can consider more realistic alternatives that might make a difference on the ground.

Wrapping Up

Throughout this discussion, we've seen the ways that the superhero mythology functions as a shared and seemingly inexhaustible resource that many different groups and movements have deployed toward their own political goals. We've seen how different elements of the superhero genre can be made to speak about questions of origins and identity, about the nature of power, about what it might mean to have a mission, to fight for truth and justice, or to defend and protect the oppressed. We've seen the image of the superhero get appropriated and remixed through different media practices—from projecting the Bat Signal on the side of a building to remixing or redrawing images from comics, from holding debates via social media to posting videos on YouTube. In some cases, the superhero has been used to inspire speculations within the movement and in other cases, it has been used to help bridge between groups who have very different social experiences but shared affective investments in these characters. In some cases, what results is only talk, though such talk may provide mechanisms for translating political concerns into a language that speaks to young people who may never have seen themselves as part of the political process before, and in other cases, the superhero gets embodied and performed as part of various forms of ethical spectacle. Read side by side, these multiple examples give us some snapshots of the ways popular culture becomes part of the civic imagination and helps to inspire participatory politics.

As we share these examples, we suspect they will do little to resolve ongoing debates in cultural studies around the relationship between culture and politics. Some may well feel that these examples do not yet constitute the political or, worse, that they are simply another manifestation of consumer culture. Institutional politics often depicts civic participation as a special event and isolates the process of governance from other aspects of our lives; participatory politics, on the other hand, incorporates politics into our ordinary interactions with each other as politics becomes part of our overall lifestyle. We would argue that each of these examples constitutes some step, small or large, into civic and political life: they provide the participants with a means of asking core questions, envisioning themselves as civic agents who have the capacity to change the world; they encourage young people to play a role in some of the core political debates of our time (from immigration reform to wealth inequality, from feminism to human rights issues). And they have done so at the precarious intersection between the grassroots communication system and the commercial broadcast media system, helping us to better understand the ways that civic media practices might build on the infrastructure and visibility of commercial entertainment to expand the public for grassroots messages.

References

Ali, Aman. 2012. "First Knight of Ramadan—A Muslim Nerd's Dilemma." https://www.youtube.com/watch?v=2k1aiUIT13Y.

Andrae, Thomas. 1987. "From Menace to Messiah: The History and Historicity of Superman." In *American Media and Mass Culture: Left Perspectives*, ed. Donald Lazare, 124–138. Berkeley: University of California Press.

Banaji, Shakuntala, and David Buckingham. 2013. *The Civic Web: Young People, The Internet and Civic Participation*. Cambridge, MA: MIT Press.

Bennett, W. Lance. 2008. *Civic Life Online: Learning How Digital Media Can Engage Youth*. Cambridge, MA: MIT Press.

Buckingham, David. 2000. *The Making of Citizens: Young People, News and Politics*. London: Routledge.

Castells, Manuel. 2012. *Networks of Outrage and Hope: Social Movements in the Internet Age*. London: Polity.

Cohen, Cathy J., and Joseph Kahne. 2012. "Participatory Politics: New Media and Youth Political Action." MacArthur Foundation Youth and Participatory Politics Research Network. http://ypp.dmlcentral.net/content/participatory-politics-new-media-and-youth-political-action-ypp-survey-report.pdf.

Couldry, Nick. 2010. *Why Voice Matters: Culture And Politics After Neoliberalism*. London: Sage.

Duncombe, Stephen. 2007. *Dream: Re-Imagining Progressive Politics in an Age of Fantasy*. New York: New Press.

Duncombe, Stephen. 2012 a. "Imagining No Place." "Transformative Works and Fan Activism," ed. Henry Jenkins and Sangita Shresthova, special issue, *Transformative Works and Cultures* 10. doi:.10.3983/twc.2012.0350

Duncombe, Stephen. 2012 b. "Theory: Ethical Spectacle." In *Beautiful Trouble: A Toolbox for Revolution*, ed. Andrew Boyd and Dave Oswald Mitchell. New York: OR Books. http://beautifultrouble.org/theory/ethical-spectacle.

Engle, Gary. 1987. "What Makes Superman So Darned American?" In *Superman at Fifty: The Persistence of a Legend*, ed. Dennis Dooley and Gary Engle. Cleveland, OH: Octavia.

Gibson, Cynthia. 2003. "The Civic Mission of Schools." Report from Carnegie Foundation and CIRCLE: The Center for Information and Research on Civic Learning and Engagement. http://www.civicyouth.org/PopUps/CivicMissionofSchools.pdf.

Gomez, Julian. 2013. "Immigrants Are the American Way." *Huffington Post,* July 16. http://www.huffingtonpost.com/julian-gomez/superman-is-an-immigrant_b_3606264.html.

Harris, Franklin. 2009. "We Don't Need Another Hero." *Young Americans for Liberty Blog,* October 30. http://www.yaliberty.org/node/13083.

Hills, Carol. 2014. "Captain America Is a Sikh. You Got a Problem With That?" *PRI's   The World (Oakland, CA),* October 17. http://www.pri.org/stories/2014-10-17/captain-america-sikh -you-got-problem.

Huerta, Eric. 2013. "Superman and His Immigration Status." *Just a Random Hero,* June 11. http://justarandomhero.blogspot.com/2013/06/superman-and-his-immigration-status.html.

Institute for the Future. 2013. "Framework: Public Imagination." *Reconstitutional Convention.* http://reconcondev.govfutures.org/?recent_works=frameworks8.

Ito, Mimi, Elisabeth Soep, Neta Kliger-Vilenchik, Sangita Shresthova, Liana Gamber-Thompson, and Arely Zimmerman. 2015. "Learning Connected Civics: Narratives, Practices, Infrastructures." *Curriculum Inquiry* 45 (1): 10–29.

Ito, Mizuko, Kris Gutierrez, Sonia Livingstone, Bill Penuel, Jean Rhodes, Katie Salen, Juliet Schor, Julian Sefton-Green, and S. Craig Watkins. 2013. "Connected Learning: An Agenda for Research and Design." MacArthur Foundation. http://dmlhub.net/publications/connected-learning -agenda-research-and-design.

Jenkins, Henry. 1992. *Textual Poachers: Television Fans and Participatory Culture.* New York: Routledge.

Jenkins, Henry. 2006 a. *Convergence Culture: Where Old and New Media Collide.* New York: New York University Press.

Jenkins, Henry. 2006 b. "Captain America Sheds His Mighty Tears: Comics and September 11." In *Terror, Culture, Politics: Rethinking 9/11,* ed. Daniel J. Sherman and Terry Nardin, 69–102. Indianapolis: Indiana University Press.

Jenkins, Henry. 2012. "'Cultural Acupuncture': Fan Activism and the Harry Potter Alliance." *Transformative Works and Cultures* 10.

Jenkins, Henry, with Katie Clinton, Ravi Purushotma, Alice J. Robinson, and Margaret Weigel. 2007. "Confronting the Challenges of Participatory Culture: Media Education for the 21st Century." John D. and Catherine T. MacArthur Foundation. http://www.macfound.org/media/article_pdfs/JENKINS_WHITE_PAPER.PDF.

Jenkins, Henry, Sam Ford, and Joshua Green. 2013. *Spreadable Media: Creating Meaning and Value in a Networked Culture*. New York: New York University Press.

Jenkins, Henry, and Wyn Kelley, with Katie Clinton, Jenna McWilliams, Ricardo Pitts-Wiley, and Erin Reilly. 2013. *Reading in a Participatory Culture: Remixing Moby-Dick in the Literature Classroom*. New York: Teacher's College Press.

Jenkins, Henry, and Sangita Shresthova. 2012. "Up, Up and Away!: The Power and Potential of Fan Activism." *Transformative Works and Cultures* 10.

Kahne, Joseph, Jessica Timpany Feezell, and Namjin Lee. 2011. "The Civic and Political Significance of Online Participatory Cultures Among Youth Transitioning to Adulthood." DMLcentral Working Paper. http://ypp.dmlcentral.net/publications.

Kligler-Vilenchik, Neta. 2013. "Decreasing World Suck: Fan Communities, Mechanisms of Translation, and Participatory Politics." Working Paper. MacArthur Foundation. Accessed June 10, 2014. http://dmlhub.net/publications/decreasing-world-suck-fan-communities-mechanisms -translation-and-participatory-politics.

Know Your Meme. 2014. "The Hawkeye Initiative." http://knowyourmeme.com/memes/the -hawkeye-initiative.

Levine, Peter. 2007. *The Future of Democracy: Developing the Next Generation of American Citizens*. Medford, MA: Tufts University Press.

Litz, Stacey. 2010. "Iron Man 2 Depicts Struggle Between Libertarian Super Hero and Intrusive Government." *Examiner.com*, May 8. http://www.examiner.com/article/iron-man-2-depicts -struggle-between-libertarian-super-hero-and-intrusive-government.

Lopez, Lori Kido. 2011. "Fan Activists and the Politics of Race in *The Last Airbender*." *International Journal of Cultural Studies* 15 (5): 431–445.

Pahle, Rebecca. 2014. "Hijab-Wearing Superhero Fan Draws Herself as Various Comic Book Characters." *The Mary Sue*, July 3. http://www.themarysue.com/hijab-marvel-dc-superheroes.

Papacharissi, Zizi. 2014. *Affective Publics: Sentiment and the New Political*. Oxford: Oxford University Press.

Phillips, Forrest. 2013. "Captain America and Fandom's Political Activity." *Transformative Works and Cultures* 13. doi:.10.3983/twc.2013.0441

Pinzon, Dulce. 2010. "The Real Story of the Superheroes." http://www.dulcepinzon.com/en _projects_superhero.htm.

Putnam, Robert D. 1995. "Tuning In, Tuning Out: The Strange Disappearance of Social Capital in America." *PS: Political Science and Politics* 28 (4): 664–683.

Read, Mark. 2012. "Case Study: 99 Percent Bat Signal." In *Beautiful Trouble: A Toolbox for Revolution*, ed. Andrew Boyd and Dave Oswald Mitchell. New York: OR Books; http://beautifultrouble.org/ case/99-bat-signal.

Roeder, Fred. 2014. "16 Libertarian Sci-Fi Heroes." *Students for Liberty Blog*, June 16. http://studentsforliberty.org/blog/2014/06/16/16-libertarian-sci-fi-heros.

Slack, Andrew. 2010. "Cultural Acupuncture and a Future for Social Change." *Huffington Post*, July 2. http://www.huffingtonpost.com/andrew-slack/cultural-acupuncture-and_b_633824.html.

Thompson, S. Leigh. 2011. "Superman as Immigrant Rights Activist." *Colorlines*, October 10. http://colorlines.com/archives/2011/10/superman_as_immigrant_rights_activist.html.

Wattenberg, Martin P. 2008. *Is Voting for Young People?* New York: Pearson Longman.

Whitbrook, James. 2015. "Islamophobic Bus Ads in San Francisco Are Being Defaced with Kamala Khan." Toybox blog, January 27. http://toybox.io9.com/islamaphobic-bus-ads-in-san-francisco-are-being-defaced-1681857271.

Yockey, Matt. 2012. "Wonder Woman for a Day: Affect, Agency, and Amazons." *Transformative Works and Cultures* 10. doi: Accessed August 11, 2014.10.3983/twc.2012.0318

18   Case Study: Mashnotes

Roy Bendor

Over a period of two weeks in spring 2011, Vancouver residents were invited to voice their opinion on the city's urban design by interacting with three kiosks that were placed at central locations in the city's downtown (see figure 18.1). Each kiosk featured a different question pertaining to one of the city's high-profile urban design issues, inviting people to vote by pressing one of two clearly marked buttons located immediately below a slender screen (see figure 18.2).

The kiosk on Granville Street provided a choice between inner-city densification and expansion of the highway system that links Vancouver with other Lower Mainland communities. The question read, "Should we create more density in the city and expand laneway housing or create projects like the Gateway to make it easier to get to the suburbs?" and the two potential answers were "laneway" and "gateway." The kiosk at the Woodward's Building atrium offered a choice between high-rise and low-rise architectural styles, asking: "Vancouver is a young city whose look has shifted with the trends. What should be our signature architectural style?" The two alternatives were "super-tower" and "low-rise." And the kiosk at the Roundhouse Community Centre provided a choice between green and social public spaces, inquiring: "What is more important, spaces like the seawall or places where we can see wall to wall people?" Possible choices were "sea" and "be seen."

The three kiosks were part of an installation titled *Mashnotes*, named after the childhood game of "Mansion, Apartment, Shack, and House." It was commissioned by the Museum of Vancouver (MOV), funded by a grant from the Canada Council for the Arts, and created by Vancouver-based design outfit, Tangible Interaction. Votes cast through the kiosks were collected using the Arduino open source microcontroller platform, sent over the cellular (GSM) network, and collated with the votes sent by text messages (SMS) and through the project's (now defunct) website. All votes were then aggregated and displayed as a set of live data visualizations projected on large screens at the MOV's main gallery space (see figure 18.3). The museum's gallery also featured a light table that allowed visitors to pose open-ended questions and interact with them by using

Figure 18.1
Voice It kiosk on Granville Street. Image credit: Tangible Interaction.

Figure 18.2
Voice It kiosk. Image credit: Tangible Interaction.

natural hand gestures (figure 18.4). Altogether, more than 2,000 votes were cast, tallied, and visualized.[1]

Mashnotes was timely. Not only was Vancouver celebrating its 125th anniversary, the city was also in the process of revisiting its growth strategy and revising several of its long-term development plans. These coincided with the city's ambitious plan to become "the world's greenest city by 2020."[2] Taking advantage of this momentum, the installation was meant to "hold a mirror up to the city and lead provocative conversations about its past, present and future."[3] And indeed, as told by the installation's designer, Alex Beim, "On the city streets in particular, we noticed people didn't just walk up to the Mashnotes Voice It kiosks, read the question and simply press an answer

Figure 18.3
Data visualization at Museum of Vancouver. Image credit: Roy Bendor.

button. They'd actually start debating the topic with their friends or family right there. We've no way of knowing if those conversations continued or if they led to any action but it's a pretty good indication that the installations sparked something."[4]

While the kiosks may have provoked lively conversations about some of the dilemmas facing Vancouver's urban design and city planning, one may ask whether that was all they provoked. Could it be that the installation sparked curiosity about civic policy-making in general, or a sense of agency, evoked by the kiosks' voting mechanism and invitation "to have a direct say"? The noticeable lack of information regarding the issues would indicate that the installation served more to instigate than to educate. Additionally, the fact that the City was not involved in funding or designing Mash-notes, and was not committed to integrating any of the opinions expressed through the kiosks into actual policy, would militate against a perception of the installation as an official surveying device or a direct channel between citizens and policymakers. Perhaps a shift in attention from the installation's context to its actual affordances, would reveal a different kind of politicizing potential at play here. In this vein, while bearing in mind Anthony Dunne and Fiona Raby's (Dunne and Raby 2013, 37)

Figure 18.4
Light Table at Museum of Vancouver. Image credit: Tangible Interaction.

cautioning that "the power of design is often overestimated," it could be suggested that what the installation sparked was a sense of urban design *itself* as a space of contention, that is, an object of politics.

In this reading the installation's rudimentary interactive affordances take on new significance. When considering the kiosks' provocative phrasing of the questions, the avoidance of engineering or bureaucratic jargon, and the way choices were posed as contrasting dyads, Mashnotes can be seen as an instance of what Carl DiSalvo (2012, 2) calls "adversarial design": "a kind of cultural production that does the work of agonism through the conceptualization and making of products and services and our experiences with them." So while the installation may have stripped away some of the complexity and ambiguity that are inherent to Vancouver's urban design, it also signified the latter as a set of irreducible trade-offs, revealing the tensions that underlie it as an essentially contested space. In this sense, the installation provided the public with an opportunity to perform the conflictual nature of urban design, and to experience it as an element of civic politics.

Notes

1. Hanna Cho, Museum of Vancouver's curator for engagement and dialogue, email message to author, April 12, 2013.

2. "Vancouver 2020 A Bright Green Future," http://vancouver.ca/files/cov/bright-green-future .pdf.

3. "MOV Asks: Mansion, Apartment, Shack or House?," http://www.museumofvancouver.ca/ sites/default/files/FOR%20IMMEDIATE%20RELEASE%20-%20MOV%20MASH%20NOTES.pdf.

4. V.I.A, "Tangible Interaction and Mashnotes at MOV," *Vancouver Is Awesome*, April 8, 2011, http://vancouverisawesome.com/2011/04/08/tangible-iteraction-and-mash-notes-at-mov.

References

DiSalvo, Carl. 2012. *Adversarial Design*. Cambridge, MA: MIT Press.

Dunne, Anthony, and Fiona Raby. 2013. *Speculative Everything: Design, Fiction, and Social Dreaming*. Cambridge, MA: MIT Press.

19   Case Study: From #destroythejoint to Far-Reaching Digital Activism—Feminist Revitalization Stemming from Social Media and Reaching Beyond

Jessica McLean and Sophia Maalsen

Civic engagement in digital activism involves diffuse yet powerful networks of individuals and organizations uniting under a common interest. This case study of Destroy the Joint, a largely online group of over 74,000 people on Facebook and 17,500 on Twitter, shows how what began as a humorous turnaround of sexist comments on national talkback radio, is now a broad-based and effective, unified but not uniform, organization that aims to shine a light on sexism and misogyny. In analyzing its origins and accounting for its ongoing relevance more than three years after the birth of #destroythejoint, we show how feminist revitalization in social media and elsewhere is growing in Australia, and in other parts of the world.

The Origins of Destroy the Joint

The #destroythejoint movement began after a conservative Australian radio host, Alan Jones, declared on August 31, 2012, that several leading women in politics were "destroying the joint" by their efforts to support gender equality and other miscellaneous acts. He said:

She [the Prime Minister] said that we know societies only reach their full potential if women are politically participating. Women are destroying the joint—Christine Nixon in Melbourne, Clover Moore here. Honestly. (Totaro, 2012)

Jill Tomlinson, a surgeon and writer, ignited the campaign in conversation with education activist and writer Jane Caro, with the tweet exchange shown on the next page in figures 19.1 and 19.2.

Caro and Tomlinson were inviting others to contribute and originated the new hashtag: Destroy the Joint.

Within one day, thousands had tweeted their own versions of acts and intentions to quash sexism and misogyny and a new digital activism moment and movement had begun (McLean and Maalsen, 2013).

Jane Caro @JaneCaro   1d
Got time on my hands tonight so
thought I'd spend it coming up with
new ways of "destroying the joint"
being a woman & all. Ideas
welcome.

Figure 19.1

Jill Tomlinson @jilltomlinson   22h
Bored by Alan Jones' comments
on women destroying Australia?
Join with @JaneCaro & suggest
ways that women #destroythejoint

Figure 19.2

First Destroy the Joint Actions

Initially, the Destroy the Joint (DTJ) hashtag was an online meeting point for people reflecting on the absurdity of claims that women in political life were destructive forces because of their gender, but it grew to encompass critiques of gender inequality and to lampoon sexist and misogynistic acts.

The popularity of DTJ can in part be linked to the political climate at the time of its creation and a wider discontent with gender inequality. Australia's first female Prime Minister, Julia Gillard, experienced frequent public sexism, from conservative commentators and politicians alike. In early October 2012, during a debate in parliament about the behavior and role of Peter Slipper (then the Speaker of the House), the leader of the Opposition, Tony Abbott, accused Gillard of sexism. This accusation prompted the renowned anti-misogyny speech where Gillard declared to Tony Abbott that "I will not be lectured on misogyny and sexism by this man … and the Leader of the Opposition should think seriously about the role of women in public life and in Australian society because we are entitled to a better standard than this." (Gillard, 2012)

Being entitled to a better standard of gender equality is reflected in DTJ's activism. The first substantial intervention Destroy the Joint contributed to was against Alan Jones's radio station, campaigning for advertisers to withdraw support for his show in response to his ongoing sexist behavior, particularly directed against Gillard. Over 100,000 people signed an online petition within a week and Jones's radio station lost between AUD 1 and 1.5 million. The feminist campaign action enacted through social media thus affected a corporation in a material sense.

Micro-Campaigns under a Unified Anti-Sexism and Anti-Misogyny Collective

Multiple micro-campaigns characterize the ongoing productive space that is Destroy the Joint, and extend its reach contributing to a feminist revitalization that operates in social media and beyond. While DTJ started as a hashtag, now there is also a Twitter and Facebook presence for this digital activist collective.

Some of the micro-campaigns DTJ organized are shown in table 19.1.

Digital Activism in DTJ: Connections to Global Campaigns

Currently, feminist moments and movements are proliferating around the world, many emerging in digital spaces, such as #everydaysexism and #yesallwomen and often spring-boarding from these to other activist modes, including book publications, anti-corporate interventions, walks, and gatherings. For the Facebook supporters of DTJ, a prominent campaign to stop violence against women presently focuses DTJ activity (see figure 19.3).

Revitalizing Feminism?

Similarly to #destroythejoint, #everydaysexism and #yesallwomen provide meeting points for further engagement with feminist issues. The feminist revitalization has global reach and works to reinforce simultaneous campaigns and interventions. For instance, Destroy the Joint social media pages frequently cross-reference #everydaysexism and #yesallwomen and invite followers to contribute to these globally linked discursive feminist spaces. In this way they allow for distributed feminist networks to converge in online spaces to focus support on contemporary gender issues and create a community around this. Furthermore, despite being "online" their campaigns have physical and material effects as demonstrated in table 19.1, suggesting that campaigns facilitated through new media are effective and useful ways of producing change.

Table 19.1

Early acts of intervention DTJ organized and promoted (from McLean and Maalsen, 2013)

Date	Issue	Actions/ interventions	Result
November 2012	Sexist and violent slogans on t-shirts sold by Amazon	Public shaming, emails, comments on websites	T-shirts removed from sale
November 2012	Melbourne comedy debate "There's nothing funny about rape"	Calls to venue management, public shaming, emails to organizers	Debate cancelled
December 2012	"Guess the celebrity boobs" competition run by Fox FM Melbourne	Calls to Fox FM, emails to management, comments on website	Competition pulled
January 2013	David Koch's comments on Sunrise that breastfeeding near a pool is not classy	Nurse-in at Sunrise, protester discussion of issue with Koch on live television	No retraction but qualified opinion with assertion that people should be able to breastfeed anywhere
February 2013	Telstra charging victims of domestic violence for using silent numbers	Emails to Telstra	Change in policy and now people in circumstances where privacy is a must, are not charged
March 2013	Radio DJ John Laws's on-air comments to survivor of child abuse, asking if it was her fault	Petition with GetUp, emails, comments on webpages of radio stations that air Laws; 40,000 signatures	Dr Kezelman, president of Adults Surviving Child Abuse, spoke with Laws on-air about the impact of his comments; Laws attested to being "better informed" now
Ongoing	Equal pay for equal work	Sharing information about inequities, multiple means	Unknown
Ongoing	Critiquing "rape culture"	Sharing stories of people's experiences with rape, questioning lenient sentences	Unknown

Figure 19.3
Current Facebook home page for Destroy the Joint.

References

Destroy the Joint on Facebook. https://www.facebook.com/DestroyTheJoint.

Destroy the Joint on Twitter. https://twitter.com/jointdestroyer.

Gillard, Julia. 2012. "Transcript of Julia Gillard's speech," September 18. http://www.smh.com.au/federal-politics/political-news/transcript-of-julia-gillards-speech-20121009-27c36.html.

McLean, Jessica, and Sophia Maalsen. 2013. "Destroying the Joint and Dying of Shame? A Geography of Revitalised Feminism in Social Media and Beyond." *Geographical Research* 51:243–256. doi:.10.1111/1745-5871.12023

Totaro, Paola. 2012. "Australian Radio Host Says Female Leaders Are 'Destroying The Joint.'" *Guardian,* September 4. http://www.theguardian.com/world/2012/sep/04/australian-radio-host-female-leaders.

20   Case Study: The "It Gets Better Project"

Laurie Phillips Honda

Examples of twenty-first century social media–based activism are plentiful, but few have garnered 50 million YouTube views; launched affiliates in nearly 20 countries; and brought bullying to the forefront of mainstream media coverage and public policy debates. The "It Gets Better Project" (IGBP) is an ongoing campaign to prevent suicide among lesbian, gay, bisexual, transgender, and queer (LGBTQ) youth comprised of videos created by LGBTQ individuals and allies of all ages. Blending global citizen engagement and digital technologies, the IGBP phenomenon is an effective form of modern civic participation.

"It Gets Better Project" Overview

Prompted by a reader's desire to prevent LGBTQ youth suicide, Dan Savage[1] and Terry Miller filmed a video about the harassment and bullying they were subjected to as youth and about their adult familial and economic successes.[2] Savage and Miller uploaded the video to YouTube on September 21, 2010, and invited LGBTQ adults to contribute similar user-generated messages of hope.[3] Setting an initial goal of 100 messages, they received more than 1,000 videos in one week's time, exceeding the channel's limits and prompting YouTube engineer Carol Chen to hack into the mainframe and allot them more space.[4] Logistical constraints necessitated the launch of itgetsbetter.org on October 6, 2010, to accommodate the flood of submissions,[5] and soon after the IGBP registered as a 501(c)3 nonprofit organization.

Since inception, "celebrities, organizations, activists, politicians, media personalities," and non-famous LGBTQ individuals and allies alike have contributed more than 50,000 videos.[6] The IGBP's breadth extends far beyond the original YouTube channel to include a multiplatform traditional and social media presence (BETTERMedia), legal support services (BETTERLegal), and merchandise.[7] Additionally, the IGBP has spawned other LGBTQ-centric social change projects, including the "Make it Better Project"[8] and "Not All Like That"[9].

IT GETS BETTER: Elder Rev. Kevin E. Taylor (Black, Gay, Christian and Proud!)

Kevin E. Taylor

5,282

Figure 20.1
Screenshot taken 5/7/15 from "It Gets Better: Elder Rev. Kevin E. Taylor" on YouTube, http://bit.ly/1x4soAO.

It Gets Better: Kaali in New Jersey

Kaali

119 views

Figure 20.2
Screenshot taken 5/7/15 from "It Gets Better: Kaali in New Jersey" on YouTube, http://bit.ly/1IjMwHr.

It Gets Better - Thomas in Ypsilanti Michigan

tproa

Subscribe 2

293 views

Figure 20.3
Screenshot taken 5/7/15 from "It Gets Better: Thomas in Ypsilanti Michigan" on YouTube, http://bit.ly/1bATbOY.

It Gets Better - Portland, ME - Jill B.

PortlandPhoenix

Subscribe 29

1,295

Figure 20.4
Screenshot taken 5/7/15 from "It Gets Better: Portland, ME—Jill B." on YouTube, http://bit.ly/1RgTqzT.

The IGBP as Contemporary Civic Engagement

Online participatory culture researchers have found that individuals' motivations for civic participation are varied and multifaceted,[10] and IGBP video contributors reported doing so because of viewer camaraderie, desires for rectification, determination to broaden LGBTQ media representation, and the ease of participating in the project.[11] The timeless quest for civic engagement takes both new and reimagined forms, and digital technologies such as YouTube continue facilitating more efficient global participation and engagement in activities once hindered by temporal, spatial, and other barriers to entry. Nevertheless, it is important to critically examine why the IGBP has been so successful in mobilizing citizens when most online-based social change initiatives routinely fail to garner substantial initial and/or long-term support.

As a long-time contributor to Seattle's alternative newspaper *The Stranger*, Savage is a vocal—and controversial—activist with media access not afforded to most. Accordingly, Savage was able to use his celebrity status to solicit others' support and action when launching the IGBP. Rather than embark on a K–12 school speaking tour to combat LGBTQ youth bullying and suicide, Savage opted to broadcast his message via a platform youth regularly use—YouTube[12]—igniting what would soon become an extensive compilation of videos from diverse voices worldwide.[13] Unsolicited celebrity backing bolstered the IGBP early on, and the nonprofit organization strategically used mainstream media outlets and maximized corporate support to draw public attention to the issue.

LGBTQ harassment and bullying remain pervasive problems in the U.S.: Among 13–21-year-old LGBTQ-identified middle and high school students, approximately 74 percent report being verbally harassed; 36 percent physically harassed; and 17 percent physically assaulted.[14] Moreover, Centers for Disease Control and Prevention (CDC) research showed that suicide is one of the top three leading causes of death among 10–34-year-olds,[15] and LGB-identified youth are "four times more likely to attempt suicide as their straight peers."[16] While this epidemic and related interdisciplinary scholarly research on LGBTQ suicide are not new,[17] in-depth international media coverage of it is a more recent development.

Media coverage is intimately tied to U.S. cultural shifts pertaining to LGBTQ individuals, including public figures' highly publicized coming out stories, same-sex marriage legislation, and the repeal of "Don't Ask, Don't Tell." All topics received extensive media attention within the last decade, and according to Gallup, U.S. citizens' tolerance of lesbian and gay individuals has never been higher.[18] In addition to garnering international media coverage of LGBTQ harassment, bullying, and suicide, the IGBP was bolstered by corporate support from YouTube's parent company. Google officially sanctioned the IGBP one month after its launch; made a $50,000 contribution to IGBP benefactor The Trevor Project;[19] and partnered with ad agency Bartle Bogle Hegarty (BBH) to develop and nationally broadcast a commercial spotlighting the IGBP.[20]

Undoubtedly, civic awareness of and citizen engagement with the IGBP were strengthened by mainstream media coverage and corporate buy-ins. Additionally, the nonprofit organization has strategically planned for its future through the marriage of numerous online and offline ventures, and Savage intends to make the IGBP a long-term resource for youth.[21] Amid early criticisms of his video and the project overall, Savage stated that his overarching goal was for the IGBP to be a vehicle for nationwide LGBTQ policy change amid ongoing battles for equal rights.[22]

While battles for safe school legislation and LGBTQ equality are ongoing, the Webby award–winning IGBP has facilitated meaningful online and offline civic participation and contribution to U.S. political action.[23] President Obama's administration declared LGBTQ equality a focal point of international policy on December 6, 2011,[24] bolstered by White House–led anti-bullying conferences, summits, panels, and workshops;[25] Presidential endorsement of the Student Non-Discrimination & Safe Schools Improvement Acts;[26] and former Secretary of State Hillary Clinton's United Nations proclamation that "gay rights are human rights."[27] Although federal LGBTQ-inclusive anti-bullying policies still do not exist, local and state policies have multiplied since the IGBP's inception.[28] While causality between the IGBP's development and an increase in LGBTQ-inclusive anti-bullying policies has not been proven, the momentum for civic engagement and social change that the project fostered certainly contributed to the lengthy process of bills becoming laws. Thus, the IGBP has lived up to journalistic labeling as "a new kind of activism," unquestionably serving as a contemporary model of civic participation.[29]

Notes

1. See theStranger.com for information about columnist Dan Savage, www.thestranger.com/authors/259/dan-savage.

2. "It Gets Better: Dan and Terry," YouTube, September 21, 2010, http://bit.ly/1rGvdFY.

3. Dan Savage, "Give 'em Hope," *The Stranger*, September 24, 2010, www.thestranger.com/seattle/SavageLove?oid=4940874.

4. Laurie Phillips Honda, "It Was a Matter of Life and Death: A YouTube Engineer's Decision to Alter Data in the 'It Gets Better Project,'" Data & Society, 2016.

5. "A New Website and a New Partnership for It Gets Better," *Blue State Digital* (blog), October 9, 2010, www.bluestatedigital.com/news/entry/a-new-website-and-new-partnership-for-it-gets-better.

6. "About the It Gets Better Project," ItGetsBetter.org, accessed October 1, 2014, http://www.itgetsbetter.org/pages/about-it-gets-better-project.

7. See "About the It Gets Better Project" for more information.

8. "About," MakeItBetterProject.org, accessed June 13, 2014, http://bit.ly/1E4dhJd.

9. "About the NALT Christians Project," NotAllLikeThat.org, accessed June 13, 2014, http://www.notalllikethat.org/about/.

10. Daren C. Brabham, *Crowdsourcing* (Cambridge, MA: MIT Press, 2013); Henry Jenkins, *Convergence Culture: Where Old and New Media Collide* (New York: New York University Press, 2006); Clay Shirky, *Cognitive Surplus: Creativity and Generosity in a Connected Age* (New York: Penguin Press, 2010); Howard Rheingold, *Smart Mobs: The Next Social Revolution* (Cambridge, MA: Perseus, 2002).

11. Laurie M. Phillips, "A Multi-method Examination of Race, Class, Gender, Sexual Orientation, and Motivations for Participation in the YouTube-based 'It Gets Better Project'" (doctoral dissertation, University of North Carolina at Chapel Hill, 2013).

12. Kristen Purcell, "Teens 2012: Truth, Trends, and Myths about Teen Online Behavior," *PewInternet.org*, July 11, 2012, http://www.pewinternet.org/2012/07/11/teens-2012-truth-trends-and-myths-about-teen-online-behavior/.

13. Mary Louise Kelly and Melissa Block, "Dan Savage's Message to Gay Youth: 'It Gets Better,'" *NPR*, October 12, 2010, http://www.npr.org/templates/story/story.php?storyId=130519806.

14. Joseph G. Kosciw, Emily A. Greytak, Neal A. Palmer, and Madelyn J. Boesen, "2013 National School Climate Survey," GLSEN.org, 2014, http://www.glsen.org/article/2013-national-school-climate-survey; see also "Playgrounds and Prejudice: Elementary School Climate in the United States," GLSEN.org, 2012, http://www.glsen.org/article/lgbt-issues-elementary-schools.

15. "Ten Leading Causes of Death and Injury," CDC.gov, accessed June 13, 2014, http://www.cdc.gov/injury/wisqars/leadingcauses.html.

16. "Facts about Suicide," TrevorProject.org, accessed June 13, 2014, http://www.thetrevorproject.org/pages/facts-about-suicide; see also Laura Kann, Emily O'Malley Olsen, Tim McManus, Steve Kinchen, David Chyen, William A. Harris, and Howell Wechsler, "Sexual Identity, Sex of Sexual Contacts, and Health-Risk Behaviors among Students in Grades 9–12—Youth Risk Behavior Surveillance, Selected Sites, United States, 2001–2009," CDC.gov, June 10, 2011, http://www.cdc.gov/mmwr/preview/mmwrhtml/ss6007a1.htm?s_cid=ss6007a1_w.

17. Anthony R. D'Augelli and Scott L. Hershberger, "Lesbian, Gay, and Bisexual Youth in Community Settings: Personal Challenges and Mental Health Problems," *American Journal of Community Psychology* 21, no. 4 (1993): 421–448; Mickey Eliason, "Introduction to Special Issue on

Suicide, Mental Health, and Youth Development," *Journal of Homosexuality* 58, no. 1 (2010): 4–9; Ann P. Haas, Mickey Eliason, Vickie M. Mays, Robin M. Mathy, Susan D. Cochran, Anthony R. D'Augelli, Morton M. Silverman, Prudence W. Fisher, Tonda Hughes, Margaret Rosario, Stephen T. Russell, Effie Malley, Jerry Reed, David A. Litts, Ellen Haller, Randall L. Sell, Gary Remafedi, Judith Bradford, Annette L. Beautrais, Gregory K. Brown, Gary M. Diamond, Mark S. Friedman, Robert Garofalo, Mason S. Turner, Amber Hollibaughy, and Paula J. Clayton, "Suicide and Suicide Risk in Lesbian, Gay, Bisexual, and Transgender Populations: Review and Recommendations," *Journal of Homosexuality* 58, no. 1 (2010): 10–51; Heather E. Murphy, "Suicide Risk among Gay, Lesbian, and Bisexual College Youth" (doctoral dissertation, University of Washington, 2007); Yue Zhao, Richard Montoro, Karine Igartua, and Brett D. Thombs, "Suicidal Ideation and Attempt among Adolescents Reporting 'Unsure' Sexual Identity or Heterosexual Identity Plus Same-sex Attraction or Behavior: Forgotten Groups?," *Journal of the American Academy of Child & Adolescent Psychiatry* 49, no. 2 (2010): 104–113.

18. Rebecca Riffkin, "New Record Highs in Moral Acceptability," Gallup.com, last modified May 30, 2014, http://www.gallup.com/poll/170789/new-record-highs-moral-acceptability.aspx.

19. Megan Smith and Laszlo Bock, "Working to Stop Bullying, National Ally Week and Navigating Online LGBTQ Resources," Google (blog), October 22, 2010, http://googleblog.blogspot.com/2010/10/working-to-stop-bullying-national-ally.html.

20. Claire Cain Miller, "Google Takes to TV to Promote Browser," *NYTimes.com*, May 3, 2011, http://www.nytimes.com/2011/05/04/technology/04chrome.html?_r=1.The video can be seen here: http://bit.ly/1t9ENOP.

21. Dan Savage, "Dan Savage at the UNC Memorial Hall," (presentation, University of North Carolina, Chapel Hill, NC, February 2, 2012).

22. Dan Savage, "Welcome to the It Gets Better Project," It Gets Better Project (blog), October 7, 2010, http://www.itgetsbetter.org/blog/entry/welcome-to-the-it-gets-better-project/.

23. Max Gouttebroze, "Webby Awards to Honor Dan Savage for It Gets Better Project," GLAAD.org, June 13, 2011, http://www.glaad.org/2011/06/13/webby-awards-to-honor-dan-savage-for-it-gets-better-project.

24. Office of the Press Secretary, "Presidential Memorandum—International Initiatives to Advance the Human Rights of Lesbian, Gay, Bisexual, and Transgender Persons," WhiteHouse.gov, December 6, 2011, https://www.whitehouse.gov/the-press-office/2011/12/06/presidential-memorandum-international-initiatives-advance-human-rights-l.

25. Jesse Lee, "President Obama & the First Lady at the White House Conference on Bullying Prevention," WhiteHouse.gov (blog), March 10, 2011, https://www.whitehouse.gov/blog/2011/03/10/president-obama-first-lady-white-house-conference-bullying-prevention.

26. "President Obama Endorses Critical Safe Schools Bills," Human Rights Campaign (press release), April 20, 2012, http://www.hrc.org/press-releases/entry/president-obama-endorses-critical-safe-schools-bills.

27. Igor Volsky and Zack Ford, "Secretary Clinton to UN: 'Gay Rights are Human Rights, and Human Rights are Gay Rights,'" ThinkProgress.org, December 6, 2011, http://thinkprogress.org/lgbt/2011/12/06/383003/%20sec-clinton-to-un-gay-rights-are-human-rights-and-human-rights-are-gay-rights/.

28. See "About the It Gets Better Project," http://www.itgetsbetter.org/pages/about-it-gets-better-project/.

29. Peter Mongillo, "It Gets Better Project Takes Off via Social Media," *Austin American-Statesman*, October 25, 2010, http://www.statesman.com/news/lifestyles/it-gets-better-project-takes-off-via-social-media/nRy3K.

21   Case Study: Terra Incognita—Serendipity and Discovery in the Age of Personalization

Catherine D'Ignazio

This case study describes "Terra Incognita: 1000 Cities of the World," a serendipitous global news recommendation system designed to help people out of their personalized media filter bubbles.

As Herbert Simon argued in his prescient 1969 essay, "A wealth of information creates a scarcity of attention."[1] In a world of hundreds of cable channels, free news dailies, personalized websites, algorithmically curated feeds, and interactive apps, how do people—with limited attention—fulfill their information needs? And what are the public repercussions for personal media decisions, particularly in relationship to our notions of "the informed citizen" in a representative democracy?

Numerous critics have articulated concerns about the shifting media landscape and its potential impact on informed decision making. Algorithms may suppress content that corporations have decided an individual will not like.[2] Individuals may self-select only information that is agreeable to them and end up in informational gated communities,[3] a phenomenon known as "selective exposure." Our tendency toward homophily—seeking out people like us—is as true in cyberspace as it is in face-to-face interactions.[4] The scholarship investigating these concerns is not conclusive. While there is some support for the idea that we tweet and blog in echo chambers,[5,6,7] particularly in relationship to partisan politics,[8,9] other studies show that our online interactions are actually more diverse than our offline interactions.[10,11] What is true is that the work of gate keeping and agenda setting in a "high-choice"[12] media environment increasingly rests on the individual and her social networks. While we may imagine ourselves to be cosmopolitan, our news increasingly comes from what we directly seek through search, curate through feeds, and find through friends.[13]

Isn't There an App for That?

At the end of his book *Rewire*, Ethan Zuckerman introduces the provocative idea of *engineering serendipity* as a possible way to encounter information that we otherwise wouldn't. Unintended information encountering happens regularly in online

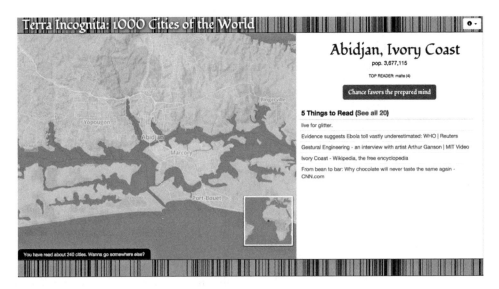

Figure 21.1
The main screen for Terra Incognita. Each new browser window the user opens shows a new city.

environments.[14] But can we intentionally design information systems to introduce us to new information outside what we know we want or what our social networks offer up?

Terra Incognita: 1000 Cities of the World is a speculative design intervention that took up this challenge in relation to the geographic diversity of information an individual reads. The central conceit is the term *terra incognita,* which was used on maps in the Age of Discovery to denote unexplored territories. It's a perspectival term. Because, of course, there were people like the Tupinambá actually living in those seemingly unexplored lands on Martin Waldseemüller's map (above). The places the Tupinambá knew intimately—where they fished or hunted or celebrated or slept—were not terra incognita to them. But to the Europeans embarking on their voyages, each new cove or settlement was a curve or mark to be made on a map, a way of demarcating the limits of their peoples' understanding. And, in a way, the main goal of Terra Incognita: 1000 Cities of the World is the same: to introduce the user to the vastness of the world that is unknown to them through making news recommendations about the top 1,000 most populous global cities.

The main user experience of Terra Incognita is an intervention into your Internet browsing experience. Technically, it is an extension for the Chrome browser which you can download from the Chrome Web Store.

Once installed, Terra Incognita becomes the default screen for every new browser window you open. Each time you open a new tab, Terra Incognita shows you a city that

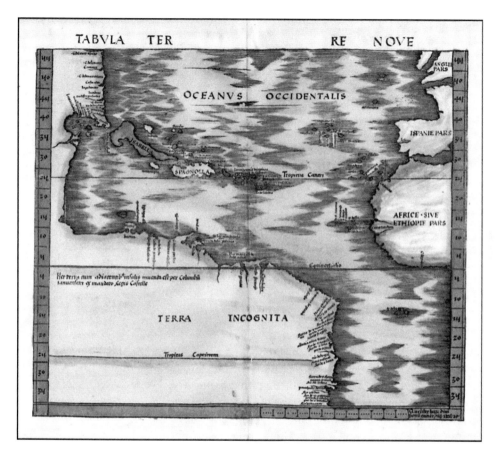

Figure 21.2
"Terra Nova" (the Americas), by Martin Waldseemüller, 1513.

you have not yet read about and gives you options for reading about it. Chelyabinsk (Russia), Hiroshima (Japan), Belo Horizonte (Brazil), and Abidjan (Ivory Coast) are a few of the places where you might end up.

You can click to read a news recommendation or take your chances with the big red button, which will take you to a news story drawn by chance. In the interface you can also see which of the 1,000 cities you have read about and navigate to other cities through the bar on the bottom. There are some lightweight social features, including a call-out for which user in the system has read the most about that city and a count for how many cities the user has read about.

Terra Incognita presents news recommendations for each city from a variety of sources, including stories other users in the system have read, stories trending online

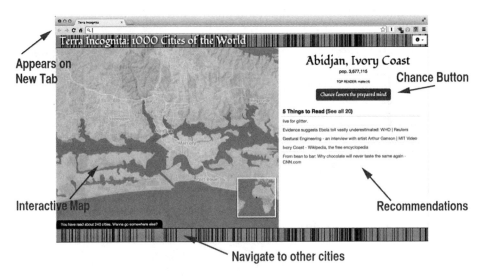

Figure 21.3
The main screen for Terra Incognita (annotated).

for that place, stories specifically retrieved from the Global Voices community, stories we crowdsourced through an open call, and stories sourced from Instapaper[15] saves. Even with these multiple sources of recommendations there were many blank spots in the recommendation system that we had to address. For example, China accounts for about 20 percent (or 200) of the cities in Terra Incognita, but there was very little information in English about many medium-sized Chinese cities available through our recommendation channels. In this case, we worked with Chunhua Zhang, a media scholar from China, to manually compile a list of English-language news sources by city.

Findings

From May 2014 to July 2014 we ran a user study with 170 users that examined their global news browsing patterns prior to using Terra Incognita and after using Terra Incognita. We surveyed users about their transnational ties and attitudes toward global news, collected both qualitative and quantitative data, and found some interesting results:

1. While Terra Incognita did not shift the aggregate diversity of users' reading it was a positive micro-learning and reflection experience for the majority of users.
Though the app may not have shifted user behavior in aggregate, the vast majority of users (87.5 percent) say that they learned about a new place from Terra Incognita. Most users clicked at least 5 recommendations and 43 percent shared a recommendation

that they found through Terra Incognita. Most of them (63 percent) think that Terra Incognita prompted them to reflect on the geography of their news reading. It broadened users' horizons, piqued their curiosity, and helped some feel "more connected" to unknown places. "It was a constant reminder that there's a larger world than my screen" (User 3).

2. Users with more transnational ties read more diverse geographic information.

We surveyed users with the Transnationality Index developed by Mau, Mewes, and Zimmerman[16] which assesses people's transnational social ties and personal experiences, and found that for every 10 percent increase in an individual's score on the index, the user showed a 2 percent increase in geographic diversity of reading. This is a finding that confirms an intuitive assumption (people with global experiences will read globally). This could be leveraged in future designs that combine online and offline transnational encounters as we discuss below.

Conclusion

We offer several takeaways extrapolated from these findings that may inform the design of information diversity technologies. While the user study was originally conceived to examine behavior shift in reading patterns, Terra Incognita did not magically shift all users into reading more about Chelyabinsk, Hiroshima, Belo Horizonte, and Abidjan. Moreover, it was unrealistic to have behavior change expectations for such a modest insertion into users' daily information routine. What it did do is provide small, repeated opportunities for people to engage with unknown places. For many users, the value of the experience was in enlarging their sense of what they don't know. "I found myself wondering about parts of the world (China!!) that I don't usually think of in much depth" (User 47).

So rather than starting with narrow, quantitatively based metrics for success, it may be useful to see encounters with the unknown as a process that stretches from awareness to curiosity to engagement to aggregate behavior shift. Design goals and metrics may be devised for one or more of these stages and scaled appropriately to the scale of the intervention. In the case of Terra Incognita, by design a small and easily ignorable disruption, the tool was most effective at raising awareness of unknown places and at piquing the curiosity of users. There is more work to be done to explore exactly how best to achieve design goals at each of these stages and when is the opportune moment for introducing new information. Here we may look to the fields of persuasive technology and public relations for deep and possibly creepy sources of insight into media messages, technology, and human behavior.

Additionally, we see design implications for the finding that correlates an individual's transnationality index with more diverse reading habits. This finding supports the common sense idea that people who have traveled abroad, lived abroad, and/or have friends and family in far-flung locations read about more places. Given that an individual's life experience and the spatial configuration of their loved ones matters so much to the geography of the media they consume (accounting for 16 percent of the variation in the geographic diversity of their reading), it seems wise to consider how to architect offline encounters as well as informational experiences. Face-to-face social encounters with geographic difference need not entail traveling to a foreign country. For example, Conflict Kitchen invites hungry people in Pittsburgh, PA, to eat takeout food from places the US is in conflict with.[17] Food wrappers are printed with first-person stories and interviews. WATCH CDC, a community development corporation in my hometown of Waltham, MA, hosts an annual event called "The Immigrant Experience" that introduces the local community to new members through storytelling and potluck dinner.[18] Combining information delivery with face-to-face social encounters that produce reasons to care and be curious about the world seems like a particularly fruitful next avenue of inquiry.

Try It Out

Download Terra Incognita: 1000 Cities of the World from the Chrome Web Store. Currently only available for the Chrome browser. Terra Incognita was designed and implemented by Catherine D'Ignazio with contributions from Ethan Zuckerman and Matt Stempeck.

Notes

1. Herbert A. Simon, "Designing Organizations for an Information-Rich World," 1969, in *The Economics of Communication and Information*, ed. Donald M. Lamberton (Elgar Reference Collection, International Library of Critical Writings in Economics, vol. 70, 1996), 187–202.

2. Eli Pariser, *The Filter Bubble: How the New Personalized Web Is Changing What We Read and How We Think* (New York: Penguin Books, 2012).

3. C. R. Sunstein, *Republic.com* (Princeton, NJ: Princeton University Press, 2002).

4. E. Zuckerman, *Rewire: Digital Cosmopolitans in the Age of Connection* (New York: W. W. Norton & Company, 2013).

5. D. Schkade, C. R. Sunstein, and R. Hastie, "What Happened on Deliberation Day?," *California Law Review*, 95(3), 2007, 915–940.

6. Beth Simone Noveck, "Paradoxical Partners: Electronic Communication and Electronic Democracy," *Democratization* 7, no. 1 (2000): 18–35, doi:10.1080/13510340008403643.

7. William A. Galston, "If Political Fragmentation Is the Problem, Is the Internet the Solution?," in *The Civic Web: Online Politics and Democratic Values,* ed. David M. Anderson and Michael Cornfield (Oxford: Rowman & Littlefield Publishers, Inc., 2003), 35–44.

8. Lada A. Adamic and Natalie Glance, "The Political Blogosphere and the 2004 U.S. Election: Divided They Blog," in *Proceedings of the 3rd International Workshop on Link Discovery,* LinkKDD '05 (New York: ACM, 2005), 36–43, doi:10.1145/1134271.1134277.

9. Bruce Allen Bimber and Richard Davis, *Campaigning Online: The Internet in U.S. Elections* (New York: Oxford University Press, 2003).

10. M. Gentzkow and J. M. Shapiro, "Ideological Segregation Online and Offline (NBER Working Paper No. 15916)," National Bureau of Economic Research, 2010. http://www.nber.org/papers/w15916.

11. Keith Hampton, Lauren Sessions Goulet, Eun Ja Her, and Lee Rainie, "Social Isolation and New Technology," Pew Research Center, November 4, 2009, http://www.pewinternet.org/2009/11/04/social-isolation-and-new-technology.

12. Markus Prior, *Post-Broadcast Democracy: How Media Choice Increases Inequality in Political Involvement and Polarizes Elections* (New York : Cambridge University Press, 2007).

13. Kristen Purcell, Lee Rainie, Amy Mitchell, Tom Rosentiel, and Kenny Olmstead, "Understanding the Participatory News Consumer," Pew Research Center's Internet & American Life Project, March 1, 2010, http://www.pewinternet.org/2010/03/01/understanding-the-participatory-news-consumer.

14. Sanda Erdelez, "Investigation of Information Encountering in the Controlled Research Environment," *Information Processing and Management* 40, no. 6 (November 2004): 1013–1025, doi:10.1016/j.ipm.2004.02.002.

15. Instapaper is a "read it later" service. Articles saved by Instapaper users tend to be longer. Our hypothesis here is that longer articles already saved by others can be used as a signal for higher quality.

16. Steffen Mau, Jan Mewes, and Ann Zimmermann, "Cosmopolitan Attitudes through Transnational Social Practices?," *Global Networks* 8, no. 1 (January 1, 2008): 1–24, doi:10.1111/j.1471-0374.2008.00183.x.

17. Conflict Kitchen, http://conflictkitchen.org.

18. WATCH CDC, flyer for "The Immigrant Experience Potluck Dinner and Discussion," December 4, 2014, http://watchcdc.org/images/pdfs/breaking_barrier_flyer.pdf.

22 Case Study: Innovation in the Absence of a State—Civic Media and the Inclusion of the Marginalized in the Somali Territories

Nicole Stremlau

Somalia is often described as "lawless" and the world's worst "failed state." Twenty years of continued violent conflict has left a legacy of destruction, crumbling infrastructure, and a lack of formal government institutions. This absence of regulation and of a formal economic system has also given rise to the piracy, shadow networks, and vibrant trade that have become characteristic of Somalia's surprisingly functional informal economy. Despite significant interventions and efforts by the international community, by the UN in particular, to create and implement structures of governance, from the presidency to the army, most initiatives remain largely symbolic. The Federal government's authority does not extend far beyond the capital city of Mogadishu, with the rest of the Somali territories controlled and governed by a patchwork of forces. These groups include the al-Qaeda–allied Islamist group Al Shabaab in south-central Somalia; the self-governing state of Puntland, and its northern neighbor, Somaliland, which is actively seeking independence partly by virtue that it has its own governance institutions and is largely stable, peaceful, and relatively democratic.

In this varied political and economic context there has been a fascinating experiment—the growth of a vibrant Information Communications Technology (ICT) sector despite the absence of a legal and regulatory environment, and without the state institutions and framework that would normally support the development of such media.[1] The growth of this sector has leveraged social networks, particularly with the diaspora, and has helped develop services that would normally be provided by the government or formal institutions. Private companies have proliferated, providing telecommunications and Internet infrastructure and creating products uniquely suited to the Somali context. Given the complexity of operating in such a varied political environment, and with pressing security concerns, investment has been led almost exclusively by Somalis, both from the diaspora and within the country. This is a substantially different environment than telecommunications in countries across the rest of the continent, which have been dominated by multinational companies such as India's Bharti Telecom or France's Orange.

While many parts of the ICT sector have experienced significant growth, from phone-in radio shows to Internet cafés, one of the most innovative platforms to emerge has been mobile money, a service that is accessible through mobile phones and allows customers to send and receive money, or even in the case of Somaliland, hold money in e-wallets. Kenya has the most vibrant mobile money market on the planet with almost 70 percent of adults using their mobiles for payments, while Somalia and Uganda are close behind.[2] Mobile money has become a crucial tool for poor people that do not have access to bank accounts and are excluded from the global and national economies.[3]

With the proliferation of cell phones in Somalia and across the continent, mobile money has become an important tool for civic engagement. The study of civic media, which looks at citizen involvement through new forms of technology and media, has tended to overlook what media usage looks like in informal, and often highly unstable, contexts. Cell phones in Somalia are a way to manage finances, connect with community, and access information. Similar to the well-known M-Pesa in neighboring Kenya, mobile money in Somalia has grown to occupy a central role in increasing citizen participation and inclusion in the local and international economies. It has, however, taken on very local characteristics and has also adapted to the particularities of the Somali context.

Somalia may lack a formal banking system but the dynamic *hawalah* (money transfer) system that has developed provides many financial services, including facilitating the flow of an estimated 1.6 billion USD in remittances from the diaspora, making this transfer method one of the most important contributors to the country's GDP.[4] The remittance industry, in partnership with a relatively inexpensive yet strong telecommunications network, much of which they own, has encouraged the growth of the mobile money sector. Hormuud, known as Telesom in Somaliland and as Golis Telecom in Puntland, has the market share through the remittance company Zaad payment system, which allows users to pay for items in shops (including informal markets), transfer money, and pay bills. It has even been adopted by some institutions to manage payrolls; for example, Amoud University, one of Somaliland's leading institutions, not only accepts course fees using mobile phone payments but also pays its hundreds of employees with Zaad.

Zaad's more comprehensive approach to mobile money and banking has, along with its competitors both contemporary and aspirational, encouraged the move to a more cashless economy. While M-Pesa has tended to focus on person-to-person payments, mobile money in Somalia has filled a more traditional banking need. Somalis use mobile money as e-wallets, holding money in the system and saving it securely for larger purchases or transfers, in essence acting as a bank account. It has been further adapted to the Somali context in that it is free for all users, in contrast with other mobile money companies that are more commonly fee based. Furthermore, mobile money in Somalia functions in USD rather than Somali (or Somaliland) shillings, the effects of which are not always considered positive. While USD has always been a major currency in the Somali territories, its growing use through Zaad has also been seen to encourage inflation and penalize civil servants who are among those primarily paid in local currency.[5]

The growth of mobile money has been completely reliant on local dispute resolution mechanisms, including customary (or *xeer*) law and networks of trust, which have both helped facilitate and support the remittance industry. This more bottom-up approach to innovation, whereby technology has succeeded in starting to address challenges of everyday governance and service delivery, is also an important lesson for the importance of taking a context-based approach to understanding innovation and the potential of new technologies to engage marginalized communities.

Notes

1. Nicole Stremlau, "Somalia Media Law in the Absence of a State."

2. Claire Penicaud and Fionan McGrath, "Innovative Inclusion: How Telesom ZAAD Brought Mobile Money to Somaliland," Mobile Money for the Unbanked, 2013, http://www.gsma.com/mobilefordevelopment/wp-content/uploads/2013/07/Telesom-Somaliland.pdf.

3. Ibid.

4. Central Intelligence Agency, "Somalia Country Page," *CIA World Factbook*.

5. Gianluca Iazzolino, "Somaliland Has Embraced Mobile Money—but at What Price?,"

References

Central Intelligence Agency. 2015. "Somalia Country Page." *CIA World Factbook*. https://www.cia.gov/library/publications/the-world-factbook/geos/so.html.

Iazzolino, Gianluca. 2014. "Somaliland Has Embraced Mobile Money—but at What Price?" *The Guardian Online,* May 19. http://www.theguardian.com/global-development/2014/may/19/somaliland-mobile-money-zaad-inflation-economy-banking-remittance.

Stremlau, Nicole. "Somalia Media Law in the Absence of a State." 2012. *Journal of Media and Cultural Politics* , 8 (2), 159–174.

IV Learning + Engagement

23 Capitalists, Consumers, and Communicators: How Schools Approach Civic Education

Renee Hobbs

The ability to listen to others and express oneself is fundamental to the practice of democracy because effective communication skills are the building blocks of civic competence. Today there is renewed interest in how young people acquire the ability to investigate the problems in their communities, neighborhoods, and world, circulate information, spark dialogue, produce content, and prod others to take action (Soep 2014). Scholars have offered significant documentation of the ways in which new media can support participatory politics and the practice of civic engagement (Kahne, Middaugh, and Allen 2014). Programs that encourage youth civic engagement have generally occurred in non-school settings, through youth media programs in nonprofit organizations and libraries.

Sadly however, U.S. educational reforms of the past 20 years have generally not encouraged youth to be active participants in the civic life of their communities. Civics has not been part of the "Race to the Top" testing regime that emphasizes academic improvement in English language arts and mathematics (Reich 2012). Indeed, the Common Core, with its focus on close reading "without attention to the identities of students and the context in which texts are written," may even trivialize what it means to learn how to be a citizen in contemporary democracy and push the purpose of education toward individual economic competitiveness and away from preparation for citizenship in a democracy (Strauss 2014, 1).

In U.S. secondary schools, as in most other nations, civics is traditionally taught as a content-focused curriculum. When most Americans remember their own experiences with civic education, they recall learning about the three branches of government, how a bill becomes law, and the role of regulatory agencies. They recall student government elections that mirror the popularity contests of electing a homecoming king and queen. If a school newspaper existed, it printed generally inoffensive stories on the wins and losses of the school's athletic program and profiles of new teachers. Unfortunately, this portrait still accurately captures what civic education is like in many American schools.

But in a small but increasing number of schools, programs that connect the classroom to the culture are on the rise. In addition, digital media and technology are creating opportunities for civic education to undergo a transformation that enables students—in and out of school—to discover how to use the power of information and communication to make a difference in the world. In this chapter, I frame up the practice of civic education in U.S. schools by briefly considering its historical and educational context and then by examining the positioning of young people in relation to three forms of civic agency: as capitalists, as consumers of news and information, and as communicators with stories to tell. I will show that although all three approaches do increase the perceived relevance of schooling in ways that support some fundamental practices of contemporary civil society, there are important gaps and blind spots that challenge educators to advance genuine civic education in a digital age.

Civic Education in Schools

Although theoretically education has long been understood as a form of empowerment, helping people move away from complacency and toward active citizenship in a democracy (Dewey 1927), the reality of American public education is more rooted in the model of the factory, where large groups of students are prepared for the workplace through a series of sorting and winnowing practices tied to social class, racial identity, and performance on standardized tests. However, school reform initiatives occurring at various times throughout the twentieth century have helped the American public to recognize how the activities that happen in schools shape the practice of democracy. Today, many young people in both high school and college get civic learning that includes the practice of open discussion, participation in passionate debates, and practices of service learning and community activism. Participation in collaborative, real-world projects reveals the power of small but meaningful civic actions to transform personal, social, and civic identity.

In some schools, teachers themselves have developed innovative approaches to connect technology, media, and civic engagement. For example, in Montgomery Blair High School in Silver Spring, Maryland, a media literacy initiative, the Communication Arts Program (CAP) has been in place for more than 20 years, offering a select group of students multi-faceted opportunities to develop voice and agency through media literacy activities, including the school newspaper, video production program, and rich civic education curriculum that includes plenty of real-world learning opportunities that address civic issues. Quasi-experimental research shows that participation in this media literacy program is associated with higher levels of civic engagement (Martens and Hobbs 2015).

Thanks to generous funding from technology firms like Mozilla and philanthropies like the McArthur Foundation, in some urban schools, public school students have the opportunity to participate in after-school programs in digital media. One organization, Global Kids, works in several dozen schools to bring digital media and civic engagement programs to learners. Global Kids trains urban youth to become critical thinkers, media producers, and global citizens by developing their film production and leadership skills. Teens learn skills such as storyboarding, script writing, and acting to create socially conscious, original stories and produce their own films on topics like child soldiers in Uganda, access to education, and sex trafficking.

In still other schools, high school students may use project-based learning curricula like Project Citizen, created by the Center for Civic Education, where students use discussion to identify a problem in their community, conduct research, and monitor and influence public policy in their communities. Such programs have been measurably effective, as quasi-experimental field research with a matched control group showed that such a process enables students to develop persuasive writing skills, gain knowledge of public policy, and activate problem-solving skills (Root and Northup 2007).

But despite these impressive examples, most educators would agree that these practices are not yet normative. Instead, in most American schools, we would find a teacher lecturing about history or government, with students sitting, listening, and taking notes. Perhaps students will be watching a video or taking a multiple-choice test. Because the general pedagogy of many social studies classes is based on a teacher-centered transmission model of education, a knowledge-based focus still offers "dry portrayals of the formal structure of our federal government, charts on how a bill becomes law, and sometimes idealized portraits of the heroes of our political history" (Quigley 1999, 1), all presented with PowerPoints and lectures by someone who knows more to fill up the heads of those who know less.

While many teachers recognize the value of using student-centered learning approaches, they work in institutional contexts with a variety of structural features that may limit and challenge their work. Approaches to civic education that emphasize inquiry, collaboration, reasoning, and problem solving have faced substantial resistance from school administrations, teachers, and community leaders for many years. Back in the 1940s, for example, Harold Rugg's innovative and popular textbook, *Man and His Changing Society*, was attacked for espousing socialist values. Fifty years later, in 1994, the U.S. Congress voted 99–1 to reject the National History Standards developed by the National Center for History in the Schools on the grounds that they were too critical of American government and political institutions (Rubin 2012).. Although the National Council for the Social Studies (NCSS) has embraced progressive concepts including experiential education, media literacy, and project-based learning, such work is only slowly gaining traction as part of the civic education curriculum in most schools.

The impact of a content-centered pedagogy is all too evident in the results of the National Assessment of Educational Progress (NAEP), which measures civic knowledge, intellectual skills, and civic dispositions. Students at Grade 4 are expected to be able to recognize that taxes are the main source of funding for government, identify a purpose of the U.S. Constitution, and explain two ways that countries can deal with shared problems. At Grade 8, students are expected to know some of the rights protected by the First Amendment, recognize a role performed by the Supreme Court, and name two actions that citizens can take to encourage Congress to pass a law. At Grade 12, students are expected to be able to interpret a political cartoon and define the term "melting pot" and argue whether it applies to the U.S. They are expected to compare the citizenship requirements of the U.S. to other countries. As measured by these tests, American students fail to demonstrate good understanding of civics. In 2010, test scores showed that only 25 percent of American fourth, eighth, and twelfth grade students were proficient in civics. Fifty percent of Grade 8 students could not correctly interpret a question that required the interpretation of a political cartoon. The NAEP tests also showed substantial disparities in civic knowledge between white students and minority students. Educators may attempt to shovel content knowledge into the minds of learners through lectures and textbook reading, but it does not seem to be effective. Many students graduate without a firm conceptual understanding of the legal, regulatory, and civic dimensions of being a citizen in a democracy.

There are many reasons for this. Throughout the twentieth century and until today, civic education has been a political football. Elites from all sectors aim to convey their own understanding of society and cultural values, and criticize the ideologies, content, methods, and approaches used by others to teach about civic life. In general, the content of textbooks is a source of continuing struggle (Loewen 1995).

Fortunately, innovative curriculum approaches to promoting citizenship in the context of social studies education have proved to be effective. One example is National History Day, where students create video documentaries, develop websites, conduct oral histories, and plan and execute community-based projects. Research comparing students who participated in the program to those who did not found students who participated are better writers, more confident and capable researchers, and have a more mature perspective on current events and civic engagement than their peers. Collaboration skills, time-management, and perseverance also are reported to be higher.

But such programs require deep investment by faculty (National History Day 2011). Because a social studies teacher may face as many as 150 students per week, innovative initiatives, when they do occur, take colossal reserves of teacher time and energy, and as a result, are sometimes tacked on to traditional curriculum approaches which tend to emphasize a chronological content focus to learning about government.

Sadly, it is an open question whether innovative teaching approaches like the ones described here can shift this longstanding tension about the content, pedagogy, and thematic focus of civic education curricula in American public education. Some conservatives have attempted to address some of the failures of civic education by identifying new problems, including American's generally low levels of knowledge about economics, banking. and finance. To be an effective worker *and* citizen, it is argued, young Americans need to be able to balance a checkbook, evaluate interest rates, and understand how money moves in a global economy.

Youth as Capitalists

Learning about capitalism is a key part of civic education because of the closely interconnected and overlapping relationship between the social roles of family member, worker, and citizen. For a growing international community of civic leaders, financial education, social education, career education, and financial inclusion are seen as the building blocks of personal and social empowerment. In a sense, being able to participate actively in the financial dimensions of capitalism underpins citizenship in Western democracies. Financial literacy is viewed as a life skill that supports individuals and institutions at the same time. As stated in the mission statement of Child and Youth Finance International, a Dutch NGO, "When children … experience financial inclusion, or real access to appropriate financial products and services along with the opportunity to practice using those services," they invest in their own futures (CYFI 2014).

In Britain and Canada, financial literacy is conceptualized as a strategy to help create self-sufficient citizens who do not need to rely on the welfare state and are thus not a burden to their fellow citizens. In the UK, a curriculum resource entitled "My Money: Citizenship Teacher Handbook" emphasizes self-sufficiency, charity, and ethical buying as elements of civic duty (Arthur 2012).

The rise of interest in financial literacy in the United States developed from an appreciation of its absence in the context of public school education. Although economics is offered as an elective course in some American high schools, social studies educators often feel unqualified to teach the practical business knowledge and competencies that directly relate to life skills, like opening up a checking account, balancing a budget, or getting a loan. Particularly in poor, minority, immigrant, and underserved communities with many non-working adults, adolescents may be unfamiliar with basic fiscal concepts that are part of everyday life for the children of middle-class workers. In 2012, the U.S. Financial Literacy and Education Commission gathered a group of experts to assess what is needed to improve the overall state of financial literacy among young people in the United States. They recognized the need to better understand the current state of financial literacy education, attitudes of educators and other stakeholders, and the impact of risk and financial shocks on the attitudes, beliefs, and behaviors of teens and young adults.

To be a citizen is to be aware of how all our fiscal choices, at both the micro- and macro-level, affect our short- and long-term quality of life. Today many adults are mired in debt; the employment situation is dire for teenagers and young adults, and the changing economics of higher education has had a dramatic influence on the financial situation of youth. Yet few efforts to promote civic agency include a focus on financial literacy. In the context of young people's identities as workers, consumers, and entrepreneurs, financial literacy is generally provided using a "stand and deliver" approach, where expert knowledge about best practices for spending, saving, and investing is offered to learners. Typical curricula include "Money Talks," which is a monthly newsletter targeting teens, who read and discuss the newsletter during class time.

Because financial literacy curricula are developed by members of the business community, they place great emphasis on framing up personal economic practices as fundamentally rational choices. There is little emphasis on providing critiques of capitalism or alternative framing that positions individual behavior within a larger global and structural economic context. Few programs make use of constructivist learning principles. Notably, educational and instructional strategies are described as "delivery systems" with focus on how media, including print and digital technology, could be used to deliver information and affect behaviors of learners.

Little emphasis is placed upon situating lessons about financial literacy in the context of the lived experience of the learner. Instead, information about cash flow, savings, and investment are provided but little attention is given to instructional strategies used to engage learner interests, build knowledge, and develop skills that connect to real life. Professionals in finance cannot be expected to understand the needs, interests, and capabilities of teens and young adults. Fortunately, there is a growing understanding of this problem. A review of leading financial literacy curricula emphasized the problems of pedagogy, noting the gap between providing information and providing education (Varcoe et al. 2005).

For these reasons, educational media, interactive games, and other approaches that engage students in project-based learning around financial literacy can be important sources of learning for children and young people. Some efforts to advance financial literacy through media and communication have been notable: Entrepreneur Ray Martinez's company, Ever-Fi has created financial literacy interactive programs where private industry, wealthy individuals, businesses, and foundations sponsor middle school and high school students to enroll in digital education programs where edu-tainment videogames introduce concepts like risk and reward, profit and loss. Students playing these interactive games get to practice balancing a checkbook, keeping track of credit card expenses, and deciding how best to finance a major purchase like a car. When the program rolled out in a summer program in Chicago in 2013, students learned about business fraud, personal finances, and banking, and were able to receive stipends for participating in the program, which was supported by a local bank.

Another initiative, *Biz Kid$*, is a PBS TV show about money and business, produced by the team who created *Bill Nye, the Science Guy*. Funded by a coalition of credit unions, it uses a clever blend of entertainment and education; each *Biz Kid$* episode shows kids how to make and manage money by introducing concepts of financial literacy and entrepreneurship. The program offers a fast-paced mix that includes actors, sketch comedies, animation, and feature stories featuring young entrepreneurs. In one episode, a vampire dad has a conversation with his daughter about getting into the family business and this video clip inspires discussion about the concepts of entrepreneurship and succession. In another clip, we see Dorothy with the Tin Man, Cowardly Lion, and Scarecrow, each of whom reveals different "money personalities," including being oblivious about the future, over-spending to assuage self-esteem, and making impulsive financial decisions. And the "King of Ka-Ching" explains how marketers use various persuasive strategies to promote consumption. Lesson plans and at-home materials make it possible for teachers to advance an understanding of key financial literacy topics, including credit and debt, entrepreneurship, saving and investing, and careers.

Despite the availability of engaging curricular resources, in some communities, school leaders are ambivalent about teaching financial literacy in the context of civic or mathematics education. Some teachers often don't feel comfortable with these topics because of their own conflicted perspective on capitalism. Some teachers are adamantly opposed to teaching about capitalism on principle. Others may see financial literacy as essentially a form of propaganda, where "money creates more money," leading young people to see individual consumers as morally responsible for managing economic forces that are essentially out of their control (Arthur 2012).

Other educators are aware that all financial literacy curricula have a distinctive point of view that requires careful scrutiny and interrogation. However, it may not be easy for high school teachers to recognize the full scope of ideological implications embedded in a financial literacy curriculum. For example, in many financial literacy programs, personal money management is treated as if it were an effective solution to socially created economic risks. As Arthur (2012) notes, for genuine financial literacy to occur, students should be "able to reflect on and alter the very conditions that give rise to consumer choice" (p. xvii). Merely focusing on and promoting individual responsibility is insufficient for understanding how money flows in a global economy. For financial literacy to be conceptualized as a form of civic education, it must be paired with a deep understanding of news and current events in a global context.

Youth as Consumers of News Media

During the fall of 2014, when a grand jury failed to indict the white police officer who shot and killed Michael Brown in Ferguson, Missouri, many teachers compiled, traded, and shared articles, handouts, and other resources to help them address the news story with their students. Although at least one school district warned teachers not to address the news event, many teachers engaged in dialogue with students about the case. Jesse Hagopian put it on his blog in a post on teaching about Ferguson, "If education is not dedicated to empowering our youth to solve the problems they face in their communities, in our nation, and in our world, then it isn't really an education at all—it is an indoctrination designed to reproduce oppression" (Desmond-Harris 2014).

But apart from blockbuster news events like this, the reading and discussion of news and current events has been challenged during the twenty-first century as the profession of journalism has faced monumental challenges to its business model as a result of the rise of the Internet and digital culture. Today, an increasing number of people engage in surveillance of their environment through Facebook, YouTube, and Twitter, not through reading the *Providence Journal,* the *Chicago Tribune,* or the *Houston Chronicle,* or watching FOX News, CNN, or ABC's *World News Tonight.*

Research shows that regular news reading and viewing of television news not only builds language, reading and viewing comprehension, critical thinking, oral expression, and listening skills, but it directly models expectations in preparing students for adult life, where attention to local, national, and international events is expected as a core tenet of informed citizenship (Rubin 2012). But although one in three American middle school and high school students watch *Channel One News* each school day, researchers have little faith in the power of the journalistic marketplace to meet the genuine needs of children and teens. In a recent study of the journalistic quality of adolescent-targeted newscasts in the United States, researchers compared *Channel One News, CNN Student News*, and the *CBS Evening News.* Content analysis revealed that *Channel One News* had significantly more references to commercially oriented websites than *CNN Student News* or the *CBS Evening News* (Scott, Chansior, and Dixon 2014). In the U.S., it seems, child and adolescent audiences are just another market for the now-struggling field of journalism, whose leaders have only recently recognized that without a focus on the "demand side" of news, there may be little opportunity for growth on the supply side.

Recently, nonprofit organizations and university programs, well-funded by charitable foundations, have begun programs in news literacy. The most well-known programs include the Stony Brook news literacy program, led by former *Daily News* editor Howard Schneider, and the News Literacy Project, led by former *Washington Post* journalist Alan Miller. Some of these programs emphasize how journalists verify information by looking for high-status sources to confirm facts; other programs feature classroom visits from journalists who describe their experiences in constructing the news. In these programs, students listen and ask questions, presumably inspired by the opportunity to meet a journalist who has contributed to creating "the first draft of history" by gathering information from multiple sources.

News literacy certainly represents an advance upon even more traditional approaches like the Newspaper In Education (NIE) programs, which were widely promulgated during the 1970s and '80s and included activities such as looking for active verbs in news headlines and summarizing a single news article. Sadly, using the newspaper often has little to do with reading and discussing news and current events, as some curriculum approaches include activities like searching through a newspaper to find adjectives from A to Z (Rubin 2012). Such activities might naturally discourage students' interest in news and journalism, and are certainly no substitute for regular sustained reading and discussion of current events.

Perhaps the entrance of former journalists into the classroom is indeed an improvement over the sporadic or occasional use of news and current events as a curriculum resource. Research shows that American students do not generally discuss current events in school during class time. In a study of a nationally representative sample of ninth grade students, Kahne and Middaugh (2007) found that low-income students, non-college bound students, and students of color are the groups least likely to discuss current events in class. As Rubin (2012) explains, "most social studies classes are not structured to take into account or build upon students' varying experiences with civic life; many educators choose to avoid controversial social and civic issues their classrooms" (7).

Researchers have identified a variety of reasons why news and current events are not routinely used in American high schools. Passe and Fitchett (2013) write, "Whether it is because of a desire to get through the curriculum, prepare for standardized tests, or simply avoid anything that might be deemed controversial, teachers often do not engage students" in discussions of news and current events (249). Teachers say there is simply no time in the typical content-heavy social studies curriculum for reading and discussion of the news (Rubin 2012). News articles, in fact, are too episodic in nature to be of much educational value to children and youth, as they lack background information and context to be easily comprehensible to young people. And because many teachers themselves are not active news consumers, they may lack the needed background information to scaffold and support students' emerging interpretation of the news. It might be noted that teachers' expertise is too easily challenged when using news media resources with their dynamic and ever-changing content. Furthermore, teachers may avoid teaching about current events because these discussions can be too controversial. For example, some teachers have experienced backlash from administrators when teaching about the Iraq War (Burgos 2008).

As traditional mainstream journalism continues to decline, it's possible that user-generated content may provide fresh opportunities for learners to engage in discussion and dialogue about news and current events across geographic and cultural divides. One powerful example of how online producers are addressing children and youth as news consumers comes from the work of Brad Montague, founder of the YouTube channel "Soul Pancake." One of the channel's videos, "Kid President—How to Change the World" features an African American boy, Robby Novak, age 9, as Kid President, commenting on why people don't think they can change the world, followed by his charming and insightful reflections. Kid President offers a playful, optimistic perspective on small actions that people can take to respond to the news and current events in the world around them. "Things don't have to be the way they are," Kid President notes, offering small, kid-friendly ideas for solving social problems (like donating socks to homeless families for Socktober). With optimism and off-beat energy, amateur and local producers on YouTube may provide meaningful opportunities for children and young people to experience and engage with diverse others, using compelling content to explore differences and promote genuine dialogue, helping to counter the increasingly re-segregated communities in which we live.

Youth as Communicators

The use of media and technology in education has received much attention as a result of deep investment by venture capitalists and charitable foundations, who are aware of the changing economic context of K–12 and higher education and the need for approaches that meet the needs of learners today. Although most economic analyses project that, by 2018, more than 60 percent of the workforce will need to have some form of higher education, fewer than 35 percent of the population are expected to have attained degrees by that time (Tierney and Rodriquez 2014). Along with the rise of for-profit higher education, a variety of forms of online and social media are now being explored in the hopes that they may emerge as a potentially disruptive force.

There is no shortage of idealism among those in the area of digital media and learning. Aiming for a sea change in American public education, some media and education scholars, practitioners, and advocates consider the near-limitless possibilities of digital media education to be vital dimensions of educational transformation (Davidson and Goldberg 2009; Gee 2010; Jenkins 2009). To provide digital media courses in civic engagement will mean overcoming several challenges, including a lack of time, funding, and training.

But when young people discover a sense of agency from participating in a meaningful form of public communication, where their voices are part of a strategy to create social change, the impact can be transformative. One example of this is the PBS Student Reporting Labs, a school-based news media literacy initiative which connects middle and high school students to local PBS stations and broadcast news professionals in their communities to report on critical issues from a youth perspective. Through a project-based, active learning model, students learn how to synthesize information and investigate important topics, while building media literacy, communication, and problem-solving skills. In 2013–2014, the program involved more than 50 schools across the country, with each site adapting the program as needed to meet the particular educational needs of its students, faculty, and community. In quantitative research conducted with nearly 500 high school students who participated in the program, we measured the development of media production skills that involved gathering and synthesizing information, using digital media and technology to communicate ideas in the format of a broadcast news package, and engaging in cycles of revision and feedback to polish their work. We found statistically significant increases in collaboration and teamwork competencies, including intellectual curiosity, the ability to give and receive feedback, and confidence in self-expression and advocacy. We also found increases in media literacy analysis skills, more selectivity in media use choices, and a shift toward high-quality news sources over entertainment-type news. Students had a less apathetic view of news and journalism, as well as orientation toward journalism careers. We also observed increased commitment to civic activism and an interest in civic engagement activities, particularly ones that are digital and collaborative (Hobbs et al. 2013).

Still, some have wondered whether simply creating, composing, or making civic media is enough—especially if there is no one to watch or respond to it (Weiland 2014). "Students must find appropriate audiences for their work in a crowded media environment dominated by commercial products," notes Levine (2008, 119). Is real civic agency achieved if young people create videos that nobody watches? Indeed, critics of life in "the late age of print" wonder about the depth of readers' engagement and comprehension with screen media (Carr 2010; Striphas 2013). Perhaps the values of entertainment culture have eclipsed any educational or civic value of amateur and youth media video.

However, educators are developing creative approaches to activate youth civic engagement while developing communication, collaboration, and critical thinking skills. Some of these skills may be learned as part of general education and are not specifically tied to civic education. For example, in a large-scale study of California high school and college students, Kahne, Lee, and Feezell (2012) found that about 50 percent of students self-reported that they had learned how to assess the trustworthiness of online information, were required to use the Internet to get information about political or social issues, were required to use the Internet to find different points of view about political or social issues, or were given an assignment where they had to create something to put on the Web.

A number of civic education programs rely on external partnerships—including university faculty or nonprofit organizations—to stimulate and support innovation. For example, Rubin (2012) documented her work with three social studies teachers, as she used design-based research to generate, implement, and track new approaches to civic education. Her work encouraged teachers to make active use of discussion, writing and expression, current events, and civic action research. By re-organizing the history curriculum into thematic units undergirded by essential questions, Rubin found that teachers were able to more effectively integrate the teaching of current events in the context of history. Simple instructional practices that promoted authentic discussion were effective; a strong focus on writing and creative expression became a means for students to represent their knowledge and emerging understanding. Similarly, in another example of a university–school partnership that aimed to integrate media literacy into an urban elementary school, skills of critical analysis of the news media were activated through a range of creative media production activities that included critically analyzing the representation of courts and law enforcement, talking back to the news media, and analyzing news media portrayals of youth (Hobbs and Cooper Moore 2013).

Digital media tools can support the deep integration of reading and writing into the civic education classroom. Research shows that students need extensive instruction to develop online reading comprehension (Coiro 2011), and organizations like the National Writing Project are exploring how to use digital media for multimedia (or multimodal) composition and self-expression. An online learning program called Drafting Board helps students develop policy analysis and argumentation skills. Created by iCivics, the nonprofit organization founded by former Supreme Court justice Sandra Day O'Connor, Drafting Board involves students in gathering information about a controversial topic, matching evidence to support their position on the issue. A digital tool, Paragraph Constructor, helps students create grammatically correct and sequentially logical paragraphs, while Critic Crusher helps them recognize weaknesses in the arguments of the opposition. Research with 1,500 middle school students showed statistically significant gains in writing skills using the California Writing Standards evaluation rubric (Kawashima-Ginsberg 2012).

In addition to discussion and writing activities, simulations are sometimes used as expressive activities in which writing is used to deepen students' understanding of a historical or current event. In these forms of learning, students role play particular characters and converse with others as a way to demonstrate their knowledge. Some students play the part of journalists, asking probing questions to gather information and provide opportunities for evaluating ideas (Rubin 2012).

There are many strategic assumptions embedded in how digital media learning addresses learners in how to be voters, consumers, and global citizens. One concern is that some new initiatives engage learners directly in ways that do not offer a role for a classroom teacher. Instead, mentors from the community provide support services to youth. For this reason, civic education initiatives that include digital media may receive strong support from philanthropies, university researchers, and nonprofit organizations, but considerably less support from K–12 educators and public school leaders.

Conclusion

This chapter has explored how schools have addressed youth as capitalists, as consumers of news, and as communicators. To help young people learn about capitalism, initiatives in financial literacy have been introduced in schools. The practice of reading news and current events and the development of effective communication skills, including students' use of media as a vehicle for advocacy, are small but key dimensions of civic education in the U.S. public education system.

But given that we have not reached the tipping point with any of these initiatives, I wonder: Are educators' attitudes toward youth voice partly to blame? When students speak out, they can say things that make adults uncomfortable. They can point out adult hypocrisy and make astute observations about the gaping divide between our democratic ideals and the actuality of contemporary life. But they can also say things that are out of context, uninformed, and mean-spirited. The paradox of youth voice is a subject that requires deep interrogation within the context of financial literacy, discussions of news and current events, and youth as media makers.

Because most schools are essentially undemocratic institutions, it's a risk to teach civic education with any point of view that emphasizes empowerment. When students are conceptualized as products whose value is measured with standardized tests, and where learning how to follow orders trumps the cultivation of intellectual curiosity, students learn to tolerate or submit to injustice because they lack any meaningful form of social power, despite the presence of mock institutions like student government and school newspapers, which sadly no longer serve to help them learn how democracy should work. Instead, students capitulate to an image-conscious, status-driven, "brand-me" world, where individual achievement leads to entry into selective and exclusionary institutions of higher education, followed by further burnishing of the personal brand in college and beyond.

Financial literacy, teaching about news and current events and empowering young people as communicators in their own communities can be key dimensions of civic education that aim to address the limits of the currently dominant paradigm of teaching civics through a focus on content knowledge about how government works. But because teachers are largely disempowered to effect curricular change in the U.S., text-book publishers, testing companies, and state departments of education work with private industry and large charitable foundations as de facto shapers of curriculum. School administrators, controlled by local government, are influenced by fads and fashions that result from non-professional community leaders reacting to crisis rather than pro-actively and strategically using best practices. But this bleak perspective does not fully represent the full complexity of what is happening in American public education in both high schools and institutions of higher education.

So we have no choice but to be optimistic. There is a need for creative new approaches that help teachers and students, in schools, use the power of information and communication to make a difference in the world. It's possible that a combination of financial literacy, media literacy focused on news and current events, and youth media initiatives that combine project-based learning with community activism can be effective in cultivating the range of citizenship skills needed for full participation in work, civic, community, and cultural life, locally, nationally, and internationally.

References

Arthur, C. 2012. "Financial Literacy Education: Neoliberalism, the Consumer and the Citizen." In *Educational Futures: Rethinking Theory and Practice 53*. Rotterdam: Sense Publishers.

Burgos, R. 2008. "Teaching the Iraq War." *PS: Political Science & Politic s* 1(1): 173–178. doi:10.1017/S1049096508080268.

Carr, N. 2010. *The Shallows: What the Internet Is Doing to Our Brains*. New York: Norton.

Child and Youth Finance International Research Group. 2012. Children and Youth As Economic Citizens: Review of Research on Financial Capability, Financial Inclusion and Financial Education. http://csd.wustl.edu/Publications/Documents/RR13-02.pdf.

Coiro, J. 2011. "Talking About Reading as Thinking: Modeling the Hidden Complexities of Online Reading Comprehension." *Theory into Practice* 50:107–115.

Davidson, C., and T. Goldberg. 2009. *The Future of Learning Institutions in a Digital Age*. New York: Viking.

Desmond-Harris, J. 2014. "Do's and Don'ts for Teaching About Ferguson." *The Root*, September 2. http://www.theroot.com/articles/culture/2014/09/teaching_about_ferguson_do_s_and_don_ts.html.

Dewey, J. 1927. *The Public and Its Problems*. New York: Holt.

Gee, J. 2010. *New Digital Media and Learning as an Emerging Area and "Worked Examples" As One Way Forward*. Cambridge, MA: MIT Press.

Graham, D. 2014. "Lil John's Goofy Rock the Vote Video Might Actually Work." *Atlantic* 9 (October). http://www.theatlantic.com/politics/archive/2014/10/what-if-lil-jons-goofy-rock-the-vote-video-actually-works/381202.

Hobbs, R., K. Donnelly, J. Friesem, and M. Moen. August. 2013. *Evaluation of PBS NewsHour Student Reporting Labs*. Kingston, RI: Media Education Lab. University of Rhode Island.

Hobbs, R., and D. C. Moore. 2013. *Discovering Media Literacy: Digital Media and Popular Culture in Elementary School*. Thousand Oaks, CA: Corwin/Sage.

Ito, Mizuko, Elisabeth Soep, Neta Kligler-Vilenchik, Sangita Shresthova, Liana Gamber-Thompson, and Arely Zimmerman. 2015. "Learning Connected Civics: Narratives, Practices, Infrastructures." *Curriculum Inquiry* 45 (1).

Ito, M., S. Baumer, M. Bittanti, D. Boyd, R. Cody, B. Herr-Stephenson, H. Horst, 2009. *Hanging Out, Messing Around and Geeking Out: Kids Living and Learning with New Media*. Cambridge, MA: MIT Press.

Jenkins, H. 2009. *Confronting the Challenges of Participatory Culture: Media Education for the 21st Century*. Cambridge, MA: MIT Press.

Kahne, J., E. Middaugh. 2009. "Democracy for Some: The Civic Opportunity Gap in High School." In J. Youniss, J. and P. Levine, eds. *Engaging Young People in Civic Life*. Nashville, TN: Vanderbilt University Press.

Kahne, J., E. Middaugh, and D. Allen. 2014. "Youth New Media, and the Rise of Participatory Politics." YPP Research Network Working Paper #1, March 2014. http://ypp.dmlcentral.net/sites/default/files/publications/YPP_WorkinPapers_Paper01.pdf.

Kahne, J., N. Lee, and J. T. Feezell. 2012. "Digital Media Literacy Education and Online Civic and Political Participation." *International Journal of Communication* 6:1–24.

Kahne, J., E. Middaugh, N. Lee, and J. T. Feezell. 2012. "Youth Online Activity and Exposure to Diverse Perspectives." *New Media & Society* 14 (3): 492–512. doi:.10.1177/1461444811420271

Kawashima-Ginsberg, K. 2012. "Summary of Findings from the Evaluation of iCivics Drafting Board Intervention." Center for Information and Research on Civic Learning and Engagement. Working Paper 76. Tufts University.

Levine, P. 2008. "A Public Voice for Youth: The Audience Problem in Digital Media and Civic Education." In *Civic Life Online: Learning How Digital Media Can Engage Youth*, ed. W. Bennett, 119–138. The John D. and Catherine T. MacArthur Foundation Series on Digital Media and Learning. Cambridge, MA: The MIT Press, 2008. doi: .10.1162/dmal.9780262524827.119

Lindsay, J., and V. Davis. 2012. *Flattening Classrooms, Engaging Minds: Move to Global Collaboration One Step at a Time*. Upper Saddle River, NJ: Pearson.

Loewen, J. 1995. *Lies My Teacher Told Me*. New York: Simon & Schuster.

Lusardi, Annamaria, Olivia S. Mitchell, and Vilsa Curto. 2010. "Financial Literacy Among the Young: Evidence and Implications for Consumer Policy." CFS Working Paper, No. 2010/09. http://nbn-resolving.de/urn:nbn:de:hebis:30-78626.

Martens, H., and R. Hobbs. 2015. "How Media Literacy Supports Civic Engagement in a Digital Age." *Atlantic Journal of Communication, April*. doi:.10.1080/15456870.2014.961636

National History Day. 2011. National Program Evaluation. Accessed December 1, 2014. http://www.nhd.org/NHDworks.htm.

Passe, J., and P. Fitchett. 2013. *The Status of Social Studies*. New York: Information Age Publishing.

Quigley, C. 1999. "Civic Education: Recent History, Current Status and the Future." American Bar Association Symposium, Washington, D.C. February 25. http://www.civiced.org/papers/papers_quigley99.html.

Reich, J. 2012. "Civic Education in the Online Space." *Educational Leadership* 70 (6). Association for Supervision and Curriculum Development. http://www.ascd.org/publications/educational-leadership/mar13/vol70/num06/Civic-Education-in-the-Online-Space.aspx.

Root, S., and J. Northup. 2007. "The Impacts of Project Citizen on U.S. Middle and High School Students: A 2005–2006 Study." *Center for Civic Education*. http://www.civiced.org/pdfs/PC/ProjectCitizen%20FullReport%202007.pdf.

Rubin, B. 2012. *Making Citizens: Transforming Civic Learning for Diverse Social Studies Classrooms*. New York: Routledge.

Scott, D., M. Chansior, and J. Dixon. 2014. "Analysis of Television Adolescent Classroom News in the United States." *Journal of Children and Media* 8 (4): 457–473.

Soep, E. 2014. *Participatory Politics: Next-Generational Tactics to Remake Public Spheres. The John D. and Catherine T. MacArthur Foundation Research Reports on Digital Media and Learning*. Cambridge, MA: MIT Press.

Strauss, V. 2014. "Why the Common Core Flunks of Civic Education." *Washington Post*, March 12. http://www.washingtonpost.com/blogs/answer-sheet/wp/2014/03/12/why-the-common-core-flunks-on-civic-education.

Striphas, T. 2013. *The Late Age of Print*. New York: Columbia University Press.

Tierney, W. G., and B. A. Rodriguez, eds. 2014. The Future of Higher Education in California: Getting In and Getting Through—Problems and Solutions. Los Angeles: Pullias Center for Higher Education. http://web-app.usc.edu/web/rossier/publications/85/The%20Future%20of%20Higher%20Education%20in%20CA%20Monograph.pdf.

Varcoe, K., A. Martin, Z. Devitto, and C. Go. 2005. *Using a Financial Education Curriculum for Teens*. Association for Financial Counseling and Planning Education.

Weiland, S. 2014. "How Much Technology Is Enough? "In *Postsecondary Play: The Role of Games and Social Media in Higher Education*, ed. W. Tierney, Z. Corwin, T. Fullerton and G. Ragusa. Baltimore: Johns Hopkins University Press.

24   Connecting Pedagogies of Civic Media: The Literacies, Connected Civics, and Engagement in Daily Life

Paul Mihailidis and Roman Gerodimos

Youth and Civic Engagement in Digital Culture

A host of large-scale civic movements over the past decade have employed digital technologies as facilitators for the organization, engagement, and participation of citizens in democratic processes. The Arab Spring, (Eltantawy and Wiest 2011; Khondker 2011), the Obama 2008 and 2012 campaigns (Gerodimos and Justinussen 2014), Occupy Wall Street, the Ice Bucket Challenge, and the Kony 2012 movement are often cited as major catalysts for driving interest into the role of young people and social networks in civic engagement (Castells 2012; Milner 2010). Recent protest movements in Turkey, Greece, Ukraine, and Hong Kong have codified a certain category of civic uprising that, while not dictated solely by social media, utilizes social media to organize and facilitate the sharing of information, and to document actions and events for the world to see.

These large-scale events, however, overshadow compelling local grassroots uses of connective technologies for engagement in civic life.

In 2012, in Scotland, a 9-year-old student named Martha Payne started a blog where she documented her school lunches visually through photos and commentary. She began to share her blog, "NeverSeconds," with her friends and community, and soon her photos about the poor conditions of school food spread far and wide. She gained over 2 million followers and raised over 5,000 GBP for a school cafeteria in Africa. Her popularity, however, exposed conditions that were uncomfortable for local officials, who ordered the blog to be removed citing privacy issues and the use of a camera in the school (Russell 2012). As Martha's followers heard about the decision to close down Martha's site, they took to Twitter to voice their concerns and put pressure on local officials to reverse their decision. Within weeks, Scottish council leader Roddy McCuish "instructed senior officials to immediately withdraw the ban on pictures from the school dining hall" (Bryant 2012). Since then, Martha's blog has reached over 10 million people, she has traveled to Malawi to visit the schools where her funds reached, and she has put pressure on Scottish officials to improve their school lunch offerings.

Around the same time in Sanford, North Carolina, 12-year-old Marshall Reid had been struggling with his weight for years, and suffered from bullying at school as a result. After seeing the movie *Super Size Me*, Marshall decided to try and reduce the portions of his meals for 30 days, in an effort to lose weight. Instead of simply trying to implement his plan, Marshall and his family wanted to show the positive impact that healthy lifestyles could have on daily life. They chose to create YouTube videos that documented Marshall's new diet, and to use the platform as a space for Marshall to express his frustrations, joys, and the challenges that accompanied his journal. After posting more than 140 videos on YouTube (Hoffman 2012), a large community of supporters, followers, and friends offered support and encouragement, and shared in the plight of Marshall's attempt to lose weight. As Marshall's community grew and embraced his initiative, The Portion Size Me project launched a contest for portion control, published a book, and garnered media attention that led to community discussions on portions, healthy food, and youth in schools and communities (Hoffman 2012).

Just one year earlier, in 2011, 22-year-old Molly Katchpole, upon hearing of Bank of America's implementation of a $5/month banking fee, took to the nonprofit Change. org site to mount a participatory campaign to protest the fee. Katchpole composed a letter (see figure 24.1) expressing her concerns about the fee, calling out banks' role in the recession of 2008–2009 to support her point. She ended the letter by urging Bank of America to remove its fee, and asked the Change.org community to sign and support the letter to Bank of America. In very short time, Katchpole's petition garnered over 300,000 signatures, which led to mainstream media coverage, spinoff campaigns against Bank of America, and a widespread condemnation of the fee imposed by the bank. Within one month of Katchpole's campaign, Bank of America announced it was dropping its new fee, and a host of other national banks followed suit by dropping fees they had implemented or were planning to implement.

Stories of young people using their voices to fight against social oppression grow more common with each passing year. The well-documented DREAMer movement provides a strong example of young activists using their voices to repurpose narratives of immigration into calls for civic and political awareness (Zimmerman 2012). Their activism, in the form of videos, images, art, and text, provides a space for marginalized voices to gather, interact, and advocate for reform and rights. Citizens also utilized social networks to react to the events of racial injustice, oppression, violence, and death in Ferguson, New York City, Florida, and beyond. Hashtags were created to collate conversations and call for direct action in response to such injustices. #Blacklivesmatter continues to provide a space for resistance, support, and expression, and corresponds with Attorney General Eric Holder's call for a federal inquiry into the legal actions acquitting an officer in the death of Eric Garner in New York City. The hashtags #ICantBreathe, #Iamtrayvon, #HandsUpDontShoot, and #iftheygunnedmedown brought

To:

Brian T. Moynihan, President and CEO, Bank of America

I'm writing to express my deep concern over Bank of America's decision to charge customers $5 a month to use their debit cards when making purchases.

The American people bailed out Bank of America during a financial crisis the banks helped create. You paid zero dollars in federal income tax last year. And now your bank is profiting, raking in $2 billion in profits last quarter alone. How can you justify squeezing another $60 a year from your debit card customers? This is despicable.

American consumers can't afford these additional fees. We reject any claims by BofA that this latest fee is somehow necessary.

Please, do the right thing. Reverse your decision to charge customers $5 each month for using their debit cards to make purchases.

Sincerely,

{Your name]

Figure 24.1
The petition letter written by Molly Katchpole and uploaded to Change.org. Credit: Molly Katchpole.

together a nation of voices in protest against violence against black citizens. Other examples of meaningful hashtag activism, like #yesallwomen, #bringbackourgirls, and #umbrellarevolution, have led to a surge of research and inquiry into how this type of expression and activism can gather diverse civic voices in defense of social justice, equality, and tolerance (Constanza-Chock 2014; Gerbaudo 2012).

These examples are but a few of a what is a vastly expanding list of cases from around the world that show how communities are using media and networks to engage in civic life. Shumow (2014) argues that "from the leveraging of social media by protesters during the Arab Spring to the more recent use of a walkie-talkie phone app developed in Austin, Texas, and used by protesters in Ukraine and Venezuela (Parker 2014), the past decade has seen an explosion of grassroots, popular movements that use horizontal communication to bypass traditional power structures" (3). Civic media are bypassing not only traditional power structures, but also the "transaction costs" (Shirky 2010) that constrain civic voices to participate in traditional media outlets.

This growing presence of digital technologies as primary facilitators for participation in civic life brings about important questions about the competencies—or literacies— needed to effectively navigate digital spaces for civic engagement in digital culture. How young people learn to engage in civic life is a question that has historically been explored by the ability to transfer rote knowledge of government structure, process, and function, and tangible actions that are situated in the physical world and rooted in measurable outcomes like voting, volunteering, paying taxes, and attending town hall meetings. While such metrics still play an important role in understanding the myriad of ways people engage in civic life, the increasing centrality of digital technologies in daily life necessitates the re-imagining of how we approach teaching and learning about civic engagement today (Gerodimos 2008, 2012; Mihailidis 2014b, 2013).

This chapter explores the role of pedagogy in preparing young people for active and inclusive participation in civic life. It argues for a need to insert more explicit attention to civic voice—the dispositions and modalities of expression that young people use to participate in daily life—in media and digital literacy pedagogies that can support both formal and informal spaces of learning. The examples above reinforce the need to centralize participatory culture in teaching and learning about media's role in civic life. Young people are using media for information and knowledge transfer, but also as tools for advocacy, participation, and engagement in daily life. Adults should acknowledge these uses accordingly and integrate them into the core of a civics education within and beyond the classroom walls.

The Role of Literacies in Civic Learning

It is often assumed that being "born digital" confers an instinctive understanding of and adaptability to digital tools. Research has shown, however, that young people have difficulty negotiating the wide range of information made available via those digital tools (Killi, Laurinen, and Marttunen 2008). They often lack the critical awareness to differentiate quality, intent, and bias across the myriad of converged platforms within which they are exposed to information (Fieldhouse and Nicholas 2008). At the same time, the simple connotation of the "digital native" assumes a level of sophistication that has not been supported by scholarship. Research has found that young people are often prone to overconfidence about their ability to critically navigate the Web with an alarming level of blind trust in search engines (Bartlett and Miller 2011). Overconfidence in information consumption also led students to project a level of cynicism toward media outlets without warranted inquiry into the content and scope of the messages themselves (Mihailidis 2009).

In response to growing ubiquitous digital culture, a range of literacies has proliferated in the past decades, premised on providing a range of skills and dispositions aimed at teaching and learning about critical evaluation, inquiry, analysis, and production for savvy media and information consumption. Media literacy, perhaps the literacy with the most widespread application and appeal, emerged from an effects tradition incorporating the work of the Frankfurt School (Horkheimer 1937); critical theories of political economy and hegemony (Schiller 1975); and more recent work by Neil Postman (1985) and contemporaries, who argue for the need to offer a way to combat media messages and systems to facilitate young people in "deconstructing injustices, expressing their own voices, and struggling to create a better society" (Kellner and Share 2007, 20). This work embraces Freire's (1970) *conscientização*—or "critical consciousness"—in which:

individuals develop the ability to perceive their social reality "not as a closed world from which there is no exit, but as a limiting situation which they can transform" (49). Media literacy education, then, prepares citizens for democratic participation by helping them analyze mediated *representations of* their communities, as well as address *issues within* their communities (Mihailidis, 2014a).

In response to collapsing media industries, a post–print media culture for youth, and a need to understand media in a more holistic context, media literacy advocates for pedagogies of "empowerment" (Buckingham 2005) that place the learner at the center of the mediated equation, and emphasizes that individuals must learn about media in the context of the situated political, social, and cultural ecosystems in which they are embedded (Buckingham 2003; Carlsson 2008). Empowerment narratives advocate for a set of skills and dispositions for young people to embrace media and digital literacies (Glister 1997)—Internet searching, hypertext navigation, knowledge assembly, content evaluation (Bawden 2008)—as a way to build constructive competencies in critical inquiry and expression online that are "fundamentally implicated in the practice of citizenship" (Hobbs 2011a, 16). Hobbs (2011a) argues that digital literacies have capacity to "turn people from passive spectators to active citizens, where people generate ideas that are relevant to their own communities. Technologically speaking, every person can be a pamphleteer" (154).

Digital literacies necessarily embrace participation in digital culture. In their seminal white paper entitled "Confronting the Challenges of a Participatory Culture," Henry Jenkins et al., (2009) advocate for a cross-pollination of skills, dispositions, competencies, and modes of engagement that transcend any set approach to learning about media and offer a diverse set of constructs—from play and curation to transmedia navigation, simulation, and performance, among others—that support diverse avenues to engagement and participation in daily civic life. These "new media literacies" incorporate DIY maker movements (Lankshear and Knobel 2011), online navigation of texts (Coiro et al. 2014), and creation-based pedagogies that focus on a new set of digital fluencies for young people to "acquire multimedia communication skills and know how to use these skills to engage in the civic life of their communities" (Hobbs 2010, vii).

The emergence of the literacies provides a rich space for building deeper and more meaningful experiences that approach the civic potential of young people in digital culture. For decades, scholars, starting as far back as Dewey and de Tocqueville, have waxed poetic about the democratic potential of media literacy. British media education pioneer Len Masterman wrote back in 1985 that "media education is an essential step in the long march toward a truly participatory democracy and the democratization of our institutions" (13).

While these big picture modes of thinking have helped promote the literacies as central spaces for civic learning and engagement, they carry with them a set of constraints that has restricted how we understand their potential. Jenkins (2006) positioned his new set of literacies as a way to "encourage greater reflection and public discussion on how we might incorporate these core principles systematically across curricula and across the divide between in-school and out-of-school activities." By and large, these discussions have been happening at the periphery of formal education spaces, and are largely lacking in underserved communities. Further, the impact of the literacies as avenues for meaningful civic learning has been largely anecdotal.

In *Net Smart*, Howard Rheingold (2012) notes the difficult position that formal spaces of education find themselves in relation to evolving technology and youth engagement with networks for informal collaboration, learning, and engagement. "Educational institutions," notes Rheingold, "cannot change swiftly and broadly enough to match the pace of change in digital culture ... " (252). Not only are schools limited by testing standards tied to learning measurements, but also the space of the literacies is relegated to peripheral curricular spaces and implemented only by champion teachers. At the same time, civic education in secondary schools remains in the domain of what Ito et al. (2015) refer to as "in the head" work (for example, knowing who controls the judiciary branch or which party holds the majority in the U.S. Senate) (12). What results from this is a series of constraints that limits the application of the literacies into meaningful discussions about civic learning and civic engagement today.

First, the literacies are only peripherally associated with civic engagement as a direct outcome of their work, and at best assume civic learning as an implicit byproduct of their pedagogies. Studies have shown that media literacy education can result in more attention paid to news and politics (McDevitt and Kiousis 2006; Kahne et al. 2010), greater awareness about violence depicted in the media (Scharrer 2002), media's implicit bias (Vraga et al. 2009), critical analysis of news content (Mihailidis 2009), and more knowledge about news and civics (Hobbs et al. 2013; Craft et al. 2013). These studies focus on young people and attainment of new skills or dispositions, but connections to any behavior changes or direct forms of engagement in civic life are often assumed. There have been few studies that approach the literacies as directly impacting civic learning or civic participation. Those that explore civics as part of work in the literacies often promote inquiry through a duty-based citizenship (Bennett 2007; Dalton 2009) frame, asking mainly about voting, volunteering, and paying attention to news and current events. (Hobbs et al. 2013; Bennett and Segerberg 2011; Walgrave et al. 2011; Buckingham 2007, 2008; Kahne et al. 2012, 2011).

Second, work in the literacies often suffers from its relative slippage between and across many disciplines. Media literacy's conceptual home oscillates between education and communication fields, while its content emerges from humanities, social sciences, life sciences, and in general across disciplines. This conceptual vagueness has helped the literacies gain attention and appeal as applied modes of inquiry. The growth of information literacy, news literacy, political literacy, digital literacy, health literacy, and so on, has brought attention to how young people learn to use skills to better understand content, practice, and praxis. At the same time, the diffusion of the literacies has limited their ability to grow in unified ways and to be considered a distinct space of inquiry. Potter (2010) noted the conceptual vagueness in a piece called "The State of Media Literacy" where he wrote, "Media literacy is a term that means many different things to different people—scholars, educators, citizen activists, and the general public." He went on to critique the field as catering to different constituencies and failing to build an identity or cohesive body of work that moves beyond educational application. Hobbs (2011b), in an essay responding to Potter, makes note of the many contributions to the literacies that are proliferating around the world, noting "slowly but surely, digital and media literacy now are becoming a basic part of contemporary discourse" (421).

Lastly, because the literacies often encompass the formal space of education, they have been less willing to embrace explicit civic action as an outcome of their work. Formal education has long struggled with how to build effective approaches to teaching about citizenship while being wary of the complex political, social, and cultural constraints that are embedded in pedagogical design and approval. Civic action that is seen as overtly political in some way is harder to justify as a learning outcome. As a result, the work of the literacies can be agnostic toward social justice, inequality, underserved populations or communities, and the role of civic voice as a change agent. Ito (2008) sees this as a friction between an increasingly participatory youth and traditional pedagogical models. Learning in digital culture, Ito (2008) argues, should be about "more than being able to access serious online information and culture. Youth could benefit from educators being more open to forms of experimentation and social exploration that are generally not characteristic of educational institutions" (2). Working within the constraints of formal education spaces leaves advancement in the literacies vulnerable to large-scale bureaucracy, standardized testing, and alignment with rigid outcomes, and to problems of inequality that befall public school systems. This has made the work of the literacies a noble endeavor, but one that struggles to keep pace with the digital realities of individuals' worlds and with the need to be agile, dynamic, and responsive.

The civic potential of literacies, then, must rely on an ability to build more connected, inclusive, and justice-oriented narratives for young people to engage with in daily civic life. The examples laid out in the introduction of this chapter highlight the potential that digital technologies have to bridge formal schooling and the online spaces that allow learning to be made active around social and civic issues.

Connected Civics and Civic Media

In their recent paper, "Learning Connected Civics," Ito et al. (2015) build on the work of MacArthur-funded research groups in Connected Learning and Youth and Participatory Politics to advance the idea of "connected civics," which they define as "a form of learning that mobilizes young people's deeply felt interests and identities in the service of achieving the kind of civic voice and influence that is characteristic of participatory politics." (11). They go on to qualify the learning aspect of this idea by noting:

learning connected civics does not entail individually driven "transfer" between the personally meaningful cultural projects young people actively create and modes of concerted political engagement, but is centered instead on building shared contexts that allow for what we elaborate below as "consequential connections" between these spheres of activity (11).

Connected civics builds three support structures for consequential connections—*hybrid narratives, shared civic practices,* and *cross-cutting infrastructure*—that collectively move the space of civic learning beyond rote knowledge retention and toward dynamic capacities for civic voice, in which young people are now more often "expressing or in some cases organizing resistance to institutions and ideologies they deem problematic, obsolete, or oppressive." (Ito et al. 2015, 12).

Young people are also circulating content frequently and freely across connective networks that are not inherently political, and are exercising forms of citizenship in their support of a wide array of cultural and social interests (Jenkins, Ford, and Green 2013). Research in support of connected civics shows that such networks offer places of belonging (Deuze 2006; Turkle 2012), spaces for collaborative production (McPherson, Smith-Lovin, and Brashears 2006; Musick and Wilson 2008; Benkler and Nissenbaum 2006), and a participative potential for engagement in daily civic life (Brabham 2008; Jenkins et al. 2009). The general correlation between social media and participation in civic life is positive, though not necessarily transformative (Boulianne 2015).[1]

At the same time, Ito et al. (2015) acknowledge that "young people's everyday experiences of agency in their social worlds, and of citizenship and community involvement, turn out to be largely disconnected from what most educators might think of as sites of civic and political engagement" (13). The experience of agency in lived social worlds is reinforced by scholarship showing that young people's civic activity in digital spaces can promote constructive civic behavior offline: from supporting causes, to advocating for movements and raising local awareness about social issues (Fowler and Christakis 2010; Musick and Wilson 2008; Romer et al. 2009). While a range of research has highlighted the expansion of learning cultures to support participatory youth (Riley and Literat 2012; Middaugh 2012; Kligler-Vilenchik and Shresthova 2012; Williamson 2013), these remain somewhat removed from spaces of formal education.

By advocating for connecting participatory politics, participatory culture, and civic interests, connected civics embraces "diverse routes to civic and political participation as well as learning" that focus on "peer culture, personal interests and identities and opportunities for young people to be recognized in sites of power in the wider world" (Ito et al. 2015, 16). The literacies focus on skill attainment and youth development in order to, according to Hobbs (2011a), "not [teach] students what to think; rather, [media literacy] emphasizes the process of helping people arrive at informed choices that are consistent with their own values through the active, reflective, collaborative, and self-actualizing" (427–428). This perspective assumes that pedagogies focus on value formation and informed decision making in the context of the situated self in society. While arriving at an informed choice is an indication of active engagement in civic life, it rarely embraces a specific direction toward active civic participation, and we believe this limits the true civic potential of the literacies.

Connected civics, while not focusing explicitly on the space of formal education, advocates for pedagogies that do the explicit work of turning audiences into participants, users into makers, and citizens from those who fulfill duties to those who exercise their voices to become empowered in their daily lives. Central to this process is the realization that traditional forms of political participation, while still crucial, cannot adequately represent the complexity of agendas, richness of issues, and dispersion of power into networks that are characteristic of contemporary liberal democracies. Global flows and technologies of communication and information have become integral, if not the primary, elements of contemporary politics, which means that those who lack the means to follow and participate in this process are profoundly disenfranchised.

The Work of Pedagogies for Civic Media

Contrary to previous forms of explicit disenfranchisement—such as not having the right to vote—today's inequalities are obscure precisely because the processes of voice

Figure 24.2
Engaged research design for civic media. Credit: Salzburg Global Seminar/Ela Grieshaber.

aggregation, representation, and decision making are less formalized and explicit. Therefore, pedagogies that support civic media become not just tools for critical thinking but essential components of the civic process; not just the means for exercising one's democratic power, *but also for finding out where that power lies and how to exercise it*. In other words, this entails acquiring and exercising agency, both individual and social, and negotiating the boundaries between the two, so that young people realize the affordances and limitations of individual actions, recognize the need to balance competing agendas and manage limited resources, and respect and are respected so as to coexist with others within the civic commons. That means that pedagogies for civic media have to become embedded parts of young people's political socialization and, as such, may start in, but cannot be limited to, formal pedagogy or education.

The paradigm of engagement outlined here is not about a particular political stance or skill set, but about the importance, value, and multiple benefits that exercising one's voice has in itself, both for the individual and for the community. Redressing injustice and tackling inequality are not the exclusive properties of any particular political or media space, but the foundations of a healthy and sustainable citizenry. However, adapting to this new paradigm so as to exploit its full civic potential requires shifting our mindset from a conceptualization of power as a top-down and zero-sum game. In some contexts, one agent's (e.g., the citizens') acquisition of power may indeed require another agent's (e.g., an authoritarian regime's) loss of power. And in some contexts, situations require the top-down exercise of force so as to, for example, maintain law and order.

Yet, an alternative conceptualization, and one that is more connected to the complex realities of highly interdependent digital communities, would be to view pedagogies for civic media as *facilitators of civic voice*—that is, the realization of one's potential and incorporation into the body politic, which rather than reducing another actor's ability to make decisions, actually creates an environment of pluralism and interaction that has benefits for *all* actors within the system (Gerodimos et al. 2013, 2). In practical terms this means that pedagogical approaches to civic media are not just about formal learning or personal growth—i.e., about the absolute resources of individuals—but about an open and engaged attitude toward others in the community that benefits both; an approach to cultivating civic voice that is not solely based on either romantic notions of duty or cynical perceptions of self-interest, but on the willingness and ability to reach out to others so as to address real-life problems, as was the case with the grassroots cleanup movement (using the hashtag #riotscleanup and the account @riotcleanup) following the 2011 riots in England, the immediate aftermath of the 2013 Boston Marathon attacks, or the recent #blacklivesmatter movement in the United States.

Pedagogical models for civic media confront the common criticism of civic engagement online: that it creates a false sense of empowerment or that it lacks substance and impact. Bialski (2008) argued that "consuming the social web and sharing that content for others to consume is not, in fact, using the social web to its potential. Even content-creation, if it is not truly reflexive, is just a mechanic reproduction of a consumer product. ... [W]hat are these individuals sharing? What are they communicating? How are the countless social operating systems on Facebook, such as the 'What Prostitute Are You?' actually being productive?" While it is true that the excessive hype by over-eager commentators or stakeholders can create unrealistic or just plain irrelevant expectations about what technological applications or innovations can achieve, it is also true that, in an effort to tackle citizens' perceived deficits of efficacy and link civic issues to their daily lives, pedagogies for civic media imply that action by an individual citizen should, can, or always will lead to tangible social or global change. Liking a Facebook post, retweeting a link, signing an e-petition, or donating to a campaign may not, and in fact probably will not, lead to noticeable change.

However, the impact of civic voices on social and civic problems takes different forms and is the result of both short- and long-term actions and interactions. In the aftermath of the January 7, 2015, terrorist attack against the French satirical weekly newspaper *Charlie Hebdo* in Paris, the slogan "Je suis Charlie" ("I am Charlie") was launched. Within hours, millions of people used the hashtag on Twitter, changed their profile photos on Facebook, and reproduced the slogan in solidarity with the victims of the attack. Four days after the attack, millions of people participated in some of the largest-ever peace and unity rallies in Paris and across the world. While that outpouring of support was largely symbolic, it was also a moment that seems to have profoundly affected the identities, values, motivations, hopes, and fears of citizens not just in France but also across the globe. It sent a robust message of support of democratic values, while also sparking debate about freedom of speech and religious tolerance. That incident was a useful reminder that collective action, the intermingling of personal and public expression, and the use of connective technologies to share symbols and emotions are potent drivers of both engagement and change in civic life.

Furthermore, while from a rational perspective the impact of one citizen expressing their voice in social media or signing one e-petition may be negligible, surely the same could be, and has been, argued to be the case with voting or joining a political party. Yet, apart from the very real and very substantive benefits in terms of emotional investment, identity formation, and sense of belonging that engagement has for the individual concerned, the aggregate of those "clicks," "likes," votes, emails, or voices can ultimately create significant local, national, or even global change. Avaaz is a global Web movement promoting civic action on issues such as climate change, human rights, poverty, conflict, and government transparency founded in 2007 by a group of digital activists. It now has more than 40 million members in 194 countries (a community base that political parties in democratic countries could only dream of). Over the last eight years, Avaaz has made impactful and rapid-response interventions around the world, from banning bee-killing pesticides in the European Union and promoting worker safety plans in Bangladesh to organizing the biggest climate march in history, which took place in 2,000 communities around the world in September 2014.

These examples demonstrate that, as digital media coexist and in some cases replace "traditional" media, so will new forms of expression complement and coexist with more traditional ones. However, civic engagement in digital culture is not a linear process moving along a predetermined path. It depends on the extent to which citizens learn to use media to step out of their routines and comfort zones, experiment, fail, innovate, interact, argue, and learn. The pedagogy of civic media, then, requires addressing structural barriers that are ingrained both in human nature and in the architecture of digital culture (see Milan, chapter 4).

We argue that the role of pedagogies, stemming from work in the literacies and in connected civics, opens up the digital realities of civic life for young people, and finds ways to connect the classroom and the community to bring teaching and learning with and about civic media into relevant and applied social worlds of young people. One initiative that has influenced our work in pedagogies of civic media is at the Salzburg Academy on Media & Global Change, a summer activist pedagogy and action research incubator where teaching and learning blend theory and practice, inquiry and expression, to advocate for inclusive engagement and participation in civic life.

Civic Media Pedagogy in Action: The Salzburg Academy on Media & Global Change

The Salzburg Academy on Media & Global Change was founded in 2007, and since then it has gathered more than 600 young people and 100 scholars, educators, and practitioners from around the world to engage in the development and implementation of projects that advocate for social change in local communities across the world. The Academy's objective is to lead the creation of media action plans, multimedia storytelling, and comparative research that collectively embrace the teaching and learning of media as an act of civic engagement.

Over the past ten years, we have seen our case studies implemented in rural schools in sub-Saharan Africa, and we have led media action projects in rural communities in Mexico and in the buffer zone of Cyprus. We have implemented active storytelling projects in Slovakia, used games for development in Egypt, and supported the launch

Figure 24.3
A global cohort of young people engaged in applied research for civic action. Credit: Salzburg Global Seminar/Ela Grieshaber.

of a project on digital and media literacy in Beirut. Out of this work we have identified a framework that guides a pedagogy of civic media.

Our approach aims to enable participants to be part of positive change at local, national, and global levels, and to bridge divides, cross boundaries, and overcome deficits. The process of becoming an active citizen and being able to encounter and interact with the Other is intrinsically linked to the development of one's identity, one's relationship to community, and one's personal values. Our experience with various curricular iterations and interactions with people from all over the world has reinforced our conviction that change starts first and foremost with oneself and then moves outward, so we encourage our students to start by reflecting on their own identity, cultural "baggage," life goals, and values (the "Me" story). We then ask students to reflect on how they interact with, affect, and are affected by the communities to which they belong (the "We" story), before examining issues and causes that are important to them and the ways and means of taking action.

We present this framework not as a prescriptive approach to pedagogies that support civic media, but as a set of constructs that may guide considerations of how pedagogies can better embrace civic media and civic voice as explicit aims for teaching and learning with and about media, participation, and civic life. We focus on three steps that are key to developing and exercising civic voice in global digital culture:

(a) **LISTEN:** How do citizens encounter and make sense of diverse voices? And how do they process stimuli so as to develop their identities and open up to change? These questions guide the situated space of listening that we advocate. Stepping out of one's comfort zone so as to encounter voices and opinions that challenge beliefs and preconceptions is key to developing empathy, rejecting stereotypes both about the self and the Other, and questioning assumptions that drive conflict and inequality. This can be done online, using news curation tools, so as to access and evaluate multiple perspectives on a given issue, as well as offline, in the safe and "unplugged" space of a room in which people from diverse, often clashing, backgrounds are encouraged to speak out and explore their differences. Creating a micro-environment of respect and tolerance is paramount to enabling young people to talk, listen, and appreciate the value of open interaction.

(b) **SHARE:** How can young people articulate their voices so as to reach out to the community and make an impact? Storytelling is key to articulating and sharing one's ideas, grievances, and visions and to becoming empowered. In addition to practical skills, such as multimedia production, storytelling entails reflecting on the factors that enable civic campaigns and messages to become successful and drive change, including the emotional and symbolic elements of civic engagement highlighted earlier. A common issue identified in our students' early attempts to produce and share is that they often do not appreciate the potential power of their own thoughts and words. Realizing the extent to which simple, everyday stories told with empathy, positivity, and wisdom can affect others is a very empowering experience.

(c) **ACT:** In what ways and through which means can citizens take meaningful action to address problems of inequality, injustice, and lack of freedom? While listening to others and participating in the dialogue is important, the civic potential of the literacies can only be fulfilled through participation and the realization of agency. Despite the linguistic, cultural, and socioeconomic barriers that divide young people, we have repeatedly and consistently observed in such diverse cohorts a profound ability to come together and design small-scale community interventions that harness the power of crowds, are based on emerging modes of collaboration and co-creation, and are able to address real-life concerns.

Most of the examples of civic media mentioned earlier in this chapter are *reactions* to events such as natural and humanitarian disasters, conflict, oppression, and crisis. However, meaningful civic action can also be *proactive*, starting at the local (and even

Figure 24.4
Students at Salzburg Academy using Art for Public Expression. Credit: Salzburg Global Seminar/ Moses Itani.

individual) level. The space of civic media continues to open up new ways for young people to advocate for their rights, to support issues that matter to them, and to engage in active forms of participation to better their communities. Our argument incorporates work already done in the literacies and in connected civics, to call for pedagogies aimed at cultivating diverse and vibrant civic voices that contribute to a virtuous cycle of engagement and empowerment. This is not so much a matter of scale, as one of motivation and determination. Or, as anthropologist Margaret Mead put it, "Never doubt that a small group of thoughtful, committed citizens can change the world; indeed, it's the only thing that ever has."

Note

1. Boulianne (2015) notes "… the metadata raise questions about whether the effects are causal and transformative. Only half of the coefficients were statistically significant. These findings raise doubts about transformative effects" (534).

References

Bartlett, J., and C. Miller. 2011. "Truth, Lies and the Internet: A Report into Young People's Digital Fluency." *Demos,* September. http://www.demos.co.uk/files/Truth_-_web.pdf?1317312220 pdf.

Bawden, D. 2008. "Origins and Concepts of Digital Literacy." In *Digital Literacies: Concepts, Policies and Practices,* ed. C. Lankshear and M. Knobel, 17–32. New York: Peter Lang.

Benkler, Y., and H. Nissenbaum. 2006. "Commons-based Peer Production and Virtue." *Journal of Political Philosophy* 14:394–419.

Bennett, W. L. 2007. "Changing Citizenship in the Digital Age." Prepared for OECD/INDIRE Conference on Millennial Learners, Florence, March 5–6, 2007. http://spotlight.macfound.org/resources/Bennett-Changing_Citizenship_in_Digital_Age-OECD.pdf.

Bennett, W. L., and A. Segerberg. 2011. "Digital Media and the Personalization of Collective Action: Social Technology and the Organization of Protests against the Global Economic Crisis." *Information Communication and Society* 14 (6):770–799.

Bialski, P. 2008. "Searching for True Productiveness on the Social Web." *Re-public.* http://www.re-public.gr/en/?p=286.

Brabham, D. C. 2008. "Crowdsourcing as a Model for Problem Solving: An Introduction and Cases." *Convergence (London)* 14 (1): 75–90.

Bryant, M. 2012. "Ban on 9-year-old School Food Blogger Is Reversed." *The Next Web*, June 15. http://thenextweb.com/uk/2012/06/15/ban-on-9-year-old-school-food-blogger-is-reversed.

Boulianne, S. 2015. "Social Media Use and Participation: A Meta-Analysis of Current Research." *Information, Communication & Society* 18 (5): 524–538.

Buckingham, D. 2003. *Media Education: Literacy, Learning and Contemporary Culture*. Cambridge: Polity Press.

Buckingham, D. 2005. "Will Media Education Ever Escape the Effects Debate?" *Telemedium: The Journal of Media Literacy* 52 (3): 17–21.

Buckingham, D. 2007. *Beyond Technology: Children's Learning in the Age of Digital Culture*. Cambridge: Polity Press.

Buckingham, D., ed. 2008. *Youth, Identity, and Digital Media*. Cambridge, MA: MIT Press.

Carlsson, U., ed. 2008. *Empowerment Through Media Education: An Intercultural Dialogue*. International Clearinghouse on Children, Youth and Media, Nordicom. Göteborg University.

Castells, M. 2012. *Networks of Outrage and Hope: Social Movements in the Internet Age*. Cambridge: Polity Press.

Coiro, J., M. Knobel, C. Lankshear, and D. J. Leu, eds. 2014. *Handbook of Research on New Literacies*. New York: Routledge.

Constanza-Chock, S. 2014. *Out of the Shadows, Into the Streets: Transmedia Organizing and the Immigrant Rights Movement*. Cambridge, MA: MIT Press.

Craft, S., A. Maksl, and S. Ashley. 2013. "Measuring News Media Literacy: How Knowledge and Motivations Combine to Create News-Literate Teens." White Paper Report, McCormick Foundation. http://www.whynewsmatters.org/wp-content/uploads/2014/10/MeasuringNewsMedia Literacy.pdf.

Dalton, R. 2009. *The Good Citizen: How a Younger Generation Is Reshaping American Politics*. Washington, DC: CQ Press.

Deuze, M. 2006. "Participation, Remediation, Bricolage: Considering Principal Components of a Digital Culture." *Information Society* 22 (2): 63–75.

Eltantawy, N., and J. B. Wiest. 2011. "The Arab Spring: Social Media in the Egyptian Revolution: Reconsidering Resource Mobilization Theory." *International Journal of Communication* 5: 1207–1224.

Fieldhouse, M., and D. Nicholas. 2008. "Digital Literacy as Information Savvy." In *Digital Literacies: Concepts, Policies and Practices*, ed. C. Lankshear and M. Knobel, 47–72. New York: Peter Lang Publishing, Inc.

Fowler, J., and N. Christakis. 2010. "Cooperative Behavior Cascades in Human Social Networks." *Proceedings of the National Academy of Sciences of the United States of America* 107 (12): 5334–5338.

Freire, P. 1970. *Pedagogy of the Oppressed*. New York: Seabury Press.

Gerbaudo, P. 2012. *Tweets and the Streets: Social Media and Contemporary Activism*. London: Pluto Press.

Gerodimos, R. 2008. "Mobilising Young Citizens in the UK: A Content Analysis of Youth and Issue Websites." *Information, Communication & Society* 11 (7): 964–988.

Gerodimos, R. 2012. "Online Youth Civic Attitudes and the Limits of Civic Consumerism: The Emerging Challenge to the Internet's Democratic Potential." *Information, Communication & Society* 15 (2): 217–245.

Gerodimos, R., and J. Justinussen. 2014. "Obama's 2012 Facebook Campaign: Political Communication in the Age of the Like Button." *Journal of Information Technology & Politics*. doi:.10.1080 /19331681.2014.982266

Gerodimos, R., R. Scullion, D. G. Lilleker, and D. Jackson. 2013. "Introduction." In *The Media, Political Participation and Empowerment*, ed. R. Scullion, R. Gerodimos, D. Jackson, and D. Lilleker. London: Routledge.

Glister, P. 1997. *Digital Literacy*. New York: Wiley.

Hobbs, R. 2010. "Digital and Media Literacy: A Plan of Action." White Paper on the Digital and Media Literacy Recommendations of the Knight Commission on the Information Needs of Communities in a Democracy. Washington, DC: The Aspen Institute.

Hobbs, R. 2011 a. *Digital and Media Literacy: Connecting Culture and Classroom*. Thousand Oaks, CA: Corwin Press.

Hobbs, R. 2011 b. "The State of Media Literacy: A Response to Potter." *Journal of Broadcasting & Electronic Media* 55 (3): 419–430.

Hobbs, R., K. Donnelly, J. Friesem, and M. Moen. 2013. "Learning to Engage: How Positive Attitudes about the News, Media Literacy, and Video Production Contribute to Adolescent Civic Engagement." *Educational Media International* 50 (4): 231–246.

Hoffman, J. 2012. "A Child's Helping Hand on Portions." *New York Times*, April 24. http://www.nytimes.com/2012/04/25/dining/a-child-offers-plan-on-portion-control-for-dieters.html?_r=0.

Horkheimer, M. 1937. "Traditional and Critical Theory." In *Critical Theory: Selected Essays*, ed. M. Horkheimer. New York: Continuum.

Ito, M. 2008. *Living and Learning with New Media: Summary of Findings from the Digital Youth Project*. Cambridge, MA: MIT Press.

Ito, M., E. Soep, N. Kligler-Vilenchik, S. Shresthova, L. Gamber-Thompson, and A. Zimmerman. 2015. "Learning Connected Civics: Narratives, Practices, Infrastructures." *Curriculum Inquiry* 45 (1): 10–29.

Jenkins, H. 2006. *Convergence Culture: Where Old and New Media Collide*. New York: NYU Press.

Jenkins, H., S. Ford, and J. Green. 2013. *Spreadable Media: Creating Value and Meaning in a Networked Age*. New York: New York University Press.

Jenkins, H., R. Purushotma, M. Weigel, K. Clinton, and A. J. Robinson. 2009. "Confronting the Challenges of Participatory Culture: Media Education for the 21st Century." A Report for the MacArthur Foundation. Cambridge, MA: MIT Press.

Kahne, J., N. Lee, and J. Feezell. 2010. "The Civic and Political Significance of Online Participatory Cultures Among Youth Transitioning to Adulthood." DML Central Working Paper. http://dmlcentral.net/sites/default/files/resource_files/OnlineParticipatoryCultures.WORKINGPAPERS.pdf.

Kahne, J., N. Lee, and J. T. Feezell. 2012. "Digital Media Literacy Education and Online Civic and Political Participation." *International Journal of Communication* 6:1–24.

Kahne, J., J. Ulman, and E. Middaugh. 2011. *Digital Opportunities for Civic Education*. Washington, DC: American Enterprise Institute.

Kellner, D., and J. Share. 2007. "Critical Media Literacy, Democracy, and the Reconstruction of Education." In *Media Literacy: A Reader*, ed. D. Macedo and S. R. Steinberg, 3–23. New York: Peter Lang.

Khondker, H. H. 2011. "Role of the New Media in the Arab Spring." *Globalizations* 8 (5): 675–679.

Kiili, C., L. Laurinen, and M. Marttunen. 2008. "Students Evaluating Internet Sources: From Versatile Evaluators to Uncritical Readers." *Journal of Educational Computing Research* 39 (1): 75–95.

Kligler-Vilenchik, N., and S. Shresthova. 2012. "Learning through Practice: Participatory Culture Practices." Digital Media & Learning Research Hub. http://dmlhub.net/publications/learning-through-practice-participatory-culture-practices.

Lankshear, C., and M. Knobel. 2011. *New Literacies: Everyday Practices and Social Learning*. New York: McGraw-Hill International.

Masterman, L. 1985. *Teaching the Media*. London: Routledge.

McDevitt, M., and S. Kiousis. 2006. "Deliberative Learning: An Evaluative Approach to Interactive Civic Education." *Communication Education* 55 (3): 247–264.

McPherson, M., L. Smith-Lovin, and M. E. Brashears. 2006. "Social Isolation in America: Changes in Core Discussion Networks Over Two Decades." *American Sociological Review* 71 (3): 353–375.

Middaugh, E. 2012. "Service & Activism in the Digital Age: Supporting Youth Engagement in Public Life." MacArthur Research Network on Service and Activism in the Digital Age. http://dmlcentral.net/sites/default/files/resource_files/sa.pdf.

Mihailidis, P. 2009. "Beyond Cynicism: Media Education and Civic Learning Outcomes in the University." *International Journal of Media and Learning* 1 (3): 1–13.

Mihailidis, P. 2013. "Exploring Global Perspectives on Identity, Community and Media Literacy in a Networked Age." *Journal of Digital and Media Literacy* 1 (1).

Mihailidis, P. 2014 a. *Media Literacy and the Emerging Citizen: Youth, Participation and Engagement in Digital Culture*. New York: Peter Lang.

Mihailidis, P. 2014 b. "A Tethered Generation: Exploring the Role of Mobile Phones in the Daily Life of Young People." *Mobile Media & Communication* 2 (1): 58–72.

Milner, H. 2010. *The Internet Generation: Engaged Citizens or Political Dropouts*. Medford, MA: Tufts University Press.

Musick, M., and J. Wilson. 2008. *Volunteers: A Social Profile*. Bloomington, IN: Indiana University Press.

Parker, K. 2014. "Texas-based App Fueling Protests in Ukraine, Venezuela." *San Antonio Express-News*, February 26. http://www.mysanantonio.com/news/us-world/world/article/Texas-based-app-fueling-protests-in-Ukraine-5270453.php.

Postman, N. 1985. *Amusing Ourselves to Death: Public Discourse in the Age of Show Business*. New York: Penguin.

Potter, W. J. 2010. "The State of Media Literacy." *Journal of Broadcasting & Electronic Media* 54 (4): 675–696.

Reilly, E., and I. Literat, eds. 2012. "Designing with Teachers: Participatory Approaches to Professional Development in Education." USC Annenberg Innovation Lab. http://dmlhub.net/publications/designing-with-teachers-participatory-approaches-to-professional-development-in-education.

Rheingold, H. 2012. *Net Smart: How to Thrive Online*. Cambridge, MA: MIT Press.

Romer, D., K. Hall Jamieson, and J. Pasek. 2009. "Building Social Capital in Young People: The Role of Mass Media and Life Outlook." *Political Communication* 26:65–83.

Russell, J. 2012. "Let Them Eat Cake, but No Camera: British Council Gags 9-year-old School Lunch Blogger." *The Next Web*, June 15. http://thenextweb.com/uk/2012/06/15/let-them-eat-cake-but-no-cameras-british-council-gags-9-year-old-school-lunch-blogger.

Scharrer, E. 2002. "Third-Person Perception and Television Violence: The Role of Out-Group Stereotyping in Perceptions of Susceptibility to Effects." *Communication Research* 29 (6): 681–704.

Schiller, H. 1975. *The Mind Managers*. Boston, MA: Beacon Press.

Shirky, C. 2010. *Cognitive Surplus: How Technology Makes Consumers into Collaborators*. New York: Penguin.

Shumow, M., ed. 2014. *Mediated Communities: Civic Voices, Empowerment and Media Literacy in the Digital Era*. New York: Peter Lang.

Turkle, S. 2012. *Alone Together: Why We Expect More from Technology and Less from Each Other*. New York: Basic Books.

Vraga, E. K., M. Tully, and H. Rojas. 2009. "Media Literacy Training Reduces Perception of Bias." *Newspaper Research Journal* 30 (4).

Walgrave, S., W. L. Bennett, J. Van Laer, and C. Breunig. 2011. "Multiple Engagements and Network Bridging in Contentious Politics: Digital Media Use of Protest Participants." *Mobilization: An International Quarterly (San Diego, CA)* 16 (3): 325–349.

Webster, J. G. 2014. *The Marketplace of Attention: How Audiences Take Shape in a Digital Age*. Cambridge, MA: MIT Press.

Williamson, B. 2013. *The Future of the Curriculum: School Knowledge in the Digital Age. The John D. and Catherine T. MacArthur Foundation Reports on Digital Media and Learning*. Cambridge, MA: MIT Press; http://dmlhub.net/publications/future-curriculum.

Zimmerman, A. M. 2012. "Documenting Dreams: New Media, Undocumented Youth and the Immigrant Rights Movement." http://ypp.dmlcentral.net/sites/all/files/publications/Documenting%20DREAMs%20-%20Working%20Paper-MAPP%20-%20June%206%202012.pdf.

25 Youth Agency in Public Spheres: Emerging Tactics, Literacies, and Risks

Elisabeth Soep

Introduction

In 2012, 24-year-old Pendarvis Harshaw was finishing up college credits and working as a mentor for the local school district. Over spring break, he set off on a road-trip to visit his father, whom he hadn't seen in 18 years. It was via Facebook that Pen tracked down his dad, through an uncle. Pen flew from Oakland to Chicago and then joined a friend with a car for the 12-hour drive to the Alabama prison where his father lived. Pen tweeted the whole way, regularly updating his growing community of 2,250-plus followers. A couple months later, he wrote a story about the experience. An emerging journalist who'd spent his teen years at Youth Radio, a youth-driven production company in Oakland, Pen set out to get the story distributed. The week before Father's Day, he published the story online, hoping a big outlet would pick it up. No takers. So when Father's Day arrived, he posted the piece on his own Tumblr, *OG Told Me*, a photo-rich oral history site chronicling his encounters with black male elders and their advice to young men.

Soon after, he took to Facebook: "After pitching my piece about my journey to meet my father to multiple outlets that report on 'Black news'—and getting no response ... I decided to post it on my personal blog. In turn, the response from my circle of friends has been amazing. ..." Pen's friends had commented on and spread the link, urging others to do the same. They reflected on how the story touched them personally, and connected it to issues including mass incarceration, drug policies, the role of journalism in public affairs, race and masculinity and fatherhood. What really got him, though, were the in-person responses. When he was jogging around Lake Merritt one day, an acquaintance stopped him to say, "I didn't want to react online, but I wanted to tell you in person how much I appreciated your being so transparent and open." On Facebook, Pen wrote, "Conversations, texts, emails, tweets, facebook shares & likes ... all from a lil sumn I decided to write ... that's love. Thanks."

Pen didn't overturn a government, get an official hired or fired, or change a policy by producing, sharing, and stoking conversation through his story about his father. He did, however, engage in some of the key activities that drive youth involvement in civic life today. This emerging set of activities fuels what colleagues and I are calling "participatory politics" (Kahne, Middaugh, and Allen 2014; Cohen et al. 2012; Jenkins et al., forthcoming).

Though sometimes disavowing "politics" as an apt description of what they're doing, civically engaged young people are using every means and media at their disposal to carry out the core tasks of citizenship. Through a mix of face-to-face and digital encounters, they deliberate on key issues, debate with peers and powerbrokers, and in some cases change the structures of joint decision making and the course of history (Allen and Light, 2015). Like Pen, many young people who are coming into their political selves today both distrust public institutions and want in. They get excited about alternative means to make a difference, and they seek access to traditional channels into power. Through their interactions with peers and elites, they're redefining some key dynamics that govern civic life.

This chapter delves into these shifting dynamics to ask: What specific tactics are young people experimenting with to exercise agency and intervene in public affairs? How can these activities grow in quality? What work is required to ensure that opportunities to engage in participatory politics are equitably distributed among youth, including those marginalized from digital and other forms of privilege? I'll draw from insights in the existing literature; my own collaborative practice with teens co-producing media with them over the past 14 years (see for example, Soep 2005 and 2012; Soep and Chávez 2010); as well as a set of studies that are part of the Youth and Participatory Politics (YPP) Research Network, an initiative supported by the John D. and Catherine T. MacArthur Foundation. YPP research includes two national surveys of young people, interviews with civically engaged youth, large-scale inventories of digital sites and platforms, design research efforts aimed to maximize equitable access to high quality learning environments, meta-analyses of existing research, and international comparative case studies of youth activism (Allen and Light, 2015; Cohen et al. 2012; DeVoss, Eidman-Aadahl, and Hicks 2010; Earl 2013; Gardner and Davis 2013; Jenkins et al. forthcoming; Soep 2013; Zuckerman 2015).

The list of tactics identified here emerge from this collaborative body of research and from sustained, direct collaboration with youth. The five tactics are: (1) Pivot Your Public; (2) Create Content Worlds; (3) Information-Forage; (4) Code Up; (5) Hide and Seek.

I will focus on youth-driven activities in the United States, though in many cases they will be transnational in origin and/or effect. After detailed discussion of each of the five tactics, I will identify the key literacies that communities will need to organize themselves around if they want to help cultivate meaningful roles for young people shaping public affairs. Following a discussion of literacies is a section on the risks associated with participatory politics, and concluding thoughts on implications for future research and on-the-ground activity.

Participatory Politics: What Sets It Apart?

Consider some of the activities Pen and his community carried out in his storytelling project. They *circulated information*, activating various channels including self-publication via personal outlets while also pursuing third-party distribution. They *sparked dialogue*, not only telling but also hearing; Pen deliberately stoked conversation by joining in comment streams and publicly recognizing "link-love" when others reposted his piece, and by warmly receiving acknowledgment of what he'd shared in his story. Both he and his readers *produced content*, using digital tools and platforms to craft compelling narratives and responses that addressed potent social themes. They *investigated* sources of information, connection, and opportunity, not only in the service of crafting the story, but also to discover and track channels for reaching and activating significant audience. Finally, they *prodded others to act*. Peers confessed that they were motivated to reach out to members of their own families and continue their work on issues relevant to Pen's story, based on his words.

These five activities powering Pen's project are the core features of participatory politics (Kahne, Middaugh, and Allen 2014). None is brand new. Young people have always circulated media in various forms, engaged in dialogue, produced content, investigated their worlds for information and insights, and mobilized peers toward shared goals. Likewise, as documented for decades by cultural studies scholars, young people marginalized from institutional politics have long leveraged subcultural domains to exercise voice and agency (Ginwright, Noguera, and Cammarota 2006; Willis 1990). What is new is evidence suggesting that young people's civic and political activities have become less centralized and more prominent, due in large part to dynamics of digital and social media, which include closer connections between culture and politics, as well as diminished costs and easier access to far-flung collaborators and impact at scale (Bakardijeva 2009; Bennett and Segerberg 2012; Earl and Kimport 2011).

These hold promise for youth engagement in digital-age civics, but these same conditions also breed new inequalities, which can block access to the knowledge and networks that drive today's change. Freedom, after all, is not possible without equity, argues Danielle Allen (2012). Politics are a kind of art, Allen goes on to say, and participation requires mastery of techniques through which citizens can understand shared experience, see and pursue alternative paths, "take turns accepting losses in the public sphere, and ... acknowledge and honor the losses that others have accepted" (1). Interdependence along these lines is required to produce democracy, hence the focus in participatory politics on collective tactics across a range of tools and platforms aimed to promote freedom, equity, and democratic deliberation.

Five Tactics of Participatory Politics

1. Pivot your public: Mobilizing civic capacity within networks that form out of shared personal and cultural interests and communities

The opening example of Pendarvis Harshaw's distribution strategy for a story rejected by mainstream news outlets is an instance of pivoting his public. As noted above, Pen's friends and followers shared many personal, social, and cultural interests. That much is obvious, from his social media posts about upcoming poetry events and bicyclist gatherings, and photos of extreme hairstyles. By interspersing news of his journey within his ongoing social media updates—where he also cheered the Oakland As and planned his upcoming birthday—Pen enlisted a network of already connected friends and associates to examine issues with relevance to public affairs. Personal and playful updates were intercut with links to Pen's own critical writing, as well as conversation about President Obama's responsibilities as a mentor to the next generation, and provocations such as, "Confused. So ... They're closing public schools across the Nation & privatizing education? What does it mean?" He converted these online activities into meaningful offline interactions, defying the troubling extent to which observers tend to bifurcate young people's digital and real-life activities (and to argue about whether e-politics "count" without acknowledging the constant criss-crossing of virtual and face-to-face encounters in most civic and political activities). What's at work here is the tactic of marshalling the shared history and sensibility that can form inside a network of mutual interest, to motivate engagement in topics and activities with civic import.

Civic and political potential within these networks may appear to be latent, but a great deal of work goes into maintaining communities so they are ready to mobilize behind collective efforts, under the right conditions (Kligler-Vilenchik 2013). When peers pursue their popular culture interests together, they can produce highly sophisticated creative products and develop robust literacies in the process (Barron et al. 2014; Jenkins et al. 2009; Ito 2009; Vossoughi and Bevan 2014). The value of these activities should not be judged exclusively on the basis of whether they translate directly into political outcomes. That said, we have seen that through their interest-driven activities, young people are often crafting, feeding, and nurturing a community that will be prepared to think and act, in civic and political ways, when the time comes.

Survey data from Cathy Cohen and Joe Kahne's national study of youth and participatory politics provides further evidence for how interest-driven activities can power civic engagement, perhaps especially in the digital age. It appears that such activities lay a foundation for participatory politics by cultivating "digital social capital" (Cohen et al. 2012). Pursuing interests can build knowledge, skills, and networks that support subsequent (or simultaneous) civic and political organizing. Cohen, Kahne, and their colleagues found that young people who were highly involved in interest-driven activities were five times as likely as those without such involvements to engage in participatory politics, and nearly four times as likely to participate in all political acts measured in their survey (see also Barron et al. 2014). Findings along these lines expose the hidden significance of activities easily dismissed as recreational or "only" driven by shared interest, when it comes to organizing civic-minded collective action (see also Ito and Soep et al, forthcoming).

The Harry Potter Alliance (HPA) is one of the case studies published from the YPP network that offers an example of what pivoting your public can look like on an organizational level (Kligler-Vilenchik 2013, Kligler-Vilenchik and Shresthova 2012). Established in 2005, HPA was inspired by the fictional student activist group, "Dumbledore's Army," which appeared in the Harry Potter narratives. In real life, HPA has organized more than 100,000 U.S. fans to work on political and philanthropic issues such as literacy, equality, and human rights. Campaigns include "Accio books, an annual book drive, in which members have donated over 87,000 books to local and international communities; Wizard Rock the Vote, registering 1100 voters in Wizard Rock concerts across the nation; Wrock 4 Equality, a phone-banking campaign to protect marriage equality rights in Maine, and many others" (Kligler-Vilenchik and Shresthova 2012, 11). HPA has managed to pivot a fan community's energetic identification with a make-believe world, and turn that engagement toward civic ends. Though members might gather behind overseas relief efforts or marriage equality campaigns, the social and creative bond remains a key factor: "I think there's this balance," reports one HPA chapter organizer. "It's equal parts making a difference and equal parts meeting more people, and connecting with people that probably are kinder to them in a way or just more similar to them."

That said, just because someone's your friend, that doesn't mean he or she will necessarily take kindly to the injection of political themes when young people are just trying to hang out. In the Harvard-based interview study of civically engaged youth, some young people reported keeping offline civic activities outside their digital social networks, an approach Emily Weinstein (2013) and her colleagues call "fragmented." Others limit their civic sentiments to only a select number of the various platforms they use—a "bracketed" pattern of identity expression. And still others—the largest of the three groups—integrate their civic views and participation into their online identities, favoring what Weinstein calls a "blended" approach.

But even the most careful strategizing doesn't always work. Another YPP site is a Chicago-based civic organization that engages high school students in the political process through elections, activism, and policy-making efforts. Interviews there reveal that it's not always easy to strike the balance between socializing and organizing with peers. One young person from the Chicago program confessed that some of her

Facebook friends started hiding her in their newsfeeds, because they found her political posts annoying; her remarks interrupted the fun social flow (James 2012). Clearly, knowing how to read your face-to-face and online peer network and edge it forward is among the key forms of literacy required for civically engaged youth.

2. Create content worlds: Using inventive and interactive storytelling to achieve public attention and influence

In 2012, we saw a sensational and highly controversial example of young people enlisted into what Henry Jenkins and his colleagues call a "content world"—this one containing an explicit political call-to-action. Content worlds are deeply engaging, multi-faceted narratives that invite active participation, and the one I am referring to is *Kony 2012*.

Kony 2012 is a half-hour, highly produced documentary that shows more than 99 million views on YouTube at the time of this writing. The film was created by Invisible Children, a US-based organization that members of the YPP network have been researching for three years.[1] Founded by three film students from the University of Southern California in 2003, Invisible Children aims to "use the power of media to inspire young people to help end the longest running war in Africa." The goal of the *Kony 2012* film was to make one man famous—Joseph Kony, leader of the Ugandan Lord's Resistance Army—in order to take him down for his crimes against humanity, which included kidnapping children, conscripting them as soldiers, and forcing them into slavery.

Kony 2012 was not, by any means, an overnight media sensation. It built on Invisible Children's explicit, longstanding strategy of mobilizing public action through storytelling and social media spread. Four years prior to their video sensation, Invisible Children was one of 17 organizations convened by the U.S. State Department as part of its efforts to fight "extremism." The organization reported 2012 net liabilities and assets of more than $17 million and has received significant support from entities ranging from right-wing Christian organizations to Hollywood celebrities (Kron 2012).

Invisible Children's tactics, says Lana Swartz (2012), include "visually-arresting films, spectacular event-oriented campaigns, provocative graphic t-shirts and other apparel, music mixes, print media, blogs, and more. To be a member of Invisible Children means to be a viewer, participant, wearer, reader, listener, commenter of and in the various activities, many mediated, that make up the Movement. It is a massive, open-ended, evolving documentary 'story.'" Swartz describes these activities as "world-making" in the sense that they contain varied points of entry for audiences to co-create and collaborate in the production of "the movement's" master narratives.

While trending at record-breaking rates across leading digital platforms, *Kony 2012* sparked intense criticism from a range of sources for the "world" it produced. The

Invisible Children solution was totally out of step with Kony's current status in the region, argued some African commentators and others, who saw in Invisible Children's call to action a familiar assumption that the solution would originate in the west and deny Ugandans agency in their own fight for justice. Building on his provocative series of Tweets, the writer Teju Cole published a critique in the *Atlantic* of *Kony 2012* as a product of what he dubbed the White Savior Industrial Complex, which "is not about justice," said Cole. "It's about having a big emotional experience that validates privilege." That "big emotional experience" is one we need to take seriously as a force within content worlds formed through participatory politics. World-making content is emotional—that's part of what draws people in, makes them "enthusiastic," to use Cole's term, to get involved and make a difference. And yet, as Ethan Zuckerman (2012a) argued in his own widely distributed response to *Kony 2012*, sometimes content resonates and spreads because of the story's simplicity, and simplified stories can, despite good intentions, cause serious harm.

While I have spent considerable time in this discussion of content worlds on a highly resourced and professionally produced video that captured global attention, smaller-scale storytelling efforts, supported by tiny budgets and little-to-no infrastructure, are equally important to consider as we explore content creation as political work—both its merits and risks. User-generated content streams invite more and more media makers into public dialogue, which is a core activity within participatory politics. And yet there are downsides, with respect to sustaining a critical message. Given the fact that memes often set a clock ticking, before long clever tropes turn into tired gimmicks, effectively retiring messages whose substance might still deserve serious attention long after the meme has timed out. Achieving "virality" is fun to aspire to but extremely hard to pull off. More problematically, the same mechanisms that enable viral spread—for example, users' ability to riff off of online postings—can also invite deeply disturbing activities like bullying, savage mockery, and "RIP trolling," in which anonymous commenters harass contributors to memorial pages dedicated to deceased loved ones, a phenomenon researcher Whitney Phillips (2011) argues has an "accidental politics" of its own. Creating content worlds involves a whole lot more than making and posting a piece of media. Production of the story, as a meaningful tool for civic and political activity, extends into a "digital afterlife" that endures well beyond the moment any one publication goes live (Soep 2012).

3. Information-Forage: Finding and sharing information via public data archives to discover trends, fact-check, and juxtapose claims with evidence

With this third tactic of participatory politics, young people and their mentors leverage emerging tools and platforms to discover, organize, and share untapped stores of information, in the process upsetting conventional assumptions about who normally "handles" original data and in what ways. Foraging implies that not only accredited experts are in a position to glean public assets, that resources reside all around us, and that there shouldn't be a million obstacles, nor should it require a million dollars, to access those goods. Young people are increasingly involved in gathering data that's hiding in plain sight, within social networking sites they rely on for civic and political news, and through public information repositories they can tap to identify patterns officials might rather obscure.

Journalism is one field where young people's investigations through digital and social media have made a serious civic impact. I work as part of one such effort, Youth Radio, where I first met our chapter's opener, Pendarvis Harshaw. At Youth Radio in downtown Oakland, young people—the majority youth of color from low-income communities—collaborate with professional producers and editors on content for outlets including National Public Radio, American Public Media, the *Huffington Post*, *National Geographic*, local and commercial public radio stations around the country, and a slew of online sites (Soep and Chávez 2010). Some of the organization's most ambitious work in the last few years has come out of its Investigative Desk, including two series that were recognized with major national honors (the Robert F. Kennedy and George Foster Peabody Awards respectively). In *Navy Abuse*, Youth Radio investigated a U.S. Navy base in the Persian Gulf where a culture of hazing and abuse targeted a young gay sailor and others in the unit. In *Trafficked*, the newsroom dedicated several months to tracking the social and policy dynamics that drive underage girls into commercial sexual exploitation, through a legal system that criminalizes teens who've been trafficked and makes it exceedingly difficult to prosecute their abusers.

I was a member of the production teams behind both of these projects and have written previously about them (Soep 2011 and 2012). For my purposes here, I am struck by the ways in which digital and social media surfaced information that was pivotal to each story's production and dissemination. In *Navy Abuse*, at one point the fate of the story hinged on whether the reporter could verify the unit's Chief Petty Officer's whereabouts, and the fact that he'd been promoted after abuse allegations came to light. For a long time, we couldn't locate him—until a source told the youth reporter about a social media site for military personnel and vets. That website provided crucial information about the Chief Petty Officer's rank and deployment status, which enabled Youth Radio finally to get official confirmation of the facts, and to send questions directly to him.

In the second Youth Radio investigation, *Trafficked*, digital and social media surfaced as central forces in the story itself. The reporting team uncovered a network of local photography studios and PR consultancies that had sprung up to help clients, including teens, produce digital profiles for websites that sold girls for sex. Moreover, efforts to crack down on prostitution sites—a move some researchers say might erase traces of perpetrators' activities that are actually useful to law enforcement (boyd et al.

2011)—were an important backdrop to Youth Radio's reporting and showed up through heated comment streams that scrolled from the story after publication.

In both of these examples, young reporters and their colleagues deployed digital and social media tools to forage for crucial information, while reporting on how those very tools factored in the stories themselves. Producers then exploited the same tools to spread the news.

That said, per usual, new opportunities also created new challenges. No one wants unflattering information to surface unexpectedly, and the dynamics can get especially intense when multiple power discrepancies are in play. In one YPP study of a large urban school district's youth advisory committee, researcher Margaret Rundle, part of the Harvard team, learned about students' efforts to have a role in teacher evaluation. In a meeting the youth group had captured on video, the superintendent had, in their view, expressed support for these efforts. But when the group went public with that endorsement, the superintendent backed off and sought to distance herself from that position. The fact that the young people had video documentation of the original meeting strengthened their position for sure, but it also rendered them a greater threat. Information is power, but it can also get you in trouble. Moreover, sometimes the veneer of transparency can be more dangerous than obvious efforts to distort or block access to information, because it makes institutions that are actually keeping secrets appear forthcoming.

4.   Code Up: Designing tools, platforms, and spaces that advance public good

In 2010, Youth Radio launched a new arm of its production company, the Mobile Action Lab.[2] The Lab partnered young people with professional designers and developers to create mobile apps. Motivating the work was the realization that it was no longer enough for young people to create content using existing tools, or to deliver their stories via available platforms. They needed to be the ones engineering those tools and designing those platforms, which increasingly determine who knows what, how information circulates, and what sparks change.

Youth Radio's Mobile Action Lab is part of a growing movement to engage young people in efforts to design software that supports transparency, democracy, and justice. Youth App Lab was another early effort along these lines, founded at Youth Uplift in Washington DC by engineer Leshell Hatley, who aimed to create pathways for black youth into computer science. Iridescent is a national program that builds tech literacy in girls, in part through the Technovation Challenge, in which the girls learn to produce mobile apps and launch start-up companies. By exposing students to computer science and technology, the San Francisco-based Black Girls Code sets out to increase the number of women of color "in the digital space" and enable them to be leaders and builders of their own futures. The Hidden Genius Project in Oakland strives to unlock pathways for young black males into careers in software development and design.

Many early efforts drew inspiration from Apps4Good, a UK-based project that was perhaps the first to engage teens in app-making. Many used tools like App Inventor, built by Google Labs and now run out of MIT, which enables people with no computer science training to create apps. And many of these organizations are now in the process of iterating not only on apps in their portfolios, but also on the structure and scope of their own programs. They're graduating from start-up mode into periods of establishing consistent and sustainable frameworks for engaging youth and communities through mobile software design.

Whether based in contexts centered on app development, game design, robotics, or other maker-oriented activities, "coding up" activities tend to share a belief that young people are creators and not just users of technology and media, and that their activities and products have the potential to bring good to their own lives and communities. As this work builds momentum, the challenges are significant. Any maker knows, while creating a prototype can happen fast, building a friction- and glitch-free project that totally delivers on its promise and gains runaway traction with users is rare, and takes time, luck, stamina, and money. Along the way is plenty of failure, which start-up types like to celebrate, but which can be deeply demoralizing for young people whose humanity and intelligence are often already under assault, and for organizations whose existence can depend on cheerful grant reports touting success.

There's a lot to learn from youth app development and other digital maker spaces about new models for mentorship or "collegial pedagogy" between novices and experts (Soep and Chávez 2010), as there's a huge gap between what it takes to create the simplest app, robot, e-textile garment, or digitized contraption, and the work required to bring a sophisticated product to market—not to mention one intended to achieve civic good. Great projects get started through the increasingly popular phenomenon of the youth-oriented hackathon, which can immerse young people in the world of community-driven design. And yet even hackathon enthusiasts are seeking new models for promoting youth learning over time and for launching sustainable projects that advance beyond one-off designs, which rarely evolve into fully developed tools with measureable impact on local lives. Even when those tools make it to the stage of community usage, standard metrics like download counts fall far short of capturing nuanced measures of the impact of these projects. We are only beginning to frame analytics that assess quality of product design, learning experience, and outcomes for the makers and their communities, while enabling the developers to maintain independence and agency with respect to their code, content, and craft. The work of developing these new methodologies and analytics is key, as expressing voice and influence in public spheres increasingly requires not only use but also development of digital tools. Knowing how to create and assess the impact of those tools, products, and environments isn't simply a set of technical skills. It's a mandate for civic learning.

5. Hide and Seek: Covering tracks and protecting information from discovery as actors engage in politics that only selectively surface into public awareness

On November 11, 2011, two Latino students in their early twenties walked into a border patrol office in Mobile, Alabama, in hopes that they wouldn't freely walk back out. "Last words?" one asked the other, as they fired up the cell phone camera in the car and prepared to step inside. The video of their encounter with two white border patrol officers has the now-familiar look of an engineered confrontation "caught" on amateur video (it's unclear from the footage whether the people on camera know they're being taped). From the point of view of one of the young men, you see a non-descript office space, with the requisite flags, framed head-shots, and couches lit from above by over-exposed rectangles of fluorescent light. He tells a woman who greets them that he and his companion are lost. "Hang on a second," she says, sounding nervous. The woman slides her security card through a reader, unlatching a door, and exits to find help. Two officers emerge from the other room. "Hey what's going on? How you doing? Can we help you with something?" one asks. "Yeah, you know what? I'm actually not lost. I'm just kinda pissed off. What are you all doing here?" one of the students responds. "Doing our job, why?" "What's your job?" "To enforce immigration laws." "That what you do?" "Yeah, that's what we do. ... What's it to you?" The young man with the camera says, "I'm illegal too." "Oh you're illegal?" "So you think I should get deported?" The officers ask for ID. The one in uniform looks at the card, flips it over to examine the back, and asks, "How'd you get to the United States?" "Cross the border." "When did you do that?" "Long time ago." The following words flash on the screen: "After the cell phone signal dropped, Jonathan and Isaac were detained and transferred to the Basile Detention Center in southern Louisiana. Inside the detention center, they're meeting many people like them—immigrants who've committed no crimes. The administration is lying when they tell us they are only deporting serious criminals."

YPP ethnographers Arely Zimmerman (2012) and Sangita Shresthova are considering this video as part of their research on undocumented youth and their allies' use of participatory media to oppose US immigration policy and advocate for the DREAM Act, legislation that grants conditional legal status to college students who were brought to the US before they turned 16. This tense scene of entry into a space of policed authority is a trope as prominent within activist videos as the "arrival stories" anthropologists use to introduce their ethnographies of far-away cultures (Pratt 1991). In this particular video, Jonathan and Isaac come across as kind of scared, as if maybe they hadn't fully thought through what they were about to do when they hatched the plan to turn themselves in to border control. But like many documentary-style confrontations of this sort, it turns out there's a mix here of genuine and dramatized affect. In a subsequent interview, Jonathan told the website CultureStrike (2011), "We went undercover and decided to *pretend* we were afraid, *pretend* we are not connected in any way" (emphasis added), as part of a strategy that would get them sent to a detention center, where the two could continue their organizing from inside (Chen 2011).

At first glance, this video would seem to be consistent with the other cases of participatory politics I've considered above. All four sets of tactics—pivoting public discussion toward political ends, creating content worlds designed to instigate action, foraging for information, and developing digital tools to express voice and exert influence in public spheres—center on proclaiming civic positions. But what's striking in Jonathan and Isaac's story is the play of disclosure and cover, voice and silence, activities that take place in the full light of public awareness and those that happen in the shadows of digital life. The power of this video, and the larger phenomenon of youth "coming out" as undocumented, without papers and at risk of detention and deportation, resides in the tension these public gestures create against the backdrop of a larger expectation of secrecy and silence.

Studies of politics in the digital age tend to focus on speech—new ways that technology enables overt, amplified, and ever-escalating civic expression and action. We would be remiss not to account also for the tactics young people deploy to mix authorship and anonymity, vocalization and silence, especially under digitally enabled conditions of heightened surveillance.

"The re-conceptualization of the public sphere around silence, instead of speech, provides the tools necessary for grasping the political significance of anonymous speech," says political philosopher Danielle Allen (2010, 2). The conceit of anonymity, if not its reality, is of course a hallmark feature of digital identity. Public spheres are made up of rituals and mechanisms that foster discovery and disclosure, for sure. But there are also proliferating ways to close off, cover up, and disguise certain kinds of conversation. Tactical silence, Allen (2010, 9) argues, can have important political value as a destabilizing and deceptive force. It "can serve as a political weapon when it is used to mislead powerholders about the truth of their situation; not knowing the truth of their situation, they will fail to make sound practical judgments about it."

Research with communities that are targets of intensified state-backed suspicion, including undocumented youth activists and Muslim American youth organizers, has found that the young people in these communities have learned to "hide and seek" inside systems of surveillance. Sangita Shresthova interviewed participants in an incident at the University of California Irvine in 2010, when a group of students associated with the Muslim Student Union disrupted the speech of Israel's ambassador during his visit to campus (the students were later convicted and their club suspended). One interviewee confessed that she found it difficult to figure out what to reveal about herself, and when to keep silent. "It's hard," she said. "I try not to post too much personal information just because you don't know who—I'm sure there are people that don't agree with my viewpoint that are friends with me on Facebook. ... So you don't want to post too much personal information. ... I mean, we ... [get] death threats and stuff, hate emails and stuff. … Like one of the things I try not to do is to post like where I am … like physical location. I try to limit things."

Managing visibility and invisibility, speech and silence, is itself a participatory activity in the digital age. Under the old system of institutional politics, established gatekeepers were better positioned to control the flow of information, delineate the conditions where dialogue occurs, and determine which people's identities and activities are revealed and concealed. In an era of participatory politics, elites continue to play important roles in all of these areas. But institutions operate alongside young people and their peers, who actively pursue, analyze, and critique information about issues of public concern; shape the creation and flow of news; mobilize others through social networks and organized groups to accomplish political goals; and help decide what information enters the public record and what stays unattributed and hidden from public view (Kahne, Middaugh, and Allen 2014).

Literacies That Support Participatory Politics

When it comes to the play of "hide and seek" and every other tactic I have presented here, the trick, of course, is knowing how to leverage these activities in ways that achieve the desired impact on issues of public concern. Which brings me to literacies. What forms of know-how power participatory politics? My aim in this section of the chapter is to identify some of the emerging literacies that seem most relevant to the tactics of participatory politics, with some exploratory ideas for how they might be cultivated through learning activities.

Literacies are best conceived as practices honed through participation and situated within social contexts, rather than discrete, transferable skill-sets. Think verb, not noun, and imagine collective orchestration versus individual knowledge acquisition (Heath, Flood, and Lapp 2008; Varenne and McDermott 1999; Street 2001). The rising salience of participatory politics both forces us to rethink core literacies and our conventional ways of teaching (DeVoss, Eidman-Aadahl, and Hicks 2010) and offers a useful starting point for educators seeking to build learning environments that spark civic engagement (Ito and Soep, et al. 2015).

Let's start with the literacy demands behind our first tactic, pivoting your public, which entails mobilizing (apparently) latent civic capacity within networks that originate in popular culture. In order to activate peers on issues of public concern, young people need to know how to feed their social networks and forecast the ways in which their activities in the here-and-how will play out in any given project's digital afterlife. To maximize this tactic, young people need to understand the tacit etiquette, and to build the stamina and habits that undergird networks poised for mobilization. Standards of reciprocity are rarely spelled out within the terms and conditions of websites or mobile apps. And yet mastering those protocols can make all the difference, for users

who reach the point of wanting to leverage the power of their networks to raise awareness about issues related to justice, equality, and sustainability.

Pendarvis Harshaw's highly active and receptive community of friends and followers provides a model of an informal network that is well fed, well held, and poised to
share. Again and again, though, we see clumsy pivots. Someone misjudges the social
dynamic and introduces an issue in ways that inspire eye-rolls or outright resentment,
rather than productive action. Educators seeking to help young people get smarter
about pivoting their publics might start by collecting cases of efforts along these lines
that were wildly successful as well as flaming disasters, and to identify what features
and design principles distinguished the two. There are thorny ethical questions that
could spark meaningful discussion as young people work to develop literacy in this
area. Is it okay to fake interest in other people's work, or to contrive token gestures of
digital solidarity, if the real intent of these moves is to set yourself up for reciprocal
support for the efforts you care about? Also, there is the crucial matter of dissent. How
can young people galvanize a community with shared popular culture passions, for
example, without alienating those whose political views don't line up with the majority or the most vocal within the group? Key here is not just how you pivot your network toward issues relevant to public affairs, but also how you effectively pivot back.

The second tactic presented here is creating content worlds: using inventive and
interactive storytelling to achieve public attention and influence. This one can call for
some very specific technical skills. To create compelling media that triggers concerted
action, young people need to know how to plot, cast, and enact storylines that translate issues and arguments into provocative narratives that enlist others as co-producers.
There is tremendous value in knowing how to record and edit media in sophisticated
ways. But content worlds don't always require advanced technical skills. Also important are platforms that make it easy for a community to post up a quick site or polish
snapshots captured by cell phone, as well as learning environments that support the
rhetorical skills of conversational storytelling, or cultivate the drawing skills to create
posters for rallies or craft skills to make masks and costumes. Above all, content worlds
thrive on curiosity and the conceptual capacity to "map" popular culture onto the
political, often through remix and appropriation.

There's nothing particularly new about this core set of activities. What's remarkable
is the increasingly important role they play not as expendable extracurricular talents,
but as capacities that are key to active citizenship. There are still considerable numbers
of youth without easy access to the forms of high-speed connectivity and mobility that
support content creation anytime and anywhere. Even media designed to look quick-
and-dirty can require sophisticated staging and editing that take lots of practice and
mentorship. Equally if not more importantly, especially in schools with high concentrations of families living in poverty, we see too many examples of cases where the
equipment might be there, but there is no curriculum that uses those resources to

support higher-order thinking, critical engagement, and opportunities to apply lessons to novel situations—a cluster of abilities S. Craig Watkins (2010, 2012) defines as "critical design literacy."

The third tactic of participatory politics is information foraging: finding, sharing, and interpreting data available through proliferating social media and public archives to advance understanding and justice. To glean and package actionable information from a dizzying array of minimally vetted sources, young people need active support systems that help them tap and mine meaningful insights from complex data sets, including some that are walled off from easy public access, and to deliver these insights to target audiences. Suddenly some of the academic subjects seen by many youth as deadly, based on how they're typically taught in school (for example, math and statistics) can start to feel vital to them in new ways. To raise awareness and instigate action on issues they care deeply about, young people will increasingly be called upon to "show me the data," in rigorous and provocative displays. As Lindsay Grant (2012) has argued, though, "datafication" is only freeing to the extent that it enables young people to keep asking new and worthwhile questions. Debates about interpretation can be as productive and mind-shifting as the conclusions that make their way into public spheres, and we need curriculum models that foster that spirit of iterative analysis.

Beyond identifying and negotiating access to information troves, building the skills to fact-check and track patterns, and triangulating contradictory information, young people deploying the tactic of information foraging are also in the business of data *representation*. Here's where we start to see the exciting possible melding of technical and creative subjects (admittedly already a specious dichotomy). The ability to design a compelling infographic that people are inspired to share with friends, or a clever way to sonify, for example, environmental pollution data into a musical soundtrack, emerges not as a neutral design assignment but as the possible fulfillment of a civic mandate. Often, data young people need access to in order to move their issues forward will be proprietary. Key to any curricular approach that supports this tactic will be mechanisms for youth to understand digital rights and advocate collectively for transparency, with respect to the platforms and data sets from which the public has the most to gain and learn.

By coding up, the fourth tactic in our series, young people program tools and platforms that advance public good. To do so, they need not only the concrete skills of computer programming, but also capacity for some specific forms of collective intelligence. Cathy Davidson (2012a and 2012b) has made the case that a fourth "r" should be added to the standard required literacy line-up of reading, 'riting and 'rithmetic: 'rithms, as in algorithms, which she sees as the basis of computational thinking, coding, and "webcraft." Extending the technical definition of algorithm into a metaphor for the kind of thinking that enables young people to develop and not just use existing digital tools and platforms, Davidson says literacy in this realm can't be postponed and reserved for college-going kids. "What could be more relevant," she asks (2012b), "to the always-on student of today than to learn how to make apps and programs and films and journalism and multimedia productions and art for the mobile devices that, we know, are ubiquitous in the United States?" We need better systems and incentives to draw allies with engineering expertise into mentoring relationships with youth, and we need curricula that support the production of civic software. Algorithms, after all, can do both harm and good.

I would add a second kind of literacy to this discussion of coding up. Young people need practice thinking algorithmically, for sure, but also "constellationally." I'm borrowing a term here from the writer Teju Cole (2012), who uses the phrase "constellational thinking" to conclude his critique I've already cited of *Kony 2012*, which he published in the *Atlantic* shortly after that film caught fire (see also Rheingold and Weeks 2012). Especially when political activity interferes in the lives of others, constellational thinking means always and only acting "with awareness of what else is involved." Privilege and distance too often block constellational thinking, by allowing us to impose solutions that ignore how even our best intentions can hurt people, and that obscure how some of us benefit from the way things are. Coding can feel politically neutral, and algorithms can appear to offer tidy formulas for right answers (Wilson 2012). But if there's one thing we learn from the logic of programming, it's that everything is connected to everything else. When young people aim to promote democracy, equity, and freedom, they deserve to be held to a standard that pushes them not just to fiddle with product design but also to interrogate the constellation of experiences their technology solutions can both create and trample.

The final tactic of participatory politics offered here is what I'm calling hide and seek, which involves engaging in civic activities that only selectively surface into public awareness. To express political speech while staying safe and managing privacy, young people need to understand what it takes to maintain diverse digital identities across networks governed by distinct and often non-transparent protocols for connection, encryption, and discovery. These protocols can, of course, obliterate best-laid boundaries and juxtapose young people's varied civic commitments side-by-side on a list of search results. I have had direct experience with this dilemma, especially with young people who've been publishing revealing content about themselves and their politics starting at an early age. Every once in awhile, a colleague or I will get a call at Youth Radio from a graduate of the program requesting that we unpublish a commentary on a sensitive topic that aired years prior, sometimes because the author's positions have changed, sometimes out of fear of professional or social fall-out, and sometimes for reasons I don't fully understand. The beauty of radio as a space for youth learning used to be that the story "evaporated into the ether," as my boss used to say, after the broadcast. Of course now the post associated with the story persists forever, permanently attaching young people to their own teenaged sentiments, and to the comment streams their stories sparked.

In my view, among the best ways to support literacy development in this area is to learn from young people with the most at stake. The DREAMing Out Loud symposium in 2011 brought immigrant youth activists together to discuss their work at the inter-section of digital media, art, and social justice (see also the Storytelling and Digital-Age Civics webinar series, http://connectedlearning.tv/storytelling-and-digital-age-civics). More convenings along these lines, where youth organizers and media producers with a range of ideologies can share their experiments in participatory politics, are needed. Through these kinds of gatherings, both in real life and online, we can start to learn from young people's own best practices, as well as their mistakes, when it comes to deciding what to expose and how to protect information that could damage lives and movements for justice. And we can build organizations that expressly and strategically support these best practices, making them accessible to greater numbers of youth. Adult allies need to be prepared to support young people as they figure out where to draw their lines, personally and collectively, as they occupy sites where surveillance is there but not always obvious, and where sometimes hyper-visibility offers protection, and other times poses its own dangers. Those same allies also need to be willing to provide "vertical support" grounded in seasoned ethics and to absorb at least some of the risks faced by young people who take a stand without a lot of institutional protec-tion (Gardner 2013).

In closing out this discussion of literacies associated with participatory politics, I want to be careful not to create three false impressions. First, we tend to associate litera-cies with skill-sets taught by adults in formal educational institutions. As evident in the above discussion, young people themselves often mentor one another in the kinds of habits and practices that support effective forms of digital civics. Second, my hesitation in even using the term literacy is that too often, lists like these are seen as exhaustive and, more perniciously, immediately used to rank and rate students on their relative levels of knowledge acquisition, highlighting deficiencies among those with fewer opportunities to learn. That is the last thing we need. Literacies are not skill-sets pos-sessed by individuals but practices we can cultivate within learning environments where young people are doing some of their most robust work advancing understand-ing and justice in public spheres. Third, literacies imply goodness. Throughout this paper, with each tactic I have tried to highlight its potential and also point to ways in which efforts to express voice and exert influence in public spheres can backfire, mak-ing things worse. Building literacy in every case means learning how to carry out some of the most promising tactics within participatory politics, and knowing how to re-group when efforts derail.

Mind the Risks

Toward that end, I'll run through a series of concerns that merit serious attention as we work to leverage the strengths and minimize the risks of digital-age civic engagement.

Digital tools remove some of the barriers to civic participation, but they also knock out some of the safeguards that have traditionally been in place to mitigate harm, and they can invite their own problems.

Simplification

Digital media conventions for production and circulation can compel citizens to sacrifice important nuance in the messages that drive movements. Whether it's the 140-character limit of Twitter, or the assumption that videos won't "go viral" if they're more than a couple minutes long, often brevity is blamed for the dumbing down of civic discourse. But time and again, we see politically trenchant Twitter feeds that manage to spark profound debate through short bursts of expression. On the flipside, hourlong videos can be dismayingly and dangerously simplistic. The underlying problem is not the inherent limits of any given format or genre. It's the belief that for a message to spread, it's got to lack complexity or internal contradiction. It's true that any one media product in isolation will never capture all there is to say, acknowledge every caveat, or consider every possible point of view. That's why studies of participatory politics need to account for bodies of work over time, for media that is both "spreadable" and "drillable" (Jenkins, Ford, and Green 2013), and for actions that don't reduce enduring conflicts with deep roots and far-flung implications to battles between good guys and bad guys. The tools and tactics of participatory politics are, in fact, uniquely set up to reveal the hidden harms of what looks virtuous, and the underlying logic that can hide underneath something too easily dismissed as all wrong. That said, with more and more movements targeting change at the level of discourse, we run the risk of pursuing simple attention as the ultimate political currency, sometimes foregoing or at least postponing efforts to change something more concrete, like a law or policy (Zuckerman, 2015).

Sensationalization

Related to above, the pressure to simplify often triggers an urge to sensationalize. Let's find the most extreme, grotesque, and riveting manifestation of whatever civic issue that's motivating our politics, and heighten that story through digital media production and spread. This phenomenon is as old as media itself. What's new is that young people are increasingly the ones creating the news, and so they need to be aware of the ways in which their own productions can reify these familiar patterns. Sensational stories can make for great media, but they distort the truth. In creating compelling content worlds, we can't lose sight of scale. How representative is this story? Who benefits from this telling? What will it mean for those profiled in any given account to be presented in this light? Just because young people are among those who've suffered the most from media sensationalization doesn't mean they're immune to the instinct to tell the most attention-grabbing story. What can get lost are efforts to dislodge more mundane realities that reinforce the status quo, and the less glamorous grind of pursuing legislative and policy change.

Slippage

For civically engaged youth who follow a range of political thought-leaders and movements, any given day's social media feed can play like a surreal simulcasting of disparate struggles, local, national, and global. The challenge that comes with this weird juxtaposition of dispatches is that it gets easy to assume the dynamics that govern the causes you actually know a lot about are universally relevant. Conditions that differentiate struggles and call for specific forms of organizing can slip out of focus. With many of the most politically charged issues in recent memory, there's been a curious pattern of community members claiming a kind of one-click solidarity that moves beyond a message that "I get you" or "I'm with you" and goes all the way to "I am you," or even "We are all you." The sentiment echoes through the "We are the 99%" discourse of the Occupy movement; photos of white people in hoodies to signal their support for Trayvon Martin, the black teen who was killed by neighborhood watch; and even the controversy surrounding a blog post called "I am Adam Lanza's mother" in the wake of the 2012 Newtown Elementary School shootings, written by a woman who believed her own mentally ill son to be capable of chilling violence. It can be advantageous and humanizing to focus on commonalities that unite our struggles, and to insist on the possibility of empathy across disparate identities and experiences. But there is also the risk here that conventions in digital shorthand gloss over inequalities with respect to categories like class, race, geography, and disability that need to be seen for what they are, if participatory politics are to advance freedom and justice in public spheres.

Unsustainability

Like many things in life, when it comes to participatory politics, getting started is often a lot easier than keeping something going. In the wake of a specific crisis, like Hurricane Sandy in New York, we can see an intense and hopeful flurry of public response that peters out quickly as people return to their daily lives. Even with persistent community problems, like inaccessibility of high-quality, affordable, fresh food in low-income communities, sometimes developers or funders will get energized to create prototypes for solutions but fall short of resources—human and monetary—to build levels of enduring engagement necessary to make those interventions take root and grow. The challenge is to manage expectation from the outset of an undertaking, and to set a realistic scope and plan for any given effort's "end of life decisions" (as my Youth Radio colleague dramatically calls the need for a clear hand-off and post-launch strategy for every app created out of our Lab). Otherwise, under-resourced communities already subjected to inadequate and inconsistent public support find themselves navigating the aftermath of empty platforms, glitchy sites, stalled efforts, and broken commitments.

Saviorism

When distance shrinks and young people are exposed to faraway struggles without sufficient context, saviorism can set in. Through well-meaning civic engagements, those who are already relatively empowered to "do good" and "make a difference" can lead with their own needs, reproducing privilege and worse. That much has been established, I hope, throughout the paper, so I won't repeat the points here. But I would just add that dynamic isn't only something to keep an eye on in cases of global activism like the events surrounding *Kony 2012*. Consider, for example, another 2012 video sensation, *Caine's Arcade*. It's the story of a nine-year-old kid who cobbled together a magnificent arcade out of cardboard, stuffed animals, and plastic toys, all of it held together with a dazzling hodgepodge of pipe cleaners, pushpins, colored yarn, and see-through duct tape. Caine operated the arcade out of his dad's East Los Angeles auto-body shop. A local filmmaker happened into the shop, saw Caine's installation, and was totally inspired. You'd pretty much need to have a heart of stone not to be. So he decided to create a film about it. The filmmaker got the idea to surprise Caine with a huge crowd of visitors. In cahoots with Caine's dad, he arranged for a humongous meet-up of Angelenos to descend on the auto-body shop while Caine was out for lunch. In the video, you watch the little boy arrive on the scene strapped into the backseat of car, giggling and beaming when he sees the cheering crowd. The filmmaker greets Caine with a mic and says to the throngs, "Welcome to Caine's arcade, man." It's a genius, chills-inducing cinematic moment and might very well be a main reason the video became such a sensation, launching a scholarship campaign that is likely to make a real difference in Caine's life. Without taking anything away from that achievement or the filmmaker's commitment or brilliance, it's also a moment when Caine's position shifts from host to interviewee, from a maker who masterminded an elaborate invention to a kid arriving at his own surprise party. (To be fair, another way to look at it is, Caine got to be all four of these things at once.) The larger point is, in our efforts to join forces with young people at their most creative and powerful, it's probably worthwhile to watch for moments like these, so we're aware of the new dynamics media attention and adult involvement can set in motion, when young people's voices enter public spheres in a big way.

Concluding Thoughts

In this paper, I identify a set of emerging tactics young people are using to engage with and remake public spheres, often deploying digital and social media tools in intriguing ways. I have linked those tactics to a series of literacies that young people will increasingly rely on as they exercise civic agency. And I have highlighted some concerns related to participatory politics—risks that can cause even well-intentioned efforts to do inadvertent harm.

The table on the following page shows how the various dimensions of participatory politics can work together.

This configuration is just one snapshot of how features, tactics, literacies, and risks can line up. For example, in the first row I've posited a scenario where young people create content worlds primarily to circulate civic media, and where to do so they leverage an ability to collaborate in the making of stories that engage audiences in strategic ways, and where they'd need to be very intentional about not sacrificing complexity and understanding for the sake of spread. That same tactic, creating content worlds, is also of course extremely relevant to *production*, and hopefully invites substantive *dialogue*, and can require *investigation* to get the story straight, and can be a part of a larger campaign designed to *mobilize* a particular form of collective action. Likewise, young people seeking to create content worlds for civic ends would need to look out for all of the risks associated with participatory politics, not just simplification. Content worlds can feed sensationalization; can ultimately be unsustainable and in that sense set up participants for disappointment, resentment, cynicism and missed opportunity; can reveal a kind of saviorism that denies agency to those with direct knowledge and the most to lose; and can invite slippage to the extent that participants eager to connect with the widest possible audience sometimes obscure the specificity of particular struggles. The fluidity in how these features, tactics, literacies, and risks connect helps explain the potential power of participatory politics at its most fully realized. There are multiple possible points of entry that tap a range of capacities within individuals and communities to create positive change. The flexibility within the model also highlights the challenges involved, in that those risks in the right hand column are always hovering and require vigilance if those involved are, at minimum, to do no harm.

The digital age creates conditions that strengthen ties between politics and everyday creativity, lower barriers to entry in civic efforts, create opportunities for greater recognition for young people as producers of media and culture, and enable young people to leverage traditional organizations in new ways, sometimes bypassing or installing new gatekeepers. Individuals accrue trust, credibility, and influence differently today, not so much through official certification but more and more by way of association with valued networks and searchable track records of activity. A defining feature of participatory politics is its center of gravity in peer relationships. Young people can find civic resources within their own communities, and not all of their efforts necessarily aim toward the usual targets. With widespread distrust of the formal institutions of government and conventional mechanisms for creating change, we're seeing young people experiment with bottom-up tactics to challenge the social order. In carrying out civic

Table 25.1

Feature	Tactic	Literacy	Risk
Circulation	Create Content Worlds	How to participate in transmedia storytelling that inspires sharing and action	Simplification: Nuance in the message can get lost and spread can get out of control.
Dialogue	Hide and Seek	How to structure collective interaction in ways that *selectively* disclose personal and other forms of highly sensitive information in order to generate substantive conversation within ideologically diverse communities	Sensationalization: Stories with the most epic and still palatable themes capture public attention. Everyday experiences of ordinary lives shadowed by fear and constrained by unfair policies don't rise to that level of attention and slip from debates and decisions.
Production	Code Up	How to design and develop platforms that invite and constrain modes of engagement towards desired ends, balancing openness and the aim to engineer specific forms of user response	Unsustainability: Civic software projects can require ongoing iteration over extended periods of time—a never-ending cycle that is hard to maintain with limited resources; even the most promising abandoned experiments can do more harm than good.
Investigation	Information-Forage	How to glean insights from dense databases that aren't always set up to invite access or scrutiny, and then how to represent findings in accurate and compelling ways	Saviorism: The zeal for "making a difference" on behalf of others perceived as vulnerable can lead young people (and any of us) with incomplete understanding of a complex situation to misconstrue information and release it in ways that can be dangerous to self and others.
Mobilization	Pivot Your Public	How to support peers and others in ways that invite reciprocity when the time is right to enlist one's network to take action with respect to a specific issue or cause	Slippage: The desire to leverage shared interests in order to mobilize peers behind a deeply felt cause can blind us to consequential differences, gaps in our own understanding, and limits to our solidarity.

work today, young people are seizing every tool, platform, and structure they can find or create. That said, face-to-face, sustained adult mentoring is still key to young people's stories of political becoming. Allies who contribute time, expertise, and humility into collaborative civic work with youth are indispensible (Gardner, James, Knight, and Rundle 2012). We live together, after all, in these public spheres.

Acknowledgments

This chapter is adapted from my 2012 report, *Participatory Politics: Next-Generation Tactics to Remake Public Spheres*, Cambridge, MA: MIT Press.

I am so grateful to be part of the network that co-developed the concept of participatory politics offered here, produced key studies, and offered crucial feedback as I prepared this piece: Danielle Allen, Cathy Cohen, Jennifer Earl, Elyse Eidman-Aadahl, Howard Gardner, Mimi Ito, Henry Jenkins, Joseph Kahne, and Ethan Zuckerman. The research could not have happened without exceptional vision and support from Connie Yowell and An-Me Chung from the John D. and Catherine T. MacArthur Foundation's Digital Media and Learning Initiative. Sangita Shresthova, Ellen Middaugh, and Carrie James—all leaders of Youth and Participatory Politics study teams—have been enormously generous and thoughtful in guiding me through their projects and sharing the most striking early findings they and their colleagues have been discovering over the last few years of concerted research. Ellen Seiter, editor for the MIT Reports series, read and re-read the longer version of this piece at various stages and seriously pushed my thinking—thank you! Pendarvis Harshaw, Rebecca Martin, and Shirin Vossoughi shared reflections that have been instrumental in my efforts to get it right. Of course, I take full responsibility for all that's here.

Notes

1. Invisible Children research is supported by the John D. and Catherine T. MacArthur Foundation and the Spencer Foundation, through funding to Henry Jenkins and his colleagues at the University of Southern California.

2. The Lab is funded in part by the MacArthur Foundation and the National Science Foundation.

References

Allen, D. 2010. "Anonymous: On Silence and the Public Sphere." In A. Sarat, ed. *Speech and Silence in American Law*, 106–133. Cambridge: Cambridge University Press.

Allen, D. 2012. "Toward Participatory Democracy." *Boston Review*, April 16.

Allen, D., and J. Light, eds. 2015. *From Voice to Influence: Understanding Citizenship in a Digital Age*. Chicago: University of Chicago Press.

Bakardijeva, M. 2009. "Subactivism: Liveworld and Politics in the Age of the Internet." *Information Society* 25 (2): 91–104.

Barron, B., K. Gomez, N. Pinkard, and C. Martin. 2014. *The Digital Youth Network*. Cambridge, MA: MIT Press.

Bennett, L., and A. Segerberg. 2012. "The Logic of Connective Action." *Information, Communication & Society* 15 (5): 739–768.

Bourdieu, P. 1977. *Outline of a Theory of Practice*. Cambridge: Cambridge University Press.

boyd, d. 2010. "Privacy and Publicity in the Context of Big Data." Paper presented at *WWW*. Raleigh, North Carolina, April 29.

boyd, d., H. Thakor, M. Casteel, and R. Johnson. 2011. "Human Trafficking and Technology: A Framework for Understanding the Role of Technology in the Commercial Sexual Exploitation of Children in the U.S." http://research.microsoft.com/en-us/collaboration/focus/education/htframework-2011.pdf.

Chaiklin, S., and J. Lave, eds. 1996. *Understanding Practice: Perspectives on Activity and Context*. Cambridge: Cambridge University Press.

Chen, M. 2011. "Activists Enter Detention and Emerge Inspired." *CultureStr/ke*, December 16, 2011. http://culturestrike.net/activists-enter-detention-and-emerge-inspired.

Chun, W. 2015. "The Dangers of Transparent Friends: Crossing the Public and Intimate Spheres." In *From Voice to Influence*, ed. D. Allen and J. Light. Chicago: University of Chicago Press.

Cohen, C., J. Kahne, B. Bowyer, E. Middaugh, and J. Rogowski. 2012. "Participatory Politics: New Media and Youth Political Action" (YPPSP Research Report). http://ypp.dmlcentral.net/sites/default/files/publications/Participatory_Politics_Report.pdf.

Cole, T. 2012. "The White-Savior Industrial Complex." *Atlantic* (March). http://www.theatlantic.com/international/archive/2012/03/the-white-savior-industrial-complex/254843.

Davidson, C. 2012 a. *Now You See It: How Technology and Brain Science Will Transform Schools and Business for the 21ˢᵗ Century*. New York: Penguin.

Davidson, C. 2012 b. "A Fourth R for 21ˢᵗ Century Learning." *Washington Post*, January 2.

DeVoss, D. N., E. Eidman-Aadahl, and T. Hicks. 2010. *Because Digital Writing Matters: Improving Student Writing in Online and Multimedia Environments*. San Francisco: Jossey-Bass.

Dougherty, D. 2012. "Maker Spaces in Education and DARPA." *Makezine*, April 4. http://makezine.com/2012/04/04/makerspaces-in-education-and-darpa/.

Earl, J. 2013. "Spreading the Word or Shaping the Conversation: 'Prosumption' in Protest Websites." In *Research in Social Movements, Conflicts and Change*, ed. P. G. Coy, 3–38. Emerald Group Publishing Limited.

Earl, J., and K. Kimport. 2011. *Digitally Enabled Social Change: Activism in the Internet Age*. Cambridge: MIT Press.

Gamber Thompson, L. 2012. "The Cost of Engagement: Politics and Participatory Practices in the U.S. Liberty Movement" (Working Paper). http://ypp.dmlcentral.net/sites/all/files/publications/The_Cost_of_Engagement-Working_Paper-MAPP_12.10.12.pdf.

Gardner, H. 2013. "Re-Establishing the Commons for the Common Good." *Daedalus* 142 (2): 199–208.

Gardner, H., and K. Davis. 2013. *The App Generation*. New Haven, CT: Yale University Press.

Gardner, H., C. James, D. Knight, and M. Rundle. 2012. "Diverse Pathways of Participatory Politics." Presentation to the April Meeting of the Youth and Participatory Politics Research Network.

Ginwright, S., P. Noguera, and J. Cammarota, eds. 2006. *Beyond Resistance!* London: Routledge.

Glassman, J., and J. Cohen. 2008. "Special Briefing to Announce the Alliance of Youth Movement." United States Department of State Archive. http://2001-2009.state.gov/r/us/2008/112310.htm.

Grant, L. 2012. "Datafication: How the Lens of Data Changes How We See Ourselves." *DML Central*, December 31. http://dmlcentral.net/blog/lyndsay-grant/datafication-how-lens-data-changes-how-we-see-ourselves.

Grossman, J., C. Chan, S. Schwartz, and J. Rhodes. 2012. "The Test of Time in School-Based Mentoring: The Role of Relationship Duration and Re-Matching on Academic Outcomes." *American Journal of Community Psychology* 49:43–54.

Heath, S. B., J. Flood, and D. Lapp. 2008. *Lawrence Handbook for Literacy Educators: Research in the Visual and Communicative Arts, 2*. New York: Earlbaum.

Hing, J. 2011. "Alabama DREAMers Speak from Detention: ICE Is 'Rogue Agency.'" *Colorlines*, November 18. http://colorlines.com/archives/2011/11/dreamers_in_detention_expose_obamas_deportation_lies.html.

Howard, P. 2010. *The Digital Origins of Dictatorship and Democracy: Information Technology and Political Islam*. Oxford: Oxford University Press.

Ito, M. 2009. *Hanging Out, Messing Around, and Geeking Out: Kids Living and Learning with New Media*. Cambridge, MA: MIT Press.

Ito, M., E. Soep, N. Kligler-Vilenchik, S. Shresthova, L. Gamber-Thompson, and A. Zimmerman. Forthcoming. *Curriculum Inquiry*.

James, C. 2012. Personal communication.

Jenkins, H. 2008. *Convergence Culture: Where Old and New Media Collide*. New York: New York University Press.

Jenkins, H. 2012. "DREAMing Out Loud! Youth Activists Spoke about Their Fight for Education, Immigrant Rights, and Justice through Media and Art." *HenryJenkins.org*. http://henryjenkins.org/2012/01/dreaming_out_loud_youth_activi.html.

Jenkins, H., S. Ford, and J. Green. 2013. *Spreadable Media: Creating Value and Meaning in a Networked Culture*. New York: New York University Press.

Jenkins, H., L. Gamber-Thompson, N. Kligler-Vilenchik, S. Shresthova, and A. M. Zimmerman. (forthcoming). *By Any Media Necessary: Mapping Youth and Participatory Politics*. New York: NYU Press.

Jenkins, H., R. Purushotma, K. Clinton, M. Weigel, and A. J. Robison. 2009. *Confronting the Challenges of Participatory Culture: Media Education for the 21st Century* (Occasional paper on digital media and learning). Chicago, IL: John D. and Catherine T. MacArthur Foundation.

Jones, J. 2012. "The Network Society after Web 2.0: What Students Can Learn from Occupy Wall Street." DML Central. December 24. http://dmlcentral.net/blog/john-jones/network-society-after -web-20-what-students-can-learn-occupy-wall-street.

Kahne, J., E. Middaugh, and D. Allen. 2014. "Youth, New Media and the Rise of Participatory Politics." Youth and Participatory Politics Working Papers #1. http://ypp.dmlcentral.net/sites/ default/files/publications/YPP_WorkinPapers_Paper01_1.pdf.

Kron, J. 2012. "Mission from God: The Upstart Christian Sect Driving Invisible Children and Changing Africa." *Atlantic* (April). http://www.theatlantic.com/international/archive/2012/04/ mission-from-god-the-upstart-christian-sect-driving-invisible-children-and-changing-africa/ 255626/.

Kligler-Vilenchik, N. 2013. "Decreasing World Suck": Fan Communities, Mechanisms of Translation, and Participatory Politics. http://dmlhub.net/publications/decreasing-world-suck -fan-communities-mechanisms-translation-and-participatory-politics:

Kligler-Vilenchik, N., and S. Shresthova. 2012. "Learning Through Practice: Participatory Culture Civics." http://dmlcentral.net/sites/default/files/resource_files/learning_through_practice_kligler -shresthova_oct-2-2012.pdf.

Lenhart, A. 2012. "Cell Phone Ownership." *Pew Internet and American Life Project*. March 19, http://pewinternet.org/Reports/2012/Teens-and-smartphones/Cell-phone-ownership/ Smartphones.aspx.

Middaugh, E. 2012. "Service and Activism in the Digital Age: Supporting Youth Engagement in the Public Life" (DML Central Working Papers). http://www.civicsurvey.org/Service_Activism _Digital_Age.pdf.

Niemeyer, G., A. Garcia, and R. Naima. 2009. "Black Cloud: Patterns Towards Da Future." Proceedings of the Seventeenth ACM International Conference on Multimedia. Beijing: Association for Computing Machinery, 1073–1082.

Ortner, S. 1984. "Theory in Anthropology Since the 60s." *Comparative Studies in Society and History* 26 (1): 126–166.

Phillips, W. 2011. "LOLing at Tragedy: Facebook Trolls, Memorial Pages, and Resistance to Grief Online." *First Monday* 16 (12).

Rheingold, H., and A. Weeks. 2012. *Net Smart: How to Thrive Online*. Cambridge, MA: MIT Press.

Schrock, A. 2011. "Hackers, Makers and Teachers: A Hackerspace Primer." *Andrew Richard Schrock*, July 27. http://andrewrschrock.wordpress.com/2011/07/27/hackers-makers-and-teachers -a-hackerspace-primer-part-1-of-2.

Sefton-Green, J. 2013. *Mapping Digital Makers: A Review Exploring Everyday Creativity, Learning Lives and The Digital*. Nominet Trust State of the Art Reviews.

Shresthova, S. 2013. *Between Storytelling and Surveillance: American Muslim Youth Negotiate Culture, Politics and Participation*. http://ypp.dmlcentral.net/publications/161.

Soep, E. 2005. "Making Hard-Core Masculinity: Teenage Boys Playing House." In *Youthscapes: The Popular, the National, the Global*, ed. S. Maira and E. Soep, 173–191. Philadelphia: University of Pennsylvania Press.

Soep, E. 2011. "All the World's an Album: Youth Media as Strategic Embedding." In *International Perspectives on Youth Made Media*, ed. J. Fisherkeller, 246–262. New York: Peter Lang.

Soep, E. 2012. "The Digital Afterlife of Youth-Made Media." *Comunicar* 38 (19): 93–100.

Soep, E. 2013. *Participatory Politics: Next Generation Tactics to Remake Public Spheres*. Cambridge, MA: MIT Press.

Soep, E., and V. Chávez. 2010. *Drop that Knowledge: Youth Radio Stories*. Berkeley. CA: University of California Press.

Street, B., ed. 2001. *Literacy and Development: Ethnographic Perspectives*. New York: Routledge.

Swartz, L. 2012. "Invisible Children Working Paper." http://civicpaths.uscannenberg.org/ wp-content/uploads/2012/03/Swartz_InvisibleChildren_WorkingPaper.pdf.

Thompson, L. G. 2012. *The Cost of Engagement: Politics and Participatory Practices in the U.S. Liberty Movement*. http://civicpaths.uscannenberg.org/wp-content/uploads/2012/03/Swartz _InvisibleChildren_WorkingPaper.pdf.

Varenne, H., and R. McDermott. 1999. *Successful Failure: The School America Builds*. Boulder, CO: Westview Press.

Vossoughi, S., and B. Bevan. 2014. *Making and Tinkering: A Review of the Literature* (White Paper). National Research Council Committee on Out of School Time STEM.

Watkins, S. C. 2012. "From Theory to Design: Exploring the Power & Potential of 'Connected Learning,' Part Two." *The Young and The Digital*, October 9. http:/theyoungandthedigital .com/2012/10/09/from-theory-to-design-exploring-the-power-potential-of-connected-learning -part-2/.

Watkins, S. C. 2010. *The Young and the Digital: What the Migration to Social Network Sites, Games, and Anytime, Anywhere Media Means for Our Future*. Boston: Beacon Press.

Weinstein, E. 2013. "Beyond Kim Kardashian on the Middle East: Patterns of Social Engagement among Civically-Oriented Youth." *The Good Project*, February 25. http://www.thegoodproject.org/

beyond-kim-kardashian-on-the-middle-east-patterns-of-social-engagement-among-civically
-oriented-youth.

Willis, P. 1990. *Common Culture*. Boulder, CO: Westview Press.

Wilson, G. 2012. "On Algorithmic Thinking." *Third Bit*, February 1. http://www.third-bit.com/
2012/02/01/on-algorithmic-thinking.html.

Zimmerman, A. 2012. "Documenting Dreams: New Media, Undocumented Youth and the Immigrant Rights Movement." *DML Central*, June 6. http://dmlcentral.net/sites/dmlcentral/files/
resource_files/documenting_dreams_-_working_paper-mapp_-_june_6_20121.pdf.

Zuckerman, E. 2008. "The Cute Cat Theory Talk at ETech." Retrieved from http://www
.ethanzuckerman.com/blog/2008/03/08/the-cute-cat-theory-talk-at-etech.

Zuckerman, E. 2012 a. "Unpacking Kony 2012." *Ethan Zuckerman*, March 8. http://www
.ethanzuckerman.com/blog/2012/03/08/unpacking-kony-2012.

Zuckerman, E. 2012 b. "Attention Activism and Advocacy in the Digital Age." Connected Learning. http://connectedlearning.tv/ethan-zuckerman-attention-activism-and-advocacy-digital-age.

Zuckerman, E. 2015. "Cute Cats to the Rescue? Participatory Media and Political Expression." In
From Voice to Influence, ed. D. Allen and J. Light. Chicago: University of Chicago Press.

26   Case Study: Tracking Traveling Paper Dolls—New Media, Old Media, and Global Youth Engagement in the Flat Stanley Project

Katie Day Good

In the last two decades, thousands of students around the world have communicated with each other using homemade paper cutouts called Flat Stanleys. They are participants in the Flat Stanley Project (FSP), a letter-writing and digital literacy campaign launched in 1994 that has since "gone viral" in the education world. The Flat Stanley Project has taken many forms, but it typically involves a young person creating his or her own paper doll—a Flat Stanley (or Flat Stella or Stacie)—and sending it, along with a blank journal and note of introduction, to a faraway student, relative, or celebrity in the mail.[1] Recipients then take the paper figures on "adventures" in their schools, communities, and workplaces, photographing them in front of notable landmarks, documenting their travels in the journal, and often gathering local mementos before returning the materials to the sender. In addition to carrying out these postal exchanges of physical materials, many FSP participants make use of digital tools to track Flat Stanley's journeys and share them with a wider audience online, including email correspondence, blog entries, YouTube videos, Google Maps, and photos posted on social media websites.

With its emphasis on combining material and virtual forms of exchange, the FSP is a unique artifact of educational media culture at the turn of the millennium, evidencing both the integration of digital media tools into instruction and the increasing emphasis on cultivating new literacies and global citizenship among youth.[2] While educators' discourses about the FSP often focus on its value as a project with technological applications and a novel form of global virtual exchange, many also praise its "old media" elements—e.g., handwritten letters and journals, material mementos, and, most importantly, the handmade, mobile avatar of the child in the Flat Stanley doll—for establishing a palpable sense of connection among far-flung youth. My aim here is to suggest that the FSP's preservation of these material and localized forms of international exchange, deployed in conjunction with efforts to involve students in the participatory networking potentials of virtual and digital technology, offers a unique and promising model for cultivating global youth engagement in the digital age.

Figure 26.1
Many participants in the Flat Stanley Project create physical maps or bulletin boards to track
Stanley's travels. This display case at the Middleburg Heights Branch Library in Cleveland, Ohio,
shows the pictures, postcards, and souvenirs that accompanied Flat Stanley on his return from different parts of the United States and the world. Source: Cuyahoga County Public Library Middleburg Heights Branch.

The FSP began in 1994 when Dale Hubert, a 3rd-grade teacher in Ontario, Canada,
read *Flat Stanley*, a 1964 children's book by Jeff Brown in which a young boy is flattened
by a falling bulletin board and subsequently mailed to California in an envelope. The
story inspired Hubert to assign his students to create their own paper Flat Stanleys and
exchange them with faraway peers in the mail, an activity that he believed would not
only promote writing and literacy, but also engage them with the new technology of
the Internet. After creating a simple HTML website, Hubert began coordinating
exchanges of Flat Stanleys between Canadian and American schools. Soon, his website
became a hub for teachers and students to post pictures of the Stanleys' travels and

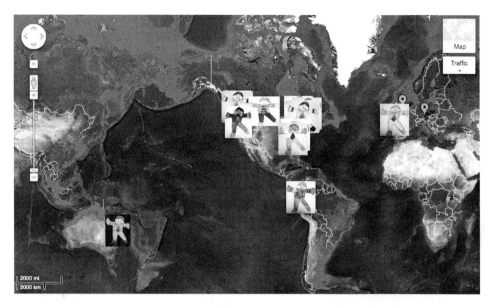

Figure 26.2
A digital plot of Flat Stanley's journeys created in Google Maps. From Lisa Thumann, "Flat Stanley: The 21st Century Version," *Thumann Resources: 21st Century Ideas to Help Facilitate Good Teaching and Learning*, September 6, 2011. http://thumannresources.com/2011/09/06/flat-stanley-the-21st-century-version.

share curriculum ideas. Within a few years, Hubert was inundated with requests from educators around the world seeking to participate in the project. By 2005, Flat Stanleys were being exchanged by as many as 10,000 classes in 62 countries. They had ridden aboard Air Force One and the space shuttle *Discovery*, visited Tibet, Antarctica, and the Taj Mahal, and posed with Presidents Bill Clinton and George W. Bush.[3]

As the FSP has grown along with the surge of new media devices in education, it has been lauded for its adaptability to teaching the new literacies of the twenty-first century.[4] Teachers now use the exchange of Flat Stanleys not just to improve students' proficiencies with new technology—whether by conducting Web projects, creating and navigating digital maps, tracking traveling items online through geocaching, or participating in cross-cultural conversations through videoconferencing[5]—but also to develop students' global awareness, intercultural competencies, and interest in government and international affairs.[6] Educators also highlight the *collaborative* nature of the FSP's virtual exchanges, drawing parallels between the participatory, networked features of the digital media involved and the active global citizenship they hope to cultivate in students through its use.[7]

Despite this enthusiasm for the digital applications of the FSP,[8] discourses about the *material* aspects of the exchange—the letters, dolls, and souvenirs sent through the mail—suggest that physical objects continue to provide a meaningful complement to virtual tools in expanding children's global networks and knowledge in the twenty-first century.[9] For instance, some have mused that the paper-based FSP revives the "lost art" of letter writing and the excitement of waiting for, and eventually opening, a package that has made a long journey. Against the backdrop of instant connectivity and communicative convenience afforded by the Internet, the mailing and hand-to-hand

Figure 26.3
A participant in the Flat Stanley Project documents Stanley's visit to the Ice Palace at the Winter Carnival in St. Paul, Minnesota. Flat Stanley Project Picture Archive, 2004. http://www.flatstanleyproject.com/saintpaul-wintercarnival.htm.

Figure 26.4
Students in West Java, Indonesia, pose with their own version of a Flat Stanley, a Flat "Kuda Lumping," before sending him on a trip to Turkey. Flat Stanley Project Picture Archive, n.d. http://www.flatstanleyproject.com/indo/atriptoturkey2/turkey2.htm.

passing of physical artifacts and handwritten texts between contacts conveys a valuable sense of intentionality, *communitas*, and care.[10] Teachers have also cited the value of students handling tactile objects that traveled from afar, or seeing the dolls they made themselves standing in front of faraway landmarks, in giving them a "vicarious tour" of the world.[11] While Hubert has suggested that the FSP is effective in both its digital and material variations, he has also reflected on the "pleasantly low-fi" aspect of the mail exchanges and observed how the handmade avatar is especially effective at creating "shared experiences" among distant people because "[s]tudents can write about how they made the Stanley, explain any rips or damage in a creative way, and talk to the other person using Flat Stanley's voice."[12]

The global circulation of paper Flat Stanleys is representative of a trend that folklorist Lynne McNeill calls "serial collaboration," or "the process of passing an object from person to person and place to place in order to see how far around the world it can travel." McNeill argues that in a world where virtual relations are increasingly the norm, the exchange of material objects creates meaningful, physical connections among distanced people and "reassures people that the other beings they interact with ephemerally are still present and real—as tangible and as solid as the object sent out."[13] These tangible aspects of material exchange are worth keeping in mind as educators move to integrate new technologies into lessons on global citizenship and engagement. Perhaps a combination of "new" and "old" media devices can enhance virtual

Figure 26.5
A participant in the Flat Stanley Project poses with the souvenirs that his Flat Stanley paper doll collected over the course of his journey abroad. Flickr user loopy1, 2006. https://www.flickr.com/photos/loopy1/140906977. Used with permission.

exchanges by anchoring them in a tangible sense of connection and community between far-flung youth.

Notes

1. Another variation of the FSP involves students passing on, via mail or by hand, their Flat Stanleys to friends and relatives who are about to undertake trips to faraway places. Alternatively, some participate in the project entirely online through the Flat Stanley mobile application developed by Flatter World, Inc. (see note 8).

2. Sarah Guth and Francesa Helm, eds., *Telecollaboration 2.0: Language, Literacies and Intercultural Learning in the 21st Century* (Bern: Peter Lang AG, 2010); Douglas Kellner, "New Media and

New Literacies: Reconstructing Education for the New Millennium," in *Handbook of New Media: Social Shaping and Consequences of ICTs*, ed. Leah A. Lievrouw and Sonia Livingstone (London: SAGE Publications, 2002); Laurie A. Henry and Clarisse O. Lima, "Promoting Global Citizenship through Intercultural Exchange Using Technology: The Travel Buddies Project," in *Computer-Mediated Communication: Issues and Approaches in Education*, ed. Sigrid Kelsey and Kirk St. Amant (Hershey, PA: IGI Global, 2012), 100–116.

3. Dale Hubert, "The Flat Stanley Project," *Education Canada* 43, no. 2 (2003): 34; Sam Miller, "Flat Stanley Goes Everywhere," *Orange County Register*, April 7, 2004, sec. Local; Dale Hubert, "The Flat Stanley Project and Other Authentic Applications of Technology in the Classroom," in *Innovative Approaches to Literacy Education: Using the Internet to Support New Literacies*, ed. Rachel A. Karchmer et al. (Newark, DE: International Reading Association, 2005); email correspondence with Dale Hubert, June 17, 2014.

4. New literacies are defined here as the combination of technological, multimodal, and intercultural communication skills and competencies deemed necessary for citizens to be able to critically consume and communicate information and actively participate in a globalized, technology-dependent, and media-rich society. Adapted from Julie L. Coiro et al., eds., *Handbook of Research on New Literacies* (New York: Taylor & Francis, 2008), 11–12.

5. Donald Leu, "Flat Stanley Goes Cyber: Easy Web Projects to Motivate Kids to Use New Technologies to Read, Write, and Go Global," *Instructor* 112, no. 5 (2003): 28; Angie McCune, "Our Project—Following Flat Stanley with Google Earth," 2011, https://sites.google.com/site/geflatstanley/my-project; Burt Lo, *GPS and Geocaching in Education* (Eugene, OR, USA: ISTE, 2010); Ganan Fannin, "Skype/ Flat Stanley Project and Program Reviews," *Mrs. Fannin's Fabulous Class*, April 2014, http://mrsfannin.blogspot.com/p/social-studies-class-business_22.html; "Flat Stanley Goes Hi-Tech," n.d., http://www.chesterfield.k12.sc.us/Jefferson%20Elementary/FlatStanley/stanleypage_3.htm.

6. The image archive of the FSP (www.flatstanleyproject.com/picture_gallery.php) shows that students have sent Flat Stanleys to people and places to illuminate civic issues in both the national and international arenas, including military combat zones, disaster relief sites, government agencies, and prominent political figures and world leaders. On teaching intercultural competencies and global citizenship, see Paul C. Gorski, "Multicultural Education and Progressive Pedagogy in the Online Information Age," *Multicultural Perspectives* 6, no. 4 (2004): 37–48; Anonymous, "Flat Stanley: Global Traveler," *Lifelong Learner*, June 14, 2010, http://wilkes.discoveryeducation.com/balbright/2010/06/14/flat-stanley-global-traveler/; Homa Sabet Tavangar and Becky Mladic-Morales, *The Global Education Toolkit for Elementary Learners* (Thousand Oaks, CA: Corwin Press, 2014), 25–26; Linda L. Carpenter, Jennifer J. Fontanini, and Linda V. Neiman, *From Surviving to Thriving: Mastering the Art of the Elementary Classroom* (Dayton, OH: Lorenz Educational Press, 2010), 42.

7. Michael Graffin et al., "Learning, Sharing and Collaborating Globally in the Early Years: Stories from the Global Classroom Project," *R.I.C. Publications*, 2013, http://ricpublications.co.za/primary/learning-sharing-and-%E2%80%A8collaborating-globally-in-the-early-years-stories

-from-the-global-classroom-project/; Gorski, "Multicultural Education and Progressive Pedagogy in the Online Information Age"; Leu, "Flat Stanley Goes Cyber: Easy Web Projects to Motivate Kids to Use New Technologies to Read, Write, and Go Global."

8. The interest in mobilizing the FSP to foster a virtual global network of youth is especially visible in the recent launch of a popular Flat Stanley mobile app, created by the Silicon Valley startup Flatter World, Inc., in 2010. Describing the FSP as "one of the earliest social networks for children," the app enables teachers and students to find exchange partners online, design and swap Flat figures either online or in the mail, and share digital photos, maps, and texts through a kid-friendly interface.

9. On the history of intercultural media and material exchanges in education, see Katie Day Good, "Bring the World to the Child: Grassroots Media and Global Citizenship in American Education, 1900–1965" (Ph.D. Thesis, Communication Studies, Northwestern University, 2015); on the role of material artifacts in user-driven communication with new media, see Leah Lievrouw, *Alternative and Activist New Media* (Malden, MA: Polity Press, 2011), 7–8, 15–16.

10. Michael Stoll, "Flat Stanley's Excellent Adventure: With Letters from Abroad, Marcus Hook Students Get a Vicarious Tour of the World," *Philadelphia Inquirer*, February 28, 2000, B1; Rachel Buxton, "Pemayetv Emahakv Students Travel the World Through the Eyes of Flat Stanley," *Seminole Tribune*, January 28, 2011, sec. Education, 1B, 2B; Allison Hoewisch, "Creating Well-Rounded Curricula with 'Flat Stanley': A School-University Project," *The Reading Teacher* 55, no. 2 (2001): 154–68; Angie Favot, "'Flat Stanley' Lands on American Idol Stage," *The News Herald*, April 23, 2010, http://thenewsherald.com/articles/2010/04/22/news/doc4bd0af11578dd181941578.txt; Loretta Waldman, "Obama's Letter Was Answer To A Little Boy's Request," *Courant.com*, October 30, 2008, http://www.courant.com/news/connecticut/hc-flatobama1030.artoct30,0,5018994.story; Skype interview with Dale Hubert, June 13, 2014.

11. Shari Y. Ehly, *The Learning-Centered Kindergarten: 10 Keys to Success for Standards-Based Classrooms* (Thousand Oaks, CA: Corwin Press, 2009), 28–35; Tom Long, "Where in the World Is Flat Stanley?," *Boston.com*, May 11, 2008, http://www.boston.com/travel/explorene/specials/family/articles/2008/05/11/where_in_the_world_is_flat_stanley/?page=full; Mary Beth Bishop, "Travels with Flat Stanley Follow Little Globe-Trotter's Paper Trail," *The Atlanta Journal-Constitution*, August 29, 2005, sec. Living, C8; Stoll, "Flat Stanley's Excellent Adventure."

12. "Squashing Flat Stanley: A Grassroots Online Community Is Threatened by Trademark Issues," *Edutopia*, accessed April 16, 2014, http://www.edutopia.org/flat-stanley-pen-pals; Hubert, "The Flat Stanley Project," 34; Skype interview with Dale Hubert, June 13, 2014.

13. Lynne McNeill, "Portable Places: Serial Collaboration and the Creation of a New Sense of Place," *Western Folklore* 66, no. 3/4 (2007): 282, 297.

27 Case Study: From Website to Weibo—New Media as a Catalyst for Activating the Local Communication Network and Civic Engagement in a Diverse City

Daniela Gerson, Nien-Tsu Nancy Chen, Sandra Ball-Rokeach, and Michael Parks

Elections were canceled in the predominantly immigrant Los Angeles suburb of Alhambra in 2010. Nobody entered the race to unseat five incumbents. The city faced a challenge that is increasingly common across the United States: How to engage diverse residents and instill in them a sense of community (Ramakrishnan and Bloemraad 2008).

Two years earlier, a research group from University of Southern California's Annenberg School for Communication and Journalism began investigating how a local news product could improve civic engagement in Alhambra. The group, the Alhambra Project, defined civic engagement in three ways—residents' feelings of attachment to their local community and neighborly behaviors (neighborhood belonging), their belief that neighbors can be counted on to solve shared problems (collective efficacy), and their involvement in civic activities (civic participation). This research was informed by the communication infrastructure theory (CIT), which elucidates the role of networked local communication agents (e.g., residents, local media, community organizations, and public institutions) in enhancing engagement (Kim and Ball-Rokeach 2006; Kim, Jung, and Ball-Rokeach 2006).

Within weeks of the elections being canceled, the Alhambra Project launched the Alhambra Source. This local news outlet was set up to achieve several objectives, principally to promote a more engaged population and create connections across linguistic and cultural barriers (Chen et al. 2012). Alhambra is 53 percent Asian, 33 percent Hispanic, and 11 percent Anglo, according to the American Community Survey 2012 3-year summary data. Seventy-five percent of the population speaks a language other than English at home, with nearly half speaking an Asian language—primarily Mandarin or Cantonese—and 30 percent speaking Spanish. Research indicated that residents had overlapping local interests, but ethno-linguistic barriers had prevented them from engaging in information-sharing and civic dialogue. Without this type of communication, it is difficult to develop a sense of community and the capability for collective problem-solving (Anderson 1991, Friedland 2001). Consequently, the site's coverage has focused on topics diverse residents identified as common concerns such as crime, education, and city government—and these topics provided the basis for building virtual "communities of interest" across ethnicities.

To further cross language and cultural barriers, Alhambra Source provides select trilingual content through original reporting and translation. To reach the area's substantial Chinese population, Alhambra Source editors created connections with the Chinese ethnic media in the area. More than a half dozen Asian outlets covered the site's launch; content exchanges were created with the leading Chinese language press in Southern California, World Journal; and the editorial staff hosted multilingual community forums. Within three years, the site has developed a network of 90 community contributors who speak 10 languages. They have written hundreds of articles, attended scores of editorial meetings, and been critical for meeting the objective of enabling participatory local storytelling through new technologies. Still, while content contributors and readership come from diverse backgrounds, both groups remain primarily English dominant.

Another objective was to help create connections among communication agents in the area, and this has led to one of the most interesting outcomes of the project. The strengthened communication network was the catalyst for the first US local law enforcement agency to launch a Sina Weibo account. Weibo is the Chinese equivalent of Twitter, and one of the most utilized social media platforms by Chinese at home and abroad.[1] The Alhambra Police Department, in launching its Weibo account, added a linguistic and cultural layer to a practice that public agencies across the country are increasingly adapting to reach marginalized residents.[2]

The use of Weibo is an example of how connecting with immigrant residents via their preferred social media platforms can impact civic engagement. Five days after launching, it attracted more than 5,000 followers, about five times the "likes" for the Facebook account the police department had spent more than a year building. Within four months, followers grew to more than 11,000. The immediate impact is clear: Cantonese and Mandarin calls to the department requiring translation increased 64 percent since launching.[3] In an email survey of users, more than 90 percent said they felt closer to and know more about local policing as a result of Weibo.[4]

The Weibo initiative was triggered after Alhambra Police Chief Mark Yokoyama read an article in Alhambra Source on engagement techniques to reach the Chinese community. The chief asked for a meeting with the editorial staff and the author, courts interpreter and site community contributor Walter Yu. To reach younger and more recent immigrants, Yu suggested the department develop Weibo. He also offered to help make it happen by sharing his social media skills.

While many of the recent Chinese immigrants in Alhambra did not read the site, some influential ones did. Yu is an example of how incorporating local voices into the communications outreach strategy can help activate and enhance Chinese local storytelling and connect it with mainstream outlets and government officials.

Figure 27.1
The images are Weibo messages sent from the Alhambra Police Department. Photo by Brett Van
Ort of Chi Zhang, a USC Annenberg doctoral student, in Alhambra California.

The Alhambra Source, Yu, and the police chief developed a system for taking in questions, translating them, and sharing them with the public, and Yu also created an #AskAmericanPolice campaign for the Alhambra Police Department. When questions arrive, at the height of dozens a day, Yu and a team of volunteer translators[5] translate them into English and send them to the police chief. Yokoyama responds and sends them to Alhambra Source staff for a copy edit. Once approved, Yu translates them back into Chinese for Weibo and for cross-posting on the Alhambra Source.

The Alhambra Police Weibo is both local and global in nature. The questions come from immigrants living in Alhambra, Los Angeles, across the country, and from people in China curious about how American policing works. Various local residents expressed relief, and sometimes surprise, to learn that they could actually call the police for help. "We're answering those questions that have probably been on the minds of people for a long time. They just didn't know how to ask or who to ask," Yokoyama said. "It tells me people have some sense of trust in at least asking the question of the police."

With the dialogue also started to come tips, as the police realized this was a key population segment that could be activated to help solve crimes. When there was a Southern California Edison phone call scam, the police department put out a warning on Weibo. Soon people were reporting that they had been scammed. Others reported prostitution and drug sales. "I believe sometimes people are just afraid to report to the police because of repercussions," Yu said, referring to different relationships with the police in China.[6]

The impact of the Weibo initiative has spread beyond social media to provide a bridge for the ethnic media to increase coverage of the police department and Alhambra. One prominent LA-based Asian-language TV station, for example, produced a feature story by shadowing the Alhambra police department for a day. The Weibo initiative is one of the many ways in which the Alhambra Project has put into practice the network perspective of CIT, where a participatory local news website helps forge connections between a key public agency and a major population group previously underserved due to ethno-linguistic barriers. As illustrated, this type of virtual connection has offline consequences, and it can be beneficial to creating an informed, active citizenry while enabling public institutions to better serve their diverse constituency.

Notes

1. Clayton Dube, Director US-China Institute, University of Southern California. Interview by Daniela Gerson, Los Angeles, CA, May 12, 2014.

2. Nancy Kolb, Senior Program Manager, International Association of Chiefs of Police. Interview by Daniela Gerson via phone, May 9, 2014.

3. Mark Yokoyama, Alhambra Police Chief. Interview by Daniela Gerson, Alhambra, CA, April 18, 2014.

4. This was a voluntary survey conducted with 121 Alhambra Weibo followers in March 2014.

5. These volunteers have been recruited via Weibo.

6. Walter Yu, courts interpreter and Alhambra Source community contributor. Interview by Daniela Gerson, Alhambra, CA, April 18, 2014.

References

Anderson, B. 1991. *Imagined Communities: Reflections on the Origin and Spread of Nationalism*. New York: Verso.

Chen, N.-T. N., F. Dong, S. J. Ball-Rokeach, M. Parks, and J. Huang. 2012. "Building a new media platform for local storytelling and civic engagement in ethnically diverse neighborhoods." *New Media & Society*, 14(6), 931–950.

Friedland, L. A. 2001. "Communication, Community, and Democracy: Toward a Theory of the Communicatively Integrated Community." *Communication Research*, 28(4), 358–391.

Kim, Y.-C., and S. J. Ball-Rokeach. 2006. "Community Storytelling Network, Neighborhood Context, and Civic Engagement: A Multilevel Approach." *Human Communication Research*, 32(4), 411–439.

Kim, Y.-C., J.-Y. Jung, and S. J. Ball-Rokeach. 2006. "'Geo-Ethnicity' and Neighborhood Engagement: A Communication Infrastructure Perspective." *Political Communication*, 23(4), 421–441.

Ramakrishnan, S. K., and I. Bloemraad, eds. 2008. *Civic Hopes and Political Realities: Immigrants, Community Organizations, and Political Engagement*. New York: Russell Sage Foundation.

28   Case Study: Becoming Civic—Fracking, Air Pollution, and Environmental Sensing Technologies

Jennifer Gabrys, Helen Pritchard, Nerea Calvillo, Nick Shapiro, and Tom Keene

Within the broader context of civic media, a number of environmental sensing technologies and practices are emerging that seek to enable citizens to use DIY and low-tech monitoring tools to understand and act upon environmental problems. Such "citizen sensing" projects intend to democratize the collection and use of environmental sensor data in order to facilitate expanded citizen engagement in environmental issues. But how effective are these practices of citizen sensing not just in providing "crowd-sourced" data sets, but also in giving rise to new modes of environmental awareness and practice?

The Citizen Sense project investigates the relationship between technologies and practices of environmental sensing and citizen engagement.[1] Environmental sensors, which are an increasing part of digital communication infrastructures, are commonly deployed for monitoring within scientific study, as well as in urban and industrial applications.[2] Practices of monitoring and sensing environments—or citizen sensing—have migrated to a number of everyday participatory applications, where users of smart phones and networked devices are able to undertake environmental observation and data collection. While environmental citizenship and citizen science are established areas of research, citizen sensing is an environmental practice that has not yet been analyzed in detail—although many claims are made about the capacities of digital monitoring technologies to enhance and enable democratic participation in environmental science and politics.

Through three project areas, the Citizen Sense project examines environmental sensing practices, and tests their capacities for generating new types of civic engagement. The first project area, "Pollution Sensing," concentrates on citizen-sensing practices that use sensors to detect environmental disturbance, with a particular focus on air pollution. The second project area, "Urban Sensing," examines urban sustainability or "smart city" projects that implement citizen-sensing practices along with sensor technologies often to realize more efficient or environmentally sound urban processes. The third project area investigates "Wild Sensing," and focuses on citizen-sensing practices that map and track flora and fauna activity and habitats, as well as engage with organisms as organic sensors of sorts. This brief case study describes Citizen Sense project work from the first project area of "pollution sensing" in relation to monitoring air quality near infrastructure of unconventional natural gas extraction in the form of hydraulic fracturing (or fracking) of shale gas in northeastern Pennsylvania. We consider both how citizen-sensing practices are already underway in this region, and how to contribute to this process through further participatory and practice-based citizen-sensing initiatives.

Environmental Monitoring and Fracking

Pennsylvania has a long history of oil and gas extraction. The world's first oil well was drilled there in 1859. Since then, some 350,000 wells have been drilled in the state. Nearly 8,000 of these wells are in operation or under development as sites of fracking-based extraction, which has been underway in its current mode of operation on the Marcellus Shale since 2003. The process of fracking involves using water, sand, and a proprietary mix of chemicals, which are pounded into deep shale formations to release reserves of natural gas. A mesh of pipelines, condensate tanks, frack chemical

Figure 28.1
Particulate Matter (PM 2.5) environmental sensor kit, tested on Citizen Sense "Air Walk."

impoundments, and compressor stations assemble into landscapes of natural gas extraction. The round-the-clock activity, including a constant stream of freight-truck traffic and the din of heavy machinery, generates considerable concerns about environmental disturbance, particularly in the form of water and air pollution. At every step along the course of this infrastructure, chemicals can leak into the air or be released intentionally as permitted emissions. Monitoring activities undertaken by any number of corporate, governmental, or advocacy groups in different ways may struggle to give a clear indication of what is in the air.

In the case of fracking, environmental monitoring may become a source of indeterminate and even contentious data. At the disjuncture of official monitoring data and the experiences of residents living on the shale field, citizens are attempting to engage with environmental monitoring to begin to generate evidence that speaks to their particular experiences. Citizen Sense fieldwork has raised multiple questions about what citizen monitoring practices might sense and be able to sense, and within what larger landscape of environmental monitoring might the findings of pollution monitoring be located, questioned, and differently mobilized.

Civic Technology and Practice-Based Research

The Citizen Sense project has both undertaken a review of existing citizen-sensing practices attentive to air pollution near fracking sites in northeastern Pennsylvania and collaborated with these communities to identify pollutants and issues of concern in order to develop monitoring kits and practices. The methods of the Citizen Sense project are practice-based and participatory, and consist of intensive fieldwork, making and remaking of environmental sensor technologies, site-specific walks to test devices, and charettes and workshops to trial and learn about environmental monitoring techniques.

Multiple "kits" have been developed in the course of this practice-based research, from a "Logbook of Monitoring Practices" given to residents that asks them to document their particular concerns and questions about fracking and environmental monitoring; to off-the-shelf digital and analog sensors that capture volatile organic compounds (VOCs) and particulate matter (PM); to bespoke digital sensors and Web platforms for testing how sensed variables, experience, and collective monitoring data might come together to form new understandings of air pollution. These methods set out to multiply understandings and possibilities of democratized environmental action through citizen-sensing practices. In this way, the Citizen Sense project seeks to generate new interpretive understandings of citizen sensing through an iterative relationship between theory, practice, and field-based investigations, and to put forward new models for understanding citizen sensing.

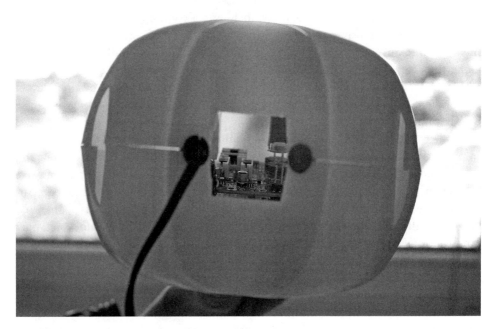

Figure 28.2
Air Quality Egg testing.

Becoming Civic: Environmental Sensing as a Political Technology in Process

The Citizen Sense project is equally invested in exploring how environmental sensors *become* technologies of action or civic engagement. A common assumption may exist that technologies developed for civic engagement will seamlessly unfold into participatory encounters. Sensors for environmental monitoring are often presented as tools that will facilitate the generation of data on pollution, for instance, which are meant to lead to political engagement and efficacy. Our research has suggested that these are not technologies that are immediately "civic," however, but that may become civic in specific ways through involvement with communities and concrete environmental problems such as air pollution related to fracking. What are the standards and conditions that lend political effect to sensing practices and data? How does pollution data circulate so as to have effect? How do communities form to convey the importance of monitoring practices and data? These are questions that ask about the civic attachments that may form in relation to technologies, but are not solved by technologies alone.

Many environmental sensor devices, from the Air Quality Egg to AirCasting to Smart Citizen Sensor and more, primarily exist as proof-of-concept technologies, with the

Figure 28.3
Fieldwork in northeastern Pennsylvania: unconventional natural gas drill site.

sensing capacities of these technologies producing more or less accurate data. Yet the capacities of these technologies in realizing new modes of environmental citizenship often remain untested, even while this is a recurring way in which these technologies are promoted. The Citizen Sense project has set out to put these existing technologies to work in order to understand the social, political, and technical problems with which they are entangled; and to test how environmental sensing technologies operate in contexts where more emphasis is placed on the civic and political capacities of these kits in comparison to their technical inventiveness as such.

In other words, the invention of technologies does not automatically lead to the invention of civic engagement. These technologies need to become civic, often in quite different ways depending upon the projects in which they would be put to work. The Citizen Sense project is raising distinct questions about the politics and practices of sense that emerge at the intersection of sensor technologies, citizen participation, and environmental change. It is our contention that civic-ness does not automatically follow development of sensors for environmental monitoring. Instead, pollution-sensing

Figure 28.4
Fieldwork in northeastern Pennsylvania: unconventional natural gas compressor station and participant monitoring with FLIR camera.

technologies are provocations for thinking about how—in this case—environmental monitoring data on air pollution might be collected, communicated, and acted upon, and to what effect. Citizen sensing is not just made up of observations of environmental change, but also involves technical and political practices that form a complex ecology of sensing. Environmental sensors and DIY platforms may not offer up a simple pathway from citizen-collected data to effective political action, but they do open up an expansive set of questions about how civic engagement forms attachments in and through particular technologies, how communities might assemble to address distinct environmental problems, and how digital technologies are but one part of this larger effort to invent new modes of environmental and political practice.

Notes

1. For more information on the Citizen Sense project, see http://www.citizensense.net.

2. For an extended study on environmental sensors, see Jennifer Gabrys, *Program Earth: Environmental Sensing Technology and the Making of a Computational Planet* (Minneapolis: University of Minnesota Press, 2016).

V Community + Action

29 Activist DDoS, Community, and the Personal

Molly Sauter

Crowd-based actions, such as blockades and public marches, are not based on the discreet identities of individual participants to be successful. Distributed denial of service (DDoS) actions, a coordinated series of actions wherein many individual computers target a central server, flooding it with requests until it is unable to properly function, rely on a similar dynamic to achieve their activist ends. The visual spectacle of the mass (or, in the case of DDoS, the imagined mass behind the signal flood) is more valuable than the individual as a self-contained entity in the greater campaign. Organizers rely on the visual image of streets crowded with marchers to convey the commitment of their supporters, or directly reference huge numbers of potential and actual activists in how they refer to their movements and actions, through evocative titles such as the Million Mom March. Tocqueville called this coming together of individuals the moment when "they are no longer isolated men but a power seen from afar …" (Tocqueville 2002). As a communicative act, it is the coming together as a community of action that is of importance. For each individual within that community, however, there is still a granularity of identity to be contended with, including the questions of anonymity, performed identity, responsibility, and technological elitism.

DDoS actions, which have been used as a form of digital activism since the mid-1990s, are hardly the only instance wherein the malleability and concealment of activist identities have become an issue. Recent attempts in the US, the UK, France, Germany, Spain, Switzerland, Denmark, and Austria (some successful, some not) to implement anti-mask legislation demonstrate both the popularization of identity concealment within certain activist communities as well as the state's deep distrust of the tactic. Canada's Bill C-309 is the most recent example of this type of restrictive legislation, which carries a potential penalty of 10 years in prison for wearing a mask during a riot or unlawful assembly. The assumed ease with which online activists can conceal their identities often attracts criticism. Leaders of the tech industry are often the source of these critiques, as when Randi Zuckerberg, then Director of Market Development at Facebook, stated that "Anonymity on the Internet has to go away," arguing that anonymity leads to bad behavior and abusive speech (CBS News 2011). Google CEO Eric

Schmidt has made similar statements in the past. Anonymous political speech is seen as not carrying the same weight as named political speech because it is widely perceived as less risky or allowing the speaker to avoid accountability. The opposition of tech executives to anonymous speech on, ostensibly, grounds of moral and political responsibility is striking due to their control of the very structures and platforms of expression that many rely on for political organizing. Moreover, this critique, though popular, often runs counter to the historical deployment of identity within activist actions, including DDoS actions.

Critiques of anonymous activism also reveal a tension at the base of the Western conception of political responsibility. Though anonymity can be granted to mainstream political activities, such as the use of the anonymous ballot, those political minorities whose democratic participation has been hamstrung by a failure of the public discourse to seriously consider a specific set of issues, or by outright disenfranchisement, are denied the protection of anonymous participation. Instead they are forced into legally and sometimes physically precarious situations as a type of public "authenticity" gauntlet, as the public abusively tests the depth of their commitment to their claims. Similarly, there is little credence given to the idea that moral and political responsibility can attach to protest when performed under identities that are not state sanctioned. This combination leaves only the Western state in a position to determine the validity of its critics, not based on the content of their criticism but on the performance of their critical identity. What's more, the simultaneous refusal to accept the validity of anonymous protest coupled with punitive overreaching on the part of the judicial system in response to innovative forms of disruptive civil disobedience has a distinctly chilling effect on the ability of many individuals to participate in the public political discourse. Rather, it encourages the expression of dissent only by those individuals willing to risk everything for the sake of a political point, or in Hannah Arendt's words, it fosters "single-minded fanaticism ... mak[ing] impossible a rational discussion of the issues at stake" (Arendt 1972).

In short, the emphasis on identity-tied "responsibility," as determined and retributed by the state, which has an interest in discouraging novel forms of dissent, actively suppresses opportunities for wide political participation, discourse, and enfranchisement, rather than encouraging them. Civil disobedience, rather than being welcomed as an alternative mode of political participation, is pushed to the fringes of public political life where its practice becomes more extreme and fanatical, and easier for the political mainstream to dismiss.

This chapter is an attempt to bring to the fore the tensions of identity, responsibility, performance, and exclusion that sit at the core of the political use of DDoS actions. These tensions exist within the use of the tactic itself and in the tactic's interplay with the political processes of a discursive democracy in general.

A Technical Note on the DDoS and Its Role in Digital Protest

A denial of service action is a purposeful attempt to render a targeted computer server inaccessible to those looking to communicate with it for legitimate purposes. The action can originate from a single source, as with an exploit-based action, or it can be the result of a coordinated act coming from multiple sources. In the latter case, the action is known as a *distributed* denial of service action. Unlike other tactics of digital disruption like website defacement or data exfiltration, complicated tools or sophisticated skills are not necessary to wage a DDoS action. A group of people simultaneously refreshing the same webpage over and over could be considered a manual DDoS action, if their intention is to bring the webpage down for political reasons. However, modern Web infrastructure makes it extremely unlikely that such a "manual" DDoS would be effective against a major corporate or government website. More often, small programs called tools are used to dramatically multiply the number of requests that can be sent from a given machine in a short period of time. These tools can also include graphical user interfaces (GUIs), messaging functionalities, or even information about the activist action itself. Botnets, or networks of computers being controlled by a central command-and-control machine, have also been employed in activist DDoS actions. These machines may have been volunteered for duty by their owners, or, more problematically, may have been illicitly infected with a virus that allows them to be remotely controlled by someone other than their owners.

In its modern implementation, activist DDoS actions can serve as an easily accessible first step into engagement with disruptive online activism. DDoS actions have been used as a tactic of activism essentially since the arrival of the public network, with public-facing DDoS actions starting at least as far back as 1995 with the Italian Strano Netstrike action (Sauter 2014). DDoS tools like FloodNet and Low Orbit Ion Cannon (LOIC), developed by the Electronic Disturbance Theater and Anonymous-affiliated coders in the late 1990s and mid 2000s respectively, have accessible, point-and-click interfaces that allow participants with relatively low levels of technological sophistication to take part in activist DDoS actions. Both these tools have been open sourced, giving other activists and organizations the chance to build on the technology, adapting them for different activist populations. As the user population shifts, so too can the technological affordances of these open tools, enabling them to be used in the service of a variety of activist ends. Activist DDoS actions can be deployed as tactics of direct action, such as the 1999 *electrohippies* action targeting the email servers of the WTO Ministerial Conference in Seattle, or as tactics of media manipulation, such as the actions of the Electronic Disturbance Theater or Anonymous, or as tools of popular education, biographical impact, and recruitment.

DDoS and Impure Dissent

DDoS actions and the theatrics that surround them, particularly those indulged in by groups like the infamous hacker/trickster collective Anonymous (Coleman 2012), can and have often been dismissed as apolitical or antipolitical. The disruptive, trollish nature of the actions, and their seeming incapability, at the most fundamental, functional level, to contribute meaningfully to the public democratic discourse, makes the dissent practiced though DDoS actions easy to dismiss. In this way, activist DDoS actions can fall under the umbrella of what Tommie Shelby calls "impure dissent" (Shelby 2015). Impure dissent is that which does not take the form of traditional, morally exemplary civil disobedience or other anticipated forms of protest. Shelby's main subject of analysis is hip hop, but his analysis leaves room for confrontational, disruptive forms of street activism as well. To Shelby, impure dissent contains a mash-up of legitimate, meaningful political content, and other speech and conduct elements that dramatically break from the norms of typical political speech. It is these other elements that have the potential to undermine or counteract the political content of impure dissent. Shelby notes that these nonpolitical elements can include profanity, epithets, negative stereotypes, or violent or pornographic images (Shelby 2015).

By both design and practice, activist DDoS actions directly confront the privatized, communicative nature of the modern online space. Jodi Dean's theory of communicative capitalism gives us a framework that allows us to work through the specific impact of DDoS actions as a collective action. Dean's theory reveals as irrelevant the constant flow of additive communication that dominates the online environment. While the Web 2.0 community framework gives many people the chance to "participate," that participation is ultimately recursive and irrelevant to the structures of power which dominate the current landscape. While individuals may satisfy their "participation" itch with a constant flow of likes, retweets, comments, and shares, and may even build personally meaningful relationships and communities in the process, these actions and relationships are ultimately politically impotent (Dean 2009). While it is the nature of the online space to facilitate the additive flow of information, it is the nature of the DDoS action to disrupt that flow and to draw explicit attention to that disruption. DDoS actions can be seen as destructive, antisocial, and informatically deviant enough to completely undermine the intended political message of the action. The continued existence and practice of DDoS actions can be interpreted as dangerously undermining the stability of the online space to such an extent that any use is seen as deeply irresponsible at best, and acutely criminal and threatening at worst. This view can be seen reflected in news coverage of activist DDoS actions, particularly of early groups like the Electronic Disturbance Theater (EDT), who were active in the late 1990s and early 2000s. Press coverage of their pro-Zapatista actions would often associate the group with criminals or terrorists, often not acknowledging their explicit activist claims (Sauter 2014).

In a more extreme manifestation of this, Anonymous, and other such groups, purposefully cultivate popular associations with antisocial hacker and trollish personas. The use of the stereotyped hacker persona by Anonymous has a number of uses within the culture, including creating greater community cohesion through performance, aligning the group with a romantic and compelling history, and providing a ready-made hook for the media to latch on to in their reporting of Anonymous actions. However, by taking on such an outlaw persona, Anonymous also recuses itself from the pantheon of traditional civic actors. The hacker outlaw is a politically impure actor, a potential threat who lives on the fringes of respectable society. By taking on that character's mantle, Anonymous renders their dissent both politically and morally "impure." The inflection or tone of their outward messaging is also seen as deeply problematic, as it often incorporates cursing, vulgar humor, epithets, and a host of content unsuitable to polite conversation. Anonymous's status as impure dissenters makes it difficult for them to communicate their political message to those outside the culture, but should not in and of itself invalidate their dissent.

The interruptive nature of DDoS actions means that the role they can serve within a discursive democratic sphere is limited. Those who use the tactic are functionally incapable *in that moment* from participating in the democratic process as a discussant. It is here that DDoS actions are often criticized as a "heckler's veto" or an attempt to merely shout down the opposition without making any productive contribution to the public discourse (Ruffin 2000). But a disruptive political act of civil disobedience serves to alert the wider public that the normal channels of participation have failed for a certain population. The lack of signal that is the external manifestation of an activist DDoS action should be interpreted as making space for unheard dissent. That making-of-space, the creation of an awkward silence in the constant whirl of communicative capitalism, is not a breakdown of "authentic deliberation" but a chance to "reinstate a deliberative environment" which has suffered a participatory breakdown (Smith 2013).

A primary motivation for early practitioners of activist DDoS actions like the EDT and *the electrohippies*, a British group active in the early 2000s, was to establish the Internet as a viable space for civil disobedience and dissent. *the electrohippies* stated in one of their initial papers defending the use of DDoS actions:

Whilst the Internet was originally a place of discussion and networking, the invasion of corporate interests into this space has changed the perceptions of what the purpose of the Internet is. Some believe that the Internet is no longer a "public" space—it has become a domain for the large corporations to peddle their particular brand of unsustainable consumerism. For many this is unacceptable. ... Whatever the views of particular people about the development of e-commerce on the 'Net, we must not ignore the fact that as another part of society's public space the Internet will be used by groups and individuals as a means of protests. There is no practical difference between cyberspace and the street in terms of how people use the 'Net. (DJNZ/electrohippies 2000)

However, despite their aspirations, the commercialization and privatization of the Internet continued. As of 2013, the online space is, as it stands, thoroughly privatized. Public spaces, as they are understood to exist in the physical world under the guise of parks, sidewalks, and roadways, do not exist online. As such, the expectations of speech rights online follow, not the norms of public spaces, but the norms of private property. In the United States, "public forum doctrine" governs both the law and the social norms here.

Of the three, sometimes four, broad categories identified by the U.S. Supreme Court, the most permissive in terms of speech restrictions is the "traditional public forum": streets, parks, sidewalks, town commons, and other areas traditionally recognized as being held in common for the public good. The most restrictive is private property, in so much as the owners of private property are relatively free in the restrictions they can place on the speech of others when it takes place on their property (McPhail et al. 1998).

The Internet is not a "traditional public forum." Online outlets for speech, such as blogging platforms, social networks, forums, or other wellsprings of user-generated content are privately owned. US-based ISPs could be subject to liability if they do not properly police their users' content. The Internet has developed into a zone of modern life lacking some crucial First Amendment protections. While the freedom of the press is relatively well protected in the online space, the rights of assembly and speech of the average individual remains unprotected. Given the Internet's current role as a basic outlet of personal expression, association, and communication, this is deeply troubling. While protests taking place in the various public fora in the physical world have a foundation of history and legal doctrine to support their legitimacy as valid and protected political speech, actions that take place in the online sphere can only ever infringe on privately held property. The architecture of the network does not, as of yet, support spaces held in common.

As a privately held public sphere, disruptive acts of civil disobedience online will always be in conflict with dearly held doctrines of private property. This conflict has a physical-world parallel. The initial Occupy Wall Street camp was established at Zucotti Park, a "privately held public space" that is ostensibly available for public use but still subject to the potential restrictions of private property. The free speech obligations/ protections provided by such spaces are legally murky. Without substantial legal precedent supporting the rights of activists to stage potentially disruptive political actions, the use of DDoS as a tactic in and of itself has the potential to render the activist action impure by coming into conflict with private property rights, without the established cultural and legal protections that have developed around physical-world civil disobedience. This is disastrous for the development of civil disobedience online. By being continually compared with activism in a sphere with substantially different norms of property and speech (i.e., the physical world), civil disobedience online consistently comes out tainted by perceived criminality or bullying behavior. In this case, it is primarily the evolved constraints of the network itself that render DDoS activist actions impure.

Early groups explicitly revealed and advertised the identity of the organizers of DDoS actions. This followed the position of the EDT and *the electrohippies* that DDoS actions were a direct adaptation of sit-ins and other street-based tactics, which incorporate a give-and-take with the state and law enforcement into their operational logic. However, this view of identification, responsibility, and state participation hasn't held in more recent DDoS actions. In particular, Anonymous, which maintains anonymity as an aspect of their culture, refuses to buy the claim that the state is engaging with digital activism in good faith. Moreover, Anonymous for the most part refuses to acknowledge that national governments, particularly that of the United States, have any legitimate role in governing the Internet at all.

Both the EDT and *the electrohippies* explicitly revealed and advertised their identities as organizers of DDoS actions. This tactic of preemptive identification was yet another aspect of their adaptation of physical-world protest tactics for the online space. As articulated by *the electrohippies*:

> We have nothing to hide, as we believe that our purpose is valid, and so we do not seek to hide it from any authorities who seek to surveil us. Likewise, we do not try to bury our identities from law enforcement authorities, any authority could, if it chose to, track us down in a few hours. ... The right to take action against another entity on the 'Net must be balanced with the principle of accountability. (DZNJ/electrohippies 2000)

the electrohippies claimed that by openly revealing their identities as organizers, they could be held accountable by the public whose participation they were seeking. Further, they claimed that such accountability ensured that the tactic would only be used in "justifiable" situations: "If the group using the tool do not feel they can be open about its use then we consider that their action cannot be considered justifiable. A justifiable action cannot be mounted from behind the mask of anonymity" (DZNJ/electrohippies 2000). They also viewed the practice as a hedge against accusations of terrorism or criminality by the state or in the press.

In their essay analyzing their use of "client-side distributed denial of service" and in other writings, *the electrohippies* repeatedly frame their use of DDoS as a natural continuation of existing constitutional rights. Like the EDT, they saw the online space as a complementary, equally valid theater of activism to the physical world, and approached it as such with the assumption that if previously accepted activist practices, like sit-ins, were symmetrically adapted to the online space, the reactions of the state could be predicted.

These groups did not require participants to publicly identify themselves to the same degree as organizers; *the electrohippies* recommended the use of anonymous, throw-away email addresses for their WTO email bombing campaign. However, the groups did acknowledge the likelihood and potential consequences of being identified as participants in these actions, as stated on the EDT's website, still using street activism as the dominant frame of reference:

WARNING: This is a Protest, it is not a game, it may have personal consequences as in any off-line political manifestation on the street:

Based on critiques from the Heart Hackers and other individuals about FloodNet:

1. Your IP address will be harvested by the government during any FloodNet action. When you click and enter FloodNet your name and political position will be made known to the authorities.

(Similar to having your picture taking [sic] during a protest action on the street.)

2. Possible damage to your machine may occur because of your participation in the FloodNet action.

(Just as in a street action—the police may come and hurt you.)

3. FloodNet clogs bandwidth and may make it difficult for many individuals using small pipelines around the world to get information. FloodNet may not impact the targeted website specifically as much as it disrupts traffic going to the targeted website, i.e., problems for Internet routes to the site.

(This also happens when people take to the streets. Individuals may find themselves unable to get to work or buy a newspaper because of the action. FloodNet actions are short term and only disturb bandwidth during the time of the manifestation. The Electronic Disturbance Theater feels that even if FloodNet only functions as a symbolic action, that is enough to make the collective presence of activists felt beyond the electronic networks.)

We hope that when you join our Virtual Sit-in's in support of global communities of resistance, you will take the above information to heart. (Karasic and Stalbaum 1998)

The EDT and *the electrohippies'* reliance on physical-world structures of accountability indicate a belief that the assumptions of physical-world activism would hold true for activism in the online space as well, particularly assumptions around interactions with the state and its agents. The EDT's warning acknowledges the expected role law enforcement typically plays in street activism. In this conception, the state serves as a theatrical antagonist and legitimator of dissent by virtue of its reaction: as stated by Jerry Rubin in 1969, "The cops are a necessary part of any demonstration theater. When you are planning a demonstration, always include a role for the cops. Cops legitimize demonstrations" (Rubin 1969). Similarly, in his original conception of civil disobedience, when Thoreau says, "Under a government which imprisons any unjustly, the true place for a just man is also a prison" (Thoreau 1849), he values the spectacle of the state imprisoning a just man for its value as an illustration of the injustice of the state, to which others may react. William Smith calls this a "moral dialogue with authorities" in which the protestors, law enforcement, and general citizenry are all participants (Smith 2013). Insomuch as activists can provoke a punitive reaction from the state, they can in turn also trigger a public dialogue as to the appropriateness of that response (Smith 2013).

Symbolic activism of the type practiced by the EDT and other co-temporaneous groups requires an interaction with the state to be effective. Though the reaction of the state to novel forms of dissent is not entirely predictable, it's clear from their writings that the EDT expected the state's response to fit broadly within the mold of its typical responses to street activism. They expected to be treated as activists. Like street activists, the EDT's actions were occasionally met with a militarized response: one of the EDT's FloodNet-powered actions prompted an aggressive "counter-hack" from the Pentagon, an action that was criticized as being an unreasonable cyber-attack against US-based civilians (Meikle 2002). This notwithstanding, the EDT maintained through its literature and practice an assumption that their actions would be treated as political in nature. By refusing to conceal their own legal identities, and by not providing their participants with the technical knowledge and means to evade identification, the EDT maintained a space for the state to participate as a useful actor in the processes they were trying to impact.

Contrary to this, Anonymous holds anonymity to be a core aspect of its culture. Anonymity is the default assumption, both in interpersonal interactions and particularly when engaging in public-facing actions. Individuals who out themselves are derisively referred to as "name-fags" and can sometimes receive a quite aggressive reaction (Coleman 2012). David Auerbach lays the credit for this cultural development at the feet of the technological systems upon which the Anonymous culture was built: fast-moving message boards that maintained no archive and were ephemeral and unsigned by nature (Auerbach 2012). While this explains where the value originated, it does not explain why it has penetrated so deeply into the culture's activist activities, nor why it has persisted at the levels of both technological systems and cultural practice.

Anonymous's maintenance of anonymity in the face of established activist practice in part indicates a refusal to accept the assumptions of earlier groups. While the EDT and *the electrohippies* inherently granted the rights of states to govern the online space as they govern the physical world, Anonymous does not. Anonymous's political conception of the Internet, insomuch as it coherently stands, is more akin to that articulated by John Perry Barlow in his 1996 "A Declaration of the Independence of Cyberspace":

Governments of the Industrial World, you weary giants of flesh and steel, I come from Cyberspace, the new home of Mind. On behalf of the future, I ask you of the past to leave us alone. You are not welcome among us. You have no sovereignty where we gather.

We have no elected government, nor are we likely to have one, so I address you with no greater authority than that with which liberty itself always speaks. I declare the global social space we are building to be naturally independent of the tyrannies you seek to impose on us. You have no moral right to rule us nor do you possess any methods of enforcement we have true reason to fear.

Governments derive their just powers from the consent of the governed. You have neither solicited nor received ours. We did not invite you. You do not know us, nor do you know our world. Cyberspace does not lie within your borders. Do not think that you can build it, as though it were a public construction project. You cannot. It is an act of nature and it grows itself through our collective actions. (Barlow 1996)

Anonymity, in this context, becomes a political response to the perceived illegitimacy of state governance online. During the Operation Chanology street protests against the Church of Scientology, Anonymous encouraged participants to wear masks to protect themselves against later harassment by the Church. During Operation Payback and later actions, the use of anonymity during a DDoS action incorporates within it a refusal to engage with traditional scripts of activism that inherently legitimize the role of the state and of law enforcement within the action.

In addition to simply denying the legitimacy of the state in governing dissent online, anonymity as an online activist practice contains within it a belief that the state and corporate actors targeted by the activists will not respond in good faith (Shelby 2015). Earlier groups drew on the history and scripts of street activism to anticipate interactions with states and law enforcement. Anonymous, operating some 10 years later, draws on a much different history of state antagonism toward hackers, DRM battles, and post-9/11 War on Terror surveillance and policing of dissent. Given the tradition in the United States of frankly ridiculous, overreaching Computer Fraud and Abuse Act-enabled computer crime prosecutions, this assumption of bad faith is not unreasonable. This is similar to the rationale behind the use of masks by Black Bloc actors during street actions. Thompson quotes Black Bloc activists citing "protect[ing] ourselves from illegal police surveillance" and "provid[ing] cover for activists engaged in illegal actions during the demo" (Thompson 2010) as reasons for the use of masks during street protests. The logic is clear: if your aim is to commit a political act not recognized as a privileged political act by the state, then taking actions to prevent yourself, as a political actor, from being assigned the role of criminal actor by the state is reasonable.

Anonymity as an outward-facing cultural practice strengthens the "relational equality" between the individual participant and the greater cultural movement (Thompson 2010). Anonymous relies on the perception of an inexhaustible mass for much of its rhetorical bite. The identical-ness of its masked, technologically anonymized participants fosters a sense of omnipresence, the type of "improperly named" mob noted by Deseriis (Deseriis 2013). Outward-facing anonymity prevents outside actors, like the media, from focusing on and privileging charismatic actors. Anonymous values the optics of the mass, the "hive," while simultaneously continuing to value internally individuality and individual initiative (Coleman 2012).

That said, though anonymity is the goal during these actions, it is not always achieved. The most popular versions of the LOIC DDoS tool used by Anonymous during its 2010 Operation Payback made no effort to cover their users' digital tracks. More sophisticated

DDoS tools will "spoof" IP addresses, generating a fake IP address to assign to the packets the program sends out, or take other steps to prevent the target of an action from tracing the packets back home. However, all packets sent with LOIC are tagged with the IP address of the sender. ISPs maintain records of the IP addresses of computers on their network and can match those IP records to the real names and addresses of their subscribers. Law enforcement can and often does subpoena those records when pursuing computer crime prosecutions. It was possible for an individual using LOIC, without taking additional security measures, to be identified on the basis of information contained in the packets he or she sent. The EDT's FloodNet tool and the adapted version used by *the electrohippies* also did not utilize any measures to mask the identities of participants. However, this should be seen as an extension of those groups' integration of physical-world/legal identity into their actions. Given Anonymous's history of anonymous action and the emphasis placed on anonymity within Anonymous culture, that LOIC does not conceal users' identities is more likely to be a mistake or hallmark of an inexperienced developer rather than an intentional decision.

For a sophisticated user, this security flaw is relatively easy to detect by glancing at the tool's source code or by testing the tool against a known machine (such as one's own server). However, most of those participating in the December 2010 DDoS campaign were not sophisticated users. They were recent additions to the Anonymous DDoS army, "n00bs" or "newfags" in Anonymous parlance. Whereas an experienced user may have been aware that running LOIC through a proxy or a spoofed IP address would provide some measure of protection from the security flaws in the tool, it is unlikely that someone new to digital activism would be aware those tools existed or would understand how to operate them. Very few of the tutorials available online made mention of any of these options. In fact, many of the FAQs and tutorials reassured users that they were unlikely to be caught using the tool as is, or if they were caught, they were unlikely to face any serious trouble. These statements were often factually inaccurate and based on a faulty understanding of how servers operated. One FAQ reads, in part:

Q: Will I get caught/arrested for using it?

A: *Chances are next to zero.* Just blame [sic] you have a virus, or simply deny any knowledge of it. (Operation Payback Setup Guide 2010) (emphasis added)

The media also picked up this line, and repeated it extensively, as in this article by Joel Johnson of *Gizmodo*:

What is LOIC? It's a pushbutton application that can be controlled by a central user to launch a flood of killer internet packets with *little risk to the user*. Because a DDoS knocks everything offline—at least when it works as intended—*the log files that would normally record each incoming connection typically just don't work*. And even if they do, many LOIC users claim that another user was on their network or that their machine was part of a bot net—a DDoS client delivered by [sic] virus that performs like a hivemind LOIC, minus the computer owner actually knowing they are participating. (Johnson 2010; emphasis added)

In this article, Johnson mistakenly states that a server targeted by a DDoS action would not log the IP addresses on the incoming packets, a statement that is simply inaccurate. In fact, PayPal and other Operation Payback targets kept extensive logs of traffic to their websites, logs that law enforcement used to target participants for searches and arrests.

As a result, it is probable that many newly recruited Anons used LOIC to join in on large-scale DDoS actions against financial institutions, such as PayPal, Visa, and MasterCard, without taking any security precautions whatsoever. In the coming months, dozens of those individuals would be arrested and charged under the Computer Fraud and Abuse Act (Zetter 2011). It was later revealed that those arrests were based on a master list of IP addresses collected by PayPal as its servers were struck by a massive wave of DDoS actions on December 9 and 10, 2010 (Poulsen 2011), something sites such as Gizmodo had previously claimed was impossible. Despite criticism that activist DDoS actions are cheaper or easier or "less risky" than other forms of activism, these actions can be extremely legally risky, due to an insistence on the part of the judicial system that activist DDoS actions be treated as criminal felonies, not political acts.

An insistence that legal identity be tied to dissenting speech or disruptive activism benefits a state with an interest in tracking and suppressing those activities. The U.S. Supreme Court has noted the value of anonymous political speech, going so far as to recognize a right to anonymous pamphleteering, in the tradition of the anonymous and pseudonymous writings of Thomas Paine and the founding fathers (McIntyre v. Ohio Elections Comm'n, 1995). Just as an interruptive DDoS can open an opportunity for dissenting speech, the ability to engage in anonymous activism can create for individuals the opportunity to dissent. A chance to protest that is tracked and monitored is, for most of the public, no chance at all. It restricts the opportunities for dissent and disruption to the few who can bear the state-determined cost. As Tressie McMillan Cottom notes, "The penalty for raising hell is not the same for everyone" (Cottom 2014). An insistence on exposing oneself to legal threat as a cost to dissenting speech prices most people out of the discursive democracy market, regardless of their views. A democratic society that recognizes the right of citizens to political participation, and recognizes the value of civil disobedience as a reasonable and necessary manifestation of that right, must in turn recognize that anonymous civil disobedience and dissent is vital to the expression of those rights. Otherwise, we are using the excuse of "responsibility" to deny individuals their right to full political participation.

Accessibility in Technologically Defined Tactical Spaces

DDoS actions were taken up by digitally enabled activists as a more accessible, less geographically bounded tactic for activist expression than physical-world actions. While the CAE saw the move to the online space as tracking the movements of structures of power to their new abode (Critical Art Ensemble 1996), later groups saw it as a way to lower the barriers to entry. As mass DDoS actions have continued to develop tactically over the years, different groups have continued to adapt it so that it is easier for individuals to participate. This adaptation occurs both on the level of tool design and information distribution, but also at a community level. During Operation Payback, for example, LOIC tutorials began popping up on YouTube and other locations around the Web. Though it would be impossible to get an exact figure, a YouTube search conducted in April 2013 for "LOIC tutorial" yields thousands of results. One video, "How to Use LOIC (Low Orbit Ion Cannon)," uploaded in mid-November 2010, had been viewed over 80,000 times by December 12, 2010, and had been viewed over 250,000 times by April 2013.

However, any efforts to further spread the tactic will be hampered by its very nature as a high bandwidth digital tactic. Its use is restricted to relatively affluent populations with unrestricted access to digital technology and high-quality, reliable Internet connectivity. Most DDoS tools in use from 2010 on must be downloaded and run from a computer, though other, less popular versions exist that can be run from a website or a smart phone. This automatically excludes potential participants in areas with poor Internet connectivity, or those who don't own their own computers and must rely on machines at schools, libraries, or cybercafes where they aren't able to download and install new programs.

In some ways, the earlier webpage-based tools like the EDT's FloodNet may have been more diversely accessible than tools like LOIC or its successors. The early actions were also scheduled to last for only short amounts of time, at most an hour or two, to accommodate the restrictions and expense of participating in an action over a dial-up connection. The "occupation"-style DDoS actions organized by Anonymous, conversely, have run for days through broadband, cable, DSL, or fiber connections. So though advances in connectivity and computing power have made it possible for actions to last longer (and potentially have a greater impact on their target), taking advantage of those advancements can severely limit the potential participant pool.

This has resulted in natural narrowing of trigger events for activist DDoS actions to mostly Internet- or technology-oriented events. While the EDT, *the electrohippies*, and others targeted the online representations of state governments and multinational organizations, responding to cross-border issues of policy and globalization, Anonymous and its kin most frequently respond to events that occur in the online space itself. Operation Chanology was triggered by the Church of Scientology's attempts to remove a video of Tom Cruise from various websites. Operation Payback, both in its initial and Avenge Assange segments, was provoked by actions taken online which affected "internet native" entities, like Pirate Bay or WikiLeaks. This focus results in a further narrowing of the potentially interested participant pool. So while DDoS actions were and are often now deployed with intentions of dramatically expanding the activist population, accessibility and cultural issues often create severe barriers to that goal.

DDoS Actions and the Law: A Conclusion

Activist DDoS actions are one of the few tactics of disruptive digital activism that rely on the bringing together of a coherent community of individuals in order to function. Due to their technological simplicity and the diffusion of easily adaptable tools, activist DDoS actions have become accessible, public-facing disruptive tactics capable of bringing together groups of novice activists, and introducing them to the methods and working theories of digital disruption as a valid form of political activism.

However, there are many aspects of disruptive digital activism in general, and activist DDoS actions in particular, which make it difficult for the broader political community to swallow. The anonymous or semi-anonymous nature of most activist DDoS actions are often seen as detracting from any serious political point such actions wish to convey. But anonymity itself plays a layered role within activist DDoS action, a role that has shifted over time and among the different groups that have made use of the tactic. These groups have often deployed anonymity tactically, revealing or withholding their identities to support differing philosophies of identity, accountability, and the role of the state in protest and the online space in general.

Similarly, the antics of groups like Anonymous, while often useful for internal culture-construction and group cohesion, can render attempts at public political dissent "impure," as described by the theories of Tommie Shelby. Ironically, the anti-social, trickster-like hacker persona that Anonymous intentionally casts in public has made them a much more attractive figure for media attention than earlier groups who also used the tactic of activist DDoS but whose public activist personas were more sedate, more fitting with the traditional view of a political actor. So Anonymous's public role play has had the contradictory effects of making them appealing targets of news media while at the same time delegitimizing them as valid political actors in the eyes of most of the public.

Finally, though activist DDoS actions have in many ways opened a door for genuinely accessible crowd-based activism in the online space, that accessibility is still shrouded in privilege. DDoS tools like LOIC must often be downloaded and run from a personal computer or phone, unlike earlier webpage-based tools like FloodNet. Whereas in the past actions were scheduled many days in advance and ran for a few hours at most, the actions coordinated by Anonymous occur on the fly and can run for many hours or even days. This requires that participants have access to an always-on Internet connection, a consistent power supply, and the financial means to support both. While Anonymous may have expanded the potential pool of participants through its media savvy and LOIC's volunteer botnet capabilities, they are still drawing from the same technologically literate, web savvy, comparatively wealthy, and well-educated population. As a technologically based form of activism, DDoS remains inaccessible to huge swathes of the global population, and the issues that trigger its use are often those of specific interest to that privileged group.

It is useful in this context to consider whether disruptive digital activist tactics like DDoS can use the online space to transcend state lines, becoming truly transnational forms of activism. Certainly, early activist DDoS actions like the Strano Netstrike actions against French government websites or the EDT's pro-Zapatista actions or even *the electrohippies'* WTO actions carried activists' actions across borders. Groups operating under the Anonymous brand have staged actions with globally distributed participants, though some of Anonymous's subgroups have claimed distinct national identities, focusing primarily on issues and topics within those countries, like Anonymous Brazil's focus on the 2014 World Cup.

Despite the transnational sympathies of digital activists, however, activists are still subject to the laws of the jurisdiction in which they reside, or on occasion where the target is headquartered. These laws can vary widely between jurisdictions, with those in the US being particularly harsh. In 2013 the PayPal 14, a group of Anonymous-affiliated activists who had participated in Anonymous's 2010 Operation Payback DDoS action again PayPal, faced charges in the US which could have resulted in 15 years in prison and up to $500,000 in fines and restitution payments each. Ultimately the group received a plea deal that involved only a fraction of those threatened penalties, but the chilling effect is clear. While activist DDoS actions are inherently community- and group-based actions, state powers, particularly in the US, have a demonstrated interest in discouraging the evolution of this type of activism. So while DDoS actions themselves by their nature may encourage the construction and maintenance of transnational communities of digital activists, these communities are re-divided by both the divergent local and national interests of the participants as well as the legal regimes they may have to contend with if they are apprehended.

In the US, prosecutors are enabled to threaten defendants with massive, disproportionate penalties in order to encourage them to take a plea deal or to turn state's evidence. Because the US legal system relies on precedent, or previous legal decisions, to progress, the emphasis on plea bargaining actively prevents precedent from being established. Every activist DDoS case which is pled out by defendants who have been reasonably intimidated by the threat of unreasonably harsh penalties is a missed opportunity to set the legal precedent that activist DDoS actions are a rational, legitimate form of civil disobedience, and should be accorded the same level of political, social, and legal respect as a sit-in or an occupation in the physical world.

Author's Note

A version of this chapter was previously published in *The Coming Swarm: DDoS Actions, Hacktivism, and Civil Disobedience*, published by Bloomsbury Academic in October 2014.

References

Arendt, Hannah. 1972. *Crises of the Republic*. San Diego: Harcourt Brace.

Auerbach, David. 2012. "Anonymity as Culture: Treatise," Triple Canopy 15. http://canopycanopycanopy.com/15/anonymity_as_culture__treatise.

Barlow, John Perry. 1996 "A Declaration of Independence for Cyberspace." https://projects.eff.org/~barlow/Declaration-Final.html.

CBS News. 2011. "Facebook: 'Anonymity on the Internet Has to Go Away.'" *CBS News*, August 2. Accessed April 3, 2015. http://www.cbsnews.com/news/facebook-anonymity-on-the-internet-has-to-go-away/.

Coleman, Gabriella. 2012. "Our Weirdness Is Free." *Triple Canopy*. Accessed February 25, 2014. http://www.canopycanopycanopy.com/contents/our_weirdness_is_free.

Cottom, Tressie McMillan. 2014. "Academic Cowards and Why I Don't Write Anonymously." http://tressiemc.com/2014/01/21/academic-cowards-and-why-i-dont-write-anonymously.

Critical Art Ensemble. 1996. *Electronic Civil Disobedience and Other Unpopular Ideas*. Brooklyn, NY: Autonomedia.

Dean, Jodi. 2009 "Technology: The Promises of Communicative Capitalism. In *Democracy and Other Neoliberal Fantasies: Communicative Capitalism and Leftist Politics*, 26–27. Durham, NC: Duke University Press.

Deseriis, Marco. 2013. "Is Anonymous a New Form of Luddism? A Comparative Analysis of Industrial Machine Breaking, Computer Hacking, and Related Rhetorical Struggles." *Radical History Review* 117: 35.

DJNZ/electrohippies. 2000. "Client-side Distributed Denial-of-Service: Valid campaign tactic or terrorist act?" Electrohippies Occasional Paper, February. Last accessed February 25, 2014. www.fraw.org.uk/projects/electrohippies/archive/op-01/html.

Johnson, Joel. 2010. "What Is LOIC?" *Gizmodo.com*, December 8. Last accessed February 25, 2014. http://gizmodo.com/5709630/what-is-loic.

Karasic, Carmin, and Brett Stalbaum. 1998. "FloodNet Warning." Thing.net, September. Last accessed February 25, 2014. Archived at http://www.thing.net/~rdom/zapsTactical/warning.htm.

McIntyre v. Ohio Elections Comm'n (93–986), 514 U.S. 334 (1995).

McPhail, Clark, David Schweingruber, and John Mccarthy. 1998. "Policing Protest in the United States: 1960–1995." In *Policing Protest*, ed. Donatella Della Porta and Herbert Reiter. Minneapolis, MN: University of Minnesota Press.

Meikle, Graham. 2002. *Future Active*. New York: Routledge.

"Operation Payback Setup Guide." December 2010. Accessed February 27, 2014. http://pastehtml.com/view/1c8i33u.html.

Perry, John B. 1996. "A Declaration of Independence for Cyberspace." February 8. Accessed February 25, 2014. https://projects.eff.org/~barlow/Declaration-Final.html.

Poulsen, Kevin. 2011. "In Anonymous Raids, Feds Work from List of Top 1,000 Protesters," *Wired*, June. Last accessed February 25, 2014. http://www.wired.com/threatlevel/2011/07/op_payback/.

Ruffin, Oxblood. 2000. "hacktivismo." *Cult of the Dead Cow Blog.* http://w3.cultdeadcow.com/cms/2000/07/hacktivismo.html.

Rubin, Jerry. 1969. "Yippie Manifesto." In *Free Pamphlet Series #1*. Vineyard Haven, MA: Evergreen Review, Inc.

Sauter, Molly. 2014. *The Coming Swarm: DDoS Actions, Hacktivism, and Civil Disobedience on the Internet*. New York: Bloomsbury Academic.

Shelby, Tommie. 2015. "Impure Dissent: Hip Hop and the Political Ethics of Marginalized Black Urban Youth." In *From Voice to Influence: Understanding Citizenship in a Digital Age*, ed. Danielle Allen and Jennifer Light. Chicago: University of Chicago Press.

Smith, William. 2013. *Civil Disobedience and Deliberative Democracy*. London: Routledge.

Thompson, A. K. 2010. *Black Bloc, White Riot: Antiglobalization and the Genealogy of Dissent*. Oakland, CA: AK Press.

Thoreau, Henry David. 1849. *Civil Disobedience*.

de Tocqueville, Alexis. 2002. *Democracy in America*. Trans. H. C. Mansfield and D. Winthrop. Chicago: University of Chicago Press.

Zetter, Kim. 2011. "Feds Arrest 14 'Anonymous' Suspects over PayPal Attack, Raid Dozens More." *Wired*, June. Last accessed February 25, 2014. http://www.wired.com/threatlevel/2011/07/paypal-hack-arrests/.

30 Partnering with Communities and Institutions

Ceasar McDowell and Melissa Yvonne Chinchilla

Introduction

In contemporary society, diversity has moved from the margins to the center of public experience. By and large we expect the public sphere to be heterogeneous, a mixture of cultures, races, sexual orientations, etc. While we may not know how to negotiate this demographic complexity, it is a fact of our day-to-day lives. Yet, in general, heterogeneity does not lead to greater civic or social engagement. Instead, diversity decreases trust, which is an essential catalyst for civic participation (Putnam 2007; Stolle et al. 2008; Costa and Kahn 2003). People participate more in civic activities when they live and connect with people who are more like themselves. Moreover, our institutional arrangements tend to further segregate people, not only from each other—the poor go to welfare offices for housing vouchers, the rich to real estate brokers—but from themselves. For instance, when an individual seeks Section 8 housing, the office assigned to support the process does not simultaneously assist with the individual's health care, their employability, or their child's education. This sense of fragmentation carries over into our civic life and the tools we create to support civic participation. Our current systems for engagement keep us apart from one another and ask us to section our lives in order to address issues that are fundamentally interrelated.

We live in a multi-layered segregated society with the hope that civic technology can help us stitch together a true "public." Civic technologies promise new avenues for engagement. However, like their analog equivalents, they are not always based on democratic principles that ensure all members of the public an equal voice, and they may also continue to parse out our lives by issue areas. Accordingly, civic technologies often do not succeed in creating a system able to function amid a diverse society in which many people, especially those at the margins, are denied power, privilege, and voice. Proponents of civic engagement often refer to the "public" as though it comprises a unified body of people. By doing so, they fail to acknowledge that supporting civic participation in demographically complex societies requires more than engaging people across their differences. What is needed are approaches that have the primary purpose of helping all members of the public learn from one another, amplify their collective voice, and define the agenda and future they want (McDowell and Otero 2011).

This chapter is based on the simple assertion that, to promote democracy in a diverse society, civic technology must design for civic inclusion instead of civic engagement. We refer to civic technology by the Knight Foundation's definition—"technology that spurs citizen engagement, improves communities, and makes governments more effective." As the foundation notes, civic technology represents the "nexus of technology, civic innovation, open government, and resident engagement."[1] We pull from the social inclusion framework forged by European scholars to argue for a shift from civic engagement to one of civic inclusion (Room 1995, 1999; Stewart and Askonas 2000; Chapman et al. 1998; Commins 1993). Social inclusion shifted the conversation on inequality from distributional issues, such as a lack of income, to one addressing relational concerns including efficacy, social participation, and integration (Room 1995; 1999). We use the term civic inclusion to refer to the process by which groups, previously excluded, are incorporated into democratic processes as full citizens.

Civic inclusion requires that all individuals learn to engage with established organizational structures, and that institutions become adept in serving an increasingly heterogeneous membership. Pivotal to this process are the intentional efforts made to bring people into conversation with one another and to reduce asymmetries of power (Eckstein 1984). Civic inclusion recognizes that an individual's ability to engage in civic action is impacted by his or her resources and that, as a result of such constraints or due to social and cultural differences, individuals participate in varying ways. Additionally, civic inclusion emphasizes the importance of sustainable engagement patterns and the role that relationship building plays in enabling these. While civic inclusion is a contested issue—perhaps best illustrated by contemporary immigration debates—we believe that an inclusive framework is the only way democracy can flourish in an increasingly diverse world.

In the rest of this chapter we explore five design and implementation challenges that impact democratic processes, and should be of concern to those utilizing technology to increase civic inclusion. These challenges are: connecting digital and analog worlds, bridging social division, supporting full frame action, addressing the hyperlocal, and shifting the locus of (technology) design. The five challenges were identified through our professional work, case study research, and a review of current literature. The first three challenges—connecting digital and analog worlds, bridging social division, and supporting full frame action—are based on an acknowledgment that true civic inclusion strives to break down the silos that separate us from our various concerns and from each other. Our emphasis on addressing the hyper-local and shifting the locus of design represent important ways to think about engagement efforts and civically inclusive design practices. In each section we illustrate how organizations are rising to meet these challenges. The recommendations presented are targeted toward local organizations involved in efforts to promote civic inclusion at the scale of the city and below.

Bridging the Digital and Analog Worlds

Civic technology segments people by access and patterns of usage; not all citizens have access to the same technologies or are able to benefit from them in the same way. While access is the first step toward assuring participation, efforts aimed at public engagement must also consider whether or not individuals have the skills needed to utilize technology and fully engage in civic action. Social inclusion is highly correlated with digital inclusion, which functions as a catalyst for incorporation (Warschauer 2004; DiMaggio et al. 2004; Selwyn and Facer 2007; Notley 2009; Al-Jaghoub and Westrup 2009).

What we know about civic technology utilization largely stems from research on Internet Communication Technologies (ICTs). Accessing and knowing how to utilize ICTs are key to economic and social inclusion in under-served communities (Norris 2001; Warschauer 2004). Digital access is increasingly becoming the basis for participation in knowledge societies, which raises concerns of potentially widening social and economic disparities (Hoffman and Novak 2000; Norris 2001; Selwyn et al. 2001). Those that have access to and the skills to navigate digital technologies are likely to earn more, benefit from public goods at a higher rate, and are more politically and civically engaged (DiMaggio and Hargittai 2001; Katz and Rice 2002; Kennard 2001; Oden and Rock 2004; Tufekcioglu 2003). The potential benefits of technology have led to concerns over access and usage patterns, particularly among poor and marginalized populations. In large part, this conversation centers on unequal access, referred to as the "digital divide."

The digital divide focuses on the roles of "race, gender, age, income, education, physical and mental ability, and spatial location" in determining access to technology (Hoffman and Novak 2000; Norris 2001; Servon 2002 as cited in Tapia, Kvasny, and Ortiz 2011, 3). Prevalent differences exist in the types of technology used by varying groups. For instance, there are gender gaps in the use of computers, mobile phones, and the Internet. Men are using ICTs at higher rates than women, and the gap is more prevalent in developing than in developed countries (International Telecommunication Union 2013). Furthermore, some technologies may be used at higher rates than others. For example, developing countries have experienced the most rapid growth among mobile broadband subscriptions compared to other technologies, with subscriptions doubling over the past two years. In fact, subscriptions in developing countries now outnumber those in developed countries (International Telecommunication

Union 2013). Thus, mediums for engagement may differ by demographic characteristics and by geographic context.

Increasing access to technology is frequently thought to be the primary solution for bridging the digital divide. However, the divide runs much deeper than access. For instance, municipalities stressing a direct access model to reduce social exclusion have found that wireless broadband initiatives fall short of meeting social goals. While increasing the availability of technology, these efforts may not generate greater usage or increase social capital as expected (Hudson 2010; Kvasny and Keil 2006; Tapia and Ortiz, 2010; Tapia, Kvasny, and Ortiz 2011). In some cases, the introduction of technology actually creates an added barrier for marginalized communities that already have trouble with information access, increasing the gap between the digital and analog worlds. Consequently, efforts to expand usage must take into account the need to build capacity through skilled support (Mervyn, Simon, and Allen 2014).

Technology alone cannot address the deeply rooted, long standing, and systemic patterns of spatial, political, and economic disadvantage that are responsible for communities' civic exclusion (National Democratic Institute 2013). Jenkins suggests that increasing access to technology is only one step toward closing the participation gap. He stresses three core flaws in a laissez-faire approach to digital skills acquisition: (1) it does not address fundamental inequalities in access to new technologies and the varying opportunities for participation that different forms of access may represent; (2) it assumes that users actively reflect on their experiences with new media and can articulate what they learn from their participation; and (3) it presumes that users naturally develop ethical norms for interacting in a complex and diverse online social environment (Jenkins et al. 2009).

The digital divide is a symptom of the broader problem of persistent inequality, which goes further than access to encompass digital inclusion (Powell 2011; Servon and Nelson 2001). An inclusive framework considers the way that usage is shaped by social and economic stratification, and emphasizes that the ability to fully utilize technologies is crucial (Warschauer 2004; Gurstein 1999). To be effective, proponents of civic technology must consider longstanding social inequalities that shape beliefs and expectations about technology's value in individuals' lives and that influence usage patterns (Kvasny 2006). They must understand how access and usage function to include or exclude people from society. Intentionality and responsiveness are necessary to ensure that voices are heard and have political impact. This necessitates a political process focused on organizing, leadership skills, and political analysis (National Democratic Institute 2013). In addition, there is growing evidence that the most powerful applications merge online and face-to-face interaction (Bittle, Haller, and Kadlec 2009).

Local organizations are increasingly recognizing the need to incorporate vulnerable and marginalized populations into key civic conversations. These organizations focus on promoting digital inclusion through varying processes and technologies aimed at making information and participation more accessible. There are several organizational efforts to increase digital inclusion, but here we have chosen to highlight the past work of the Dev. Kalpana project in India, which was developed by the Center for Development Imageries (CDI).[2]

CDI was established in New York in 1995, as an information and communication technologies for development (ICT4D) research and consulting organization that advocated for low-cost communications. The center strongly critiqued random access to Internet communication technologies in rural communities, which is believed to perpetuate the current digital divide by bringing opportunities to only a subsection of the population. CDI believed that "understanding local needs and the aspirations of the whole community first and offering digital solutions to tackle those needs, can eliminate digital divides in some of the poorest and most technology-challenged communities in the world."[3]

The Dev. Kalpana project used mobile phone–based technology to engage rural women and marginalized communities in governance. The interactive voice-based system was developed through a participatory methodology, which allowed the organization to understand the needs of the target beneficiaries. The mobile phones allowed low-literate and rural women to listen to information on maternal and child health, sexual and reproductive health, and other campaigns through their mobile phones. Participants were also able to record and share their life stories on physical coercion and violence.

Dev. Kalpana "over[came] literacy divides, language divides, technology (digital) divides, and many other socio-political divides in India."[4] The use of mobile phone technology increased accessibility, as these devices were highly available throughout India. Notably, the project aimed to develop communication skills among marginalized communities by encouraging women to communicate with one another. It created a space, both real and virtual, for collective action among rural women. In addition, information collected through the system was used to advocate for health, education, and legal policy changes.

In order to be civically inclusive, local organizations need to meet the challenge of bridging digital and analog worlds. This requires an understanding of who is being left out of the conversation and why. It also necessitates a strong commitment to assuring that civic efforts include a diverse constituency.

Bridging Social Divides

There are important links between political participation and the development of bridging social capital that function to connect diverse groups and characterize cohesive societies (Putnam 2002). For instance, voting may make citizens more respect-ful of each other's rights (Smith 2002), and public participation can help people learn to communicate with others, facilitating an understanding of different perspectives and respect for other peoples' positions (Barnes, Newman, and Sullivan 2007).

Civic technology makes it easier for individuals to connect with like-minded people. However, bringing disparate groups together requires much effort and commitment. Limited research has been done on the demographic patterns of users, but social psy-chology literature suggests that divisions among groups occur naturally and there must be intentionality behind efforts to address these fissures (Brewer 1991; 1993).

People are segmented by socioeconomic status, race, and/or ethnicity. Before we can build civic technologies that are able to motivate entire communities to engage, we must comprehend what brings people together and what keeps them apart. Studies have found that increased levels of diversity challenge civic and redistributive values. Greater heterogeneity results in lower levels of trust, participation in social activities, and community attachment (Alesina and La Ferrara 2002; Delhey and Newton 2005; Uslaner 2002; Alesina and La Ferrara 1999; Rice and Steele 2001). Ethnic and racial dif-ferences discourage substantive engagement with community members, reducing trust and the capacity for cooperation and collective action (Messick and Kramer 2001). Separation by race, ethnicity, and class is socially constructed, yet these categorical dif-ferences have serious repercussions for how people understand their identities and interact with one another. Various theories in social psychology have arisen to explain inter-group relationships. These theories primarily focus on the construction of group identity, patterns of interaction, and intergroup conflict.

According to social categorization theory, individuals cope with diversity by devel-oping categorical thinking, which simplifies differences and results in stereotype-based judgment. Categorization minimizes perceived dissimilarities within categories and accentuates inter-category differences (Tajfel 1969). This results in a failure to recognize in-group differences, while perpetuating the false notion that individuals belonging to varying groups are always dissimilar. While categorization is responsible for group identity, trust formation explains why individuals prefer to interact with people that most resemble them in terms of income, race, or ethnicity. Homogeneity theory pro-poses that it is easier to develop trust when we are familiar with the people around us, and familiarity is based on the degree to which others appear to be similar to ourselves (McPherson, Smith-Lovin, and Cook 2001; Alesina and La Ferrara 1999; Costa and Kahn 2003).

While ethnic and racial neighborhood diversity results in negative short-term effects on trust, civic attitudes, and behaviors (Putnam 2007), in the long run, individuals who talk regularly with neighbors are less influenced by racial or ethnic differences than people who lack frequent social interaction. Therefore, it is possible that social ties can mediate the negative effects of diversity on trust. If social ties exist, diversity may not be as threatening to levels of interpersonal trust (Stolle, Soroka, and Johnston 2008). How then can collaboration and cohesion be increased?

Optimal distinctiveness theory posits that social identity is derived from two opposing motivational systems that govern relations between self-concept and membership in social groups. In other words, the way in which individuals understand their identities within groups will impact their relationships with out-group members. The theory recognizes that individuals have both a need to belong and a need to differentiate themselves. Within this framework, group difference must first be addressed through in-group identity formation, and then must move toward establishing out-group cooperation. According to optimal distinctiveness theory, groups are not nested in hierarchies but are characterized by crosscutting social categories that maintain distinctiveness while moving toward mutual cooperation (Brewer 1991; 1993).

Optimal distinctiveness theory is perhaps best exemplified by organizations that aim to build coalitions to enact policy change. Coalition building unites diverse interest groups to engage in conversation with the aim of achieving a common goal. One notable example is the Right to the City (RTTC) Alliance. RTTC is a national organization with the goal of establishing a unified response to gentrification and halting the displacement of low-income and marginalized groups. Its frame of action is tied to Lefebvre's belief that we "need to restructure the power relations that underlie the production of urban space, fundamentally shifting control away from capital and the state and toward urban inhabitants" (Purcell 2002).

RTTC is a national alliance composed of local racial, economic, and environmental justice organizations. Member organizations work on varying issues and with a variety of constituents at the local level, yet are all brought together under the RTTC umbrella. The alliance uses various tactics, both online and on the ground, to create a unified voice among disparate groups. Locally, RTTC hosts urban congresses so that stakeholders can share models and strategies for organizing in their city. In this way, each group makes a unique contribution to the coalition's learning. Online tools include blogs, a local events calendar, petitions, opportunities to upload content, and interactive tools to learn more about the nationwide housing crises.[5]

We know that the Internet enables like-minded individuals to connect with one another. Yet, it is still unclear how civic technologies might help build capacity and momentum for inclusive, collaborative, and boundary-crossing problem solving (National Democratic Institute 2013). What is known is that facilitating interaction among diverse groups is challenging, and civic technology aimed to bridge social divides must understand group formation and identification if it is to create an inclusive system. For now, interactions among diverse groups have primarily been seen through coalition-building efforts that strive to use technology to create greater coordination and cooperation among groups (National Democratic Institute 2013).

Supporting Full Frame Thinking

Organizations that undertake local engagement efforts frequently identify topics and set the parameters for civic action. They are largely bounded by organizational goals that may or may not align with community needs. Furthermore, community members are often left out of initial agenda setting. As a result, campaigns can fail to address people's lives holistically and instead segment them by issue areas. Efforts to engage individuals in inclusive civic action recognize that effective change to the status quo requires that people's lives be understood in their entirety.

Today, most campaigns to drive engagement largely focus on increasing participation through issue-based efforts. Asking people to become politically engaged by issue area is particularly difficult when dealing with low-income and marginalized populations, whose lives are constantly in flux. One campaign may look to address health while another addresses economic stability. However, these issues may be intertwined, with one affecting or causing the other—work instability may lead to stress-related health problems. When an individual has co-occurring concerns it is difficult for him or her to take civic action. Among other things, participation may be constrained by an absence of free time, a lack of transportation to community meetings, and familial obligations such as caring for children (McBride et al. 2006). People have multi-dimensional lives with competing interests and concerns, which makes it difficult for them to focus on one issue.

Of course, this is not limited to marginalized communities. It is true for everyone. Accordingly, civic technology needs to support the notion of community put forth by Carl Moore, who suggests that inclusive communities are able to "struggle (successfully) with the traditions that bind them and the interests that separate them so that they can realize a future that is an improvement on the past" (Moore 2000). The challenge is to support what Fells-Smith calls "full frame thinking" (Smyth, Goodman, and Glenn 2006). This framework looks at "the environment, the relationships, the events, and the interactions" that impact an individual's life. It is guided by a principle of creating lasting change by addressing the full context of peoples' lives and undertaking efforts at the individual and community levels.[6] To do so requires the creation of analog and digital spaces that allow the public to simultaneously hold competing values that cut across different issues as they try to find a common solution to a specific problem.

The Orton Family Foundation's Heart and Soul Process exemplifies a full frame civic inclusion effort. It seeks to engage diverse stakeholders in community change efforts that use emotional attachment to place as the primary driver for action. Heart and Soul is founded on three principles: 1) involve everyone; 2) focus on what matters; and 3) play the long game. It strives to assure that diverse stakeholders are able to fully participate in local engagement efforts. It brings people together around a common cause by

identifying shared interests and values. Heart and Soul emphasizes participatory decision making and priority setting. This creates a sense of ownership and commitment,
which is necessary to achieve long-range goals.[7]

It is important that engagement tools allow people to express their integrated
lives. This includes a focus on empowering local residents to enact change across
concerns. Deliberative democratic principles suggest that in order to have a lasting
impact, public participation must move beyond projects and events, to capacity-
building efforts that increase a community's ability to address its needs and garner
resources. This assures that civic practices become embedded in community life
(Carcasson 2009).

Addressing the Hyper-Local

One of the challenges to increasing civic action involves connecting people to where
they live, and understanding their community needs. Civic issues are frequently framed
as citywide engagement, without much effort to understand the varying degrees of
importance these issues may have at the local level. Whether or not a matter is considered a primary concern is shaped by individuals' lived experiences, which often revolve
around their local community. Engaging people locally means that they are able to
participate in civic actions that impact their everyday lives.

Engagement at the local level raises a community's ability to meet individual and
neighborhood challenges through increased levels of social capital (Putnam 2000).
Social capital is understood as arising from relationships between individuals, families,
groups, or communities that provide access to valuable resources (Manza 2006). For
years, scholars have documented the benefits derived from social capital, including its
impacts on employment and occupational attainment, crime prevention, and health
outcomes (Portes 2000). Conversely, a lack of social capital perpetuates poverty, welfare
dependency, and crime (Curley 2005). Social capital is built over time through social
interactions. Local organizations can play an important role in facilitating social capital
gains by helping people form social ties and by serving as bridges to other organizations and resources (Small 2009).

Proponents of civic technology must recognize the importance of place by facilitating engagement at the hyper-local level. Technology that aims to foster civic inclusion
must allow individuals to connect with one another and define themselves. This
includes providing citizens with information that gives them the opportunity to act in
their communities.

Information technologies are playing a growing role in helping communities
share information and in promoting interaction among local residents and organizations. Sirianni and Friedland (2001) argue that civic journalism focusing on community-
level news can function to inform and, potentially, increase local civic engagement.

However, outlets providing information on community issues may not always allow individuals to interact with one another. Instead these efforts serve to push information, rather than create dialogue. On the other hand, place-based virtual groups use computer-mediated communication tools (CMC), such as email lists, message boards, and social network sites, to enable people to connect with their neighbors and learn about their community. Place-based virtual groups have the potential to support community-building efforts and increase civic engagement. They allow people to connect with greater ease than previously possible. Additionally, CMCs help support and further strengthen social ties established through face-to-face interactions (Ellison et al. 2007; Ellison 2007; Virtanen and Malinen 2008), and have been associated with increases in social capital and civic engagement (Hampton and Wellman 2003; Mesch and Levanon 2003; Mesch and Talmud 2010). However, these online communities do not develop spontaneously. They require significant time, effort, and resources to succeed (Bittle, Haller, and Kadlec 2009).

To successfully engage individuals at the local level, civic technologies must be used as tools to understand and address community concerns. PlaceMatters, a Denver-based nonprofit think tank that specializes in civic engagement and process, provides some useful models.

PlaceMatters believes that information accessibility is key for increasing meaningful participation. Technical jargon makes it difficult for non-professionals to take part in the process, while oversimplified information results in feedback that lacks the specificity needed to impact goals. Acknowledging this dilemma, PlaceMatters strives to facilitate inclusive decision making in local community-planning efforts by utilizing new technologies aimed at creating a more inclusive civic process. These tools help community members visualize and explore data, giving them a better understanding of key issues and the implications of planning decisions.

Likewise, CrowdGauge, one of the web-based tools used by PlaceMatters, is a game that allows individuals to set priorities, make action and policy recommendations, and construct budget proposals. The game was created to provide users with an understanding of the impact of their choices. In addition to facilitating a deeper awareness of planning decisions and processes, CrowdGauge collects demographic and geographic information that helps planners understand community choices.

PlaceMatters also developed WALKscope, an online tool for crowdsourcing data about walkability. Local community members can access WALKscope through mobile devices and report pedestrian amenities and conditions. Community members are able to engage in a dialogue about walkability, and the data that is collected is utilized to advocate for pedestrian infrastructure improvements.

In addition, PlaceMatters developed the Placeways' CommunityViz scenario-planning tool that allows individuals to allocate jobs, housing, and transportation on a digital map. Users are able to see how their proposed scenarios would perform through easy-to-understand charts and visual representations. Feedback makes it possible to have conversations about complex issues.[8]

PlaceMatters is a prime example of an organization using civic technology to engage local residents in community issues that impact their everyday lives. The organization facilitates community-planning efforts across the country, striving to ensure that local residents are able to truly understand and contribute meaningfully to neighborhood change. Technological innovation allows for a better understanding of community concerns, while data visualizations and in-person workshops bring people together to engage in conversation and communicate concerns.

Shifting the Locus of Design

"Process is often overshadowed by outcome, yet without appropriate processes, good (i.e., appropriate) outcomes are unlikely." (Light and Luckin 2008)

All too often functionality and usability of civic technology are considered after applications have been created. However, the goal of civic inclusion must inform both the design and use of digital tools if they are to be successfully adopted. Civic inclusion is part of a broader conversation to promote relationship building and self-definition. Using civic technology to support civic inclusion requires an understanding of how Internet ICTs shape social relationships and engagement patterns. Efforts to use civic technology to promote civic inclusion must acknowledge that moving toward this framework requires recognition of the need to change the status quo. This includes ensuring that civic technologies foster inclusive communities, understanding usage may vary among groups, and using civic technologies to actively connect people to one another to build socially cohesive societies. In order to do this, it is important to understand how power structures function to exclude and disadvantage some groups, limiting their ability to have an equal voice in civic engagement efforts. This entails working to change how hundreds of years have structured interactions. The only way to do this is by changing the principles that govern relationships among groups.

Deliberative democracy, rooted in Habermasian communication strategies, which stress rational discourse and deliberative intent, pays insufficient attention to pluralism and difference. It has also been accused of being disciplinary to disadvantaged groups (Bächtiger et al. 2010). Sanders and Young argue that deliberative theorists stress rational discourse and process, which emphasizes uniformity in deliberation (Sanders 1997; Young 2001). Constraining methods for deliberation means that some, usually disadvantaged people, are left out of the conversation because they are unable to engage in "idealized" forms of deliberation that may only privilege a few (Sanders 1997). Yet, differences may actually enrich the deliberative process if an effort is made to recognize the equal value of all contributions (Coleman and Gotze 2001). Sanders and Young both call attention to a need to incorporate wider forms of communication, such as storytelling, to facilitate greater participation (Sanders 1997; Young 2001). This requires that individuals and groups be viewed as diverse stakeholders with a diverse set of entitlements to representation in the private and public sphere (Rustin 1997).

Co-design is a method for developing technologies aimed at increasing civic action. It dates back to 1970, when Norwegian iron and metalworkers partnered with computer professionals to influence the design and introduction of computer systems into the workplace. Co-design is a collaborative process in which everyone involved is aware of all aspects of development, including established goals and progress made. All those involved are considered "experts," with no one person or group viewed as more knowledgeable than the other. Engaging various stakeholders in the process ensures a range of viewpoints while building community relationships among those involved. Co-design creates an environment in which the input of every group or individual is given the same legitimacy and value (Bradwell and Marr 2008). It broadens participation and allows for the exploration of how social values can be embedded in design (Flanagan, Howe, and Nissenbaum 2008). Under this framework, technologies are thought to consist of human networks and practices rather than merely hardware and software tools.

Given that groups use technology differently, there is a need to make sure that content created benefits all communities, not just some. Design efforts must involve stakeholders in envisioning the potential role of new technology. Co-production of technology is particularly important for efforts aimed at promoting social justice, which can only truly be successful when anchored in a democratic vision for development (Bradwell and Marr 2008). From an interventionist standpoint, design that aims to promote social justice turns ideas of a better society into actual structures and systems (Light and Luckin 2008). This can include the transformation of people themselves (Light and Miskelly 2008).

Co-design processes require significant resources, yet their potential benefits should far outweigh the costs. Participatory design can lead to a greater understanding of the design process, increasing participants' skills and spotlighting their own agency (Light and Luckin 2008). In addition, when social change is a central outcome, processes should encourage maximum stakeholder involvement. This not only increases ownership of the final product (Greenbaum and Kyng 1991), but also ideally brings together a diverse set of users. Social complexity and increasing diversity create greater demands on our systems for civic engagement. While not only crafting systems that are more efficient and better able to meet the needs of users, co-design fosters social cohesion by empowering communities and strengthening individual relationships (Bradwell and Marr 2008).

VozMob, an open source media project that supports immigrant and low-wage workers in Los Angeles, California, illustrates the values embodied by co-design practices. From 2008 to 2010, Drupal (i.e., open source) developers, Instituto de Educacion Popular del Sur de California's (IDEPSCA) Popular Communication team (a team of day laborers and household workers), IDEPSCA staff, University of Southern California researchers, media activists, and volunteers worked together to design a system that would enable wageworkers to create and share stories about their lives and communities. Working together, they developed an open source program known as the *VozMob Drupal Distribution*, a system that makes it easy for people to share content through their mobile phones. Participants use cell phones to record messages that are uploaded to VozMob's website. This system was created at the request of users who did not have access to Internet technologies, but wanted a way to be virtually engaged.

VozMob supports the visibility of stories of those that have been excluded by traditional media. The project aims to increase low-income and marginalized communities' participation in the digital public sphere by allowing them to tell their personalized narratives. The popularity of the VozMob platform has resulted in its appropriation by various organizations and causes. It has been used for Hurricane Sandy recovery efforts, participatory budget initiatives, community design projects, and even local endeavors to address domestic violence. The system was built to allow users the ability to adapt the application to their needs. Consequently, the tool is constantly being altered to meet the demands of a diverse set of users (VozMob, 2011).

Conclusion

Our democratic ideals currently function in a system defined by exclusion. At its inception, the United States allowed only white males who owned property the right to vote. Women did not receive the right to vote until 1920, and it was not until 1965 with the passage of the Voting Rights Act that government was prohibited from racial discrimination in voting. Our democratic structures emerged from systematic efforts to exclude specific groups of people. In order to create a system based on principles of civic inclusion, we must produce a civic process that operates within a different framework.

Those that seek to increase civic participation must consider the fundamental differences between engagement and inclusion. Civic inclusion requires that proponents of civic technologies develop a deep understanding of individuals' needs and motivations. In this chapter we have suggested that proponents of civic technologies take a five-pronged approach:

Bridging the digital and analog: The public lives in both the digital and analog worlds and needs to be engaged equally in both realms. In addition to digital access, we must consider empowerment for utilization.

Bridging social divides: Challenge our tendency to connect only with those who are similar to ourselves.

Thinking full frame: Engage people in all the ways they experience and know the world so they can bring their full selves to the public realm.

Being hyper-local: Engagement must attend to the everyday lives of people and the immediate spaces they live and work in.

Shifting the locus of design: In designing civic technologies and interventions, design first for those at the margins of society.

Proponents must understand how power structures create impediments to participation; the difference between access and usage; the importance of local communities; and the need to generate conversations and connections among an increasingly diverse public. They must also approach the design of civic technologies through collaboration, working to create technologies that are best able to meet the needs of users.

Organizations are beginning to realize the importance of civic inclusion. Various groups are incorporating key principles that aim to create strong partnerships with local communities. The goal of a civic inclusive framework—functional, cohesive, and inclusive community engagement across differences—is almost within reach, but there is still much work to be done.

Notes

1. "Knight Foundation's Civic Tech Report: Why It Matters," http://knightfoundation.org/blogs/knightblog/2013/12/9/knight-foundations-civic-tech-report-why-it-matters.

2. The Center for Digital Inclusion (CDI) was founded in 1995 and appears to have been active until early 2015. CDI was set up as a social entrepreneurship project with a focus on overcoming the digital divide. The organization consisted of various international centers that ran local initiatives to help disadvantaged groups use Information and Communication Technologies (ICTs). DevKalpana was an effort based in India. Although it appears to no longer be active, we reference this effort as an example of how ICTs can be used as a tool for digital inclusion and on the ground change.

3. "DevKalpana: What We Do," https://en.wikipedia.org/wiki/Center_for_Digital_Inclusion.

4. "DevKalpana: Swara Sanjog," https://en.wikipedia.org/wiki/Center_for_Digital_Inclusion.

5. Right to the City, "About," http://righttothecity.org/about/.

6. Full Frame Initiatives, "Our Work," http://fullframeinitiative.org/breaking-cycles/.

7. Orton Family Foundation, "What We Do," http://www.orton.org/what-we-do.

8. Place Matters, "About," http://placematters.org.

References

Al-Jaghoub, Saheer, and Chris Westrup. 2009. "Reassessing social inclusion and digital divides." *Journal of Information, Communication and Ethics in Society* 7 (2/3): 146–158.

Alesina, Alberto, and Eliana La Ferrara. 1999. "Participation in Heterogeneous Communities." NBER Working Paper No. 7155, National Bureau of Economic Research.

Alesina, Alberto, and Eliana La Ferrara. 2002. "Who Trusts Others?" *Journal of Public Economics* 85 (2): 207–234.

Bächtiger, André, Simon Niemeyer, Michael Neblo, Marco R. Steenbergen, and Jürg Steiner. 2010. "Symposium: Toward More Realistic Models of Deliberative Democracy: Disentangling Diversity in Deliberative Democracy: Competing Theories, Their Blind Spots and Complementarities." *Journal of Political Philosophy* 18 (1): 32–63.

Barnes, Marian, Janet Newman, and Helen C. Sullivan. 2007. *Power, Participation and Political Renewal: Case Studies in Public Participation*. Bristol, UK: Policy Press.

Bittle, Scott, Chris Haller, and Alison Kadlec. 2009. "Promising Practices in Online Engagement." Occasional Paper No. 3, Center for Advances in Public Engagement.

Bradwell, Peter, and Sarah Marr. 2008. *Making the Most of Collaboration: An International Survey of Public Service Co-design*. London: Demos.

Brewer, Marilynn B. 1991. "The Social Self: On Being the Same and Different at the Same Time. *Personality and Social Psychology Bulletin* 17 (5): 475–482.

Brewer, Marilynn B. 1993. "The role of distinctiveness in social identity and group behaviour." *Journal of Multivariate Analysis*.

Carcasson, Martín. 2009. "Beginning with the End in Mind: A Call for Goal-Driven Deliberative Practice." Occasional Paper No. 2, Center for Advances in Public Engagement.

Chapman, Polly, Euan Phimister, Mark Shucksmith, Richard Upward, and E. Vera-Toscano. 1998. "Poverty and Exclusion in Rural Britain: The Dynamics of Low Income and Employment." Joseph Rowntree Foundation.

Coleman, Stephen, and John Gotze. 2001. *Bowling Together: Online Public Engagement in Policy Deliberation*. London: Hansard Society.

Commins, Pat. 1993. *Combating Exclusion in Ireland 1990–1994: A Midway Report*. Brussels: Observatory on National Policies to Combat Social Exclusion, Commission of European Countries.

Costa, Dora L., and Matthew E. Kahn. 2003. "Civic Engagement and Community Heterogeneity: An Economist's Perspective." *Perspectives on Politics* 1 (1): 103–111.

Curley, Alexandra. 2005. "Theories of Urban Poverty and Implications for Public Housing Policy." *Journal of Sociology and Social Welfare* 32:97.

Delhey, Jan, and Kenneth Newton. 2005. "Predicting Cross-National Levels of Social Trust: Global Pattern or Nordic Exceptionalism?" *European Sociological Review* 21 (4): 311–327.

DiMaggio, Paul, and Eszter Hargittai. 2001. "From the 'Digital Divide' to 'Digital Inequality': Studying Internet Use as Penetration Increases." Princeton University Center for Arts and Cultural Policy Studies, Working Paper No. 15.

DiMaggio, Paul, Eszter Hargittai, Coral Celeste, and Steven Shafer. 2004. "Digital Inequality: From Unequal Access to Differentiated Use." In *Social Inequality,* ed. Kathryn M. Neckerman, 355–400. New York: Russell Sage Foundation.

Eckstein, Harry. 1984. Civic Inclusion and Its Discontents. *Daedalus* 113 (4): 107–145.

Ellison, Nicole B., Charles Steinfield, and Cliff Lampe. 2007. "The Benefits of Facebook 'Friends": Social Capital and College Students' Use of Online Social Network Sites." *Journal of Computer-Mediated Communication* 12 (4): 1143–1168.

Ellison, Nicole B. 2007. "Social Network Sites: Definition, History, and Scholarship." *Journal of Computer-Mediated Communication* 13 (1): 210–230.

Flanagan, Mary, Daniel Howe, and Helen Nissenbaum. 2008. "Embodying Values in Technology: Theory and Practice." In *Information Technology and Moral Philosophy,* ed. Jeroen van den Hoven and John Weckert., 322–353. Cambridge: Cambridge University Press.

Greenbaum, J., and M. Kyng, eds. 1991. *Design at Work: Cooperative Design of Computer Systems.* Hillsdale, NJ: Lawrence Erlbaum Associates.

Gurstein, Michael, ed. 1999. *Community Informatics: Enabling Communities with Information and Communications Technologies.* IGI Global.

Hampton, Keith, and Barry Wellman. 2003. "Neighboring in Netville: How the Internet Supports Community and Social Capital in a Wired Suburb." *City & Community* 2 (4): 277–311.

Hoffman, Donna L., and Thomas P. Novak. 2000. "The Growing Digital Divide: Implications for an Open Research Agenda." In *Understanding the Digital Economy: Data, Tools, and Research,* eds. Erik Brynjolfsson and Brian Kahin. Cambridge, MA: MIT Press.

Hudson, Heather E. 2010. "Municipal Wireless Broadband: Lessons from San Francisco and Silicon Valley." *Telematics and Informatics* 27 (1): 1–9.

International Telecommunication Union. 2013. "Measuring the Information Society." http://www.itu.int/en/ITU-D/Statistics/Documents/publications/mis2013/MIS2013_without_Annex _4.pdf.

Jenkins, Henry, Ravi Purushotma, Margaret Weigel, Katie Clinton, and Alice J. Robison. 2009. *Confronting the Challenges of Participatory Culture: Media Education for the 21st Century.* Cambridge, MA: MIT Press.

Katz, James Everett, and Ronald E. Rice. 2002. *Social Consequences of Internet Use: Access, Involvement, and Interaction.* Cambridge, MA: MIT press.

Kennard, William E. 2001. "Equality in the Information Age." In *The Digital Divide: Facing a Crisis or Creating a Myth?,* ed. Benjamin M. Compaine, 195–198. Cambridge, MA: MIT Press.

Kvasny, Lynette. 2006. "Cultural (Re)production of digital inequality in a US community technology initiative." *Information, Communication & Society* 9 (2): 160–181.

Kvasny, Lynette, and Mark Keil. 2006. "The challenges of redressing the digital divide: A tale of two US cities." *Information Systems Journal* 16 (1): 23–53.

Light, Ann, and Rosemary Luckin. 2008. "Designing for social justice: people, technology, learning." Futurelab. http://www2.futurelab.org.uk/resources/documents/opening_education/Designing_for_Social_Justice.pdf

Light, Ann, and Clodagh Miskelly . 2008. "Brokering Between Heads and Hearts: An Analysis of Designing for Social Change." In *Undisciplined! Design Research Society Conference 2008,* Sheffield Hallam University, Sheffield, UK, July 16–19.

Manza, Jeff. 2006. "Social Capital." In *The Cambridge Dictionary of Sociology, ed. Bryan S. Turner.* New York: Cambridge University Press.

McBride, Amanda Moore, Margaret S. Sherraden, and Suzanne Pritzker. 2006. "Civic Engagement Among Low-Income and Low-Wealth Families: In Their Words." *Family Relations* 55 (2): 152–162.

McDowell, Ceasar, and Vanessa Otero. 2011. "A Model for Inclusive Engagement." *Communities & Banking,* Fall, 29–31.

McPherson, Miller, Lynn Smith-Lovin, and James M. Cook. 2001. "Birds of a Feather: Homophily in Social Networks." *Annual Review of Sociology* 27 (August):415–444.

Mervyn, Kieran, Anoush Simon, and David K. Allen. 2014. "Digital inclusion and social inclusion: a tale of two cities." *Information, Communication & Society,* 17 (9): 1086–1104.

Mesch, Gustavo S., and Yael Levanon. 2003. "Community Networking and Locally-Based Social Ties in Two Suburban Localities." *City & Community* 2 (4): 335–351.

Mesch, Gustavo S., and Ilan Talmud. 2010. "Internet Connectivity, Community Participation, and Place Attachment: A Longitudinal Study." *American Behavioral Scientist,* 53 (8): 1095–1110.

Messick, David M., and Roderick M. Kramer. 2001. "Trust as a Form of Shallow Morality." In *Trust in Society,* ed. Karen S. Cook. New York: Russell Sage Foundation.

Moore, Carl. 2000. "What Is Community?" In *Across the Great Divide: Explorations in Collaborative Conservation and the American West,* eds. Philip Brick, Donald Snow, and Sarah Van de Wetering. Washington, DC:Island Press.

National Democratic Institute. 2013. *Citizen Participation and Technology.* https://www.ndi.org/files/Citizen-Participation-and-Technology-an-NDI-Study.pdf

Norris, Pippa. 2001. *Digital Divide: Civic Engagement, Information Poverty, and the Internet Worldwide.* Cambridge: Cambridge University Press.

Notley, Tanya. 2009. "Young People, Online Networks, and Social Inclusion. *Journal of Computer-Mediated Communication* 14 (4): 1208–1227.

Oden, Michael, and C. Rock. 2004. *Beyond the Digital Access Divide, Developing Meaningful Measures of Information and Communications Technology Gaps.* Austin, TX: The University of Texas at Austin Press.

Portes, Alejandro. 2000. "Social Capital: Its Origins and Applications in Modern Sociology." In *Knowledge and Social Capital*, ed. Eric L. Lesser, 43–67. Boston: Butterworth-Heinemann.

Powell, Alison. 2011. "Metaphors for Democratic Communication Spaces: How Developers of Local Wireless Networks Frame Technology and Urban Space." *Canadian Journal of Communication* 36 (1).

Purcell, Mark. 2002. "Excavating Lefebvre: The right to the city and its urban politics of the inhabitant." *GeoJournal* 58:99–108.

Putnam, Robert D. 2000. *Bowling Alone: The Collapse and Revival of American Community.* New York: Simon and Schuster.

Putnam, Robert D. 2007. "*E Pluribus Unum:* Diversity and Community in the Twenty-first Century. The 2006 Johan Skytte Prize Lecture." *Scandinavian Political Studies* 30 (2): 137–174.

Putnam, Robert D., ed. 2002. *Democracies in Flux: The Evolution of Social Capital in Contemporary Society.* New York: Oxford University Press.

Rice, Tom W., and Brent Steele. 2001. "White Ethnic Diversity and Community Attachment in Small Iowa Towns." *Social Science Quarterly* 82 (2): 397–407.

Room, Graham. 1995. "Poverty in Europe: competing paradigms of analysis." *Policy and Politics* 23 (2): 103–113.

Room, Graham J. 1999. "Social exclusion, solidarity, and the challenge of globalization." *International Journal of Social Welfare* 8 (3): 166–174.

Rustin, Mike. 1997. "Stakeholding and the Public Sector." In *Stakeholder Capitalism,* ed. Gavin Kelly, Dominic Kelly, Andrew Gamble, 72–81. New York: St. Martin's Press, Inc.

Sanders, Lynn. 1997. "Against Deliberation." *Political Theory* 25: 347–376.

Selwyn, Neil, and Keri Facer. 2007. "Beyond the Digital Divide: Rethinking Digital Inclusion for the 21st Century." Opening Education Reports. Bristol: Futurelab. www2.futurelab.org.uk/resources/documents/opening_education/Digital_Divide.pdf

Selwyn, Neil, Stephen Gorard, and Sara Williams. 2001. "Digital Divide or Digital Opportunity? The Role of Technology in Overcoming Social Exclusion in U.S. Education." *Educational Policy* 15 (2): 258–277.

Servon, Lisa J., and Marla K. Nelson. 2001. "Community Technology Centers: Narrowing the Digital Divide in Low-Income, Urban Communities." *Journal of Urban Affairs* 23 (3–4): 279–290.

Sirianni, Carmen, and Lewis Friedland. 2001. *Civic Innovation in America: Community Empowerment, Public Policy, and the Movement for Civic Renewal.* Berkeley: University of California Press.

Small, Mario Luis. 2009. *Unanticipated Gains: Origins of Network Inequality in Everyday Life.* New York: Oxford University Press.

Smith, Mark A. 2002. "Ballot Initiatives and the Democratic Citizen." *Journal of Politics* 64 (3): 892–903.

Smyth, K. F., L. Goodman, and C. Glenn. 2006. "The full-frame approach: a new response to marginalized women left behind by specialized services." *American Journal of Orthopsychiatry* 76 (4): 489–502.

Stewart, Angus, and Peter Askonas. 2000. *Social Inclusion: Possibilities and Tensions.* London: Palgrave MacMillan.

Stolle, Dietlind, Stuart Soroka, and Richard Johnston. 2008. "When Does Diversity Erode Trust? Neighborhood Diversity, Interpersonal Trust and the Mediating Effect of Social Interactions." *Political Studies* 56 (1): 57–75.

Tajfel, Henri. 1969. "Cognitive Aspects of Prejudice." *Journal of Biosocial Science* 1 (no. S1): 173–191.

Tapia, Andrea H., and Julio Angel Ortiz. 2010. "Network Hopes: Municipalities Deploying Wireless Internet to Increase Civic Engagement." *Social Science Computer Review* 28 (1): 93–117.

Tapia, Andrea H., Lynette Kvasny, and Julio Angel Ortiz. 2011. "A Critical Discourse Analysis of Three US Municipal Wireless Network Initiatives for Enhancing Social Inclusion." *Telematics and Informatics* 28 (3): 215–226.

Tufekcioglu, Z. 2003. *In Search of Lost Jobs: The Rhetoric and Practice of Computer Skills Training.* Austin, TX: University of Texas.

Uslaner, Eric M. 2002. *The Moral Foundations of Trust.* Cambridge: Cambridge University Press.

Virtanen, Tytti, and Sanna Malinen. 2008. "Supporting the sense of locality with online communities." In *Proceedings of the 12th international conference on Entertainment and media in the ubiquitous era*, 145–149. ACM.

VozMob. 2011. "Mobile Voices: Projecting the voices of immigrant workers by appropriating mobile phones for popular communication." *Communications Research in Action: Scholar-Activist Collaborations for a Democratic Public Sphere,* ed. Philip M. Napoli and Minna Aslama, 177–196. New York: Fordham University Press.

Warschauer, Mark. 2004. *Technology and Social Inclusion: Rethinking the Digital Divide.* Cambridge, MA: MIT Press.

Young, Iris Marion. 2001. "Activist Challenges to Deliberative Democracy." *Political Theory* 29 (5): 670–690.

31 Community Media Infrastructure as Civic Engagement

Colin Rhinesmith

Facebook, Twitter, and YouTube allow people to create and share videos with anyone in the world with access to a computer and the skills needed to participate in our globally networked society. Citizens around the world have used these digital media tools not only for entertainment but also to document human rights abuses and to advocate for social movements. As a result, these "netizens" are working together across distance to change the ways that governments and corporations control the terms in which their access and participation online are decided (e.g., see MacKinnon 2012). At times, it's difficult to believe that widespread use of online video production and distribution tools, as a phenomenon, is only a decade old.

As the use of Web video platforms continues to spread through the use of mobile devices, additional challenges facing netizens continue to rise. Threats to our online privacy, in the wake of the Edward Snowden leaks, have given a new urgency to involving ordinary citizens in Internet policy. In the past, debates about the future of the Internet were often delegated to expert technologists and politicians behind closed doors in Washington. However, since the outrage over the Stop Online Privacy Act and Protect IP Act (*Washington Post* 2012), there has been much broader engaged debate and public interest in these mundane Internet policy discussions. These free and open forums for public debate have led to a much broader discussion of how the Internet should be governed to prevent censorship and to provide everyone with access to the communication tools needed to participate fully in a democratic society.

In this chapter, I argue that it's critical to look beyond Facebook, YouTube, and other participatory media platforms in order to focus on the underlying civic communications infrastructure that makes free speech possible in many communities around the world. In doing so, I highlight the case of public, educational, and government (PEG) access television in the United States as an example to show how ordinary people can engage with their local governments to determine the shape of their local media landscape and to promote open access to communication technology. Unfortunately, this vital form of community media infrastructure has been under attack in recent years in the transition from cable to broadband Internet access. I join recent calls from scholars (e.g., Fuentes-Bautista 2014; Goodman and Chen 2009) who have argued for the need to rethink localism and self-determination in discussions of Internet policy in order to engage more people in deciding the future of free speech in the digital age. While Internet policy continues to be important in national and global debates, I argue that the history and present of PEG access in the U.S. provides a model for determining how local communities can shape their civic communication spaces. This model of localism in civic communications infrastructure development, I argue, provides important lessons for our thinking about the future of the Internet at home and around the world.

Why the History of PEG Access TV Matters

Twenty-eight years before the first blogs appeared on the Internet, public access to cable television emerged as a revolutionary and disruptive new medium. Many groups in the early 1970s saw cable television as having the potential to democratize the media by allowing "ordinary" people to participate. Public access cable television is a form of community media, which are often best understood in relation to what they are not: commercial mainstream media. Alternative, citizens', or radical media are closely aligned terms. As Downing (2001) argued, "radical media are quite often referred to as community media and as democratic alternatives to media monopolies" (38). Community media appear in many forms and practices, including low-power radio and public access television. Although each medium has its own distinct set of social and technical infrastructures, all are "dedicated to principles of free expression and participatory democracy" (Howley 2005, 2). Therefore, one might define community media as (1) an alternative to mass media, (2) concerned with self-determination (i.e., local ownership and control), and (3) noncommercial. It's important to note that community media are often deeply committed to "human rights, social justice, the environment, and sustainable approaches to development" (World Association of Community Radio Broadcasters 2002, 2). Community media practitioners are fundamentally concerned with issues of power and frequently ask: Who ultimately gains, and who does not, from access to and participation in local media production and distribution?

Public access to cable television during the 1970s "was viewed as a means to address some of the social problems of the period, many of which grew from a fundamental distrust of social institutions and a widespread belief that people had lost the power to influence the direction of society" (Higgins 1999, 625). Community activists joined educators and policymakers during this time to rally for public access to cable television as a medium by, for, and of the people. Public access to cable television was rooted in the activism of the era, "a time when public access advocates enjoyed a mutually supportive environment with an emerging cable industry eager to demonstrate its potential to diversify television" (Johnson 2007, 7). The Federal Communications Commission (FCC) also saw the potential in cable technology to serve local communities through noncommercial television (Linder 1999, 19). In response, in its 1972 Cable Television Report and Order, the FCC required cable operators to provide channel space for local origination in the form of public, educational, and government (PEG) access channels, as well as funding for equipment and facilities for PEG channel productions. This period laid an important foundation for the tremendous growth of public access television—and the cable industry—over the next decade. However, as Engelman (1990) argued, "early support for public access by the cable industry should be understood in the context of the bitter struggle between broadcasters and cablecasters over the future of cable television in the United States" (23).

The Midwest Video Corporation later challenged the FCC's rules, bringing their case before the Supreme Court in 1979 in *FCC v. Midwest Video*. The Court decided that the FCC did not have the authority to require the commercial cable companies to provide channels, equipment, and facilities for PEG access television. However, it was not until the Cable Communications Policy Act of 1984 that Congress finally "developed a national policy for cable television, which codified the ability of the franchising authority to require PEG channels, facilities, and equipment" (Rennie 2006, 55). The legislation required cable operators to provide these resources, but only when negotiated for by municipalities as part of the franchise agreements. Linder (1999) underscored, "if the franchisers did not require public access, the cable operators would not have to provide it" (26).

The Cable Communications Policy Act of 1984 later mandated that cable television operators in the 100 largest U.S. markets must set aside channels, equipment, and facilities for PEG access television in exchange for the cable company's commercial use of "public rights-of-way" (i.e., city streets and sidewalks). In many states, a local franchise authority (LFA) negotiates with the cable company to establish the terms of the cable license agreement. The LFA may also conduct a *community needs assessment* to gain input from community members to inform how the social and technical infrastructure of cable television can be used to enhance civic life. Cable operators in many states are still required to negotiate with the LFA in return for their commercial use of public rights-of-way: "Included in the grant of a franchise to a cable system are rights relating to the construction of the system, including the local franchising authority's authorization to use public rights-of-way, easements, and to establish the areas to be served" (Federal Communications Commission 2010). However, in several states today there is no negotiation at all. Here is a summary by the Benton Foundation about the impact of statewide franchising legislation on PEG access centers:

Since 2005, PEG access centers in 100 communities have closed. The overwhelming majority of these are public access centers, rather than educational or government channels seen on local cable systems. California has been particularly hard-hit, with 51 closures throughout the state. Nearly half of those survey respondents who provided financial information for the five-year period of the study (2005–2010) reported an average funding decrease of nearly 40 percent.

Also, 20 percent of those who reported in-kind support from their cable operators reported that in-kind materials and services had been cut back or eliminated during this five-year period. (Garcia 2011)

The negotiations that do still exist create franchise fees to help fund channels, equipment purchases, and facilities for PEG access television. However, telephone companies, such as AT&T and Verizon, that are interested in providing video service (along with broadband and voice) have fought against this local model in recent years, leaving the future of PEG access television to hang in the balance of heavily lobbied state and federal legislators.

From Public Access TV to Community Media Centers

For many years PEG access centers have offered more than just access to cable television. In the section entitled "From Cable Access to Community Media Centers" in the 1995 issue of the *Community Technology Center News & Notes*, George Preston of the Lowell Telecommunications Corporation and Dirk Koning of the Grand Rapids Community Media Center described how their centers embraced public computers. As Koning envisioned, "The Community Media Center will be an amalgam of brick and mortar and bits and bytes" (Koning 1995, 13). Over the years, more and more PEG access stations have embraced the term *community media centers* to describe the shift from a focus on cable access television to a multiplicity of forms, including broadband Internet platforms (e.g., see Rhinesmith 2010b). This rebranding of public access television in the age of YouTube has also made it possible for community media centers to connect with new partners and constituents who use video-sharing platforms and other participatory media today as a taken-for-granted part of everyday life.

Since the early days of cable television, civic organizations have been close, natural allies with community media centers. Civic and community groups understood that public access television provided a space where ordinary citizens could engage with other local residents to raise awareness about the important issues of the day—a function that PEG access television still serves on both cable and broadband Internet platforms. Devine's foundational scholarship on PEG access television continues to be an important reminder of the civic mission of PEG access TV. As Devine (1995) explained:

Public access brings private citizens into public life. It creates associations, forges coalitions, and transforms private concern into public activism. It stimulates and supports public expression and dialogue and provides a forum for discussion of the issues of concern in two thousand communities across the country. (32)

Viewed in this way, public access television can be understood as a process or a means, rather than simply an end (e.g., a program aired on a public access television station). This conceptualization has always been at the core of public access philosophy. As Higgins (1999) explained, "community television as a process conceptualizes constant change within individuals and the collectivities within which they participate" (639). This is a process that brings "civil society into view" to highlight the ways in which community media can negotiate group needs as well as individual freedoms (Rennie 2006, 59). Because community media often exist outside the market and the state, they represent "an important site for the growth and development of civil society" (Howley 2013, 823). Civil society in a global context is often referred to as the space between the market and the state that provides the "conditions under which people, individually and collectively, are willing and able to engage as members of communities" (Kim and Ball-Rokeach 2006, 173). In this way, Oldenberg's (1999) concept of "third places" outside of work and home where people can socialize and engage in public debates is also an important concept for understanding the role that PEG centers play in fostering local civic engagement. This shift in thinking has also opened the door to reimagine the role of PEG access centers in the digital age.

Community-Building Access Centers

Devine (2000) outlined seven ways that public access television stations can be viewed as "community-building access centers" (2–3). In describing a public access center as a community center "for public (not just individual) benefit," Devine argued:

It provides an accessible place where people can learn and practice the virtues of being a community, where they can come together to interact and collaborate with others across lines of difference, and thereby develop the sort of social capital which extends well beyond the actual access activity into the larger community. (2)

Devine challenged individuals to look beyond public access programming "as the singular measure of access success" (2). Rather, he explained that public access centers, as community-building access centers, should focus their goals on "fostering significant public discourse, engaging diverse voices, and contributing to the overall texture of democratic life" (2). In this way, many public access centers share a common mission with telecenters and community technology centers worldwide (e.g., see Miller 2013).

Community media centers in the broadband age remain focused on their community-building roles and continue to foster what Higgins (1999) referred to as a growing "awareness of self, others, and society" (634) among community media producers. In his 1993–1994 study of "the implementation of the public access empowerment vision as a method of evaluating the viability of the vision itself" (630) at ACTV21, Higgins found that "a new awareness of self is an outcome of the public access experience for some of the respondents; most also experience a new awareness of others. An understanding of oneself is enhanced by a heightened awareness of others and a broader society" (632). He wrote that it is this process that leads public access producers to "move outward from the self, to others, and to society" (632).

Higgins's study is significant and relevant to my focus on infrastructure because his findings show how participation in public access television becomes "part of a process of societal change that begins at a personal level" and that moves away from the idea of individualism toward "a dynamic process of interaction between the individual and the collectivity" (639). This approach, as Higgins wrote, provides a way of understanding community media as the application of the tools that enable "social change and truly democratic purposes rather than the tools themselves" (641). This contribution is useful because it moves the discussion away from technological deterministic perspectives of public access television and toward an appreciation of community media as a means for civic engagement and social change. As Halleck (2002) argued, "perhaps the most significant development of the public access movement has been the informed practice of thousands of individuals who have taken an active role not only in the production of their own television, but in the implementation, nurturing, and the defending of local telecommunications structures" (108). This movement should serve as a model to ensure that *all* residents have an opportunity to shape their civic communications infrastructure.

Community Media Infrastructure in the Digital Age

The most important thing is for the user of the infrastructure to first become aware of the social and political work that the infrastructure is doing and then seek ways to modify it (locally or globally) as need be.
—Star and Bowker (2010, 246)

The social, technical, and regulatory dimensions of PEG access provide a space within which local residents have an opportunity to engage in civic life. Here, I define *community media infrastructure* as both the material aspects (e.g., facilities, equipment, channels) as well as the less visible factors (e.g., federal and state legislation, telecommunication lobbyists, local franchise authorities) that play an equally vital role in shaping civic communications infrastructure and its consequences. In doing so, I call attention to the often hidden dimensions that are not always seen on cable access television. I draw upon Star and Ruhleder's (1996) theory of infrastructure as a foundation for advancing the concept of community media infrastructure.

What Is Infrastructure?
Infrastructure is commonly referred to as something that exists in the background, such as bridges, railroads, and highways. Because of its role in supporting other social processes, infrastructure is often taken for granted (Star and Ruhleder 1996, 113). Rather than looking at infrastructure as being separate from social, political, and economic processes, residents in local communities should think about infrastructure as inseparable from those social, institutional, and technical forces that shape its development and consequences. This vision of infrastructure takes a long view of

community media evolution that looks "beyond human versus technological components" and moves toward "a set of interrelated social, organizational, and technical components or systems" (Bowker et al. 2010, 99). By making infrastructure visible, I maintain that individuals in local communities can gain a better grasp of the political and ethical values embedded in the design of community media systems and the ways in which individuals and groups claim ownership and control over their development.

Jackson et al. (2007) provide a concise summary of Star and Ruhleder's conceptualization of infrastructure in the following list:

- *Embedded* in other structures, social arrangements, and technologies
- *Transparent* (and largely invisible) once established, "reappearing" only at moments of upheaval or breakdown
- Defined by its *reach* beyond particular spatial or temporal locations
- *Learned* as a part of membership within particular professional, social, or cultural communities
- Deeply linked with *conventions of practice* and other forms of routinized social action
- Built on, shaped, and constrained by its relationship to an already *installed base*
- *Fixed and changed in modular increments*, through complex processes of negotiation and mutual adjustment with adjacent systems, structures, and practices

Star and Ruhleder (1996) explained that infrastructure often becomes visible upon breakdown. In the community media context, infrastructure appears in the form of signal loss on PEG access television or white noise on low-power FM radio. These infrastructural breakdowns are the visual and audible outcomes of a broad range of social, institutional, and technical processes that are often out of view from everyday sight and consideration. The cables, wires, and antennae that support community media practices are often something that we take for granted, again because they are unseen. Infrastructure studies scholars have emphasized the fact that infrastructure is not simply technical. It is always considered to be more relational or dependent on a variety of social and technical, as well as political, economic, cultural, and historical factors. In other words, "infrastructure is then not a thing but a question: what does this activity depend on?" (Sandvig 2013, 92).

Community media infrastructure can be understood as involving its physical or material attributes, but it is always connected to the broader social and institutional forces that shape its development and consequences in local settings. Because infrastructure is taken for granted, Jackson et al. (2007) argued this fact makes it difficult "to recall what is at stake with infrastructure (which turns out to be quite a lot)." For example, telecommunications companies in the United States have been colluding with federal policymakers to restrict community-owned broadband infrastructure

(Fung 2014). These developments have important implications for community media centers and their ability to operate community media forms and practices beyond PEG access TV.

Community Media Infrastructure

Infrastructure has always been at the core of public access television. As Halleck (2002) explained, "One effort to create local media democracy in the United States has been the public access movement ... a unique experiment in creating an infrastructure for open access to communication technology" (73). The cables that provided access to this new medium were at the very foundation of the cultural, technological, and legal arguments that provided cable access television in the first place. More recently, Breitbart et al. (2011) argued that public access advocates should look beyond cable television and toward multiple community media forms. The authors maintained that the Alliance for Community Media (ACM), the national nonprofit organization that "represents over 3,000 Public, Educational, and Governmental (PEG) access organizations and community media center throughout the country" (Alliance for Community Media 2014), should focus their public policy efforts on expanding "the definition of 'public access' so that it refers not only to a type of content that is locally produced and reflects the diversity of a community, but also to a type of communications infrastructure that is governed by the people who use it" (1).

Breitbart et al. (2011) maintained that the PEG access transition from cable television to broadband networks should include an emphasis on a "multiplatform" approach that includes low-power FM radio, community wireless, and other mobile platforms (1). The authors recommended that the ACM should develop a bold public policy approach that puts community-controlled communications infrastructure at the center of its advocacy efforts in Washington, D.C. The legacy of PEG access television, and in particular the cable franchise renewal process, provides a standard upon which civic and community engagement into our local communications infrastructure can be promoted as a potential for reinvigorating the debate over who ultimately controls the Internet as well as who determines our First Amendment rights. In this fragile period of crumbling information privacy and increased digital surveillance, PEG access history provides an essential social and civic mechanism for engaging everyday citizens in decisions about their local technology infrastructure.

The Community Needs Assessment as an Infrastructural Process

I argue that the cable franchising process is the civic mechanism that allows ordinary citizens to participate in determining the form and outcome of their local media and technology environment. However, this civic process is under attack in many states across the U.S. The cable franchising process should grow, not diminish, to include a much more expansive view of community infrastructure and its interconnection with global networks. As Johnson (1998) argued, "cable franchising is no longer simply about receiving television and access to television. It is now about how our communities are going to be organized in relationship to a global economy and culture" (8). This vision for community-controlled infrastructure is perhaps more relevant now than ever. The steps are important to review.

During the cable franchise renewal process, a local government may decide to conduct a formal process to assess the performance of the local cable operator(s) as well as the community needs and interests related to PEG access television. As Buske (1998) explained, "The communities with the most successful results approach renewal as an opportunity to undertake a community-wide communications planning process" (13). The Cable Communications Policy Act of 1984 established the premise upon which the local franchising authority can determine a cable company's past performance and "identify the community's future cable-related needs and interests" (Buske 1998, 13). Community input is therefore critically important in establishing the basis upon which the franchise renewal is determined. "The needs assessment should include not only current needs, but also future needs, such as broadband capacity for distance learning or equipment for multimedia production" (Fischer and Hardenbergh 2004, 39).

Community input is sought from a variety of local constituents to gain a deeper understanding of the past performance of the cable operator(s) as well as the community's needs and future interests related to PEG access television. Focus groups are often used to gather information from the following groups: government departments and agencies; educational institutions; current access users; nonprofit organizations in areas such as community service, social service, health care, youth, and senior citizen services; minority groups; local neighborhood associations and business organizations; arts, culture, and heritage groups and organizations; and church groups and religious organizations (The Buske Group 2014, 4).

Several methods are recommended as techniques for gathering this important information. For example, the research conducted in the needs assessment process (e.g., telephone and online surveys, review of PEG operations, and interviews with community organizations that use PEG services) provide local governments with the data they need to make key decisions about their community's cable systems and to understand their constituents' unique and often innovative visions for how community infrastructure can be used to enhance the civic life of the community (The Buske Group 2014). However, big cable and telecommunications companies have threatened these processes because they argue it's too time consuming to negotiate with each individual franchise authority. These large corporations have hired lobbyists to convince state governments to make it easier for them to profit off the public rights-of-way and have even eliminated this process altogether in most cases, as I describe below. In the next section, I will detail the impact of these lobbying efforts at a time when local communities need political and corporate accountability perhaps more than ever, particularly given the revelations about the NSA's spying program through which telecommunications companies have collaborated with government agencies to share people's personal digital communications.

Threats to Community Media Infrastructure

Significant challenges lay ahead in determining the appropriate funding mechanisms for the sustainability of community media centers in the broadband age. I now briefly review some of these ongoing struggles before describing some of the more recent and exciting opportunities for community media centers given their adequate legal and financial support. I begin by elaborating on some of the cultural, political, and technical challenges facing community media centers over the past decade.

Cultural Challenges

Since the beginning, public access television has faced numerous challenges at the local, state, and national levels (e.g., see Fuller 1994; Linder 1999). In the early years, raising awareness about public access within the community was no small task. As Theodora Sklover, Director of Open Channel, told the *New York Times* in 1971: "Our biggest problem is informing the public that they can go on television and say whatever is on their minds. People are used to thinking of TV as something someone else does, not as something they do. We have to overcome that inertia" (Gent 1971). Lack of financial resources, as well as "fierce competition for the more professional, fast-paced production, of commercial broadcasting" (Fuller 1994, 33), contributed to challenges of reaching the public.

Commercial television programming benefits from built-in advertising while public access suffers from a lack of commercial publicity via telecommunications and cable providers. Images of "vanity" and controversial programming have also stigmatized public access as a medium only for the "fringe" of society, as exemplified in the 1992 film *Wayne's World.* While these and other stereotypes continue to prevent its vision from becoming fully realized, other more recent and challenging barriers may perhaps be the most threatening to the future of PEG access television.

In June 2006, city commissioners in Alacheu County, Florida, convened a public hearing to discuss local support for public access television. The meeting followed several failed attempts by local groups and elected officials to come to consensus. Disagreements over franchising details with cable operators and squabbles between advocates and officials were among the many roadblocks. But during the hearing in June, a new factor became the focus of debate. Commissioners argued that online video-sharing websites such as YouTube eliminate the need for public access television (Swirko 2006). If anyone with a portable video-recording device and the means to self-publish can participate on the Web, why should cities and towns across the U.S. continue to fund community access to cable television?

The answer to this question can be found in the fact that community media organizations provide the local capacity building that YouTube, as a Web-based commercial platform, can never address. In addition, many community media centers provide access to computers and technology training, which provides individuals in low-income communities with the resources to develop professional skills and to engage in the public life of their community. These and other benefits that I described above can not be matched by online video-sharing platforms alone.

Political Challenges

Media scholars have described public access television as a struggle for access and democratic participation in an age of increasing consolidation and commercialism in U.S. media, culture, and society (e.g., see Downing et al. 2001; Fuller 1994; Halleck 2002; Howley 2005; Kellner 1992; Linder 1999). More recently, the convergence of voice, television, and Internet services has created additional challenges for public access advocates. Commercial providers of these convergent services have spent enormous sums of money to influence telecommunications policy and lawmaking at the state and national levels.

After unsuccessful attempts by cable and telephone companies to change the video franchising laws at the national level in the mid-2000s, these same companies hired lobbyists to challenge the rules at the state level. During this period, state legislation was introduced as an attempt to take the video franchising authority away from local officials and move it into the hands of state legislators. The result ultimately allowed the telephone and cable companies, with the assistance of state legislators, to create a one-size-fits-all cable franchise model—despite the fact that every local community is different and each has a different set of needs and interests related to their own communications infrastructure. American Community Television (2012) reported the following in 2012: "Statewide/State Issued franchising in ten states either completely eliminated PEG support funding or set a shot clock on when PEG support funding would end." Today, the number of states with statewide franchising models is believed to be much higher.

The cable franchise model has come under an unprecedented attack over the past ten years because of the reasons I've described in this chapter. In addition, press reports from across the country detailed these statewide lobbying efforts. For example, Tennessee is one of the many states that has struggled with statewide video franchising legislation laws. On February 18, 2008, *The Tennessean* wrote: "This is the second year AT&T has pushed for a bill at the Capitol that would let the San Antonio–based company sell TV services statewide without getting franchise agreements with individual communities" (Snyder 2008). AT&T argued that the legislation would bring increased competition to the video service market and additional choice to consumers. Opponents, however, argued that if the bill passed, local control over the video franchising process would be lost, allowing AT&T to pick and choose the neighborhoods it wished to serve. The fear was that wealthier communities would be served with enhanced video, broadband, and phone services and low-income communities would be left behind, a process also known as *redlining*. Community media advocates worried that the legislation would reduce or eliminate funding for public access television, leaving the future of local media in the hands of heavily lobbied state legislators. Unfortunately, for many communities, this fear has since become a reality in many states across the country.

Technical Challenges

Technical dimensions have added to the cultural and political challenges discussed, particularly during community media's transition from cable to broadband Internet platforms. Even though many communities across the United States do not yet have high-speed Internet access, broadband has become the new mass medium and the commercial market has reflected this change. Many cable subscribers have traded in their set-top boxes for Internet delivery systems that offer Hulu, YouTube, and other online video playback services. This shift in consumer culture has created enormous challenges for cable companies and PEG access centers. Many cable companies have been forced to create their own digital apps to compete with Google, Apple, and other software companies.

In addition, community media workers have faced significant difficulties in the transition from analog to digital video systems. Many understaffed and under-resourced centers have not had the capacity needed to incorporate many of the following broadband-enabled facilities. These challenges only begin to paint a picture of the ongoing cultural, political, and technical needs facing community media centers in the age of broadband.

A Way Forward

Online distribution is bringing audiences and producers closer, enabling new ways of dialogue about common interests and local issues.
—Fuentes-Bautista (2009, 37)

Local Engagement in Community Media Infrastructure

The digital culture that we live in today demands that residents have access to high-speed broadband communication tools along with the training and support needed to adopt computers and the Internet. It is best to view cable access television as one of the many community media services provided by PEG access/community media centers.

These tools should be protected, built upon, and reimagined within broadband spaces and infrastructures. As quiet murmurs about the eventual rewrite of the Telecommunications Act of 1996 are softly heard behind closed doors in Washington, D.C. (e.g., see Eggerton 2014; Glassman 2013), now is the time to begin laying out a framework for community media infrastructure in the broadband age, building on the existing scholarship and past recommendations of scholars and practitioners.

As many PEG access advocates have pointed out, broadband networks are just the next phase in the evolution of community media infrastructure. And it's critical for community media scholars, practitioners, and activists to engage with the public policy issues in this evolving broadband landscape.

For four decades, PEG access/community media centers have been important community service providers on cable TV systems. The only thing that has changed is the bandwidth capacity of the systems, stemming from the migration from analog to digital delivery of voice, video, and data services. We will continue to be on the wireline and wireless broadband networks of the future. But that will happen only if we understand our valuable past and ensure our future value through our participation in ongoing local, state, and national policy and planning processes as these broadband networks are developed around the country. If we don't tell our story, who will? (Sherwood 2010, 6)

Fuentes-Bautista (2014) suggested that one way for PEG access centers to build on their mission is to embrace the "resources of digital video franchise to revamp PEG services and promote residents' use of advanced broadband applications, through their active involvement in the creation, curation, and exchange of PEG digital content" (76). These suggestions should be strongly considered along with nationwide efforts to expand the regulatory space for PEG access in the digital age.

Community Broadband Infrastructure

Since the early days of public access television, community media practitioners and advocates have always looked at the potential of networked information systems to advance community development. For example, Sklover (1970) wrote: "Due to the broadband capability of cable which can carry voice, television, and record information simultaneously into the home, office, or classroom, what has appeared as plans for a tomorrowland may well be made available today" (3). The advent of high-speed broadband Internet has more recently made it possible for community media advocates to design, develop, and implement exciting new participatory platforms to advance community engagement in both physical and virtual spaces.

There are a number of exciting community media initiatives worth noting, including open source software projects that are supported across several community media centers. Denver Open Media (DOM) was one of the earliest examples of a public access center that not only lost its cable franchise fees, but also reinvented itself as a result.

Denver's Open Media Project was "a collaborative project among six public access facilities across the nation to implement open source and web-based tools for public access producers and staff." DOM received a grant from the Knight Foundation "to make these tools accessible to other centers to create a Nationwide Public Access Network that employs web capabilities for its operations" (Fuentes-Bautista 2014, 70). Digital Redwoods (2014) and Civic Cloud (2014) are two more recent examples of the potential for PEG to exist alongside other broadband services. These projects represent innovative examples that build upon the original mission and vision of public access television. They also show the potential of civic broadband applications to support community-defined development goals, including the use of public access facilities to promote sustainable broadband adoption.

One thing is certain in today's community media climate: local communities require high-speed, reliable, and sustainable broadband infrastructure through which communication services can be provided. To secure a strong future for community media, communities themselves need access to robust information and communication infrastructure upon which PEG and other services can be built. "In the U.S., local governments and communities have taken the lead in building next generation broadband infrastructure. In more than 100 cities and towns across America, a public entity provides services to homes and businesses throughout the community." These community-owned and operated Internet service providers are also becoming a popular option that provides "some of the fastest connections to residents, businesses, and community anchor institutions" (Lennett, Lucey, Hovis, and Afflerbach 2014, 5). In addition to community broadband infrastructure, local residents need access to technology training that respects people's everyday experiences with technology.

Community Technology Integration and Training

As I mentioned above, a number of PEG access centers realized in the early days of the Internet that cable television is just one of the many available community media tools. Computers and broadband platforms today play a significant role in the daily operations and management of PEG access centers as well as other cross-platform models of community media infrastructure, such as PEG access centers that have launched radio stations and mesh wireless networks operated by community-run Internet service providers. Several public access television stations also decided years ago to open "community technology centers" for residents to gain access to computers and the Internet along with their cable television offerings. These public computing facilities within community media centers continue to provide exciting opportunities to support local journalism projects, digital literacy training, and broadband adoption, particularly for residents within low-income areas (e.g., see Rhinesmith 2010b).

The community technology center movement in the 1990s played a significant role in helping to bridge the "digital divide," or the gaps between the information "haves" and "have nots." Early initiatives such as the Playing to Win Network were part of a "growing trend among community-based organizations, social service agencies, churches, and community centers for acquiring and integrating computers into their programs" (Miller 1994, 5). The legacy of these initiatives can be found in many PEG access centers today, as well as within other movement building organizations including the Media Mobilizing Project (MMP). As their website explains:

MMP exists to build a media, education and organizing infrastructure that will cohere and amplify the growing movement to end poverty. We use media to organize poor and working people to tell our stories to each other and the world, disrupting the stereotypes and structures that keep our communities divided. (Media Mobilizing Project 2015a)

MMP's mission to provide access to communication technology involves running a network of six community technology centers as part of the Philadelphia KEYSPOTs program (Media Mobilizing Project 2015b). A vibrant community-building access center should not only encompass the facilities and training needed to meet the social and technical challenges facing communities today, but should also serve as a bridge to other community-based organizations working toward community revitalization.

Community media centers should also resemble advances in local libraries that have embraced makerspaces, or "places to create, build, and craft" (American Library Association 2014), and other spaces to promote informal learning in science, technology, engineering, arts/design, and math (STEAM). All centers therefore should be equipped with public facilities that provide access to a range of broadband-enabled production and distribution channels, facilities, equipment, and training. Scholars and activists alike have argued that community media centers have long supported access to computers and the Internet, including opportunities for community members to gain digital literacy skills. As McConnell (2010) explained:

While the hardware and software may have changed in the last several decades from analog to digital, and new distribution platforms have emerged on the Internet, the core need for community media centers remains the same: the public needs access to the tools, training, and distribution channels to make media that matters to them and their communities. Community media centers should be first in line to benefit from—and advocate for—recommendations that could provide funding and capacity for broadband infrastructure and adoption programs. (8)

The FCC should build on the recommendations found in its National Broadband Plan (2010) by providing support for public computing facilities within all PEG access centers. In addition, federal policymakers should recognize community media centers as community anchor institutions, much like public libraries. Similar to libraries, broadband community media centers should have the capacity they need to foster digital inclusion and promote sustainable broadband adoption community-wide. To make this happen, residents in local communities across the U.S. must get engaged in local media policy debates to ensure access to their local communications infrastructure. The future of free speech depends upon this struggle.

Broadband infrastructure can help community media centers serve as connectors between civic organizations and local residents as well as to broader social movements. These networked models of community media organizing and infrastructure building are reflected in other non-PEG examples, such as the Digital Stewards Project in Detroit.

The Digital Stewards program prepares teams of community organizers, people with construction skills and techies to design and deploy communications infrastructure with a commitment to the Detroit Digital Justice Principles. Through the program, Digital Stewards learned about mesh wireless technology, which allows neighbors to form their own local network and share an Internet connection. (Allied Media Projects 2013)

The program is rooted in the concept of "Digital Stewardship," which emphasizes self-governance and sustainability in communication infrastructure development. "Digital Stewards grow and maintain the technology their communities need to foster healthy relationships, build resilience, and increase access to critical information" (Open Technology Institute 2014). By connecting principles of digital justice (Detroit Digital Justice Coalition 2015) and stewardship to communications infrastructure building, these community media models offer innovative approaches to engage local residents in helping to build and sustain broadband community networks.

Conclusion

The Internet has transformed how people engage in civic life in many parts of the world. At the same time, many residents in communities across the United States, for example, still do not have access to the twenty-first-century information and communication technologies, particularly in low-income communities. PEG access centers with public access computer labs help connect those residents most in need and provide opportunities to engage in making decisions about their civic communications infrastructure. The Cable Communications Policy Act of 1984 provided the foundation upon which community needs assessments can be used to gain input from a wide range of constituents about the state of their local media environment and future direction for community media engagement. I described how the concept of community media infrastructure provides an alternative to for-profit driven communication platforms, such as YouTube and Facebook, that have threatened our privacy as they partner with the U.S. government in the name of national security. Community media infrastructure is a form of civic engagement that allows local residents in many communities to imagine and implement a more robust and ecological foundation for free speech and digital rights. It is within this space that the less visible aspects of this civic communications infrastructure come into view and provide opportunities for private citizens to move into public life. The examples and suggestions found within this chapter are contributed as a vision for a vibrant and sustainable future for free speech and human rights in the broadband age.

References

Alliance for Community Media. 2013. "The Community Access Preservation Act (CAP Act)." http://www.allcommunitymedia.org/policy-advocacy/community-access-preservation-act-cap-act.

Alliance for Community Media. 2014. "About Us." http://www.allcommunitymedia.org/about-us.

Allied Media Projects. 2013. "Digital Stewards Launch Community Wireless Networks in Detroit." https://www.alliedmedia.org/news/2013/07/19/digital-stewards-launch-community-wireless-networks-detroit.

American Community Television. 2012. "For Many States, Time Is Running Out. …" http://www.acommunitytv.org/actnow/troubleinthestates.html.

American Library Association. 2014. "Makerspaces." Accessed December 4, 2014. http://www.ala.org/tools/makerspaces.

Bowker, Geoffrey C., Karen Baker, Florence Millerand, and David Ribes. 2010. "Toward Information Infrastructure Studies: Ways of Knowing in a Networked Environment." In *International Handbook of Internet Research*, ed. Jeremy Hunsinger, Lisbeth Klastrup, and Matthew M. Allen, 97–117. Berlin: Springer.

Breitbart, Joshua, Tom Glaisyer, Bincy Ninan, and James Losey. 2011. "Full Spectrum Community Media: Expanding Public Access to Communications Infrastructure." http://newamerica.net/publications/policy/full_spectrum_community_media.

Buske, Sue. 1998. "Demystifying the Cable Franchise Renewal Process." *Community Media Review* 21 (1): 13–15.

The Buske Group. 2014. "Cable Communications Policy Act of 1984." http://www.buskegroup.com/Conducting_a_Community_Needs_Assessment.pdf.

Civic Cloud. 2014. "Civic Cloud Platform for Civic Collaboration." http://codeforbtv.org/collaborations/civic-cloud.

Community Technology Center News & Notes. 1995. "Libraries, Cable Access, and New Media Centers." https://app.box.com/shared/2vejroltcl.

Detroit Digital Justice Coalition. 2015."Digital Justice Principles." http://detroitdjc.org/?page_id=9.

Devine, Robert H. 1995. "Discourses on Access: The Marginalization of a Medium." Paper presented at the Speech Communication Association's 81st Annual Convention, San Antonio, TX, November.

Devine, Robert H. 2000. "Access and Community Building." Brief summary of a presentation given at the Alliance for Community Media National Conference, Tucson, AZ, July 10.

Digital Redwoods. 2014. "Digital Redwoods." http://www.accesshumboldt.net/wp/digitalredwoods.

Downing, John D. H., with Tamara Villarreal Ford, Geneve Gil, and Laura Stein. 2001. *Radical Media: Rebellious Communication and Social Movements*. Thousand Oaks, CA: Sage.

Eggerton, John. 2014. "House to Hear from Former FCC Chairs." *Broadcasting & Cable*, January 8. http://www.broadcastingcable.com/news/washington/house-hear-former-fcc-chairs/128366.

Engelman, Ralph. 1990. "The Origins of Public Access Cable Television 1966–1972." *Journalism Monographs (Austin, TX)* 123: 1–47.

Federal Communications Commission. 2010. "National Broadband Plan." http://www.fcc.gov/national-broadband-plan.

Fischer, Saskia, and Margot Hardenbergh. 2004. *Media Empowerment: A Guide to Understanding Media Power and Organizing for Media Justice in Your Community*. Cleveland, OH: United Church of Christ.

Fuentes-Bautista, Martha. 2009. "Beyond Television: The Digital Transition of Public Access." SSRC Necessary Knowledge Program.

Fuentes-Bautista, Martha. 2014. "Rethinking Localism in the Broadband Era: A Participatory Community Development Approach." *Government Information Quarterly* 31 (1): 65–77.

Fuller, Linda K. 1994. *Community Television in the United States*. Westport, CT: Greenwood Press.

Fung, Brian. 2014. "Net Neutrality Was Just the Start. Can the FCC Keep States from Banning Public Internet?" *Washington Post*, July 17. http://www.washingtonpost.com/blogs/the-switch/wp/2014/07/17/net-neutrality-was-just-the-start-can-the-fcc-keep-states-from-banning-city-funded-internet.

Garcia, Ceclia. 2011. "PEG Access Centers Closing at Alarming Rate." Benton Foundation, April 13. http://benton.org/node/55372.

Gent, George. 1971. "Public Access TV Here Undergoing Growing Pains." *New York Times*, October 26, 83.

Glassman, James. 2013. "A Re-Write of the 1996 Communications Act? That's Exactly What I Wanted for Christmas!" Tech Policy Daily, December 5. http://www.techpolicydaily.com/communications/re-write-1996-communications-act-thats-exactly-wanted-christmas.

Goodman, Ellen P., and Anne Chen. 2009. "Digital Public Media Networks to Advance Broadband and Enrich Connected Communities." http://papers.ssrn.com/sol3/papers.cfm?abstract_id=1569677.

Halleck, DeeDee. 2002. *Hand-Held Visions: The Impossible Possibilities of Community Media*. New York: Fordham University Press.

Higgins, John W. 1999. "Community Television and the Vision of Media Literacy, Social Action and Empowerment." *Journal of Broadcasting & Electronic Media* 43 (4): 625–644.

Howley, Kevin. 2005. *Community Media: People, Places, and Communication Technologies*. Cambridge: Cambridge University Press.

Howley, Kevin. 2013. "Community Media Studies: An Overview." *Sociology Compass* 7 (10): 818–828.

Jackson, Steven J., Paul N. Edwards, Geoffrey C. Bowker, and Cory P. Knobel. 2007. "Understanding Infrastructure: History, Heuristics and Cyberinfrastructure Policy." *First Monday* 12 (6).

Johnson, Fred. 1998. "Cable Franchising: Notes on Creating Public Space." *Community Media Review* 21 (1): 8.

Johnson, Fred. 2007. "What's Going On in Community Media?" Benton Foundation. http://benton.org/sites/benton.org/files/CMReport.pdf.

Kellner, Douglas. 1992. "Public Access Television and the Struggle for Democracy." In *Democratic Communications in the Information Age*, ed. Janet Wasko and Vincent Mosco, 100–113. Toronto: Garamond Press.

Kim, Y., and Sandra J. Ball-Rokeach. 2006. "Civic Engagement from a Communication Infrastructure Perspective." *Communication Theory* 16: 173–197.

Koning, Dirk. 1995. "Cable Access II: The Grand Rapids Community Media Center," *Community Technology Center News & Notes*. http://peterbmiller.wordpress.com/ctrfall95.

Lennett, Ben, Patrick Lucey, Joanne Hovis, and Andrew Afflerbach. 2014. "The Art of the Possible: An Overview of Public Broadband Options." http://www.newamerica.net/sites/newamerica.net/files/policydocs/ArtofPossible-OverviewPublicBroadband_NAFOTI-CTC_0.pdf.

Linder, Laura. 1999. *Public Access Television: America's Electronic Soapbox*. Westport, CT: Praeger.

MacKinnon, R. 2012. *Consent of the Networked: The Worldwide Struggle for Internet Freedom*. New York: Basic Books.

McConnell, Beth. 2010. "What's the Role of Community Media Centers in the FCC's National Broadband Plan?" *Community Media Review* 33 (2): 8–11.

Media Mobilizing Project. 2015 a. "Who We Are." http://mediamobilizing.org/who-we-are/updates.

Media Mobilizing Project. 2015b. "Computer Center Locations." http://mediamobilizing.org/trainings-centers/computer-center-locations.

Miller, P. B. 2013. "From the Digital Divide to Digital Inclusion and Beyond: Update on Telecentres and Community Technology Centers (CTCs)." Social Science Research Network. http://papers.ssrn.com/sol3/papers.cfm?abstract_id=2241167.

Oldenberg, R. 1999. *The Great Good Place: Cafes, Coffee Shops, Bookstores, Bars, Hair Salons, and Other Hangouts at the Heart of a Community*. New York: Marlowe & Company.

Open Technology Institute. 2014. "Digital Stewardship and Your Community." http://www .newamerica.org/oti/digital-stewardship-and-your-community.

Rennie, Ellie. 2006. *Community Media: A Global Introduction*. Lanham, MD: Rowman & Littlefield Publishers.

Rhinesmith, Colin. 2010a. "How Public Access TV Evolved into Community Media Centers." *Mediashift*, November 20. http://www.pbs.org/mediashift/2010/11/how-public-access-tv-evolved -into-community-media-centers324.

Rhinesmith, Colin. 2010b. "Community Media Centers Support Broadband Adoption." http:// mediapolicy.newamerica.net/blogposts/2010/community_media_centers_support_broadband _adoption-34467.

Sandvig, Christian. 2013. "The Internet as an Infrastructure." In *The Oxford Handbook of Internet Studies*, ed. William H. Dutton, 86–108. Oxford: Oxford University Press.

Sherwood, Chuck. 2010. "Are Broadband Networks Just Another Phase of Our Ongoing Communications Revolution?" *Community Media Review* 33 (2): 6.

Sklover, Thea. 1970. "CATV—April Conference in Chicago." *Radical Software* 1: 1–2.

Snyder, Naomi. 2008. "AT&T Video Debate Heats Up." *The Tennessean*, February 18. http://rghm. wordpress.com/category/red-lining/.

St. Paul Neighborhood Network. 2014. "Community Technology Empowerment Project (CTEP)." http://spnn.org/ctep.

Star, Susan Leigh, and Geoffrey B. Bowker. 2010. "How to Infrastructure." In *Handbook of New Media: Social Shaping and Social Consequences of ICTs, Updated Student Edition*, ed. L. A. Lievrouw and S. M. Livingstone, 230–246. London: Sage.

Star, Susan Leigh, and Karen Ruhleder. 1996. "Steps Toward an Ecology of Infrastructure: Design and Access for Large Information Spaces." *Information Systems Research* 7 (1): 111–134.

Swirko, Cindy. 2006. "Public Access TV Kept Off the Air." *The Gainesville Sun*, June 25. http:// www.gainesville.com/article/20060625/LOCAL/206250339?Title=Public-access-TV-kept-off-the-air.

Washington Post . 2012. "SOPA Bill Shelved After Global Protests from Google, Wikipedia and Others." January 20. http://www.washingtonpost.com/business/economy/sopa-bill-shelved-after -global-protests-from-google-wikipedia-and-others/2012/01/20/gIQAN5JdEQ_story.html.

World Association of Community Radio Broadcasters. 2002. "Draft Declaration of Principles." https://www.itu.int/dms_pub/itu-s/md/03/wsispc3/c/S03-WSISPC3-C-0107!!PDF-E.pdf.

32   Case Study: The #YoSoy132 Movement in Mexico

Emiliano Treré

EPN's Black Friday: The Emergence of #YoSoy132

The movement #YoSoy132 emerged less than two months before the Mexican federal elections, at a time when Mexico seemed ready for a change after 12 years under the National Action Party (PAN). Before these two mandates of the PAN government, the Institutional Revolutionary Party (PRI) had ruled the country for seven decades, and leading up to the 2012 elections the PRI was credited by polls as the favored party, with Enrique Peña Nieto (EPN) leading the coalition "Commitment for Mexico." The other contenders were Andrés Manuel López Obrador (AMLO), who led a coalition of the left parties, while Josefina Vázquez Mota and Gabriel Quadri were the candidates of the PAN and the PANAL parties, respectively.

On Friday, May 11, 2012, EPN arrived at the Universidad Iberoamericana in Mexico City to give a conference. During the candidate's presentation, students began to question him with posters regarding the police repression that occurred in 2006 in San Salvador Atenco, when EPN was governor of the state of Mexico. When EPN justified the police's violent repression, the tension rose and he had to leave the university surrounded by a security cordon. The triggers that led students to organize were the subsequent statements released by some PRI politicians who qualified students as thugs—violent, fascist, and intolerant—going so far as to deny the students' affiliation with the university. Mexican television networks and the newspaper chain Organización Editorial Mexicana presented versions of the event where EPN was portrayed as a hero against a boycott organized by the left (see figure 32.1).

Facing manipulative media coverage, 131 university students published a video on YouTube[1] in which they exhibited their university credentials of the Universidad Iberoamericana and read their names to criticize the politicians who had accused them of being violent and not affiliated with the university (see figure 32.2).

This act of reclamation of identity marked the beginning of the movement. These 11 minutes of the video are so powerful because they build an event where individual responsibility is assumed and students talk from a "place of identity" (Reguillo 2012),

MÉXICO, D.F., SÁBADO 12 DE MAYO DE 2012

El Sol de México

DÓLAR $13.68
CENTENARIO $25,912.00

ORGANIZACIÓN EDITORIAL MEXICANA   AÑO XLVII   No. 16,613   http://www.elsoldemexico.com.mx   MARIO VÁZQUEZ RAÑA, PRESIDENTE Y DIRECTOR GENERAL

PRECIO: $10.00

Vengo a decirles lo que pienso, si no les parece no pasa nada; esta es nuestra pluralidad

CRÓNICA DE MIGUEL REYES RAZO

Enrique Peña Nieto se encerró ayer con varios cientos de jóvenes estudiantes de la Universidad Iberoamericana en los rumbos de Santa Fe. Ahí saludó inquietudes y diferencias.

VEA 3A

ÉXITO DE PEÑA EN LA IBERO, PESE A INTENTO ORQUESTADO DE BOICOT

》 ENRIQUE PEÑA Nieto, candidato presidencial de la coalición Compromiso por México, convocó a superar encinos y dar paso a la unidad para concretar las reformas estructurales que requiere el país, durante su participación en el Encuentro buen ciudadano Ibero.

■ Ante universitarios destacó los valores de la democracia, la libertad y pluralidad

■ Jamás rechazaré la oportunidad de oír a la sociedad, mucho menos a los jóvenes

■ Increpa un grupo de alumnos de esa casa de estudios al candidato priísta

POR CARLOS LARA

INFORMACIÓN: 4A

ENCUESTA MITOFSKY

48%

Peña Nieto

27%

Vázquez Mota

23%

López Obrador

2%

Gabriel Quadri

PREFERENCIA EFECTIVA QUE NO CONTABILIZA EL "NINGUNO", "NO SABE" Y "NO CONTESTA"

INFORMACIÓN: 11A

Llega el quinto gasolinazo de 2012; la Magna sube 9 centavos

INFORMACIÓN: FINANZAS

Investiga el Vaticano a sacerdotes seguidores de Maciel por pederastia

■ Confirma el vocero de la Santa Sede casos de abuso sexual de 7 religiosos

JORGE SANDOVAL
CORRESPONSAL

CIUDAD DEL VATICANO (OEM-Informex).- El Vaticano investiga a siete sacerdotes de la Congregación "Legionarios de Cristo", organización fundada por el padre Marcial Maciel Degollado, quien también, en vida, fue acusado insistentemente por abusos sexuales. El vocero de la Santa Sede, padre Federico Lombardi, dijo que fueron los mismos Superiores de los Legionarios de Cristo, encabezados por el cardenal Velasio De Paolis, quienes presentaron la denuncia.

INFORMACIÓN: MUNDO

FRACASA EN GRECIA INTENTO DE FORMAR GOBIERNO DE COALICIÓN

INFORMACIÓN: MUNDO

Concreta Med Atlántica compra de 95% de Mexicana

■ Se convierte prácticamente en la nueva dueña de la aerolínea

POR SALVADOR GUERRERO

INFORMACIÓN: FINANZAS

ATACAN SEDES TRIBUTARIAS EN ITALIA

》 UN SALDO de 10 policías y dos funcionarios heridos fue el resultado de fuertes enfrentamientos con manifestantes que atacaron sedes de la agencia tributaria en Italia, en protesta por las políticas de pago de impuestos. (FOTO: AFP)

INFORMACIÓN: MUNDO

No hay forma de evitar dinero del narco en campañas: obispos

■ Hay una gran cantidad de recursos de partidos que se oculta a la autoridad, advierten los purpurados de El Bajío

POR JUDITH GARCÍA

INFORMACIÓN: 6A

》 Detienen a "El Chilango", líder del grupo delictivo "Los Zetas" en Veracruz

INFORMACIÓN: 13A

OFRECE PGR 50 MDP POR 11 PERSONAS DESAPARECIDAS

INFORMACIÓN: 13A

EJECUCIONES

★ EN EL SEXENIO   52,214
★ AYER   13

Figure 32.1

The May 12, 2012, cover of the Mexican newspaper *El Sol de México* (*The Sun of Mexico*) of the Organización Editorial Mexicana (Mexican Editorial Organization) reads "Success of Peña, despite orchestrated attempt of boycott."

131 Alumnos de la Ibero responden

Figure 32.2
The YouTube video that started it all: 131 students of the Universidad Iberoamericana respond to the critiques by exposing their university credentials.

contrasting the official media discourse, reclaiming their agency, and using mass self-communication (Castells 2009) to trigger collective identification processes. The phrase "131 Students from Ibero" quickly became one of the trending topics on Twitter in Mexico and worldwide.[2] Other students began to join the protest, stating, "I'm one more of you," "I'm 132," thus leading to the creation of the Twitter hashtag #YoSoy132, which went on to identify the whole movement.

Media Democratization and Mexican Telecracy

From its emergence, the central concern of the #YoSoy132 movement has been the democratization of the Mexican media. As stated in their manifesto[3], the movement "wants the democratization of the mass media, in order to guarantee transparent, plural, and impartial information to foster critical consciousness and thought" (see figure 32.3).

This emphasis on media democratization is perfectly understandable in the Mexican context, where two media giants (Televisa and TV Azteca) encompass 99 percent of the

Figure 32.3
The manifesto of the #YoSoy132 movement.

audience and advertising market (Huerta-Wong and Gómez 2013), and where 76 percent of the population acquires political information through television (INEGI-SEGOB 2012, 2). Televisa, the most powerful media corporation in the country, is considered the central agent within what has been defined as the Mexican *telecracy*— i.e., the imposition of the interests of the advertising dealers of the TV monopolies over the interests of the whole Mexican society and the public interest (Esteinou Madrid and Alva de la Selva 2011). As Villamil has shown, the PRI party and Televisa carefully constructed the image of EPN over a period of six years (Villamil 2010). His findings were supported by other evidence presented by the *Guardian* that exposed how Televisa designed an undercover strategy to present EPN in various TV programs in a positive way, while at the same time developing a strategy against AMLO (Tuckman 2012).

Civic Media and Youth Agency

#YoSoy132 embodies the perfect example of a contemporary networked movement: to fight against the concentrated Mexican media system and to reclaim media

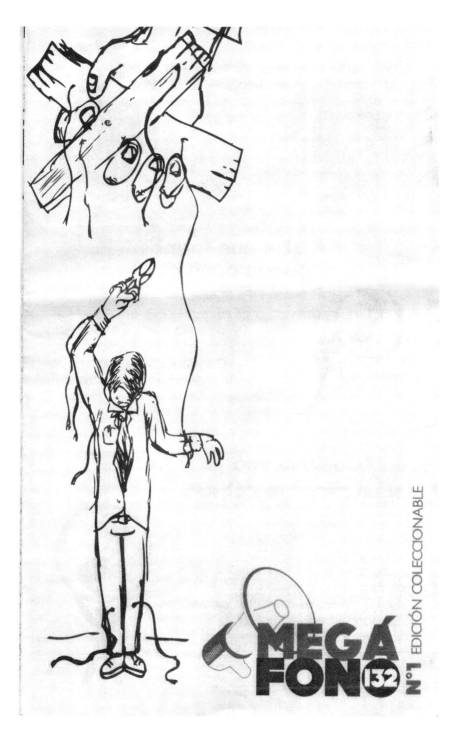

Figure 32.4
(a) The first issue of the *Megáfon132* gazette of #YoSoy132;

Figure 32.4 (continued)
(b) the second issue of the *Megáfon132* gazette of #YoSoy132;

Figure 32.4 (continued)
(c) the number 0 of the *Cientotreintaydos* (*132*) magazine;

Figure 32.4 (continued)

(d) the number 1 of the *Cientotreintaydos* (*132*) magazine.

democratization and pluralism, it unleashes the full potential of social media such as Twitter, Facebook, and YouTube, in order to spread critical messages, organize and coordinate mobilizations, cultivate collective identities, build counter-hegemonic spaces, forge transnational connections, and increase civic engagement and participation (Treré 2013). Corporate social networking platforms have been appropriated by the Mexican movement as civic media,[4] and are used to strengthen youth agency. In recent years, a vibrant digital sphere has emerged in Mexico, where young urban middle classes, especially university students, are increasingly using social media to acquire and spread critical content. In 2011, Internet World Stats estimated that Internet penetration in Mexico was 36.9 percent.[5] According to AMICPI (Mexican Internet Association), in the same year 90 percent of Mexican Internet users used social media (Facebook being the most used online platform).[6]

Activists of #YoSoy132 also created their own citizens' media (Rodríguez 2001), such as magazines, gazettes, alternative radio stations, and fanzines (see figure 32.4).

Furthermore, the movement represented an occasion for young Mexican artists to apply their skills to the production of graffiti, posters, and performances; many of these artistic productions also signal the power of civic media to travel beyond the technical

Figure 32.5
Esperanza (Hope) by artist Luis Emilio Lepine.

limitations of the online realm and infiltrate other territories, as the creation of *HASHTAG* magazine[7] and other forms of art indicate (see figure 32.5).

#YoSoy132 is part of a cycle of contention (Tarrow 1998) that has shaken the world since 2011, from the Arab Spring to the Brazilian revolts. Like many of these uprisings, #YoSoy132 was mainly comprised of a young, urban, and networked middle class that successfully merged online and offline actions in order to fight against the worn mechanisms of contemporary neoliberal democracies. Its original trait has been identifying the dangerous interconnections between media and politics as the central obstacle to the production of an informed and conscious citizenry.

Notes

1. "131 Alumnos de la Ibero responden," YouTube, May 14, 2012. Accessed June 19, 2014. http://www.youtube.com/watch?v=P7XbocXsFkI.

2. Accessed June 15, 2014. http://goo.gl/zo5C8B.

3. Manifiesto #YoSoy132," YouTube, May 29, 2012. Accessed June 20, 2014. http://www.youtube.com/watch?v=igxPudJF6nU (my translation from the original Spanish).

4. I follow here Henry Jenkins's definition of civic media as "any use of any technology for the purposes of increasing civic engagement and public participation, enabling the exchange of meaningful information, fostering social connectivity, constructing critical perspectives, insuring transparency and accountability, or strengthening citizen agency." Henry Jenkins, "Civic Media: A Syllabus," July 5, 2010. Accessed June 22, 2014. http://henryjenkins.org/2010/07/civic_media_a_syllabus.html#sthash.7TKbv3c9.dpuf.

5. Internet World Stats: Usage and Population Statistics. Accessed June 19, 2014. http://www.internetworldstats.com/stats.htm.

6. Accessed June 22, 2014. https://www.amipci.org.mx/es/estudios.

7. *Revista Hashtag*. Accessed 20 June 2014. http://www.revistahashtag.net.

References

Castells, Manuel. 2009. *Communication Power*. Oxford: Oxford University Press.

Esteinou Madrid, Javier, and Alma Rosa Alva de la Selva. 2011. *Los medios electrónicos de difusión y la sociedad de la información*. Mexico, DF: Dirección General del Acervo Histórico Diplomático, Secretaría de Relaciones Exteriores.

Huerta-Wong, Juan Enrique, and Rodrigo Gómez. 2013. "Concentración y diversidad de los medios de comunicación y las telecomunicaciones en México." *Comunicación y Sociedad* 19: 113–152.

INEGI-SEGOB. 2012. *Encuesta Nacional Sobre Cultura Política y Prácticas Ciudadanas ENCUP 2012*. Mexico: Segob.

Reguillo, Rossana. 2012. "Reflexiones iniciales en torno a #YoSoy132." *Magis*, May 28. http://www.magis.iteso.mx/redaccion/reflexiones-iniciales-en-torno-yosoy132.

Rodríguez, Clemencia. 2001. *Fissures in the Mediascape. An International Study of Citizens' Media.* Creskill, NJ: Hampton.

Tarrow, Sidney. 1998. *Power in Movement: Collective Action, Social Movements and Politics.* Cambridge: Cambridge University Press.

Treré, Emiliano. 2013. "#YoSoy132: la experiencia de los nuevos movimientos sociales en México y el papel de las redes sociales desde una perspectiva crítica." *Educación Social. Revista de Intervención Socioeducativa* 55: 112–121.

Tuckman, Jo. 2012. "Mexican media scandal: secretive Televisa unit promoted PRI candidate." *Guardian*, June 26. Accessed June 16, 2014. http://www.guardian.co.uk/world/2012/jun/26/mexican-media-scandal-televisa-pri-nieto.

Villamil, Jenaro. 2010. *El sexenio de Televisa: Conjuras del poder mediático.* Mexico: Grijalbo.

33 Case Study: An #EpicFail #FTW—Considering the Discursive Changes and Civic Engagement of #MyNYPD

Sarah Whitcomb Lozier

The focus of this case study is the "hijacking" of the #MyNYPD hashtag by Twitter users on April 22, 2014.[1] Over the course of that day, #MyNYPD was used to spread images and tweets of police brutality all over the country. As will become clear throughout this study, this particular instance of "hashtag activism" changes the terms of this highly criticized form of early twenty-first-century political, civic engagement. #MyNYPD demonstrates that, while a hashtag may not be able to effect physical change in the world in the way that a march, a sit-in, a rally, or the act of voting may be able to, it can effect significant change at the level of discourse and rhetoric. That is, this event shows the potential for hashtags and their function throughout digital social media to provide a model of political activism, of civic participation, aligned with staging a conversation, opening a dialog, or delivering a speech.

On April 22, 2014, the New York Police Department experienced, first hand, the power of a well-placed (some may say *misplaced*) hashtag on Twitter. At 10:55 a.m., @NYPDnews tweeted: "Do you have a photo w/ a member of the NYPD? Tweet us & tag it #myNYPD. It may be featured on our Facebook."

Accompanying the tweet was an image of two NYPD officers and a smiling member of their public, posing for a picture in front of a squad car. As the model photo demonstrates, the expectation of this social media campaign was to elicit photographs of the New York citizenry being protected and served by New York's Finest. Some Twitter users, like Lindsay Dixon (@poshwonderwoman) and JP Quinn (@JPQ904), responded with the expected photos and tweets. At 11:34 a.m., Dixon provided a picture of herself, smiling, surrounded by three uniformed officers with the 140 character caption: "@NYPDnews my photo from the ride along with the boys from the 90th pct #myNYPD" (see figure 33.2), and at 10:59 a.m., Quinn tweeted a photo of a delightfully smirking Yankees fan posing with an equally jolly uniformed officer, captioned: "@NYPDnews #MyNYPD #MyBrother #YankeeStadium" (figure 33.3).

Little more than an hour after @NYPDNews's original tweet, however, the tide turned as Twitter users co-opted the #myNYPD hashtag, mobilizing it to flood Twitter with photos of alleged police brutality. Sincere photos like Dixon's and Quinn's were

 NYPD NEWS @NYPDnews · Apr 22
Do you have a photo w/ a member of the NYPD? Tweet us & tag it #myNYPD. It may be featured on our
Facebook. pic.twitter.com/mE2c3oSmm6
↩ Reply ↻ Retweet ★ Favorited   Flag media

Figure 33.1
Original tweet by the NYPD, demonstrating the goal of the #MyNYPD campaign. (Source: NYPD
News, Twitter post, April 22, 2014, 10:55 a.m., https://twitter.com/NYPDnews.)

quickly drowned by this continuous wave of violent images accompanied by biting,
sarcastic captions. Occupy Wall Street (@OccupyWallStreetNYC), for example, posted
an image of an officer in the act of forcefully swinging a baton at protestors with the
caption "Here the #NYPD engages with its citizenry, changing hearts and minds one
baton at a time. #MyNYPD."

Similarly, Casey Aldridge (@CaseyJAldridge) tweeted an image of a man lying on the
ground screaming as his leg is trapped under a police motorcycle. The caption accompanying this photo reads, "'And we're going to have to run you over, just for good
measure.' #MyNYDP."

By the end of the day, #MyNYPD was the top trending conversation on Twitter, having sparked a viral visualization of police brutality that raged across the country: from
#MyNYPD to #MyLAPD and #MyOPD (Oakland), to #MyAPD (Albuquerque) and
#MyCPD (Chicago). The original invitation to tweet a photo with a member of the
NYPD with the hashtag #MyNYPD became an invitation to "post police brutality

Lindsay Dixon @poshwonderwoman · Apr 22
@NYPDnews my photo from my ride along with the boys from the 90th pct
#myNYPD pic.twitter.com/vwv7KQjLFD

↩ Reply ⇄ Retweet ★ Favorite   Flag media

Figure 33.2
One of the few tweets responding to @NYPDnews' call for images featuring the NYPD as sincere civil servants. (Source: Lindsay Dixon, Twitter post, April 22, 2014, 11:34 a.m., https://twitter.com/poshwonderwoman.)

photos … that reveal the reality of your local police department, with the hashtag #My(Insert Your Corrupt Police Department Here)."[2]

In what has become known as the NYPD's comically disastrous #EpicFail, the NYPD did indeed learn a valuable lesson in viral media campaigning or "asking the internet to use a Twitter hashtag."[3] The lesson, of course, is that police officers may wield power in the physical world where, as the images make clear, they can make and break physical bodies. However, in the virtual world, in the "Twitterverse," the power belongs to the tweeters, the hashtag users. As has been exhaustively observed in conversations about the relationship between hashtags and political activism—hashtag activism or *slacktivism* as it is has been called—the use of a hashtag does not, in itself, have any effect on the physical world. #MyNYPD cannot break bodies like a baton, it cannot blind eyes like pepper spray, and it cannot stop hearts like bullets. Similarly, it cannot

Figure 33.3
Another early tweet featuring the NYPD as a civil servants. (Source: J.P. Quinn, Twitter post, April 22, 2014, 10:59 a.m., https://twitter.com/JPQ904.)

revive the bodies and rebuild the lives damaged by those tools, nor can it change the standards and laws governing police weaponry and their use. As Shonda Rhimes succinctly sums it up: "A hashtag does not make you Dr. King. A hashtag does not change anything. It's a hashtag."[4] The course of the #MyNYPD event, however, demonstrates the danger of this kind of dismissal for those whose power stands to be usurped by a surge of hashtaggers. Over the course of April 22, 2014, the balance of power shifted: the NYPD was no longer in charge of that hashtag, its meaning, or its usage. Indeed, more than two months after the event, the hashtag continued to be used to tag and signify police brutality rather than civil service.

The pivot in the ability of the hashtag to signify is what marks this event as key in our discussions and considerations of civic media, or civic engagement through digital

Occupy Wall Street @OccupyWallStNYC · Apr 22
Here the #NYPD engages with its community members, changing hearts and
minds one baton at a time. #myNYPD pic.twitter.com/GErbiFFDvY
↰ Reply ↻ Retweet ★ Favorite   Flag media

Figure 33.4
Occupy Wall Street's tweet demonstrating #MyNYPD's pivot from a tag marking service to a tag
marking brutality. (Source: Occupy Wall Street, Twitter post, April 22, 2014, 12:12 p.m., https://
twitter.com/OccupyWallStNYC.)

social media. Over the course of April 22, Twitter users wrested rhetorical and discursive
power from the NYPD by changing the meaning of the #MyNYPD signifier. In other
words, this event, mobilized by and around a hashtag, is significantly more than just
"typing into your computer and going back to binge-watching your favorite show."[5] It
is typing into your computer and changing the very terms of what you have just typed.
This is change bound to the level of the abstract and the virtual, certainly, but the
abstract and the virtual is precisely the realm where public rhetoric functions, the space
where discourse is located. That this iteration of discursive change was accompanied by
a shift in power dynamics, an insistence on visibility and transparency, and a form of
civic participation, housed in the Twitter conversations of young people that spanned
and continues to span beyond the United States, only marks it as that much more significant. What may have been an #EpicFail for the NYPD's public relations team was an
#EpicWin for the Twitterverse and its hashtagging "slacktivists."

 Casey Aldridge @CaseyJAldridge · Apr 22
"And we're going to have to run you over, just for good measure." #myNYPD
pic.twitter.com/q6JMNAajxb
↩ Reply   ↻ Retweet   ★ Favorite   Flag media

Figure 33.5
Casey Aldridge's tweeted photo illustrating the way #MyNYPD's meaning fully shifted to one marking police brutality rather than civil service. (Source: Casey Aldridge, Twitter post, April 22, 2014, 3:30 p.m., https://twitter.com/CaseyJAldridge.)

Notes

1. This term, "hijack," was originally used by Dana Ford in her article featured on CNN's website that described this event. I use it here to signal the level of rhetoric used in public discourse to describe this Twitter phenomenon—rhetoric that signifies the potential violence of an inarguable power shift, as well as the ubiquity of militarized surveillance in the post-9/11 United States. Both rhetorical connotations of the term "hijack" take on a particularly charged resonance in an event wherein Twitter users wrested power from the NYPD in order to show the NYPD's abuse of that power. See Ford's article here: Dana Ford, "D'oh! NYPD Twitter Campaign Backfires," *CNN Tech*, April 24, 2014, accessed June 29, 2014, http://www.cnn.com/2014/04/22/tech/nypd-twitter-fail/index.html.

2. Cassius Methyl, blog post, "#MyNYPD Police Brutality Goes Global Worldwide #My(InsertCorruptPD) Twitter Storm Underway," April 23, 2014.

3. Ryan Broderick, "The NYPD Learned a Very Valuable Lesson about Asking the Internet to Use a Twitter Hashtag," *BuzzFeed News,* April 22, 2014, 3:22 p.m., http://www.buzzfeed.com/ryanhatesthis/the-nypd-just-learned-a-very-valuable-lesson-about-asking-th.

4. Shonda Rhimes, "2014 Dartmouth Commencement Address," Commencement Address, Dartmouth College 2014 Commencement, Dartmouth College, Hanover, NH, June 8, 2014.

5. Ibid.

34 Case Study: Pivot—Surreptitious Communications Design for Victims of Human Trafficking

Tad Hirsch

Introduction

Pivot is an outreach tool that provides rescue information to human trafficking victims by hiding messages in generic-looking menstrual pads, which can be discretely distributed by medical workers, social service providers, and other civic groups (figure 34.1). Pivot is a low-tech, interventionist civic media project that enables citizens to take direct action addressing a pressing public issue. It exemplifies surreptitious communications design, a strategy that emphasizes concealment and obfuscation to deliver messages to intended audiences without detection or interference by adversaries (Hirsch, 2016).

Background

Human trafficking refers to the illegal trade in human beings for forced or compulsory labor (International Labour Organization 2012). Human trafficking is most commonly associated with prostitution and sexual exploitation, but it also occurs in a variety of industrial, agricultural, and domestic labor contexts. Although precise numbers are difficult to come by, there are an estimated 20.9 million victims globally, of which 75 percent are women and girls (United Nations Office on Drugs and Crime 2012).

Human trafficking has emerged as a key global human rights issue. The United Nations Office on Drugs and Crime marked July 30, 2014, the first "United Nations World Day Against Trafficking in Persons."[1] In the United States, President Obama has made human trafficking a top human rights priority, declaring "our fight against human trafficking is one of the great human rights causes of our time" (The White House 2012).

There have been numerous print, broadcast, and social media campaigns to raise awareness of human trafficking and solicit donations for anti-trafficking groups (see, for example, the United Nations' "Blue Heart"[2] and New York City's "Let's End Human

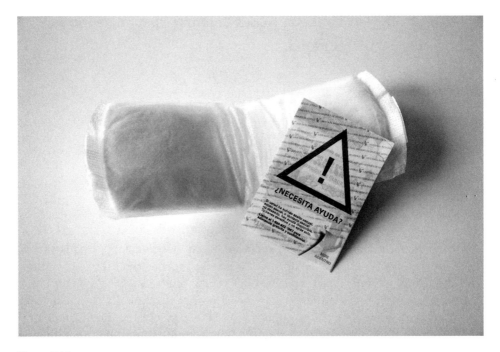

Figure 34.1
Anti-human trafficking messaging, printed on water-soluble paper and inserted into generic sanitary pad packaging.

Trafficking"[3] campaigns). The Pivot project complements these efforts, but focuses on direct intervention by outreach workers and civic organizations.

Stakeholders

Pivot was developed by the Public Practice Studio,[4] a multi-disciplinary design and research studio at the University of Washington. Students and faculty worked closely with the Washington Anti-Trafficking Network (WARN),[5] a network of organizations across Washington state that advocate against human trafficking and provide direct relief to victims. WARN serves all victims of human trafficking regardless of age, country of origin, legal status in the United States, or industry in which the trafficking occurred. WARN provides clients with free, confidential access to a variety of critical services including medical and mental health treatment, immigration and legal assistance, interpretation services, and access to safe housing, food, and clothing.

WARN has developed a robust organizational and communications infrastructure that enables the network to provide critical services to victims anywhere across Washington state, usually within 24 hours. However, victim response organizations like WARN struggle with outreach and continually seek innovative, effective ways to connect with victims who remain under their captors' control.

Design Challenges

Pivot is intended to help victims free themselves. According to anti-trafficking experts, victims are rarely rescued through outside intervention but rather via "self-rescue," when they have the opportunity and are prepared to take action (Morris 2012). Victims face many barriers in extricating themselves from captivity. Many victims don't recognize their situations as trafficking, and may not know that they are entitled to legal protection. They may hail from countries with weak human rights protections, or may be culturally predisposed to distrust law enforcement and other government agencies. In some cases, victims may feel compromised, because of their immigration status or participation in illegal activity (including prostitution). Perhaps the most important barrier to self-rescue is the extreme surveillance and control that captors exert over victims. Victims' movements are highly restricted, and their access to information and use of communications technologies are closely monitored.

To be effective, rescue information must be provided in ways that elude their captors' notice, address social and cultural issues that deter victims from seeking help, and mitigate significant lag times between when the information is encountered and when a victim has the opportunity to act.

Design

To develop an effective outreach tool, PPS designers employed a "surreptitious communications design" strategy. Surreptitious communication design is concerned with creating communications channels and messages that are accessible and legible to intended audiences, but which remain unnoticed or inscrutable to others. Surreptitious communications occupy a middle space between broadcast media and private messaging, targeting largely anonymous audiences while simultaneously avoiding detection and interference by adversaries.

Pivot was designed to encourage victims to seek help, and to provide on-demand access to a hotline number that could connect them with vital services. Given the tight surveillance and restricted access to communications technologies that characterize victims' lives, designers sought ways of embedding information into everyday products that could be accessed by victims without raising captors' suspicions. After an extensive review of potential artifacts, the design team focused on feminine hygiene products because the majority of victims are female, and because feminine hygiene practices often go unsupervised. Menstrual pads were seen as particularly inconspicuous because they are routinely distributed by nurses and healthcare professionals, who are often the primary or sole point of contact between victims and service agencies (Sabella 2011).

Designers developed a water-soluble information sheet that is inserted into sealed, nondescript packages of sanitary pads. The insert encourages human trafficking victims to call the National Human Trafficking Resource Center's 24-hour hotline, which provides referrals to victim service agencies. To help victims understand their circumstances and the options available to them, the information sheet portrays a variety of trafficking scenarios including sexual, agricultural, and domestic labor. To mitigate linguistic and literacy concerns, information is presented in a highly visual, comic-strip format which can be easily adapted to a variety of languages. The information sheet also includes a tear-away tab that features the hotline number disguised as a fortune-cookie insert (figure 34.2). This tab can be discretely kept and accessed for later use, while the remainder of the information sheet can be safely flushed down a toilet.

Figure 34.2
Tear-away tab featuring the National Human Trafficking Resource Center's hotline number, disguised as a fortune cookie insert.

Work to Date

Approximately 20,000 pads have been distributed to organizations across the United States. The project has also received awards from several international design associations, including the Industrial Designers Society of America and the Interaction Design Association. An evaluation study is nderway to examine the project's efficacy in supporting anti-human trafficking intervention efforts.

Conclusion

The Pivot project helps human trafficking victims escape captivity by providing crucial information and facilitating access to vital services. The designers adopted a surreptitious communications design strategy that emphasized low-tech, disposable materials, embedding critical content in everyday products, and encoding messages in familiar, unthreatening formats. While Pivot employed print media and focused on human trafficking, surreptitious communications design approaches are applicable to a broad range of civic media campaigns and formats that attempt to reach well known but anonymous audiences, while simultaneously avoiding detection or interception by adversaries.

Notes

1. United Nations Office on Drugs and Crime, "World Day against Trafficking in Persons," http://www.unodc.org/endht.

2. United Nations Office on Drugs and Crime, "Have a Heart for Victims of Human Trafficking," http://www.unodc.org/blueheart.

3. City of New York, "Let's End Human Trafficking," http://www.nyc.gov/html/endht/html/home/home.shtml.

4. Public Practice Studio, http://www.publicpractice.org.

5. Washington Anti-Trafficking Response Network, http://www.warn-trafficking.org.

References

Hirsch, Tad. 2016. "Surreptitious Communication Design.: *Design Issues* Spring (32:2).

International Labour Organization (ILO). 2012. "ILO Global Estimate of Forced Labour 2012: Results and Methodology. http://www.ilo.org/global/topics/forced-labour/publications/WCMS_182004/lang--en/index.htm.

Morris, Kathleen. 2012. Interview with Kathleen Morris, Program Director Washington Anti-Trafficking Response Network (WARN). Interview by Tad Hirsch.

Sabella, Donna. 2011. "The Role of the Nurse in Combating Human Trafficking. *AJN The American Journal of Nursing* 111 (2): 28–37.

United Nations Office on Drugs and Crime. 2012. *Global Report on Trafficking in Persons: 2012.* Vienna: United Nations Office on Drugs and Crime.

White House. 2012. "Fact Sheet: The Obama Administration Announces Efforts to Combat Human Trafficking at Home and Abroad." http://www.whitehouse.gov/the-press-office/2012/09/25/fact-sheet-obama-administration-announces-efforts-combat-human-trafficki.

35 Case Study: MídiaNINJA and the Rise of Citizen Journalism in Brazil

Stuart Davis

Beginning in June 2013, Brazil was struck by a series of explosive, chaotic, and oft-violent protests. Rallying around the slogan "A Gigante Accordou" ("The Giant Has Awakened"), these protests were the largest displays of citizens taking to the street since the end of the military dictatorship in the 1980s.[1] Though the demonstrators raised multiple grievances including reckless public spending on mega-events like the Olympics and the World Cup, entrenched governmental corruption, and the arbitrary raising of public transportation fares, one of the most common claims was an intense dissatisfaction with the way the nation's news media were failing to represent the views of the Brazilian citizenry. When observing this situation, international commentators writing for media outlets from the *Wall Street Journal* to the *Guardian* observed that the protests were throwing into clear relief a dissatisfaction over oligopoly control of mainstream media and its impact on information access and news production. In turn, the protests offered what many international journalists called the "beginning of an alternative media sphere in Brazil."[2]

At the center of the shifting media landscape was a social media–based citizen journalism project calling itself "MídiaNINJA." Launched in late 2012, NINJA (a Portuguese acronym for "Independent Narratives, Journalism, and Action) has received copious attention for using footage recorded on mobile phones and aired via social media to record police violence and unsanctioned arrests during the 2013 protests. Publically besmirching mainstream news conglomerates like the Globo Network, NINJA claims that it is opening up a new space for Brazilian citizens to make media.[3]

While it officially "launched" in 2012, NINJA grew directly out of and was incubated by Fora do Eixo (FDE), a much larger arts and culture organization. While FDE initially focused more on organizing music festivals and public art installations than promoting citizen journalism, its explicit focus on opening chapters and sponsoring events outside of preexisting cultural hubs like Rio, São Paulo, and Recife laid a foundation that NINJA would use to establish many of its own regional centers. On the technological level, NINJA draws heavily on both the recording functions of smart phones and the distributional capabilities of social networking sites including TwitCasting, Twitter,

Figure 35.1
A journalist from MídiaNINJA confronts a member of the Rio de Janeiro Military Police in the wake of the June 17, 2013, protest. The group's street-level coverage of this event and other protests in Rio drew international attention both to police treatment of protestors and to NINJA's unique style of coverage. Photo courtesy MídiaNINJA Facebook page.

Facebook, and Instagram. The process begins when the group's reporters (or "NINJAs" as they call them) record street-level footage of demonstrations or public events. This material is then uploaded directly onto the group's TwitCasting site.[4] From here it is re-screened in chunks on the group's websites, called "Pos-TV" (or "Post-TV.") Videos from the group's sites are then re-posted on NINJA's Facebook page and Twitter account. By developing a multi-faceted approach to distribution NINJA is able to capitalize on the unique capabilities of a variety of social networking sites.

Potential Innovations and Limitations of MídiaNINJA

Though it launched less than two years ago, NINJA has caused major ripples both within the field of independent media production and in public security. Building off of Fora do Eixo's attempt to support cultural production nationwide, NINJA is consistently trying to find new locations to start chapters. Since the protests began in June 2013, the group has established projects in cities including Boa Vista, Cuiaba, Fortaleza, João Pessoa, Londrina, Manaus, and Uberlândia. While some of these cities have vibrant

Figure 35.2
This screen capture provides an example of the group's use of the TwitCasting platform to live stream its coverage. Taken from a June 19, 2014, demonstration launched in Rio during the first game played in Maracanã Stadium, this image illustrates the basic functionalities of the site: NINJA collaborators stream footage and site users are given the option to comment in real time or share links to coverage via Twitter and other social networking sites.

histories of alternative and community-based journalism, many of them have been historically serviced primarily by mainstream newspapers and television networks.

Beyond its attempt to popularize citizen journalism, NINJA has also played an enormous role in the protection of civil rights during mobilizations. Starting with the first events of the Brazilian Spring, NINJA reporters were on the front lines of every major protest from the June 17, 2013, gathering in Rio to the 2014 World Cup protests. By recording simultaneously with the protests and quickly disseminating footage through social media, NINJA has been able to spread material that has bolstered accusations of police violence and exonerated protestors unduly arrested or detained.

Figure 35.3
Citizen journalists from NINJA film an April 24, 2014, march through the Sá Freire Alvim Tunnel connecting Ipanema and Copacabana to protest the death of a popular dancer from the Cantagalo favela at the hands of the police's favela pacification unit. Recording at a short distance from demonstrators and police allows NINJA to simultaneously circulate coverage of events and create a visual record that has been used in some cases to expose police brutality and exonerate protestors accused of crimes—though the group has consistently struggled with archiving its footage for later retrieval. Photo courtesy Rio Olympics Neighborhood Watch (www.rioonwatch.org).

Though NINJA offers novel tactics, it also raises questions about how loosely networked and geographically dispersed citizen journalism groups maintain both the financial and human resources needed to survive. More specifically, NINJA has faced problems related to fundraising and to its ability to maintain a nationwide network while competing with other TwitCasting news sites developed for specific regions or political factions. From a financial perspective, NINJA faces a difficult and potentially paradoxical situation. While the group largely consists of unpaid volunteers, NINJA does have a board of directors consisting exclusively of FDE members. This board is responsible for maintaining equipment, covering traveling costs for trainings, paying for data storage, and providing legal fees accrued by arrested NINJAs. Though critics don't dispute the idea that a project like NINJA with expansive aspirations needs a sizable operational budget, they have expressed concern about both the source of the group's financial resources and how finances are distributed.[5] In 2012 FDE founder Pablo Capilé faced a wave of public scrutiny when it became public that the group had received a substantial amount of money from Coca Cola to sponsor its annual "Marcha da Liberdade" ("Liberty March").[6] FDE's fundraising strategies became subject to even more intense scrutiny when numerous rumors began to circulate claiming that the group received large financial contributions from political parties on the right and the left. NINJA's financial situation became even more contested when opponents started to accuse group leadership of being highly secretive about NINJA's budget. Along with these financial considerations, NINJA's commitment to non-partisan, nationwide coverage has in some cases led to a drop in membership as collaborators have stopped contributing in order to start their own TwitCasting channels including Mídia-CAPOEIRA in Salvador, MídiaGEISHA in São Paulo, and Colletivo Carranca in Rio. Former collaborators have also left to work with groups that are more directly aligned with political or social movements such as the increasingly popular Black Bloc anarchist movement. According to NINJA co-coordinator Felipe Altenfelder, the rise of these new groups has pushed NINJA to a point where it has to reconsider its role as an autonomous media producer.[7]

As a case, NINJA offers novel strategies for encouraging participation in media production and using citizen journalism to protect the right to openly gather and protest in public spaces. However, it also highlights fundamental obstacles that citizen journalism projects face related to fundraising and preserving volunteer interest. These pitfalls, as community media theorist Clemencia Rodriguez and co-authors have recently argued, are two of the major problems that can damage and ultimately destroy citizen journalism initiatives.[8]

Notes

1. Venicio A. Lima, "Mídia, rebeldia urbana, e crise de representação."

2. Loretta Chao, "Brazil Protests Prompts Shift in Media Landscape."

3. Luke Bainbridge, "How Social Media Gives New Voice to Brazil's Protests."

4. The TwitCasting service was developed by the Japanese Moi Corporation in early 2013 as a way for using Twitter feeds to stream content from smart phones directly onto a "channel" developed and maintained by individual users.

5. George Yúdice, "New Social and Business Models in Latin American Musics."

6. André Forresteri, "Uma entrevista com Pablo Capilé, do Fora do Eixo."

7. Euler de França Belém, "Mídia Ninja lança portal interativo pra competir com mídia dominante."

8. Clemencia Rodriguez, Benjamin Ferron, and Kristin Shamas, "Four Challenges in the Field of Alternative, Radical, and Citizen's Media Research."

References

Bainbridge, Luke. 2014. "How social media gives new voice to Brazil's protests." *Guardian*, April 27. Accessed May 1, 2014. http://www.theguardian.com/world/2014/apr/27/social-media-gives -new-voice-to-brazil-protests.

Belém, Euler de França. 2014 "Mídia Ninja lança portal interativo pra competir com mídia dominante." *Jornal Opção*, June 20. Accessed June 26, 2014. http://www.jornalopcao.com.br/colunas-e -blogs/imprensa/midia-ninja-lanca- portal-interativo-pra-competir-com-midia-dominante-7648.

Chao, Loretta. 2013. "Brazil Protests Prompts Shift in Media Landscape." *Wall Street Journal*, June 29. Accessed May 01, 2014. http://online.wsj.com/news/articles/SB100014241278873238 73904578570244226440374.

Forresteri, André. 2013. "Uma entrevista com Pablo Capilé do Fora do Eixo." *Noticias R7*, August 16. Accessed June 26, 2014. http://noticias.r7.com/blogs/andre-forastieri/2013/08/16/uma -entrevista-com-pablo-capile-do-fora-do-eixo-parte-3.

Lima, Venicio A. 2013. "Mídia, rebeldia urbana, e crise de representação." In *Cidades Rebeldes: Passe livre e as manifestações que tomaram as ruas do Brasil*, ed. Racquel Rolnik, 65–72. São Paulo: Editora Buotempo.

Rodriguez, Clemencia, Benjamin Ferron, and Kristin Shamas. 2014. "Four challenges in the field of alternative, radical, and citizen's media research." *Media Culture & Society* 36 (2): 150–166.

Yúdice, George. 2012. "New Social and Business Models in Latin American Musics." In *Consumer Culture in Latin America*, ed. John Sinclair and Ana Cristiana Pereira, 17–41. New York: Palgrave and Macmillan.

36 Case Study: Hacking Politics—Civic Struggles to Politicize Technologies

Sebastian Kubitschko

Despite the longstanding equating of hacking as infused with political significance, the scope and style of hackers' engagement with *institutionalized politics* remains poorly understood. Based on face-to-face interviews, participant observations, and media analysis over three years (2011–2014), this case study of the Chaos Computer Club (CCC) fills part of this gap—the CCC is Europe's largest and one of the world's oldest hacker organizations. It shows that hackers practice a wide range of insider and outsider tactics related to media technologies and infrastructures (MTI). The rationale is to examine hackers as actors that practice politics *through*, *with*, and *about* MTI, and by doing so, to deepen the understanding of contemporary civic engagements. By considering the CCC as a civic organization that emphatically engages with democratic constellations, this case study challenges common sense assumptions that guide understandings of the intersection of civic culture, technologies, and institutionalized politics.

Considering transformations of civic engagement and politics, hackers might not necessarily be the first actors that come to mind. "Hacking" is often used as a catchall term to describe almost any computer-related crime and hackers tend to be portrayed as anti-social, possibly dangerous individuals, who attack systems, invade privacy, and even threaten national security (Coleman 2012). Governments' and mainstream media's obsession with the activities of particular hacker groups—most prominently Anonymous and WikiLeaks—further reinforces this labeling. Founded in 1981 in Germany and with a membership figure of around 5500, the CCC stands in stark contrast to such stereotyping and criminalization. The Club is a heterogeneous collection of multi-socialized and multi-determined citizens that bring together knowledge, experience, and skills related to the functioning and political consequences of MTI (Kubitschko 2015). For over three decades its members have been engaging in the area of conflict between technological and social developments.

While the Club's organizational structure is based on decentralized local groups, prominent spokespersons and long-term members ensure that the collective communicates its political aims (more or less) coherently beyond the circle of like-minded

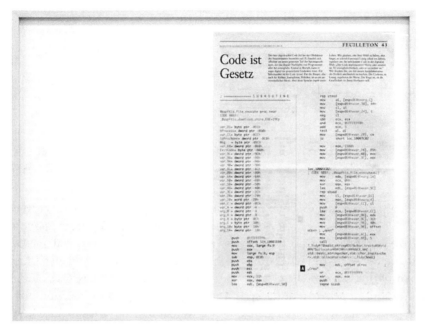

Figure 36.1
How to turn code into art: artistic extract of the Staatstrojaner program code originally published
in the Frankfurter Allgemeine Zeitung, October 9, 2011. Courtesy of Aram Bartholl.

people. Accordingly, the CCC acts as an organized civic collective or what can be
referred to as a civil society organization. Ever since its establishment, the Club does
not only practice so-called hacktivism (Jordan 2008), but in fact engages in a plurality
of political activities by acting *through*, *with*, and *about* MTI. In more concrete terms the
three attributes indicate the following practices.

First, the hackers are acting *through* MTI. This denotes that similar to most political
organizations nowadays (Rucht 2013, 249–268), the Club's internal modes of organization and coordination starkly rely on mediated communication among its members. At
the same time, the CCC acts through MTI by utilizing contemporary technologies in
explorative, reflective, or subversive ways. By reverse-engineering a suspicious hard
drive in October 2011, for example, the organization's so-called Staatstrojaner (Federal
Trojan) hack disclosed that German government agencies were illegally using surveillance software. Conceptual artist Aram Bartholl turned the hack into art by exhibiting
the Staatstrojaner program code that was published in the Frankfurter Allgemeine
Zeitung.

Second, the CCC critically engages *with* MTI by supporting and sustaining alternative communication infrastructures like The Onion Router (Tor)—a client software that

enhances online anonymity by directing internet traffic through a global volunteer network of servers. In addition, the CCC is running one of the most used Extensible Messaging and Presence Protocol (XMPP) servers worldwide—an open technology, which powers a wide range of applications including instant messaging, multi-party chat, and voice and video calls. It is important to note that "alternative" in this context should not be treated synonymously with "autonomous." As Chris Kelty puts it, "independence from power is not absolute; it is provisional and structured in response to the historically constituted layering of power and control within the infrastructures of computing and communication" (Kelty 2008, 9).

Third, CCC members are acting *about* MTI by articulating their knowledge, skills, and experiences. On the one hand, this is achieved by communicating to the general public via popular platforms and mainstream media channels. On the other hand, the Club has increasingly direct interactions with relevant actors like legislators and judges. Given the growing relevance of media technologies and infrastructures for political constellations, mainstream media continue to be exceptionally significant for actors to publicly voice their concerns (Chadwick 2013). Over recent years, both the amount of

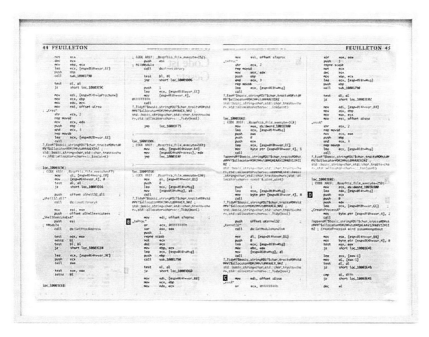

Figure 36.2
How to turn code into art: a continuation of the artistic extract of the Staatstrojaner program displayed in figure 36.1. Originally published in the Frankfurter Allgemeine Zeitung, October 9, 2011. Courtesy of Aram Bartholl.

media coverage as well as the frequency of access by CCC members to mainstream media has increased drastically. Besides writing articles and maintaining blogs for quality outlets, CCC members are regular interview partners to various well-established media and act as sources to numerous news media. In 2013 alone, the Club's spokespersons had 8,973 requests by media representatives via email. Parallel to these media-related practices, interactions with institutionalized politics continue to grow in quantity and quality. Over the past decade, the CCC has been requested as an official expert by the German constitutional court on five occasions—among others, related to the use of computerized voting machines. At the same time, the Club is advising all major political parties in Germany and two CCC members took part in the German parliament's committee on "Internet and Digital Society."

Acting *with*, *through*, and *about* MTI are interlocking arrangements that enable the CCC not only to question and supervise (Rosanvallon 2008) technological developments, but also to practice both "defensive" and "offensive" modes of engagement (Cohen and Arato 1992, 548–563). On the one hand, their engagements are directed inward to civil society by supporting emancipatory practices related to communicative infrastructures. On the other hand, their activities are directed outward to institutionalized politics. By doing so the Chaos Computer Club politicizes issues that otherwise might be understood as solely technological and are part of defining the predominant conception of what is understood as political.

References

Chadwick, Andrew. 2013. *The Hybrid Media System: Politics and Power*. Oxford: Oxford University Press.

Cohen, Jean, and Andrew Arato. 1992. *Civil Society and Political Theory*. Cambridge: Polity Press.

Coleman, Gabriella. 2012. *Coding Freedom: The Ethics and Aesthetics of Hacking*. Princeton, NJ: Princeton University Press.

Jordan, Tim. 2008. *Hacking: Digital Media and Technological Determinism*. Cambridge: Polity Press.

Kelty, Christopher. 2008. *Two Bits: The Cultural Significance of Free Software*. Durham, NC: Duke University Press.

Kubitschko, Sebastian. 2015. "Hackers' Media Practices: Demonstrating and Articulating Expertise as Interlocking Arrangements." *Convergence* 21 (3): 388–408.

Rosanvallon, Pierre. 2008. *Counter-Democracy: Politics in an Age of Distrust*. Cambridge: Cambridge University Press.

Rucht, Dieter. 2013. "Protest Movements and Their Media Usages." In *Mediation and Protest Movements*, ed. Bart Cammaerts, Alice Mattoni and Patrick McCurdy, 249–268. Bristol, UK: Intellect.

VI   Research + Funding

37 Revisiting the Measurement of Political Participation for the Digital Age

Benjamin Bowyer and Joseph Kahne

This chapter explores the implications of changes in information and communication technologies for the measurement of civic and political engagement. A growing body of research indicates that online forms engagement may be adding to more traditional forms of participation. These technological developments also have the potential to enable a broader change in the character of political participation in the twenty-first century. In particular, the widespread adoption of new ICTs has created a possibility of political and civic engagement that is more participatory; that is, more interactive, more independent of elites and formal organizations, and more peer-based than traditional, institutionally oriented actions. In this chapter, we explore the implications of these changes for survey researchers seeking to measure these emerging civic and political practices. Adapting survey measures in response to the developments requires not only additional questions that measure traditional forms of participation that are now occurring online, but also a shift in the conceptualization of political participation to encompass the broader range of activities through which individuals make themselves heard politically in the Digital Age.

The chapter begins with a discussion of the various definitions of political participation that have been applied in the literature. It then traces the history of how civic and political engagement have been operationalized in survey research, focusing on how changes in measures have adapted as the repertoire of political action has evolved over time. We find that researchers have had to confront the challenges of including emerging forms of participation in standard batteries of political participation. Beginning in the 1960s, surveys sought to incorporate a widening range of activities as political action increasingly took place outside the regularity of electoral campaigns and has been directed beyond governmental targets to include corporations and other non-representative institutions. More recently, the emergence of online forms of participation has required researchers to adapt their approach to the measurement of civic and political behavior. Ultimately, we contend that researchers need to attend not only to whether political activities are taking place online or offline, but also to the degree to which they can be considered participatory. Whereas some activities represent a simple translation of traditional political activities into an online context, other emerging actions signify a more fundamental shift in the locus of engagement. Instead of engaging in political and civic life through formal institutions, individuals are connected in politics through their social networks, a practice that is greatly facilitated by digital and social media. We suggest a number of survey items that can be used to gauge these participatory dynamics, including the circulation and production of political content through the Internet and social media. The chapter concludes with a discussion of the challenges facing researchers seeking to chronicle civic and political engagement in a rapidly evolving media landscape.

Defining Political Participation

The first step in measurement of political participation, of course, is to define it. Verba, Schlozman, and Brady (1995, 38) provide an influential definition of political participation as, "activity that has the intent or effect of influencing government action—either directly by affecting the making or implementation of public or indirectly by influencing the selection of people who make those policies." They further focus their attention on "voluntary" political participation; in other words, participation that is neither forced nor that receives substantial financial compensation. Though the latter qualification can be murky, the conceptual focus on the behavior of non-elites is almost unanimously agreed upon by all studies of political participation. Their focus on "activity" is also widely accepted, but here there is more disagreement between researchers as to where the lines should be drawn. As Brady (1995, 737) put it, this means that political participation "is something that a person does." Concepts like political interest, political knowledge, and political efficacy might be strongly related to political participation, but they do not constitute participation, as they are not actions. Verba, Schlozman, and Brady also exclude communicative activities like discussing politics with friends and writing a letter to the editor on the grounds that they are not targeted at a public official. However, other scholars include expressions of "public voice" in their conceptualization of political engagement (Zukin et al. 2006). The rise of new ICTs makes this sort of expressive political behavior more relevant (Gil de Zúñiga et al. 2010), and Cohen et al. (2012, vi) include acts that attempt to "exert voice and influence" within their definition of participation.

Perhaps the most controversial aspect of Verba, Schlozman, and Brady's conceptualization of political participation is their definition of "political." Their definition is rather restrictive and Brady (1999, 738) lays it out even more stringently: actions "do not become political activity itself until they directly attempt to affect governmental action." Collective efforts to influence corporations, religious institutions, unions, or other institutions of power in society are excluded from this conceptualization. Following this approach, Zukin et al. (2006, 7) distinguish political engagement from civic engagement, the latter defined as "organized voluntary activity focused on problem solving and helping others." Verba et al. (1995) acknowledge that the line between civic and political is rather blurry, but are part of a long tradition of scholarship that has emphasized the importance of civic activity as a gateway to political engagement (Putnam 2000; Tocqueville 1848).

Yet, to limit the definition of political participation to those activities that target the government is to ignore the changing ways that political power is exercised and contested in contemporary societies. As Norris (2002, 193) argues, "the diffusion of power resulting from both globalization and decentralization means that this represents an excessively narrow conceptualization." Rosenstone and Hansen (1994, 4) include all "action directed explicitly toward influencing the distribution of social goods and social values" within their more expansive definition of political participation. This opens the possibility for political activity to be focused at non-governmental targets, which will be discussed in more depth below, and allows the pressure to be indirect as well as direct (Kinder 1998). The more open-ended definition of politics does run the risk of opening a Pandora's box where every human behavior could be construed as political (see van Deth 2013, for a discussion). Nonetheless, it seems to more adequately represent a political world in which "decisions over the authoritative allocation of values for society" (Teorell, Torcal, and Montero 2007, 336) are no longer the exclusive purview of the nation-state (if they ever were).

However expansive or restrictive a definition of political participation a study adopts, a major challenge in operationalizing the concept is that the realm of activity that it potentially encompasses becomes nearly infinite as soon as one moves beyond an exclusive focus on the formal channels of participation legally established by the political system (e.g., voting). In practice, though, political participation tends to be restricted to a certain range of actions determined by cultural and historical forces; that is, it "usually takes well-defined and established forms" (Kinder 1998). Here Charles Tilly's concept of a political repertoire is especially helpful in identifying those activities that are most likely: "on the whole, when people make collective claims they innovate within limits set by the repertoire already established for their place, time, and [claimant-object] pairs" (Tilly 2010, 35). Would-be political participants do not select their activities in a vacuum, rather they do so in ways that are bounded by cultural, economic, social, and political structures.

The challenge for survey researchers, in particular, is that political repertoires are not static, as changes in society are often associated with transformations in the forms of political participation. As we will describe in detail below, changes in cultural norms in advanced industrial democracies in the decades after World War II were associated with the emergence of forms of political action directed outside the formal channels of representative government. More recently, the rise of the Internet has helped to create the possibility of a politics that is more peer-based and interactive. The failure of survey researchers to adapt their measures to the changing times can have profound implica-tions for conclusions that are drawn about the level and distribution of political partici-pation in society. For example, where one set of scholars notes the decline of voter turnout and other forms of political engagement in American society in recent decades, especially among younger generations (Macedo et al. 2005; Putnam 2000; Wattenberg 2008), another group sees a generational shift in value priorities and preferred forms of participation—a change, not a decline (Dalton 2008a; 2009; Inglehart 1997; Zukin et al. 2006). Similarly, studies of online political participation that focus only on those activities that have offline parallels (e.g., petition signing) run the risk of missing fun-damental developments in the ways that individuals can exert political voice and influ-ence that are enabled by changes in information and communication technologies. Below we chronicle some of the major challenges that survey researchers have grappled with over the past several decades in adapting their conceptual and operational defini-tions to an expanding repertoire of political activity.

History of the Survey Measurement of Political Participation

Brady (2000, 47) argues that, "Surveys ... have revolutionized social science since their introductions in the 1940s." Applied in a multitude of places and time periods, across countless populations and sub-populations to a wide range of topics, the sample survey has been a foundation of social science research. Nowhere is this truer than in the study of mass political participation. Surveys allowed for the systematic collection of data about the level of political activity among ordinary citizens that was impossible for all but a few forms of participation, such as voting, on which official statistics were kept. Furthermore, even in those few areas where systematic data was previously available, such as official election returns, surveys allow for the testing of individual-level theo-ries of behavior that are free from concerns about ecological inference that arise in the analysis of aggregate data.

Of course, as with any methodology, survey research has its critics and its limita-tions. Small differences in question wording can result in very different patterns of response, which can render comparisons across surveys or time periods difficult (Bishop 2009; Brady and Orren 1992). Social desirability biases mean that survey respondents tend to over-report their involvement in activities like voting (Belli et al. 1999; Burden 2000; Traugott and Katosh 1979). More recently, the decline in response rates among face-to-face and telephone samples and the rise of opt-in Internet panels has led to concerns about the representativeness of the sample survey (American Association for Public Opinion Research 2010; Berinsky 2004; Blumberg and Luke 2007; Keeter et al. 2007; Keeter et al. 2006; Yeager et al. 2011). While these are all correctly seen as major threats to the accuracy of survey measurements, an even more fundamental challenge to their validity arises if they do not cover the full range of activity through which individuals engage with politics. Surveys remain the primary tool by which social scientists attempt to measure political participation; however, to retain validity, measures need to be updated to reflect changes in the political repertoire. In the following sections, we chronicle the ways by which survey researchers have sought to adapt their instruments to reflect developments in the scope of political participation.

Early Survey Research on Political Participation

As in so many areas of survey research in political science, the agenda for the study of political participation was largely shaped by the American National Election Studies (ANES). The ANES has been collecting data on voter turnout since 1948 and other forms of participation since 1952. Its measures of political participation have been enormously influential not just in the in study of political participation in the United States but also in the many other countries that adopted their own election study. One of the most comprehensive early studies that used the ANES to focus on political participation beyond voter turnout was Milbrath (1965). Respondents were ranked along on a "hierarchy of political involvement" based on their responses to questions about voting and six other forms of electoral participation (see Milbrath 1965, figure 3, p. 18). See table 37.1 for a list of the questions used to construct this scale.

Subsequent research sought to extend the measurement of political participation beyond that which took place in the context of electoral campaigns, and called into

Table 37.1

Items from American National Election Study used in Campaign Activity Index (Milbrath 1965)

	Hierarchy of Involvement
In talking to people about the election we find that a lot of people weren't able to vote because they weren't registered or they were sick or they just didn't have time. How about you, did you vote this time?	Least involved
Did you talk to any people and try to show them why they should vote for one of the parties or candidates?	
Did you wear a campaign button or put a campaign sticker on your car?	
Did you give any money or buy tickets or anything to help the campaign for one of the parties or candidates?	
Did you go to any political meetings, rallies, dinners, or things like that?	
Did you do any other work for one of the parties or candidates?	
Do you belong to any political club or organization?	Most involved

question the assumption that political participation could be operationalized as a unidimensional spectrum. The Political Participation and Equality Surveys (Verba and Nie 1972; Verba, Nie, and Kim 1979) made the case both conceptually and empirically that rather than a single spectrum ranging from political inactivity to activity, political participation should be classified into distinct modes. These modes of activity differ in their fundamental characteristics in ways that affect which citizens are likely to be involved in them, including the type of influence that the act has over political leaders, the narrowness or breadth of the outcome of that is expected of the act, the amount of conflict inherent in the activity, the degree of initiative required of the participant, and the amount of cooperation with others that the act requires (Verba and Nie 1972; Verba, Nie, and Kim 1979). Verba and Nie's (1972) factor analysis of survey data collected in the United States in 1967 largely confirmed the expectations derived from their theoretical model and indicated the presence of four modes of participation: voting, campaign activity, communal acts, and personalized contacts. Table 37.2 displays the survey questions used to measure the activities found to belong to each mode. In a subsequent volume, Verba, Nie, and Kim (1979) extended this analysis to an additional six countries—Austria, India, Nigeria, Yugoslavia, Japan, and the Netherlands—in which parallel surveys to that conducted in the US were fielded between 1966 and 1971. The factor analyses run for each of the countries identified the same four modes of participation as did the analysis of the American data, confirming the "multidimensionality of political participation" (Verba et al. 1979).

These basic findings have been largely replicated, with a few refinements and caveats, in more recent surveys of the American public. The 1987 General Social Survey replicated Verba and Nie's participation questions and in his analysis of these data, Brady (1999) found that the four modes identified in the 1967 survey continued to constitute distinct dimensions twenty years later. Verba, Schlozman, and Brady's (1995) study provides one of the most comprehensive detailing of Americans' participatory habits. One of their key conceptual insights for the study of participation is that political acts vary in the types and amount of resources that they require of actors, and that operationally it is necessary to include questions that measure this variation. For example, donating to a campaign requires money, while volunteering for a campaign requires time, and donors and volunteers vary in how freely they give of their respective resources. The importance of this distinction regarding the type and amount of resources required by various forms of participation is demonstrated in Claggett and Pollock's (2006) analysis of thirty-one participation items that appeared in the ANES from 1980 to 2004. Their confirmatory factor analysis indicates Verba and Nie's multidimensional model of participation fits the data better than a unidimensional model, but it also suggests that the typology needs to be refined such that campaign activities and donating money constitute distinct modes.

Table 37.2

Items and Modes of Participation in 1967 Participation in America Survey (Verba and Nie 1972)

Item	Mode of Participation
Can you tell me how you voted in the 1964 presidential election—did you vote for Johnson or Goldwater or perhaps you did not vote.	Voting
And how about in 1960—can you tell me how you voted in the presidential election—did you vote for Kennedy or Nixon or perhaps you did not vote.	Voting
What about local elections—do you always vote in those, do you sometimes miss one, or do you rarely vote, or do you never vote?	Voting
During elections do you ever try to show people why they should vote for one of the parties or candidates? (If yes), Do you often, sometimes, rarely, or never?	Campaign Participation
In the past three or four years have you attended any political meetings or rallies?	Campaign Participation
In the past three or four years have you contributed money to a political party or candidate or to any other political cause?	Campaign Participation
Have you ever done (other) work for one of the parties or candidates in most elections, some elections, only a few, or have you never done such work?	Campaign Participation
Now we would like to know something about the groups and organizations to which individuals belong—here is a list of various kinds of organizations: What about *political groups* such as Democratic or Republican clubs, or political action groups? (If yes), Are you an active member, that is, do you regularly attend meetings and play an active role in the organization?	Campaign Participation
Have you ever worked with others in this community to try to solve some community problem?	Communal Activity
Have you ever taken part in forming a new group or a new organization to try to solve some community problem?	Communal Activity
We were talking earlier about problems that you and the people of this community have—have you ever personally gone to see, or spoken to, or written to—some member of the local community about some need or problem?*	Communal Activity / Particularized Contacting
What about some representative of governmental official outside of the local community—on the county, state, or national level—have you ever contacted or written to such a person on some need or problem?*	Communal Activity / Particularized Contacting

*Responses to the questions about contacting officials were coded as communal activity if in response to a follow-up question about the subject matter of the contact, the respondent indicated it regarded an issue of broad concern to a group of citizens or the community as a whole. If the contact involved an issue relevant only to the individual or her family, then it was coded as particularized contacting.

The Rise of "Unconventional" Political Participation

While the works of Verba, Nie, and their colleagues were trail-blazing in moving the field away from an almost exclusive focus on voting, they were criticized for focusing too restrictively on activities taking place in electoral campaigns and, in particular, for ignoring protest and other forms of "unconventional" participation. The neglect of these activities in the Political Participation and Equality in Seven Nations surveys was perhaps partially a product of the timing of the surveys, which went into the field at the end of a long period of relative political quiescence in most of the advanced, industrial democracies, especially the United States. However, by the time the findings from the surveys appeared in print in the 1970s, the repertoire of political action in these societies had changed in ways that were undeniable. The "new social movements" that grew in strength and prominence from the mid-1960s, around issues like civil rights, women's rights, and the Vietnam War, were associated with new (or, at least, re-discovered) forms of political action. As boycotts, sit-ins, and other forms of protest grew in prominence, survey researchers sought to identify ways to measure them.

One of the earliest and most ambitious of these efforts to incorporate this expanded political repertory into survey measurements of political participation was undertaken in the Political Action Study (PAS) fielded in 1974 in five Western democracies (Austria, Great Britain, the Netherlands, the United States, and West Germany) (Barnes and Kaase 1979). At the core of their argument was the notion that while "direct, noninstitutionalized political action" had been regarded previously as unconventional and illegitimate, "Western liberal democracies are experiencing a process of change in political culture exhibited by, among other things, the increasing inclination of the citizenry to participate in such acts" (Kaase and Marsh 1979, 31). However, studying this sort of activity systematically through survey research presented a host of challenges. For one thing, unlike electoral campaigns, which typically provide opportunities for participation at regular and predictable intervals, political protest is rather episodic in nature and many citizens may have few opportunities to become involved. Consequently, rather than measuring whether individuals actually got involved in protest, the Political Action Surveys instead sought to gauge "protest potential," which was defined as, "the individual propensity to engage in unconventional forms of political behavior as a means of political redress" (Marsh and Kaase 1979, 51). To measure this potential, they constructed Guttmann scales based on responses to questions about seven forms of protest: signing a petition, lawful demonstrations, refusing to pay rent, boycotts, unofficial strikes, obstructing traffic, and occupying buildings. The scales included items that asked not only whether the respondents "have actually done" each of the acts "during the past ten years," but also whether they "would do" or "might do" each and whether they approved of the acts. The scales assumed an underlying continuum from least extreme (petitions and legal demonstrations) to most extreme (occupations and political violence).

The protest potential index came under criticism for measuring attitudes toward behavior rather than actual political behavior (Budge 1981) and little subsequent research adopted the protest potential measurement approach of combining measures of approval and activity (Brady 1999). However, elements of the protest activity battery have been repeated in several studies, perhaps most notably in the World Values Survey (WVS) that has been fielded in multiple waves since 1981 in dozens of countries. The WVS has generally followed the PAS format, asking respondents whether they "have actually done," "might do," or "would never, under any circumstances," do each of five activities that are assumed to fall along a continuum of increasing extremity: signing a petition, joining in boycotts, attending lawful demonstrations, joining unofficial strikes, occupying buildings or factories. In practice, most studies only count those respondents who have actually done the activity when analyzing these questions. Factor analyses of these five WVS items have found that they do form a single dimension that is distinct from the civic activism (belonging to a political party or a civic organization) and voting modes (Dalton, Van Sickle, and Weldon 2009; Inglehart and Welzel 2005; Norris 2002).

In addition, the over-time trends in the WVS data indicate that these activities had become quite commonplace by the 1980s and 1990s, suggesting that their classification as unconventional was no longer appropriate (Dalton 2008a; Inglehart 1997; Inglehart and Welzel 2005; Norris 2002). As alternatives, Inglehart (1997) prefers "elite challenging" participation to encompass these acts; Dalton (2008a) refers to them as "contentious"; and Marien, Hooghe, and Quintelier (2010) uses the term "non-institutionalized" participation.[1] These labels draw attention away from the question of how commonplace these activities have become and focus it instead on the expanded range of targets that these forms of action seek to influence: "participants in non-institutionalised forms of political participation keep some distance from the political system by trying to have an indirect impact on political decision making or by circumventing the political system altogether" (Marien et al. 2010, 188). Drawing on survey data from twenty-six countries that participated in the 2004 International Social Survey Program, Marien et al. (2010) construct scales of institutionalized participation and non-institutionalized participation that are both shown to be reliable and distinguishable empirically.

Other studies similarly identify an expanded range of targets for political action beyond government. Stolle, Hooghe, and Michelleti (2005, 251) argue the case that, "as states tend to lose control or meet with competition from other spheres over the authoritative allocation of values in society, citizens seek new arenas for political participation." In particular, political consumerism—the "consumer choice of producers and products based on political or ethical considerations" (Stolle et al. 2005, 246)—is a way to circumvent traditional political structures in order to exert direct pressure on companies and markets. A challenge in measuring such activity is that it requires not just an indicator of an individual's behavior (i.e., buying or not buying a product), but also of whether this behavior is "motivated by ethical or political considerations" and if it reflects an "ingrained and habitual commitment" (Stolle et al. 2005, 255). Consequently, the six-item index of political consumerism constructed by Stolle et al. includes items that ask respondents to rate the importance of ethical considerations when they buy various consumer goods, as well as questions that ask about whether they have actually engaged in activities like boycotting or buycotting in the past twelve months. Along similar lines, Shah et al. (2007) employ an index of political consumerism that combines reports of past participation with intentions to engage in such activity in the future. Specifically, their scale is constructed from three agree-disagree items on DDB-Chicago's Life Style Study: "I will not buy a product from a company whose values I do not share," "I have boycotted products or companies in the past," and "I make a special effort to buy from companies that support charitable causes" (Shah et al. 2007, 223).

Other measures of political consumerism rely on solely on questions about past behavior. The National Civic Engagement Survey (NCES) included two items that asked whether the respondent had engaged in boycotting or buycotting—see table 37.4 later in the chapter for the full list of items from the NCES. Similarly, Newman and Bartels (2011, 7) use two items from the 2005 United States Citizenship, Involvement, Democracy Survey that asked respondents whether they had "boycotted certain products" or "deliberately bought certain products for political, ethical, or environmental reasons." In many respects, these provide more straightforward measures of actual participation in political consumerism than the scales that include separate items about motivations or intentions. However, these may also be quite challenging to survey respondents, who are being asked to recall not just whether they engaged in a consumer behavior but also the motivations for that behavior.

In any event, Zukin et al. (2006) see political consumerism as part of a broader category of participatory activities. Based on a factor analysis of items from the 2002 NCES, they group nineteen activities from the survey into four categories: civic activities, political activities, public voice, and cognitive engagement (see table 17.3 for a list of all the items included in each group). One concern with this classification is that the categories are data-driven: since the four categories were created by a factor analysis based on one specific dataset, it is unclear how generalizable they are. More fundamentally, the distinctions between the categories, especially between "political activities" and "public voice," often lack a theoretical basis and they produce some inconsistent classifications. For example, volunteering for a candidate or political organization falls under the "political activity" label, but canvassing for a party or candidate is put in the "public voice" category. On the other hand, the category of civic engagement is

Table 37.3

Indicators of Civic and Political Engagement from 2002 National Civic Engagement Survey (Zukin et al. 2006)

Item	Type of Engagement
Have you ever worked together informally with someone or some group to solve a problem in the community where you live? [IF YES] Was this in the last 12 months or not?	Civic
Have you ever spent time participating in any community service or volunteer activity, or haven't you had time to do this? By volunteer activity, I mean actually working in some way to help others for no pay. [IF YES] Have you done this in the last 12 months? I'm going to read a list of different groups that people sometimes volunteer for. As I read each one, can you tell me if you have volunteered for this type of group or organization within the last 12 months? [IF YES] Thinking about your work for [type of group] over the last 12 months—Is this something you do on a regular basis, or just once in a while?	
• A political organization or candidates running for office	Political
• An environmental organization	Civic
• A civic or community organization involved in health or social services. This could be an organization to help the poor, elderly, homeless, or a hospital.	Civic
• An organization involved with youth, children, or education	Civic
• Is there any other type of group I haven't mentioned that you have volunteered for in the last 12 months?	Civic
We know that most people don't vote in all elections. Usually between one-quarter to one-half of those eligible actually come out to vote. Can you tell me how often you vote in local and national elections? Always, sometimes, rarely, or never?	Political
When there is an election taking place do you generally talk to any people and try to show them why they should vote for or against one of the parties or candidates, or not?	Political
Do you wear a campaign button, put a sticker on your car, or place a sign in front of your house, or aren't these things you do?	Political
In the past 12 months, did you contribute money to a candidate, a political party, or any organization that supported candidates?	Political
Now I'm going to read you a quick list of things that some people have done to express their views. For each one I read, please just tell me whether you have ever done it or not. [IF YES] And have you done this is the last 12 months, or not?	
• Contacted or visited a public official—at any level of government—to ask for assistance or to express your opinion?	Public voice
• Contacted a newspaper or magazine to express your opinion on an issue?	Public voice
• Called in to a radio or television talk show to express your opinion on a political issue, even if you did not get on the air?	Public voice
• Taken part in a protest, march, or demonstration?	Public voice
• Signed an e-mail petition?	Public voice

Table 37.3 (continued)
Indicators of Civic and Political Engagement from 2002 National Civic Engagement Survey (Zukin et al. 2006)

Item	Type of Engagement
• And have you ever signed a written petition about a political or social issue?	Public voice
• NOT bought something because of conditions under which the product is made, or because you dislike the conduct of the company that produces it?	Public voice
• Bought a certain product or service because you like the social or political values of the company that produces or provides it	Public voice
• Personally walked, ran, or bicycled for a charitable cause—this is separate from sponsoring or giving money to this type of event?	Civic
• Besides donating money have you ever done anything else to help raise money for a charitable cause?	Civic
• Have you worked as a canvasser—having gone door to door for a political or social group or candidate?	Public voice

conceptually well defined, and the finding that younger generations tend to be drawn more to these types of activities is consistent with the general argument that changes in values are associated with a shift in political repertoire.

Teorell, Torcal, and Montero (2007) provide an alternative typology to incorporate these newer political activities. In their conceptualization, various forms of political participation can be classified along two primary dimensions. The first, the "channel of expression," distinguishes between those acts that attempt to work through the institutions of representative democracy (e.g., voting or working for a party) and those that work through "extra-representational" channels (e.g., demonstrations or boycotts). The second dimension is the "mechanism of influence," which separates activities that are "exit based" from those that are "voice based." The former includes activities that are based on a revealed preference (e.g., voting or buycotting), while the latter involves activity that makes the activists' demands known directly. The voice-based activities are further subdivided into those that are narrowly targeted (contacting) and those that are not (e.g., party work or protest). The resulting typology identifies five modes of participation: voting, consumer participation, party activity, protest activity, and contacting. The empirical test of this typology is conducted using the Citizenship, Involvement, and Democracy Survey (CID), which was fielded in twelve European countries between 1999 and 2003. The survey included twenty-five items that tapped into political participation. A principal component factor analysis largely confirms the conceptual distinctions between the five modes of participation across all the countries (Teorell et al. 2007).

New ICTs and Political Participation

If change in the value priorities in advanced, industrial democracies appears to have led, at least in part, to an expansion of the political repertoire in the last half of the twentieth century (Dalton 2008b; Inglehart 1997; Inglehart and Welzel 2005; Norris and Inglehart 2009), then the question for the early twenty-first century is whether (and how) technological change is being accompanied by changes in the ways that individuals engage in politics. Just as economic affluence and the expansion of higher education encouraged and enabled an expansion of political expression in the Baby Boom generation, the rise of interactive media and participatory cultures may lead to new norms and expectations for political engagement among the Millennial generation. Moreover, just as (quantitative) political scientists were charged with failing to notice the emergence of non-institutional forms of participation in the 1960s, so too they recently have been criticized for being slow to recognize the implications of the Internet for political engagement (Farrell 2012). For example, Teorell, Torcal, and Montero (2007) do not consider how online activities might fit in their typology, and the CID survey contained just one question pertaining to the use of the Internet for politics.[2] Similarly, Zukin et al. (2006) include signing email petitions among their indicators of "public voice," but do not really explore at either a conceptual or empirical level whether and how new ICTs might be changing the repertoire of political action.

A growing body of research identifies several ways by which new ICTs might alter or amplify existing forms of political participation and create altogether new means of exerting political influence or voice. Because the Internet lowers "barriers to citizen political activity, it would seem to provide multiple avenues by which political participation might be enhanced" (Schlozman, Verba, and Brady 2010, 488). Beyond this potential to increase the amount of political participation, an even more fundamental question has to do with whether developments in information and communications technologies have altered the forms of engagement. Social media allow individuals to use their networks to circulate political content, post original opinions, and mobilize others without having to navigate institutional gatekeepers. As noted by Anduiza, Cantijoch, and Gallego (2009), a complete consideration of consequence of the Internet for political participation requires attention to three types of political acts: "those which are only possible online, those which could be carried out equally in the real world and via the Internet, and those which can only be carried out offline" (Anduiza et al. 2009, 862). Given the scope of this chapter, we do not explore the consequences of the Internet for the latter type of participation here (Boulianne 2009), but instead concentrate on what the growth of the first two forms means for those seeking to measure political participation in the Digital Age.

These developments have led scholars to consider and measure a separate online dimension of political participation. For example, in the fifth edition of his text *Citizen*

Politics, Dalton (2008a) described a new mode of participation that he dubbed "wired activism" and distinguished from the four modes also included in previous editions. While the ability to communicate with others and gather news online provides "a new way for people to carry on traditional political activities" (52), "the Internet is creating political opportunities that had not previously existed" (53), such as advocacy groups on Facebook. Other studies adopt a similar approach in constructing separate scales of online political activity and offline political activity. Best and Krueger (2005) construct a scale of Internet political participation that includes four items and a scale of conventional political participation that aggregates four offline activities. Nam (2012) combines eleven measures of offline participation and three items of online activity, respectively, from the 2005 United States Citizenship, Involvement, Democracy Survey.

Similarly, in one of the more influential studies in the field, Schlozman, Verba, and Brady (2010) use seventeen items in a 2008 survey conducted by the Pew Internet and American Life Project to construct three scales. As shown in table 37.4, five items gauge offline political activity, five items measures online political activity, and an overall index of political activity is constructed from eleven activities (which may be online or offline and includes most of the items in the other two scales). In addition, the Pew survey also included several items relating to political activity on social networking sites, which the authors identify as having the potential to bring about an even more fundamental change:

the possibilities for political engagement through social network sites such as Facebook do not simply reproduce participation as we have always known it but instead reflect some of the distinctive civic tastes of post-Boomer cohorts: their preference for participatory forms that are anchored in non-hierarchical and informal networks and that eschew such traditional political intermediaries as campaigns, parties, and interest groups. (Schlozman, Verba, and Brady 2010, 498)

Ultimately, though, Schlozman et al. are cautious in their interpretation of this phenomenon, as many activities on social networking sites do not match their definition of political participation, and they see it more as a potential pathway to participation than as a form of political participation in its own right. We believe that this constitutes too narrow a construction of politics, as discussed above, and that it also fails to recognize the ways that new ICTs are enabling a new set of practices that are expanding the repertoire of political action.

Additionally, the integration of these technologies into day-to-day life means that the distinction between online and offline spheres of activity has become less relevant, thus calling into question the assumption that online participation should be distinguished from other forms. Oser, Hooghe, and Marien (2013) explore the question of whether online and offline participation can be distinguished empirically with the same 2008 Pew data analyzed by Schlozman et al. (2010). Specifically, they perform a

Table 37.4

Items from Pew Internet and American Life Project (Schlozman et al. 2010; Smith et al. 2009)

Item	Type of Engagement
Here's a list of activities some people do and others do not. For each, please tell me if you have done this in the past 12 months or not.	
• Attended a political rally or speech	Overall
• Attended an organized protest of any kind	Overall
• Attended a political meeting on local, town, or school affairs	Overall
• Worked or volunteered for a political party or candidate	Overall
• Made a speech about a community or political issue	Overall
• Been an active member of any group that tries to influence public policy or government, not including a political party	Overall
• Worked with fellow citizens to solve a problem in your community	Overall
Thinking about the political or community group in which you are MOST involved ... In the past 12 months, have you communicated with others in this group by	
• having a face-to-face meeting	Offline
• email	Online
• print letter or newsletter	Offline
• telephone	Offline
• using the group's website	Online
• instant messaging	Online
• using a social networking site	Online
Now, here is another list of activities some people do and others do not. For each, please tell me if you have done this in the past 12 months or not.	
• Contacted a national, state, or local government official in person, by phone, or by letter about an issue that is important to you?	Offline; Overall
• Sent an email to a national, state, or local government official about an issue that is important to you?	Online; Overall
• Signed a paper petition?	Offline; Overall
• Signed a petition online?	Online; Overall
• Sent a "letter to the editor" through the U.S. Postal Service to a newspaper or magazine?	Offline; Overall
• Emailed a "letter to the editor" or your comments to a newspaper or magazine?	Online; Overall
Have you contributed money to a political candidate or party, or any other political organization or cause in the past 12 months, or have you not done this? [IF YES] Thinking about the political contributions you have made in the past 12 months ...	
• Did you make those contributions online	Online; Overall
• or did you make those contributions offline, say, in person, by phone, or through the mail	Offline; Overall
• or have you made contributions both online and offline?	Offline; Online; Overall

latent class factor analysis of ten measures of political participation (five online and five offline) and find that four clusters of respondents emerge. The largest group by far is disengaged from political activity, while the second largest group specializes in contacting and petitioning (both online and offline). Another group generally displays higher than average participation offline and low participation online. The remaining cluster is distinctive in its high probability of engaging in online political activities. Even though this group does not appear to avoid offline participation, it does appear that online participation is a distinctive type of participation (Oser et al. 2013). The relatively small number of online activities analyzed from the Pew survey, however, makes it difficult to assess whether online participation is multidimensional, and the finding that both online and offline contacting and petitioning cluster together raises the possibility that mode of participation might matter more than medium.

Additional research further calls into question the assumption that Internet political participation is one dimensional and suggests that clusters of activities are emerging without regard to the increasingly blurry online/offline border. Hirzalla and Zoonen (2011) perform a confirmatory factor analysis on sixteen items from a 2007 survey of Dutch youth and show that these political activities can be grouped into four modes: "politics," "consumption," "activism," and "sharing." Some of the items (e.g., "visiting websites about politics" or "buying products that use recycled packaging") might fall short of our definition of political participation; however, the primary lesson is that, at least for youth, the online/offline distinction is not particularly helpful. That is, the findings indicate that "online participation, as a theoretical construct, is too 'narrow' when considered as an action repertoire isolated from offline activities and too 'broad' ... when it lumps together online activities that have different functions and forms" (Hirzalla and Zoonen 2011, 492).

This finding is confirmed and expanded upon by Gibson and Cantijoch (2013) in perhaps the most comprehensive test of the dimensionality of online and offline participation to date. They analyze a survey conducted in the United Kingdom in 2010 that included eighteen questions relating to political participation, including thirteen online activities. A simultaneous confirmatory factor analysis indicates that online participation is multidimensional in ways similar to offline participation: specifically, online activities cluster into distinct modes of campaign or party activities, contact-related activities, expressive actions, and passive attention to politics (Gibson and Cantijoch 2013, 710). In addition, when both online and offline activities are included in the analysis, there is some evidence of integration between online and offline participation. In particular, "targeted" forms of participation (e.g., donating, contacting an official, signing a petition) display a blending between online and offline acts, similar to the findings of Oser et al. (2013) in the US. At the same time, for both the news consumption and expressive activities there is evidence of independence between the online and offline spheres. Gibson and Cantijoch (2013, 714) speculate that "this might be due to these behaviors taking on a more active, collective, and networked quality in the online environment."

This last possibility was taken up in more depth by Youth and Participatory Politics Surveys (YPP) conducted among nationally representative samples of American youth in 2011 and 2013. These surveys sought to measure "participatory politics," defined by Kahne, Middaugh, and Allen (2014, 41) as "interactive, peer-based acts through which individuals and groups seek to exert both voice and influence on issues of public concern." This notion of participatory politics has its roots in Jenkins's (2009) concept of a "participatory culture."[3] While participatory political activity defined this way does not have to take place online and has a long history prior to the advent of the Internet, "these acts are often facilitated through online platforms" (Cohen et al. 2012, 3). To capture the range of these activities, the 2013 survey included twenty questions about a variety of activities that are grouped into "participatory" and "institutional" politics, each of which includes some acts that occur in online settings and some that occur offline—see table 37.5 for a full list of the items grouped into categories. This categorization of participation thus appears to have much in common with the categories between "institutionalized" and "non-institutionalized" participation (Marien et al. 2010); however, the key difference between the two conceptualizations is that where the latter distinction is based on the targets of the political activities, the distinction between "participatory" and "institutional" has to do with the nature of the relationships among the participants. For example, an activity like petition signing might be regarded as "institutional" or "participatory," respectively, depending on whether the petition was initiated by political elites and circulated through traditional channels or whether it was created by ordinary citizens who spread it through their own social networks. This can create a degree of ambiguity that is difficult to penetrate in a standard battery of survey items. Thus it better to conceptualize of the difference between "institutional" and "participatory" politics as a continuum, rather than a sharp distinction (Kahne et al. 2014). For instance, the Obama Administration has sought to use digital media to amplify its messages, sending communications to its supporters who are encouraged to circulate the messages through their own social networks. While these activities are "institutional" in the sense that they are elite-driven attempts to set the public agenda, they also are "participatory" to the extent that that act of re-circulating the message allows individuals to express their own opinion in a ways that affords them a degree of agency. That said, some activities are clearly at the participatory end of this spectrum and the YPP survey includes five items designed specifically to measure online participatory politics. These five online participatory politics activities appear to form a reliable scale, and 42 percent of young people between the ages of fifteen and twenty-seven indicate that they had done at least one of these activities over the past twelve months. The affordances of social media, in particular, enable a quantitative increase in individuals' engagement with politics, as well a qualitative

Table 37.5

Items from 2013 Youth and Participatory Politics Survey

Item	Mode of Politics	Medium of Participation
We find that many people participate in politics in other ways besides voting. Please tell us if you have supported a candidate, political party, or political issue during the **past 12 months** by:		
• Attending a meeting, rally, speech, or dinner	Institutional	Offline
• Working on an election campaign	Institutional	Offline
• Wearing a campaign button, putting a campaign sticker on your car, or placing a sign in your window or in front of your home	Institutional	Offline
• Expressing support through a social network site such as Facebook, IM, or Twitter (for example, by liking or becoming a fan)	Either	Online
• Donating money to a candidate, party, or political organization	Institutional	Either
• Raising money from your friends and network for a candidate, party, or political organization	Institutional	Either
• Starting or joining a political group on a social network site (like MySpace or Facebook)	Participatory	Online
People use a variety of methods to gather and share information about political candidates, campaigns, or political issues. Please tell us how often you have done the following during the **past 12 months:**		
• Forwarded, re-tweeted, or posted someone else's article, blog, picture, or video about a political campaign, candidate, or issue	Participatory	Online
• Created and circulated your own article, blog, picture or video about a political campaign, candidate or issue to an online site	Participatory	Online
• Commented online or tweeted about an article, blog, picture, or video you saw about a political campaign, candidate, or issue	Participatory	Online
• Posted a status update or sent an email, Tweet, or instant message about a political campaign, candidate, or issue	Participatory	Online
• Followed someone on Twitter for political information, news, or opinions	Institutional	Online
• Signed up to receive information from candidates or campaigns via email or text	Institutional	Online
Many people try to have influence in ways that aren't directly related to campaigns or elections. Please indicate whether you have done the following in the **past 12 months**:		
• Taken part in a protest, demonstration, or sit-in	Participatory	Offline

Table 37.5 (continued)
Items from 2013 Youth and Participatory Politics Survey

Item	Mode of Politics	Medium of Participation
• Participated in a **boycott**, that is not buying something because of the conditions under which the product is made or because you dislike the conduct of the company that produces it	Participatory	Offline
• Engaged in **buycotting**, that is buying a certain product because you like the social or political values of the company that produces or sells the product	Participatory	Offline
• Signed a paper petition	Institutional	Offline
• Signed an e-mail, Facebook, or other online petition	Institutional	Online
• Participated in an event where young people express their political views (such as a poetry slam, musical event, etc.)	Participatory	Offline
• Been active in or joined a group that meets face to face to address social or political issues	Participatory	Offline

shift in the locus of engagement from institutions to social networks. Coupled with the studies cited above, there is thus evidence that new and important forms of political participation are emerging that take advantage of the interactive nature of new ICTs.

Conclusions and Future Directions

While this review has concentrated exclusively on the survey measurement of political participation, we are by no means advocating for surveys as the only, or even the best, way to measure these activities. For one thing, changes in information and communication technologies offer not just the potential for new forms of political activity, but also new opportunities for research as these activities leave behind digital artifacts that represent an almost infinite amount of data. As King (2011) notes, social scientists are only just beginning to come to grips with the sheer amount of available data that was not imaginable even twenty years ago. At the same time, scholars of political participation awash in the sea of Big Data will need to depend on qualitative research to make sense of the changing tides. As the history of survey measurement reported in this chapter demonstrates, survey researchers struggle to keep up with changes to the repertoire of political action. Indeed, many of imperatives of survey research—the development of reliable measures, comparability with previous surveys, ensuring sufficient variation for statistical analysis—impart a sort of conservative bias to the measurement of political participation that makes it difficult to spot emerging trends. Qualitative research is better suited for identifying changes forms of participation, particularly among activists, youth, and other individuals and groups who are likely to be at the vanguard of future expansions of the repertoire of political action.

Nevertheless, we would argue for the continued relevance of survey research for the measurement of political participation and believe that the emergence of new ICTs opens many important questions that survey researchers are uniquely positioned to explore. An emerging body of research addresses concerns that are critical to the functioning of democracy in the twenty-first century. Is there a "digital divide" that is creating new forms of political inequality as political activity moves online (Norris 2001; Schlozman et al. 2010)? Can new media serve to mobilize segments of the population that are under-represented, or will they be used to reinforce the advantages of those who are already active (Norris 2001)? Before these questions can be answered, though, researchers must first come to grips with the nature of the change in contemporary political engagement. This requires not only changes in how political participation is operationalized in survey research, but also in how it is conceptualized. As new ICTs are integrated into people's day-to-day lives, simple dichotomies between online and offline activities rapidly become obsolete, and what is required instead is a more thorough understanding of the ways in which these new technologies allow and how they encourage entirely new ways to address issues of public concern.

Notes

1. As described in more detail, Cohen et al. (2012) draw a similar distinction between "institutional" and "participatory" political activity.

2. Specifically, at the end of the battery of offline participation items, respondents were asked, "Did you use the Internet in connection with any of these activities?"

3. See Kahne et al. (2014) for a discussion of how this use of participatory politics compares to other uses of term, including that of Barber (1984).

References

American Association for Public Opinion Research. 2010. "AAPOR Report on Online Panels." www.aapor.org/AAPORKentico/AAPOR_Main/media/MainSiteFiles/AAPOROnlinePanelsTFReport FinalRevised1.pdf .

Anduiza, E., M. Cantijoch, and A. Gallego. 2009. "Political Participation and the Internet." *Information Communication and Society* 12 (6): 860–878.

Barber, B. R. 1984. *Strong Democracy: Participatory Politics for a New Age.* Berkeley, CA: University of California Press.

Barnes, S. H., and M. Kaase. 1979. *Political Action: Mass Participation in Five Western Democracies.* Beverly Hills, CA: Sage Publications.

Belli, R. F., M. W. Traugott, M. Young, and K. A. McGonagle. 1999. "Reducing Vote Overreporting in Surveys: Social Desirability, Memory Failure, and Source Monitoring." *Public Opinion Quarterly* 63 (1): 90–108.

Berinsky, A. J. 2004. *Silent Voices: Public Opinion and Political Participation in America.* Princeton, NJ: Princeton University Press.

Best, S. J., and B. S. Krueger. 2005. "Analyzing the Representativeness of Internet Political Participation." *Political Behavior* 27 (2): 183–216.

Bishop, G. F. 2009. *The Illusion of Public Opinion: Fact and Artifact in American Public Opinion Poll.* Lanham, MD: Rowman & Littlefield.

Blumberg, S. J., and J. V. Luke. 2007. "Coverage Bias in Traditional Telephone Surveys of Low-Income and Young Adults." *Public Opinion Quarterly* 71 (5): 734–749.

Boulianne, S. 2009. "Does Internet Use Affect Engagement? A Meta-Analysis of Research." *Political Communication* 26 (2): 193–211.

Brady, H. E. 1999. "Political Participation." In *Measures of Political Attitudes*, ed. J. P. Robinson, P. R. Shaver, and L. S. Wrightsman. New York: Academic Press.

Brady, H. E. 2000. "Contributions of Survey Research to Political Science." *PS, Political Science & Politics* 33 (1): 47–57.

Brady, H. E., and G. R. Orren. 1992. "Polling Pitfalls: Sources of Error in Public Opinion Surveys." In *Media Polls in American Politics*, ed. T. E. Mann and G. R. Orren, 55–94. Washington, DC: Brookings Institute.

Budge, I. 1981. "Review of *Political Action: Mass Participation in Five Western Democracies*, by Samuel H. Barnes; Max Kaase and Associates." *American Political Science Review* 75 (1): 221–222.

Burden, B. C. 2000. "Voter Turnout and the National Election Studies." *Political Analysis* 8 (4): 389–398.

Claggett, W., and P. H. Pollock. 2006. "The Modes of Participation Revisited, 1980–2004." *Political Research Quarterly* 59 (4): 593–600.

Cohen, C., J. Kahne, B. T. Bowyer, E. Middaugh, and J. Rogowski. 2012. *Participatory Politics: New Media and Youth Political Action.* Retrieved from http://ypp.dmlcentral.net/sites/default/files/publications/Participatory_Politics_Report.pdf.

Dalton, R. J. 2008 a. *Citizen Politics: Public Opinion and Political Parties in Advanced Industrial Democracies.* 5th ed. Washington, DC: CQ Press.

Dalton, R. J. 2008 b. "Citizenship Norms and the Expansion of Political Participation." *Political Studies* 56 (1): 76–98.

Dalton, R. J. 2009. *The Good Citizen: How a Younger Generation Is Reshaping American Politics.* Revised ed. Washington, DC: CQ Press.

Dalton, R., A. Van Sickle, and S. Weldon. 2009. "The Individual–Institutional Nexus of Protest Behaviour." *British Journal of Political Science* 40 (1): 51–73.

Farrell, H. 2012. "The Consequences of the Internet for Politics." *Annual Review of Political Science* 15 (1): 35–52.

Gibson, R., and M. Cantijoch. 2013. "Conceptualizing and Measuring Participation in the Age of the Internet: Is Online Political Engagement Really Different to Offline?" *Journal of Politics* 75 (3): 701–716.

Gil de Zúñiga, H., A. Veenstra, E. Vraga, and D. V. Shah. 2010. "Digital Democracy: Reimagining Pathways to Political Participation." *Journal of Information Technology & Politics* 7 (1): 36–51.

Hirzalla, F., and L. V. Zoonen. 2011. "Beyond the Online/Offline Divide: How Youth's Online and Offline Civic Activities Converge." *Social Science Computer Review* 29 (4): 481–498.

Inglehart, R. 1997. *Modernization and Postmodernization: Cultural, Economic, and Political Change in 43 Societies*. Princeton, NJ: Princeton University Press.

Inglehart, R., and C. Welzel. 2005. *Modernization, Cultural Change, and Democracy: The Human Development Sequence*. New York: Cambridge University Press.

Jenkins, H. 2009. *Confronting the Challenges of Participatory Culture: Media Education for the 21st Century*. Cambridge, MA: MIT Press.

Kaase, M., and A. Marsh. 1979. Political Action: A Theoretical Perspective. In S. H. Barnes and M. Kaase, eds. *Political Action: Mass Participation in Five Western Democracies*, pp. 27–56. Beverly Hills, CA: Sage Publications.

Kahne, J. E., E. Middaugh, and D. Allen. 2014. Youth, New Media, and the Rise of Participatory Politics. In D. Allen and J. S. Light, eds. *From Voice to Influence: Understanding Citizenship in a Digital Age*, pp. 35–58. Chicago: University of Chicago Press.

Keeter, S., C. Kennedy, A. Clark, T. Tompson, and M. Mokrzycki. 2007. "What's Missing from National Landline RDD Surveys?: The Impact of the Growing Cell-Only Population." *Public Opinion Quarterly* 71 (5): 772–792.

Keeter, S., C. Kennedy, M. Dimock, J. Best, and P. Craighill. 2006. "Gauging the Impact of Growing Nonresponse on Estimates from a National RDD Telephone Survey." *Public Opinion Quarterly* 70 (5): 759–779.

Kinder, D. R. 1998. "Opinion and Action in the Realm of Politics." In *The Handbook of Social Psychology*, ed. D. T. Gilbert, S. T. Fiske, and G. Lindzey, 778–867. New York: McGraw-Hill.

King, G. 2011. "Ensuring the Data-Rich Future of the Social Sciences." *Science* 331 (6018): 719–721.

Macedo, S., Y. Alex-Assensoh, J. M. Berry, M. Brintnall, D. E. Campbell, L. R. Fraga, A. Fung, 2005. *Democracy at Risk: How Political Choices Have Undermined Citizenship and What We Can Do About It*. Washington, DC: Brookings Institution Press.

Marien, S., M. Hooghe, and E. Quintelier. 2010. "Inequalities in Non-institutionalised Forms of Political Participation: A Multi-level Analysis of 25 countries." *Political Studies* 58 (1): 187–213.

Marsh, A., and M. Kaase. 1979. Measuring Political Action. In *Political Action: Mass Participation in Five Western Democracies*. S. H. Barnes and M. Kaase, eds., 57–96. Beverly Hills, CA: Sage Publications.

Milbrath, L. W. 1965. *Political Participation: How and Why Do People Get Involved in Politics?* Chicago: Rand McNally.

Nam, T. 2012. "Dual Effects of the Internet on Political Activism: Reinforcing and Mobilizing." *Government Information Quarterly* 29 (1): S90–S97.

Newman, B. J., and B. L. Bartels. 2011. "Politics at the Checkout Line: Explaining Political Consumerism in the United States." *Political Research Quarterly* 64 (4): 803–817.

Norris, P. 2001. *Digital Divide: Civic Engagement, Information Poverty, and the Internet Worldwide*. New York: Cambridge University Press.

Norris, P. 2002. *Democratic Phoenix: Reinventing Political Activism*. New York: Cambridge University Press.

Norris, P., and R. Inglehart. 2009. *Cosmopolitan Communications: Cultural Diversity in a Globalized World*. New York: Cambridge University Press.

Oser, J., M. Hooghe, and S. Marien. 2013. "Is Online Participation Distinct from Offline Participation? A Latent Class Analysis of Participation Types and Their Stratification." *Political Research Quarterly* 66 (1): 91–101.

Putnam, R. D. 2000. *Bowling Alone: The Collapse and Revival of American Community*. New York: Simon and Schuster.

Rosenstone, S. J. and Hansen, J. M., 1993. *Mobilization, Participation, and Democracy in America*. New York: Macmillan.

Schlozman, K. L., S. Verba, and H. E. Brady. 2010. "Weapon of the Strong? Participatory Inequality and the Internet." *Perspectives on Politics* 8 (2): 487–509.

Shah, D. V., D. M. McLeod, E. Kim, Sun Young Lee, M. R. Gotlieb, S. S. Ho, and H. Breivik. 2007. "Political Consumerism: How Communication and Consumption Orientations Drive 'Lifestyle Politics.'" *Annals of the American Academy of Political and Social Science* 611 (1): 217–235.

Smith, A., K. L. Schlozman, S. Verba, and H. E. Brady. 2009. *The Internet and Civic Engagement*, 1–66. Pew Internet & American Life Project. http://www.pewinternet.org/2009/09/01/the-internet-and-civic-engagement/.

Stolle, D., M. Hooghe, and M. Micheletti. 2005. "Politics in the Supermarket: Political Consumerism as a Form of Political Participation." *International Political Science Review* 26 (3): 245–269.

Teorell, J., M. Torcal, and J. R. Montero. 2007. "Political Participation: Mapping the Terrain." In *Citizenship and Involvement in European Democracies: A Comparative Analysis*, vol. 17, ed. J. W. van Deth, J. R. Montero, and A. Westholm, 334–357. New York: Routledge.

Tilly, C. 2010. *Regimes and Repertoires*. Chicago: University of Chicago Press.

Tocqueville, A. de 1848. *Democracy in America*. 8th ed. New York: Pratt, Woodford, & Co.

Traugott, M. W., and J. P. Katosh. 1979. "Response Validity in Surveys of Voting Behavior." *Public Opinion Quarterly* 43 (3): 359–377.

Verba, S., and N. H. Nie. 1972. *Participation in America: Political Democracy and Social Equality*. Chicago: University of Chicago Press.

Verba, S., N. H. Nie, and J. O. Kim. 1979. *Participation and Political Equality: A Seven-Nation Comparison*. New York: Cambridge University Press.

Verba, S., K. L. Schlozman, and H. E. Brady. 1995. *Voice and Equality: Civic Voluntarism in American Politics*. Cambridge, MA: Harvard University Press.

Wattenberg, M. P. 2008. *Is Voting for Young People? With a Postscript on Citizen Engagement*. 2nd ed. New York: Longman.

Yeager, D. S., J. A. Krosnick, L. Chang, H. S. Javitz, M. S. Levendusky, A. Simpser, and R. Wang. 2011. "Comparing the Accuracy of RDD Telephone Surveys and Internet Surveys Conducted with Probability and Non-Probability Samples." *Public Opinion Quarterly* 75 (4): 709–747.

Zukin, C., S. Keeter, M. Andolina, K. Jenkins, and M. X. Delli Carpini. 2006. *A New Engagement? Political Participation, Civic Life, and the Changing American Citizen*. Oxford: Oxford University Press.

38 Participatory Action Research for Civic Engagement

Marcus Foth and Martin Brynskov

Introduction

The future of civic engagement is characterized by both technological innovation and new technological user practices that are fueled by trends toward mobile, personal devices; broadband connectivity; open data; urban interfaces; and cloud computing. These technology trends are progressing at a rapid pace, and have led global technology vendors to package and sell the "Smart City" as a centralized service delivery platform predicted to optimize and enhance cities' key performance indicators—and generate a profitable market. The top-down deployment of these large and proprietary technology platforms have helped sectors such as energy, transport, and healthcare to increase efficiencies. However, an increasing number of scholars and commentators warn of another "IT bubble" emerging. Along with some city leaders, they argue that the top-down approach does not fit the governance dynamics and values of a liberal democracy when applied across sectors. A thorough understanding is required of the socio-cultural nuances of how people work, live, and play across different environments, and how they employ social media and mobile devices to interact with, engage in, and constitute public realms.

Although the term "slacktivism" is sometimes used to denote a watered down version of civic engagement and activism that is reduced to clicking a "Like" button and signing online petitions, we believe that we are far from witnessing another Biedermeier period[1] that saw people focus on the domestic and the non-political. There is plenty of evidence to the contrary, such as post-election violence in Kenya in 2008, the Occupy movements in New York, Hong Kong, and elsewhere, the Arab Spring, Stuttgart 21, Fukushima, the Taksim Gezi Park in Istanbul, and the Vinegar Movement in Brazil in 2013. These examples of civic action shape the dynamics of governments, and in turn, call for new processes to be incorporated into governance structures. Participatory research into these new processes across the triad of people, place, and technology is a significant and timely investment to foster productive, sustainable, and livable human habitats. With this chapter, we want to reframe the current debates in academia and priorities in industry and government to allow citizens and civic actors to take their rightful centerpiece place in civic movements. This calls for new participatory approaches for co-inquiry and co-design. It is an evolving process with an explicit agenda to facilitate change, and we propose *participatory action research* (PAR) as an indispensable component in the journey to develop new governance infrastructures and practices for civic engagement.

This chapter proposes participatory action research as a useful and fitting research paradigm to guide methodological considerations surrounding the study, design, development, and evaluation of civic technologies. We do not limit our definition of civic technologies to tools specifically designed to simply enhance government and governance, such as renewing your car registration online or casting your vote electronically on election day. Rather, we are interested in civic media and technologies that foster citizen engagement in the widest sense, and particularly the participatory design of such civic technologies that strive to involve citizens in political debate and action as well as question conventional approaches to political issues (DiSalvo 2012; Dourish 2010; Foth et al. 2013).

Following an outline of some underlying principles and assumptions behind participatory action research, especially as it applies to cities, we will critically review case studies to illustrate the application of this approach with a view to engender robust, inclusive, and dynamic societies built on the principles of engaged liberal democracy.

The rationale for this approach is an alternative to smart cities in a "perpetual tomorrow" (cf., e.g., Dourish and Bell 2011), based on many weak and strong signals of civic actions revolving around technology seen today. This approach seeks to emphasize and direct attention to active citizenry over passive consumerism, human actors over human factors, culture over infrastructure, and prosperity over efficiency.

First, we will have a look at some fundamental issues arising from applying simplistic smart city visions to "the kind of problem a city is" (cf. Jacobs 1961). We focus on the touch points between "the city" and its civic body, the citizens. In order to provide for meaningful civic engagement, the city must provide appropriate interfaces.

Civic Engagement and Urban Interaction Design

Cities are vast and complex systems, and over the years many professions have specialized in taking care of all parts of urban life, in more or less collaboration with other actors, including the people who simply live there. Part of this specialization has been around the interfaces, that is, designing the points where the system meets the end-user, either in the form of a person or a physical touch point. We may refer to the making of urban interfaces as urban interaction design (Brynskov et al. 2014), which has emerged as a field with a discourse sensitive toward civic engagement.

Citizen service facilities, digital or not, are urban interfaces, but so are pavements, paper letters, websites, mobile radio waves, signage, sushi bars, electricity plugs, libraries, and "desire paths" (where people *actually* would like to walk).[2] It is difficult to underestimate the complexity of a city. However, the level of civic support offered by a specific city is the result of years and years of fine tuning or, using another register, of cultural development.

The city as material, as technology, as medium, in McLuhan's (1964) broad sense, is a culture machine that no simple plan could devise, but which developed networks of human practices can maintain and continuously co-create, what Brynskov et al. (2014) refer to as *city making*—desire paths with institutional support, as it were. As digital technologies and globalization have reshaped geographies and economies, these complex urban systems struggle to catch up and rewire (Zuckerman 2003). What was once an optimized workflow or accepted practice has now become impractical or obsolete.

Licenses for hotels and taxi cabs, which were once a practical instrument to manage supply and demand, balanced against the welfare of both drivers and passengers, are undermined by the gray zones of ad hoc car-pooling. To name two seminal and concrete examples: Airbnb facilitates access to providers of temporary housing and short-term letting much as hotels do, but focusing on making the connection between customers and private proprietors a shared experience. Similarly, Uber is a service which does the same with cars, offering the same service as licensed taxis, but on an ad hoc basis.

While at first glance these two examples of services in the sharing economy (Benkler 2004) appear to be a formidable success of resource sharing, the same can actually be said of the incumbents, hotels and taxis. Airbnb and Uber's point of difference and innovation is not the sharing of resources in a market economy per se, but the way these service providers understand and take advantage of new urban dynamics that govern these interactions.

Increasingly, Airbnb and Uber have become professionalized to the extent that they can no longer sustain the romanticism of peer-to-peer interactions, that is, private citizens opening the doors of their homes and automobiles to friendly strangers. Airbnb valued at $10 billion (TPG) and Uber at $18 billion (Fidelity), have become dominant economic forces in the territories where they operate, both disrupting systems which were ripe for disruption, while also hindering prudent governance of core public goods: land use and mobility infrastructure.

The most dominant technological catalyst of this trend in urban space, the mobile phone, is a convergence point of this struggle that provides appropriate interfaces for all links in the value chain. As the umbilical cord to a networked society, it is the stuff which allows Airbnb and Uber to challenge centuries of practiced privileged government, by, in fact, reverting urban interactions to much more engaged and personal forms known to communities since the dawn of settlements.

Some would claim it is a de-civilization (Morozov 2013). Others say it is a welcome removal of unnecessary friction in society (Schmidt and Cohen 2013). It is most likely a bit of both. However, the point of our argument here is that "engagement" is not a goal in itself. "Heal yourself" government is certainly engaging, but not desirable to those who lack the institutional support to act, e.g., a well-functioning hospital or home (e.g., Dawson 2012).

Taken on face value, Airbnb and Uber represent civic engagement that takes a short-cut between identifying and fulfilling needs and minimal overheads. What is more engaging than acting to find immediate fulfilment? It spurs further engagement. And when this real-time, ad hoc, empowerment-centric governance model is scaled up, e.g., to a city level, it is in a way easy to view all these needs, resources, and possible configurations as a solution space which is most efficiently governed by a now-possible, albeit complex, digital model or approximation by data and simulations (Koonin, Dobler, and Wurtele 2014).

That is the simple tenet of the smart city: to optimize, broker, and moderate. This proposition, however, fails in two ways: It is singular, and it is utopian—some may say, dystopian.[3]

First, the singular narratives of optimized systems background the fact that cities are zones of conflicting interests. The republican (in the Machiavellian sense) dynamics cannot be abstracted away into algorithms and an optimized model-based solution, in the singular. These dynamics are potential conflicts and need to be treated as such, including providing the means for conflict identification and resolution (DiSalvo 2012). If the system is a near-universal arbitrator, like a traffic light or a parent to infants, then the city would not be in line with what an adult citizen has come to expect from a liberal democracy—this of course varies depending on the development context.

What pre-digital cities have developed to support is infinitely fine-grained distribution and arbitration of power, with an endless array of means to take action against perceived wrongs, and including assistance in many cases to do so.

The simplest example is "taking the streets," protesting, occupying, that is, taking place and giving voice. Smart city visions are hopelessly singular and apolitical, non-republican. That is the first fault in the proposition of the smart city as a civic technology (Greenfield 2013; Townsend 2013; Sassen 2012).

The second problem is that many first-wave digital urban systems were highly specialized and directed at certain sectors (e.g., traffic or energy distribution), and so were—and are—non-particular with regards to the actual city in which they operate: utopian (dystopian), i.e., non-placed. That may be fine for traffic lights. They are culturally attuned, but that has taken decades. It also works for leakage sensors in water pipes and air pollution controls. Yet, that is just about the upper limit of complexity. When systems start to become interlinked, across sectors, and especially when they evolve into an urban interface, then these utopian systems break under the weight of the need to adapt to specific sociocultural nuances and circumstances (Williams, Robles, and Dourish 2009).

What about the mobile phone, then? That is a highly generalized interface which works in just about any cultural and climatic context. In fact, the mobile phone is incredibly amenable to adaptation and appropriation. Its chameleon-like features of skins and services, from text messaging to audio-visual appearance, are a marvel of flexibility (Chipchase, 2014) and convergence—on the one hand.

On the other hand, mobile phone practices are shaping human behavior: We get distracted when we walk and drive, we have a hard time not looking up information when we are unsure, we get stressed (Satchell 2009). Yet, we can also accomplish numerous tasks almost simultaneously that were unthinkable before the mobile: last-minute coordination of meeting points, checking price points in shops—in short, optimizing behavior in real time. This smacks of a regimenting smart city, but it bears some affinity to civic ideals of participation, because the interface itself is personal, down to our shared microbiome (the microbes inhabiting a human body).[4]

The utopian nature of many IT systems stems from the fact that it takes time to fine tune complex systems, and by the time the fine tuning is starting to happen, the technological development has moved on. Unless it is traffic lights which are too expensive to change more often than every other decade. Utopias are yesterday's tomorrows (cf. Bell and Dourish 2007), not tomorrow's embodied history.

The singular and utopian natures of smart cities are a problem because of their scale. The slowly developed expressiveness and understandability that well-understood technologies offer is lacking, and there is no plan that points to the best solution. In fact, there is no plan as much as there is crystallized practice, as activity theorists within human–computer interaction have put it (Berthelsen and Bødker 2003). Such practices take time to be formed, and they are continuously still being formed.

If we are to have systems that are, in fact, perceived as smart, they must work toward our, different, goals. A spraypaint can in the hands of a graffiti street artist has proven to be a smart technology or medium. It offers the artist a voice, the possibility to claim space on an urban scale. As such, it is a civic technology or civic media (Iveson 2011). What is the equivalent to graffiti in the digital realm? What are our digital soapboxes (Foth, Parra Agudelo, and Palleis 2013)? It could be the hacking and defacing of a website. Or it could be an open annotation system to communicate idiosyncrasies and identity of the creator (de Souza e Silva 2013), or citizen news reporting systems such as ushahidi.com (Hirsch 2011). In our own work focusing on civic technologies, we have looked at the visualization of city maintenance issues on public buildings (*City Bug Report*; Korsgaard and Brynskov 2014; figure 38.1), as well as the situated engagement on public displays for urban planning (*Discussions in Space*; Schroeter, Foth, and Satchell 2012; figure 38.2).

Figure 38.1
City Bug Report. Photo: Rasmus Steengaard/Media Architecture Biennale 2014.

We argue that the focus is not on whether urban computing technology allows us to aspire toward utopian or dystopian outcomes in a perpetual tomorrow, it is whether we have the possibility to judge for ourselves as competent members of a community or society, and whether our judgments and consequent actions scale up by linking to others' judgments in finely tuned networks of actors, if not actor networks (Latour 2005; Dourish 2010).

This leads us to a first conclusion about urban interaction design of civic technologies: They need time and resources to develop and mature in a specific cultural context. They cannot be developed and figured out in a vacuum, they need to be grown, as it were. Organicity is impossible to plan. We have known for a long time that community development is about "human horticulture" rather than social engineering (Gilchrist 2000).

Second, both establishing a baseline of many perspectives (non-singularity) and providing the cultural context for urban interaction design (topianism) call for participation from potential stakeholders—that means everyone. However, taking part also means being responsible, and able, to contribute in a community of urban interaction design practice.

Figure 38.2
Discussions in Space at Federation Square, Melbourne, Australia.

In the following we will take a closer look at the ontology and epistemology of communities of practice underlying our conception of participatory action research.

Participatory City Making: The View from Everywhere

The way that the idea of a smart city is communicated in a commercial context is usually accompanied by the promise of innovation across a range of areas. Smart city–induced innovation is often heralded to make the life of urban dwellers easier, safer, faster, cheaper, more convenient, efficient, enjoyable. At the core of the smart city notion are three distinct but related disciplines: the social, the spatial, and the technical. It is the constellation and configuration of this triad that makes for variations in the way the smart city is not only perceived but how it eventually plays out in the lived experience of urban residents.

The aforementioned community of practice around urban interaction design as well as affiliated communities of academics and practitioners subscribing to related terms such as urban computing and urban informatics (Foth, Choi, and Satchell 2011) seek to establish a dialogue connecting people, place, and technology. Overcoming disciplinary boundaries requires a genuinely transdisciplinary approach that overcomes the risk of these core disciplines merely sitting alongside each other. In order to deliver a better understanding of the way knowledge and innovation are created, studied, communicated, applied, shared, and deployed in urban settings, epistemological and methodological flexibility, fluidity, and innovation are required.

Knowledge, or even knowing, is the justified belief that something is true. Knowledge is thus different from opinion. Epistemology is the investigation of what distinguishes knowledge from opinion. Before we propose participatory action research as a useful concept in the context of civic technologies, we first want to critique the apparently universal applicability of the dominant epistemology in technology and engineering. Although there are strong reasons in support of how the dominant model in technology and engineering is applied to many urban civic projects, we ask whether civic engagement in urban environments may require a different, complementary epistemological model for understanding knowledge and civic media in community contexts.

The combination of people, place, and technology opens up a variety of significant questions. Aurigi, for example, asks whether socio-technical innovation in cities should be directed toward improving, augmenting, and enhancing: "information for an audience, services for customers, or networks for citizens?" (2006, 19). These options imply different power relationships between the actors and non-human agents of the city as well as different self- and externally imposed identities. Questioning the spatial as well as social assumptions that have prevailed in urban sociology to date, Amin draws on Latour (2005) to propose a trans-human urban sociology where

the social is considered to exist as an arena of enactment involving varied human and nonhuman inputs given life, meaning, and purpose through processes of enrolment and alignment, rather than as a purely human field structured and differentiated by abstract rules, hidden essences, dehumanized structures, nature, and technology held apart. (Amin 2007, 108)

Illustrating the inanimate, non-human elements, he explains that "code, timetables, traffic signals, zoning patterns, lists, databases, grids, and the like, have become the indispensable 'hidden hand' of everyday organization" (Amin 2007, 110).

These nonhuman agents and artifacts store and embed the codified and universally true knowledge of cities. If rethinking the urban social requires a consideration of nonhuman forms, in reverse, we argue that an urban epistemology requires a re-consideration of human—that is, social—knowledge.

Feminist Juli Eflin (2008) uses Nagel's (1986) phrase "the view from nowhere" to characterize traditional, that is, positivist epistemology:

Epistemologists in the traditional mold believe that the only way to achieve certainty is to strip away all but the bare reasoning needed to make inferences. It is also believed that anyone can achieve a close approximation of this ideal state, so it is perspective-less. All that is needed is careful reasoning in which you deliberately set aside any complicating emotions, goals, or history. Hence, your context—socially, historically, and economically—is irrelevant as are your individual goals and your emotions. In traditional epistemology, the perspective of the idealized knower is a "view from nowhere." (Nagel 1986)

We set out to understand the impact that a view from nowhere has on the "urban social" (Amin 2007) with a view to providing the rationale for a participatory approach to city making that participatory action research can deliver. The two key questions guiding this discussion are: What forms and appearances of knowledge exist in an urban context? And how are these forms of knowledge typically assessed and managed? Applying a traditional epistemological stance to the urban environment recognizes objectified and codified knowledge as true and valid. The pool of data that is stored and represented by traffic signals, timetables, retail signage, official displays, and urban screens provides a means to read publicly accessible and visible information which is universally applicable and supposedly the same for every recipient, that is, the collective city audience. Logos and emblems are placed in prominent positions to indicate knowledge authority. This is coupled with design strategies, such as consistency, hierarchy, repetition, and a mass communication approach of one-to-many. Official office bearers such as policemen and tourist guides wear uniforms and badges to indicate that the city information they communicate can be trusted.

What this view fails to recognize is the wealth of knowledge, wisdom, and experiences collectively and privately held by each urbanite. Similarly to how Bannon (1992) at the time called for a profound shift in attention "from human factors to human actors," more and more commentators these days critique the established hegemony of the engineering- and technology-centric epistemology and have started to consider alternative approaches that focus on "smart citizens" and their not just vital but crucial participation in the city-making enterprise (Townsend 2013; Greenfield 2013; Hemment and Townsend 2014; de Waal 2014). Part of the reason why this view is not congruent with the "view from nowhere" is the inherent difficulty of codifying tacit knowledge; for "we can know things, and important things, that we cannot tell" (Polanyi 1966, 22). Non-codified knowledge cannot be universally and centrally assessed and managed. However, this does not mean it must be discarded. Cross and Borgatti (2004, 137) provide a quote of an informant illustrating that it is specifically the potential of personalized and tacit knowledge which makes it worthwhile to explore means to tap into the collective intelligence—or *civic intelligence* as Schuler (2008, 2009) would call it—of the people around us:

Despite all the technology we have and the huge investment we make as a firm into it, people are the only way I get information that matters to me. … Learning how to use the constellation of people around you requires understanding what they can and will do for you. In part this means knowing what they are good at and can be relied on for, but just as importantly, it means knowing to what degree you can trust someone or how to get them to respond to you in a timely fashion.

"Information that matters" can be the universally codified knowledge that a view from nowhere advocates. However, there are many situations where finding information that matters requires contextualization; that is, the specific, individual circumstances and factors of the situation as well as the personal attributes of the actors and agents and their impact on the significance and relevance of information choices. Knowledge that is passed on through civic media and social networks of urban residents is not about universality. The diversity of strong and weak ties in urban social networks is a strength of cities and a source of both explicit and tacit knowledge which can ripple from its origin to the distant capillary fringes (Granovetter 1973; Kavanaugh et al. 2005).

Congruent with this emphasis is Eflin's (2008) call for an epistemology that is relevant to lived experience based on the following four principles:

1. Understand "context" robustly but avoid the extreme of naïve relativism;
2. Be cognizant of and attempt to avoid epistemic blindness;
3. Make values transparent as well as the relations between values and social policy, and;
4. Share cognitive authority.

In other words, Eflin asks that a range of epistemic voices be listened to; something like a democracy of ideas. This stance is consistent with a trend toward local, democratic, and alternative modes of knowledge production. It is corroborated by Nancy Odendaal, an urban planner with a track record in community informatics and digital city research interested in the marginalized urban populations, particularly in South Africa. Odendaal (2006, 36) says:

Writers such as Sandercock (1995) remind us that the terrain in which we plan is populated by diverse needs and "other ways of knowing"; we need to be sensitive to the needs and voices of the marginalized. An understanding of local conditions and sensitivity to local knowledge is, therefore, required. The access to this information is not necessarily through reports and documents, but may have to be gained through oral histories, story-telling, and poetry, for example.

The central concerns are about institutional changes and new methodological approaches needed to facilitate bringing together the people, information, strategies, infrastructure, facilities, and other resources necessary to solve some of the complex problems we now face. Movements toward civic engagement in urban design and planning, as well as citizen science approaches to solving environmental and health problems, are undergirded by social media such as Twitter, Facebook, and YouTube to create new models of researching and solving urban problems (Foth, Forlano, Satchell, and

Gibbs, 2011; Gordon and de Souza e Silva 2011; Paulos, Kim, and Kuznetsov 2011). One of these approaches is participatory action research.

Participatory Action Research

A long held, and at the time rarely questioned, assumption in scientific inquiry and scholarly pursuit has been the separation of researcher and research subject. Objectivity is still regarded by some as the prime imperative necessary to produce verifiable insights with academic rigor that are backed up by reproducible empirical evidence. This stance resonates with the aforementioned "view from nowhere" and is certainly appropriate for mathematics, science, and other positivist disciplines. However, when applied to research involving humans, people, communities, and culture, it causes tensions when trying to reconcile the exact and accurate precision required to produce logical or mathematical proof, and the fuzzy qualities of human behavior, cultural practices, and social interactions.

This conundrum shows some resemblance with the old division of roles between teacher and student that was questioned and eventually corrected by the critical pedagogy movement led by Paulo Freire (1993) and others. Participatory action research borrows from the principles and philosophies of critical pedagogy insofar as it seeks to overcome the conventional delineation of researcher and research subject. There are no subjects. In recognition of their domain expertise and contribution, their status and authority is elevated to that of study participant, and in the most emancipated versions of action research, to that of co-investigator. Reason and Bradbury (2001, 1) define action research as follows:

A participatory, democratic process concerned with developing practical knowing in the pursuit of worthwhile human purposes. [...] It seeks to bring together action and reflection, theory and practice, in participation with others, in the pursuit of practical solutions of pressing concern to people, and more generally the flourishing of individual persons and their communities.

Hearn et al. (2009, 10–11) explain the overarching approach taken in action research:

The imperative of an action research project is not only to understand a problem, but also to provoke change (Dick, 2002; Reason & Bradbury, 2001; Smith, Willms, & Johnson, 1997). [...] action research is a generic term that covers a wide range of methodologies and approaches. However, at its core, action research is an approach that "focuses on simultaneous action and research in a participative manner" (Coghlan & Brannick, 2001, p. 7). ... Action research is operationalised by constant cycles of planning, acting, observing, and reflecting. Findings and theory-building, which the researcher drives, are balanced by the phase of planned action, which benefits the participants by giving them a solution to their problem or at least by making a step toward a solution.

Many variations of action research have been proposed, developed, and tested over time, some of which stem from customizing and tailoring action research to specific community settings and circumstances. However, there is a set of underlying principles that usually apply to all of them:

• The project tends to conduct "applied research"—as opposed to pure, basic, or strategic research—with the aim of producing actionable knowledge that in turn informs action and change with a measurable impact.
• The project is concerned not only with meeting the needs and "key performance indicators" of the academic project participants (such as peer reviewed publications), but also the needs—identified through co-inquiry research—of the people or community participating in the project.
• Academic and community representatives participate in the project as equals with mutual respect.
• Iterative cycles of planning, acting, observing, and reflecting are conducted.

We briefly discuss three variations of action research: Ethnographic action research, network action research, and anticipatory action research.

Ethnographic action research (EAR), as proposed and applied by Tacchi, Slater, and Hearn (2003), combines anthropological principles and methods of ethnography with action research. Ethnography is useful particularly for the first phase of immersion and sense making, but also for the later phases of observing and reflecting once action is being implemented. Tacchi and colleagues have used EAR for various projects in media and communication studies, particularly looking at the use of information and communication technology for development (ICT4D) projects in South Asia (Tacchi and Lennie 2014).

Network action research was proposed and used by Foth (2006) as a way to embed and embrace the use of then newly emerging digital media and communication tools in action research projects. Using such tools offers the ability to complement the typically collective, communal approach to action research with a social network strategy and, thus, alleviate some of the reported challenges of conventional collective-only action research projects. Some of these challenges include:

• Improve representation to better reflect community diversity
• Ease participation in order to encourage more people to have a say
• Balance community hegemony by encouraging marginalized voices to be heard on their own terms
• Extend the outreach and impact of the project by connecting with existing social networks
• Invite situated participation "in the wild" by allowing participants to act and reflect on their own work, living, or urban environments

Anticipatory action research, pioneered by Hearn et al. (2009), combines future studies and action research, and aims at anticipating the ways in which innovations, new socio-technical practices, or environmental conditions could impact on existing social structures. The objective is to enable participants to use anticipatory action research in order to plan, prepare, make choices, and take responsibility for such future impacts. An example in the context of civic engagement is the Institute for the Future study commissioned by the Rockefeller Foundation that studied worldwide "weak signals" to examine novel ways of harnessing data for development and inclusion (Townsend and Maguire 2010).

From Participation and Engagement to Sustainable City Making

There are strong and valid reasons for putting a heavy emphasis on participation in the pursuit of rigorous action research. Reason (1998) outlines the political, epistemological, ecological, and spiritual dimensions of participation. His thoughts corroborate the principles of participation in related methodologies, such as participatory design (Foth and Axup 2006), which is particularly relevant to the domains of civic technologies, urban interaction design, and urban informatics (Bilandzic and Venable 2011).

With participation comes the need to customize and tailor action research to the specific circumstances and settings of the project under study—and rightly so. However, in the extreme case, this may lead to an agglomeration of singular, unrelated case studies that shy away from attempting to discuss transferability of their results, since the findings are so unique and idiosyncratic to the case being studied. It also voids any endeavor to collaboratively work across different case studies in order to contribute to the building of robust theory. Gustavsen (2003, 93) articulated some of these challenges and encouraged action researchers to develop new research platforms and to seek new alliances with other branches of research.

An example of a new research platform pertinent to participatory action research is the way that Schuler (2008) adopted Christopher Alexander's pattern language for use in community informatics, social change, and civic engagement. Problematic as they can be in isolation, the patterns help to overcome the problem of the single case pointed out by Gustavsen (2003) by introducing a method for describing and cataloguing the insights gained from action research studies. By using a collection of patterns in conjunction with syntax and grammar, Schuler is able to produce a repository of knowledge that is both transferable and extensible.

With regards to Gustavsen's call for new alliances with other branches of research, the transdisciplinary combination of social, spatial, and technical research domains has already led to a number of successful projects fostering civic engagement (Foth, Forlano, Satchell, and Gibbs 2011). The Urban Informatics Research Lab is an example of a transdisciplinary research team, "in that it comprises and collaborates with architects with degrees in media studies, software engineers with expertise in urban sociology, human-computer interaction designers with a grounding in cultural studies, and urban planners with an interest in digital media and social networking" (Foth, Choi, and Satchell 2011, 1).

The challenges for participatory action research articulated by Gustavsen (2003) have started to be addressed, but the work is not over yet. Furthermore, new challenges but also opportunities have emerged. In previous work (Foth, Parra Agudelo, and Palleis 2013), we argued that there are at least two significant issues for us to consider when creating, using, and studying the next generation of civic technologies: First, the disconnect between citizens participating in *either* digital *or* physical realms has resulted in a neglect of the hybrid role that public urban space and situated technology can play in contributing to civic engagement. Second, under the veneer of many social media tools, hardly any meaningful strategies or approaches are found that go beyond awareness raising and allow citizens to do more than clicking a "Like" button. We call for an agenda to design the next generation of "digital soapboxes" that contributes toward a new form of polity helping citizens not only to have a voice but also to appropriate their city in order to take action for change, and to be able to institutionalize and grow communities of socio-technical practice in dosed symbiosis with other systems and institutions. Two examples are our attempts to give people the tools not only to participate in movements of civic engagement, but to create and use their own in order to establish a DIY (do-it-yourself) mode of fostering civic innovation (Caldwell and Foth 2014), and the overall attempt to formulate a field of practice and research which addresses this organic city making: urban interaction design (Brynskov et al. 2014).

Notes

1. Definition of "Biedermeier period," Wikipedia, https://en.wikipedia.org/wiki/Biedermeier.

2. Definition of "desire path," Wikipedia, http://en.wikipedia.org/wiki/Desire_path.

3. "Human dystopia," YouTube, August 30, 2011. http://youtu.be/h1BQPV-iCkU.

4. Definition of "microbiota," Wikipedia.http://en.wikipedia.org/wiki/Microbiota.

References

Amin, A. 2007. "Re-thinking the Urban Social." *City* 11 (1): 100–114.

Aurigi, A. 2006. "New Technologies, Same Dilemmas: Policy and Design Issues for the Augmented City." *Journal of Urban Technology* 13 (3): 5–28.

Bannon, Liam. 1992." From Human Factors to Human Actors: The Role of Psychology and Human-Computer Interaction Studies in System Design." In Joan Greenbaum and Morten Kyng, eds., 25–44. *Design at Work*. Hillsdale, NJ: L. Erlbaum Associates.

Benkler, Y. 2004. "Sharing Nicely: On Shareable Goods and the Emergence of Sharing as a Modality of Economic Production." *Yale Law Journal* 114 (2): 273–358.

Bilandzic, M., and J. Venable. 2011. "Towards Participatory Action Design Research: Adapting Action Research and Design Science Research Methods for Urban Informatics." *Journal of Community Informatics* 7 (3).

Bell, G., and P. Dourish. 2007. "Yesterday's Tomorrows: Notes on Ubiquitous Computing's Dominant Vision." *Personal and Ubiquitous Computing* 11 (2): 133–143.

Berthelsen, O., and S. Bødker. 2003. "Activity Theory." In *HCI Models, Theories, and Frameworks: Toward a Multidisciplinary Science*, ed. J. Carroll, 291–324. San Francisco: Morgan Kaufman.

Brynskov, M., Juan Carlos Carvajal Bermúdez, Manu Fernández, Henrik Korsgaard, Ingrid Mulder, Katarzyna Piskorek, Lea Rekow, and Martjin de Waal. 2014. *Urban Interaction Design: Towards City Making*. UrbanIxD.eu. issuu.com/urbanixd/docs/urbanixd_towardscitymaking.

Caldwell, G., and M. Foth. 2014. "DIY Media Architecture: Open and Participatory Approaches to Community Engagement." In *Proceedings of the Media Architecture Biennale 2014*, Aarhus, Denmark, November 19–22. New York, NY: ACM.

Chipchase, J. 2014. JanChipchase.com.

City Bug Report. 2012. http://citybugreport.projects.cavi.dk.

Coghlan, David, and Teresa Brannick. 2001. *Doing Action Research in Your Own Organization*. Thousand Oaks, CA: SAGE Publications.

Cross, R., and S. P. Borgatti. 2004. "The Ties That Share: Relational Characteristics That Facilitate Information Seeking." In *Social Capital and Information Technology*, ed. M. Huysman and V. Wulf, 137–161. Cambridge, MA: MIT Press.

Dawson, M. 2012. "Against the Big Society: A Durkheimian Socialist Critique." *Critical Social Policy* 33 (1): 78–96.

de Souza e Silva. A. (2013). "Mobile Narratives: Reading and writing urban space with location-based technologies." In N. K. Hayles, and J. Pressman, eds., 33–52. *Comparative Textual Media: Transforming Humanities in the Postprint Era*. Minneapolis: University of Minnesota Press.

de Waal, M. 2014. *The City as Interface: How New Media Are Changing the City*. Rotterdam, NL: nai010 publishers. http://www.thecityasinterface.com.

Dick, B. 2002. *Action Research and Action Learning for Community & Organisational Change*. Retrieved Sep 16, 2014. http://www.aral.com.au.

DiSalvo, Carl. 2012. *Adversarial Design*. Cambridge, MA: Mit Press.

*Discussions in Spa*ce. 2015. http://urbaninformatics.net/dis.

Dourish, P. 2010. "HCI and Environmental Sustainability: The Politics of Design and the Design of Politics." In *Proceedings of the 8th ACM Conference on Designing Interactive Systems (DIS '10)*, 1–10. New York: ACM. doi:.10.1145/1858171.1858173

Dourish, P., and G. Bell. 2011. *Divining a Digital Future*. Cambridge, MA: MIT Press.

Eflin, J. 2008. "Women and Cognitive Authority in the Knowledge Economy." In *Knowledge Policy: Challenges for the 21st Century*, ed. G. Hearn and D. Rooney, 45–58. Cheltenham, UK: Edward Elgar.

Foth, M. 2006. "Network Action Research." *Action Research* 4 (2): 205–226.

Foth, M., and J. Axup. 2006. "Participatory Design and Action Research: Identical Twins or Synergetic Pair?" Paper presented at the Participatory Design Conference (PDC), Trento, Italy, July 31– August 5. http://pdcproceedings.org/

Foth, M., J. H. Choi, and C. Satchell. 2011. "Urban Informatics." In *Proceedings of the ACM 2011 Conference on Computer Supported Cooperative Work (CSCW '11)*, 1–8. New York: ACM. doi:.10.1145/1958824.1958826

Foth, M., L. Forlano, C. Satchell, and M. Gibbs, eds. 2011. *From Social Butterfly to Engaged Citizen: Urban Informatics, Social Media, Ubiquitous Computing, and Mobile Technology to Support Citizen Engagement*. Cambridge, MA: MIT Press.

Foth, M., L. Parra Agudelo, and R. Palleis. 2013. "Digital Soapboxes: Towards an Interaction Design Agenda for Situated Civic Innovation." In *Proceedings of the 2013 ACM conference on Pervasive and ubiquitous computing adjunct publication (UbiComp '13 Adjunct)*, 725–728. New York: ACM. doi:.10.1145/2494091.2495995

Freire, P. 1993. *Pedagogy of the Oppressed*. New York: Continuum.

Gilchrist, A. 2000. "The Well-Connected Community: Networking to the Edge of Chaos." *Community Development Journal: An International Forum* 35 (3): 264–275.

Gordon, E., and A. de Souza e Silva. 2011. *Net Locality: Why Location Matters in a Networked World*. Chichester, UK: Wiley-Blackwell.

Granovetter, M. 1973. "The Strength of Weak Ties." *American Journal of Sociology* 78 (6): 1360–1380.

Greenfield, A. 2013. *Against the Smart City (The City Is Here for You to Use)*. New York: Do projects. http://foryoutou.se/againstthesmartcity.

Gustavsen, B. 2003. "Action Research and the Problem of the Single Case." *Concepts and Transformation* 8 (1): 93–99.

Hearn, G., J. Tacchi, M. Foth, and J. Lennie. 2009. *Action Research and New Media: Concepts, Methods and Cases*. Cresskill, NJ: Hampton Press.

Hemment, D., and A. Townsend. 2014. *Smart Citizens*. Manchester, UK: FutureEverything Publications; http://futureeverything.org/ideas/smart-citizens-publication/.

Hirsch, T. 2011. "More Than Friends: Social and Mobile Media for Activist Organizations." In *From Social Butterfly to Engaged Citizen: Urban Informatics, Social Media, Ubiquitous Computing, and Mobile Technology to Support Citizen Engagement*, ed. M. Foth, L. Forlano, C. Satchell, and M. Gibbs, 135–150. Cambridge, MA: MIT Press.

Iveson, K. 2011. "Mobile Media and the Strategies of Urban Citizenship: Control, Responsibilization, Politicization." In *From Social Butterfly to Engaged Citizen: Urban Informatics, Social Media, Ubiquitous Computing, and Mobile Technology to Support Citizen Engagement*, ed. M. Foth, L. Forlano, C. Satchell, and M. Gibbs, 55–70. Cambridge, MA: MIT Press.

Jacobs, J. 1961. *The Life and Death of Great American Cities*. New York: Random House.

Kavanaugh, A. L., D. D. Reese, J. M. Carroll, and M. B. Rosson. 2005. "Weak Ties in Networked Communities." *Information Society* 21 (2): 119–131.

Koonin, S. E., G. Dobler, and J. S. Wurtele. 2014. "Urban Physics." *American Physical Society News* 23 (3): 8.

Korsgaard, H., and M. Brynskov. "City Bug Report: Urban Prototyping as Participatory Process and Practice." In *Proceedings of the Media Architecture Biennale, Aarhus, Denmark*, 21–29, 2014. New York: ACM.

Latour, B. 2005. *Reassembling the Social: An Introduction to Actor-Network-Theory*. Oxford: Oxford University Press.

McLuhan, M. 1964. *Understanding Media: The Extensions of Man*. New York: McGraw-Hill.

Morozov, Evgeny. 2013. *To Save Everything, Click Here: Technology, Solutionism, and the Urge to Fix Problems that Don't Exist*. London: Penguin.

Nagel, T. 1986. *The View from Nowhere*. Oxford: Oxford University Press.

Odendaal, N. 2006. T"owards the Digital City in South Africa: Issues and Constraints." *Journal of Urban Technology* 13 (3): 29–48.

Paulos, E., S. Kim, and S. Kuznetsov. 2011. "The Rise of the Expert Amateur: Citizen Science and Micro-Volunteerism." In *From Social Butterfly to Engaged Citizen: Urban Informatics, Social Media, Ubiquitous Computing, and Mobile Technology to Support Citizen Engagement*, ed. M. Foth, L. Forlano, C. Satchell, and M. Gibbs. Cambridge, MA: MIT Press.

Polanyi, M. 1966. *The Tacit Dimension*. Gloucester, MA: Peter Smith.

Reason, P. 1998. "Political, Epistemological, Ecological and Spiritual Dimensions of Participation." *Studies in Cultures, Organizations and Societies* 4 (2): 147–167.

Reason, P., and H. Bradbury, eds. 2001. *Handbook of Action Research: Participative Inquiry and Practice*. London: Sage.

Sassen, S. 2012. *Urbanizing Technology*. Paper presented at the Urban Age Electric City conference, LSE Cities, London, December 6–7.

Satchell, C. 2009. "From Social Butterfly to Urban Citizen: The Evolution of Mobile Phone Practice." In *Handbook of Research on Urban Informatics: The Practice and Promise of the Real-Time City*, ed. M. Foth, 353–365. Hershey, PA: IGI.

Schmidt, Eric, and Jared Cohen. 2013. *The New Digital Age: Reshaping the Future of People, Nations and Business*. London: John Murray.

Schroeter, R., M. Foth, and C. Satchell. 2012. "People, Content, Location: Sweet Spotting Urban Screens for Situated Engagement." In *Proceedings of Designing Interactive Systems*, Newcastle, UK, June 11–15, 146–155. New York: ACM.

Schuler, D. 2008. *Liberating Voices: A Pattern Language for Communication Revolution*. Cambridge, MA: MIT Press.

Schuler, D. 2009. "Communities, Technology, and Civic Intelligence." In *Proceedings of the 4th International Conference on Communities and Technologies (C&T '09)*, 61–70. New York: ACM. doi:.10.1145/1556460.1556470

Smith, S. E., D. G. Willms, and N. A. Johnson, eds. 1997. *Nurtured by Knowledge: Learning to Do Participatory Action-Research*. New York: Apex Press.

Tacchi, J., and J. Lennie. 2014. "A Participatory Framework for Researching and Evaluating Communication for Development and Social Change." In *The Handbook of Development Communication and Social Change*, ed. K. G. Wilkins, T. Tufte, and R. Obregon, 298–320. West Sussex, UK: Wiley-Blackwell.

Tacchi, J., D. Slater, and G. Hearn. 2003. *Ethnographic Action Research Handbook*. New Delhi, India: UNESCO.

Townsend, A. 2013. *Smart Cities: Big Data, Civic Hackers, and the Quest for a New Utopia Hardcover*. New York: W. W. Norton & Company. http://www.smartcitiesbook.com/.

Townsend, A., and R. Maguire. 2010. "A Planet of Civic Laboratories." Paper presented at the Future of the Crowdsourced City conference, Rockefeller Foundation, New York, NY, December 16.

Williams, A., E. Robles, and P. Dourish. 2009. "Urbane-ing the City: Examining and Refining the Assumptions behind Urban Informatics." In *Handbook of Research on Urban Informatics: The Practice and Promise of the Real-Time City*, ed. M. Foth, 1–20. Hershey, PA: IGI.

Zuckerman, E. 2013. *Rewire: Digital Cosmopolitans in the Age of Connection*. New York: W. W. Norton.

39   Field-Building in Stages: Funding and Sustainability in Civic Innovation

Valerie Chang and Beth Gutelius

In 2012, the U.S. was home to 86,192 foundations with $715 billion in assets and $52 billion in giving.
—The Foundation Center, Preview of Key Facts on U.S. Foundations, 2014

If you've seen one foundation, you've seen one foundation.
—Anonymous

Introduction

Philanthropy has played a central role in the development of the field of civic innovation, understood here as the use of new communications technologies to connect residents and institutions of government and governance.1 Using the distinct set of tools and resources at their disposal, namely financial resources, convening power, and relationships, foundations provide backing for a broad range of activities. For civic innovation in the United States, the focus of this chapter, support has meant helping to recognize, define, and promote the field in its earliest days, and pushing for greater attention to evaluation and impact as tech-supported innovation matures.

The potential for civic innovation to transform relationships, improve institutional effectiveness, and bolster democratic participation continues to draw the attention of foundations, even as new forms of communication technologies bring both positive potential and unintended consequences. Philanthropy's longstanding commitment to trying to solve intractable problems like poverty means that funders bring considerable knowledge to the challenges of institutional transformation; this commitment to civic improvement drives the interest in exploring and understanding how best to advance civic innovation as a powerful force for improved outcomes.

Yet philanthropy is not a permanent solution to funding the continued development of more effective and collaborative governance. Foundations are sometimes criticized for their shifting priorities and seemingly mysterious methods of developing strategies and selecting grantees; their support may not seem like a natural fit for a field concerned with participation and transparency, but it also signals an appreciation on the part of many foundations for the fundamental precepts of civic innovation.

Civic innovation has grown over the last decade and has attracted the attention and support of a relatively small number of philanthropic funders. With increasing engagement from the public sector, the private sector, nonprofit organizations, and the public at large, technology-enabled collaboration is growing. Is there an ongoing role for philanthropy? As civic innovation continues to mature, how will funding for the field be sustained over time? In this chapter, we consider these questions based on our philanthropic experience, in addition to a series of interviews with grant recipients and with other grant makers who have funded civic innovation projects.[2] This chapter provides insight into the sometimes enigmatic world of philanthropy and characterizes foundation support for innovation initiatives. We then propose a lifecycle framework to better understand the stages of field building in civic innovation and to contextualize funding activities in each stage. Finally, we suggest a set of three core themes for foundations to consider throughout the lifecycle: evaluation, diversity, and equality.

The lifecycle framework suggests that, while philanthropic support will continue to guide the field in particular ways, long-term sustainability will be predicated on the widespread diffusion of an open, participatory political culture, within and outside of government institutions. As civic innovation evolves, practitioners, academics, and funders need to continue to identify the infrastructure necessary to sustain the field in the long term, beyond the horizon of philanthropic investment.

Throughout this chapter, we use the term civic innovation to encompass the range of activities that are re-shaping government interaction and processes, often aided by technology. Black and Burstein (2013) detail the significant debate over the terminology used to describe new approaches to civic participation, technology, and the public good. Following Sirianni and Friedland (2001), Black and Burstein propose civic innovation as an organizing principle, acknowledging that while constituencies interpret the term differently, it "has the advantage of encompassing institutional change, not just a set of disparate programs, and includes a wide variety of communities" (Ibid., 3). This emphasis on shifts in process and practice has been central to MacArthur's approach to grant making in this field, which is comprised of government, technologists, nonprofits, researchers, and residents.

Methodology

This chapter draws on the experience of the authors and a series of interviews we undertook in 2014, both in person and over the phone, lasting 30 to 60 minutes. Semi-structured interviews were conducted with leaders of four grantee organizations and six funders, both within and outside of the MacArthur Foundation. Topics included philanthropy's role in the development of civic innovation, key issues facing funders and practitioners, and future phases of development and maturation. The interviews were transcribed and data were coded to draw out both the common and divergent ideas. We used this analysis to inform our argument about the state of funding sustainability, as well as the lifecycle we propose.

The Philanthropic Sector

Philanthropy is difficult to characterize as a whole, given the size and diversity of the field: foundation approaches to grant making, strategy development, and internal culture vary widely. Yet some broad stroke characterizations are useful for the purposes of this chapter. According to the Foundation Center (2014), 16 percent of all private giving in the U.S. in 2012—roughly $50 billion—came from foundations. Philanthropy plays an important role in funding and sustaining the work of organizations in the social sector in diverse areas—from education and health to arts and the environment. Foundations can be broadly characterized by their type (corporate, community, operating, or independent) and asset size. The latter ranges from multi-billion dollar endowments at the largest foundations (the Bill & Melinda Gates Foundation has the largest total assets of U.S. foundations, at roughly $35 billion) to small independent foundations with a few thousand dollars (Foundation Center 2011).

These categories offer somewhat crude methods of differentiating among the very diverse range of grant-making institutions, and while foundations tend to defy neat typologies, research has suggested that these characteristics are associated with particular outlooks and strategies (Ostrower 2006). For example, Frumkin (2006) differentiates between what he characterized as instrumental versus expressive giving, and suggests that these approaches tend to correlate to the asset size of the institution. Instrumental giving hones in on a particular problem or issue and attempts to make tangible, measurable headway through significant investments over time. Frumkin suggests that large foundations with substantial resources often pursue instrumental grant making, because they possess the wherewithal to tackle large-scale problems—issues like neighborhood poverty or educational opportunity. Expressive giving, more commonly associated with smaller foundations or individual donors, has more modest aims because of the size of grants these foundations are able to make.

Yet small foundations often have impact in important ways, particularly when work is narrowly focused or when partnerships among foundations coalesce around particular problems. And large foundations, despite their resources, do not always succeed in their attempts to solve large, complex problems. Fleishman (2009) suggests that while expressive and instrumental giving styles are distinct approaches to grant making, the choice is less a product of foundation size than their approach to strategy formulation. Foundation staff and boards are constrained and guided by the mission established by the donors, but beyond that they exercise considerable discretion as they establish the priorities of their grant making, selecting issue areas, populations, geographic boundaries, and different tools and levels of support.

The best-known resources that foundations provide are monetary: grants to organizations and individuals are the hallmark of philanthropy, but other financial tools, like program-related investments (PRIs) and mission-related investments (MRIs) can be equally catalytic. PRIs and MRIs provide low interest rate capital to social ventures considered too risky or unproven for the mainstream capital markets. In the past, the MacArthur Foundation's PRI program, for example, focused on financing nonprofit multi-family housing development as part of a broader program to preserve quality, affordable housing. For the field of civic innovation, these financial tools may offer more options for long-term sustainability, particularly for projects that include a potential revenue stream.

Philanthropic support can also come in forms other than monetary. Alongside financial resources, foundations provide technical assistance, convening power, networking, and operational guidance to their grantees and to broader fields. In addition, foundations of all sizes engage in collaborations, both formally and informally, in order to leverage a cumulative effect that their own grant making alone might not achieve.

Philanthropy performs a range of functions: using private wealth to affect social change, seeding innovation, carrying out redistribution, encouraging pluralism, and fulfilling the needs and wishes of donors themselves (Frumkin 2006). These functions are not mutually exclusive, and they point to a longstanding tension in philanthropy: the relationship between private giving and public purposes. Philanthropies are agenda-setting institutions with the capacity to incentivize certain behaviors and practices, not unlike government, but without the public oversight. While this requires foundations to be very thoughtful about their investments and assessments and to take pains to maintain high ethical standards, it also represents one of philanthropy's unique advantages. Foundations operate largely outside of political pressure, which creates unique opportunities for experimentation.

Of the functions above, seeding social innovation has been a particularly important activity for philanthropy in the field of civic innovation. A common perception of government is that it is often slow to innovate, in part because of the high stakes of implementing programs and projects that potentially affect millions of lives. Philanthropy can help seed new innovative ideas, piloting them at smaller scales and funding iterations of program models. The ability to take risks and to take the long view is a particular strength of foundations: even if a project fails, the survival or legitimacy of the institution is usually not in jeopardy, as it might be with a business, nonprofit, or government. In the civic context, philanthropy acts as a catalyst for experimental social ventures that aim to affect other institutions by providing an independent source of funding, outside of government or the market. One long-term goal of funders in civic innovation is to help the public sector understand the benefits and constraints of technological tools in the process of improving governance.

Recent Trends in Philanthropy

Perhaps the most significant trend in philanthropy since the 1990s is the rise of so-called "strategic philanthropy," which marked a shift toward data-driven strategies with carefully designed "theories of change," quantifiable goals with metrics, and rigorous evaluations in order to improve the effectiveness of foundation giving. The results of strategic philanthropy have been mixed, and some critics suggest that the trend has drawn foundations away from funding innovation and experimental projects that may carry more risk and potentially higher rates of failure (Kasper and Marcoux 2014).

There is a healthy debate in philanthropic circles about how to ensure the relevance of foundations in tackling the interconnected, complex problems of the twenty-first century. In order to avoid the rigidity that strategic philanthropy can impose, some argue that foundations need to adopt a more flexible approach—termed "emergent philanthropy" (Kania, Kramer, and Russell 2014). Emergent philanthropy calls on funders to adapt strategies to changing circumstances, co-create solutions with partners, and become more comfortable with less control and certainty. Others make the case that the increasing scale and complexity of social challenges requires funders to work in different ways: instead of funding discrete programs or individual organizations, funders need to become more open to working with networks (Grantmakers for Effective Organizations and Monitor Institute 2011). The latter suggests that new communication technologies should aid philanthropies in becoming more open, engaging in co-creation and sharing. Sound familiar? These same principles, common in attempts to improve efficacy and transparency in government, are beginning to percolate in the funding world.

Beyond broader, sector-wide trends like strategic philanthropy, individual foundations periodically re-assess their grant making in order to make decisions about funding priorities. This occurs when a program area comes to the end of a time-limited strategy and foundation staff evaluates the progress of the work, but can also happen at other, less predictable junctures, such as when new leadership enters the foundation. Midcourse assessments can lead to pivots in strategies or partners, a shift in expectations, or to the exit of the foundation from the issue area.

The criteria that foundation staff uses to determine whether an idea has salience will vary depending on the institution, but overall ideas must fit within the mission of the organization. Foundation missions are often broad, reflecting the need for relevance over a long time span. Beyond this initial test of fit, foundations consider whether they have the expertise to carry out the work and the timeliness of the proposed approach. Philanthropic choices about areas of work to pursue and grantees to support tend to be guided by the logic models to which foundation staff and leadership adhere. These models, commonly referred to as theories of change, are not always explicit, however, and can require both careful research on stated strategies and, where possible and appropriate, conversations with program staff themselves.

At the MacArthur Foundation, grant making and the use of other philanthropic approaches are anchored in an approach that invests in creative people and in research, experimentation, policy analysis, and practical, on-the-ground efforts to bring about positive change, helping to create a deep reservoir of ideas, to connect people and organizations to increase the power of their actions, and to provide evidence of what is possible and what works. This "research, policy, practice" cycle makes it possible to work on multiple dimensions of an issue, with each element informing the other. In U.S. immigration policy work, for example, the Foundation has supported research to understand the economic and fiscal impacts of immigration, at the federal, state and local levels. The results of this research can help inform and shape on-the-ground responses in states and communities experiencing an influx of immigrants. Both the research and the practice will inform the development of policy that is based on data, evidence, and work on the ground. Changes in policy may spur additional research to understand better the impact of new policies and their implications for practice. In this way, the foundation supports ongoing knowledge development, experimentation, and innovation.

Philanthropic Support for Civic Innovation

There have been few attempts to comprehensively scan the funding landscape of civic innovation. In 2013, the Knight Foundation issued a report that sought to answer questions about the amount of investment and characteristics of investors, and to define clusters of innovation activity. The authors point out that the boundaries of "civic technology," their preferred term, are loosely defined, which makes quantification difficult, and the report includes peer-to-peer consumer networks like Airbnb that fall outside of the definition of technology-supported civic projects considered for this chapter. Still, it offers an initial glimpse into the field's financial support ecosystem. Under the wide definition of civic technology employed, the authors catalog 32 philanthropic funders of civic tech projects between 2011 and 2013, and suggest that civic engagement and participation are some of the least well-funded activities in the sector. Among the most prominent philanthropies in civic technology were the Knight, MacArthur, Hewlett, and Rockefeller foundations. While the report represents a valiant initial attempt to characterize an amorphous field, the questions of how to track investment trends and share learnings remain a central challenge.

Broadly speaking, civic innovation possesses a number of characteristics that make it appealing to foundations: an emergent field with creative, dynamic individuals; new technology and tools, with the potential to engage people around public challenges and improve their lives; and involvement with the public sector, with the potential to improve government and governance. Civic innovation also cuts across and has the potential to transform engagement and participation in multiple domains—from journalism and education to urban planning and civic participation.

Beyond broad strokes, interviewees offered a variety of reasons aligned with their institutional worldviews for being drawn to civic innovation, among them that it has the potential to reshape and open up institutions of democracy and change their relationship to citizens; that it can promote community-level engagement and thereby strengthen democracy; that it may make government more effective and legitimate; that it can have large-scale impact at low cost; and that it is forward looking and bridges to a younger generation. Several funders emphasized that civic innovation holds the promise for large-scale change that can affect a wide cross section of people; at its best, it is not technology for its own sake, but a tool that can help create beneficial impact on communities.

Within the MacArthur Foundation, funding for civic innovation cuts across multiple issue areas, including work in education, community, and economic development, human rights, and democracy. In each of these areas, technology is changing the interaction between individuals and institutions, creating new pathways and norms for engagement, and shifting existing paradigms about expertise, privacy, participation, and collaboration. Funded projects, to name a few, include the Aspen Institute Task Force on Learning and the Internet, the Smart Chicago Collaborative, the MacArthur Research Network on Opening Governance, Code for America, and Ushahidi.

Civic Innovation Lifecycle

In a relatively short period of time, the field of civic innovation has flourished. Interviewees noted that perhaps the most important role of philanthropy over the last decade has been to develop the concept of civic innovation and to promote it as part of a larger field. While a cohesive, shared definition of technology-supported civic collaboration across groups of stakeholders and participants has not yet solidified, it no longer takes a three-minute conversation to describe the work. Civic innovation conjures a set of ideals and practices that put technology to work in service of improving outcomes for people and for the places where they live. As the field evolves and practices become more widely adopted, we suggest that it goes through a lifecycle marked by three stages: early, middle, and late. Each stage is defined by a different context, possesses different characteristics, and has a particular set of needs. In each stage of the lifecycle, there is a distinct role for philanthropy to play in shaping and supporting the changing nature of the field.

Figure 39.1 depicts a stylized three-stage maturity lifecycle for civic innovation in which we identify some of the key characteristics at each stage and corresponding foundation investments; it also points toward what more may need to be done. In identifying the field's characteristics, we considered traits such as stage of diffusion, mode of operating, orientation, locus of activity, perception, and visibility. We attempt to map the types of philanthropic activity in each stage, which is responsive to the ongoing shifts. We believe that civic innovation has matured from its early stage and is transitioning into the middle stage. We take some liberties as we suggest shifts in both the field and foundation activity and recognize that processes of development do not necessarily follow a teleological path. Yet the lifecycle has the potential to be a useful organizing logic to grapple with the long-term sustainability of civic innovation.

Early Stage

In the characteristics of the civic innovation field in the early stage, the level of practice and project diffusion is very limited. Here we employ Everett Rogers' (1962, 2003) theory of the diffusion of innovation to capture the breadth of adoption. Diffusion theory posits a process by which an innovation spreads through certain channels over time, among either the members of a connected social network or a societal sector of disconnected but similar members. Rogers suggests that those who adopt innovations can be characterized by when they adopt: there are innovators and early adopters; early and late majority adopters, and finally, laggards. The distribution follows a standard bell-shaped distribution.

The spread of civic innovation is still limited in the early stage, but those who engage with it are innovators and early adopters, many of whom have the potential to influence others and encourage broader take up. In this stage, we characterize the mode of working as one focused on experimentation, often by creative innovators who are incubating different ideas and projects. The Boston Office of New Urban Mechanics is a good example of this: a locally-focused project using new technological tools to deliver improved city services to Boston's residents. Products and ideas in this phase are frequently driven by supply, like the release by cities of troves of data without a clear understanding of demand: the "if we build it, they will come" phenomenon. The locus of activity is more individualized and fractured at the early stage in pockets of activity. From the perspective of the public, where technology-aided institutional innovation has any visibility at all, it remains a novelty—a new and largely marginal set of activities that may or may not have staying power.

In figure 39.1 we also consider the roles that philanthropies play during each stage in the lifecycle. In the early stage, foundations must work to understand their potential role in the civic innovation landscape, as a partner, catalyst, or driver of activities. In this stage, a foundation's tolerance for risk and failure sometimes becomes clear, as the

	Early Stage	Middle Stage	Optimal Late Stage
Characteristics of the Field			
Diffusion	Innovators, early adopters	Early majority	Late majority
Mode	Experimentation	Iteration	Openness
Locus of activity	Individualized	Networked	Broadly distributed and inclusive
Perception	Novelty	Potential	Demonstrated value
Visibility	Nascent	Increasing	Ubiquitous
Orientation	Driven by supply	Growing demand side	Embedded in institutions and practices
Philanthropic Activity			
Philanthropic niche	Learn how foundations can be valuable	Ensure diversity, broad inclusion, and connection to real life issues	Secure and sustain advances
Funding activities	• Seed experiments • Convene stakeholders • Support research • Identify key thought leaders	• Refined experimentation based on learning • Build networks • Develop evaluations • Test business models • Support research	• Widespread knowledge diffusion • Attract new forms of capital to build long-term organizations • Stimulate partnerships and new business models
Foundation involvement	Very few foundations	• Growing foundation support • Philanthropic collaboration	?

Figure 39.1
Maturity lifecycle for civic innovation.

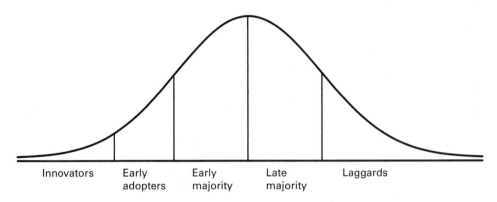

Figure 39.2
Rogers' diffusion of innovation theory.

rapid cycling through ideas and projects can engender doubt and fatigue, even as it also produces a better understanding of the efficacy of particular approaches. Beyond financial resources, foundations can convene different sets of stakeholders—both to learn how philanthropy can add value and to help advance relationships and deliberation in the field. In terms of "field building," a common activity in philanthropy (see, for example, Hirschhorn and Gilmore 2004), civic innovation presents particular challenges. Both in our experience and in what we heard in interviews, there are disconnects between set of actors and constituencies that can complicate collaborative governance. Relationships between researchers and advocates, particularly around open, free Internet and digital freedom, but across a plethora of other domains, have not been as productive they could be. Government employees who focus on delivering services and implementing policies have a different set of guiding principles than those of application developers and other technologists. The priorities and lived experiences of application engineers can differ dramatically from residents experiencing entrenched problems like lack of access to transportation and affordable housing, educational and health disparities, and a host of other issues. Foundations, at their best, have worked to align these disparate interests around common goals, aided in no small part by philanthropic staff's familiarity with the underlying problems. The gulfs between these groups have sometimes made communication difficult, and foundations have a role to play in helping to facilitate productive exchanges. The work of convening stakeholders is ongoing and likely to continue throughout philanthropy's involvement in civic innovation.

Because philanthropy can take more risks with fewer consequences for failure, foundations can fund experimentation and support a wide array of promising new ideas and projects. Beyond funding initial "beta" or pilot projects, some funders also support the next iterations of these projects as they move past the prototype phase. Foundations also contribute to building essential infrastructure, examples of which include the Berkman Center for Internet and Society and Creative Commons. Research in this stage is focused on data gathering, implementation evaluation, and outcomes analysis.

In the early stage foundations leverage their financial and reputational assets to help gain attention for the field. This helps the field establish credibility, legitimacy, and voice and takes various forms, including communication and outreach strategies that engage prominent personalities.

Middle Stage

In the middle stage of the lifecycle, diffusion spreads beyond the innovators and early adopters, and is taken up by those Rogers called the "early majority." This stage, which we argue civic innovation has entered, is marked by iteration and learning from earlier experiments. From the point of view of a philanthropist, networks are forming where work had been more isolated and individualized. This trend is evident in the municipal innovation initiatives. Cities across the United States are developing the capacity to use technology tools to improve the delivery of services and engage differently with their residents. Led by cities such as New York, Boston, Chicago, and San Francisco, where technologists and public policymakers have created communities of practice to collaborate, learn from each other, and co-create solutions, the momentum has grown and more cities are beginning to work in this way.

There is increasing recognition that the demand side—not just the supply side— must be bolstered and supported. It is not enough to develop new tools and applications. These tools must be connected to issues and challenges that matter to broad sections of the population, and that capacity exists inside government to understand and act upon information. Funders should be cautious to assume that increased participation translates into institutional evolution. Visibility and legitimacy are on the rise among groups of stakeholders, and there is growing awareness of the field and a healthy optimism about its potential for transformation.

In the middle stage, foundations may continue to provide funding for experimentation, but they may narrow their experimental focus, based on what has been learned in the early stage. With tremendous amounts of action and "doing" in the early stage, the middle stage is characterized by more maturity and a need to understand what is working, why, under what conditions, and the potential for scale. There is an increased focus on research to identify successes, to derive lessons from failure, and to share those findings with the field.

There is also a critical need in this stage to understand the unintended consequences and the potential "dark side" of civic innovation. Are there ethical dimensions that should be considered in the use of big data? What are the implications of these tools and practices for notions of privacy? Are there downsides to philanthropic engagement in the field? How do dissenting voices and perspectives get brought into the field? Will innovation help level the playing field or exacerbate inequality? These questions should be—and are being—researched, soundly debated, and considered.

Convenings in the middle stage of the cycle continue, with an increased emphasis on seeding and supporting networks and communities of practice. These are forums for shared learning, problem solving, and co-creation. Funders may find they are jointly funding projects or organizations, and may seek to collaborate explicitly on shared interests. In this stage, philanthropy can look to bridge gaps and deficits and continue to build the case for government investment in participatory political culture. Funding modalities may include fellowships and space to test business models.

Late Stage

The late stage of the civic innovation lifecycle is undetermined. Here, we present an optimal scenario of the field's maturation process, marked by widespread adoption both by residents and institutions. If civic innovation reaches its transformational potential, broad and inclusive participation will become normalized in a democratic system marked by long-term dynamism. The use of technology to improve collaboration in governance will lose its novelty and become a common civic experience. Both the effective and failed experiments, along with rigorous evaluations, will have demonstrated the value and impact of civic innovation in re-legitimizing and defining twenty-first-century governance institutions. In this stage, the role of philanthropy shifts again, focusing on securing the long-term infrastructure and diffusing the knowledge base. Activities in this stage could include supporting academic and popular journals that provide a platform for the dissemination of research and debate; attracting and providing new forms of capital to support organizations over the long term; stimulating partnerships and launching new business models. It is uncertain whether foundation support would be growing, shrinking, or in stasis—this question depends, in part, on how the field progresses in the coming years, the emergence of other sources of revenue and support, especially from the public sector, and on philanthropy's continued investment in a context of increasingly urgent competing priorities.

The maturing of civic innovation is not without challenges, and in order to reach the idealized late stage we sketch, those invested in the success of the field have to attend to a set of themes that arise repeatedly in conversations about civic innovation. Across the lifecycle, there are three cross-cutting themes that should undergird philanthropy's involvement in the field's development: evaluation, diversity, and equality.

Evaluation in civic innovation has focused largely on more easily measureable metrics: the number of people using an app, tweets sent, or projects produced. These can be useful statistics to gather, but are not sufficient to understand if and how civic innovation is making life qualitatively better for residents—technology alone does not guarantee more people will participate, or that their engagement is deep or of high quality. Evidence is lacking across the board: rigorous evaluation, both quantitative and qualitative, will help clarify whether new technology-enabled transactions have produced transformations, and determine whether a model is successful enough to be disseminated. Philanthropy has an important role to play in helping to illuminate whether projects are making progress toward more open governance, or more meaningful participation. Until these shifts are evaluated, the transformative potential of civic innovation will be unproven, and efforts at diffusion may be stymied.

As detailed above, people who understand technology, those who understand government, and those who understand communities lack a shared language and fundamental agreement on priorities and approaches. Scholarship on Internet usage demonstrates that a digital divide persists, based largely on education, income, and age but with disproportionate effects on African Americans, Latinos, and Native Americans, who lag whites and Asians in Internet access (Fairlie 2005; Mossberger, Tolbert and Stansbury 2003). There remains a persistent gap in civic engagement, too, where the likelihood of participation is less among individuals with lower levels of education and income (Jacobs and Skocpol 2005). Almost all of our interviewees cited the demographics of the field of civic innovation, which they believe are likewise skewed toward well-educated white men, as a challenge to longer-term sustainability. Foundations can use their resources to broaden participation, prioritizing diverse voices and communities and ensuring that programs and projects address issues of interest to different constituencies.

Finally, the equality theme is one of anticipating and reconciling unintended consequences. In the same moment, civic innovation possesses both the potential to undermine and to calcify inequalities that exist in society, and it needs to be coupled with strategies to reduce barriers to participation while broadening and stabilizing access. For low-wage workers who struggle to pay their smart phone bill every month, the potential of phone apps to encourage democratic participation remains out of reach. Issues of privacy and open Internet also raise ethical quandaries. Philanthropy's engagement in issues of inequality and poverty aligns well with the need for a continuous focus on whether civic innovation is benefitting society as a whole.

Evaluation, diversity, and equality are cross-cutting themes that can form an underpinning of philanthropic engagement, regardless of the stage of field maturity and the actual funding activities of the foundation. These themes are crucial to the ability of civic innovation to reach the late stage of maturity, and can help ensure that the promise of institutional transformation that normalizes openness, collaboration, and engagement is fulfilled.

Future Funding and Sustainability

Where civic innovation will culminate is, at this juncture, unclear; yet we are optimistic that it can play an important role in a new, more inclusive vision for democratic practice and governance. There is growing enthusiasm for the power of technology and data to change how public institutions work and how those institutions interact with the people they are meant to serve. On the other hand, the challenges are daunting: institutional evolution is a slow and sometimes arduous process; there is skepticism about the effectiveness and legitimacy of government; and in order to sustain any movement toward better governance, new social practices have to be introduced and supported alongside technological advances.

Philanthropy's involvement in the development of civic innovation has provided essential resources during the early stages of the lifecycle, but the nature of philanthropy is that support for particular areas of funding almost always ebbs. As the field moves into a new stage of evolution, it's a good time to step back and consider the role of philanthropy over the long term. At some point in the future—when the value and impact of civic innovation have been more firmly demonstrated to government, when practices are more equitably established, when a business model emerges that could allow some projects to generate revenue—philanthropy should be able to step away. In order for this to happen, government will have to recognize the benefits of new tools, processes, and practices and commit resources to their continued development. It's imperative, then, that the value proposition of civic innovation is proven to the public sector.

For this reason, at a time when institutions of governance risk being perceived as irrelevant and peoples' relationships to them are changing, philanthropy may need to make a concerted push to help residents connect to government and governance in new ways. Civic innovation is one means of encouraging engagement, rebuilding confidence, and ushering institutions of governance into a twenty-first-century sense of legitimacy. Funders should seek new models for public-philanthropic partnerships to ensure that the third sector, operating outside of government and the market, has a place in shaping the progression of civic innovation.

Notes

1. We use both government and governance in this paper. *Governance* describes how an organization or a society makes collective decisions and acts to realize its objectives. The use of the term "governance" acknowledges that a range of institutions, participants, rules, and norms, often

operating across geopolitical boundaries, come together to influence, negotiate, and arrive at shared decisions. *Government* is an institution with formal authority in a geopolitical jurisdiction run by a combination of public servants and elected political leaders who have the power to enforce their decisions.

2. While this article is informed by our experience working at the John D. and Catherine T. MacArthur Foundation, the views expressed are ours alone and do not represent the views of the institution.

References

Black, Alissa, and Rachel Burstein. 2013. *The 2050 City: What Civic Innovation Looks Like Today— and Tomorrow*. Washington, D.C.: New America Foundation.

Fairlie, Robert W. 2005. "Are We Really a Nation Online?: Ethnic and Racial Disparities in Access to Technology and Their Consequences." *Leadership Conference on Civil Rights Education Fund,* September 20.

Fleishman, Joel L. 2009. *The Foundation: A Great American Secret*. New York: PublicAffairs.

Foundation Center. 2011. "Foundation Stats: Guide to the Foundation Center's Research Database." http://data.foundationcenter.org/#/foundations/all/nationwide/total/list/2011.

Foundation Center. 2014. "Preview of Key Facts on U.S. Foundations, 2014 Edition." http:// foundationcenter.org/gainknowledge/research/pdf/keyfacts2014.pdf.

Frumkin, Peter. 2006. *Strategic Giving: The Art and Science of Philanthropy*. Chicago: University of Chicago Press.

Grantmakers for Effective Organizations and Monitor Institute. 2011. *Catalyzing Networks for Social Change: A Funder's Guide*. Washington, D.C.: Grantmakers for Effective Organizations. http://www.monitorinstitute.com/downloads/what-we-think/catalyzing-networks/Catalyzing _Networks_for_Social_Change.pdf.

Hirschhorn, Larry, and Thomas Gilmore. 2004. "Ideas in Philanthropic Field-Building: Where They Come from and How They Are Translated into Actions." Foundation Center, March. http:// folio.iupui.edu/handle/10244/19.

Jacobs, Larry, and Theda Skocpol eds. 2005. *Inequality and American Democracy: What We Know and What We Need to Learn*. New York: Russell Sage Foundation.

Kania, John, Mark Kramer, and Patty Russell. 2014. "Strategic Philanthropy for a Complex World." *Stanford Social Innovation Review,* Summer. Accessed September 29, 2014. http:// www.ssireview.org/up_for_debate/article/strategic_philanthropy.

Kasper, Gabriel, and Justin Marcoux. 2014. "The Re-Emerging Art of Funding Innovation." *Stanford Social Innovation Review,* Spring. Accessed September 29, 2014. http://www.ssireview.org/ articles/entry/the_re_emerging_art_of_funding_innovation.

Knight Foundation. 2013. "The Emergence of Civic Tech: Investments in a Growing Field." http://www.knightfoundation.org/media/uploads/publication_pdfs/knight-civic-tech.pdf.

Mossberger, Karen, Caroline J. Tolbert, and Mary Stansbury. 2003. *Virtual Inequality: Beyond the Digital Divide*. Washington, D.C.: Georgetown University Press.

Ostrower, Francie. 2006. "Foundation Approaches to Effectiveness: A Typology." *Nonprofit and Voluntary Sector Quarterly* 35 (3): 510–516. doi:.10.1177/0899764006290789

Rogers, Everett M. 2003. *Diffusion of Innovations*. 5th ed. New York: Free Press.

Sirianni, Carmen, and Lewis Friedland. 2001. *Civic Innovation in America: Community Empowerment, Public Policy, and the Movement for Civic Renewal*. Berkeley: University of California Press.

40   Case Study: Guerrilla Research Tactics—Alternative Research Methods in Urban Environments

Glenda Amayo Caldwell, Lindy Osborne, Inger Mewburn, and Ben Kraal

Guerrilla Research Tactics (GRT) involves the use of unexpected design interventions to actively engage participants in the co-creation of data within the urban fabric (Caldwell et al. 2015). Extending Gauntlett's definition of "new creative methods ... an alternative to language-driven qualitative research methods" (Gauntlett 2007), GRT is an important contribution to the growing body of literature on creative and participatory approaches to data collection. GRT is an evolution of participatory action research (Kindon et al. 2008) and unobtrusive research methods (Kellehear 1993). Researchers can use GRT as an alternative, creative approach to data acquisition that allows them to engage with the public as active co-creators of knowledge. In this case study we briefly offer a summary of some of the previous work in this area to illustrate what GRT is and how it might be used.

The GRT project drew out of small-scale experiments such as *Print + Talk = Love* (PTL) undertaken in Brisbane, Queensland, in 2012 . This was a situated paper-based intervention that invited ordinary citizens to discuss place-based topics which had no connections to digital devices or Web-based platforms. PTL was constructed of a large piece of corrugated cardboard that had pinned pieces of paper with printed questions relating to the event or place in which the intervention was located, as seen in figure 40.1. Clips and string were used to attach colored pens to the board. The pieces of paper had blank space allowing for participants to write their responses to such questions as, "What's your great idea for Grey St.?" (Parra-Agudelo et al. 2013). The board was interactive, allowing participants to express themselves on paper through their own personalized way of manipulating, writing, drawing, or repositioning the pieces of paper.

PTL was purposely designed to be easy to use and easy to interact with. When deploying PTL, its location and setup were considered carefully, along with its visibility and content, all of which contributed to the ability of researchers to stand back and allow for unobtrusive observation (Parra-Agudelo et al. 2013).

Another experiment involving an interactive application on urban screens is *Discussions in Space* (DIS), a public participation tool for urban public places (Schroeter 2012; Schroeter et al. 2012), which continues to be used in various locations around

Figure 40.1
Print + Talk = Love at the Changing Lanes event in Brisbane, Queensland, May 2012. Photo: Mark Bilandzic.

Brisbane and Melbourne, Australia. DIS allows situated users to respond to context-specific questions such as "Brisbane's laneways need more ...?" through SMS, Twitter, and a website, as shown in figure 40.2. The responses and messages are revealed on the dynamic screen in an animated way. DIS has demonstrated that when it is situated within the right parameters it can be a useful tool in collecting urban planning data from young people who generally do not participate in typical community consultation processes (Schroeter 2012; Schroeter et al. 2012).

Researchers employing PTL and DIS extended their data beyond the comments collected; they also conducted unobtrusive observations, took photographs, and made video recordings to examine how users interacted with the displays. In the case of DIS, geo-locative data was available through some of the Twitter comments.

Confronted with the challenge of engaging research participants, a group of researchers from The Queensland University of Technology, Brisbane, Australia, began to interrogate the impact of activating PTL and DIS in public spaces and test their effectiveness as potential research tools. Providing researchers with both analogue and digital examples of experimental interventions allowed for researchers to trial and experiment with

Figure 40.2
Discussions in Space collects citizen input for ideas to improve city life, Brisbane, Queensland, May 2012. Photo: Glenda Caldwell.

a range of research approaches. Analogue, digital, and hybrid (analogue and digital) variations of PTL and DIS were implemented in Australia and New Zealand, encouraging participants to engage with both the physical intervention and accompanying digital websites and surveys.

Figure 40.3 is a photo of a variation of PTL used to engage with fashion design students in a study about studio-based learning environments. The researcher designed the pieces of paper to resemble Polaroid photographs. The papers also had a mix of a few different questions, and the researcher ultimately used this approach to collect data instead of a survey or questionnaire. Another adaptation of PTL, shown in figure 40.4, is called the Puzzle of Collaboration, where the researcher was examining the motivation behind interdisciplinary collaboration. This adaptation used colored pieces of paper that were cut into puzzle pieces on which participants could write their responses to targeted questions. The papers were pinned on the board and fit together as a large puzzle.

A hybrid adaptation of PTL, called the Mural Wall, was used to engage with the public to question their preferences among design ideas of a third place for an underutilized railway underpass (Caldwell et al. 2013). Five hand-drawn vignettes of potential uses for that location were posted on a large corrugated cardboard, and participants were invited to vote for their preferred design idea by using sticky dots and Post-it

Figure 40.3
Situated paper-based design intervention. Photo: Louise Barbour.

notes. The Mural Wall also included QR codes which linked to a WordPress site that included more information about the research project such as ethical clearance, survey and social media links, and research team information (Caldwell et al. 2013).

More projects began to be conceived in the same GRT mode, for example a hybrid approach we call "Poll Bombing": the strategic placement of physical artifacts with embedded QR codes linked to Web-based surveys and polls. Figure 40.5 is an example of an origami paper crane that was placed in targeted locations. The paper used text and words to express the research topic in question. It also had a sign asking for the participant to unfold the crane and look inside it. On the inside a QR code was found which when scanned would take the user to the survey.

A similar approach was the use of carefully designed stickers placed in urban spaces, as shown in figure 40.6. The stickers used bright colors and simple graphics and text to ask open-ended and location-specific questions, such as, "This space needs. …" The

Figure 40.4
The Puzzle of Collaboration. Photo: Lindy Osborne.

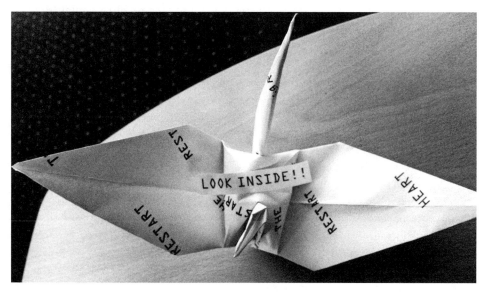

Figure 40.5
A paper crane with a QR code inside. Photo: Glenda Caldwell.

Figure 40.6
Pink stickers placed in urban environments. Photo: Leonardo Parra Agudelo.

sticker also included a QR code taking the participant to a website that contained more information about the research project.

Social media, predominately Facebook and Twitter, were employed as means to disseminate links to websites, surveys, and blogs, extending the access to research participants well beyond the physical location in which the interventions were placed.

The success of guerrilla research tactics relies on the ability of researchers to appropriate and adapt their methods to create context-specific applications and interventions. This is not a straightforward or easy process. Guerrilla research tactics requires creative design thinking, the desire to make tangible artifacts as well as clever use of social media, ubiquitous technologies, and a willingness to explore alternative research methodologies. GRT should be easy to implement and easy to use. Influenced by guerrilla activism, the key characteristics of GRT are a political agenda, the use of the unexpected, and the unconventional design that created opportunities for interactive, unique, and thought-provoking experiences for the researcher and participant alike (Caldwell et al. 2015). Burgess et al. (2006) argue that active citizenship is practiced by everyday people through their day-to-day life, leisure, and entertainment activities as much as through formal political debate and engagement. GRT draws on these everyday practices to provide researchers tools for gathering information from larger parts of society.

As a form of participatory action research, GRT encourages the collaboration of researchers and participants in reviewing and questioning problems pertaining to space and place, social and natural environments. As such we can understand GRT as a "bottom up process" where data emerges from interactions with the urban fabric itself (Kindon et al. 2008; Caldwell et al. 2015). The process of generating data encourages participants to reflect upon local issues that are directly related to them and consider actions that are required to create positive change (Kindon et al. 2008). Through GRT, civic research has the capacity to promote active citizenship (Burgess et al. 2006) and effect positive change in urban environments.

Part of the GRT framework involves implementing unexpected design interventions in urban locations so that passersby are confronted with an element of surprise and intrigue. By luring people to participate and interact with the intervention, researchers can increase the possibility that passersby become involved in the discussion and advocate for their opinions and ideas. Motivation and empowerment for participants are also critical elements of GRT. The collection of information from people, how and for what purposes it is used, and how that information is revealed to others, does, however, need careful consideration.

We acknowledge that GRT faces many challenges. Of foremost concern is to ensure that data is collected ethically and that participants are aware of their actions. This comes into tension with the ability to conduct unobtrusive observations where the researchers do not influence the actions of participants. GRT may also be difficult to understand by users who do not recognize the intention of the interventions and are not aware of how they can participate or interact with them. Environmental factors such as inclement weather and lighting also have to be acknowledged and considered when designing and deploying GRT. In windy or wet conditions, how does the researcher ensure the stability and security of its implementation? Ultimately it is understood that this approach to research is not suitable to all researchers or contexts, however it may be adapted to suit a range of different areas of investigation beyond creative-based disciplines.

Not only is GRT a useful, fun, and creative data collection tool, but the actual process of developing unique applications of GRT and transferring it into other domains will ensure its evolution. Motivated by the open sourcing of information, we created the GRT website (GuerrillaResearchTactics.com) with the intention to share our experience with others, to invite them to continue to evolve, adapt, appropriate, and share their versions of GRT. Together we can learn from each other and continue to creatively activate the collection of information and the co-creation of knowledge.

References

Burgess, Jean E., Marcus Foth, and Helen G. Klaebe. 2006. "Everyday Creativity as Civic Engagement: A Cultural Citizenship View of New Media." Presented at the Communications Policy & Research Forum, Sydney, AU, September 25–26.

Caldwell, Glenda Amayo, Marcus Foth, and Mirko Guaralda. 2013. "An urban informatics approach to smart city learning in architecture and urban design education." *IxD&A (Interaction Design and Architecture[s])* 17, Summer: 7–28.

Caldwell, Glenda Amayo, Lindy Osborne, Inger Mewburn, and Philip Crowther. 2015. "Guerrillas in the [urban] midst: Developing and using creative research methods—guerrilla research tactics." *Journal of Urban Technology*. 22 (3) 21-36.

Gauntlett, David. 2007. *Creative Explorations: New Approaches to Identities and Audiences*. New York: Routledge.

Kindon, Sara, R. Pain, and M. Kesby. 2008. "Participatory action research." In *International Encyclopaedia of Human Geography*, ed. Rob Kitchin and Nigel Thrift, 90–95. Elsevier Science.

Kellehear, A. 1993. *The Unobtrusive Researcher: A Guide to Methods*. St Leonards, Australia: Allen & Unwin Pty Ltd.

Parra Agudelo, L., G. A. Caldwell, and R. Schroeter. 2013. "Write vs. Type: Tangible and digital media for situated engagement." Paper presented at the 5th IASDR Conference: Consilience and Innovation in Design Conference, Tokyo, Japan, 4818–4829.

Schroeter, R. 2012. "Engaging new digital locals with interactive urban screens to collaboratively improve the city." In *Proceedings of the ACM 2012 Conference on Computer Supported Cooperative Work*, 227–236. New York: ACM Press.

Schroeter, R., M. Foth, and C. Satchell. 2012. "People, content, location: sweet spotting urban screens for situated engagement." In *Proceedings of the Designing Interactive Systems Conference*, 146–155. New York: ACM Press.

41 Case Study: Hackathons as a Site for Civic IoT—Initial Insights

Carl DiSalvo and ken anderson

Over the past several years we have taken a research-through-design approach to civic hackathons, engaging them as organizers, hosts, and participants. Of late, we have become interested in using civic hackathons to explore the civic potentials of the Internet of Things (IoT). With its focus on IoT, the 2014 National Day of Civic Hacking provided an opportunity to do just this. We approached this hackathon as a design experiment. We were curious to see how we might use the hackathon as an opportunity to prototype services in support of an in-progress civic IoT system. Such a product-service approach (Morelli 2002), we believed, might fit well with the practices of hackathons. Through this design experiment we were able to glean insights into tactics for mediating the design process for IoT in hackathons and reflect on the character of participation in civic hackathons.

Our in-progress civic IoT system was being developed to support foraging. Foraging is the practice of collecting fruits and vegetables from sites other than farms or orchards, such as from trees or plants in public parks, private yards, or abandoned lots. Sometimes the foraged food is for personal consumption, other times it is sold at markets, and still other times it is donated to food banks. Foraging is an interesting civic practice because it can serve a common good, but it operates orthogonally to standard structures for governance and the care of citizens. The fruits and vegetables collected through foraging augment the food resources available to those in need, and contribute to the resilience of a local food system. As foraging is a volunteer endeavor, the timing and organization of activities is essential to manage involvement. One of the challenges is knowing when fruit is ripe, so that picks can be organized to collect the fruit. At the suggestion of a local foraging group, we decided to explore the use of sensing mechanisms to alert foragers that a given apple tree might be ready for picking. The idea was relatively simple: as apples become ripe they gain weight and the tree limb bends. If we could detect a change in the bend of the limb, we could surmise that a tree might be ready for picking and notify the foragers.

For the 2014 National Day of Civic Hacking, our goal was not to have attendees contribute to the sensing mechanism itself, but to contribute to the product-service

Figure 41.1
Testing sensing hardware at the 2014 National Day of Civic Hacking.

system through the development of software. In part this was because the sensing mechanism did not require extensive engineering. But, moreover, this was because we wanted to explore civic IoT as a problem of product-service integration: to focus on the ecology of components that comprise an IoT system and how they work together. So, we took the hardware as a given and sought to explore how services might make that hardware more useful to practice.

On the first evening of the event we presented the challenge and a small group gathered together to work on the project. While one of us worked on tweaking the branch-bending sensor (for demo purposes and to establish a material connection between the hardware and the software, to make present the components of the product-service system) the rest of the team began brainstorming software applications and features in support of the sensor's capabilities and the practices of the foragers. The brainstorming process was lead by a team member with expertise in User Experience (UX). He asked questions of us (the researchers representing the foragers) to better understand foraging and began to gather requirements. He also served as the project director for the rest of the team, who had technical backgrounds ranging from machine learning to Web development.

Over the course of the 24-hour hackathon the team prototyped a mapping service to document and monitor a distribution of sensors across the city. The prototype displayed mock-sensor data at actual locations of apple tress, basic digital cartography features (such as visual clustering associated with levels of zoom), and basic data management and interactivity (such as the ability to sort by fields). The data structures and framework were designed so future versions could support tracking alerts, sensor calibration at site, and comparative tracking of trees over time.

The 2014 National Day of Civic Hacking thus served as a worthwhile site to prototype services in support of an in-progress civic IoT system. Taking the hardware as a given allowed the team to focus on software capabilities that would bolster the usefulness of the product-service system overall. One insight drawn from the event was the value of UX in mediating between software and hardware prototyping of IoT. Though perhaps obvious in retrospect—as UX is a generalist design concerned with

Figure 41.2
De-bugging a map interface for sensor data at the 2014 National Day of Civic Hacking.

integration—the UX expert was able to convert an understanding of the practices of foraging into desirable system features, and then manage the prototyping process.

Beyond being a site for ad-hoc design, what insights can be gleaned from this case study to reflect on the character of participation in civic hackathons?

To begin with, in addition to UX as project management, we might acknowledge the role of UX in organizing a coalition of effort at the hackathon. In effect, the UX role made the practice technically tractable. One might argue this has an effect of stripping a civic practice into a mere set of design requirements. To an extent that is true. There was only minor engagement with foraging as a practice, or local food systems as an issue. But this minor engagement is not entirely problematic when it occurs in participation with a network of commitment—a collective. In civic contexts we might want to realize a kind of collective engagement that includes but is not limited to individuals. *The individual participates in the collective. The collective participates in the issue.* This is not to suggest to that there is no individual responsibility. Nor is it an embrace of solutionism (Morozov 2013). Rather, it is recognition that the kinds of ad-hoc design practices that comprise civic hackathons require new appreciations for what constitutes civic engagement.

References

Morelli, Nicola. 2002. "Designing Product/Service Systems: A Methodological Exploration." *Design Issues* 18 (3): 3–17.

Morozov, E. 2013. *To Save Everything, Click Here: The Folly of Technological Solutionism.* New York: PublicAffairs.

Rodrigo Davies

Crowdfunding, the raising of money from large numbers of small donors using online platforms such as Kickstarter and IndieGoGo, has emerged as a very popular means of supporting a wide range of projects in the past five years: from film and music releases, to consumer technology products and scientific experiments. The practice is also beginning to be applied to projects that provide services to communities, such as public parks, community centers, and grass-roots civic groups (Davies 2015). Brazil offers one of the best examples of how civic crowdfunding can be used as a powerful movement-building mechanism: Pimp My Carroça (Pimp My Wagon) was a public art campaign to highlight the condition of waste pickers in São Paulo and to advocate for worker protections. It leveraged the emergent practice of civic crowdfunding both to gather financial resources and to build a popular movement around its civic goals.

São Paulo, a city of more than 11 million people, recycles less than 1 percent of its 17,000 tons of daily waste. Ninety percent of the recycling activity that occurs is carried out by waste pickers, or *catadores* (Offenhuber 2012; Parede Viva 2012). Despite the contribution they make to the city, however, the catadores are either ignored, or face complaints and abuse from drivers and police officers, who blame them for blocking traffic. Angered by the treatment of the catadores, Mundano, a 27-year-old artist from the city, decided to intervene on their behalf.[1] In 2007 he began befriending waste pickers and offering to paint their carts, as a way of making them more visible to traffic, and giving each person he worked with an individual identity. He painted 160 carts over five years, in cities around Brazil (Mundano 2012b). The murals often contained political messages, such as "One catadore does more than an environmental minister" and "*Se eu pudesse eu reciclava os politicos*" ("If I could I would recycle the politicians"), although his primary goal was to increase public awareness of the catadores and their contribution to the sustainability of Brazilian cities (Parede Viva 2012). More often, he painted messages such as "*Eu carro não pollu*" ("My car does not pollute") and "*Eu reciclo, e você?*" ("I recycle, what about you?") (PauloV2 2009).

These people … support their families through a living based on our waste. They work in the middle of the city, silently. They do work for everybody and nobody notices them. Or if they do, they say, "there's a homeless person." It's totally wrong. … They're employed people, working honestly. I painted carts … to make people think about this problem. This is my life's mission. (Mundano 2012b)

But his one-man mission needed greater scale in order to have a larger impact, so in early 2012 Mundano created a crowdfunding campaign on the São Paulo–based platform Catarse in order to grow the movement. Mundano and the three other local graffiti artists with whom he runs *Parede Viva* (Living Wall), a graffiti collective and education program, named the campaign Pimp My Carroça (Pimp My Wagon, or PMC), echoing the MTV series *Pimp My Ride*, in which contestants' cars are refitted and redecorated by professionals. The group's goal was to raise BRL 38,200 (USD 17,260) to fund supplies to paint 20 waste pickers' carts at a public event. The catadores would also be given free medical consultations from local doctors. They also planned to make a documentary film about the movement and the public art event (Mundano 2012a). They offered backers credits in the documentary, vinyl stickers, t-shirts, recycled bottles, and artwork.

Contagious Success

The PMC campaign opened on March 27, 2012, and during its first five days raised almost a quarter (22 percent) of its target. By the end of April the campaign had raised just over half of the total, and the median donation was between BRL 20 and 30 (USD 5–8) throughout this period. On May 3, the campaign received its biggest donation by far up to that point—BRL 3,000 (USD 800)—from a backer in Rio de Janeiro. It was the third-largest pledge the project received overall. A week later, two days before the deadline of May 11, the campaign met its target after the 704th backer pledged BRL 100. The success of the campaign was contagious. In the three days after reaching the funding target, PMC raised BRL 25,669, more than it had raised in March and April combined.[2] While the three largest backers, two of whom participated in the final three days of the campaign, accounted for almost a third of the overall raise, most donations were clustered around BRL 30.

The large volume of relatively small donations suggests that the PMC outreach strategy, which focused on email, in-person communication, and social media accounts of the members of Parede Vida (PV), was very successful. Mundano tweeted 93 times about the campaign on his Twitter handle @mundano_sp, receiving mentions and retweets from Brazilian celebrities with large Twitter followings, such as Sergio Marone (399,000 followers) and film director and television host Marcelo Tas (5,000,000).[3] The campaign's reach was also highly localized: four out of five backers (631) listed their address as being in São Paulo. Nevertheless, the project received nationwide attention and attracted backers from 17 of Brazil's 27 states. The PMC campaign was a great success in terms of surpassing its goal and achieving broad-based, small-dollar support for a civic issue. It's notable that close to half of the campaign's 792 backers—346—were first-time users of the Catarse platform.[4]

On June 5, 2012, over 1,000 supporters of the campaign gathered in Sao Paulo for the "pit-stop" event, at which Mundano and the PV team painted the carts of 50 waste pickers. Following the event, waste pickers and their supporters marched to the center of São Paulo for a rally at which they presented a manifesto calling for labor protections for waste pickers (Parede Viva 2012). The group was invited to participate in several events and exhibitions across Brazil, and as planned, made a short documentary film, which was released and circulated online.

To Curitiba and Beyond

In September 2013, PV opened a second PMC crowdfunding campaign on Catarse, for catadores in Curitiba. It raised BRL 44,888, 117 percent of its target, from 502 donors. Backers for the campaign were split between Curitiba's state, Parana, and São Paulo, which contributed two-fifths of the backers. The Curitiba "pit stop" event attracted 29 catadores and their families, and 150 volunteers and doctors.

PMC São Paulo and its Curitiba spinoff are effective examples of tactical civic, urban interventions that can attract broad-based support from crowdfunders. PV has been able to grow and retain its digital community since the first campaign, and has 10,000 followers on Facebook, even though the group had not used the platform prior to the end of the São Paulo campaign. Although the campaign did not elicit a public response from policymakers, this was not the campaign's primary intention. Mundano and PV are happy to make rhetorical challenges to the political establishment, but their theory of change is rooted in public engagement and education, changing the discourse around waste pickers. In this respect the campaign was successful in using crowdfunding to support the building of a movement around sustainability issues. PV continues to use the PMC Sao Paulo Catarse page as a place to engage supporters and has posted fourteen updates as of September 2015. In May 2014 the group held a second event in Sao Paulo's Luz subway station, involving 50 catadores. An update posted in January 2014 suggests that they are considering crowdfunding events for catadores in other Brazilian cities in the coming years: "We once again appreciate your involvement ... continue watching our movement, which only continues to grow and has no ambition of stopping anytime soon."[5] (Parede Viva 2012).

Notes

1. Elements of this case study were adapted from Rodrigo Davies, "Civic Crowdfunding: Participatory Communities, Entrepreneurs and the Political Economy of Place" (May 9, 2014). Available at SSRN: http://ssrn.com/abstract=2434615 or http://dx.doi.org/10.2139/ssrn.2434615.

2. One backer was recorded on May 14 due to a delay in payment processing.

3. The social media analytics service Topsy recorded 100 mentions of the phrase "Pimp My Carroça" during the campaign, citing Marone and Tas as two of the biggest drivers of posts featuring that string, alongside Mundano. http://topsy.com/s?q=%22pimp%20my%20Carro\c{c}a%22\& mintime=1332867659\&maxtime=1336755619.

4. The data used to analyze pledging amounts nd behavior was anonymized; the Catarse site shows backer identities where available, but does not reveal individual backers' pledge amounts. In order to preserve the privacy of that information, no comparison of the two datasets was made. The past activity of the 36 backers who chose to remain anonymous is unknown.

5. Original text: "Agradecemos o envolvimento ... continuar acompanhando o nosso movimento, que felizmente só cresce e não tem ambições de parar tão cedo!"

References

Davies, Rodrigo. 2015. "Four Civic Roles for Crowdfunding." In *Crowdfunding the Future: Media Industries, Ethics, and Digital Society*, ed. Lucy Bennett, Bertha Chin, and Bethan Jones. London: Peter Lang.

Mundano. 2012 a. "Custos—Pimp My Carroça 2012." https://docs.google.com/spreadsheet/ccc?key=0Ao8hmRpvVO_PdGdwZGlWVmVBZmR0Sm9OTVo4WjJDc0E#gid=0.

Mundano. 2012 b. "Mundano: Pimp My Carroça: A Street Artist Celebrates Trash Collectors." *TEDTalentSearch*. YouTube, June 28, 2012. http://www.youtube.com/watch?v=X0AydRnNnlM.

Offenhuber, Dietmar. 2012. "Tracking Trash with Waste Pickers in Brazil." MIT CoLab Radio. http://colabradio.mit.edu/tracking-trash-with-waste-pickers-in-brazil/.

Parede Viva. 2012. "PIMP MY CARROÇA." Catarse. http://catarse.me/en/pimpmycarroca.

PauloV2. 2009. "Graffiti Brazil: Mundano." *Abduzeedo*. http://abduzeedo.com/street-art -mundano.

Contributors

ken anderson is an iconoclast by nature and a symbolic anthropologist by training. He is an Anthropologist at the Cultural Transformations Lab at Intel, and over the last 20 years his research has explored the relationship among identity, culture, and technology (ICTs). ken is spearheading efforts to develop worldwide university collaborations with Intel around "green information and communication technologies (ICTs)." ken's career has included positions in the labs of AT&T, MediaOne, US West, and Apple Computer. He has taught at Brown University, UCHS, and Bethel College. He is founder and currently president of the board of directors for EPIC and on the governing board of National Association for the Practice of Anthropology.

Sandra Ball-Rokeach is a Professor of Communication and Sociology in the Annenberg School for Communication and Journalism, at the University of Southern California. She is also the Principal Investigator of the Metamorphosis Project. Sandra is author or editor of six books: *Violence and the Media* (with R. K. Baker), *Theories of Mass Communication* (with M. L. DeFleur), *The Great American Values Test: Influencing Belief and Behavior through Television* (with M. Rokeach and J. W. Grube), *Media, Audience and Society* (with M. G. Cantor), *Paradoxes of Youth and Sport* (with M. Gatz and M. Messner), and *Technological Visions: The Hopes and Fears That Shape New Technologies* (with M. Sturken and D. Thomas). Her published articles appear in such journals as *Communication Research, Journalism Quarterly, Mass Communication and Society, American Sociological Review, Public Opinion Quarterly, Journal of Communication, New Media & Society, Social Problems*, and *The American Psychologist*. She has been co-editor (with C. R. Berger) of *Communication Research* from 1992 to 1997, a Fulbright scholar at the Hebrew University, and a Rockefeller Fellow at the Bellagio Study Center. She also serves on the advisory boards of the McCune Foundations, Southern California Public Radio, and the Research and Learning Group, BBC World Service Trust.

Roy Bendor explores the cultural and political significance of digital media. He teaches at Simon Fraser University's School of Communication, and is a Postdoctoral Research Fellow at the University of British Columbia, where he examines the ways in which interaction design can help shift the place sustainability occupies in the social imaginary. His recent writing appears in *Techne: Research in Philosophy and Technology*, and *Interactions*.

Lance Bennett received his PhD in political science from Yale University and now teaches at the University of Washington, where he is Ruddick C. Lawrence Professor of Communication, Professor of Political Science, and director of the Center for Communication and Civic Engagement. Bennett's work focuses on the importance of media and information systems in civic life. Current research interests include: press–government relations, changing patterns of citizenship, the quality of public information, and digital media and the organization of social movements. He has received career achievement awards from the American Political Science Association, the National Communication Association, and the International Communication

Cheryl Blake served as 2013–2015 e-Government Fellow at the Cornell e-Rulemaking Initiative (CeRI) at the Cornell Law School, where she supported CeRI's efforts to facilitate meaningful public participation in complex policymaking through the Regulation-Room discussion platform. Cheryl received her JD cum laude from Cornell Law School in 2013, where she served as Managing Editor of the *Cornell International Law Journal* and associate editor of the Legal Information Institute's *Supreme Court Bulletin*.

Benjamin Bowyer is Senior Researcher with the Civic Engagement Research Group at Mills College. He received his PhD in Political Science from the University of California, Berkeley. His research interests center around the effects of social context on political attitudes and behavior. His current research draws upon data from the Youth Participatory Politics Survey—a three-wave, nationally representative survey of American youth—to investigate the ways in which digital and social media are transforming civic and political engagement, including the effects that online communities have on young people's participatory norms.

Martin Brynskov, PhD (Computer Science/Human-Computer Interaction), is associate professor in interaction technologies at Aarhus University in Denmark. He is also director of the Digital Design Lab, research director of AU Smart Cities, coordinator of the Danish Smart City Network, chair of the Connected Smart Cities Network (Open & Agile Smart Cities), general chair of the Media Architecture Biennale 2012 and 2014, research fellow at Participatory IT Centre (PIT) and Center for Advanced Visualization and Interaction (CAVI), and former director of the Civic Communication group at the Center for Digital Urban Living. He also holds an MA in Information Studies and Classical Greek.

Bob Buttigieg is a PhD candidate at Griffith University in Australia. His doctoral project examines how queer youth engage with the people and spaces of the Gold Coast, and looks at what it means to "be" queer at this time and in this place. The project includes a "mapping" of the spatial practices of queer young people on the Gold Coast; a consideration of these spatial practices with regard to local, state, and federal government policies and their impact on the lives of queer young people; and the production of a set of recommendations for the various levels of government to take queer young people and their welfare into account.

Glenda Amayo Caldwell is a lecturer in Architecture at the Queensland University of Technology, Brisbane, Australia, and a PhD candidate in the Urban Informatics Research Lab, QUT. Through her research and teaching, she questions the effect of media and technology have on the design of architecture and urban environments. Her investigations explore the connection between the digital and the physical layers of the city, particularly through Media Architecture, to promote community engagement.

Nerea Calvillo is an architect, a Design Studio Lecturer at the Universidad de Alicante, and a curator. Her research interests are centered on the relation among the urban environment, humans, and more-than-humans; architecture; STS; sensing; media studies; feminist theories; non-representational cartographies; citizen science; and smart cities, with the air, digital façades, and tender infrastructures as main case studies. She primarily focuses on the agencies of the microscopic components of the air. Part of this research has been exhibited in Medialab-Prado, (Spain, 2008–2009), Kitchen Budapest (Hungary, 2009), the Museum of Contemporary Art of Santiago de Chile (Chile, 2010), and the Canadian Centre of Architecture (Canada, 2011–2012).

Valerie Chang is the Managing Director for Programs and the Director of Policy Research at the MacArthur Foundation. Her grant making focuses on policy issues related to the MacArthur Foundation's domestic grant-making priorities and special fiscal, demographic, and analytical projects that have broad implications for national, state, and local policy. Chang joined the Foundation in 2003 after working with the national office of the Local Initiatives Support Corporation, where she was chief of staff for the Neighborhood Business Development Group. She has worked with private sector organizations, including Merrill Lynch & Co., Inc., and Salomon Brothers, Inc., where she provided research on macroeconomic and political developments in global emerging markets.

Nien-Tsu Nancy Chen is an Assistant Professor in Communication at California State University, Channel Islands. She was a Postdoctoral Scholar at the Annenberg School for Communication and Journalism at the University of Southern California when this chapter was composed, and she has been involved with the research and development of the *Alhambra Source* since 2008. In addition to new media, civic engagement, and intergroup relations, Nancy's other research interest pertains to health communication with diverse populations.

Melissa Chinchilla is a doctoral student in the Department of Urban Studies and Planning at MIT. Melissa's current research focuses on the intersection between housing, health, and community integration. She is particularly interested in exploring questions related to individual identity, group formation, and community building amongst diverse populations. Before joining the PhD program, Melissa worked on Los Angeles County's plan to end chronic and veteran homelessness—Home For Good. She also holds bachelor's degrees in Social Welfare and Mass Communications, and a master's in City and Regional Planning from the University of California, Berkeley.

The CITRIS Connected Communities Initiative at UC Berkeley: Brandie Nonnecke (Corresponding Author, CITRIS, University of California, Berkeley, nonnecke@citris-uc.org), Tanja Aitamurto (Brown Institute for Media Innovation; Electrical Engineering, Stanford University), Daniel Catterson (University of California, Berkeley, Department of Psychology), Camille Crittenden (CITRIS, University of California, Berkeley), Chris Garland (California Office of Lieutenant Governor), Allen Ching-Chang Huang (University of California, Berkeley, Industrial Engineering and Operations Research), Sanjay Krishnan (University of California, Berkeley, Electrical Engineering and Computer Science), Matti Nelimarkka (Helsinki Institute for Information Technology [HIIT], Aalto University; University of California, Berkeley, School of Information), Gavin Newsom (California Office of Lieutenant Governor), Jay Patel (University of California, Berkeley, Electrical Engineering and Computer Science), John Scott (University of California, Berkeley, Graduate School of Education), Ken Goldberg (University of California, Berkeley, Electrical Engineering and Computer Science; University of California, Berkeley, Industrial Engineering and Operations Research). The Connected Communities Initiative (CCI) at the Center for Information Technology Research in the Interest of Society (CITRIS) at UC Berkeley supports collaborative discovery, design, and governance through new technologies that enhance education, creative work, and public engagement. CCI embraces the development of experimental online platforms and novel hardware and software systems that connect peers to each other and to institutions in meaningful and productive ways. The initiative develops tools to support dynamic relationships between digital media and democratic practices, such as the use of innovative mobile, Internet, and social media applications to facilitate online deliberation, participatory decision making, and rapid mobilization. CCI seeks to enhance individual and collective awareness, understanding, and engagement for people of diverse backgrounds on critical social, political, and economic issues. CCI collaborates with faculty members and research centers on multiple University of California campuses as well as with companies, government agencies, and nonprofit organizations in the United States and internationally. More information is available at citris-uc.org.

Beth Coleman is Associate Professor of Experimental Digital Media at the University of Waterloo where she directs the City as Platform Lab. Coleman works with new technology and art to create transmedia forms of public, civic, and poetic engagement. She is the co-founder of SoundLab Cultural Alchemy, an internationally acclaimed multimedia art and sound platform. Her book *Hello Avatar* is published by the MIT Press.

Rodrigo Davies is a civic technologist and researcher who designs, builds, and analyzes tools to help communities and governments collaborate for social good. He leads the product team at Neighbor.ly, a new platform for individuals and households to invest in their community through municipal bonds. Rodrigo co-founded Build Up, an award-winning social enterprise working on technology-supported methods for resolving conflict and developing communities, and published the first large-scale study of civic crowdfunding. He earned his master's s degree at MIT's Center for Civic Media and is currently on leave from a PhD at Stanford University. He has previously served as an adviser and product manager to the mayoral offices of San Francisco and Boston, the United Nations Development Program, and the UK-based crowdfunding platform Spacehive.

Stuart Davis recently finished his PhD at the University of Texas at Austin, Department of Radio-Television-Film. In 2013, he was a William J. Fulbright Scholar in the Department of Sociology at the Federal University of Rio de Janeiro. His dissertation is "Networking the Favelas: Information and Communications Technologies and Economic Development in Rio de Janeiro's Urban Periphery."

Catherine D'Ignazio is an Assistant Professor at Emerson College, a Research Affiliate at the MIT Center for Civic Media, and a Fellow at the Engagement Lab at Emerson College. She is a researcher, artist, and software developer who investigates how data visualization, technology, and new forms of storytelling can be used for civic engagement. She has conducted research on geographic bias in the news media, developed software to geolocate news articles, and designed an application, Terra Incognita, to promote global news discovery. She is currently working with the Public Laboratory for Open Technology and Science to create an open source water-sensing toolkit for journalists. Her art and design projects have won awards from the Tanne Foundation, Turbulence. org, the LEF Foundation, and Dream It, Code It, Win It. In 2009, she was a finalist for the Foster Prize at the ICA Boston. Her work has been exhibited at the Eyebeam Center for Art & Technology, Museo d'Antiochia of Medellin, and the Venice Biennial.

Carl DiSalvo is an Associate Professor in the Digital Media Program at the School of Literature, Media, and Communication, Georgia Institute of Technology. He created the Public Design Workshop, which is a design research studio that explores socially engaged design practices and civic media. His work draws together science and technology studies, the humanities, and design research to analyze the social and political qualities of design and to prototype experimental systems and services. Carl's current work is broadly concerned with forms of collectivity and the role of design in shaping and enabling collectivity.

Dmitry Epstein is an Assistant Professor of Digital Policy at the University of Illinois in Chicago. His work focuses on Internet governance, information technology policy, and online civic engagement in policymaking. In the past he has also studied questions of information access and the digital divide. Dmitry's work is global and cross-disciplinary. While at Cornell, and as a fellow at the Lee Kuan Yew School of Public Policy in Singapore, he studied the institutionalization of Internet governance and its discourse within the UN. During his postdoc at Cornell Law School, he worked with the interdisciplinary Cornell eRulemaking Initiative investigating technology and practices behind effective online civic engagement in complex policymaking processes.

Marcus Foth is Founder and Director of the Urban Informatics Research Lab, Research Leader of the School of Design, and Professor in Interactive & Visual Design, Creative Industries Faculty, at Queensland University of Technology. Marcus's research focuses on the relationships among people, place, and technology. He leads a cross-disciplinary team that develops practical approaches to complex urban problems. Marcus has received over $4 million in national competitive grants and industry funding and was inducted by Planetizen to the world's top 25 leading thinkers and innovators in the field of urban planning and technology. Marcus has authored or co-authored over 140 publications in journals, edited books, and conference proceedings. He can be followed on Twitter: @sunday9pm and @UrbanInf.

Jennifer Gabrys is a Reader in the Department of Sociology at Goldsmiths, University of London, and Principal Investigator on the ERC-funded project, "Citizen Sensing and Environmental Practice: Assessing Participatory Engagements with Environments through Sensor Technologies." She is author of a study on electronic waste, *Digital Rubbish: A Natural History of Electronics* (University of Michigan, 2011), and a forthcoming study on environmental sensing, *Program Earth: Environmental Sensing Technology and the Making of a Computational Planet* (University of Minnesota Press, 2016). Her work can be found at citizensense.net and jennifergabrys.net.

Liana Gamber-Thompson is a Program Associate at the National Writing Project and the Community Manager for Connected Learning TV. Previously, she was a Postdoctoral Research Associate with the Media, Activism, and Participatory Politics (MAPP) Project at the Annenberg School for Communication and Journalism at the University of Southern California, where she also facilitated the Civic Paths graduate research group. Her fields of interest include politics, popular culture, and gender and feminism. Liana received her PhD in Sociology and Feminist Studies from the University of California, Santa Cruz in 2010. She is a co-author on the forthcoming book, *By Any Media Necessary: The New Activism of American Youth*.

Roman Gerodimos is a Principal Lecturer in Global Current Affairs at Bournemouth University, founder and convener of the Greek Politics Specialist Group of the UK's Political Studies Association, and a faculty member at the Salzburg Academy on Media & Global Change in Austria. He is the winner of the 2010 Arthur McDougall Fund Prize for his research on online youth civic engagement. He is the co-editor of *The Media, Political Participation and Empowerment* (Routledge, 2013) and *The Politics of Extreme Austerity: Greece in the Eurozone Crisis* (Palgrave Macmillan, 2015). He is currently researching the relationship among digital media, public space, and urban coexistence.

Katie Day Good (PhD Northwestern) is Assistant Professor of Media, Journalism & Film at Miami University in Ohio. Her research explores the history, culture, and politics of grassroots and global practices of mediated communication. Her work has appeared in *New Media & Society, Media, Culture & Society, and Communication and Critical/Cultural Studies,* and has been supported by fellowships from the Social Science Research Council and the American Association of University Women.

Daniela Gerson is community engagement editor at the *Los Angeles Times*. She previously directed the Civic Engagement and Journalism Initiative at University of Southern California's Annenberg School for Communication and Journalism. She is the founding editor of the mulitilingual local news website *Alhambra Source*, and developed Reporter Corps, a program to train young adults to report on their own communities. Daniela's reporting focuses on immigration, and she has contributed to the *Financial Times Magazine*, the *New York Times*, PRI's *The World*, *Der Spiegel*, and WNYC: New York Public Radio, and she was a staff immigration reporter for the *New York Sun*. Daniela was an Alexander von Humboldt Foundation German Chancellor Fellow and an Arthur F. Burns Fellow, researching contemporary guest worker programs in Europe.

Eric Gordon is an Associate Professor in the department of Visual and Media Arts at Emerson College, where he is the Director of the Engagement Lab. He is also a Faculty Associate at the Berkman Center for Internet and Society at Harvard University. Eric studies civic media and public engagement within the US and the developing world, with a specific focus on games and play in these contexts. He is the author of two books: *Net Locality: Why Location Matters in a Networked World* (Blackwell, 2011, with Adriana de Souza e Silva) and *The Urban Spectator: American Concept Cities from Kodak to Google* (Dartmouth, 2010).

Erhardt Graeff is a PhD researcher at the MIT Center for Civic Media and MIT Media Lab and a Fellow at the Berkman Center for Internet and Society at Harvard University. He is a sociologist, designer, and entrepreneur, whose work explores creative uses of media and technology for civic engagement and learning. He has written about evaluating media activism, designing civic drones, bots and privacy, and political memes. He regularly leads workshops on civic media and participatory design for students, teachers, and social entrepreneurs. Erhardt is also a founding trustee of The Awesome Foundation. Find him on Twitter: @erhardt.

Beth Gutelius is a PhD candidate in Urban Planning and Policy at the University of Illinois at Chicago, and Research Associate at the John D. and Catherine T. MacArthur Foundation. Her research examines the relationship between globalization and local economic development. At the MacArthur Foundation, Beth provides research to inform grant making and strategy development across a wide range of issue areas. Prior to joining MacArthur, Beth was a researcher at the Center for Urban Economic Development at the University of Illinois at Chicago, where she worked on studies related to low-wage labor markets employment policy, and urban industrial change.

Tad Hirsch is Assistant Professor of Interaction Design and Chair of Graduate Studies at the University of Washington, and director of the Public Practice Studio, a multidisciplinary, public-interest design group. He previously worked at Intel Labs and Motorola, and has taught at the Rhode Island School of Design and Carnegie Mellon University. Tad is also a founding member of the Institute for Applied Autonomy, an internationally recognized art/technology/activism collective. He holds PhD and MSc degrees in Media Arts and Sciences from the MIT Media Lab, and an MDes in Interaction Design from Carnegie Mellon University.

Renee Hobbs is Professor and Director of the Media Education Lab at the Harrington School of Communication and Media at the University of Rhode Island. Her work stands at the intersection of media studies and education. She has developed award-winning multimedia curriculua and has published more than 150 scholarly articles and books including *Discovering Media Literacy: Digital Media and Popular Culture in Elementary School* (2013), *Copyright Clarity: How Fair Use Supports Digital Learning* (2011) and *Reading the Media: Teaching Media Literacy in High School English* (2007). She is the co-editor of the *Journal of Media Literacy Education*.

Laurie Phillips Honda is an Assistant Professor of Public Relations at the University of Oregon, School of Journalism and Communication. Her research focuses on LGBTQ-targeted strategic communication efforts. Prior to completing her doctorate at the University of North Carolina at Chapel Hill, she worked in various agency, client, and research roles, most notably as a Research Manager on the Web Intelligence Research Division (WIReD) team at J.D. Power & Associates. In that role, Laurie analyzed consumers' social media–based discussion about Fortune 500 corporations, nonprofit organizations, and media outlets and served as the Account Manager for JDPA's CNN partnership. Laurie's weekly reports were published on CNN.com.

Joseph Kahne is Professor of Education, Mills College, and Chair of the MacArthur Foundation Research Network on Youth and Participatory Politics, http://YPP.dmlcentral.net. Joe's research draws on a national longitudinal survey of youth to examine the ways participation with digital media shapes youth civic and political engagement. He is also studying a district-wide initiative titled "Educating for Democracy in the Digital Age" in Oakland, CA. More generally, Kahne's research focuses on ways that online engagement, curriculum, and school policies can improve the quantity, quality, and equality of civic and political engagement. Joe Kahne sits on the steering committee of the National Campaign for the Civic Mission of Schools (see www.civicsurvey.org).

Henry Jenkins is an American media scholar and currently a Provost Professor of Communication, Journalism, Cinematic Arts and Education at the University of Southern California. Previously, he was the Peter de Florez Professor of Humanities and Co-Director of the MIT Comparative Media Studies program with William Uricchio. He is also author of several books, including *Convergence Culture: Where Old and New Media Collide, Textual Poachers: Television Fans and Participatory Culture, Spreadable Media: Creating Meaning and Value in a Networked Culture, Participatory Culture in a Networked Era*, and *By Any Media Necessary: The New Youth Activism.*

David Karpf is an Assistant Professor and Director of Graduate Studies in the School of Media and Public Affairs at George Washington University. His research focuses on the Internet and organized political advocacy. His first book *The MoveOn Effect* was published in 2012 by Oxford University Press. He is currently completing a second book on analytics and activism, which will be published in 2016. He tweets at @davekarpf and blogs at shoutingloudly.com.

Tom Keene is an outreach artist at pioneering media art gallery Furtherfield, a founding member of artist collective OSA, a freelance programmer, and a core contributor to *Avant*, a new journal launched at Transmediale, Berlin, 2014. He graduated from the MA Interactive Media: Critical Theory and Practice at Goldsmiths College, University of London, in 2012. His work has been exhibited both nationally and internationally in the form of finished pieces, contraptions, and experimental workshops. Tom researches technological histories, builds contraptions, and performs live experiments at Citizen Sense and beyond. His practice-based approach probes a technological agency that mediates our actions yet exists outside of a designed intent.

Neta Kligler-Vilenchik earned her PhD in Communication at the Annenberg School for Communication & Journalism at the University of Southern California, and is an Assistant Professor at the Hebrew University of Jerusalem. She holds an MA in Communication from the University of Haifa, Israel, and a BA in Communication and Political Science from Tel Aviv University, Israel. Neta's research interests focus on youth civic engagement in the new media environment. As a researcher in the MacArthur Foundation's Youth & Participatory Politics (YPP) Network, she is investigating how youth's involvement in participatory cultures and fan communities promotes their civic and political engagement. Neta is a co-author on the forthcoming book, *By Any Media Necessary.*

Ben Kraal is a Research Fellow with the People and Systems Lab at the Queensland University of Technology, Australia. His recent work has focused on how people experience complex systems and services, with a specific focus on airports and healthcare. His work is situated at the intersection of design and qualitative sociology and draws on both disciplines to reveal how systems and services are made and made useful.

Sebastian Kubitschko is a postdoctoral researcher at the Centre for Media, Communication and Information Research (ZeMKI), University of Bremen, where he is a member of the interdisciplinary Communicative Figurations network. His research focus is on how hacker organizations gain legitimacy and the ways they politicize contemporary technology. Sebastian holds a PhD from Goldsmiths, University of London, and is the European Editor of *Arena Magazine*. Together with Anne Kaun he is currently editing the volume *Innovative Methods in Media and Communication Research* (Palgrave Macmillan, 2016).

Derek Lackaff is an Assistant Professor at the School of Communications in Elon University, Elon, North Carolina. He is the founder of the Better Alamance Project (http://betteralamance.org), a civic technology collaboration focused on Alamance County, North Carolina. His research focuses on social media, civic technologies, creative industries, and the social psychology of communication technology use. He teaches in the iMedia (http://elon.edu/imedia) program at Elon University.

Peter Levine is Associate Dean for Research and the Lincoln Filene Professor of Citizenship & Public Affairs in Tufts University's Jonathan Tisch College of Citizenship and Public Service. Levine was previously Director of CIRCLE (The Center for Information and Research on Civic Learning and Engagement). He is the author of the book *We Are the Ones We Have Been Waiting For: The Promise of Civic Renewal in America* (Oxford University Press, 2013), five other scholarly books on philosophy and politics, and a novel.

Sarah Whitcomb Lozier is a PhD candidate in the English department at University of California, Riverside. Her dissertation titled "Hypermaterial Language Art: Digitality, Materiality and Anti-Racist Poeitcs" is a theoretical digital humanities project that examines the aesthetics and semiotics of contemporary literary, visual, and digital art production through the lens of digital materiality. She examines the push and pull of materiality and virtuality of language in these artworks, exploring the ways they provide alternative sign systems for navigating a colorblind, post-racial, post-identity. Artists whose work she engages with include Susan Howe, Harryette Mullen, Lorna Simpson, Jenny Holzer, Glenn Ligon, Jean-Michel Basquiat, and Erik Loyer.

Sophia Maalsen is a post-doctoral researcher at the University of Sydney. She has a range of interests including urban geographies, music, gender, and the spatial relations inherent in these. A particularly strong interest is in object/subject agency and the ability of technology to extend a person's agency as well as creating the possibilities for new forms of object/subject relations.

Ceasar McDowell is Professor of the Practice of Community Development at MIT. He holds an EdD and an MEd from Harvard University. Ceasar's current work is on the development of community knowledge systems and civic engagement. He is also expanding his critical moments reflection methodology to identify, share, and maintaining grassroots knowledge. He is Director of the global civic engagement organization Dropping Knowledge International, founder of MIT's former Center for Reflective Community Practice (renamed Co-Lab), co-founder of the Civil Rights Forum on Telecommunications Policy, and founding Board member of the Algebra Project.

Jessica McLean is geographer at Macquarie University, Sydney, who researches processes of social, cultural, and environmental change in a range of contexts. Her research praxis emphasizes collaborative approaches and partnerships with communities and individuals who are working toward more equitable futures. Current work involves examining digital activism in feminist and climate action contexts to improve our understanding of material and immaterial realities.

Inger Mewburn is the Director of Research Training at Australian National University. She is responsible for convening and teaching into a range of research education programs at ANU and consults on research education policy within ANU and outside of it. She is the Founder and Managing Editor of the "Thesis Whisperer" blog, which has received over 1 million hits in the last two and a half years and the associated social media feeds which collectively have over 26,000 followers and subscribers worldwide. The blog is recognized internationally for excellence in online research student support and has been archived by Trove as a blog of national significance. She also sits on the advisory board of fIRST, a multi-university organisation facilitating online supervisor training.

Paul Mihailidis is an Associate Professor in the School of Communication at Emerson College in Boston, MA, where he teaches media literacy and interactive media. He is also Principal Investigator and Associate Director of the Engagement Lab at Emerson College, and Director of the Salzburg Academy on Media and Global Change. His research focuses on the nexus of media, education, and civic voices. His book, *Media Literacy and the Emerging Citizen* (Peter Lang, 2014), outlines effective practices for participatory citizenship and engagement in digital culture. Under his direction, the Salzburg Academy on Media and Global Change, a global media literacy incubator program, annually gathers 70 students and a dozen faculty to build networks for media innovation, civic voices, and global change. Mihailidis sits on the board of directors for the National Association of Media Literacy Education. He has authored numerous books and papers exploring media education and citizenship, and has traveled around the world speaking about media literacy and engagement in digital culture. He earned his PhD from the Phillip Merrill College of Journalism at the University of Maryland, College Park.

Stefania Milan is an Assistant Professor of New Media and Digital Culture at the University of Amsterdam, the Netherlands, and the founding director of the Data J Lab, dedicated to Big Data epistemologies. Her research interests include media activism, social movements, and cyberspace governance. Her latest research project, financed by the European Research Council, investigates citizens' engagement with massive data collection. Stefania holds a PhD in Political and Social Sciences from the European University Institute, Italy (2009). Stefania is also a research associate at the Tilburg Institute for Law, Technology and Society and at the Internet Policy Observatory of the Annenberg School for Communication, University of Pennsylvania. As a consultant, she has worked for the European Commission; the Italian Ministry of Education, University and Research; and many international NGOs.

Beth Simone Noveck directs the Governance Lab and its MacArthur Research Network on Opening Governance. The Jerry Hultin Global Network Professor at New York University's Polytechnic School of Engineering, she served in the White House as the first United States Deputy Chief Technology Officer and director of the White House Open Government Initiative (2009–2011). UK Prime Minister David Cameron appointed her senior advisor for Open Government. Beth is the author of *Wiki Government: How Technology Can Make Government Better, Democracy Stronger and Citizens More Powerful* (Brookings, 2009) and *Smart Citizens, Smarter State: The Technologies of Expertise and the Future of Governing* (Harvard University Press, 2015). She tweets @bethnoveck.

Lindy Osborne is a Senior Lecturer at the Queensland University of Technology, Australia. Her research interests and PhD center on innovative design education and the design of future learning landscapes. Lindy is a member of the Design Learning Collective at QUT, a group of academics who are seeking to develop a research profile around design and architecture education. She is currently seconded to the Chancellery as a Transformation Fellow, where she is working in a team to transform future postgraduate-level online education. Lindy's teaching has been recognised at QUT with a Vice-Chancellor's Performance Award and nationally through a Citation for Outstanding Contributions to Student Learning.

Michael Parks is a journalist and educator whose assignments have taken him around the globe, and whose "balanced and comprehensive" coverage of the struggle against apartheid in South Africa earned him the 1987 Pulitzer Prize for International Reporting. From 1997 to 2000, Parks served as editor of the *Los Angeles Times*, a period during which the *Times* garnered four additional Pulitzer Prizes. Parks joined the USC Annenberg faculty in 2000 and served as Director of the School of Journalism from 2001 to 2008.

Chris Peterson works, teaches, and researches at MIT, from which he earned his MS in Comparative Media Studies with a thesis on user-generated censorship, with interests including the politics of technology, distributed cognition, and law and society. He also serves on the Board of Directors at the National Coalition Against Censorship, as a Fellow at the National Center for Technology and Dispute Resolution, and as a Fellow at the Digital Ecologies Research Partnership, and previously earned his BA in Legal Studies from the University of Massachusetts at Amherst. He also founded BurgerMap, a crowdsourced collection of the world's best burgers, on a map.

Helen Pritchard is a Research Fellow in the Department of Sociology at Goldsmiths, University of London, on the European Research Council project led by Jennifer Gabrys, "Citizen Sensing and Environmental Practice." Her interdisciplinary work brings together the fields of computational aesthetics, software studies, environmental practice, feminist technoscience, and new feminist materialisms. She is a PhD candidate at Queen Mary University of London, and her artistic works have been shown internationally, including at DA Fest International festival of Digital Art (Bulgaria), Spacex (UK), Microwave Festival (Hong Kong), ACA Florida (USA), and Arnolfini Online (UK). Helen has previously held associate lectureships in Art, Technology and Critical Studies at Plymouth University and Dartington College of Arts.

Colin Rhinesmith is an Assistant Professor of Social and Community Informatics in the School of Library and Information Studies at the University of Oklahoma and a Faculty Research Fellow with the Benton Foundation. He received his PhD in Library and Information Science from the Graduate School of Library and Information Science at the University of Illinois at Urbana-Champaign. Rhinesmith was previously a Google Policy Fellow and an Adjunct Research Fellow with the New America Foundation's Open Technology Institute. He has been nationally recognized as a leader within the field of community media and technology.

Brady Robards is a Lecturer in Sociology at the University of Tasmania. His research explores how young people use and thus produce the social Web (previously MySpace, but more recently Facebook, Instagram, and reddit). Brady's work also explores the sustained use of social media, and how digital traces come to serve as archives of self. Brady's work appears in journals including *New Media & Society*, *Continuum*, and *Sociology*. Recent books include *Youth Cultures & Subcultures: Australian Perspectives* (Ashgate, 2015), *Mediated Youth Cultures* (Palgrave, 2014) and *Teaching Youth Studies Through Popular Culture* (ACYS Publishing, 2014). For more, visit Brady's website: bradyrobards.com.

Molly Sauter is a Vanier Scholar and doctoral student in Communication Studies at McGill University in Montreal and holds a master's degree in Comparative Media Studies from MIT. Her research focuses on the sociopolitical analysis of Internet law and regulation and the political philosophy of technology. She is the author of *The Coming*

Swarm: DDOS Actions, Hacktivism, and Civic Disobedience on the Internet (2014, Blooms-bury, 2014). She is a research affiliate at the Berkman Center for Internet and Society at Harvard University and the Center for Civic Media at the MIT Media Lab.

Andrew Schrock earned his PhD from the Annenberg School for Communication and Journalism at the University of Southern California. He is currently working as a Data and Design Research Fellow for the city of Los Angeles and is active in the public sector. His research and practice considers how grassroots groups and governments can more effectively and ethically use data and mobile media to improve civic life. He is particu-larly interested in how the "civic tech" movement brings about positive outcomes of social cohesion and civic engagement. Andrew's research has appeared in *New Media & Society*, the *International Journal of Communication*, and *Information, Communication & Society*. For more on Andrew's work, please visit his website at aschrock.com.

Alexandra Segerberg is an Associate Professor in the Department of Political Science at Stockholm University, and editor of ECPR Press, the publishing imprint of the Euro-pean Consortium for Political Research. Her work centers on political, philosophical, and empirical theories of collective action, and current research interests include the role of media and information systems in action for social change. She is the co-author of *The Logic of Connective Action: The Personalization of Contentious Politics* (Cambridge University Press, 2013, with W. Lance Bennett).

Nick Shapiro is a medical and environmental anthropologist. He is currently a Matter, Materials and Culture Fellow at the Chemical Heritage Foundation. He completed his doctoral training at the University of Oxford. He is currently a postdoctoral research fellow in Goldsmiths' Department of Sociology, University of London, where he stud-ies environmental monitoring practices and technologies as a part of the European Research Council–funded "Citizen Sense" project. He is the lead researcher of an indoor air quality project with the environmental monitoring non-profit Public Lab. Shapiro's research has been featured in various media outlets from NPR to the *New Republic*.

Sangita Shresthova is a Czech/Nepali media-maker, dancer, and scholar. Sangita is the Director of Henry Jenkins' Media, Activism & Participatory Politics (MAPP) project based at the University of Southern California. Her work focuses on the intersection among popular culture, performance, new media, politics, and globalization. She is a co-author of *By Any Media Necessary*, a forthcoming book on innovative youth-led civic action. Her earlier book on Bollywood dance and globalization (*Is It All About Hips?*) was published by SAGE Publications in 2011. Sangita is also founded Bollynatyam and continues to explore dance and media through this platform. Her work has been pre-sented in academic and creative venues around the world, including the Schaubuehne (Berlin), the Other Festival (Chennai), and the American Dance Festival (Durham, NC).

Her recent research has focused on performance through digital media, storytelling and surveillance among American Muslim youth, and the achievements and challenges faced by Invisible Children pre- and post-Kony2012.

Elisabeth (Lissa) Soep is Research Director and Senior Producer at Youth Radio, a national youth-driven production company that is NPR's Youth Desk and has won multiple Peabody and Murrow Awards, and the Robert Kennedy Journalism Award. With a PhD from Stanford, she researches youth, learning, and digital media culture. She wrote *Participatory Politics* (MIT Press), co-authored *Drop that Knowledge* (UC Press), and co-edited *Youthscapes* (Penn Press). In 2010, Lissa co-founded Youth Radio's App Lab, now called Youth Radio Interactive, which she leads as a partnership with MIT Media Lab and UC Berkeley's Information School. She is a member of the MacArthur Foundation's Research Network on Youth and Participatory Politics.

Nicole Stremlau is Head of the University of Oxford's Programme in Comparative Media Law and Policy and a Fellow at Wolfson College. Her research focuses on media and governance, particularly in areas of conflict and insecurity in Africa. Her most recent projects examine the role of new media in political participation and governance; media law and regulation in the absence of government or in weak states; the role of media in conflict, peacebuilding, and the consolidation of political power; and how governments attempt to engage citizens and communicate law-making processes. Stremlau is also an Associate Fellow at the Center for Global Communications Studies, Annenberg School for Communication, University of Pennsylvania.

Emiliano Treré is an Associate Professor at the Faculty of Political and Social Sciences, Autonomous University of Querétaro (Mexico), and a Research Fellow in the Media Studies Program of the Department of Interdisciplinary Studies at Lakehead University (Canada). His research combines insights from practice theory, ecological approaches, mediation paradigms, and the sociology of culture and communication, in order to understand the multiple roles that communication technologies play within social movements. He has published extensively in top-ranked international journals and in books on digital activism, alternative media, and the challenges of digital technology for political communication. He is co-editor of "Social Media and Protest Identities" (*Information, Communication & Society*, 2015) and "Latin American Struggles & Digital Media Resistance" (*International Journal of Communication*, 2015).

Stephen Walter is a person who makes and studies media that aim to foster experiences of complexity, difference, and play. He was the founding managing director of the Engagement Lab and has worked with the United Nations Development Program, the US Department of State, the International Red Cross/Red Crescent Climate Centre, Boston EMS, the Boston Public Health Commission, the Harvard Graduate School of Education, and the PBS television shows *Frontline* and *Nova*. He has helped lead the design, development, and implementation of civic media projects in Detroit, Boston, Philadelphia, Los Angeles, Sweden, Moldova, Zambia, Egypt, and Bhutan.

Sarah Williams is currently an Assistant Professor of Urban Planning and the Director of the Civic Data Design Lab at the Massachusetts Institute of Technology's School of Architecture and Planning. The Civic Data Design Lab employs data visualization and mapping techniques to expose and communicate urban patterns and policy issues to broader audiences. Prior to MIT, Williams was Co-Director of the Spatial Information Design Lab at Columbia University. Williams has won numerous awards, including being named to top 25 planners in technology and 2012 Game Changer by *Metropolis Magazine*. Her work is currently on view in the Museum of Modern Art (MoMA), New York.

Ethan Zuckerman is Director of the Center for Civic Media at MIT, and a Principal Research Scientist at the MIT Media Lab. His research focuses on the distribution of attention in mainstream and new media, the use of technology for international development, and the use of new media technologies by activists. Through his prior work at the Berkman Center for Internet and Society, and his ongoing work with Open Society Foundation, Global Voices, and other NGOs, Zuckerman promotes freedom of expression and the use of technology for social change.

Index